CONTACTS 2016

105th EDITION

Published by Spotlight, 7 Leicester Place, Lo[...]
T 020 7437 7631   F 020 7437 5881
E questions@spotlight.com   W www.spotlight.com

POL-1985
06/16
£13.91
* * *

D0569271

What is Contacts?

Contacts is the essential handbook for everyone working or wanting to work in the entertainment industry. It has been published by Spotlight since 1947. It contains over 5000 listings for companies, services and individuals across all branches of Television, Stage, Film and Radio. These are updated annually to bring you the most accurate information available.

Also watch out for the 'Information & Advice pages', designed to tell you more about those listed and why you might want to contact them. They include valuable advice from key industry figures - especially helpful if you are just starting out in the industry.

As ever, please send any feedback or suggestions for the next edition to contacts@spotlight.com

How can I / my company appear in the next edition of Contacts?

Contacts is published annually. If you would like to appear in the next edition please visit: www.contactshandbook.com

How can I change my listing?

If you appear in this edition and wish to inform us of any changes please email: contacts@spotlight.com

How do I buy copies of Contacts?

To purchase copies of Contacts, visit www.contactshandbook.com or call 020 7440 5026. It is also available from most good bookshops.

FSC MIX Paper from responsible sources FSC® C013436

Designed by Consider: www.considercreative.co.uk
Printed and bound in Great Britain by Latimer Trend Company Ltd.

SPOTLIGHT

CEO
Ben Seale

COO
Richard Wilson

BUSINESS DEVELOPMENT
Gary Broughton – Head of Business Development

CASTING
Pippa Harrison – Head of Casting
Holly Janowski   Curtis Walton

Joe Bates – Head of Rooms & Studios
Ilayda Arden   Hannah Imrie   Nicholas Peel

DATA
Joanna MacLeod – Head of Data
Amanda Lawrence   Emma Lear   Caroline Taylor

FINANCE
Claire Adams – Chief Financial Officer
Nas Fokeerchand – Finance Manager
Amelia Barnham   Sally Pitts

HR
Marylin Peach – HR & Facilities Manager
Luke Turvey

IT
Dan Woodhead – Head of IT
Dylan Beattie – Systems Architect
Steven Carta   Nathaniel Ghilazghi   Pencho Ilchev   Adam Kosinski
Edgar Misins   Michael Seraphine   Sadia Shafiq   Adrian Wardle

Chris Monteiro   Ross Shoderu   Sukhraj Singh   Gareth Wilsdon-Tagg

MARKETING
Lauren McKinnon – Marketing Manager
Lindsay Eyers   Rachel Flenley   Faye Maitland

MEMBERSHIP
Laura Albery – Head of Membership
Emma Dyson   Natasha Leontieff

Sally Barnham
Alice Bruce-Tresnan   Charlotte Nettey   Joan Queva   Elinor Samuels

PUBLISHING
Kate Poynton – Head of Publishing
Cindy Lian   Noll Kennedy   Pete Tynan
Sara Edwards   Hannah Frankel   Nick Goldfinch   David McCarthy
Kathy Norrish – Design & Edition Layout

C →

Contents

Contents

Contents

A →

Accountants, Insurance & Law

Agents
- Agents & Personal Managers
- Children & Teenagers
- Concert & Promoters
- Dance
- Literary
- Presenters
- Voice Over
- Walk-On & Supporting Artists

Arts Centres

PMA
For information regarding membership of
the Personal Managers' Association
please contact:
E info@thepma.com
W www.thepma.com

CPMA
For information regarding membership of
the Co-operative Personal Management
Association please contact The Secretary:
E cpmauk@yahoo.co.uk
W www.cpma.coop

Members of the above organisations are
clearly marked as such in the appropriate
listings.

Accountants, Insurance & Law

Why might I need this section?

This section contains listings for a number of companies and services which exist to help performers with the day-to-day administration of their working lives. Performers need to personally manage their business affairs in ways that those in 'normal' jobs do not. For example, unlike most employees, a performer does not have an accounts department to work out their tax and national insurance, nor an HR department to take care of contracts or health insurance on their behalf. On top of which, performers can often be away on tour or on set for many months and unable to attend to these matters themselves.

Areas covered in this section include:

Accountants and other financial services

Dedicated companies exist which can help you to manage key financial issues, including national insurance, taxation, benefits, savings and pensions. Specialist mortgage companies also exist for performers and other self-employed workers within the entertainment industry. If you are a member of Equity, the main actors' union in the UK, you can ask them for free financial advice. An Equity pension scheme exists which the BBC, ITV, PACT, TV companies and West End theatre producers will pay into when you have a main part with one of them. Similar schemes also exist for dancers and other performers.

Insurance

As a performer you may often need specialist insurance for specific roles, as well as the standard life and health insurance policies held by most people. A number of specialist insurers are listed in this section. Equity also offers a specialist backstage/accident and public liability insurance policy to all of its members.

Legal

There may be times in a performer's career when he/she needs specialist legal advice or representation. This could be because of a performer's high profile, complicated contractual details, or international employment issues. Legal advisers and solicitors are listed in this section. In addition, as part of their membership, Equity performers can also obtain free legal advice regarding professional engagements or personal injury claims.

How should I use these listings?

As when looking to hire any company or individual, you should contact a number of different companies and carefully compare the services they offer. Ask others in the industry for recommendations. If you are an Equity member, don't forget to check first that the service isn't already available free of charge, as part of your annual membership. For information about joining Equity, visit www.equity.org.uk or see their case study in the 'Unions' section.

Accountants, Insurance & Law

Theataccounts are specialist accountants and tax advisers. Alex Dyer and his team are friendly, professional and dedicated to making tax simple for the entertainment industry.

Once you enter the world of freelancing, there are three important financial areas you need to think about - Tax, National Insurance Contributions (NICs) and VAT.

Firstly, you need to register with HM Revenue and Customs (HMRC) as soon as possible. Registration can be done online, or if you don't fancy braving it yourself an accountant will be able to help you. HMRC will send you your Unique Tax Reference (UTR) number, which you need to keep in a safe place.

> **"You will need to keep a record of all business income and expenditure throughout the year in order to work out your taxable profit"**

Unlike being an employee, any payment you receive for freelance work will not be taxed when you receive it. Instead, you'll need to declare it on your tax return and pay any tax and NICs due. The tax year runs from 6 April to the following 5 April, with the deadline for filing your tax return (and paying any tax due) being the end of the following January.

You will need to keep a record of all business income and expenditure throughout the year in order to work out your taxable profit.

HMRC define eligible expenditure as costs incurred 'wholly and exclusively' for the purpose of your business. This might include agent's commission, Equity/Spotlight fees, travel costs, headshots, phone bills, printing, stationery, hair and beauty costs, computer equipment, use of home as office etc. Some costs have a 'duality of purpose' (e.g. using the same phone for business and personal calls), so you need to ensure that only the accurate business proportion is included on your tax return.

Once you have calculated your profit you will need to pay 20% tax on this amount. For the 2015/16

tax year, the Personal Allowance is £10,600, so you will only be taxed on profit above this amount. For example, if your taxable profit is £12,600, you will only pay tax on £2,000 of those profits, so your tax would be £400.

There's also National Insurance Contributions to remember and there are two main classes which apply to freelancers: Class 2 and Class 4.

Class 2 NICs are charged at £2.80 per week and from April 2015 you are required to pay these at the same time as your tax and Class 4 NICs. Previously, these were automatically payable but this changed for the 2015/16 tax year. If you were previously paying by direct debit, HMRC should have cancelled this after July 2015.

There is a certain amount you can earn before you have to pay Class 2 NICs, but you may choose to pay voluntarily in order to protect your entitlement to contributory benefits. If your earnings are under the Small Profit Threshold (£5,965 for 2015/16), you no longer have to apply for exception.

You are also now required to pay Class 4 NICs which are 9% of your taxable profit, after deducting the Lower Profits Limit of £8,060. On a taxable profit of £12,600, Class 4 NICs due would be £408.60. This makes a total tax and NI bill of £808.60 excluding Class 2 NICs.

Don't forget your tax and Class 4 NIC rates change when your profit is over a certain level.

If your total tax and Class 4 NI liability was over £1,000, HMRC require you to pay payments on account for the following tax year.

As a freelancer, you will also need to consider VAT and Limited Companies. It is compulsory to be VAT registered when your income reaches £82,000 in any 12 month period, but depending on your situation it may be beneficial to register voluntarily. Depending on your level of profit, a Limited Company may also be more tax efficient for you. We would suggest that you should seek advice from an accountant to discuss your own personal situation in further detail. Most accountants will offer a free chat.

There is a lot to take in when starting out but if you need any help, please feel free to contact us for a free chat.

To find out more visit www.theataccounts.co.uk

mGm

www.mgmaccountancy.co.uk

A firm of friendly and professional accountants who offer a wide range of personalised services within a welcoming, responsive environment at a competitive rate.

Professional accounting solutions for creative people and their business

MGM Accountancy Limited Chartered Certified Accountants
3rd Floor, 20 Bedford Street
Covent Garden, London WC2E 9HP

Tel: +44 (0)20 7379 9202
Fax: +44 (0)20 7379 9101
admin@mgmaccountancy.co.uk

1505 T 020 7112 8750
Book-keeping Packages
20 Bedford Street, London WC2E 9HP
E hello@weare1505.co.uk
W www.weare1505.co.uk

ACCOUNTS ACTION LTD T 020 7437 0301
Arts & Media Accountancy
Suite 210A, Linen Hall
162-168 Regent Street, London W1B 5TB
E nick@accountsaction.net
W www.accountsaction.net

ADDERS T 01604 492534
Accountants
60 Ashley Lane, Moulton, Northants NN3 7TJ
F 01604 642290
E jim@adders.co.uk
W www.adders.co.uk

ALEXANDER JAMES & CO T 020 8398 4447
Contact: Andrew Nicholson. Chartered Certified Accountants
Admirals Quarters, Portsmouth Road
Thames Ditton, Surrey KT7 0XA
F 020 8398 9989
E actors@alexanderjames.co.uk
W www.alexanderjames.co.uk

ARCHERFIELD PARTNERS LLP T 020 7871 0596
Bespoke Legal Services
4 Pickering Place, St James's Street, London SW1A 1EA
F 020 7930 4340
E enquiries@archerfieldpartners.com
W www.archerfieldpartners.com

BAMBRIDGE ACCOUNTANTS T 020 3757 9290
1 Mercer Street, London WC2H 9QJ
E info@bambridgeaccountants.co.uk
W www.bambridgeaccountants.co.uk

BLACKMORE, Lawrence T 020 7240 1817
Production Accountant
Suite 5, 26 Charing Cross Road, London WC2H 0DG
E laurieblackmore@aol.com

BLAKE MORGAN T 020 7405 2000
Solicitors
Watchmaker Court, 33 St John's Lane, London EC1M 4DB
F 020 7814 9421
E info@blakemorgan.co.uk
W www.blakemorgan.co.uk

BLINKHORNS T 020 7636 3702
27 Mortimer Street, London W1T 3BL
E info@blinkhorns.co.uk
W www.blinkhorns.co.uk

BOWKER ORFORD T 020 7636 6391
Accountants & Business Advisers
15-19 Cavendish Place
London W1G 0DD
F 020 7580 3909
E mail@bowkerorford.com
W www.bowkerorford.com

BREBNERS T 020 7734 2244
Chartered Accountants
130 Shaftesbury Avenue
London W1D 5AR
F 020 7287 5315
E partners@brebners.com
W www.brebners.com

Accountants, Insurance & Law

BRECKMAN & COMPANY T 01273 929350
Chartered Certified Accountants. Registered Auditors
95 Ditchling Road
Brighton BN1 4ST
E info@breckmanandcompany.co.uk
W www.breckmanandcompany.co.uk

BRECKMAN & COMPANY T 020 7499 2292
Chartered Certified Accountants. Registered Auditors
49 South Molton Street
London W1K 5LH
E info@breckmanandcompany.co.uk
W www.breckmanandcompany.co.uk

CARNE, Charlie & CO T 020 8742 2001
Chartered Accountants
49 Windmill Road, London W4 1RN
E info@charliecarne.com

CARR, Mark & CO LTD T 020 7717 8474
Chartered Accountants
90 Long Acre, Covent Garden
London WC2E 9RZ
T 01273 778802
E mark@markcarr.co.uk
W www.markcarr.co.uk

**CBW
(CARTER BACKER WINTER LLP)** T 020 7309 3800
*Chartered Accountants. Financial Planning. Tax Planning.
Corporate Recovery & Insolvency. Corporate Finance*
66 Prescot Street, London E1 8NN
F 020 7309 3801
E info@cbw.co.uk
W www.cbw.co.uk

**CITY ACCOUNTANTS &
TAX ADVISORS** T 01733 777782
24 Broadway Gardens, Peterborough PE1 4DU
T 07976 244746
E info@cityaccountants.org.uk
W www.cityaccountants.org.uk

CLEARSKY ACCOUNTING T 0808 1471776
Twitter: @ClearSkyEnt
Hampton House, Oldham Road
Manchester M24 1GT
E accountinginfo@clearskybusiness.co.uk
W www.clearskybusiness.co.uk/entertainment

COLLINS & COMPANY T 020 8427 1888
Chartered Accountants
2nd Floor, 116 College Road
Harrow, Middlesex HA1 1BQ
F 020 8863 0068
E hq@collins116.com

COUNT AND SEE LTD T 020 8767 7882
Tax, Accountancy & Book-keeping Services
219 Macmillan Way, London SW17 6AW
E info@countandsee.com
W www.countandsee.com

DUB & CO T 020 7284 8686
Chartered Certified Accountants
7 Torriano Mews, London NW5 2RZ
F 020 7284 8687
E office@dub.co.uk
W www.dub.co.uk

EAM LONDON T 020 3411 1011
Media Accountants
20 Bunhill Row, London EC1Y 8UE
E shayne.savill@eam.co.uk
W www.eam.co.uk

ENCORE INSURE
Online Theatre Insurance
E enquiries@encoreinsure.com
W www.encoreinsure.com

EQUITY INSURANCE SERVICES T 01245 357854
131-133 New London Road, Chelmsford, Essex CM2 0QZ
F 01245 491641
E enquiries@equity-ins-services.com
W www.equity-ins-services.com

EVA ACCOUNTANTS T 07883 029680
Contact: Colin Eva
31 Myrtle Avenue, Ruislip, Middlesex HA4 8SA
E colin.eva@evaaccountants.co.uk
W www.evaaccountants.co.uk

**FARROW ACCOUNTING &
TAX LTD** T 020 8876 8020
95 South Worple Way, London SW14 8ND
F 020 8876 1116
E info@farrowaccounting.com
W www.farrowaccounting.com

FILM AND BUSINESS LAW LLP T 020 7129 1449
*Offices in London, Paris & Los Angeles. American Work
Visas, Contracts, Music Sync Licensing*
17 Cavendish Square, London W1G 0PH
E legal@filmandbusinesslaw.com
W www.filmandbusinesslaw.com

FINDLAY, Richard T 0131 226 3253
Entertainment Lawyer. Business Consultant
1 Darnaway Street, Edinburgh EH3 6DW
T 07850 327725
E mail@richardfindlay.biz

**FISHER PACKMAN &
ASSOCIATES** T 020 8732 5500
Chartered Accountants. In association with Simia Wall
Devonshire House, 582 Honeypot Lane
Stanmore HA7 1JS
F 020 8732 5501
E nik@fisherpackman.com
W www.fisherpackman.com

**FISHER PACKMAN &
ASSOCIATES** T 020 8732 5500
Chartered Accountants. In association with Simia Wall
Sir Robert Peel House, 178 Bishopsgate
London EC2M 4NJ
F 020 8732 5501
E nik@fisherpackman.com
W www.fisherpackman.com

FORD, Jonathan & CO LTD T 0151 426 4512
Chartered Accountants
Maxwell House, 360 Edge Lane
Liverpool Innovation Park, Liverpool L7 9NJ
E info@jonathanford.co.uk W www.jonathanford.co.uk

GALLAGHER ENTERTAINMENT T 020 3430 6952
Insurance Brokers
Pinewood Studios, Pinewood Road
Iver, Bucks SL0 0NH
E james_fox@ajg.com
W www.ajg.co.uk

H AND S ACCOUNTANTS LTD T 020 3174 1905
Chartered Accountants
90 Mill Lane, West Hampstead, London NW6 1NL
F 020 7788 2984
E hstaxplan@gmail.com
W www.hstaxplan.com

HARDWICKE T 020 7691 0056
Contact: Mark Engelman (Barrister). Media Law
Hardwicke Building, Lincoln's Inn, London WC2A 3SB
T 07720 294667
E mark.engelman@hardwicke.co.uk
W www.hardwicke.co.uk

HARIJYOT LTD T 07958 772581
Accountants
79 Portland Crescent, Stanmore, Middlesex HA7 1LY
E jignesh@harijyot.co.uk

HILL DICKINSON LLP T 0151 600 8000
International Commercial Law
1 St Paul's Square, Old Hall Street, Liverpool L3 9SJ
E mediateam@hilldickinson.com
W www.hilldickinson.com

HOOD, Karl LLP T 07916 971998
150 Tudor Drive, Kingston, Surrey KT2 5QG
E karlhood1@gmail.com

HW LEE ASSOCIATES LLP T 020 7025 4600
Accountants
New Derwent House, 69-73 Theobalds Road
London WC1X 8TA
F 020 7025 4666
E enquiries@hw-lee.com
W www.hw-lee.com

**LA PLAYA ARTS &
ENTERTAINMENT** T 01223 200650
Insurance & Financial Services
60 Cannon Street, London EC4N 6NT
T 020 7002 1007
E tracey.mccreath@laplayainsurance.com
W www.laplayainsurance.com

**LACHMAN SMITH
ACCOUNTANTS** T 020 8731 1700
16B North End Road, Golders Green, London NW11 7PH
F 020 8731 1701
E accounts@lachmansmith.co.uk
W www.lachmansmith.co.uk

**LARK INSURANCE
BROKING GROUP** T 020 7543 2800
Ibex House, 42-47 Minories, London EC3N 1DY
F 020 7543 2801
E mailbox@larkinsurance.co.uk
W www.larkinsurance.co.uk

**MARSHAM ACCOUNTANTS &
CONSULTANTS** T 07852 814845
11 Billroth Court, 3 Mornington Close
London NW9 5JQ
E info@marshams.com
W www.marshams.com

MGM ACCOUNTANCY LTD T 020 7379 9202
3rd Floor, 20 Bedford Street
London WC2E 9HP
E admin@mgmaccountancy.co.uk
W www.mgmaccountancy.co.uk

CHARTERED ACCOUNTANTS

Will Advise on Tax, Self Assessment, Accounts, Finance, Limited Companies etc **First meeting Free**

H And S Accountants LTD. 90 Mill Lane, West Hampstead, London NW6 1NL

T: 020 3174 1905 **F:** 020 7788 2984 **E:** hstaxplan@gmail.com **W:** www.hstaxplan.com

MGR WESTON KAY LLP　　**T** 020 7625 4545
Chartered Accountants. Business Administration. Touring
55 Loudoun Road, St John's Wood, London NW8 0DL
F 020 7625 5265
E contactus@mgrwk.com
W www.mgr.co.uk

MHA MACINTYRE HUDSON　　**T** 020 7429 4100
Media & Entertainment Accountants
New Bridge Street House, 30-34 New Bridge Street
London EC4V 6BJ
F 020 7248 8939
E entertainment@mhllp.co.uk
W www.macintyrehudson.co.uk

**MONEYWISE
INVESTMENTS PLC**　　**T** 020 8552 5521
Insurance Brokers
440-442 Romford Road, London E7 8DF
E aadatia@moneywiseplc.co.uk
W www.moneywiseplc.co.uk

NYMAN LIBSON PAUL　　**T** 020 7433 2400
Chartered Accountants
124 Finchley Road, London NW3 5JS
F 020 7433 2401
E entertainment@nlpca.co.uk
W www.nlpca.co.uk

O'DRISCOLL, G. & CO　　**T** 01621 893888
2 Catchpole Lane, Great Totham
Maldon, Essex CM9 8PY
T 07780 662544
E info@godriscoll.co.uk
W www.godriscoll.co.uk

**PERFORMANCE
ACCOUNTANCY**　　**T** 01344 669084
*Chartered Accountants Specialising in Performers &
the Entertainment Industry*
6 Pankhurst Drive, Harmans Water
Bracknell, Berkshire RG12 9PS
F 01344 449727
E louise@performanceaccountancy.co.uk
W www.performanceaccountancy.co.uk

PLANISPHERES　　**T/F** 020 7602 2038
Business & Legal Affairs
Sinclair House, 2 Sinclair Gardens, London W14 0AT
T 07729 144000
E info@planispheres.com
W www.planispheres.com

RALLI　　**T** 0161 832 6131
Specialising in Personal Injury, IP & Business
Jackson House, Sibson Road, Sale M33 7RR
E enquiries@ralli.co.uk
W www.ralli.co.uk

**REES ASTLEY INSURANCE
BROKERS LTD**　　**T** 01686 626019
Mostyn House, Market Street
Newtown, Powys SY16 2PQ
F 01686 628457
E performingarts@reesastley.co.uk
W www.insurance4performingarts.co.uk

**ROBERTSON TAYLOR W &
P LONGREACH**　　**T** 020 7510 1234
*Contact: Bev Hewes. Specialist Entertainment Insurance
Brokers*
America House
2 America Square
London, EC3N 2LU
E enquiries@rtib.co.uk
W www.rtworldwide.com

SLOANE & CO　　**T** 020 7221 3292
*Chartered Certified Accountants & Registered
Accountants*
36-38 Westbourne Grove
Newton Road
London W2 5SH
F 020 7229 4810
E mail@sloane.co.uk
W www.sloane.co.uk

THEATACCOUNTS LLP　　**T** 01905 823177
Twitter: @theataccounts
The Oakley, Kidderminster Road
Droitwich Spa, Worcestershire WR9 9AY
F 01905 799856
E info@theataccounts.co.uk
W www.theataccounts.co.uk

**TOWERGATE PROFESSIONAL
RISKS**　　**T** 0844 3463307
Professional Liability Insurance
Kings Court, London Road
Stevenage, Herts SG1 2GA
F 01438 735251
E new.pro.liability@towergate.co.uk
W www.towergate.co.uk/performingartsinsurance

USMAN ACCOUNTANCY　　**T** 020 3732 4685
26 York Street, London W1U 6PZ
T 07809 448969
E info@usmanaccountancy.co.uk
W www.usmanaccountancy.co.uk

**WISE & CO CHARTERED
ACCOUNTANTS**　　**T** 01252 711244
Contact: Stephen Morgan
Wey Court West, Union Road
Farnham, Surrey GU9 7PT
E smo@wiseandco.co.uk
W www.wiseandco.co.uk

**WISE & CO CHARTERED
ACCOUNTANTS**　　**T** 01753 656770
Contact: Stephen Morgan
Room 101, Pinewood Studios
Iver Heath, Bucks SL0 0NH
E smo@wiseandco.co.uk
W www.wiseandco.co.uk

WMT LLP　　**T** 01727 838255
Tax Specialists
2nd Floor, 45 Grosvenor Road
St Albans, Hertfordshire AL1 3AW
E info@wmtllp.com
W www.wmtllp.com

Arab Actors ~ Voices ~ Presenters

Recent Clients:
- BBC TV & Radio • Channel 4 • Sky • Paramount
- Left Bank Pictures • Wall to Wall • Closed Circuit (Film)

www.genuinearabcasting.com
Tel: 020 3478 9067 info@genuinearabcasting.com

GENUINE ARAB CASTING
TALENT AGENCY
Representing ARAB ACTORS for
Film, Radio, Television & Stage

**1984 PERSONAL
MANAGEMENT LTD** T 020 7251 8046
*CPMA Member. Contact: David Meyer. By Post. Accepts
Showreels. 25 Performers*
Suite 508, Davina House
137 Goswell Road, London EC1V 7ET
F 020 7250 3031
E info@1984pm.com
W www.1984pm.com

1ST TALENT AGENCY T 0845 6454000
*Contact: By e-mail. 8 Agents represent 300+ Performers.
Commercials. Film. Modelling. Television*
1 Beaumont Avenue, West Kensington, London W14 9LP
E 1sttalent@gmail.com
W www.1sttalent.com

**21ST CENTURY ACTORS
MANAGEMENT LTD** T 020 7278 3438
*CPMA Member. Contact: By e-mail. Commercials. Film.
Stage. Television*
206 Panther House, 38 Mount Pleasant
London WC1X 0AN
E 21centuryactors@gmail.com
W www.21stcenturyactors.co.uk

2MA LTD T 023 8074 1354
Sports. Stunts
Spring Vale, Tutland Road
North Baddesley, Hants SO52 9FL
E mmatt@2ma.co.uk
W www.2ma.co.uk

40 PARTNERS T 020 7637 8836
83 Great Titchfield Street, London W1W 6RH
E talent@40partners.com
W www.40partners.com

42 T 020 7292 0554
8 Flitcroft Street, London WC2H 8DL
E talent@42mp.com

**A & B PERSONAL
MANAGEMENT LTD** T 020 7794 3255
Personal Manager. Contact: By e-mail
PO Box 64671, London NW3 9LH
E b.ellmain@aandb.co.uk

A & J ARTISTS LTD T 020 8342 0542
Adults & Children
242A The Ridgeway, Botany Bay, Enfield EN2 8AP
T 020 8367 7139
E jo@ajmanagement.co.uk
W www.ajmanagement.co.uk

**A-LIST LOOKALIKES &
ENTERTAINMENTS LTD** T 0113 253 0563
Top Floor, Crank Mills
New Bank Street, Morley, Leeds LS27 8NT
E info@alistlookalikes.co.uk
W www.alistlookalikes.co.uk

A GENT THE T 07779 595194
16 Globe Row, Dafen
Llanelli, Carmarthenshire SA14 8PA
E mark@theagent.biz
W www.theagent.biz

**AARDVARK CASTING
LONDON** T 020 8667 9812
15 Deans Close, Croydon, London CR0 5PU
T 07938 942138
E london@aardvarkcasting.com
W www.aardvarkcasting.com

ABA MANAGEMENT T 01737 821348
Robert Denholm House, Bletchingley Road
Nutfield, Redhill, Surrey RH1 4HW
E admin@abacusagency.co.uk
W www.abacusaba.com

ABAKPORO, Chris T 07903 192413
Based in London,
E chrisabak@hotmail.co.uk

ABCAST T 01978 511856
5 Bowyer Street, London N1 5RR
E info@abcast.co.uk
W www.abcast.co.uk

ACA MODELS.COM T 028 9080 9809
381 Beersbridge Road
Belfast BT5 5DT
F 028 9080 9808
E bookings@ACAmodels.com
W www.acamodels.com

**ACCESS ARTISTE
MANAGEMENT LTD** T 020 7866 5444
*Contact: Sarah Bryan. By Post/e-mail. Accepts
Showreels*
71-75 Shelton Street, Covent Garden
London WC2H 9JQ
E mail@access-uk.com
W www.access-uk.com

ACTOR-MUSICIANS @ ACCESS T 020 7866 5444
*Personal Manager. Contact: Sarah Bryan. By Post/e-mail.
Specialises in Actor-Musicians*
c/o Access Artiste Management Ltd
71-75 Shelton Street
Covent Garden, London WC2H 9JQ
E mail@access-uk.com
W www.access-uk.com

Agents & Personal Managers

Who are agents and personal managers?

There are hundreds of agents and personal managers in the UK, representing thousands of performers and artists. It is their job to promote their clients to casting opportunities and negotiate contracts on their behalf. In return, they take commission usually ranging from 10-15%. Larger agencies can have hundreds of clients on their books; smaller ones may only have a handful. Agents usually try to represent a good range of artists (varying in age, gender, type) to fill the diverse role types required by casting directors. A personal manager is someone who manages an artist's career on a more one-on-one basis.

What is a co-operative agency?

Co-operative agencies are staffed by actors themselves, who take turns to handle the administrative side of the agency and promote themselves to casting opportunities as a team. If you want more control over your career and can handle the pressures and responsibility that an agent takes away from you, then you might consider joining a co-operative agency. However it is very important that you think carefully about what you are signing up for.

You will be responsible for the careers of others as well as yourself, so you must first of all be able to conduct yourself well when speaking to casting professionals. You will also have to commit some of your time to administrative jobs. You must be prepared to deal with finances and forms – all the boring paperwork you usually hand over to your agent! You must also be aware that the other performers in the agency will want to interview you and, if you are successful, to give you a trial period working with them. The Co-operative Personal Management Association (CPMA) offers advice about joining a co-operative agency on their website www.cpma.coop

Why do I need an agent?

A good agent will have contacts and authority in the entertainment industry that you, as an individual performer, would find more difficult to acquire. Agents, if you want them to, can also deal with matters such as Equity and Spotlight membership renewal. They can offer you advice on which headshots to use, what to include or exclude in your CV as you acquire more skills and experience, what a particular casting director might expect when you are invited to an audition, and so on.

How should I use these listings?

If you are an actor getting started in the industry, or are looking to change your agent, the following listings will supply you with up-to-date contact details for many of the UK's leading agencies. Every company listed is done so by written request to us. Members of the Personal Managers' Association (PMA) and the Co-operative Personal Management Association (CMPA) have indicated their membership status under their name.

Some agencies have also chosen to list other information such as relevant contact names, their preferred method of contact from new applicants, whether or not they are happy to receive showreels and/or voicereels with prospective clients' CVs and headshots, the number of performers represented by the agency, the number of agents working for the company, and/or a description of the performance areas they cover. Use this information to narrow down your search for a suitable agent.

How do I choose a new agent?

When writing to agencies, try to research the individual company instead of just sending a 'blanket' letter to every single one. This way you can target your approaches to the most suitable agencies and avoid wasting their time (and yours). As well as using the listing information provided here, look at agency websites and ask around for personal recommendations.

Unfortunately, Spotlight is not able to offer personalised advice on choosing an agent, nor are we in a position to handle any financial or contractual queries or complaints, but we have prepared some useful career advice on our website: www.spotlight.com/artists/advice. Click on our Frequently Asked Questions page for general guidance regarding agents, or you may wish to try consulting our list of Independent Advisory Services, for one-to-one tailored advice.

You can also contact The Agents' Association www.agents-uk.com or The Personal Managers' Association (PMA) www.thepma.com

If you are a member of Equity then you can contact their legal and welfare department for general information about issues including commissions, fees and contracts. However, Equity is not able to recommend specific agencies or agents.

How do I approach agencies?

Once you have made a list of suitable agencies, consult the listings again. Some agencies have indicated their preferred method of initial contact, whether by post, e-mail or telephone. Do not e-mail them, for example, if they have stated that they wish to receive your headshot, CV and covering letter by post. It is becoming far more common to e-mail agents with applications but if you are doing it by post you should always include a stamped-addressed envelope (SAE) big enough to contain your 10 x 8 photo and with sufficient postage. This will increase your chances of getting a reply. Write your name and telephone number on the back of your headshot in case it gets separated from your CV.

Remember that agents receive hundreds of letters and e-mails each week, so try to keep your communication concise, and be professional at all times. We also recommend that your covering letter has some kind of focus: perhaps you can tell them about your next showcase, or where they can see you currently appearing on stage. This should always be addressed to an individual, not "To whom it may concern" or "Dear Sir or Madam". Some agents have indicated a specific contact to whom you can direct correspondence in their listing, otherwise check the agency's website or give them a call and find out who you should address your letter or e-mail to.

Some agents have indicated that they are happy to receive a showreel and/or voicereel with your CV, but it would be best to exclude these from your correspondence if they are not mentioned. Point out in your covering letter that one is available and the agent can contact you if they want to find out more.

Should I pay an agent to join their books? Or sign a contract?

Equity (the actors' trade union) does not recommend that artists pay an agent to join their client list. Before signing a contract, you should be very clear about the terms and commitments involved. For advice on both of these issues, or if you experience any problems with a current agent, we recommend that you contact Equity www.equity.org.uk. They also produce the booklet You and your Agent which is free to all Equity members and available from their website's members' area.

How do I become an agent?

Budding agents will need to get experience of working in an agent's office; usually this is done by working as an assistant. It can be extremely hard work, and you will be expected to give up a lot of your evenings to attend productions. There are two organisations you may find it useful to contact: The Agents' Association www.agents-uk.com or the Personal Managers' Association www.thepma.com which regularly posts information regarding vacancies/opportunities on its site.

Agents & Personal Managers

CASE STUDY

Fiona Keddie-Ord started to develop Keddie Scott Associates in 2003. She works alongside a team of 5 others with offices in Manchester and Glasgow. KSA manages a group of high caliber actors working within plays, musicals, television, film and commercials.

Advice for anyone considering becoming a professional actor:

Anyone considering a career as an actor should think very carefully before making the decision to pursue this profession. It takes high levels of talent, dedication and commitment…the bar is high, the numbers are against you and the sacrifices are huge. However, the rewards are worth it and the work is inexplicably exciting and varied.

> **"Actors enjoy their job and we spend so much of life at work, enjoying it is something to be treasured, something that so many others do not have"**

Take time to research drama schools and colleges before making your careful applications. Where you train is personal to you and needs to offer the right training for your skill set, strengths and weaknesses. Training in performing arts is physically and mentally demanding, not to mention expensive. You need to be ready to cope with the intensity and be in a position to soak up every bit of knowledge you are given, you cannot waste a single hour of this precious training.

Make sure you go to the theatre as much as possible, watch current television dramas and see the latest films in the cinema. Study successful actors; they are successful for a reason.

Pros and cons of the acting industry:

The biggest pro of all is that acting is a very exciting profession to pursue. It offers a varied life, the opportunity for travel, a platform to be creative and above all, actors enjoy their job and we spend so much of life at work, enjoying it is something to be treasured, something that so many others do not have.

On the flip side, the work is not consistent and no actor (without a level of fame) can have any control over that. This brings its own frustrations and naturally, actors have to earn a living in others ways. What can often happen is that an actor can get sucked in to non-acting work due to the pressures of earning money and paying the bills. Work, which may demand a commitment and create a situation where the actor has to turn down auditions. This becomes a vicious circle. Not getting in to the audition means that offers become fewer and fewer and if the actor is not careful, can lead to being forced to leave the industry for good. Therefore, I cannot stress the importance of taking the time to find that elusive job, other than acting, that offers complete flexibility, a good financial income and doesn't make you miserable in between projects. Sounds like the impossible? Believe me, it is not. Many actors achieve this and, in my experience, it is these actors who go on to succeed.

What a performer should look for in an agent:

Research is key. In a similar way to drama school, agent choice is a personal one. First and foremost, ensure you can have a comfortable and open dialogue with the agent and that the scope of work they cover is in the direction in which you are looking to travel. You should prepare questions for your agent interview so that you can ascertain if you are both on the same page with regards to your career aspirations and personal desires. Be clear and concise about your objectives and equally, gain an understanding on how this particular agent works and what they will be expecting from you.

What an agent looks for in new clients:

First, let's state the obvious. Agents are looking for talent, but it doesn't stop there. For us, as high a level of versatility that an actor can muster will make them all the more attractive. Great actors with the ability to play a multitude of roles, great singers, great dancers, great musicians, tricks, acro, puppetry, clowning…any skill that will enhance your potential to land an exciting contract, and the more doors that are open to you, the more chance you have of working more consistently in your chosen profession.

However, it is also important that the potential client has the professional approach - confident, not arrogant, honest, but sensitive, respectful, but not a pushover. If you have a strong opinion, be ready to back it up and above all, be nice. If you are enjoyable to work with, then people will seek to work with you again. Never underestimate someone's role or position on or off stage/set. You can never know where that someone will be in years to come and you may seek an opportunity from that person one day.

How a performer might best approach a new agent:

The best way is to check the agent's website which will often detail the way in which an agent prefers to be contacted. Never call the agent's office asking this without checking a website. In fact, I personally don't think it's ever a good idea to call an agent and ask in any situation. If the website does not detail the application process then email or write. An agent's office is so busy and tying up someone's time with a call as well as tying up a phone line unnecessarily will only irritate and send the message that you haven't bothered to do some basic research or use your own initiative. Absolutely never turn up at an agent's office to hand your CV in personally. It will do nothing for you.

Be clear and concise in your application detailing your training, professional experience and your most recent headshot. Include any material you have to back this up eg. showreel link, demo, invite to a current production or notification that you will be appearing on screen with dates and times outlined.

Relationships:

The relationship between an actor and an agent is of the highest importance. Let's be clear, we do not work for our actors and they do not work for us, there is no hierarchy. We work as a team with the same goals and objectives with mutual benefits and interests. We are not only building the careers of the actors we represent, we are building our own careers as agents and striving to push our companies forward. The agent's reputation reflects the actors they represent and in turn, the reputation of those actors reflects the agent.

Naturally, we work closely with the casting community through phone calls, emails and many an evening out to watch our clients in action. Organically, these relationships can become close but regardless, it is the agent's duty to remain entirely professional when it comes to suggesting the right actor for the right role thus ensuring that no time is wasted for the casting director or the actor. It is by way of careful suggestions that trust is built between the casting director and the agent.

Talent & Hard Work:

Assuming the talent part of the equation is in place, you are trained, signed to an agent and ready to start your career. Do not simply sit back and wait for the phone to ring. Continue that all-important research into projects and directors you would like to work with. Nurture the relationships you already have and get involved in workshops and classes that will maintain, further and strengthen your skills and contacts. When you have an audition, take as much time as you can to prepare, try to be off book if there is enough notice. Stay on top of your admin, don't leave tax returns to the last minute and save your tax contributions as you go so as to avoid a shock of a bill at the end of the year. Listen and learn from those with more experience. When your agent imparts advice, take it and trust it, that advice is given for a reason that will only be good for you in the long run.

An Agent's Job:

There is often a common misconception about what an agent actually does day to day. Tasks are endless and varied in nature. It is not as simple as clicking a button to submit a client or fielding calls with availability checks on actors. Numerous meetings, plans and strategies are discussed and put in place for each and every journey a client is on. Helping with self-tapes and suggesting appropriate material for auditions. Managing the client's time, keeping administration together, updating CVs/Biogs, making submissions, calling in pushes to casting directors, giving talks at drama schools, attending client productions (which can involve extensive travel) and organising guests from the industry to see the client at work where possible. Ensuring payments are made to the actors on time, keeping careful watch on locations whilst a client is on tour so as not to miss the chance of bringing them back for audition, updating websites and social media to promote the client's work, managing offers, negotiating money and terms (sometimes even writing the contracts or re-writing clauses). The list is certainly not exhaustive and involves the agent having skills in Law, Accountancy, Business Management, Career Adviser, I.T. and even sometimes, Counsellor.

For me, to be an agent is a gift of a job and, after 12 years, I still cannot wait to get to work every morning.

To find out more visit www.keddiescott.com, follow @keddiescott on twitter or "like" our page on Facebook

ACTORS AGENCY　　T 0131 228 4040
1 Glen Street, Tollcross, Edinburgh EH3 9JD
E info@stivenchristie.co.uk
W www.stivenchristie.co.uk

**ACTORS AGENCY OF
SWEDEN THE**　　T 00 46 7 35333011
Contact: Serina Björnbom, Janna Gränesjö
Skeppsbron 32, Box 2337
103 18 Stockholm, Sweden
E janna@actorsagency.se
W www.actorsagency.se

ACTORS ALLIANCE　　T 020 7407 6028
Co-operative. CPMA Member. Contact: By Post
Disney Place House, 14 Marshalsea Road
London SE1 1HL
E actors@actorsalliance.co.uk
W www.actorsalliance.co.uk

ACTORS' CREATIVE TEAM　　T 020 7278 3388
CPMA Member
Panther House, 38 Mount Pleasant, London WC1X 0AN
F 020 7833 5086
E office@actorscreativeteam.co.uk
W www.actorscreativeteam.co.uk

ACTORS DIRECT LTD　　T 0161 277 9360
Number 5, 651 Rochdale Road, Manchester M9 5SH
T 07427 616549
E info@actorsdirect.org.uk
W www.actorsdirect.org.uk

ACTORS FILE THE　　T 020 7582 7923
Personal Manager. Co-operative. CPMA Member.
Contact: By Post/e-mail
The White House at Oval House, 52-54 Kennington Oval
London SE11 5SW
E theactorsfile@btconnect.com
W www.theactorsfile.co.uk

ACTORS' GROUP THE (TAG)　　T/F 0161 834 4466
Personal Manager. CPMA Member
Swan Buildings, 20 Swan Street, Manchester M4 5JW
E enquiries@theactorsgroup.co.uk
W www.theactorsgroup.co.uk

ACTORS IN SCANDINAVIA　　T 00 358 4 00540640
Jääkärinkatu 10, 00150 Helsinki, Finland
T 00 358 4 00260500
E laura@actorsinscandinavia.com
W www.actorsinscandinavia.com

ACTORS INTERNATIONAL LTD　　T 020 7025 8777
18 Soho Square, London W1D 3QL
F 020 7025 8001
E mail@actorsinternational.co.uk

ACTORS WORLD CASTING　　T 07960 332846
13 Briarbank Road, London W13 0HH
T 07870 594388
E katherine@actors-world-production.com
W www.voiceoverworld.eu

ACTORUM LTD　　T 020 7636 6978
The Annexe, 25 Eccleston Place, London SW1W 9NF
E info@actorum.com
W www.actorum.com

**ADA - ACTORS DIRECT
ASSOCIATES**　　T 07951 477015
Contact: Rachael Power. By e-mail. Will Accept
Showreels/Voicereels. 1 Agent represents 25 Performers.
Commercials. Film. Stage. Television.
Voice Overs
11 St George's Crescent, Rhyl, Clwyd LL18 3NN
E ada.actors@gmail.com
W www.actorsdirectassociates.net

ADVOCATE AGENCY LTD　　T 01279 850618
Contact: Kelle Bryan. By e-mail. Accepts Showreels/
Voicereels. 4 Agents represent 45 Performers.
Commercials. Disabled. Film. Musical Theatre. Stage.
Television
EAM, 20 Bunhill Row, London EC1Y 8UE
T 07828 470191
E info@advocate.agency
W www.advocate.agency

AESTHETIC CLARITY LTD　　T 07812 371225
Contact: By e-mail only. Accepts Showreels
145 Foxhole Road, Paignton, Devon TQ3 3EY
E thenamebehindtheface@yahoo.com
W www.thenamebehindtheface.com

AFA ASSOCIATES　　T 020 7682 3677
Unit 101, Business Design Centre
52 Upper Street, London N1 0QH
E afa-associates@hotmail.com

AFA MANAGEMENT　　T 07752 408201
Amanda Fairclough Actors Management
Braeside, Bottom O'th Moor, Horwich, Bolton BL6 6QH
E info@afamanagement.co.uk
W www.afamanagement.co.uk

AFFINITY MANAGEMENT　　T 01342 715275
The Coach House, Down Park
Turners Hill Road, Crawley Down, West Sussex RH10 4HQ
E jstephens@affinitymanagement.co.uk

**AGENCY / RED LETTER
FILM AGENCY LTD THE**　　T 00 353 1 6618535
Contact: Teri Hayden, Karl Hayden
9 Upper Fitzwilliam Street, Dublin 2, Ireland
E admin1@tagency.ie
W www.theagency.ie

AHA TALENT LTD　　T 020 7250 1760
PMA Member. Contact: By Post
74 Clerkenwell Road, London EC1M 5QA
E mail@ahatalent.co.uk
W www.ahatalent.co.uk

**AIM (ASSOCIATED INTERNATIONAL
MANAGEMENT) LLP**　　T 020 7831 9709
PMA Member
4th Floor, 7 Hatton Garden, London EC1N 8AD
E info@aimagents.com
W www.aimagents.com

**AIRCRAFT CIRCUS
PERFORMANCE**　　T 07946 472329
Circus Artists only
7A Melish House, Harrington Way, London SE18 5NR
E lucy@aircraftcircus.com
W www.aircraftcircus.com

AL MANAGEMENT　　T 0161 4135500
Contact: Kimberly Simpson
210 Broadway, Media City, Salford M50 2UE
E info@theactorslab.co.uk
W www.theactorslab.co.uk

ALEXANDER PERSONAL MANAGEMENT LTD
See APM ASSOCIATES

**ALL TALENT - THE SONIA SCOTT
AGENCY**　　T 0141 418 1074
Contact: Sonia Scott Mackay. By Post/e-mail/Telephone.
Accepts Showreels/Voicereels. 2 Agents represent 40
Performers. Film. Modelling. Television. Voice Overs. Walk-
on & Supporting Artists
The Hub Unit 2.7, 70 Pacific Quay, Glasgow G51 1AE
T 07971 337074
E enquiries@alltalentuk.co.uk
W www.alltalentuk.co.uk

ALLISTON & CO.
ARTIST MANAGEMENT　　　**T** 020 3390 3456
Suite 2, 3rd Floor, 207 Regent Street, London W1B 3HH
E contact@allistonandco.com
W www.allistonandco.com

ALLSORTS AGENCY　　　**T** 020 8472 3924
Waterfront Studios, 1 Dock Road, London E16 1AH
T 07950 490364
E bookings@allsortsagency.com
W www.allsortsagency.com

ALLSORTS DRAMA
FOR CHILDREN　　　**T/F** 020 8969 3249
In association with LESLIE, Sasha MANAGEMENT
34 Crediton Road, London NW10 3DU
E sasha@allsortsdrama.com

ALLSTARS ACTORS
MANAGEMENT　　　**T** 0161 702 8257
3 Agents. Television. Film. Stage. Corporate. Role Play.
Promotional
23 Falconwood Chase, Worsley, Manchester M28 1FG
T 07584 992429
E michelle@allstarsactors.tv
W www.allstarsactors.tv

ALLSTARS CASTING　　　**T** 0151 707 2100
66 Hope Street, Liverpool L1 9BZ
T 07739 359737
E sylvie@allstarscasting.co.uk
W www.allstarscasting.co.uk

ALPHA ACTORS　　　**T** 020 7241 0077
Co-operative. CPMA Member
Studio B4, 3 Bradbury Street, London N16 8JN
F 020 7241 2410
E alpha@alphaactors.com
W www.alphaactors.com

ALRAUN, Anita
REPRESENTATION　　　**T** 01253 343784
PMA Member. Contact: By Post only (SAE)
1A Queensway, Blackpool, Lancashire FY4 2DG
T 07946 630986
E anita@cjagency.demon.co.uk

ALTARAS, Jonathan
ASSOCIATES LTD　　　**T** 020 7812 6461
PMA Member
53 Chandos Place, London WC2N 4HS
T 020 7812 6462
E info@jaalondon.com

ALW ASSOCIATES　　　**T** 020 7388 7018
Contact: Carol Paul
1 Grafton Chambers, Grafton Place, London NW1 1LN
E alw_carolpaul@talktalk.net

AM PERSONAL
MANAGEMENT LTD　　　**T** 020 7244 1159
Contact: Amanda McAllister. Film, Stage & Television
Technical Personnel only
4 Archel Road, London W14 9QH
E amanda@ampmgt.com
W www.ampmgt.co.uk

AMAZON ARTISTS
MANAGEMENT　　　**T/F** 020 8350 4909
27 Inderwick Road, Crouch End, London N8 9LB
T 07957 358767
E amazonartists@gmail.com

AMBER PERSONAL
MANAGEMENT LTD　　　**T** 0161 228 0236
No.2 Planetree House, 21-31 Oldham Street
Manchester M1 1JG
E info@amberltd.co.uk
W www.amberltd.co.uk

AMBER PERSONAL MANAGEMENT LTD   T 020 7734 7887
London
E info@amberltd.co.uk
W www.amberltd.co.uk

AMC MANAGEMENT   T 01438 714652
Contact: Anna McCorquodale, Tricia Howell
31 Parkside, Welwyn, Herts AL6 9DQ
E media@amcmanagement.co.uk
W www.amcmanagement.co.uk

AMCK MANAGEMENT LTD   T 020 7524 7788
125 Westbourne Studios, 242 Acklam Road
Notting Hill, London W10 5JJ
F 020 7524 7789
E info@amck.tv
W www.amck.tv

AMERICAN AGENCY THE   T 020 7485 8883
Contact: By Post/e-mail. 3 Agents represent 81
Performers. Commercials. Corporate. Film. Musical
Theatre. Stage. Television. Voice Overs (American)
14 Bonny Street, London NW1 9PG
E americanagency@btconnect.com
W www.americanagency.tv

AMG ARTISTS   T 07889 241283
Contact: Kyra Morrison. Consulting. Film Actors.
Directors. Producers. Artists & Writers
E amgfilms@icloud.com
W www.amgcom.eu

ANA (ACTORS NETWORK AGENCY)   T 020 7735 0999
Personal Manager. Co-operative. CPMA Member
55 Lambeth Walk, London SE11 6DX
E info@ana-actors.co.uk
W www.ana-actors.co.uk

ANDREA CASTING   T 01639 648672
Actors. Supporting Artists. Crew. Dancers. Musicians.
Presenters. Voice Overs
Office NA 059A, Centerprise
Dwr-y-Felin Road, Neath SA10 7RF
T 07774 660253
E info@andreacasting.com
W www.andreacasting.com

ANDREWS, Amanda AGENCY   T/F 01782 393889
30 Caverswall Road, Blythe Bridge
Stoke-on-Trent, Staffordshire ST11 9BG
T 07711 379770
E amanda@amandaandrewsagency.com
W www.amandaandrewsagency.com

ANGEL & FRANCIS LTD   T 020 7439 3086
PMA Member
1st Floor, 12 D'Arblay Street, London W1F 8DU
F 020 7437 1712
E agents@angelandfrancis.co.uk
W www.angelandfrancis.co.uk

ANTONY, Christopher ASSOCIATES   T 020 8994 9952
Building 3, 566 Chiswick High Road, London W4 5YA
E info@christopherantony.co.uk
W www.christopherantony.co.uk

APM ASSOCIATES   T 020 8953 7377
PMA Member. Contact: Linda French. By Post/e-mail.
Accepts Showreels/Voicereels. 3 Agents represent 80
Performers
Elstree Studios, Shenley Road
Borehamwood WD6 1JG
T 07918 166706
E apm@apmassociates.net
W www.apmassociates.net

ARAENA/COLLECTIVE   T/F 020 8428 0037
10 Bramshaw Gardens, South Oxhey
Herts WD19 6XP
E info@collectivedance.co.uk

A.R.C. ENTERTAINMENTS   T 01740 631292
Contact: By e-mail. 1 Agent represents 800 Active
Performers
10 Church Lane, Redmarshall
Stockton on Tees, Cleveland TS21 1EP
E arcentscouk@gmail.com
W www.arcentertainments.co.uk

ARCADIA ASSOCIATES   T/F 020 7937 0264
Contact: Hannah Hodgkinson
18B Vicarage Gate, London W8 4AA
E info.arcadia@btopenworld.com

ARENA ENTERTAINMENT (UK) LTD   T 0113 239 2222
Regent's Court, 39 Harrogate Road
Leeds LS7 3PD
F 0113 239 2016
E info@arenaentertainments.co.uk
W www.arenaentertainments.co.uk

ARENA PERSONAL MANAGEMENT LTD   T/F 020 7278 1661
Co-operative
Room 11, East Block, Panther House
38 Mount Pleasant, London WC1X 0AN
E arenapmltd15@gmail.com
W www.arenapmltd.co.uk

A R G (ARTISTS RIGHTS GROUP LTD)   T 020 7436 6400
PMA Member
4A Exmoor Street, London W10 6BD
F 020 7436 6700
E argall@argtalent.com
W www.argtalent.com

ARGYLE ASSOCIATES   T 07905 293319
Personal Manager. Contact: Richard Argyle. By Post
(SAE)
43 Clappers Lane, Fulking
West Sussex BN5 9ND
E argyle.associates@me.com

ARROWSMITH, Martin   T 020 3598 0636
Contact: By e-mail. Accepts Showreels. 1 Agent. Film.
Stage. Television
E office@martinarrowsmith.co.uk
W www.martinarrowsmith.net

ARTEMIS AGENCY   T 020 3422 3001
South Hill Park Mansion, Ringmead
Bracknell, Berkshire RG12 7PA
T 07477 715114
E agents@artemisagency.co.uk
W www.artemisagency.co.uk

ARTIST MANAGEMENT UK LTD   T 0151 523 6222
6 Gondover Avenue, Orrell Park
Liverpool L9 8AZ
T 07948 793552
E chris@artistmanagementuk.com
W www.artistmanagementuk.com

ARTISTS PARTNERSHIP THE   T 020 7439 1456
Personal Manager. PMA Member. Contact: By e-mail
only. Accepts Showreels. 10 Agents represent 300
Performers
101 Finsbury Pavement, London EC2A 1RS
F 020 7734 6530
E email@theartistspartnership.co.uk
W www.theartistspartnership.co.uk

SHEILA BURNETT
P H O T O G R A P H Y

Simon Pegg

Imelda Staunton

Patsy Palmer

Ewan McGregor

020 7289 3058 | 07974 731391
www.sheilaburnett-headshots.com
Student Rates

ARTLEN HOUSE ASSOCIATES   T 01268 724500
Contact: Helen Havis, Victoria Busby, Sharon Page
Artlen House, 1 Eric Road
Benfleet, Essex SS13 2HY
E agency@artlenhouseassociates.co.uk
W www.artlenhouseassociates.co.uk

ART MIX MANAGEMENT   T 00 61 0418961104
PO Box 1438 Broadbeach, Gold Coast
Queensland, Australia 4218
E studio@artmixmanagement.com
W www.artmixmanagement.com

ART-T MANAGEMENT   T 00 34 93 4106537
Contact: Chrys Hobbs
Av. Mare de Déu de Montserrat 39, Barcelona
Spain 08024
E arttmanagement@gmail.com .
W www.arttmanagement.com

ARUN, Jonathan   T 020 7840 0123
*Personal Manager. PMA Member. Contact: Jonathan
Arun, Amy O'Neill, Maria Girod-Roux (Commercials)*
37 Pearman Street, London SE1 7RB
E info@jonathanarun.com
W www.jonathanarun.com

ASQUITH & HORNER   T 020 8466 5580
*Joined with Elspeth Cochrane Personal Management.
Personal Manager. Contact: By Telephone/Post (SAE)/
e-mail*
The Studio, 14 College Road
Bromley, Kent BR1 3NS
T 07770 482144
E asquith@dircon.co.uk

ASSOCIATED ARTS   T 020 8856 4958
*Designers. Directors. Movement Directors. Lighting &
Sound Designers*
8 Shrewsbury Lane, London SE18 3JF
E karen@associated-arts.co.uk
W www.associated-arts.co.uk

ASTON MANAGEMENT   T 07742 059762
Aston Farm House, Remenham Lane
Henley on Thames, Oxon RG9 3DE
E agent@astonmgt.com
W www.astonmgt.com

**ASTRAL ACTORS
MANAGEMENT**   T 020 8728 2782
22 Parc Starling, Johnstown
Carmarthen SA31 3HX
T 01267 616162
E liz@astralactors.com
W www.astralactors.com

A TOUCH OF ELEGANZE   T 07901 822973
Contact: Ashley Fielder. Modelling & Promotions
75 Archer Way, Letchworth Garden City
Herfordshire SG6 4UL
E ashley@photo-eleganze.co.uk
W www.atouchofeleganze.co.uk

**AVALON MANAGEMENT
GROUP LTD**   T 020 7598 8000
4A Exmoor Street, London W10 6BD
F 020 7598 7300
E management@avalonuk.com
W www.avalonuk.com

**AVANTI PRODUCTIONS &
MANAGEMENT LTD**   T 07999 193311
Contact: Veronica Lazar
Units 2-8, 31 St Aubyns
Brighton BN3 2TH
E avantiproductions@live.co.uk
W www.avantiproductions.co.uk

AVENUE ARTISTES LTD   T 023 8076 0930
PO Box 1573, Southampton SO16 3XS
E info@avenueartistes.com
W www.avenueartistes.com

**AVIEL TALENT
MANAGEMENT INC**   T 001 514 288 8885
1117 St Catherine Street West, Suite 718, Montreal
Quebec, Canada H3B 1H9
F 001 514 288 0768
E avieltalentinc@gmail.com

**AXM (ACTORS EXCHANGE
MANAGEMENT)**   T 020 7837 3304
Co-operative. CPMA Member
Unit J302, J Block, Biscuit Factory
100 Clements Road, Southwark, London SE16 4DG
F 020 7837 7215
E info@axmgt.com
W www.axmgt.com

B A M ASSOCIATES   T 01934 852942
Benets, Dolberrow
Churchill, Bristol BS25 5NT .
E casting@ebam.tv
W www.ebam.tv

BANANAFISH MANAGEMENT   T 0151 708 5509
The Business Hub, 40 Devonshire Road
Wirral CH43 1TW
T 07974 206622
E info@bananafish.co.uk
W www.bananafish.co.uk

**BARKER, Gavin
ASSOCIATES LTD**   T 020 7499 4777
PMA Member. Contact: Gavin Barker, Michelle Burke
2D Wimpole Street, London W1G 0EB
F 020 7499 3777
E marvin@gavinbarkerassociates.co.uk
W www.gavinbarkerassociates.co.uk

BARR, Becca MANAGEMENT   T 020 3137 2980
97 Mortimer Street, London W1W 7SU
E info@beccabarrmanagement.com
W www.beccabarrmanagement.co.uk

**BARRETT, Becky
MANAGEMENT**   T 020 8840 7828
Specialising in Musical Theatre & Dance
11 Central Chambers, The Broadway
London W5 2NR
E info@beckybarrettmanagement.co.uk
W www.beckybarrettmanagement.co.uk

BBA MANAGEMENT   T 020 3077 1400
PMA Member
1 Heathcock Court, 415 The Strand
London WC2R 0NT
F 020 7240 0503
E castings@bba.management
W www.bba.management

**BBA MANAGEMENT
MANCHESTER**   T 0161 826 9198
PMA Member
Suite 607, Piccadilly House
49 Piccadilly, Manchester M1 2AP
F 0161 228 3930
E manchester@bba.management
W www.bba.management

BDISCOVERED   T 020 3318 0962
Contact: Tina Hartery
7 Rhodfar Mor, Rhoose CF62 3LE
E casting@bdiscovered.net
W www.bdiscovered.net

icon actors mangement
tel: 0161 273 3344   fax: 0161 273 4567
tanzaro house, ardwick green north, manchester. m12 6fz
info@iconactors.net   www.iconactors.net

BEDFORD, Eamonn AGENCY   T 020 7734 9632
PMA Member
2nd Floor, 10 Warwick Street, London W1B 5LZ
E info@eamonnbedford.com
W www.eamonnbedford.agency

BELFIELD & WARD   T 020 3416 5290
PMA Member
26-28 Neal Street, Covent Garden
London WC2H 9QQ
E office@belfieldandward.co.uk
W www.belfieldandward.com

**BELFRAGE, Julian
ASSOCIATES**   T 020 7287 8544
PMA Member
3rd Floor, 9 Argyll Street, London W1F 7TG
F 020 7287 8832
E email@julianbelfrage.co.uk

BELL, Olivia MANAGEMENT   T 020 7439 3270
*PMA Member. Contact: By Post/e-mail. 6 Agents
represent 100 Performers. Commercials. Film. Musical
Theatre. Stage. Television*
193 Wardour Street, London W1F 8ZF
E info@olivia-bell.co.uk
W www.olivia-bell.co.uk

BENJAMIN MANAGEMENT LTD   T 020 7866 5412
LG06 Garden Studios
71-75 Shelton Street
Covent Garden
London WC2H 9JQ
T 07921 212360
E agent@benjaminmanagement.co.uk

BETTS, Jorg ASSOCIATES   T 020 3405 4546
PMA Member
2 John Street, London WC1N 2ES
E agents@jorgbetts.com

**BIG TIME
ENTERTAINMENT LTD**   T 020 7127 9119
196 High Road, London N22 8HH
F 020 3397 4249
E info@bigtimeentertainment.co.uk
W www.bigtimeentertainment.co.uk

**BILLBOARD PERSONAL
MANAGEMENT**   T 020 7735 9956
Twitter: @billboardpm
45 Lothrop Street, London W10 4JB
T 07791 970773
E billboardpm@btconnect.com
W www.billboardpm.com

Sarah Wyn Jones

Trevor Bishop

AJ Lewis

teresa walton **headshot** photography
07770 855807
photos@teresawalton.com   www.teresawaltonphotos.com

BILLY MARSH DRAMA LTD
See MARSH, Billy DRAMA LTD

BINGHAM FRENCH ASOCIATES LTD
Contact: David Bingham
E d.binghamfrench@gmail.com

BIRD AGENCY   **T** 07889 723995
Personal Performance Manager
Bird College, Alma Road, Sidcup, Kent DA14 4ED
T 020 8269 6862
E birdagency@birdcollege.co.uk
W www.birdcollege.co.uk

BLACKBURN MANAGEMENT   **T** 020 7292 7555
Argyll House, All Saints Passage
London SW18 1EP
E presenters@blackburnmanagement.co.uk
W www.blackburnmanagement.co.uk

**BLAIR, Michelle
MANAGEMENT**   **T** 020 3664 9897
Personal Manager
E info@michelleblairmanagement.co.uk
W www.michelleblairmanagement.co.uk

BLOND, Rebecca ASSOCIATES   **T** 020 7351 4100
PMA Member
69A Kings Road, London SW3 4NX
F 020 7351 4600
E info@rebeccablond.com
W www.rebeccablond.com

**BLOOMFIELDS WELCH
MANAGEMENT**   **T** 020 7866 8181
PMA Member. Twitter: @bwmgt
Garden Studios, 71-75 Shelton Street
London WC2H 9JQ
E info@bloomfieldswelch.com
W www.bloomfieldswelch.com

BLUE STAR ASSOCIATES   **T** 020 7836 6220
Contact: Barrie Stacey, Keith Hopkins
7-8 Shaldon Mansions, 132 Charing Cross Road
London WC2H 0LA
E bluestar.london.2000@gmail.com

BMA ARTISTS   **T** 01442 878878
*Personal Manager. Contact: Alex Haddad. By e-mail.
1200 Performers. Children. Commercials. Corporate.
Dancers. Film. Modelling. Presenters. Singers. Television.
Walk-on & Supporting Artists*
346 High Street, Marlow House
Berkhamsted, Hertfordshire HP4 1HT
F 01442 879879
E info@bmaartists.com
W www.bmaartists.com

BODENS AGENCY   **T** 020 8447 0909
*Personal Manager. Contact: Adam Boden, Sophie
Boden, Katie McCutcheon. By Post/e-mail/Telephone.
3 Agents represent 150 Performers. Children.
Commercials. Film. Television. Walk-on & Supporting
Artists*
99 East Barnet Road, New Barnet, Herts EN4 8RF
T 07545 696888
E info@bodens.co.uk
W www.bodens.co.uk/clients

BODY LONDON   **T** 020 7371 5858
21 Heathmans Road, London SW6 4TJ
E contact@bodylondon.com
W www.bodylondon.com

BODYWORK AGENCY   **T** 01223 314461
25-29 Glisson Road, Cambridge CB1 2HA
T 07792 851972
E agency@bodyworkds.co.uk

BOHEMIA GROUP   **T** 001 323 462 5800
Based in Hollywood with Offices in London and NYC
1680 N. Vine Street, Suite 518
Los Angeles, California 90028
E management@bohemiaent.com
W www.bohemiaent.com

BOHEMIA GROUP   **T** 020 3514 0888
Based in Hollywood with Offices in London & NYC
T 07400 347591

BOSS CASTING   **T** 0161 237 0100
Fourways House, 57 Hilton Street, Manchester M1 2EJ
F 0161 236 1237
E cath@bosscasting.co.uk
W www.bosscasting.co.uk

**BOSS
CREATIVE MANAGEMENT**   **T** 0161 237 0100
PMA Member
Fourways House, 57 Hilton Street, Manchester M1 2EJ
F 0161 236 1237
E info@bossmodels.co.uk
W www.bossmodelmanagement.co.uk

BOSS LIFESTYLE   **T** 0161 237 0100
Fourways House, 57 Hilton Street, Manchester M1 2EJ
F 0161 236 1237
E info@bossmodels.co.uk
W www.bossmodelmanagement.co.uk

**BOSS
MODEL MANAGEMENT**   **T** 0161 237 0100
Fourways House, 57 Hilton Street, Manchester M1 2EJ
F 0161 236 1237
E info@bossmodels.co.uk
W www.bossmodelmanagement.co.uk

BOSS TALENT MANAGEMENT   **T** 020 7836 3111
PMA Member
3rd Floor, 47 Bedford Street, London WC2E 9HA
E enquiries@bosscreativeentertainment.com
W www.bosscreativeentertainment.com

**BOX ARTIST MANAGEMENT LTD
- BAM**   **T** 07732 704431
*Choreographers. Musical Theatre. Commercial Dancers.
Corporate Entertainment*
The Attic, The Old Finsbury Town Hall
Rosebery Avenue, London EC1R 4RP
E hello@boxartistmanagement.com
W www.boxartistmanagement.com

BOYCE, Sandra MANAGEMENT   **T** 020 7923 0606
PMA Member
125 Dynevor Road, London N16 0DA
F 020 7241 2313
E info@sandraboyce.com
W www.sandraboyce.com

**BRAIDMAN, Michelle
ASSOCIATES LTD**   **T** 020 7237 3523
PMA Member
2 Futura House, 169 Grange Road, London SE1 3BN
E info@braidman.com
W www.braidman.com

**BRAITHWAITE'S
THEATRICAL AGENCY**   **T** 020 8954 5638
8 Brookshill Avenue, Harrow Weald
Middlesex HA3 6RZ

**BREAK A LEG
MANAGEMENT LTD**   **T/F** 020 7250 0662
The City College, University House, Room 33
55 East Road, London N1 6AH
E agency@breakalegman.com
W www.breakalegman.com

BRIDGES:
THE ACTORS' AGENCY　T 0131 554 3073
CPMA Member
Studio S12, Out of the Blue Drill Hall
36 Dalmeny Street, Edinburgh EH6 8RG
E admin@bridgesactorsagency.com
W www.bridgesactorsagency.com

BROAD ACTING
MANAGEMENT LTD　T 0113 246 9632
67 St Pauls Street, Leeds LS1 2TE
E katy@broadactingmanagement.co.uk
W www.broadactingmanagement.co.uk

BROAD ACTING
MANAGEMENT LTD　T 0161 834 4716
12 Lever Street, Piccadilly, Manchester M1 1LN
E info@broadactingmanagement.co.uk
W www.broadactingmanagement.co.uk

BROAD ACTING
MANAGEMENT LTD　T 020 7544 1012
Contact: Katy Edwards
223 Regent Street, London W1B 2QD
E info@broadactingmanagement.co.uk
W www.broadactingmanagement.co.uk

BROADCASTING AGENCY LTD　T 020 3131 0128
86-90 Paul Street, London EC2A 4NE
T 07729 309000
E info@broadcastingagency.co.uk
W www.broadcastingagency.co.uk

BROOD　T 020 3489 4949
PMA Member. Contact: By e-mail. Prospective Client
Applications to broodapplication@aol.com
49 Greek Street, London W1D 4EG
E broodmanagement@aol.com
W www.broodmanagement.com

BROOK, Jeremy LTD　T 020 7434 0398
Contact: James Foster
G33 Waterfront Studios
1 Dock Road, London E16 1AG
E info@jeremybrookltd.co.uk
W www.jeremybrookltd.co.uk

BROOK, Valerie AGENCY　T 0161 486 1631
10 Sandringham Road, Cheadle Hulme
Cheshire SK8 5NH
T 07973 434953
E colinbrook@freenetname.co.uk

BROWN, SIMCOCKS &
ANDREWS　T 020 7953 7484
PMA Member. Contact: Carrie Simcocks, Kelly Andrews
504 The Chandlery, 50 Westminster Bridge Road
London SE1 7QY
F 020 7953 7494
E info@bsaagency.co.uk
W www.brownsimcocksandandrews.co.uk

BRUNO KELLY LTD　T 020 7183 7331
3rd Floor, 207 Regent Street, London W1B 3HH
F 020 7183 7332
E info@brunokelly.com
W www.brunokelly.com

BRUNSKILL MANAGEMENT LTD　T 01768 881430
Personal Manager. Contact: Aude Powell. By Post only.
Accepts Showreels/Voicereels. Commercials. Corporate.
Film. Musical Theatre. Radio. Stage. Television. Voice
Overs
The Courtyard, Edenhall
Penrith, Cumbria CA11 8ST
E accounts@brunskill.com

BSA LTD
See HARRISON, Penny BSA LTD

The Trade Association
for Talent & Booking Agencies
Promoting good practice
by its Member Agents
throughout the industry

Telephone: +44 (0)20 7834 0515
Email: association@agents-uk.com

54 Keyes House, Dolphin Square
London SW1V 3NA

www.agents-uk.com

BSA MANAGEMENT T 0845 0035301
Personal Manager. Actors & Presenters. Commercials.
Film. Television
145-157 St John Street, London EC1V 4PY
E agent@bsamanagement.co.uk
W www.bsamanagement.co.uk

BURNETT CROWTHER LTD T 020 7437 8008
PMA Member. Contact: Barry Burnett, Lizanne Crowther
3 Clifford Street, London W1S 2LF
E associates@bcltd.org
W www.bcltd.org

BURNINGHAM ASSOCIATES T 020 8892 6128
Personal Management
4 Victoria Road, Twickenham
Middlesex TW1 3HW
T 07807 176287
E info@burnassoc.org
W www.burnassoc.org

BUTTERCUP AGENCY T 0843 2899063
Wyndrums, The Village
Ewhurst, Surrey GU6 7PB
E info@buttercupagency.co.uk
W www.buttercupagency.co.uk

BWH AGENCY LTD THE T 020 7734 0657
PMA Member
5th Floor, 35 Soho Square
London W1D 3QX
F 020 7734 1278
E info@thebwhagency.co.uk
W www.thebwhagency.co.uk

BYRAM, Paul ASSOCIATES T 020 3137 3385
PMA Member
Suite B0079, The Long Lodge, 265-269 Kingston Road
Wimbledon, London SW19 3FW
E admin@paulbyram.com
W www.paulbyram.com

BYRON'S MANAGEMENT T 020 7242 8096
PMA Member. Contact: By Post/e-mail. Accepts
Showreels. Commercials. Film. Musical Theatre. Stage.
Television
41 Maiden Lane, London WC2E 7LJ
E office@byronsmanagement.co.uk
W www.byronsmanagement.co.uk

C.A. ARTISTES MANAGEMENT T 020 8618 2064
26-28 Hammersmith Grove
London W6 7BA
E casting@caartistes.com
W www.caartistes.com

CAIRNS AGENCY THE T 0141 237 8580
Contact: Robert Brown
63 Bath Street, Glasgow G2 2SZ
E office@thecairns-agency.com
W www.thecairns-agency.com

CAPITAL VOICES T 01372 466228
Contact: Anne Skates. Film. Session Singers. Stage.
Studio. Television
PO Box 364, Esher
Surrey KT10 9XZ
F 01372 466229
E annie@capitalvoices.com
W www.capitalvoices.com

CAREY, Roger ASSOCIATES T 01932 582890
Personal Manager. PMA Member
Suite 909, The Old House, Shepperton Film Studios
Studios Road, Shepperton, Middlesex TW17 0QD
F 01932 569602
E info@rogercareyassociates.com
W www.rogercareyassociates.com

CAREY DODD ASSOCIATES T 020 7692 1877
PMA Member
78 York Street, London W1H 1DP
T 020 7504 1087
E agents@careydoddassociates.com
W www.careydoddassociates.com

CARNEY, Jessica ASSOCIATES T 020 7434 4143
Personal Manager. PMA Member. Prospective Client
Applications to representation@jcarneyassociates.co.uk
with Spotlight Link
4th Floor, 23 Golden Square, London W1F 9JP
E info@jcarneyassociates.co.uk
W www.jessicacarneyassociates.co.uk

CARR, Norrie AGENCY T 020 7253 1771
Holborn Studios, 49 Eagle Wharf Road
London N1 7ED
F 020 7253 1772
E info@norriecarr.com
W www.norriecarr.com

CASAROTTO MARSH LTD T 020 7287 4450
Film Technicians
Waverley House, 7-12 Noel Street
London W1F 8GQ
F 020 7287 9128
E info@casarotto.co.uk
W www.casarotto.co.uk

CASCADE ARTISTS LTD T 020 7437 3175
Contact: By e-mail (No Large File Attachments). Accepts
Links to Showreels & Casting Profiles. 2 Agents represent
25 Performers. Film. Stage. Television. Commercials.
Corporate. Voice Over. TIE. European Connections
Studio Soho, 2A Royalty Mews, (entrance by Quo Vadis)
22-25 Dean Street, London W1D 3AR
T 07866 739510
E info@cascadeartists.com
W www.cascadeartists.com

CASTAWAY ACTORS
AGENCY T 00 353 1 6719264
30-31 Wicklow Street, Dublin 2
Ireland T 00 353 1 6719059
E office@castawayactors.com
W www.castawayactors.com

CASTCALL T 01582 456213
Casting & Consultancy Service
106 Wilsden Avenue, Luton LU1 5HR
E casting@castcall.co.uk
W www.castcall.co.uk

C B A INTERNATIONAL T 00 33 2 32671981
Contact: Cindy Brace
c/o C.M.S. Experts Associés, 149 Boulevard
Malesherbes
75017 Paris, France
E c_b_a@club-internet.fr
W www.cindy-brace.com

CBL MANAGEMENT T 01273 321245
Personal Manager. PMA Member. Television. Film.
Theatre
20 Hollingbury Rise, Brighton
East Sussex BN1 7HJ
T 07956 890307
E enquiries@cblmanagement.co.uk
W www.cblmanagement.co.uk

C C A MANAGEMENT T 020 7630 6303
Personal Manager. PMA Member. Contact: By Post.
Actors. Technicians
Garden Level, 32 Charlwood Street, London SW1V 2DY
E actors@ccamanagement.co.uk
W www.ccamanagementinfo.com

AM LONDON

Simon Pegg   Julia Sawalha   Kelly-Anne Lyons   Mathew Horne

Amanda Piery   Peter Serafinowicz   Catherine Tate   Gavin Stenhouse

www.am-london.com

CCM　　　　　　　　　　　T 020 7183 3425
CPMA Member
Unit 6, 2nd Floor, Aztec Row
Berners Road, London N1 0PW
E casting@ccmactors.com
W www.ccmactors.co.uk

CDA　　　　　　　　　　　T 020 7937 2749
Personal Manager. PMA Member. Contact: By Post/
e-mail. Accepts Showreels. Film. Stage. Television
167-169 Kensington High Street, London W8 6SH
F 020 7937 5120
E cda@cdalondon.com
W www.cdalondon.com

CELEBRITY GROUP THE　　T 0871 2501234
12 Nottingham Place, London W1M 3FA
E info@celebrity.co.uk
W www.celebrity.co.uk

CENTER STAGE AGENCY　　T 00 353 1 4533599
Personal Manager. Contact: By e-mail. Accepts
Showreels. Commercials. Film. Presenters. Stage.
Television. Voice Overs
7 Rutledge Terrace, South Circular Road
Dublin 8, Ireland
E geraldinecenterstage@eircom.net
W www.centerstageagency.com

CENTRAL LINE THE　　　　T 0115 941 2937
Personal Manager. Co-operative. CPMA Member.
Contact: By e-mail/Post
11 East Circus Street, Nottingham NG1 5AF
E centralline@btconnect.com
W www.thecentralline.co.uk

CHAMBERS MANAGEMENT　　T 020 7796 3588
Comedians. Comic Actors
39-41 Parker Street, London WC2B 5PQ
F 020 7831 8598
E info@chambersmgt.com
W www.chambersmgt.com

CHAMPION TALENT　　　　T 020 8761 5395
10 Birkbeck Place, London SE21 8JU
E info@championtalent.co.uk
W www.championtalent.co.uk

CHARKHAM, Esta
ASSOCIATES　　　　　　　T 020 8741 2843
16 British Grove, Chiswick, London W4 2NL
F 020 8746 3219
E office@charkham.net
W www.charkham.net

CHARLESWORTH, Peter &
ASSOCIATES　　　　　　　T 020 7792 4600
67 Holland Park Mews, London W11 3SS
F 020 7792 1893
E info@petercharlesworth.co.uk

CHASE PERSONAL
MANAGEMENT　　　　　　T 07775 683955
Contact: Sue Sammon
2nd Floor, 3 Kew, Richmond, London TW9 2NQ
E sue@chasemanagement.co.uk
W www.chasepersonalmanagement.co.uk

CHATTO & LINNIT LTD　　T 020 7349 7222
Worlds End Studios, 132-134 Lots Road
London SW10 0RJ
E info@chattolinnit.com

CHP ARTIST MANAGEMENT　　T 01844 345630
Meadowcroft Barn, Crowbrook Road, Askett
Princes Risborough, Buckinghamshire HP27 9LS
T 07976 560580
E chp.artist.management@gmail.com
W www.chproductions.org.uk

CHRYSTEL ARTS AGENCY　　T 01494 773336
6 Eunice Grove, Chesham
Bucks HP5 1RL
T 07799 605489
E chrystelarts@waitrose.com

CIEKABAILEY ASSOCIATES　　T 0161 484 5423
7 Ridge Road, Marple
Cheshire SK6 7HL
E enquiries@ciekabailey.com
W www.ciekabailey.com

CINEL GABRAN
MANAGEMENT　　　　　　T 029 2066 6600
Personal Manager. Contact: By Post. Accepts Showreels.
40 Performers. Commercials. Corporate. Film. Musical
Theatre. Presenters. Radio. Stage. Television. Voice
Overs
Ty Cefn, 14-16 Rectory Road
Cardiff CF5 1QL
E mail@cinelgabran.co.uk
W www.cinelgabran.co.uk

CINEL GABRAN
MANAGEMENT　　　　　　T 01947 605376
Personal Manager. Contact: By Post. Accepts Showreels.
40 Performers. Commercials. Corporate. Film. Musical
Theatre. Presenters. Radio. Stage. Television. Voice
Overs
Adventure House, Newholm
Whitby, North Yorkshire YO21 3QL
E mail@cinelgabran.co.uk
W www.cinelgabran.co.uk

CINNAMON CASTING　　　T 07477 355955
The Black & White Building, 74 Rivington Street
London EC2A 3AY
E pa@cinnamoncasting.com
W www.cinnamoncasting.com

CIRCUIT PERSONAL
MANAGEMENT LTD　　　　T 0161 425 0763
Co-operative. Contact: By Post/e-mail. Accepts
Showreels. Commercials. Corporate. Film. Stage.
Television
Suite 31, Progress Centre
Ardwick Green, Manchester M12 6HS
E mail@circuitpm.co.uk
W www.circuitpm.co.uk

CITY ACTORS
MANAGEMENT　　　　　　T 020 7793 9888
CPMA Member. Contact: Nikki Everson. By Post/e-mail.
Accepts Showreels
Oval House, 52-54 Kennington Oval
London SE11 5SW
E info@cityactors.co.uk
W www.cityactors.co.uk

CLASS - CARLINE LUNDON
ASSOCIATES　　　　　　　T 07597 378995
25 Falkner Square
Liverpool L8 7NZ
E clundon@googlemail.com

CLAYPOLE MANAGEMENT　　T 0845 6501777
PO Box 123, DL3 7WA
E info@claypolemanagement.co.uk
W www.claypolemanagement.co.uk

CLIC AGENCY　　　　　　T 01248 354420
7 Ffordd Seion, Bangor
Gwynedd LL57 1BS
E clic@btinternet.com
W www.clicagency.co.uk

COCHRANE, Elspeth
PERSONAL MANAGEMENT
See ASQUITH & HORNER

COHEN MAYER, Charlie
ASSOCIATES   **T** 07850 077825
Personal Manager & Talent Agency
121 Brecknock Road, Camden
London N19 5AE
E houseofsaintjude@gmail.com

COLE KITCHENN PERSONAL
MANAGEMENT LTD   **T** 020 7427 5681
PMA Member
ROAR House, 46 Charlotte Street
London W1T 2GS
E info@colekitchenn.com
W www.colekitchenn.com

COLLINS, Shane ASSOCIATES   **T** 020 7253 1010
PMA Member
Suite 112, Davina House
137-149 Goswell Road, London EC1V 7ET
F 0870 4601983
E info@shanecollins.co.uk
W www.shanecollins.co.uk

COMMERCIAL AGENCY THE
See TCA (THE COMMERCIAL AGENCY)

COMMERCIALS@BBA   **T** 020 3077 1400
Commercials. Corporate
1 Heathcock Court, 415 The Strand
London WC2R 0NT
F 020 7240 0503
E castings@bba.management
W www.bba.management

CONTI, Italia AGENCY LTD   **T** 020 7608 7500
PMA Member. Contact: By Post/Telephone
Italia Conti House, 23 Goswell Road
London EC1M 7AJ
F 020 7253 1430
E agency@italiaconti.co.uk

CONTROL LONDON LTD   **T** 0330 133 0422
Personal Manager. Contact: Kane D. Ricca. By e-mail.
Accepts Showreels/Voicereels. 3 Agents represent 20
Performers. Corporate. Dancers. Film. Television
E hello@control-london.com
W www.control-london.com

CONWAY VAN GELDER
GRANT LTD   **T** 020 7287 0077
Personal Manager. PMA Member
3rd Floor, 8-12 Broadwick Street
London W1F 8HW
F 020 7287 1940
E info@conwayvg.co.uk

COOKE, Howard
ASSOCIATES   **T** 020 7591 0144
PMA Member. Contact: Howard Cooke. By Post. 2
Agents represent 50 Performers. Commercials. Film.
Stage. Television
19 Coulson Street, Chelsea, London SW3 3NA
F 020 7591 0155
E mail@hca1.co.uk
W www.hca1.co.uk

COOPER, Tommy
MAGICAL AGENCY   **T** 07860 290437
Comedy. Magicians
1 Chaddersley Wood Road, Poole
Dorset BH14 7PN
E info@clivestjames.co.uk
W www.clivestjames.co.uk

COOPER & CHAND
TALENT MANAGEMENT   **T** 020 3651 9405
69 Teignmouth Road, London NW2 4EA
T 07723 324828
E agents@cooperandchand.com
W www.cooperandchand.com

CORE MGMT   **T** 020 3691 0773
PMA Member. Contact: Sara Sehdev
1st Floor, Artist House, 35 Little Russell Street
London WC1A 2HH
E info@coremgmt.co.uk
W www.coremgmt.co.uk

CORNER, Clive ASSOCIATES   **T** 01305 860267
Contact: Duncan Stratton. By e-mail. Accepts Showreels
by e-mail only. 2 Agents represent 40 Performers.
Commercials. Film. Musical Theatre. Stage. Television
'The Belenes', 60 Wakeham, Portland DT5 1HN
E cornerassociates@aol.com

CORNISH, Caroline
MANAGEMENT LTD   **T** 020 8743 7337
Technicians only
12 Shinfield Street, London W12 0HN
T 07725 555711
E carolinecornish@me.com
W www.carolinecornish.co.uk

COULSON, Lou
ASSOCIATES LTD   **T** 020 7734 9633
PMA Member
1st Floor, 37 Berwick Street, London W1F 8RS
F 020 7439 7569
E info@loucoulson.co.uk

COULTER MANAGEMENT
AGENCY LTD   **T** 0141 204 4058
PMA Member. Contact: Anne Coulter, Julie Hamilton
Suite 418 The Pentagon Centre, Washington Street
Glasgow G3 8AZ
E info@coultermanagement.com
W www.coultermanagement.com

CPA MANAGEMENT   **T** 01708 766444
The Studios, 219B North Street
Romford, Essex RM1 4QA
E agency@cpastudios.co.uk
W www.cpastudios.co.uk

CRAWFORDS   **T** 020 8947 9999
PO Box 56662, London W13 3BH
E cr@wfords.com
W www.crawfords.tv

CREATIVE ARTISTS
MANAGEMENT (CAM)   **T** 020 7292 0600
PMA Member. Contact: By e-mail only
55-59 Shaftesbury Avenue, London W1D 6LD
E reception@cam.co.uk
W www.cam.co.uk

CREATIVE BLAST AGENCY   **T** 020 8123 6386
2nd Floor Viking House, Daneholes Roundabout
Stanford Road, Grays, Essex RM16 2XE
T 01375 386247
E info@cbagency.co.uk
W www.cbagency.co.uk

CREATIVE DIFFERENCES   **T** 07804 555844
Contact: Hayley J. Bacon (Agency Director).
Twitter: @CreativeDiffs
16 Carnforth Gardens, Elm Park
Hornchurch, Essex RM12 5DJ
T 01708 456090
E creativedifferences@outlook.com
W www.creativedifferences.wix.com/agent

CREATIVE KIDZ & ADULTZ   T 07980 144802
Contact: Charlie & Dani
235 Foxglove House, Fulham
London SW6 5PQ
T 020 7381 3684
E agency@creativekidzandco.co.uk
W www.creativekidzandco.co.uk

**CREATIVE MEDIA
MANAGEMENT**   T 020 8584 5363
*PMA Member. No Actors. Film, Television & Stage
Technical Personnel only*
Ealing Studios, Ealing Green
London W5 5EP
E enquiries@creativemediamanagement.com
W www.creativemediamanagement.com

CRESCENT MANAGEMENT   T 020 8987 0191
Co-operative. CPMA Member
Southbank House, Black Prince Road
London SE1 7SJ
E mail@crescentmanagement.co.uk
W www.crescentmanagement.co.uk

**CRUICKSHANK CAZENOVE
LTD**   T 020 7735 2933
*PMA Member. Contact: Harriet Cruickshank. By Post. 2
Agents. Choreographers, Designers & Directors only*
97 Old South Lambeth Road, London SW8 1XU
E mail@ccagents.co.uk

CS MANAGEMENT   T 01708 708515
35 Chase Cross Road, Romford
Essex RM5 3PJ
T 07818 050424
E linda@csmanagementuk.com
W www.csmanagementuk.com

C.S.A.   T 020 7420 9351
Contact: By Post/e-mail. Commercials
3rd Floor, Joel House
17-21 Garrick Street, London WC2E 9BL
F 0843 2905796
E csa@shepherdmanagement.co.uk

CURTIS BROWN   T 020 7393 4400
PMA Member
Haymarket House, 28-29 Haymarket
London SW1Y 4SP
E reception@curtisbrown.co.uk
W www.curtisbrown.co.uk

**CUSACK, Alex
MANAGEMENT**   T 00 353 8 7960 3138
21 Wicklow Street, Dublin 2
E acusackmanagement@gmail.com
W www.alexcusackmanagement.com

CV ACTOR MANAGEMENT   T 07989 811999
49 Percy Road, Wrexham LL13 7EB
E cvactormanagement@yahoo.co.uk
W www.cvactormanagement.co.uk

DAA MANAGEMENT   T 020 7255 6123
PMA Member
Welbeck House, 66-67 Wells Street
London W1T 3PY
F 020 7255 6128
E info@daamanagement.co.uk
W www.daamanagement.co.uk

**DALE HAMMOND
ASSOCIATES (DHA)**   T 07581 034153
60 Wilbury Way, Hitchin
Hertfordshire SG4 0TA
T 07890 260049
E info@dalehammondassociates.com
W www.dalehammondassociates.com

DALY, David ASSOCIATES   T 020 7384 1036
Contact: David Daly, Rosalind Barch
586A King's Road, London SW6 2DX
F 020 7610 9512
E agent@daviddaly.co.uk
W www.daviddaly.co.uk

**DALY, David ASSOCIATES
(MANCHESTER)**   T 01565 631999
Contact: Mary Ramsay
16 King Street, Knutsford, Cheshire WA16 6DL
F 01565 755334
E north@daviddaly.co.uk
W www.daviddaly.co.uk

DALZELL & BERESFORD LTD   T 020 7336 0351
Paddock Suite, The Courtyard
55 Charterhouse Street, London EC1M 6HA
E mail@dbltd.co.uk
W www.dalzellandberesford.com

DANCERS   T 020 7637 1487
Trading as FEATURES AGENCY
1 Charlotte Street, London W1T 1RD
E info@features.co.uk
W www.features.co.uk

DANCERS INC   T 020 7205 2316
Twitter: @dancersincworld
INC Artists Ltd, 64 Great Eastern Street
London EC2A 3QR
E miranda@international-collective.com
W www.dancersincworld.com

**DAS IMPERIUM
TALENT AGENCY**   T 00 49 151 61957519
Contact: Georg Georgi
Torstrasse 129, Berlin 10119, Germany
T 00 49 30 28879520
E georg@dasimperium.com
W www.dasimperium.com

**DAVID ARTISTES MANAGEMENT
AGENCY LTD THE**   T 020 8618 2064
26-28 Hammersmith Grove, London W6 7BA
E casting@davidagency.co.uk
W www.davidagency.co.uk

**DAVIS, Chris
MANAGEMENT LTD**   T 020 7240 2116
PMA Member
4th Floor, 80-81 St Martin's Lane
London WC2N 4AA
E smills@cdm-ltd.com
W www.cdm-ltd.com

**DAVIS, Chris
MANAGEMENT LTD**   T 01584 819005
PMA Member
Tenbury House, 36 Teme Street
Tenbury Wells, Worcestershire WR15 8AA
F 01584 819076
E smills@cdm-ltd.com
W www.cdm-ltd.com

**DAVIS, Lena, BISHOP,
John ASSOCIATES**   T 01604 891487
Personal Manager. Contact: By Post. 2 Agents
Cotton's Farmhouse, Whiston Road
Cogenhoe, Northants NN7 1NL
E admin@cottonsfarmhouse.org

**DAVIS GORDON
MANAGEMENT**   T 07989 306252
11 Eastern Avenue, Pinner
London HA5 1NU
E miriam@davisgordon.com
W www.davisgordon.com

DAVID MACKAY PHOTOGRAPHY
THE ART OF THE HEADSHOT

New York's most famous headshot photographer Peter Hurley hand picked David as an Associate. Find out why!

London based|Headshots Portfolios|Retouching

07545 657649

www.davidmackay.photography   david@davidmackay.photography

DENMARK STREET MANAGEMENT   T 020 7700 5200
Co-operative. CPMA Member. Applications via Website
Unit 77B Eurolink Office Building, 49 Effra Road
London SW2 1BZ
E mail@denmarkstreet.net
W www.denmarkstreet.net

DEREK'S HANDS AGENCY   T 020 8618 2064
Hand & Foot Modelling
26-28 Hammersmith Grove, London W6 7BA
E casting@derekshands.com
W www.derekshands.com

DEVINE ARTIST MANAGEMENT   T 0161 726 5726
Tempus Building, 9 Mirabel Street
Manchester M3 1NP
E manchester@devinemanagement.co.uk
W www.devinemanagement.co.uk

de WOLFE, Felix   T 020 7242 5066
PMA Member. Contact: By e-mail
2nd Floor, 20 Old Compton Street, London W1D 4TW
F 020 7242 8119
E info@felixdewolfe.com
W www.felixdewolfe.com

DHM LTD (DICK HORSEY MANAGEMENT)   T 01923 710614
Personal Manager. Contact: By Post/e-mail/Telephone.
Accepts Showreels/Voicereels. 2 Agents represent 40
Performers. Corporate. Musical Theatre. Stage. Television
Suite 1, Cottingham House, Chorleywood Road
Rickmansworth, Herts WD3 4EP
T 07850 112211
E roger@dhmlimited.co.uk
W www.dhmlimited.co.uk

DIAMOND MANAGEMENT   T 020 7631 0400
PMA Member
31 Percy Street
London W1T 2DD
F 020 7631 0500
E agents@diman.co.uk
W www.diamondmanagement.co.uk

DIESTENFELD, Lily   T 07957 968214
For playing ages 55+. No Unsolicited Post/e-mails/Calls
E lilydl@talk21.com

DIRECT PERSONAL MANAGEMENT   T/F 020 8694 1788
Co-operative. CPMA Member. Contact: By Post/e-mail.
Commercials. Corporate. Film. Stage. Television.
Voice Overs
St John's House, 16 St John's Vale
London SE8 4EN
E office@directpm.co.uk
W www.directpm.co.uk

DIRECT PERSONAL MANAGEMENT   T/F 0113 266 4036
Co-operative. CPMA Member. Contact: By Post/e-mail.
Film. Stage. Television. Commercials. Corporate.
Voice Overs
Space 7, Duke Studios
3 Sheaf Street. Leeds LS10 1HD
E office@directpm.co.uk
W www.directpm.co.uk

DOE, John MANAGEMENT   T 020 7871 2969 (London)
T 0161 241 7786 (Manchester)
E casting@johndoemgt.com
W www.johndoemgt.com

DOUBLE ACT T 020 8381 0151
PO Box 25574, London NW7 3GB
E info@double-act.co.uk
W www.double-act.co.uk

**DOWNES PRESENTERS
AGENCY** T 07973 601332
E downes@presentersagency.com
W www.presentersagency.com

DQ MANAGEMENT T 01273 721221
27 Ravenswood Park, Northwood, Middlesex HA6 3PR
T 07713 984633
E dq.management1@gmail.com
W www.dqmanagement.com

**DRAGON PERSONAL
MANAGEMENT** T 020 7183 5362
Leighton House, 20 Nantfawr Road
Cyncoed, Cardiff CF23 6JR
T 029 2075 4491
E casting@dragon-pm.com
W www.dragon-pm.com

**DYSON, Louise
at VisABLE PEOPLE** T 01386 555170
Contact: Louise Dyson. Artists with Disabilities
T 07930 345152
E louise@visablepeople.com
W www.visablepeople.com

EADON JAMES ASSOCIATES T 020 7859 4997
Contact: Lucie Eadon
86-90 Paul Street, London EC2A 4NE
E info@eadonjamesassociates.co.uk
W www.eadonjamesassociates.co.uk

**EARLE, Kenneth
PERSONAL MANAGEMENT** T 020 7274 1219
214 Brixton Road, London SW9 6AP
T 07711 270698
E kennethearle@agents-uk.com
W www.kennethearlepersonalmanagement.com

**EARNSHAW, Susi
MANAGEMENT** T 020 8441 5010
Personal Manager
The Bull Theatre, 68 High Street, Barnet, Herts EN5 5SJ
E casting@susiearnshaw.co.uk
W www.susiearnshawmanagement.com

EJA COMMERCIALS T 020 7859 4997
Contact: Lucie Eadon
86-90 Paul Street, London EC2A 4NE
E commercials@eadonjamesassociates.co.uk
W www.eadonjamesassociates.co.uk

EKA ACTOR MANAGEMENT T 01925 761210
*Contact: Jodie Keith (Senior Casting Agent). Accepts
Showreels. Commercials. Corporate. Film. Television.
Voice Overs*
The Warehouse Studios, Glaziers Lane
Culcheth, Warrington, Cheshire WA3 4AQ
E jodie@eka-agency.com
W www.eka-agency.com

ELECTRIC TALENT T/F 020 7202 2300
3rd Floor, Riverside Building, County Hall
Westminster Bridge Road, London SE1 7PB
E castings@electrictalent.co.uk
W www.electrictalent.co.uk

ELITE TALENT LTD T 07490 423382
London & Manchester
54 Crosslee Road, Blackley, Manchester M9 6TA
T 07787 342221
E paul@elitetalent.co.uk
W www.elitetalent.co.uk

ELLICOTT MANAGEMENT T 01483 428998
*Management Agency for the professional Adult Actors
Formerly with Wings Agency*
29 Portsmouth Road, Godalming, Surrey GU7 2JU
T 07745 443448
E admin@ellicottmanagement.com
W www.ellicottmanagement.com

ELLIOTT AGENCY LTD THE T 01273 454111
17 Osborne Villas, Hove
East Sussex BN3 2RD
E elliottagency@btconnect.com
W www.elliottagency.co.uk

ELLIS, Bill LTD
See A & B PERSONAL MANAGEMENT LTD

ELLITE MANAGEMENT T 0845 6525361
*Contact: By Post/e-mail. Accepts Showreels. 3 Agents
represent 40 Performers. Dancers*
'The Dancer', 8 Peterson Road
Wakefield WF1 4EB
T 07957 631510
E enquiries@ellitemanagement.co.uk
W www.elliteproductions.co.uk

EMPTAGE HALLETT T 020 7436 0425
PMA Member
Mappin House, 4 Winsley Street
London W1W 8HF
W www.emptagehallett.co.uk

EMPTAGE HALLETT T 029 2034 4205
PMA Member
2nd Floor, 3-5 The Balcony
Castle Arcade, Cardiff CF10 1BU
F 029 2034 4206
E cardiff@emptagehallett.co.uk

**ENGERS, Emma
ASSOCIATES LTD** T 020 7278 9980
56 Russell Court, Woburn Place
London WC1H 0LW
T 020 7837 1859
E emma@emmaengersassociates.com
W www.emmaengersassociates.com

ENGLISH, Doreen '95 T/F 01243 825968
Contact: By Post/Telephone
48 The Boulevard, Bersted Park
Bognor Regis, West Sussex PO21 5BS

EOC MANAGEMENT T 0161 724 4880
35 Plymouth Grove, Radcliffe
Manchester M26 3WU
T 07861 778330
E eocmanagement@gmail.com
W www.eoc-management.co.uk

ESSANAY T 020 8998 0007
Personal Manager. PMA Member. Contact: By Post
PO Box 56662, London W13 3BH
E info@essanay.co.uk

ETHNICS ARTISTE AGENCY T 020 8523 4242
86 Elphinstone Road, Walthamstow
London E17 5EX
F 020 8523 4523
E info@ethnicsaa.co.uk

EUROKIDS CASTING AGENCY T 01925 761210
*Contact: Jodie Keith (Senior Casting Agent). Accepts
Showreels. Children & Teenagers. Commercials. Film.
Television. Walk-ons & Supporting Artists*
The Warehouse Studios, Glaziers Lane
Culcheth, Warrington, Cheshire WA3 4AQ
E jodie@eka-agency.com
W www.eka-agency.com

AMERICAN ACTORS UK

admin@americanactorsuk.com
www.americanactorsuk.com

Need American Actors? American Actors UK is the definitive source of genuine **American** and **Canadian** actors based in the UK. We're not an agency, but a professional network which can connect you to authentic North American performers. To find out more or to join, *get in touch today*.

**EVANS, Jacque
MANAGEMENT LTD**   T 020 8699 1202
Top Floor Suite, 14 Holmesley Road, London SE23 1PJ
E jacque@jemltd.demon.co.uk
W www.jacqueevansltd.com

EVANS & REISS   T 020 8871 0788
104 Fawe Park Road, London SW15 2EA
E janita@evansandreiss.co.uk

EVOLUTION TALENT LTD   T 020 8733 8206
Continental House, 497 Sunleigh Road, London HA0 4LY
T 07908 702714
E info@evotalentltd.com
W www.evotalentltd.com

EXCEL AGENCY   T 01772 755343
1 Sandfield Street, Leyland, Preston PR25 3HJ
T 07570 112022
E XLAgency@yahoo.com
W www.xlagency.com

EXCESS ALL AREAS   T 020 8761 2384
Contact: Paul L. Martin (Director). Cabaret, Circus & Variety Entertainment
3 Gibbs Square, London SE19 1JN
E info@excessallareas.co.uk
W www.excessallareas.co.uk

**EXPRESSIONS
CASTING AGENCY**   T 01623 424334
3 Newgate Lane, Mansfield, Nottingham NG18 2LB
E expressions-uk@btconnect.com
W www.expressionsperformingarts.co.uk

EYE CASTING THE   T 020 7377 7500
1st Floor, 92 Commercial Street
Off Puma Court, London E1 6LZ
E bayo@theeyecasting.com
W www.theeyecasting.com

F4M MODELS   T 020 7025 8000
Curve Models. Commercials. Editorials. Music Videos
18 Soho Square, London W1D 3QL
E hello@face4music.com
W www.f4mmodels.com

FACE MANAGEMENT   T 0113 245 8667
3 Bowling Green Terrace, Leeds, West Yorkshire LS11 9SP
E info@face-agency.co.uk
W www.face-agency.co.uk

FARINO, Paola   T 020 7207 0858
Representing Actors
109 St Georges Road, London SE1 6HY
E info@paolafarino.co.uk
W www.paolafarino.co.uk

FD MANAGEMENT   T 07730 800679
18C Marine Square, Brighton BN2 1DN
E vivienwilde@mac.com

**FEA MANAGEMENT
(FERRIS ENTERTAINMENT)**   T 07801 493133
London. Belfast. Cardiff. Los Angeles. France. Spain
Number 8, 132 Charing Cross Road, London WC2H 0LA
E info@ferrisentertainment.com
W www.ferrisentertainment.com

FEAST MANAGEMENT LTD   T 020 7354 5216
PMA Member
1st Floor, 34 Upper Street
London N1 0PN
F 020 7354 8995
E office@feastmanagement.co.uk

FEATURES   T 020 7637 1487
1 Charlotte Street, London W1T 1RD
E info@features.co.uk
W www.features.co.uk

FFTS MANAGEMENT   T 01639 814012
Child & Adult Performers in London & South Wales
Office 4, Sandfields Business Centre, Endeavour Place
Port Talbot, South Wales SA12 7PT
E info@fftsmanagement.com
W www.fftsmanagement.com

FIELD, Alan ASSOCIATES   T 020 8441 1137
*Personal Manager. Contact: By e-mail. Celebrities.
Composers. Musical Theatre. Presenters. Singers*
3 The Spinney, Bakers Hill
Hadley Common, Herts EN5 5QJ
T 07836 555300
E alan@alanfield.com

**FILM AND BUSINESS
MANAGEMENT**   T 020 7129 1449
*Personal Manager. Contact: Julia de Cadenet (Personal
Management/Legal Advisers). Offices in London,
Paris & California*
17 Cavendish Square, London W1G 0PH
E info@filmandbusiness.com
W www.filmandbusiness.com

FILM CAST CORNWALL & SW   T 07811 253756
Falmouth, Cornwall,
E enquiries@filmcastcornwall.co.uk
W www.filmcastcornwall.co.uk

FILM RIGHTS LTD   T 020 8001 3040
Personal Manager. Contact: By Post
11 Pandora Road, London NW6 1TS
F 020 8711 3171
E information@filmrights.ltd.uk
W www.filmrights.ltd.uk

FINCH & PARTNERS   T 020 7851 7140
Top Floor, 35 Heddon Street
London W1B 4BR
E reception@finchandpartners.com
W www.finchandpartners.com

**FIRST & FOREMOST
ENTERTAINMENT LTD**   T 0800 2707567
*Contact: Chris Neilson, Peter Stanford. By Post/
e-mail. Accepts Showreels. 2 Agents represent
175+ Performers. Entertainment Agency & Corporate
Entertainment. Corporate, Musical, Speciality &
Variety Acts*
90 Longridge Avenue, Brighton
East Sussex BN2 8RB
T 07505 565635
E info@firstandforemostentertainment.com
W www.firstandforemostentertainment.com

Ned Wolfgang Kelly

CATHERINE SHAKESPEARE LANE

PORTRAITS

020 7226 7694   www.csl-art.co.uk

FIRST CALL MANAGEMENT   T 00 353 1 6798401
Beauparc House, Ballydowd
Lucan, Co. Dublin
F 00 353 1 6798353
E info@firstcallmanagement.ie
W www.firstcallmanagement.ie

**FITZGERALD, Sheridan
MANAGEMENT**   T 01842 812028
PMA Member. Contact: Edward Romfourt. By Post only
(SAE). No Phone Calls/e-mails
16 Pond Lane, Brandon
Suffolk IP27 0LA
W www.sheridanfitzgerald.com

**FLAIR TALENT MODEL &
ACTING AGENCY**   T 020 7287 0407
48 Charlotte Street, London W1T 2NS
E bookings@flairtalent.com
W www.flairtalent.com

FLETCHER ASSOCIATES   T 020 8361 8061
Personal Manager. Contact: Francine Fletcher. Corporate
Speakers. Experts for Radio & Television. Stage
Studio One, 25 Parkway, London N20 0XN
F 020 8361 8866
E info@fletcherassociates.net
W www.fletcherassociates.net

FLETCHER JACOB   T 020 3603 7340
Artist Management
162-168 Regent Street, London W1B 5TD
F 020 7038 3707
E info@fletcherjacob.co.uk
W www.fletcherjacob.co.uk

**FLICKS FILM &
TELEVISION AGENCY**   T 00 353 21 4279680
Plunkett Chambers, 21-23 Oliver Plunkett Street
Cork 1, Ireland
T 00 353 87 2147458
E info@ddmp.ie
W www.ddmp.ie

FLP MANAGEMENT   T 020 7371 0300
136-144 New Kings Road, Fulham
London SW6 4LZ
F 020 7371 8707
E info@flpmanagement.co.uk
W www.flpmanagement.co.uk

FOCUS TALENT   T 020 3240 1064
Personal Manager. Representing Actors in Feature Films,
Television, Stage & Commercials. Existing Clients only
81 Sutherland Avenue, London W9 2HG
T 07532 158818
E info@focustalent.co.uk
W www.focustalent.co.uk

FOGGIE LONDON ASSOCIATES   T 07474 037365
Theatrical Agency
Room 2, 22 Southwark Street
London SE1 1TU
E info@foggielondon.co.uk
W www.foggielondon.co.uk

**FOLEY, Kerry
MANAGEMENT LTD**   T 07703 974235
Contact: Kerry Foley
Communications House, 26 York Street
London W1U 6PZ
E contact@kfmltd.com
W www.kerryfoleymanagement.com

FOSTER, Philip COMPANY THE   T 020 3390 2063
16 Carlisle Street, London W1D 3BT
E philip@philipfosterco.com
W www.philipfosterco.com

FOSTER, Sharon MANAGEMENT   T 07919 417812
15A Hollybank Road, Birmingham B13 0RF
E mail@sharonfoster.co.uk
W www.sharonfoster.co.uk

FOX, Clare ASSOCIATES   T/F 020 7328 7494
Set, Lighting & Sound Designers
9 Plympton Road, London NW6 7EH
E clareimfox@gmail.com
W www.clarefox.co.uk

**FOX, Julie
ASSOCIATES - LONDON**   T 020 3092 1512
Personal Manager. Contact: Julie Fox. By e-mail only.
Accepts Showreels/Voicereels. 2 Agents represent
50 Performers
3rd Floor, 207 Regent Street, London W1B 3HH
E agent@juliefoxassociates.co.uk
W www.juliefoxassociates.co.uk

**FOX, Julie
ASSOCIATES - NORTH**   T 01270 780880
Personal Manager. Contact: Julie Fox. By e-mail only.
Accepts Showreels/Voicereels. 2 Agents represent 50
Performers
Office 4, 22 Jordan Street
Liverpool L1 0AH
E agent@juliefoxassociates.co.uk
W www.juliefoxassociates.co.uk

FOX, Lauren ASSOCIATES   T 07881 078669
London Office
E london@laurenfoxassociates.com
W www.laurenfoxassociates.com

FOX, Lauren ASSOCIATES   T 07729 191621
Manchester Office
E north@laurenfoxassociates.com
W www.laurenfoxassociates.com

FRENCH, Linda
See APM ASSOCIATES

FRESH AGENTS LTD   T 01273 711777
Contact: By e-mail. Accepts Showreels/Voicereels.
4 Agents
The Dock, Wilbury Villas
Brighton & Hove BN3 6AH
T 0845 4080998
E info@freshagents.co.uk
W www.freshagents.co.uk

FRESH PARTNERS LTD   T 020 7198 8478
1 Hardwick's Square, Wandsworth
London SW18 4AW
E hello@fresh-partners.com
W www.fresh-partners.com

**FRONTLINE
ACTORS AGENCY**   T 00 353 1 6359882
30-31 Wicklow Street, Dublin 2
Ireland
E contact@frontlineactors.com
W www.frontlineactors.com

**FUNKY BEETROOT
CELEBRITY MANAGEMENT LTD**   T 07814 010691
Personal Manager. Actors. Television Celebrities
PO Box 307, Herne Bay
Kent CT6 9BQ
E info@funky-beetroot.com
W www.funky-beetroot.com

FUSION MANAGEMENT   T 020 7834 6660
201A Victoria Street, London SW1W 5NE
T 07949 635921
E info@fusionmng.com
W www.fusionmng.com

GADBURY PERSONAL MANAGEMENT T 01942 635556
5 Bolton Road, Atherton, Manchester M46 9JQ
T 07791 737306
E vicky@gadbury-casting.co.uk
W www.gadbury-casting.co.uk

GAELFORCE 10 MANAGEMENT T 0141 334 6246
14 Bowmont Gardens, Dowanhill
Glasgow G12 9LR
T 07778 296002
E info@gaelforce10.com
W www.gaelforce10.com

GAGAN, Hilary ASSOCIATES T 020 7404 8794
Personal Manager. PMA Member. Contact: Hilary Gagan, Shiv Coard
187 Drury Lane, London WC2B 5QD
F 020 7430 1869
E hilary@hgassoc.co.uk

GAG REFLEX LTD T 0161 205 8739
Contact: Lee Martin
Red 16, The Sharp Project, Thorp Road
Manchester M40 5BJ
E info@gagreflex.co.uk

GALLOWAYS T 020 3770 6823
PMA Member
Suite 410, Henry Wood House
2 Riding House Street
London W1W 7FA
E info@gallowaysagency.com
W www.gallowaysagency.com

GARDNER HERRITY LTD T 020 7388 0088
PMA Member. Contact: Andy Herrity, Nicky James
24 Conway Street, London W1T 6BG
F 020 7388 0688
E info@gardnerherrity.co.uk
W www.gardnerherrity.co.uk

GARRICKS T 020 7738 1600
PMA Member
Angel House, 76 Mallinson Road
London SW11 1BN
E info@garricks.net

GAY, Noel ORGANISATION T 020 7836 3941
PMA Member
19 Denmark Street, London WC2H 8NA
E info@noelgay.com
W www.noelgay.com

GDA MANAGEMENT　T 01322 278879
Contact: By e-mail only. No Post
Suite 793, Kemp House
152 City Road, London EC1V 2NX
T 07974 680439
E info@gdamanagment.co.uk
W www.gdamanagement.com

GENUINE ARAB CASTING　T 020 3478 9067
Contact: By e-mail. Accepts Showreels/Voicereels.
Commercials. Corporate. Film. Television. Voice Overs
78 York Street, London W1H 1DP
E info@genuinearabcasting.com
W www.genuinearabcasting.com

GENUINE CASTING
TALENT AGENCY　T 020 3478 9067
Contact: By e-mail. Accepts Showreels/Voicereels.
Commercials. Corporate. Film. Television. Voice Overs
78 York Street, London W1H 1DP
E info@genuinecasting.com
W www.genuinecasting.com

GFM ASSOCIATES
PERSONAL MANAGEMENT　T 020 8878 3105
PMA Member
20 Allenford House, Tunworth Crescent
London SW15 4PG
T 07879 402409
E gillian.gfmassociates@gmail.com
W www.gfmassociates.com

GIELGUD MANAGEMENT　T 01444 447020
PMA Member
38-42A South Road, Haywards Heath
West Sussex RH16 4LA
F 01444 447030
E info@gielgudmanagement.co.uk
W www.gielgudmanagement.co.uk

GILBERT & PAYNE　T 020 7734 7505
Room 236, 2nd Floor, Linen Hall
162-168 Regent Street, London W1B 5TB
F 020 7494 3787
E ee@gilbertandpayne.com
W www.gilbertandpayne.com

GILLMAN, Geraldine
ASSOCIATES　T 07799 791586
Harris Primary Academy Crystal Palace, Malcolm Road
Penge, London SE20 8RH
E geraldi.gillma@btconnect.com

GINGERSNAP　T 0117 929 4450
2 Montpelier Central Business Park, Station Road
Bristol BS6 5EE
E info@gingersnap.co.uk
W www.gingersnap.co.uk

GLADWIN, Elizabeth
ASSOCIATES (EGA)　T 020 8936 3553
Personal Manager. Contact: By e-mail. 2 Agents represent
40 Performers
2nd Floor, 18-24 Chaseside
London N14 5PA
E info@elizabethgladwinassociates.com
W www.elizabethgladwinassociates.com

GLASS, Eric LTD　T 020 7229 9500
25 Ladbroke Crescent, Notting Hill, London W11 1PS
F 020 7229 6220
E eglassltd@aol.com

GLOBAL7　T/F 020 7281 7679
Kemp House, 152 City Road
London EC1V 2NX
T 07956 956652
E global7castings@gmail.com
W www.global7casting.com

GLOBAL ARTISTS　T 020 7839 4888
PMA Member. Contact: By e-mail. Accepts Showreels/
Voicereels. 5 Agents
23 Haymarket, London SW1Y 4DG
F 020 7839 4555
E info@globalartists.co.uk
W www.globalartists.co.uk

GLOBALWATCH
MANAGEMENT　T 020 3086 9616
1 Berkeley Street, London W1J 8DJ
F 020 3370 7916
E pandrews@globalwatch.com
W www.globalwatch.com

GLYN MANAGEMENT　T 01449 737695
The Old School House, Brettenham, Ipswich IP7 7QP
F 01449 736117
E glyn.management@tesco.net

GMM (GREGG MILLARD
MANAGEMENT)　T 020 3475 3473
2nd Floor, 312 St Paul's Road, Islington, London N1 2LF
E greggmillard.gmm@gmail.com

GOLD AGENCY LTD　T/F 01474 561200
Contact: By e-mail. Accepts Showreels. 35 Performers
Britannia House, Lower Road, Ebbsfleet, Kent DA11 9BL
T 07831 764995
E ann@goldagency.co.uk

GOLD ARTISTES COLLECTIVE　T 07958 035241
Contact: Eki Maria
2 Alric Avenue, London NW10 8RB
E info@goldartistesmanagement.com
W www.goldartistesmanagement.com

GOLDMANS MANAGEMENT　T 01323 643961
E casting@goldmansmanagement.co.uk
W www.goldmansmanagement.co.uk

GORDON & FRENCH　T 020 7734 4818
PMA Member. Contact: By Post
12-13 Poland Street, London W1F 8QB
E mail@gordonandfrench.co.uk

GRAHAM, David PERSONAL
MANAGEMENT (DGPM)　T/F 020 7241 6752
The Studio, 107A Middleton Road
London E8 4LN
E info@dgpmtheagency.com

GRANT, James MEDIA　T 020 8742 4950
94 Strand On The Green, Chiswick, London W4 3NN
F 020 8742 4951
E enquiries@jamesgrant.co.uk
W www.jamesgrant.co.uk

GRANTHAM-HAZELDINE LTD　T 020 7038 3737
PMA Member
Suite 427, The Linen Hall
162-168 Regent Street, London W1B 5TE
F 020 7038 3739
E agents@granthamhazeldine.com
W www.granthamhazeldine.com

GRAY, Darren MANAGEMENT　T 023 9269 9973
Specialising in representing/promoting Australian Artists
2 Marston Lane, Portsmouth
Hampshire PO3 5TW
F 023 9267 7227
E darrengraymanagement@gmail.com
W www.darrengraymanagement.com

GREEN & UNDERWOOD　T 020 8998 0007
In association with ESSANAY. Personal Manager. Contact:
By Post
PO Box 56662, London W13 3BH
E ny@greenandunderwood.com

Noel Samuels   Lara Honnor   Paul Herwig

PETE BARTLETT PHOTOGRAPHY
info@petebartlett.com
petebartlett.com
07971 653994

GREEN ROOM THE T 07724 518535
Contact: Siobhan Kendall. By e-mail. UK side to
LA Management Company. London/Los Angeles.
Commericals. Film. Stage. Television
86-90 Paul Street, London EC2A 4NE
E sk@thegreenroommgmt.com

GRESHAM, Carl GROUP T 07932 750512
PO Box 3, Bradford
West Yorkshire BD1 4QN
F 01274 827161
E carlgresh@yahoo.co.uk
W www.carlgresham.co.uk

GREY MODEL AGENCY T 020 3733 3390
Contact: Rebecca Valentine. UK Model Agency
representing Mature Models (35+ yrs)
19 Eastbourne Terrace, London W2 6LG
E bookings@greymodelagency.com
W www.greymodelagency.com

GROUNDLINGS
THEATRE COMPANY T 023 9273 9496
42 Kent Street, Portsmouth
Hampshire PO1 3BS
E richard@groundlings.co.uk
W www.groundlings.co.uk

GROVES, Rob
PERSONAL MANAGEMENT T 020 7125 0207
PMA Member. Contact: By e-mail
Hudson House, 8 Tavistock Street
London WC2E 7PP
T 07740 348350
E rob@robgroves.co.uk
W www.robgroves.co.uk

GUBBAY, Louise
ASSOCIATES T 01959 573080
69 Paynesfield Road
Tatsfield, Kent TN16 2BG
E louise@louisegubbay.com
W www.louisegubbay.com

GUBBAY, Louise
ASSOCIATES (LA) T 001 323 522 5545
10642 Santa Monica Boulevard, Suite 207
Los Angeles, CA 90025, USA
E louise@louisegubbay.com
W www.louisegubbay.com

HALL JAMES PERSONAL
MANAGEMENT T 020 3036 0558
12 Melcombe Place, London NW1 6JJ
E agents@halljames.co.uk
W www.halljames.co.uk

HAMBLETON, Patrick
MANAGEMENT T 020 7226 0947
Top Floor, 136 Englefield Road, London N1 3LQ
T 020 7993 5412
E info@phm.uk.com
W www.phm.uk.com

HAMILTON HODELL T 020 7636 1221
PMA Member
20 Golden Square, London W1F 9JL
E info@hamiltonhodell.co.uk
W www.hamiltonhodell.co.uk

HANCOCK AGENCY THE T 020 3488 0159
E info@thehancockagency.com
W www.thehancockagency.com

HARDING, Andrew
MANAGEMENT LTD T 07890 186213
71-75 Shelton Street, Covent Garden
London WC2H 9JQ
E office@andrewhardingmanagement.co.uk
W www.andrewhardingmanagement.co.uk

HARRIS AGENCY LTD THE T 01923 211644
71 The Avenue, Watford, Herts WD17 4NU
E theharrisagency@btconnect.com

HARRISON, Penny BSA LTD T 07886 882843
Contact: By e-mail
E harrisonbsa@aol.com

HARVEY VOICES T 020 7952 4361
49 Greek Street, London W1D 4EG
W www.harveyvoices.co.uk

HARVEY STEIN ASSOCIATES T 020 7175 7937
Contact: Lois Harvey. Television. Film. Stage. Musical
Theatre. Commercials. Radio. Motion Capture
E info@harveystein.co.uk
W www.harveystein.co.uk

HAT MANAGEMENT T 07902 579235
Contact: Laurie Rea
Salford Arts Theatre, Kemsing Walk
Salford M5 4BS
E hatactors@hotmail.co.uk
W www.hatactingmanagement.co.uk

HATTON McEWAN
PENFORD LTD T 020 3735 8278
Personal Manager. PMA Member. Contact: Stephen
Hatton, Aileen McEwan, James Penford. By Post/e-mail
Unit LF1.6, Lafone House, The Leathermarket
Weston Street, London SE1 3ER
E mail@hattonmcewanpenford.com
W www.hattonmcewanpenford.com

HAYES, Cheryl MANAGEMENT   T 020 8994 4447
85 Rothschild Road, London W4 5NT
E cheryl@cherylhayes.co.uk
W www.cherylhayes.co.uk

H C A
See COOKE, Howard ASSOCIATES

**HEADNOD TALENT
AGENCY LTD**   T 020 3222 0035
RichMix 1st Floor West
35-47 Bethnal Green Road, London E1 6LA
E info@headnodagency.com
W www.headnodagency.com

**HENRIETTA RABBIT
ENTERTAINERS AGENCY**   T 0333 000 4567
*Contact: Stephanie. By e-mail. 2 Agents represent 21
Performers. Magicians. Clowns. Jugglers. Punch & Judy.
Stiltwalkers. Balloonologists. Close-up Magicians. Face
Painters. Role Players*
The Warren, 12 Eden Close, York YO24 2RD
E mrsrabbit1070129@aol.com
W www.henriettarabbit.co.uk

**HENRY, Sharon
MANAGEMENT**   T 020 3696 0010
Room 4, 6 Great Newport Street, London WC2H 7JA
E info@sharonhenry.co.uk
W www.sharonhenry.co.uk

**HICKS, Jeremy
ASSOCIATES LTD**   T 020 7580 5741
*Personal Manager. Contact: By Post/e-mail. Accepts
Showreels. 2 Agents. Chefs. Comedians. Presenters.
Writers*
3 Stedham Place, London WC1A 1HU
F 020 7636 3753
E info@jeremyhicks.com
W www.jeremyhicks.com

HIRED HANDS   T 020 7267 9212
12 Cressy Road, London NW3 2LY
E info@hiredhandsmodels.com
W www.hiredhandsmodels.com

**HOATH, Claire
MANAGEMENT LTD**   T 020 7193 7973
70-71 Wells Street, London W1T 3QE
E enquiries@clairehoathmanagement.com
W www.clairehoathmanagement.com

HOBBART & HOBBART   T 0047 45465527
Middelthunsgt. 25A, 0368 Oslo
Norway
E braathen@hobbart.no
W www.hobbart.co.uk

**HOLLAND, Dympna
ASSOCIATES**   T 01753 647551
Casualty Cottage, Kiln Lane
Hedgerley, Bucks SL2 3UT
T 01753 644586
E dympna@dympnaholland.com

**HOLLOWOOD, Jane
ASSOCIATES LTD**   T 0161 237 9141
Apartment 17, 113 Newton Street
Manchester M1 1AE
T 020 8291 5702
E info@janehollowood.co.uk
W www.janehollowood.co.uk

**HOLMES, Kim SHOWBUSINESS
ENTERTAINMENT AGENCY LTD**   T 0115 930 5088
8 Charles Close, Ilkeston
Derbyshire DE7 5AF
E kimholmesshowbiz@hotmail.co.uk

HOPE, Sally ASSOCIATES   T 020 7613 5353
PMA Member
108 Leonard Street, London EC2A 4XS
F 020 7613 4848
E casting@sallyhope.biz
W www.sallyhope.biz

**HORNCASTLE, Alban
MANAGEMENT**   T 07557 123022
66 High Street, Sevenoaks, Kent TN13 1JR
E info@albanhorncastlemanagement.co.uk
W www.albanhorncastlemanagement.co.uk

HOWARD, Amanda ASSOCIATES LTD
See AHA TALENT LTD

HOWELL, Philippa
*See PHPM (PHILIPPA HOWELL PERSONAL
MANAGEMENT)*

**HOXTON STREET
MANAGEMENT**   T 020 7503 5131
Hoxton Hall, 130 Hoxton Street
London N1 6SH
E ben@hoxtonhall.co.uk
W www.hoxtonhall.co.uk

HR CREATIVE ARTISTS   T 020 3286 8830
Contact: By e-mail only
18 Soho Square, London W1D 3QL
E contact@hrca.eu
W www.hrca.eu

**HUDSON, Nancy
ASSOCIATES LTD**   T 020 7499 5548
PMA Member
50 South Molton Street, Mayfair
London W1K 5SB
E agents@nancyhudsonassociates.com
W www.nancyhudsonassociates.com

**HUGHES, Steve
MANAGEMENT LTD**   T 0844 5564670
E management@stevehughesuk.com
W www.stevehughesuk.com

HUNWICK HUGHES LTD   T 07936 374102
Personal Management. PMA Member
4 West Mayfield
Edinburgh EH9 1TQ
E maryam@hunwickhughes.com
W www.hunwickhughes.com

**I.A.G.
(IDENTITY AGENCY GROUP)**   T 020 7502 4670
PMA Member
59 Banner Street, London EC1Y 8PX
E casting@identityagencygroup.com
W www.identityagencygroup.com

I AM BE PRODUCTIONS LTD   T 07834 584977
Mime Artistes. Physical Comedy Specialists
17 Cromer Road, Southend on Sea, Essex SS1 2DU
E admin@iambeproductionsltd.com
W www.iambeproductionsltd.com

I AM EPIC   T 0870 4263742
9 Grosvenor Court, The Leas
Westcliff-on-Sea SS0 8ED
E info@iamepic.co.uk
W www.iamepic.co.uk

ICON ACTORS MANAGEMENT   T 0161 273 3344
Tanzaro House, Ardwick Green North
Manchester M12 6FZ
F 0161 273 4567
E info@iconactors.net
W www.iconactors.net

Matt Anker photographer
www.mattanker.com London based

07835 241835

Student discounts

IMAGE HOSPITALITY　　T 01483 243690
3000 Cathedral Hill, Guildford, Surrey GU2 7YB
E jane@i-mage.uk.com
W www.imagehospitality.co.uk

I.M.L.　　T/F 020 7587 1080
Personal Manager. CPMA Member. Contact: By Post.
Accepts Showreels. 40+ Performers. Commercials.
Corporate. Film. Stage. Television
The White House, 52-54 Kennington Oval
London SE11 5SW
E info@iml.org.uk
W www.iml.org.uk

IMPACT INTERNATIONAL
MANAGEMENT　　T 07941 269849
Personal Manager. Contact: Colin Charles. By e-mail.
Accepts Showreels/Voicereels. 1 Agent represents 10
Performers. Cruises. Musical Theatre. Speciality Acts
& Events
310 Cascades Tower, 4 Westferry Roa, London E14 8JL
E colin.charles310@gmail.com
W www.impact-london.co.uk

IMPERIAL PERSONAL
MANAGEMENT LTD　　T 0113 244 3222
102 Kirkstall Road, Leeds, West Yorkshire LS3 1JA
T 07890 387758
E katie@ipmcasting.com
W www.ipmcasting.com

IMPERIUM MANAGEMENT　　T 020 8819 3155
PMA Member
271 Upper Street, Islington, London N1 2UQ
E info@imperiummgmt.com
W www.imperiummgmt.com

IN GOOD COMPANY　　T 00 353 1 2542252 (Ireland)
Also known as IGC Talent. Personal Manager/Talent
Agent. Contact: By e-mail. Accepts Showreels/Voicereels.
2 Agents represent 20 Performers. Commercials. Film.
Stage. Television
93 St Stephens Green, Dublin 2, Ireland
T 020 7193 4579 (UK)
E info@igctalent.com　　W www.igctalent.com

IN HOUSE AGENCY　　T 07921 843508
29 Waterloo Road, Gillingham
Kent ME7 4SA
E info@inhouseagency.co.uk
W www.inhouseagency.co.uk

INC ARTISTS LTD　　T 020 7205 2316
Twitter: @dancersincworld
64 Great Eastern Street, London EC2A 3QR
E chris@international-collective.com
W www.dancersincworld.com

INDEPENDENT TALENT
GROUP LTD　　T 020 7636 6565
PMA Member. Formerly ICM, London
40 Whitfield Street, London W1T 2RH
F 020 7323 0101
W www.independenttalent.com

INDEPENDENT THEATRE
WORKSHOP THE　　T 00 353 1 2600831
8 Terminus Mills, Clonskeagh
Dublin 6, Ireland
E agency@itwstudios.ie
W www.itwstudios.ie

INFINITY ARTIST
MANAGEMENT　　T 07538 918668
146/6 McDonald Road
Edinburgh EH7 4NL
E casting@infinityartists.com
W www.infinityartists.com

INIMITABLE　　T 07913 597956
1st Floor, 22 West Mall
Clifton, Bristol BS8 4BQ
E info@theinimitables.co.uk
W www.theinimitables.co.uk

INSPIRATION MANAGEMENT　　T 020 7833 2912
Co-operative. CPMA Member. Est 1986
Unit 6, East Block, Panther House
38 Mount Pleasant, London WC1X 0AN
E mail@inspirationmanagement.org.uk
W www.inspirationmanagement.org.uk

INSPIRE MANAGEMENT T 0115 988 1800
The Attic Studio, 3rd Floor
46-48 Carrington Street, Nottingham NG1 7FG
E admin@inspireacademy.co.uk
W www.inspireacademy.co.uk

INTER-CITY CASTING T/F 01942 321969
Personal Manager. Contact: By e-mail. Accepts
Showreels. 2 Agents represent 60 Performers
27 Wigan Lane, Wigan
Greater Manchester WN1 1XR
E intercitycasting@btconnect.com

INTERNATIONAL ARTISTS
MANAGEMENT T 020 7435 8065
St Clements House, 12 Leyden Street
London E1 7LL
E info@internationalartistsmanagement.co.uk
W www.internationalartistsmanagement.co.uk

INTERNATIONAL MODEL
MANAGEMENT LTD T 020 7610 9111
Incorporating Yvonne Paul Management
Unit 20, Dean House Studios
27 Greenwood Place, London NW5 1LD
F 020 7736 2221
E bookings@immmodels.com
W www.immmodels.com

IRISH ACTORS LONDON T 020 7125 0539
Penthouse 11, Bickenhall Mansions
London W1U 6BR
E irishactorslondon@gmail.com
W www.irishactorslondon.co.uk

ISLES MANAGEMENT T 020 3740 8438
Contact: Paul Isles. Singers. Dancers. Actors.
Choreographers
Top Floor, Old Truman Brewery
91 Brick Lane, London E1 6QL
E info@islesmanagement.com
W www.islesmanagement.com

J&R TALENT T 07800 895972
Contact: Jay Cosme
Kemp House, 152 City Road
London EC1V 2NX
E enquiries@jrtalentltd.com
W www.fusion-pictures.com

JAA
See ALTARAS, Jonathan ASSOCIATES LTD

JAFFREY MANAGEMENT LTD T 01708 732350
Personal Manager. Contact: Kim Barry. By Post/e-mail.
Accepts Showreels/Voicereels (SAE). 80 Performers.
Commercials. Film. Radio. Stage. Television
74 Western Road, Romford
Essex RM1 3LP
T 07790 466206
E mail@jaffreyactors.co.uk
W www.jaffreymanagement.org.uk

JAM2000 AGENCY T 01895 624755
The Windmill Studio Centre, 106-106A Pembroke Road
Ruislip, Middlesex HA4 8NW
E info@jam2000.co.uk
W www.jam2000.co.uk

JAMES, Billie - ORIENTAL
CASTING AGENCY LTD T 020 8660 0101
Contact: By e-mail/Telephone. Accepts Showreels/
Voicereels. 1 Agent represents 200+ Performers. Afro/
Asian Artists
22 Wontford Road, Purley, Surrey CR8 4BL
E billiejames@btconnect.com

JAMES, Susan
See SJ MANAGEMENT

JB ASSOCIATES T 0161 237 1808
Personal Manager. Contact: John Basham. By Post/e-
mail. Accepts Showreels/Voicereels. 2 Agents represent
60 Performers. Commercials. Radio. Stage. Television
PO Box 173, Manchester M19 0AR
F 0161 249 3666
E info@j-b-a.net
W www.j-b-a.net

JEFFREY & WHITE
MANAGEMENT LTD T 01462 429769
Personal Manager. PMA Member
7 Paynes Park, Hitchin
Herts SG5 1EH
E info@jeffreyandwhite.co.uk
W www.jeffreyandwhite.co.uk

JERMIN, Mark MANAGEMENT T 01792 458855
Contact: By Post/e-mail. Accepts Showreels. 5 Agents
Swansea Metropolitan
University of Wales, Trinity, Saint David
Mount Pleasant, Swansea SA1 6ED
E info@markjermin.co.uk
W www.markjermin.co.uk

JERRY MANAGEMENT T 00 34 69 9281356
Contact: Clara Nieto. Representing Actors & Directors
within the Spanish Market
Calle Martín de los Heros, 19, 4 int izq
Madrid, Spain, 28008
E jerry@jerrymanagement.es
W www.jerrymanagement.com

JEWELL WRIGHT LTD T 020 7462 0790
Contact: By Post. Accepts Showreels. 2 Agents
represent 90 Performers. Commercials. Creatives. Film.
Musical Theatre. Radio. Stage. Television
17 Percy Street, London W1T 1DU
E agents@jwl-london.com
W www.jwl-london.com

JGPM T 020 7440 1850
4th Floor, 75A Berwick Street
London W1F 8TG
E victoria@jgpm.co.uk
W www.jgpm.co.uk

J.M. MANAGEMENT T 020 8908 0502
Personal Representation to a small number of Actors/
Actresses & Magicians in Film Work. No Unsolicited
Showreels/Headshots
20 Pembroke Road
North Wembley
Middlesex HA9 7PD

JOHNSTON & MATHERS
MANAGEMENT T/F 020 8449 4968
PO Box 3167, Barnet EN5 2WA
E johnstonmathers@aol.com
W www.johnstonandmathers.com

JOYCE, Michael
MANAGEMENT T 020 7544 1065
Twitter: @michaeljoycetv
6th Floor, International House
223 Regent Street
London W1B 2QP
T 07817 448635
E michael@michaeljoyce.tv
W www.michaeljoycemanagement.com

JPA MANAGEMENT T 01494 520978
PMA Member
30 Daws Hill Lane, High Wycombe
Bucks HP11 1PW
E agent@jpaassociates.co.uk
W www.jpaassociates.co.uk

Luke Estevan Photography

www.lukeestevan.co.uk
luke@lukeestevan.co.uk

Twickenham, London
Student Rates available

**K TALENT ARTIST
MANAGEMENT LTD**   **T** 020 7379 1616
*Personal Manager. Contact: By Post/e-mail. Accepts
Showreels/Voicereels. 5 Agents represent approx 200
Adult Performers. Children. Commercials. Dancers. Film.
Musical Theatre. Singers. Stage. Television*
4th Floor
43 Aldwych
London WC2B 4DN
E mail@ktalent.co.uk
W www.ktalent.co.uk

KAIRABA COMMERCIALS   **T** 020 7839 2765
Contact: Katy Wale
1st Floor
23 Haymarket
London SW1Y 4DG
E kairabacommercials@btconnect.com

KANAL, Roberta AGENCY   **T** 020 8894 2277
82 Constance Road
Twickenham
Middlesex TW2 7JA
T/F 020 8894 7952
E roberta.kanal@dsl.pipex.com

**KEDDIE SCOTT
ASSOCIATES LTD**   **T** 020 3490 1050
*PMA Member. Contact: Fiona Keddie-Ord,
Alex France. Prospective Client Applications to
info@keddiescott.com. Accepts Showreels.
2 Agents, 2 Assistants represent 100 Performers.
Commercials. Corporate. Film. Musical Theatre. Radio.
Singers. Stage. Television*
31 Hatton Garden
London EC1N 8DH
E london@keddiescott.com
W www.keddiescott.com

**KEDDIE SCOTT
ASSOCIATES - NORTH**   **T** 07708 202374
*PMA Member. Contact: Anthony Williams.
Prospective Client Applications to
info@keddiescott.com. Accepts Showreels.
1 Agent represents 65 Performers. Commercials.
Corporate. Film. Musical Theatre. Radio. Singers. Stage.
Television*
c/o 31 Hatton Garden
London EC1N 8DH
E north@keddiescott.com
W www.keddiescott.com

KEDDIE SCOTT ASSOCIATES - SCOTLAND   T 07973 235355
PMA Member. Contact: Paul Harper. Prospective Client Applications to info@keddiescott.coml. Accepts Showreels. 1 Agent represents 65 Performers. Commercials. Corporate. Film. Musical Theatre. Radio. Singers. Stage. Television
c/o 31 Hatton Garden, London EC1N 8DH
F 020 7147 1326
E scotland@keddiescott.com
W www.keddiescott.com

KENIS, Steve   T 020 7434 9055
PMA Member. Steve Kenis & Co
95 Barkston Gardens, London SW5 0EU
F 020 7373 9404
E sk@sknco.com

KEW PERSONAL MANAGEMENT   T 07876 457402
PO Box 679, Surrey RH1 6EN
E info@kewpersonalmanagement.com
W www.kewpersonalmanagement.com

KEYLOCK MANAGEMENT   T 07943 593404
Contact: By e-mail. 2 Agents represent 40 Performers. Commercials. Film. Stage. Television
58 Plymouth Road, Tavistock
Devon PL19 8BU
E mark@keylockmanagement.com
W www.keylockmanagement.com

KHANDO ENTERTAINMENT   T 020 3463 8492
1 Marlborough Court, London W1F 7EE
E info@khandoentertainment.com
W www.khandoentertainment.com

KING TALENT INC   T 001 604 713 6980
Contact: Lisa King (Personal Manager/Agent), Michael King (Executive Assistant). Film. Stage. Television
PO Box 1087, Gibsons, B.C.
Vancouver, Canada V0N 1V0
E info@kingtalent.com
W www.kingtalent.com

KMC AGENCIES   T 0845 5193071
Personal Manager. Actors. Commercials. Corporate. Dancers. Musical Theatre. Cruise & International Work
48 Great Ancoats Street
Manchester M4 5AB
E casting@kmcagencies.co.uk
W www.kmcagencies.co.uk

KMC AGENCIES   T 0845 5193071
Personal Manager. Actors. Commercials. Corporate. Dancers. Musical Theatre. Cruise & International Work
Garden Studios, 71-75 Shelton Street
Covent Garden, London WC2H 9JQ
E london@kmcagencies.co.uk
W www.kmcagencies.co.uk

KNIGHT, Nic MANAGEMENT   T 020 8527 7420
Twitter: @nicknightmgmt
The Black & White Building
74 Rivington Street
London EC2A 3AY
E info@nicknightmanagement.com
W www.nicknightmanagement.com

KNIGHT, Ray CASTING LTD   T 020 8327 4244
Contact: Tony Gerrard (Manager)
Elstree Studios, Room 38
John Maxwell Building
Shenley Road, Borehamwood
Herts WD6 1JG
E casting@rayknight.co.uk
W www.rayknight.co.uk

KNIGHT AYTON MANAGEMENT   T 020 7831 4400
Twitter: @KnightAyton
35 Great James Street, London WC1N 3HB
E info@knightayton.co.uk
W www.knightayton.co.uk

KORT, Richard MANAGEMENT   T 01522 850940
In Association with LMG
25 Old Chapel Road, Skellingthorpe
Lincoln LN6 5UB
T 07855 032843
E richardkort@playhouseproductionsltd.co.uk

KREATE   T 020 7401 9007
32 Southwark Bridge Road, London SE1 9EU
E hello@kreate.co.uk
W www.kreate.co.uk

KREMER ASSOCIATES
See MARSH, Billy DRAMA LTD

KSA - NORTH
See KEDDIE SCOTT ASSOCIATES - NORTH

KSA - SCOTLAND
See KEDDIE SCOTT ASSOCIATES - SCOTLAND

L.A. MANAGEMENT   T 020 7183 6211
T 020 7183 4911
E info@lamanagement.co.uk
W www.lamanagement.co.uk

LADA MANAGEMENT   T 020 3770 3617
Personal Manager. Contact: Richard Boschetto. By e-mail only. Accepts Showreels/Voicereels. 2 Agents represent 30 Performers. Film. Musical Theatre. Stage. Television
23 Austin Friars, London EC2N 2QP
F 020 3384 5816
E info@ladamanagement.com
W www.ladamanagement.com

LADA MANAGEMENT   T 01522 775760
Personal Manager. Contact: Richard Boschetto. CVs & Headshots by e-mail only. Accepts Showreels/Voicereels. 2 Agents represent 40 Performers. Film. Musical Theatre. Stage. Television
Sparkhouse Studios
Rope Walk, Lincoln LN6 7DQ
E info@ladamanagement.com
W www.ladamanagement.com

LAINE, Betty MANAGEMENT   T/F 01372 721815
The Studios, East Street
Epsom, Surrey KT17 1HH
E enquiries@betty-laine-management.co.uk

LAINE MANAGEMENT LTD   T 0161 789 7775
Contact: Samantha Rigby
265A Monton Road, Eccles M30 9LF
E sam@lainemanagement.co.uk
W www.lainemanagement.co.uk

LANGFORD ASSOCIATES LTD   T 020 7244 7805
Personal Manager. Contact: Barry Langford, Simon Hayes. By Post/e-mail. Commercials. Film. Stage. Television
Vicarage House, 58-60 Kensington Church Street
London W8 4DB
E barry@langfordassociates.com
W www.langfordassociates.com

LEADING LIGHTS EVENTS   T 07870 696971
Poppy Lodge, London Road
High Wycombe, Bucks HP10 9TJ
E leadinglightsevents@hotmail.co.uk
W www.leading-lights.co.uk

DOM BURKE PHOTOGRAPHY

LE BARS, Tessa MANAGEMENT   T/F 01689 837084
Existing Clients only
54 Birchwood Road, Petts Wood, Kent BR5 1NZ
T 07860 287255
E tessa.lebars@ntlworld.com
W www.galtonandsimpson.com

LEE, Nina MANAGEMENT LTD   T 020 3375 6269
PMA Member
Suite 36, 88-90 Hatton Garden, London EC1N 8PN
E nina@ninaleemanagement.com
W www.ninaleemanagement.com

LEE, Wendy MANAGEMENT   T 020 7703 5187
T 07941 797938
E wendy-lee@btconnect.com

LEHRER, Jane ASSOCIATES   T 020 7435 9118
Personal Manager. PMA Member. Contact: By Post/
e-mail. 2 Agents
PO Box 66334, London NW6 9QT
F 020 7435 9117
E jane@janelehrer.co.uk
W www.janelehrer.co.uk

LENO MARTIN ASSOCIATES   T 020 8655 7656
Personal Management. Contact: Paul Leno (Senior
Agent). By Post/e-mail/Telephone. 4 Agents
represent 100 Performers. Film. Television. Stage.
Musical Theatre. Commercials
3B Nettlefold Place, London SE27 0JW
E info@lenomartinassociates.com
W www.lenomartinassociates.com

LESLIE, Sasha MANAGEMENT   T/F 020 8969 3249
In association with ALLSORTS DRAMA FOR CHILDREN
34 Crediton Road, London NW10 3DU
E sasha@allsortsdrama.com

LHK MANAGEMENT   T 01744 808907
20 Maltby Close, St Helens WA9 5GJ
E casting@lhkmanagement.co.uk
W www.lhkmanagement.co.uk

LIGHT AGENCY & PRODUCTIONS LTD   T 020 8090 0006
Actors. Dancers
27 Mospey Crescent, Epsom, Surrey KT17 4NA
E agency@lightproductions.tv
W www.lightproductions.tv

LIME ACTORS AGENCY & MANAGEMENT LTD   T 0161 236 0827
Contact: Georgina Andrew. By Post. Accepts Showreels
Nemesis House, 1 Oxford Court
Bishopsgate, Manchester M2 3WQ
F 0161 228 6727
E georgina@limemanagement.co.uk
W www.limemanagement.tv

LINKSIDE AGENCY   T 01233 636188
Contact: By Post/e-mail. 2 Agents represent 40
Performers. Dancers. Musical Theatre. Singers. Stage.
Television
57 High Street, Ashford, Kent TN24 8SG
E info@linksideagency.com

LINTON MANAGEMENT   T 0161 761 2020
3 The Rock, Bury BL9 0JP
E carol@linton.tv

LINTON MANAGEMENT   T 020 7785 7275
27-31 Clerkenwell Close, London EC1R 0AT
E london@linton.tv

LITTLE ALLSTARS CASTING & MODELLING AGENCY   T 0161 702 8257
23 Falconwood Chase, Worsley
Manchester M28 1FG
T 07584 992429
E casting@littleallstars.co.uk
W www.littleallstars.co.uk

LIVING THE DREAM TALENT AGENCY   T 01727 751613
145-147 St John Street, London EC1V 4PW
T 07845 267501
E agency@livingthedreamcompany.co.uk
W www.livingthedreamcompany.co.uk

LMB MANAGEMENT   **T** 020 7252 4343
In association with The LMB Partnership
Daisy Business Park, 19-35 Sylvan Grove
London SE15 1PD
E lisa@lmbmanagement.co.uk
W www.lmbmanagement.co.uk

LONDON THEATRICAL   **T** 020 8748 1478
Contact: Paul Pearson
18 Leamore Street, London W6 0JZ
E agent@londontheatrical.com
W www.londontheatrical.com

LONG, Eva AGENTS   **T** 07736 700849
*Contact: By Post/e-mail. 2 Agents represent 30
Performers. Commercials. Corporate. Film. Musical
Theatre. Radio. Singers. Stage. Television. Voice Overs*
Norwood House, 9 Redwell Road
Wellingborough NN8 5AZ
F 01604 811921
E evalongagents@yahoo.co.uk
W www.evalongagents.co.uk

**LONGRUN ARTISTES
AGENCY**   **T** 01843 639747
*Contact: Gina Long, Nikki Bond. Accepts Showreels/
Voicereels & Prospective Client Applications by
e-mail. 3 Agents Represent 100+ Performers.
Commercials. Corporate. Dancers. Film. Musical
Theatre. Singers. Stage. Television*
(Postal Address), 71-75 Shelton Street
Covent Garden, London WC2H 9JQ
E longrunartistes@icloud.com
W www.longrunartistes.com

LOOKALIKES   **T** 020 7281 8029
Contact: Susan Scott
T 07905 094904
E susan@lookalikes.info
W www.lookalikes.info

LOOKS AGENCY   **T** 020 8341 4477
*Contact: By Post/e-mail/Telephone. 400 Performers.
Commercials. Corporate. Modelling. Presenters. Walk-on
& Supporting Artists*
PO Box 42783, London N2 0UF
E lookslondonltd@btconnect.com
W www.lookslondon.com

**LOTHERINGTON, Michelle
MANAGEMENT LTD**   **T** 07785 293806
*Contact: Michelle Lotherington. By e-mail.
Choreographers. Composers. Designers. Directors.
Lighting & Sound Designers. Music Technology. Musical
Directors. Orchestrators*
436 Lordship Lane, London SE22 8NE
E michelle@michellelotherington.com
W www.michellelotherington.com

LOVE RUDEYE AGENCY   **T** 020 7014 3023
18 West Central Street, London WC1A 1JJ
E info@loverudeye.com
W www.loverudeye.com

LOVETT LOGAN ASSOCIATES   **T** 0131 478 7878
Formerly PLA. PMA Member
2 York Place, Edinburgh EH1 3EP
F 0131 478 7070
E edinburgh@lovettlogan.com   **W** www.lovettlogan.com

LOVETT LOGAN ASSOCIATES   **T** 020 7495 6400
Formerly PLA. PMA Member
40 Margaret Street, London W1G 0JH
F 020 7495 6411
E london@lovettlogan.com   **W** www.lovettlogan.com

LSW PROMOTIONS   **T/F** 020 7793 9755
PO Box 31855, London SE17 3XP
E londonswo@hotmail.com

LUXFACTOR GROUP (UK) THE   **T** 0845 3700589
*Personal Manager. Contact: Michael D. Finch. By
e-mail. 1 Agent represents 20+ Performers. Creatives.
Presenters. Television. Walk-on & Supporting Artists*
Fleet Place, 12 Nelson Drive
Petersfield, Hampshire GU31 4SJ
T 05603 680843
E info@luxfactor.co.uk
W www.luxfactor.co.uk

LYNE, Dennis AGENCY   **T** 020 7272 5020
PMA Member
503 Holloway Road, London N19 4DD
E info@dennislyne.com
W www.dennislyne.com

M&C SAATCHI MERLIN   **T** 020 7259 1460
36 Golden Square, London W1F 9JG
E enquiries@mcsaatchimerlin.com
W www.mcsaatchimerlin.com

M&P ARTIST MANAGEMENT   **T** 020 7734 1051
PMA Member
29 Poland Street, London W1F 8QR
F 020 7287 4481
E info@mandpartistmanagement.com
W www.mandpartistmanagement.com

MA9 MODEL MANAGEMENT   **T** 020 7096 1191
New Bond House, 124 New Bond Street
London W1S 1DX
E info@ma9models.com
W www.ma9models.com

**MACFARLANE CHARD
ASSOCIATES LTD**   **T** 020 7636 7750
PMA Member
33 Percy Street, London W1T 2DF
F 020 7636 7751
E enquiries@macfarlane-chard.co.uk
W www.macfarlane-chard.co.uk

**MACFARLANE CHARD
ASSOCIATES IRELAND**   **T** 00 353 1 6638646
7 Adelaide Street, Dun Laoghaire
Co Dublin, Ireland
E derick@macfarlane-chard.ie

**MACFARLANE DOYLE
ASSOCIATES**   **T** 020 3600 3470
90 Long Acre, Covent Garden
London WC2E 9RZ
E office.mfd@btinternet.com
W www.macfarlanedoyle.com

**MACNAUGHTON LORD
REPRESENTATION**   **T** 020 7499 1411
*PMA Member. Choreographers. Composers. Designers.
Directors. Lighting Designers. Lyricists. Musical Directors.
Sound Designers. Video Designers. Writers*
44 South Molton Street, London W1K 5RT
E info@mlrep.com
W www.mlrep.com

MAIDA VALE SINGERS   **T** 020 7266 1358
*Contact: Christopher Dee. Singers for Recordings, Stage,
Film, Radio & Television*
7B Lanhill Road, Maida Vale
London W9 2BP
T 07889 153145
E maidavalesingers@cdtenor.freeserve.co.uk
W www.maidavalesingers.co.uk

MAITLAND MANAGEMENT   **T** 07508 919946
Personal Manager. Contact: Annie Skates (Director)
PO Box 364, Esher KT10 9XS
F 01372 466229
E info@maitlandmanagement.com
W www.maitlandmanagement.com

S.T.ARTS MANAGEMENT

Sole Agency representing diverse & talented Actors for:

Film Television Theatre
Commercials Radio Voice-Overs
Adverts Corporate
Photographic Presenting

Contact: tarquin@startsmanagement.co.uk   +44 (0)845 408 2468   www.startsmanagement.co.uk

---

MAMBAB AGENCY   T 020 3645 8617
Contact: Nichola D. Hartwell
73 Cornwall Square, Kennington, London SE11 4JP
T 07868 120709
E contacts@mrandmissblackandbeautiful.com
W www.mrandmissblackandbeautiful.com

MANAGEMENT 2000   T/F 01352 771231
Contact: Jackey Gerling. By Post. Accepts Showreels.
1 Agent represents 30 Performers. Commercials. Film.
Radio. Stage. Television
11 Well Street, Treuddyn, Flintshire CH7 4NH
E jackey@management-2000.co.uk
W www.management-2000.co.uk

MANS, Johnny PRODUCTIONS   T 01992 470907
Incorporating Encore Magazine
PO Box 196, Hoddesdon, Herts EN10 7WG
T 07974 755997
E johnnymansagent@aol.com
W www.johnnymansproductions.co.uk

MANTLE MANAGEMENT   T 01273 454111
17 Osborne Villas, Hove, East Sussex BN3 2RD
E info@mantlemanagement.co.uk
W www.mantlemanagement.co.uk

**MARCUS & McCRIMMON
MANAGEMENT**   T 020 7323 0546
Personal Manager. Contact: By Post/e-mail. Accepts
Showreels. 2 Agents represent 100 Performers.
Commercials. Film. Musical Theatre. Stage. Television
Winston House, 3 Bedford Square, London WC1B 3RA
E info@marcusandmccrimmon.com
W www.marcusandmccrimmon.com

MARKHAM AGENCY THE   T 020 7836 4111
Personal Manager. PMA Member. Contact: John
Markham. By Post/e-mail. Accepts Showreels/Voicereels
405 Strand, London WC2R 0NE
F 020 7836 4222
E info@themarkhamagency.com
W www.themarkhamagency.com

**MARKHAM, FROGGATT
& IRWIN**   T 020 7636 4412
Personal Manager. PMA Member. Contact: By e-mail
4 Windmill Street, London W1T 2HZ
E admin@markhamfroggattirwin.com
W www.markhamfroggattandirwin.com

MARLOWES AGENCY   T 07964 589148
HMS President, Victoria Embankment
Blackfriars, London EC4Y 0HJ
T 020 7193 7227
E miles@marlowes.eu
W www.marlowes.eu

**MARLOWES AGENCY:
TV, THEATRE & DANCE**   T 020 7193 4484
HMS President, Victoria Embankment
Blackfriars, London EC4Y 0HJ
E mitch@marlowesagency.com
W www.marlowesagency.com

MARMALADE MANAGEMENT   T 01628 483808
Jam Theatre Studios, Archway Court
45A West Street, Marlow
Buckinghamshire SL7 2LS
E info@marmalademanagement.co.uk
W www.marmalademanagement.co.uk

MARSH, Billy ASSOCIATES LTD   T 020 7383 9979
PMA Member
4A Exmoor Street, London W10 6BD
F 020 7598 7300
E isabell@billymarsh.co.uk
W www.billymarsh.co.uk

MARSH, Billy DRAMA LTD   T 020 3428 5171
Actors. Actresses
Amadeus House, 27B Floral Street, London WC2E 9DP
F 020 3428 5173
E info@billymarshdrama.co.uk

**MARSHALL, Ronnie
AGENCY THE**   T/F 020 8368 4958
66 Ollerton Road, London N11 2LA
E theronniemarshallagency@gmail.com
W www.theronniemarshallagency.com

**MARSHALL, Scott
PARTNERS LTD**   T 020 7637 4623
PMA Member. Contact: Amanda Evans, Suzy Kenway,
Manon Palmer
2nd Floor, 15 Little Portland Street
London W1W 8BW
F 020 7636 9728
E info@scottmarshall.co.uk
W www.scottmarshall.co.uk

**MARTIN, Carol
PERSONAL MANAGEMENT**   T 020 8348 0847
19 Highgate West Hill, London N6 6NP
E carolmartin@talktalk.net

MAY, John   T 07733 016794
46 Golborne Road, London W10 5PR
E may505@btinternet.com

MAYER, Cassie LTD   T 020 7350 0880
PMA Member
5 Old Garden House, The Lanterns
Bridge Lane, London SW11 3AD
E info@cassiemayerltd.co.uk

MBA / MAHONEY BANNON ASSOCIATES   T 01273 685970
John Mahoney Management Group
Concorde House, 18 Margaret Street, Brighton BN2 1TS
E info@mahoney.agency
W www.mahoney.agency

McDONAGH, Melanie MANAGEMENT (ACADEMY OF PERFORMING ARTS & CASTING AGENCY)   T 07909 831409
14 Apple Tree Way, Oswaldtwistle
Accrington, Lancashire BB5 0FB
T 01254 392560
E mcdonaghmgt@aol.com
W www.mcdonaghmanagement.co.uk

McKINNEY MACARTNEY MANAGEMENT LTD   T 020 8995 4747
Technicians
Gable House, 18-24 Turnham Green Terrace
London W4 1QP
E mail@mckinneymacartney.com
W www.mckinneymacartney.com

McLEAN, Bill PERSONAL MANAGEMENT LTD   T 020 8789 8191
Personal Manager. Contact: By Post
23B Deodar Road, London SW15 2NP

McLEAN-WILLIAMS LTD   T 020 3567 1090
PMA Member
Chester House (Unit 3:06), Kennington Park
1-3 Brixton Road, London SW9 6DE
E info@mclean-williams.com
W www.mclean-williams.com

McLEOD AGENCY LTD THE   T 01482 565444
1st Floor, 6 The Square
Hessle, East Yorkshire HU13 0AA
E liz@mcleodagency.co.uk
W www.mcleodagency.co.uk

McMAHON MANAGEMENT   T 020 8752 0172
28 Cecil Road, London W3 0DB
E mcmahonmanagement@hotmail.co.uk
W www.mcmahonmanagement.co.uk

MEDIA CELEBRITY SERVICES LTD   T 07946 531011
48 Dean Street, London W1B 5BF
T 07809 831340
E info@mcsagency.co.uk
W www.mediacelebrityservices.co.uk

MEDIA LEGAL   T 01732 460592
Existing Clients only
Town House, 5 Mill Pond Close
Sevenoaks, Kent TN14 5AW

MF PERSONAL MANAGEMENT   T 01798 344356 (Maggie)
26 Orchard Close, Petworth, West Sussex GU28 0SA
T 07986 045724
E margaret.ferrari@btinternet.com

MGA MANAGEMENT & CASTING   T 07595 711159
Personal Manager. Contact: Tabitha Watson. By e-mail. Accepts Showreels/Voicereels. 2 Agents represent 60 Performers. Children. Dancers. Musical Theatre. Singers
207 Balgreen Road, Edinburgh EH11 2RZ
E admin@mgamanagement.com
W www.mgamanagement.com

MIDDLEWEEK NEWTON TALENT MANAGEMENT   T 020 3394 0079
PMA Member
3rd Floor, 95A Rivington Street, London EC2A 3AY
E agents@mntalent.co.uk
W www.mntalent.co.uk

MIDWEST TALENT MANAGEMENT   T 001 310 760 1082
Contact: Margaret Guiraud. By e-mail. Accepts Showreels. 8 Agents represent 260 Performers
Admin: Management, PO Box 4475
West Hills, CA 91308, USA
E int.talent@gmail.com

MILBURN BROWNING ASSOCIATES   T 020 3582 9370
PMA Member
The Old Truman Brewery, 91 Brick Lane, London E1 6QL
F 020 3582 9377
E info@milburnbrowning.com

MINIMEN THE   T 07875 225168
Contact: Steve Redford. By e-mail. Accepts Showreels/Voicereels. Dwarf & Short Stature Actors & Event Entertainment. 2 Agents represent 32 Performers. Commercials. Corporate. Disabled. Film. Television. Walk-on & Supporting Artists. CGI. Prosthetic. Stunts. Child Stunts. Entertainers
Church Farm, School Lane
Ardeley, Hertfordshire SG2 7AH
E info@theminimen.co.uk
W www.theminimen.co.uk

MISKIN THEATRE AGENCY THE   T 01322 629422
The Miskin Theatre, Oakfield Lane, Dartford, Kent DA1 2JT
T 07709 429354
E miskintheatreagency@yahoo.co.uk

MITCHELL MAAS McLENNAN   T 020 8301 8745
MPA Offices, 29 Thomas Street
Woolwich, London SE18 6HU
T 07540 995802
E agency@mmm2000.co.uk
W www.mmm2000.co.uk

MLA TALENT   T 020 7993 8337
Formerly Mike Leigh Associates. Personal Manager. Contact: By e-mail. 2 Agents represents 35 Performers. Commercials. Corporate. Film. Radio. Stage. Television. Writers
International House, 24 Holborn Viaduct
London EC1A 2BN
E mike@mlatalent.com
W www.mlatalent.com

MLR
See MACNAUGHTON LORD REPRESENTATION

MOMENTUM ARTIST MANAGEMENT   T 020 7060 1515
Number 1, 63 Mount Ephraim
Tunbridge Wells, Kent TN4 8BG
E email@momentumtalent.co
W www.momentumtalent.co

MONDI ASSOCIATES LTD   T 07817 133349
Personal Manager. PMA Member. Contact: Michelle Sykes. By Post/e-mail. Accepts Showreels/Voicereels. 1 Agent represents 60 Performers. Children. Commercials. Corporate. Dancers. Film. Musical Theatre. Presenters. Radio. Singers. Stage. Television. Voice Overs
Unit 3 O, Cooper House, 2 Michael Road
London SW6 2AD
E info@mondiassociates.com
W www.mondiassociates.com

MONTAGU ASSOCIATES LTD   T 020 7263 3883
Ground Floor, 13 Hanley Road, London N4 3DU
E info@montagus.org

MORELLO CHERRY ACTORS AGENCY   T 020 7993 5538
T 0161 839 1429
E info@mcaa.co.uk
W www.mcaa.co.uk

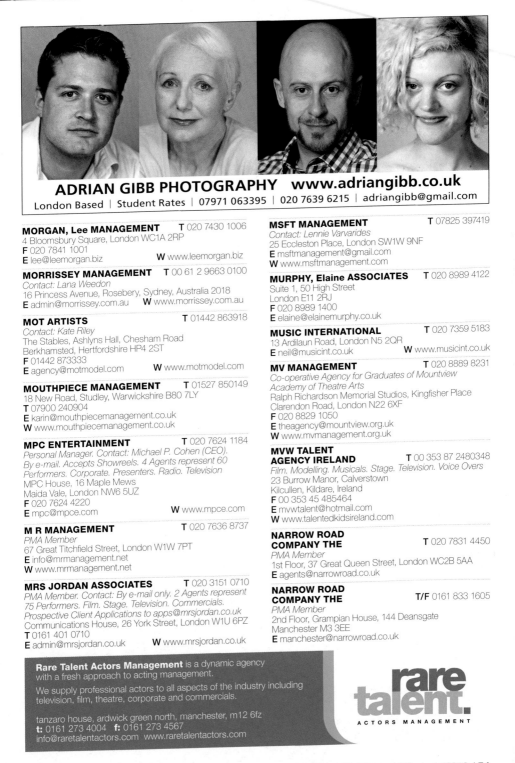

ADRIAN GIBB PHOTOGRAPHY **www.adriangibb.co.uk**
London Based | Student Rates | 07971 063395 | 020 7639 6215 | adriangibb@gmail.com

MORGAN, Lee MANAGEMENT T 020 7430 1006
4 Bloomsbury Square, London WC1A 2RP
F 020 7841 1001
E lee@leemorgan.biz
W www.leemorgan.biz

MORRISSEY MANAGEMENT T 00 61 2 9663 0100
Contact: Lana Weedon
16 Princess Avenue, Rosebery, Sydney, Australia 2018
E admin@morrissey.com.au   W www.morrissey.com.au

MOT ARTISTS T 01442 863918
Contact: Kate Riley
The Stables, Ashlyns Hall, Chesham Road
Berkhamsted, Hertfordshire HP4 2ST
F 01442 873333
E agency@motmodel.com   W www.motmodel.com

MOUTHPIECE MANAGEMENT T 01527 850149
18 New Road, Studley, Warwickshire B80 7LY
T 07900 240904
E karin@mouthpiecemanagement.co.uk
W www.mouthpiecemanagement.co.uk

MPC ENTERTAINMENT T 020 7624 1184
Personal Manager. Contact: Michael P. Cohen (CEO).
By e-mail. Accepts Showreels. 4 Agents represent 60
Performers. Corporate. Presenters. Radio. Television
MPC House, 16 Maple Mews
Maida Vale, London NW6 5UZ
F 020 7624 4220
E mpc@mpce.com   W www.mpce.com

M R MANAGEMENT T 020 7636 8737
PMA Member
67 Great Titchfield Street, London W1W 7PT
E info@mrmanagement.net
W www.mrmanagement.net

MRS JORDAN ASSOCIATES T 020 3151 0710
PMA Member. Contact: By e-mail only. 2 Agents represent
75 Performers. Film. Stage. Television. Commercials.
Prospective Client Applications to apps@mrsjordan.co.uk
Communications House, 26 York Street, London W1U 6PZ
T 0161 401 0710
E admin@mrsjordan.co.uk   W www.mrsjordan.co.uk

MSFT MANAGEMENT T 07825 397419
Contact: Lennie Varvarides
25 Eccleston Place, London SW1W 9NF
E msftmanagement@gmail.com
W www.msftmanagement.com

MURPHY, Elaine ASSOCIATES T 020 8989 4122
Suite 1, 50 High Street
London E11 2RJ
F 020 8989 1400
E elaine@elainemurphy.co.uk

MUSIC INTERNATIONAL T 020 7359 5183
13 Ardilaun Road, London N5 2QR
E neil@musicint.co.uk   W www.musicint.co.uk

MV MANAGEMENT T 020 8889 8231
Co-operative Agency for Graduates of Mountview
Academy of Theatre Arts
Ralph Richardson Memorial Studios, Kingfisher Place
Clarendon Road, London N22 6XF
F 020 8829 1050
E theagency@mountview.org.uk
W www.mvmanagement.org.uk

**MVW TALENT
AGENCY IRELAND** T 00 353 87 2480348
Film. Modelling. Musicals. Stage. Television. Voice Overs
23 Burrow Manor, Calverstown
Kilcullen, Kildare, Ireland
F 00 353 45 485464
E mvwtalent@hotmail.com
W www.talentedkidsireland.com

**NARROW ROAD
COMPANY THE** T 020 7831 4450
PMA Member
1st Floor, 37 Great Queen Street, London WC2B 5AA
E agents@narrowroad.co.uk

**NARROW ROAD
COMPANY THE** T/F 0161 833 1605
PMA Member
2nd Floor, Grampian House, 144 Deansgate
Manchester M3 3EE
E manchester@narrowroad.co.uk

NATHENSON, Zoë
AGENCY THE   **T** 020 8883 7554
Contact: Ryan Wheeler
T 07956 833850
E info@zoenathensonagency.com
W www.zoenathensonagency.com

NEALON, Steve ASSOCIATES   **T** 020 7125 0468
PMA Member
3rd Floor, International House, 1-6 Yarmouth Place
Mayfair, London W1J 7BU
T 07949 601935
E admin@stevenealonassociates.co.uk
W www.stevenealonassociates.co.uk

NELSON BROWNE
MANAGEMENT LTD   **T** 020 7970 6010
PMA Member
40 Bowling Green Lane, London EC1R 0NE
T 07796 891388
E enquiries@nelsonbrowne.com
W www.nelsonbrowne.com

NEVS AGENCY   **T** 020 7352 4886
Regal House, 198 King's Road
London SW3 5XP
F 020 7352 6068
E getamodel@nevs.co.uk
W www.nevs.co.uk

NEW CASEY AGENCY   **T** 01923 823182
129 Northwood Way, Northwood HA6 1RF
E newcaseyagency@gmail.com

NEW FACES LTD   **T** 020 7439 6900
Personal Manager. Contact: Val Horton. By Post/e-mail.
Accepts Showreels. 2 Agents represent 50 Performers.
Stage. Television. Commercials. Film
3rd Floor, The Linen Hall
162-168 Regent Street, London W1B 5TD
F 020 7287 5481
E info@newfacestalent.co.uk
W www.newfacestalent.co.uk

NFD AGENCY   **T** 01977 681949
The Studio, 21 Low Street
South Milford LS25 5AR
E info@northernfilmanddrama.com
W www.northernfilmanddrama.com

NG PERSONAL MANAGEMENT   **T** 07810 138535
Personal Manager. Contact: Natalie Giacone. By e-mail.
Accepts Showreels. 1 Agent represents 28 Performers
6 Garston Crescent, Watford
Hertfordshire WD25 0LD
E info@ngpersonalmanagement.co.uk
W www.ngpersonalmanagement.co.uk

NIC KNIGHT MANAGEMENT
See KNIGHT, Nic MANAGEMENT

NICHOLSON, Jackie
ASSOCIATES   **T** 020 7580 4422
Personal Manager. Contact: Marvin Giles (Agent).
By Post
Suite 44, 2nd Floor, Morley House
320 Regent Street, London W1B 3BD
F 020 7580 4489
E jnalondon@aol.com

N M MANAGEMENT   **T** 020 8853 4337
16 St Alfege Passage, Greenwich, London SE10 9JS
E nmmanagement@hotmail.com

NMP MANAGEMENT   **T** 01372 361004
8 Blenheim Court, Brookway
Leatherhead, Surrey KT22 7NA
F 01372 374417
E management@nmp.co.uk
W www.nmpmanagement.co.uk

NOLAN & KAY MANAGEMENT   **T** 01444 401595
Studio 35 Truggers, Handcross
Haywards Heath, West Sussex RH17 6DQ
T 07966 382766
E info@nolanandkay.co.uk   **W** www.nolanandkay.co.uk

NORTH OF WATFORD   **T** 01422 845361
CPMA Member. Twitter: @northofwatford
The Creative Quarter, The Town Hall
St Georges Street, Hebden Bridge
West Yorks HX7 7BY
T 020 3601 3372
E info@northofwatford.com
W www.northofwatford.com

NORTH WEST ACTORS -
NIGEL ADAMS   **T** 0161 761 6437
Personal Manager. Contact: Nigel Adams. By Post.
Accepts Showreels/Voicereels. Commercials. Film. Radio.
Stage. Television
64 Nuttall Street, Bury
Manchester BL9 7EW
E nigel.adams@northwestactors.co.uk
W www.northwestactors.co.uk

NORTHBRIDGE TALENT
AGENCY   **T** 01442 780550
Contact: Tom Gribby
c/o The Vyne - Berkhamsted Arts Centre
Northbridge Road
Berkhamsted, Hertfordshire HP4 1EH
T 07739 961597
E info@northbridgetalent.com
W www.northbridgetalent.com

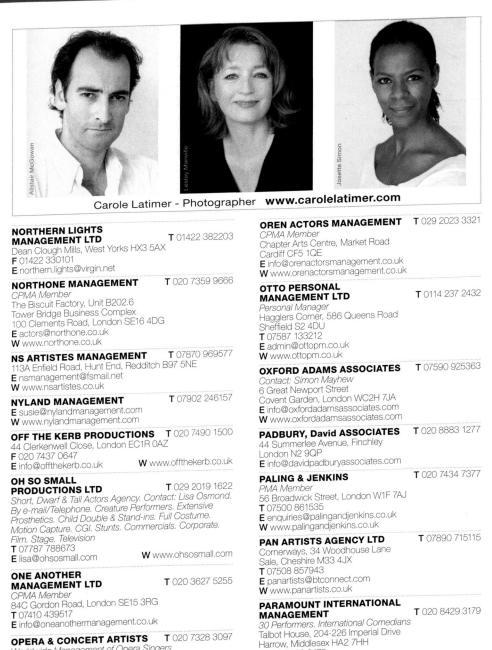

Carole Latimer - Photographer **www.carolelatimer.com**

NORTHERN LIGHTS MANAGEMENT LTD   **T** 01422 382203
Dean Clough Mills, West Yorks HX3 5AX
F 01422 330101
E northern.lights@virgin.net

NORTHONE MANAGEMENT   **T** 020 7359 9666
CPMA Member
The Biscuit Factory, Unit B202.6
Tower Bridge Business Complex
100 Clements Road, London SE16 4DG
E actors@northone.co.uk
W www.northone.co.uk

NS ARTISTES MANAGEMENT   **T** 07870 969577
113A Enfield Road, Hunt End, Redditch B97 5NE
E nsmanagement@fsmail.net
W www.nsartistes.co.uk

NYLAND MANAGEMENT   **T** 07902 246157
E susie@nylandmanagement.com
W www.nylandmanagement.com

OFF THE KERB PRODUCTIONS   **T** 020 7490 1500
44 Clerkenwell Close, London EC1R 0AZ
F 020 7437 0647
E info@offthekerb.co.uk   **W** www.offthekerb.co.uk

OH SO SMALL PRODUCTIONS LTD   **T** 029 2019 1622
Short, Dwarf & Tall Actors Agency. Contact: Lisa Osmond. By e-mail/Telephone. Creature Performers. Extensive Prosthetics. Child Double & Stand-ins. Full Costume. Motion Capture. CGI. Stunts. Commercials. Corporate. Film. Stage. Television
T 07787 788673
E lisa@ohsosmall.com   **W** www.ohsosmall.com

ONE ANOTHER MANAGEMENT LTD   **T** 020 3627 5255
CPMA Member
84C Gordon Road, London SE15 3RG
T 07410 439517
E info@oneanothermanagement.co.uk

OPERA & CONCERT ARTISTS   **T** 020 7328 3097
Worldwide Management of Opera Singers
75 Aberdare Gardens, London NW6 3AN
F 020 7372 3537
E enquiries@opera-and-concert-artists.co.uk

ORDINARY PEOPLE   **T** 020 7267 7007
Actors. Modelling
16 Camden Road, London NW1 9DP
T 07525 932227
E info@ordinarypeople.co.uk
W www.ordinarypeople.co.uk

OREN ACTORS MANAGEMENT   **T** 029 2023 3321
CPMA Member
Chapter Arts Centre, Market Road
Cardiff CF5 1QE
E info@orenactorsmanagement.co.uk
W www.orenactorsmanagement.co.uk

OTTO PERSONAL MANAGEMENT LTD   **T** 0114 237 2432
Personal Manager
Hagglers Corner, 586 Queens Road
Sheffield S2 4DU
T 07587 133212
E admin@ottopm.co.uk
W www.ottopm.co.uk

OXFORD ADAMS ASSOCIATES   **T** 07590 925363
Contact: Simon Mayhew
6 Great Newport Street
Covent Garden, London WC2H 7JA
E info@oxfordadamsassociates.com
W www.oxfordadamsassociates.com

PADBURY, David ASSOCIATES   **T** 020 8883 1277
44 Summerlee Avenue, Finchley
London N2 9QP
E info@davidpadburyassociates.com

PALING & JENKINS   **T** 020 7434 7377
PMA Member
56 Broadwick Street, London W1F 7AJ
T 07500 861535
E enquiries@palingandjenkins.co.uk
W www.palingandjenkins.co.uk

PAN ARTISTS AGENCY LTD   **T** 07890 715115
Cornerways, 34 Woodhouse Lane
Sale, Cheshire M33 4JX
T 07508 857943
E panartists@btconnect.com
W www.panartists.co.uk

PARAMOUNT INTERNATIONAL MANAGEMENT   **T** 020 8429 3179
30 Performers. International Comedians
Talbot House, 204-226 Imperial Drive
Harrow, Middlesex HA2 7HH
F 020 8868 6475
E mail@ukcomedy.com
W www.ukcomedy.com

PARKER, Cherry MANAGEMENT   **T** 01702 522647
PMA Member
T 07976 547066
E info@cherryparkermanagement.com
W www.cherryparkermanagement.com

PARKER, Cherry MANAGEMENT (RSM)
See RSM (CHERRY PARKER MANAGEMENT)

**PARSONS, Cary
MANAGEMENT**　　　　　　**T** 01926 735375
*PMA Member. Set, Costume & Lighting Designers &
Directors*
118 Plymouth Place, Leamington Spa
Warwickshire CV31 1HW
E carylparsons@gmail.com
W www.caryparsons.co.uk

PAYNE MANAGEMENT　　**T** 020 7193 1156 (London)
Contact: Natalie Payne
T 0161 408 6715 (Manchester)
E agent@paynemanagement.co.uk
W www.paynemanagement.co.uk

P B J MANAGEMENT LTD　　　**T** 020 7287 1112
*Personal Manager. PMA Member. Accepts Showreels.
11 Agents represent 115 Performers. Comedians.
Commercials. Corporate. Presenters. Radio. Stage.
Television. Voice Overs. Walk-on & Supporting Artists.
Writers*
22 Rathbone Street, London W1T 1LG
E general@pbjmanagement.co.uk
W www.pbjmanagement.co.uk

**PC THEATRICAL, MODEL &
CASTING AGENCY**　　　　　　**T** 07904 549665
Large Database of Twins
10 Strathmore Gardens, Edgware
Middlesex HA8 5HJ
T 020 8381 2229
E twinagy@aol.com
W www.twinagency.com

PELHAM ASSOCIATES　　　　**T** 01273 323010
Personal Manager. PMA Member. Contact: Peter Cleall
Albert House, 82 Queen's Road
Brighton BN1 3XE
E agent@pelhamassociates.co.uk
W www.pelhamassociates.co.uk

PEMBERTON ASSOCIATES LTD　**T** 020 7224 9036
*Contact: Barbara Pemberton. By e-mail. Showreels on
request. 5 Agents represent 130 Performers. Film. Musical
Theatre. Radio. Stage. Television. Voice Overs*
51 Upper Berkeley Street, London W1H 7QW
E general@pembertonassociates.com
W www.pembertonassociates.com

PEOPLEMATTER.TV　　　　　**T** 020 7415 7070
40 Bowling Green Lane, Clerkenwell
London EC1R 0NE
F 020 7415 7074
E tony@peoplematter.tv
W www.peoplematter.tv

PEPPERPOT PROMOTIONS　　**T** 020 7405 9108
Bands
Suite 20B, 20-22 Orde Hall Street
London WC1N 3JW
E chris@pepperpot.co.uk

**PERFORMANCE
ACTORS AGENCY**　　　　　　**T** 020 7251 5716
Co-operative. CPMA Member
137 Goswell Road, London EC1V 7ET
F 020 7251 3974
E info@performanceactors.co.uk
W www.performanceactors.co.uk

**PERFORMANCE FACTORY
MANAGEMENT THE**　　　　　**T** 01792 701570
Kemys Way, Swansea Enterprise Park
Swansea SA6 8QF
E management@theperformancefactorywales.com
W www.theperformancefactorywales.com

**PERFORMING ARTS ARTISTS'
MANAGERS LLP**　　　　　　**T** 020 7255 1362
*Personal Manager. PMA Member. Contact: By Post/e-
mail. 2 Agents represent 30 Performers. Creative Team
Members only*
6 Windmill Street, London W1T 2JB
E info@performing-arts.co.uk
W www.performing-arts.co.uk

PERRYMENT, Mandy　　　　　**T** 020 8941 7907
T 07790 605191
E mail@mandyperryment.com
W www.actorsmanagement.co.uk/mandyperrymentartists.html

PERSONAL APPEARANCES　**T/F** 020 8343 7748
20 North Mount, 1147-1161 High Road
Whetstone N20 0PH
E patsy@personalappearances.biz
W www.personalappearances.biz

PHILLIPS, Frances　　　　　　**T** 020 8953 0303
*Personal Manager. PMA Member. Contact: Frances
Zealander. By e-mail. Agency represents 50 Performers*
89 Robeson Way, Borehamwood
Hertfordshire WD6 5RY
T 07957 334328
E frances@francesphillips.co.uk
W www.francesphillips.co.uk

**PHPM (PHILIPPA HOWELL PERSONAL
MANAGEMENT)**　　　　　　**T** 020 7836 2837
405 The Strand, London WC2R 0NE
T 07790 969024
E philippa@phpm.co.uk
W www.phpm.co.uk

PICCADILLY MANAGEMENT　　**T** 0161 212 8522
Personal Manager
23 New Mount Street, Manchester M4 4DE
F 0161 953 4001
E info@piccadillymanagement.com
W www.piccadillymanagement.com

PLA
See LOVETT LOGAN ASSOCIATES

**PLATER, Janet
MANAGEMENT LTD**　　　　　**T** 0191 221 2490
*Contact: Janet Plater. By e-mail. Commercials. Film.
Radio. Stage. Television*
D Floor, Milburn House
Dean Street, Newcastle upon Tyne NE1 1LF
E info@jpmactors.com
W www.jpmactors.com

PLATINUM ARTISTS　　　　　**T** 020 3006 2242
78 York Street, Marylebone, London W1H 1DP
E mail@platinumartists.co.uk
W www.platinumartists.co.uk

PMA LONDON　　　　　　　　**T** 07714 432990
*Contact: Linda Rowley. By e-mail. Accepts Showreels.
2 Agents represents 40 Performers. Commercials.
Corporate. Film. Stage. Television*
9 Rosecroft Gardens, Twickenham, Middlesex TW2 7PT
E info@pmalondon.com
W www.pmalondon.com

PMA MANAGEMENT & AGENCY　**T** 01375 665716
Southend Road, Corringham, Essex SS17 8JT
F 01375 672353
E office@performersmanagement.co.uk
W www.performersmanagement.co.uk

POLLY'S AGENCY　　　　　　**T** 020 3696 0015
6 Great Newport Street, London WC2H 7JA
E polly@pollysagency.co.uk
W www.pollysagency.co.uk

CARL PROCTOR PHOTOGRAPHY
www.carlproctorphotography.com

t: 07956 283340   e: carlproctorphotos@gmail.com

POLLYANNA MANAGEMENT LTD   T 020 7481 1911
Rayne House, Rayne Street, London E1W 3R0
T 07801 884837
E pollyannamanagement@gmail.com
W www.pollyannatheatre.org

POOLE, Gordon AGENCY LTD   T 01275 463222
The Limes, Brockley, Bristol BS48 3BB
F 01275 462252
E agents@gordonpoole.com   W www.gordonpoole.com

POWER PROMOTIONS   T/F 0151 230 0070
PO Box 61, Liverpool L13 0EF
E tom2@powerpromotions.co.uk
W www.powerpromotions.com

PREGNANT PAUSE AGENCY   T 07970 698868
Pregnant Models, Dancers, Actresses
50 Ditton Hill Road, Long Ditton KT6 5JD
E sandy@pregnantpause.co.uk
W www.pregnantpause.co.uk

PRENELLE CASTING   T 07454 206024
17 Ambleside Terrace, Fulwell, Sunderland SR6 8NP
E barbara@prenellecasting.co.uk
W www.prenellecasting.co.uk

PRESTON, Morwenna MANAGEMENT   T 020 8835 8147
49 Leithcote Gardens, London SW16 2UX
E info@morwennapreston.com
W www.morwennapreston.com

PRICE GARDNER MANAGEMENT   T 020 7610 2111
PMA Member
BM 3162, London WC1N 3XX
F 020 7381 3288
E info@pricegardner.co.uk   W www.pricegardner.co.uk

PRINCIPAL ARTISTES   T 020 7637 2120
Personal Manager. Contact: By e-mail
Suite 1, 57 Buckingham Gate
Westminster, London SW1E 6AJ
E enquiries@principalartistes.com

PRIORITY CASTING & TALENT AGENCY   T 07468 482854
Contact: By e-mail. Accepts Showreels. 2 Agents represent 40 Performers. Commercials. Corporate. Film. Stage. Television
E casting@prioritycasting.co.uk
W www.prioritycasting.co.uk

PROSPECTS ASSOCIATIONS   T 07988 546179
Sessions. Singers
28 Magpie Close, Forest Gate, London E7 9DE
E wasegun@yahoo.co.uk

PV MEDIA LTD   T 01905 616100
County House, St Mary Street, Worcester WR1 1HB
E md@pvmedia.co.uk

QTALENT   T 020 7430 5400
PMA Member
2nd Floor, 161 Drury Lane
Covent Garden, London WC2B 5PN
E reception@qtalent.co.uk
W www.qtalent.co.uk

RAFFLES, Tim ENTERTAINMENTS   T/F 01933 741855
Personal Manager. 2 Agents represent 9 Performers. Corporate. Cruise Work. Singers. Television
22 William Trigg Close, Irthlingborough
Northamptonshire NN9 5LD
E info@timrafflesentertainments.co.uk
W www.timrafflesentertainments.co.uk

RAGE MODELS   T 020 8749 4760
Ugli Campus, 56 Wood Lane, London W12 7SB
F 020 7402 0507
E ragemodels@ugly.org
W www.ugly.org

RARE TALENT ACTORS MANAGEMENT   T 0161 273 4004
Tanzaro House, Ardwick Green North
Manchester M12 6FZ
F 0161 273 4567
E info@raretalentactors.com
W www.raretalentactors.com

RAY KNIGHT CASTING LTD
See KNIGHT, Ray CASTING LTD

RAZZAMATAZZ MANAGEMENT   T 01342 301617
Personal Manager. Contact: Jill Shirley. By e-mail/
Telephone. 1 Agent
204 Holtye Road, East Grinstead
West Sussex RH19 3ES
T 07836 268292
E razzamatazzmanagement@btconnect.com

RbA MANAGEMENT LTD   T 0151 708 7273
Personal Manager. CPMA Member. Contact: By Post/
e-mail. Accepts Showreels/Voicereels. 20+ Performers
37-45 Windsor Street
Liverpool L8 1XE
E info@rbamanagement.co.uk
W www.rbamanagement.co.uk

RBM ACTORS   T 020 7976 6021
3rd Floor, 1 Lower Grosvenor Place
London SW1W 0EJ
E info@rbmactors.com
W www.rbmactors.com

RDDC MANAGEMENT AGENCY   T 01706 211161
52 Bridleway, Waterfoot
Rossendale, Lancashire BB4 9DS
E info@rddc.co.uk
W www.rddc.co.uk

**RE-PM (RAIF EYLES
PERSONAL MANAGEMENT)**   T 020 8953 1481
Film. Stage. Television
8 Dacre Gardens
Borehamwood WD6 2JP
T 07794 971733
E info@re-pm.co.uk
W www.re-pm.co.uk

**REACH TO THE SKY
PERSONAL MANAGEMENT**   T 0843 2892503
Actors. Artistes. Entertainers. Musicians
Maxet House, Liverpool Road
Luton, Beds LU1 1RS
E info@reachtothesky.com
W www.reachtothesky.com

REACTORS AGENCY   T 00 353 1 8786833
Contact: By Post/e-mail. Accepts Showreels.
Co-operative of 24 Performers
1 Eden Quay, Dublin, Ireland
E info@reactors.ie
W www.reactors.ie

**REALITY CHECK
MANAGEMENT**   T 07546 265009
Contact: Mark Harris
Piano House, 9 Brighton Terrace
London SW9 8DJ
E mark@realitycheck-m.com
W www.realitycheck-m.com

RED 24 MANAGEMENT   T 020 7404 5722
R24, 1st Floor, Kingsway House
103 Kingsway WC2B 6QX
E miles@red24management.com
W www.red24management.com

RED CANYON MANAGEMENT   T 07931 381696
T 07939 365578
E info@redcanyon.co.uk
W www.redcanyon.co.uk

RED DOOR MANAGEMENT   T 0161 850 9989
The Greenhouse, Broadway
MediaCityUK, Manchester M50 2EQ
E mail@the-reddoor.co.uk
W www.the-reddoor.co.uk

RED SHOE MANAGEMENT   T 029 2047 3993
Contact: Andrina Amsdell-Edmunds
T-Cubed House, 319 Kingston Road
Leatherhead, Surrey KT22 7TU
T 07968 114095
E a.amsdelledmunds@gmail.com
W www.red-shoe.info

RED TALENT MANAGEMENT   T 0247 6691900
18 Earlsdon Avenue South, Earlsdon, Coventry CV5 6DT
T 07941 133812
E info@redtalentmanagement.com
W www.redtalentmanagement.com

REDROOFS ASSOCIATES   T 01628 674092
26 Bath Road, Maidenhead, Berkshire SL6 4JT
T 07531 355835 (Holiday Times)
E agency@redroofs.co.uk
W www.redroofsagency.co.uk

REDWOOD TALENT   T 0113 880 0822
Contact: Emma Helliwell
15 Queen Square, Leeds LS2 8AJ
T 07712 722282
E info@redwoodtalent.com
W www.redwoodtalent.com

**REFLECTIONS
TALENT AGENCY**   T 07412 833382
E info@reflectionstalentagency.co.uk
W www.reflectionstalentagency.co.uk

**REGAN MANAGEMENT
CARDIFF**   T 029 2047 3993
Contact: Debi MacLean, Leigh-Ann Regan
59 Mount Stuart Square, Cardiff Bay, Cardiff CF10 5LR
T 07967 488064 (Debi)
E cardiff@reganmanagement.co.uk
W www.reganmanagement.co.uk

**REGAN MANAGEMENT
LONDON**   T 020 3735 5429
Contact: Leigh-Ann Regan, George Smith
Barley Mow Centre, 10 Barley Mow Passage
Chiswick, London W4 4PH
T 07779 321954 (Leigh-Ann)
E georgesmith@reganmanagement.co.uk
W www.reganmanagement.co.uk

**REGAN MANAGEMENT
MANCHESTER**   T 0161 713 3677
Contact: Nicola Bolton, Leigh-Ann Regan
MediaCityUK, The Greenhouse
111 Broadway, Salford M50 2EQ
T 07770 236085 (Nicola)
E manchester@reganmanagement.co.uk
W www.reganmanagement.co.uk

REGAN RIMMER MANAGEMENT (CARDIFF)
See REGAN MANAGEMENT

REGAN RIMMER MANAGEMENT (LONDON)
See RIMMER, Debbie MANAGEMENT

**REPRESENTATION UPSON
EDWARDS**   T 01782 827222
Voice Coaches only
Unit 2, The Courthouse, 72 Moorland Road, Burslem
Stoke-on-Trent, Staffs ST6 1DY
F 01782 728004
E sarah.upson@voicecoach.tv   W www.voicecoach.tv

**REYNOLDS, Sandra AGENCY LTD
(COMMERCIALS)**   T 01603 623842
Bacon House, 35 St George's Street, Norwich NR3 1DA
F 01603 219825
E alex@sandrareynolds.co.uk
W www.sandrareynolds.co.uk

KM PHOTOGRAPHY HEADSHOTS
www.head-shot.photography   headshots@kamalmostofi.com   07850 219183

REYNOLDS, Sandra AGENCY LTD (COMMERCIALS)   T 020 7387 5858
Amadeus House, 27B Floral Street, London WC2E 9DP
F 020 7387 5848
E jessie@sandrareynolds.co.uk
W www.sandrareynolds.co.uk

RICHARD STONE PARTNERSHIP THE
See STONE, Richard PARTNERSHIP THE

RICHARDS, Lisa AGENCY THE   T 00 353 1 6375000
108 Upper Leeson Street, Dublin 4, Ireland
F 00 353 1 6671256
E info@lisarichards.ie   W www.lisarichards.ie

RICHARDS, Lisa AGENCY THE   T 020 7287 1441
1st Floor, 33 Old Compton Street, London W1D 5JU
E office@lisarichards.co.uk
W www.lisarichards.co.uk

RICHARDS, Stella MANAGEMENT   T 020 7736 7786
Contact: Stella Richards, Julia Lintott. Existing Clients only
42 Hazlebury Road, London SW6 2ND
E stellagent@aol.com   W www.stellarichards.com

RIDGEWAY STUDIOS MANAGEMENT   T 01992 633775
Office: 106 Hawkshead Road, Potters Bar
Hertfordshire EN6 1NG
E info@ridgewaystudios.co.uk

RIMMER, Debbie MANAGEMENT   T 020 7839 2758
1st Floor, 23 Haymarket
London SW1Y 4DG
E debbierimmer-office@btconnect.com
W www.debbierimmer.com

RKA TALENT   T 020 7287 6934
PMA Member
10 Greek Street, London W1D 4DH
E office@rkatalent.com   W www.rkatalent.com

ROAR GLOBAL   T 020 7462 9060
ROAR House, 46 Charlotte Street
London W1T 2GS
F 020 7462 9061
E info@roarglobal.com
W www.roarglobal.com

RODRIGUEZ, Anxo MANAGEMENT   T 00 34 61 9120396
Plaza de la Encarnación, No.3 Bajo Izq.
Madrid, Spain 28013
E anxo@zigguratfilms.com
W www.anxorodriguez.com

ROGUES & VAGABONDS MANAGEMENT LTD   T 020 7254 8130
Personal Manager. CPMA Member
The Print House, 18 Ashwin Street, London E8 3DL
F 020 7249 8564
E rogues@vagabondsmanagement.com
W www.vagabondsmanagement.com

ROLE MODELS   T 020 7284 4337
12 Cressy Road, London NW3 2LY
E hiredhandsmodels@gmail.com
W www.rolemodelsagency.com

RONAN, Lynda PERSONAL MANAGEMENT   T 020 7183 0017
Hunters House, 1 Redcliffe Road
London SW10 9NR
E lynda@lyndaronan.com   W www.lyndaronan.com

ROOM 3 AGENCY   T 0845 5678333
Garden Apt, 3 Blenheim Road
Redland, Bristol BS6 7JL
E kate@room3agency.com   W www.room3agency.com

ROSEBERY MANAGEMENT LTD   T 020 7684 0187
CPMA Member. Contact: Lead Agent. Prospective Client Applications should e-mail Spotlight Links only to applications@roseberymanagement.com. Otherwise Applications Accepted with CVs & Headshots by Post. Accepts Showreels. 1 Agent represents 35 Performers. Commercials. Film. Musical Theatre. Stage. Television. Voice Overs
87 Leonard Street, London EC2A 4QS
E admin@roseberymanagement.com
W www.roseberymanagement.com

ROSS, Frances MANAGEMENT   T 01726 832395
Higher Leyonne, Golant
Fowey, Cornwall PL23 1LA
T 07593 994050
E francesross@btconnect.com

ROSS-BROWN, Sandy   T 07860 558033
Personal Manager
F 020 8398 4111
E sandy@rossbrown.eu

ROSSMORE MANAGEMENT   T 020 7258 1953
PMA Member
Broadley House, 48 Broadley Terrace NW1 6LG
E agents@rossmoremanagement.com
W www.rossmoremanagement.com

ROWE ASSOCIATES   T/F 01992 640485
33 Percy Street, London W1T 2DF
T 07887 898220
E agents@growe.co.uk   W www.growe.co.uk

ROYCE MANAGEMENT　T 020 8650 1096
121 Merlin Grove, Beckenham BR3 3HS
E office@roycemanagement.co.uk
W www.roycemanagement.co.uk

RS MANAGEMENT　T 020 8257 6477
186 Waltham Way, London E4 8AZ
E info@rsmagency.co.uk
W www.rsmagency.co.uk

**RSM (CHERRY PARKER
MANAGEMENT)**　T 01702 522647
15 The Fairway, Leigh, Essex SS9 4QN
T 07976 547066
E info@rsm.uk.net
W www.rsm.uk.net

**RUSSELL, Gregory
MANAGEMENT**　T 07477 965165
60 Stanley Avenue, Birmingham B32 2HA
E info@gregory-russell.co.uk
W www.gregory-russell.co.uk

SAINOU　T 020 7734 6441
PMA Member. Twitter: @Sainou
10-11 Lower John Street, Golden Square
London W1F 9EB
E office@sainou.com
W www.sainou.com

SANDERS, Loesje LTD　T 01394 385260
*PMA Member. Contact: Simon Ash. Directors. Designers.
Choreographers. Lighting Designers. Sound Designers.
Video Designers*
The Old Rectory, Church Road
Limpenhoe, Norwich NR13 3JB
E info@loesjesanders.org.uk
W www.loesjesanders.com

SARABAND ASSOCIATES　T 020 8551 9193
Contact: Bryn Newton, Joy Jameson
PO Box 2493, Ilford, Essex IG1 8JW
E brynnewton@btconnect.com

SAROSI, Amanda ASSOCIATES　T 020 7993 6008
1 Holmbury View, London E5 9EG
F 020 7096 2141
E amanda@asassociates.biz

SASHAZE TALENT AGENCY　T 07968 762942
2 Gleannan Close, Omagh, Co. Tyrone BT79 7YA
E info@sashaze.com
W www.sashaze.com

SCA MANAGEMENT　T 01932 503285
Contact: By Post
Suite 17, Wey House
15 Church Street, Weybridge, Surrey KT13 8NA
E agency@sca-management.co.uk
W www.sca-management.co.uk

SCHNABL, Peter　T 01666 502133
The Barn House, Cutwell, Tetbury
Gloucestershire GL8 8EB
F 01666 502998
E peter.schnabl@virgin.net

**SCHWARTZ, Marie Claude -
AAMCS**　T 00 33 1 74625286
13 Av de Fouilleuse, 92210 Saint Cloud, France
E mc.schwartz@noos.fr
W www.agencesartistiques.com

SCOTT MARSHALL PARTNERS LTD
See MARSHALL, Scott PARTNERS LTD

**SCOTT, Russell
ENTERTAINMENT LTD**　T 0844 5676896
Specialises in Musical Theatre
W www.russellscottentertainment.com

SCOTT, Tim　T 020 8347 8705
PO Box 63856, London N6 9BQ
E timscott@btinternet.com

**SCOTT-PAUL YOUNG
ENTERTAINMENTS LTD**　T/F 01753 693250
Artists Representation & Promotions
SPY Record Company, Northern Lights House
110 Blandford Road North, Langley
Nr Windsor, Berks SL3 7TA
E castingdirect@spy-ents.com
W www.spy-artistsworld.com

**SCRIMGEOUR, Donald
ARTISTS AGENT**　T 020 8444 6248
Choreographers. Principal Dancers. Producers
49 Springcroft Avenue, London N2 9JH
F 020 8883 9751
E vwest@dircon.co.uk
W www.donaldscrimgeour.com

SDM　T 020 7183 8995
120 Ivor Court, Gloucester Place, London NW1 6BS
F 020 7183 9013
E admin@simondrakemanagement.co.uk
W www.simondrakemanagement.co.uk

**SEA PERSONAL
MANAGEMENT LTD**　T/F 0870 6092629
PMA Member
Moorgate House, 5-8 Dysart Street, London EC2A 2BX
T 07855 460341
E steph@seapmlondon.com
W www.seapmlondon.com

**SEA PERSONAL
MANAGEMENT LTD**　T/F 01269 870944
PMA Member
6 Bryn Tirion, Pontyberem
Llanelli, Carmarthenshire SA15 5BX
T 07855 460341
E steph@seapmlondon.com
W www.seapmlondon.com

SECOND SKIN AGENCY LTD　T/F 01494 730166
26 Wood Pond Close, Seer Green
Beaconsfield, Bucks HP9 2XG
E office@secondskinagency.com
W www.secondskinagency.com

**SEDGWICK, Dawn
MANAGEMENT**　T 020 7240 0404
3 Goodwins Court, Covent Garden, London WC2N 4LL
F 020 7240 0415
W www.dawnsedgwickmanagement.com

SELECT MANAGEMENT　T 07855 794747
*Actors. Models. Presenters. Dancers. Children. Teenagers
& Adults*
PO Box 748, London NW4 1TT
T 07956 131494
E mail@selectmanagement.info
W www.selectmanagement.info

**SHAPER, Susan
MANAGEMENT**　T 07903 196034
E info@susanshapermanagement.com

SHARKEY & CO　T 020 7287 1923
PMA Member
44 Lexington Street, London W1F 0LP
E info@sharkeyandco.com
W www.sharkeyandco.com

SHARMAN, Alan AGENCY　T 0121 212 0090
Office 6, Fournier House
8 Tenby Street, Birmingham B1 3AJ
E info@alansharmanagency.com
W www.alansharmanagency.com

SHELDRAKE, Peter AGENCY   T 020 8876 9572
Contact: By e-mail. 1 Agent represents 50 Performers.
Commercials. Film. Musical Theatre. Stage. Television
139 Lower Richmond Road
London SW14 7HX
T 07758 063663
E peter.sheldrake3@btinternet.com
W www.petersheldrakeagency.co.uk

SHEPHERD MANAGEMENT   T 020 7420 9350
PMA Member
3rd Floor, Joel House
17-21 Garrick Street
London WC2E 9BL
F 0843 2905796
E info@shepherdmanagement.co.uk
W www.shepherdmanagement.co.uk

SHEPPERD-FOX   T 020 7240 2048
PMA Member. Contact: Jane Shepperd, James Davies
2nd Floor, 47 Bedford Street
London WC2E 9HA
E info@shepperd-fox.co.uk
W www.shepperd-fox.co.uk

SHOWTIME CASTINGS   T 020 7068 6816
112 Milligan Street, Docklands
London E14 8AS
T 07908 008364
E gemma@showtimecastings.com

SILVERLEE MANAGEMENT   T 07771 194598
E info@silverleemanagement.co.uk
W www.silverleemanagement.co.uk

SIMON & HOW ASSOCIATES   T 020 7739 8865
12-18 Hoxton Street, London N1 6NG
E info@simonhow.com
W www.simonhow.com

SIMPSON FOX
ASSOCIATES LTD   T 020 7434 9167
PMA Member. Set, Costume & Lighting Designers.
Directors. Choreographers
6 Beauchamp Place, London SW3 1NG
E info@simpson-fox.com

SINGER, Sandra ASSOCIATES   T 01702 331616
Personal Manager. Contact: By e-mail. 2 Agents represent
an Adult Section (Boutique Agency). Specialising in
Children & Young Performers up to 23 yrs for Feature,
Film, Television, Commercials, Voice Over, Musical
Theatre. Choreographers
21 Cotswold Road
Westcliff-on-Sea, Essex SS0 8AA
E sandrasingeruk@aol.com
W www.sandrasinger.com

SINGERS INC   T 020 7205 2316
Twitter: @singers_inc
INC Artists Ltd, 64 Great Eastern Street
London EC2A 3QR
E lexi@international-collective.com
W www.singersincworld.com

SJ MANAGEMENT   T 020 7371 0441
8 Bettridge Road
London SW6 3QD
E sj@susanjames.demon.co.uk

SMART MANAGEMENT   T 020 7837 8822
Contact: Mario Renzullo
PO Box 64377, London EC1P 1ND
E smart.management@virgin.net

SOPHIE'S PEOPLE   T 020 8812 4999
Contact: Sophie Pyecroft. By Post/e-mail. Accepts
Showreels. 2 Agents represent 400 Performers.
Choreographers. Commercials. Corporate. Dancers. Film.
Television
40 Mexfield Road, London SW15 2RQ
T 0870 7876446
E sophies.people@btinternet.com
W www.sophiespeople.com

S.O.S.   T 020 7735 5133
Twitter: @SebHolden
85 Bannerman House, Lawn Lane
London SW8 1UA
T 07740 359770
E info@sportsofseb.com
W www.sportsofseb.com

SOUNDCHECK AGENCY THE T 020 7437 0290
PMA Member
The Soundcheck Group, 29 Wardour Street
London W1D 6PS
E castings@soundcheckentertainment.co.uk
W www.thesoundcheckgroup.co.uk

SPEAKERS CIRCUIT LTD THE T 01892 750131
After Dinner Speakers
The Country Store, The Green
Frant, East Sussex TN3 9DA
T 01892 750921
E speakers-circuit@freenetname.co.uk

SPEAKERS CORNER T 020 7607 7070
Award Hosts, Comedians, Facilitators & Keynote Speakers
for Corporate Events & Conferences
Unit 31, Highbury Studios
10 Hornsey Street, London N7 8EL
F 020 7700 8847
E info@speakerscorner.co.uk
W www.speakerscorner.co.uk

SPLITTING IMAGES
LOOKALIKES AGENCY T 020 8809 2327
25 Clissold Court, Greenway Close, London N4 2EZ
E info@splitting-images.com
W www.splitting-images.com

SPORTS OF SEB LTD T 020 7735 5133
Twitter: @Sebholden
85 Bannerman House, Lawn Lane, London SW8 1UA
T 07740 359770
E info@sportsofseb.com
W www.sportsofseb.com

SPORTS PROMOTIONS
(UK) LTD/SP ACTORS T 020 8771 4700
Contact: By e-mail/Telephone. 300+ Performers.
Commercials. Actors. Dancers. Modelling. Presenters.
Sports Models. Stunts
56 Church Road, Crystal Palace, London SE19 2EZ
E agent@sportspromotions.co.uk
W www.sportspromotions.co.uk

SPYKER, Paul MANAGEMENT T 020 7462 0046
PO Box 48848, London WC1B 3WZ
F 020 7462 0047
E belinda@psmlondon.com

SRA PERSONAL
MANAGEMENT T 020 7112 8739
Lockhart Road, Cobham
Surrey KT11 2AX
T 07766 761267
E agency@sraagency.com

SSA MANAGEMENT T 07904 817229
E info@ssamanagement.co.uk
W www.ssamanagement.co.uk

S.T. ARTS MANAGEMENT T 0845 4082468
Contact: Tarquin Shaw-Young. Actors. Actresses
Suite 2, 1st Floor Offices, Cantilupe Chambers
Cantilupe Road, Ross-on-Wye HR9 7AN
F 0845 4082464
E tarquin@startsmanagement.co.uk
W www.startsmanagement.co.uk

ST JAMES'S MANAGEMENT T 01621 772183
Personal Manager. Existing Clients only
7 Smyatts Close, Southminster, Essex CM0 7JT
E jlstjames@btconnect.com

STAGE A MANAGEMENT LTD T 07837 072775
9 Beech Grove, Midhurst
West Sussex GU29 9JA
E stageamanagement@gmail.com
W www.csa-theatreschool.co.uk

STAGE CENTRE
MANAGEMENT LTD T 020 7607 0872
Co-operative. CPMA Member. Contact: By e-mail/Post.
Commercials. Film. Musical Theatre. Stage. Television
41 North Road, London N7 9DP
E info@stagecentre.org.uk
W www.stagecentre.org.uk

STAGEWORKS WORLDWIDE
PRODUCTIONS T 01253 342426
Contact: By e-mail. Cirque Artistes. Corporate. Dancers.
Ice Skaters. Musical Theatre
525 Ocean Boulevard, Blackpool FY4 1EZ
F 01253 343702
E info@stageworkswwp.com
W www.stageworkswwp.com

STANTON DAVIDSON
ASSOCIATES T 020 7581 3388
Personal Manager. PMA Member. Contact: Geoff
Stanton, Roger Davidson. By e-mail. Accepts Showreels/
Voicereels. Commercials. Corporate. Film. Musical
Theatre. Radio. Stage. Television. Voice Overs
RADA Studios, 16 Chenies Street
London WC1E 7EX
E contact@stantondavidson.co.uk
W www.stantondavidson.co.uk

STARK TALENT T 07873 945708
Contact: Sarah McCann
Office: 13 Spark Studios, 208-210 Great Clowes Street
Salford, Manchester M7 2ZS
E sarah@starktalent.tv
W www.starktalent.tv

STENTORIAN T 07808 353611
44 Broughton Grove, Skipton BD23 1TL
E stentorian@btinternet.com
W www.stentoriantowncryer.co.uk

STEVENSON, Natasha MANAGEMENT LTD
See STEVENSON WITHERS ASSOCIATES LTD

STEVENSON WITHERS
ASSOCIATES LTD T 020 7720 3355
Personal Manager. PMA Member. Contact: By e-mail/
Telephone. 3 Agents & 1 Assistant. Commercials.
Corporate. Film. Radio. Stage. Television
Studio 7C, Clapham North Arts Centre
Voltaire Road, London SW4 6DH
F 020 7720 5565
E talent@stevensonwithers.com
W www.stevensonwithers.com

STINSON, David AGENCY T 020 3714 3393
57 Old Compton Street
London W1D 6HP
E karen@davidstinsonagency.com
W www.davidstinsonagency.com

STIRLING MANAGEMENT T 01204 848333
Contact: Glen Mortimer. By e-mail. Accepts Showreels.
3 Agents represent 100 Performers. Commercials. Film.
Presenters. Stage. Television. Corporate. Photographic
490 Halliwell Road, Bolton
Lancashire BL1 8AN
E admin@stirlingmanagement.co.uk
W www.stirlingmanagement.co.uk

STIVEN CHRISTIE
MANAGEMENT T 0131 228 4040
Incorporating The Actors Agency of Edinburgh
1 Glen Street, Tollcross
Edinburgh EH3 9JD
E info@stivenchristie.co.uk
W www.stivenchristie.co.uk

STONE, Ian ASSOCIATES T 020 8667 1627
21 Ledbury Place, Croydon CRO 1ET

KAREN SCOTT
PHOTOGRAPHY

www.karenscottphotography.com
info@karenscottphotography.com

07958 975 950
student rates

STONE, Richard PARTNERSHIP THE   T 020 7497 0849
PMA Member
Suite 3, De Walden Court
85 New Cavendish Street, London W1W 6XD
F 020 7497 0869
E all@thersp.com
W www.thersp.com

STONEHOUSE, Katherine MANAGEMENT   T 020 8560 7709
Television. Film. Musical Theatre. Stage. Commercials
PO Box 64412, London W5 9GU
E katherine@katherinestonehouse.co.uk
W www.katherinestonehouse.co.uk

STOPFORD AGENCY   T 020 8741 6158
Stage
56A Church Road, Barnes
London SW13 0DQ
E info@stopfordagency.com
W www.stopfordagency.com

STRAIGHT LINE MANAGEMENT   T 01737 353078
69 Shawley Way, Epsom Downs
Epsom KT18 5PD
E hilary@straightlinemanagement.co.uk

SUCCESS   T 020 7734 3356
Room 236, 2nd Floor, Linen Hall
162-168 Regent Street, London W1B 5TB
F 020 7494 3787
E ee@successagency.co.uk
W www.successagency.co.uk

SUMMERS, Mark MANAGEMENT   T 020 7229 8413
1 Beaumont Avenue, West Kensington
London W14 9LP
E louise@marksummers.com
W www.marksummers.com

SUPERTED.COM   T 07530 429563
TED - The Entertainment Directory
1 Berkeley Street, London W1J 8DJ
E email@superted.com
W www.superted.com

SYMPHONY TALENT GROUP   T 020 3488 0159
E us@symphonytalentgroup.com
W www.symphonytalentgroup.com

TAKE2 CASTING AGENCY   T 00 353 87 2563403
28 Beech Park Road, Foxrock
Dublin 18, Ireland
E pamela@take2.ie
W www.take2.ie

TAKE2 MANAGEMENT   T 0161 832 7715
Suite 5, Basil Chambers, 65 High Street
Manchester M4 1FS
F 0161 839 1661
E chris@take2management.co.uk
W www.take2management.co.uk

TAKE2 MANAGEMENT   T 0113 403 2930
34 Park Cross Street
Leeds LS1 2QH
E chris@take2management.co.uk
W www.take2management.co.uk

TALENT4 MEDIA LTD   T 020 7183 4330
Studio LG6, Shepherds Building Central
Charecroft Way, London W14 0EH
F 020 7183 4331
E enquiries@talent4media.com
W www.talent4media.com

TALENT AGENCY LTD THE   T 01483 281500
Contact: Mike Smith
Freshwater House, Outdowns
Effingham, Surrey KT24 5QR
F 01483 281501
E info@thetalentagencyltd.co.uk

TALENT ARTISTS LTD   T 020 7923 1119
Contact: Jane Wynn Owen. No Unsolicited Enquiries
59 Sydner Road, London N16 7UF
E talent.artists@btconnect.com

TALENT SCOUT THE   T 01924 464049
19 Edge Road, Dewsbury WF12 0QA
E connect@thetalentscout.org
W www.thetalentscout.org

TALENTED ARTISTS LTD T 020 7520 9412
Suite 17, Adam House
7-10 Adam Street, London WC2N 6AA
E info@talentedartistsltd.com
W www.talentedartistsltd.com

TALENT NORTH T 07919 181456
5 Chapel Lane, Garforth LS25 1AG
E sr@talentnorth.co.uk
W www.talentnorth.co.uk

TAVISTOCK WOOD T 020 7494 4767
PMA Member
45 Conduit Street, London W1S 2YN
F 020 7434 2017
E info@tavistockwood.com
W www.tavistockwood.com

**TCA
(THE COMMERCIAL AGENCY)** T 020 7233 8100
12 Evelyn Mansions, Carlisle Place, London SW1P 1NH
E mail@thecommercialagency.co.uk
W www.thecommercialagency.co.uk

**TCG ARTIST
MANAGEMENT LTD** T 020 7240 3600
*Contact: Kristin Tarry (Owner/Director/Agent), Cal
Griffiths (Senior Assistant), Jackie Davis (Office Manager),
Francesca Cooney (Junior Assistant). By e-mail. Accepts
Showreels. Film. Television. Stage. Musical Theatre.
Commercials*
14A Goodwin's Court, London WC2N 4LL
E info@tcgam.co.uk
W www.tcgam.co.uk

TEAM PLAYERS T 00 45 20494218
c/o The Danish Filmhouse, Vognmagergade 10, 1st Floor
DK-1120 Copenhagen K, Denmark
T 00 45 20683920
E info@teamplayers.dk
W www.teamplayers.dk

TENNYSON AGENCY THE T 020 8543 5939
10 Cleveland Avenue, Merton Park, London SW20 9EW
E agency@tennysonagency.co.uk

THEATRE EXPRESS T 01507 527140
Contact: David Kerwick
33 Queen Street, Horncastle, Lincoln LN9 6BD
E perform@theatre-express.com
W www.theatre-express.com

THOMAS, Lisa MANAGEMENT
*Contact: Lisa Thomas (Agent). 1 Agent represents 9+
Performers*
Unit 10, 7 Wenlock Road, London N1 7SL
W www.lisathomasmanagement.com

**THOMPSON, David
ASSOCIATES** T 020 8682 3083
7 St Peter's Close, London SW17 7UH
T 07889 191093
E montefioredt@aol.com

**THOMSON, Mia
ASSOCIATES** T 020 7307 5939
PMA Member
3rd Floor, 207 Regent Street
London W1B 3HH
F 020 7580 4729
E assistant@miathomsonassociates.co.uk
W www.miathomsonassociates.co.uk

**THRELFALL, Katie
ASSOCIATES** T 020 8879 0493
PMA Member
13 Tolverne Road, London SW20 8RA
E info@ktthrelfall.co.uk
W www.katiethrelfallassociates.com

**THRESH, Melody MANAGEMENT
ASSOCIATES LTD (MTM)** T 0161 457 2110
Imperial Court, 2 Exchange Quay
Manchester M5 3EB
E melodythreshmtm@aol.com

**TILDSLEY, Janice
ASSOCIATES** T 020 8521 1888
PMA Member. Contact: Kathryn Kirton
71A Grove Road, London E17 9BU
E kathryn@janicetildsleyassociates.co.uk
W www.janicetildsleyassociates.co.uk

**TINKER, Victoria
MANAGEMENT** T/F 01403 210653
Non-acting. Technical
Birchenbridge House, Brighton Road
Mannings Heath, Horsham, West Sussex RH13 6HY

**TLA BOUTIQUE
MANAGEMENT** T/F 0113 289 3433
*Formerly LAWRENCE, Tonicha AGENCY. Incorporating
Young Boutique*
T 07766 415996
E tonichalawrence@gmail.com
W www.tlaboutiquemanagement.com

TMC AGENCY T 07593 163010
*Contact: Paul Heath. Prospective Client Applications by
e-mail only. No unsolicited calls*
10A Congleton Road, Sandbach
Crewe, Cheshire CW11 1HJ
E info@tmcagency.co.uk
W www.tmcagency.net

TMG ASSOCIATES T 020 7437 1383
Previously Morgan & Goodman
4 Cavendish Square, London W1G 0PG
T 07866 589905
E tanya.greep@googlemail.com

TMP AGENCY T 020 8204 2716
Contact: Marcus Flemmings. Indian / South Asian Talent
55 Holmes Road, London NW9 5QG
E info@tmpagency.com
W www.tmpagency.com

TOP TALENT AGENCY T 01727 855903
*TTA Adults. Representing Children & Adults.
Commercials. Film. Photographic. Stage. Television*
PO Box 860, St Albans
Herts AL1 9BR
F 01727 260903
E adults@toptalentagency.co.uk
W www.ttaadults.co.uk

TOTAL VANITY T 07710 780152
15 Walton Way, Aylesbury
Buckinghamshire HP21 7JJ
E richard.williams@totalvanity.com
W www.totalvanity.com

TRENDS ENTERTAINMENT T 01253 396534
Unit 4, 9 Chorley Road, Blackpool
Lancashire FY3 7XQ
E info@trendsentertainment.com
W www.trendsentertainment.com

TROIKA T 020 7336 7868
PMA Member
10A Christina Street, London EC2A 4PA
F 020 3544 2919
E casting@troikatalent.com
W www.troikatalent.com

TTA T 01245 690080
Unit 1, Well Lane Industrial Estate, Well Lane
Danbury, Chelmsford CM3 4AB
E agents@tomorrowstalent.co.uk

TTA ADULTS LTD   T 01727 855903
Top Talent Agency Adult Division. Personal Manager.
Contact: Warren Bacci, Leoni Kibbey. By e-mail.
Accepts Showreels. 6 Agents represent 100
Performers. Commercials. Film. Musical Theatre.
Singers
PO Box 860, St Albans, Herts AL1 9BR
F 01727 260903
E adults@toptalentagency.co.uk
W www.toptalentagency.co.uk

TV MANAGEMENTS   T 01425 475544
Brink House, Avon Castle, Ringwood, Hants BH24 2BL
F 01425 480123
E etv@tvmanagements.co.uk

TWINS
See PC THEATRICAL, MODEL & CASTING AGENCY

TWO'S COMPANY   T 020 8299 3714
Existing Clients only. Directors. Stage. Writers
244 Upland Road, London SE22 0DN
E graham@2scompanytheatre.co.uk

UGLY MODELS   T 020 8749 4760
F 020 7402 0507
E info@ugly.org
W www.ugly.org

UK SCREEN ACTING ACADEMY   T 07879 846113
5 Corrie Court, Hamilton, South Lanarkshire ML3 9XE
E stuart@screenactingacademy.co.uk
W www.screenactingacademy.co.uk

UNION MANAGEMENT & COMEDY ACTORS
LONDON   T 07764 753892
Studio 13 Novello Court, 39 Dibden Street
London N1 8RH
E hello@comedyactorslondon.com
W www.comedyactorslondon.com

UNITED AGENTS LLP   T 020 3214 0800
Personal Manager. PMA Member
12-26 Lexington Street, London W1F 0LE
E info@unitedagents.co.uk
W www.unitedagents.co.uk

UPBEAT MANAGEMENT   T 020 8668 3332
Theatre Touring & Events. No Actors
Ground Floor, 10 Lindal Road
London SE4 1EJ
E info@upbeatmanagement.co.uk
W www.upbeat.co.uk

UPSON EDWARDS
See REPRESENTATION UPSON EDWARDS

URBAN COLLECTIVE LTD   T 020 7482 3282
The Basement, 17 Burghley Road
London NW5 1UG
E info@urban-collective.co.uk
W www.urban-collective.co.uk

URBAN TALENT   T 0161 228 6866
Contact: Liz Beeley
Nemesis House,
1 Oxford Court
Bishopsgate, Manchester M2 3WQ
E liz@nmsmanagement.co.uk
W www.urbantalent.tv

UTOPIA MODEL
MANAGEMENT   T 07771 884844
7 Ellerbeck
Manchester M28 7XN
F 0871 2180843
E kya@utopiamodels.co.uk

UVA MANAGEMENT LTD   T 0845 0090344
Contact: By e-mail. Commercials. Film. Presenters. Stage.
Television
Pinewood Film Studios
Pinewood Road
Iver Heath, Buckinghamshire SL0 0NH
E berko@uvamanagement.com
W www.uvamanagement.com

VACCA, Roxane
MANAGEMENT   T 020 7383 5971
PMA Member
61 Judd Street, London WC1H 9QT
E info@roxanevacca.co.uk

**VALLÉ THEATRICAL
AGENCY THE**   T 01992 622861
The Vallé Academy Studios, Wilton House
Delamare Road, Cheshunt, Herts EN8 9SG
F 01992 622868
E agency@valleacademy.co.uk
W www.valleacademy.co.uk

**VAN RENSBURG ARTIST
MANAGEMENT (VAM)**   T 07724 937331
*Contact: Michelle van Rensburg. By e-mail. 1 Agent
represents 50 Performers. Children. Film. Stage.
Television. Foreign Actors*
19 Seaview Terrace, Joppa
Edinburgh EH15 2HD
E michelle@vanartman.co.uk   W www.vanartman.co.uk

**VIDAL-HALL, Clare
MANAGEMENT**   T 020 8741 7647
*PMA Member. Choreographers. Composers. Designers.
Directors. Lighting Designers. Musical Supervisors/
Directors. Sound Designers. Video Designers*
57 Carthew Road, London W6 0DU
F 020 8741 9459
E info@clarevidalhall.com   W www.clarevidalhall.com

VINE, Michael ASSOCIATES   T 020 8347 2580
Light Entertainment
1 Stormont Road, London N6 4NS
E stephen@michaelvineassociates.com

VISIONARY TALENT   T 020 8133 4622
Suite 36, 88-90 Hatton Garden
Holborn, London EC1N 8PG
E info@visionarytalent.co.uk
W www.visionarytalent.co.uk

VJ MANAGEMENT   T 020 7237 8953
*Personal Manager. Contact: Valerie Hodson. By e-mail
with Spotlight number only. 1 Agent represents 49 Clients*
15 Jarman House, Hawkstone Road
Surrey Quays, London SE16 2PW
E valerie@vjmgt.co.uk   W www.vjmgt.co.uk

**VM TALENT LTD
(VIC MURRAY TALENT)**   T 020 7112 8938
PMA Member
Unit 40, Battersea Business Centre
99-101 Lavender Hill, London SW11 5QL
E info@vmtalent.com   W www.vmtalent.com

VSA LTD   T 020 7240 2927
PMA Member. Contact: Andy Charles, Tod Weller
186 Shaftesbury Avenue, London WC2H 8JB
E info@vsaltd.com   W www.vsaltd.com

W ATHLETIC   T 020 8948 2759
34 Hill Street, Richmond-upon-Thames
London TW9 1TW
E london@wathletic.com   W www.wathletic.com

WADE, Suzann   T 020 7486 0746
*(Casting/Production only)
Personal Manager. PMA Member. Contact: By
Post only (No Calls). Accepts Showreels via Link on
CV. Film. Musical Theatre. Stage. Television. Voice
Overs. Animation/Computer Games. Radio Drama.
Commercials. Covering UK & International Castings*
9 Wimpole Mews, London W1G 8PG
E admin@suzannwade.com
W www.suzannwade.com

**WARD, Mandy
ARTIST MANAGEMENT**   T 020 7434 3569
PMA Member
4th Floor, 74 Berwick Street
London W1F 8TE
E info@mwartistmanagement.com
W www.mandywardartistmanagement.com

WARING & McKENNA   T 020 7836 9222
PMA Member
17 South Molton Street, London W1K 5QT
F 020 7836 9186
E dj@waringandmckenna.com
W www.waringandmckenna.com

**WARRINGTON, Patrick
ASSOCIATES**   T 01765 688017
The Studio, Low Burton Hall
Masham, North Yorkshire HG4 4DQ
E patrick@pwassociates.tv   W www.pwassociates.tv

WASSERMAN MEDIA GROUP   T 020 7255 8155
PMA Member
6th Floor, 33 Soho Square
London W1D 3QU
E broadcasting@wmgllc.com
W www.wassermantvtalent.com

**WELCH, Janet PERSONAL
MANAGEMENT**   T/F 01761 463238
Contact: By Post
Old Orchard, The Street
Ubley, Bristol BS40 6PJ
E info@janetwelchpm.co.uk

WEST, Ben MANAGEMENT   T 020 7684 0060
Hoxton Hall Theatre, 130 Hoxton Street
London N1 6SH
E assistant@benwestmanagement.com
W www.benwestmanagement.co.uk

**WEST CENTRAL
MANAGEMENT**   T/F 020 7833 8134
*CPMA Member. Co-operative of 20 Performers. Contact:
By Post/e-mail*
Room 4, East Block, Panther House
38 Mount Pleasant
London WC1X 0AN
E mail@westcentralmanagement.com
W www.westcentralmanagement.com

WGM TALENT AGENCY   T 0161 850 1095
Actors. Stage. Television. Literary
82 King Street, Manchester M2 4WQ
T 07714 252026
E guy@wgmtalent.com
W www.wgmtalent.com

**WHATEVER ARTISTS
MANAGEMENT LTD**   T 020 8349 0920
PO Box 72301, London NW7 0HG
E info@wamshow.biz
W www.wamshow.biz

WHITEHALL ARTISTS   T/F 020 8785 3737
6 Embankment, Putney, London SW15 1LB
E whitehallfilms@gmail.com

**WILKINSON, David
ASSOCIATES**   T 020 7371 5188
Existing Clients only
115 Hazlebury Road, London SW6 2LX
E info@dwassociates.net

**WILLIAMS BULLDOG
MANAGEMENT LTD**   T 020 7585 1518
The Gatehouse, 24 Southend Road
Beckenham, Kent BR3 5AA
E info@williamsbulldog.co.uk
W www.williamsbulldog.co.uk

WILLIAMSON & HOLMES   T 020 7240 0407
Twitter: @WilliamsonHolme
5th Floor, Sovereign House, 212-224 Shaftesbury Avenue
London WC2H 8PR
E info@williamsonandholmes.co.uk
W www.williamsonandholmes.co.uk

'the BIG agency for short & tall actors'

Willow Management

actors from 3ft to 5ft & over 7ft
for films, TV, theatre & advertising

tel: +44 (0)1733 240392 • email: office@willowmanagement.co.uk • on-line casting directory: willowmanagement.co.uk

WILLOW PERSONAL MANAGEMENT   **T** 01733 240392
Specialist Agency for Short Actors (5 feet & under) & Tall Actors (7 feet & over)
151 Main Street, Yaxley, Peterborough, Cambs PE7 3LD
E office@willowmanagement.co.uk
W www.willowmanagement.co.uk

WILLS, Newton MANAGEMENT   **T** 07989 398381
Personal Manager. Contact: By e-mail. Accepts Showreels/Voicereels. 3 Agents represent 50 Performers. Actors. Commercials. Dancers. Film. Musical Theatre. Singers. Stage. Television
F 00 33 4 68218685
E newton.wills@aol.com
W www.newtonwills.com

WINDMILL ARTISTS MANAGEMENT   **T** 07900 735566
3 Mill End, Thaxted, Essex CM6 2LT
T 07512 998007
E info@windmillartistsmanagement.co.uk
W www.windmillartistsmanagement.co.uk

WINSLETT, Dave ASSOCIATES   **T** 020 8668 0531
4 Zig Zag Road, Kenley, Surrey CR8 5EL
F 020 8668 9216
E info@davewinslett.com
W www.davewinslett.com

WINTERSONS   **T** 020 7836 7849
PMA Member
59 St Martin's Lane, London WC2N 4JS
E info@nikiwinterson.com
W www.nikiwinterson.com

WIS CELTIC MANAGEMENT   **T** 07966 302812
Welsh, Irish & Scottish Performers
86 Elphinstone Road
Walthamstow, London E17 5EX
F 020 8523 4523

WISE BUDDAH TALENT   **T** 020 7307 1600
Contact: Sam Gregory
74 Great Titchfield Street, London W1W 7QP
F 020 730/ 1601
E sam.gregory@wisebuddah.com
W www.wisebuddah.com

WMG MANAGEMENT EUROPE LTD   **T** 020 7009 6000
Sports Management Company
5th Floor, 33 Soho Square, London W1D 3QU
F 020 3230 1053
W www.wmgllc.com

WOODS, Evie MANAGEMENT   **T** 07501 128266
Contact: Jo Hart, Hannah Cheetham
7B Jackson Road, London N7 6EN
T 07856 033205
E info@eviewoods.co.uk
W www.eviewoodsmanagement.co.uk

WYMAN, Edward AGENCY   **T** 029 2075 2351
Contact: Judith Gay. By Post/e-mail. Adults (16+ yrs). Books open for a limited number of new actors. January only. English & Welsh Language. Commercials. Corporate. Television. Voice Overs. Walk-on & Supporting Artists
23 White Acre Close
Thornhill
Cardiff CF14 9DG
E wymancasting@yahoo.co.uk
W www.wymancasting.co.uk

XL MANAGEMENT   **T** 01926 810449
Edmund House, Rugby Road
Leamington Spa
Warwickshire CV32 6EL
F 01926 811420
E office@xlmanagement.co.uk
W www.xlmanagement.co.uk

YAFTA TALENT AGENCY   **T** 07512 921934
Contact: Charlotte Armitage
16 East Park Road, Spofforth
Harrogate
North Yorkshire HG3 1BH
E agency@yafta.co.uk
W www.yafta.tv

YAT MANAGEMENT (YOUNG ACTORS THEATRE MANAGEMENT)   **T** 020 7278 2101
70-72 Barnsbury Road, London N1 0ES
E agent@yati.org.uk
W www.yati.org.uk

YT93   **T** 01580 857257
Contact: Christina Yates. By e-mail. 4 Agents represent 135 Performers. Children. Teenagers
Glassenbury Hill Farm
Glassenbury Road
Cranbrook, Kent TN17 2QF
E christina@christinayates.com
W www.yt93.co.uk

ZWICKLER, Marlene & ASSOCIATES   **T/F** 0131 343 3030
1 Belgrave Crescent Lane
Edinburgh EH4 3AG
E info@mza-artists.com
W www.mza-artists.com

Children's & Teenagers' Agents

How can my child become an actor?

If your child is interested in becoming an actor, they should try to get as much practical experience as possible. For example, joining a drama club at school, taking theatre studies as an option, reading as many plays as they can and going to the theatre on a regular basis. They could also attend local youth theatres or drama groups. Some theatres offer evening or Saturday classes.

What are the chances of success?

As any agency or school will tell you, the acting profession is highly competitive and for every success story there are many children who will never be hired for paid acting work. Child artists and their parents should think very carefully before getting involved in the industry and be prepared for disappointments along the way.

What is the difference between stage schools and agencies?

Stage schools provide specialised training in acting, singing and dancing for under 18s. They offer a variety of full and part-time courses. Please see the 'Drama Training, Schools & Coaches' section for listings. Children's and teenagers' agencies specialise in the representation of child artists, promoting them to casting opportunities and negotiating contracts on their behalf. In return they will take commission, usually ranging from 10-15%. Some larger stage schools also have agencies attached to them. A number of agents are listed in this section.

Why does my child need an agent?

While many parents feel they want to retain control over their child's career, they will not have the contacts and authority a good agent will have in the industry. Casting directors are more likely to look to an agent they know and trust to provide the most suitable children for a role than an un-represented child. This does not mean to say that a child will never get work without an agent, but it will certainly be more difficult. There are other factors like licensing and chaperoning that agents can organise and give advice on.

How should I use these listings?

This section lists up-to-date contact details for agencies specialising in the representation of children and teenagers. Every company listed is done so by written request to us. Always research agencies carefully before approaching them to make sure they are suitable for your child. Many have websites you can visit, or ask around for personal recommendations. You should make a shortlist of the ones you think are most appropriate rather than sending a standard letter to agencies. Please see the main 'Agents & Personal Managers' advice section for further guidance on choosing and approaching agents.

Can Spotlight offer me advice on choosing or changing my child's agent?

Unfortunately, Spotlight is not able to advise performers on specific agents, nor are we in a position to handle any financial or contractual queries or complaints. For agent-related queries we suggest you contact The Agents' Association www.agents-uk.com or The Personal Managers' Association (PMA) www.thepma.com, or you could try one of the independent advisers on our website www.spotlight.com/artists/advice

Who can I contact for general advice?

Your local education authority should be able to help with most queries regarding your child's education; working hours, chaperones and general welfare if they are aged 16 or under. You could also try contacting an independent adviser for advice, or for legal guidance please see the 'Accountants, Insurance & Law' section for listings.

Can my child join Equity?

Since May 2012, children aged 10 or over can apply for full Equity membership. Please see www.equity.org.uk

Should I pay an agent to represent my child? Or sign a contract?

Equity does not recommend that you pay an agent an upfront fee to place your child on their client list. Before signing a contract, you should be very clear about the terms and commitments involved. For advice on both of these issues, or if you experience any problems with a current agent, we recommend contacting Equity directly.

Why do child actors need licences?

Strict regulations apply to children working in the entertainment industry. These cover areas including the maximum number of performance hours per day/week, rest times, meal times and tutoring requirements. When any child under 16 performs in a professional capacity, the production company must obtain a Child Performance Licence from the child's local education authority.

Who are chaperones?

Child artists must also be accompanied by a chaperone at all times when they are working. Registered chaperones are generally used instead of parents as they have a better understanding of the employment regulations involved, and have professional experience of dealing with production companies.

Listings for a number of child chaperones can be found in the 'Consultants' section, but please ensure that you research any company or individual before proceeding further. Registered chaperones will have been police checked and approved by their local education authority to act in loco parentis. Always contact your local education authority if you have any questions or concerns.

What is Spotlight Children & Young Performers?

Children who are currently represented by an agent or attend a stage school can appear in the Spotlight Children & Young Performers. This is a casting resource, used by production teams to source child artists for television, film, stage or commercial work. Each child pays an annual membership fee to have their own individual online profile on the Spotlight website, searchable by casting professionals. Please speak to your child's school or agency about joining Spotlight for ongoing promotion to hundreds of casting opportunities.

For further information about the directory visit www.spotlight.com/join

Children's & Teenagers' Agents

CASE STUDY

Tarquin Shaw-Young is the Managing Director and Head of Casting for the Stagecoach Agency UK; the largest Children's and Younger Performers' Agency in the UK. Over the past 15 years he has been responsible for thousands of children's careers and auditioned well over 30,000.

Stagecoach Theatre Arts Ltd is the biggest network of acting schools in the UK with around 40,000 children attending their acting, singing and dance classes each week.

Advice on Choosing an Agent

'Tota orbis terrae theatrum est' or - *'Where all the World's A Stage'.* Shakespeare hit the nail on the head with that quote and it's more relevant now than it ever was. With more children in theatre, film and television than there has ever been, the world of the young performer has become even more competitive, with an ever evolving worldwide platform on which to perform. Finding a voice and an identity for your child is vital in an industry where nothing is guaranteed. Finding the right agent and the right path can be tricky.

> **"Always prepare children going into the industry that failure is not a reflection of ability"**

Lower your expectations

Having an amazing talent for acting is not a golden ticket to work. A child may have wowed audiences in a show, have that extra special 'X' factor appeal that everyone wants, but competition amongst child actors is just as fierce as with adults. So always prepare children going into the industry that failure is not a reflection of ability – sometimes it can be down to a specific look – in fact there are so many variables in casting that talent can sometimes be several steps down on the list.

You've got to be in it to win it

Having an agent is obviously a vital first step. Check there are no hidden fees involved – agencies shouldn't charge any up-front joining fee or any residual fee six months in. Any such charges are illegal. The only thing that they could be charging for is Spotlight entry which is an essential part of any actors' portfolio and also good professional headshots. The only money that agents earn is their commission of around 20% for children as there is obviously more work involved. As an adult this percentage will drop down to 12%-15% should they stay on in the profession. Look at the types of work an agency has done and the size of their client list. Larger agencies will have more resources and contacts than smaller agencies who might take a more personal management approach.

An honest picture

A good picture is a vital piece of the casting process. So often I have met with older actors who when they walk through the door look nothing like the person in the photo. Your photo needs to be a mirror image of the real thing. Casting Directors don't like their time being wasted. Your picture is the first port of call so a good photographer with clear honest photos is essential - most agents will have a recommended photographer.

A good level of training

Whilst working as a young performer it is vital that you continue to train. Acting is a muscle that needs a regular workout so find a good theatre club or school that gives you a consistent level of varied training that hones your skill-set and improves your capabilities.

Ask not what you can do for your Agent but what your Agent can do for you?

An agent is there to try and get jobs and opportunities for your child. When starting out in the business I am a firm believer that you should take anything that comes along – many parents demand that their children just do film and television as though that is a quick fix to fame. A good child performer will hopefully work across all areas of the industry. So typically a child might be filming for a couple of days on a commercial which is a great deal of fun, they may have their own trailer and be paid a reasonable amount of money. Next week they might be on stage in a show earning a fraction of the money and sharing a dressing room with five other children. So you should take each experience as the whole thing and treat each new role with the respect and humility it deserves.

Agents are busy people

In a typical day a busy agency can receive over a hundred castings in a day – they will be looking at many different variables that the casting directors and producers have displayed in their breakdowns. A good agent will be as accurate as possible to match the right client to the right role and send those details off with a suitable reference with a view to an audition. A good agent will make this information freely available to you. Remember that agents don't know about every casting so if you have a particular job that you have seen check with your agent first. Agents are the professionals and it is much better to have them send out your details. Your agent is there to help – they don't get paid unless you work so it's not in their best interests to sit around and do nothing.

'I love acting because it's this space where dreams can be realized, fantasy comes to life, and there are no limitations on what's possible.'
- Actress, Jessica Alba

To find our more about Stagecoach UK visit www.stagecoachagency.co.uk

alphabetkidz

TV/Film, Commercial, Photographic, Theatre and Voiceovers
Naturally talented Artists with a multitude of different skills and talents for all your casting needs.
Our philosophy is Fun, Energy, Enthusiasm, Commitment, Equality and Diversity.

t : 020 7252 4343 f: 020 7252 4341
e : contact@alphabetkidz.co.uk
w : www.alphabetkidz.co.uk

BAFTA AWARD WINNING AGENCY alphabetmanagement | alphabetagency

A & J ARTISTS LTD T 020 8342 0542
Children & Adults
242A The Ridgeway, Botany Bay
Enfield EN2 8AP
T 020 8367 7139
E info@ajmanagement.co.uk
W www.ajmanagement.co.uk

ABACUS AGENCY T 01737 821348
Robert Denholm House, Bletchingley Road
Nutfield, Redhill, Surrey RH1 4HW
E admin@abacusagency.co.uk
W www.abacusagency.co.uk

ACADEMY ARTS MANAGEMENT T 01245 422595
6A The Green, Writtle
Chelmsford, Essex CM1 3DU
E info@academyarts.co.uk
W www.academyarts.co.uk

ACORN ACTORS AGENCY THE T 01491 281321
1 The Green, Middle Assendon
Henley-on-Thames, Oxfordshire RG9 6AT
E gailrosier@hotmail.com
W www.acornmusictheatrecompany.co.uk

ACT-ON T 01379 898135
Bell Hill House, The Street
Rickinghall, Suffolk IP22 1BN
E tanya@act-on.org.uk
W www.act-on.org.uk

ACT 2 MANAGEMENT T 07939 144355
105 Richmond Avenue, Highams Park
London E4 9RR
E management@act2drama.co.uk
W www.act2drama.co.uk

ACTING KIDZ AGENCY T 0845 6458000
1 Beaumont Avenue, West Kensington
London W14 9LP
E actingkidzuk@gmail.com
W www.actingkidz.co.uk

ACT OUT AGENCY T/F 0161 429 7413
22 Greek Street, Stockport, Cheshire SK3 8AB
E ab22actout@aol.com
W www.abacademytheatreschool.webs.com

AFA MANAGEMENT T 07752 408201
Amanda Fairclough Actors Management
Braeside, Bottom O'th Moor
Horwich, Bolton BL6 6QH
E toni@afamanagement.co.uk
W www.afamanagement.co.uk

AIM (ASSOCIATED INTERNATIONAL MANAGEMENT LLP) T 020 7831 9709
Contact: Nicola Mansfield
4th Floor, 7 Hatton Garden
London EC1N 8AD
E info@aimagents.com
W www.aimagents.com

ALL EXPRESSIONS AGENCY T 020 8274 1320
218 Staines Road, Twickenham TW2 5AP
T 07581 338739
E maggie@allexpressions.co.uk
W www.allexpressions.co.uk

ALL THE ARTS CHILDREN'S CASTING AGENCY T 020 8850 2384
PO Box 61687, London SE9 9BP
T 07908 618083
E jillian@allthearts.co.uk
W www.allthearts.co.uk

ALLSORTS CHILDRENS AGENCY T 020 8989 0500
Challenge House, 1st Floor, 57-59 Queens Road
Buckhurst Hill, Essex IG9 5BU
T 07958 511647
E bookings@allsortsagency.com
W www.allsortsagency.com

ALLSORTS DRAMA FOR CHILDREN T/F 020 8969 3249
In association with LESLIE, Sasha MANAGEMENT
34 Crediton Road, London NW10 3DU
E sasha@allsortsdrama.com

ALLSTARS CASTING T 0151 707 2100
66 Hope Street, Liverpool L1 9BZ
T/F 07739 359737
E sylvie@allstarscasting.co.uk
W www.allstarscasting.co.uk

ALLSTARZ CASTING AGENCY T 01268 711180
'Glennines', Ramsden Park Road
Ramsden Bellhouse, Billericay, Essex CM11 1NS
T 07740 922956
E office@allstarzcastingagency.co.uk
W www.allstarzagency.co.uk

ALPHABET KIDZ T 020 7252 4343
Also known as Alphabet Agency
Daisy Business Park, 19-35 Sylvan Grove
London SE15 1PD
F 020 7252 4341
E contact@alphabetkidz.co.uk
W www.alphabetkidz.co.uk

ANDREWS, Amanda AGENCY T 01782 393889
30 Caverswall Road, Blythe Bridge
Stoke-on-Trent, Staffs ST11 9BG
E amanda@amandaandrewsagency.com
W www.amandaandrewsagency.com

ANNA'S MANAGEMENT T 020 8958 7636
Children. Teenagers. Young Adults
25 Tintagel Drive, Stanmore, Middlesex HA7 4SR
E annasmanage@aol.com
W www.annasmanagement.co.uk

APA AGENCY OXFORD T 01865 521168
Contact: Melissa D'Amico
3 Northfield Row, Witney, Oxfordshire OX28 1FG
E agency@authenticperformanceacademy.com
W www.authenticperformanceacademy.com

ARAENA/COLLECTIVE T/F 020 8428 0037
10 Bramshaw Gardens, South Oxhey, Herts WD19 6XP
E info@collectivedance.co.uk

ARNOULD KIDZ T 020 8942 1879
1A Brook Gardens, Kingston-upon-Thames
Surrey KT2 7ET
T 07720 427828
E info@arnouldkidz.co.uk
W www.arnouldkidz.co.uk

ARTEMIS STUDIOS PERFORMING
ARTS SCHOOL T 020 3422 3001
South Hill Park Mansion, Ringmead
Bracknell RG12 7PA
E agents@artemisagency.co.uk
W www.artemisagency.co.uk

ARTS1 MANAGEMENT T 01908 410700
The Box Studios, Sunrise Parkway
Linford Wood, Milton Keynes MK14 6LS
E info@arts1.co.uk
W www.arts1management.co.uk

ASHCROFT ACADEMY OF
DRAMATIC ART & AGENCY T 07799 791586
Harris Primary Academy Crystal Palace
Malcolm Road
Penge, London SE20 8RH
E info@ashcroftacademy.com
W www.ashcroftacademy.com

BACKGROUND WALES T 0845 4082468
Suite 2, 1st Floor Offices, Cantilupe Chambers
Cantilupe Road, Ross-on-Wye HR9 7AN
F 0845 4082464
E tarquin@backgroundwales.co.uk
W www.backgroundwales.co.uk

BANANAFISH MANAGEMENT T 0151 708 5509
The Business Hub, 40 Devonshire Road
Wirral CH43 1TW
T 07974 206622
E info@bananafish.co.uk
W www.bananafish.co.uk

BARRETT, Becky
MANAGEMENT T 020 8840 7828
11 Central Chambers, The Broadway
London W5 2NR
E info@beckybarrettmanagement.co.uk
W www.beckybarrettmanagement.co.uk

BIG TALENT SCHOOL &
AGENCY THE T 029 2046 4506
Contact: Shelley Norton. Twitter: @shellmiranda
59 Mount Stuart Square, Cardiff CF10 5LR
T 07886 020923
E info@thebigtalent.co.uk
W www.thebigtalent.co.uk

BITESIZE AGENCY T 01978 358320
Unit 6/7 Clwyd Court 2
Rhosddu Industrial Estate
Rhosrobin, Wrexham LL11 4YL
F 01978 756308
E bitesizeagency@btconnect.com
W www.bitesizeagency.co.uk

BIZZYKIDZ T 0845 5200400
Bizzy Studios, 1st Floor Hall
10-12 Pickford Lane
Bexleyheath, Kent DA7 4QW
F 0845 5200401
E bookings@bizzykidz.com
W www.bizzykidz.com

BMA ARTISTS T 01442 878878
Represents Actors, Actresses, Performers, Presenters
& Children
346 High Street
Berkhamsted
Hertfordshire HP4 1HT
E info@bmaartists.com
W www.bmaartists.com

BODENS AGENCY T 020 8447 0909
99 East Barnet Road, New Barnet
Herts EN4 8RF
T 07545 696888
E info@bodens.co.uk
W www.bodens.co.uk/clients

BONNIE & BETTY LTD T 020 8301 8333
9-11 Gunnery Terrace, Royal Arsenal
London SE18 6SW
E agency@bonnieandbetty.com
W www.bonnieandbetty.com

BOSS JUNIORS T 0161 237 0100
Fourways House, 57 Hilton Street
Manchester M1 2EJ
F 0161 236 1237
E info@bossjuniors.co.uk
W www.bossjuniors.co.uk

**BOURNE, Michelle CHILDREN'S
MULTICULTURAL ACADEMY
& AGENCY** T 07852 932473
E info@michellebourneacademy.co.uk
W www.michellebourneacademy.co.uk

BRADFORD THEATRE ARTS T 07986 713203
Daisy Hill Back Lane, Bradford
West Yorkshire BD9 6DJ
E stephanie@btapacademy.co.uk
W www.bradfordtheatrearts.webs.com

**BROAD ACTING
MANAGEMENT LTD** T 020 7544 1012
Contact: Katy Edwards
223 Regent Street, London W1B 2QD
E info@broadactingmanagement.co.uk
W www.broadactingmanagement.co.uk

BROWN AND MILLS T 020 3189 1441
Contact: Sam Brown
Suite 3, Galleon Mews
Northfleet, Kent DA11 9EE
E info@bamentertainment.co.uk
W www.brownandmills.co.uk

BRUCE & BROWN T 020 7624 7333
17 Lonsdale Road, London NW6 6RA
F 020 7625 4047
E info@bruceandbrown.com
W www.bruceandbrown.com

BRUNO KELLY LTD T 020 7183 7331
3rd Floor, 207 Regent Street
London W1B 3HH
F 020 7183 7332
E info@brunokelly.com
W www.brunokelly.com

BUTTERCUP AGENCY T 0843 2899063
Wyndrums, The Village, Ewhurst, Surrey GU6 7PB
E info@buttercupagency.co.uk
W www.buttercupagency.co.uk

BYRON'S MANAGEMENT T 020 7242 8096
Children & Adults
41 Maiden Lane, London WC2E 7LJ
E office@byronsmanagement.co.uk
W www.byronsmanagement.co.uk

CADA CASTING T 07788 765569
Contact: Robyn Beresford
Wyecroft, Beachley Road Tutshill
Chepstow, Monmouthshire NP16 7DL
E info@cadacasting.co.uk
W www.cadacasting.co.uk

CARNEY ACADEMY TALENT T 07976 869442
Montgomery Studios, Surrey Street, Sheffield S1
E talent@carneyacademy.co.uk
W www.carneyacademy.co.uk

CARR, Norrie AGENCY T 020 7253 1771
Babies, Children & Adults
Holborn Studios, 49 Eagle Wharf Road
London N1 7ED
F 020 7253 1772
E info@norriecarr.com
W www.norriecarr.com

CAVAT AGENCY T 07860 615205
16A Hook Hill, Sanderstead
Surrey CR2 0LA
E agency@cavatschool.co.uk
W www.cavatagency.co.uk

**CAVAT SCHOOL OF THEATRE
ARTS & AGENCY** T 07860 615205
16A Hook Hill, Sanderstead
Surrey CR2 0LA
E agency@cavatschool.co.uk
W www.cavatschool.co.uk

**CHARKHAM, Esta
ASSOCIATES** T 020 8741 2843
16 British Grove, Chiswick
London W4 2NL
F 020 8746 3219
E office@charkham.net
W www.charkham.net

CHEEKY MONKEY MODELS T 020 8960 6277
Unit 211, 5 Buspace Studios
Conlan Street, London W10 5AP
E dione@cheekymonkeymodels.com
W www.cheekymonkeymodels.com

**CHERIDAN, Samantha
MANAGEMENT** T 07734 964648
Contact: Samantha Smith
85 Hewson Road, Lincoln
Lincolnshire LN1 1RZ
E sam@starstruckacademy.co.uk
W www.starstruckacademy.co.uk

CHILDSPLAY MODELS LLP T 020 8659 9860
114 Avenue Road, Beckenham
Kent BR3 4SA
F 020 8778 2672
E info@childsplaymodels.co.uk
W www.childsplaymodels.co.uk

CHILLI KIDS T 0333 666 2468
1 Badhan Court, Telford TF1 5QX
F 0333 666 2469
E info@chillikids.co.uk
W www.chillikids.co.uk

CHRYSTEL ARTS AGENCY T 01494 773336
6 Eunice Grove, Chesham
Bucks HP5 1RL
T 07799 605489
E chrystelarts@waitrose.com

CIEKABAILEY ASSOCIATES T 0161 484 5423
7 Ridge Road, Marple
Cheshire SK6 7HL
E enquiries@ciekabailey.com
W www.ciekabailey.com

CONTI, Italia AGENCY LTD T 020 7608 7500
Italia Conti House
23 Goswell Road
London EC1M 7AJ
F 020 7253 1430
E agency@italiaconti.co.uk

CPA AGENCY T 01708 766444
The Studios, 219B North Street
Romford, Essex RM1 4QA
E agency@cpastudios.co.uk
W www.cpastudios.co.uk

CREATIVE KIDZ & ADULTZ   T 07908 144802
235 Fox Glove House, Fulham Road
London SW6 5PQ
T 020 7381 3684
E agency@creativekidzandco.co.uk
W www.creativekidzandco.co.uk

CS MANAGEMENT   T 01708 708515
Children & Young Adults
35 Chase Cross Road, Romford
Essex RM5 3PJ
T 07818 050424
E linda@csmanagementuk.com
W www.csmanagementuk.com

CTC AGENCY   T 01473 725822
Contact: Susan Rowe
31 Bucklesham Road, Ipswich
Suffolk IP3 8TH
E susan@thectc.co.uk
W www.ctcagency.co.uk

CUPCAKE MANAGEMENT   T 07583 295898
8 South Drive, Wokingham
Berkshire RG40 2DH
E cupcake_management@yahoo.co.uk

CURTAIN UP   T 01225 448050
3 Englishcombe Rise, Bath BA2 2RL
T 07974 014490
E admin@curtainup.org.uk
W www.curtainup.org.uk

D & B MANAGEMENT   T 020 8698 8880
Central Studios, 470 Bromley Road
Bromley, Kent BR1 4PQ
E bonnie@dandbmanagement.com
W www.dandbperformingarts.co.uk

DAISY & DUKES LTD   T 01707 377547
30 Great North Road, Stanborough
Herts AL8 7TJ
T 07507 545894
E michelle@daisyanddukes.com
W www.daisyanddukes.com

**DALE HAMMOND
ASSOCIATES (DHA)**   T 07581 034153
60 Wilbury Way, Hitchin
Hertfordshire SG4 0TA
T 07890 260049
E info@dalehammondassociates.com
W www.dalehammondassociates.com

DALY, David ASSOCIATES   T 01565 631999
Contact: Mary Ramsay
16 King Street, Knutsford WA16 6DL
E north@daviddaly.co.uk
W www.daviddaly.co.uk

DD'S CASTING AGENCY   T 020 8502 6866
6 Acle Close, Hainault
Essex IG6 2GQ
T 07957 398501
E ddscasting@ddtst.com
W www.ddtst.com

**DEVINE ARTIST
MANAGEMENT**   T 0161 726 5726
Tempus Building, 9 Mirabel Street
Manchester M3 1NP
E manchester@devinemanagement.co.uk
W www.devinemanagement.co.uk

**DODD, Emma SCHOOL OF
PERFORMING ARTS THE**   T 07903 588137
6-18 yrs
75 Westerfield Road, Ipswich IP4 2XP
E enquiries@emmadodd.com
W www.emmadodd.com

DRAGON DRAMA   T 07590 452436
Improvisational Drama for Children
347 Hanworth Road, Hampton TW12 3EJ
E askus@dragondrama.co.uk
W www.dragondrama.co.uk

**DRAMA STUDIO
EDINBURGH THE**   T 0131 453 3284
19 Belmont Road, Edinburgh EH14 5DZ
E info@thedramastudio.com
W www.thedramastudio.com

**EARACHE KIDS
(VOICE OVERS)**   T 020 7287 2291
73 Beak Street, London W1F 9SR
F 020 7287 2288
E julie@earachevoices.com
W www.earachevoices.com

**EARLE, Kenneth
PERSONAL MANAGEMENT**   T 020 7274 1219
214 Brixton Road, London SW9 6AP
E kennethearle@agents-uk.com
W www.kennethearlepersonalmanagement.com

**EARNSHAW, Susi
MANAGEMENT**   T 020 8441 5010
The Bull Theatre, 68 High Street
Barnet, Herts EN5 5SJ
E casting@susiearnshaw.co.uk
W www.susiearnshawmanagement.com

**ELITE ACADEMY OF
PERFORMING ARTS**   T 07976 971178
City Studios, 4 Sandford Street
Lichfield, Staffs WS13 6QA
E agency@eliteacademy.co.uk

ENGLISH, Doreen '95   T 01243 825968
Contact: Gerry Kinner
48 The Boulevard, Bersted Park
Bognor Regis, West Sussex PO21 5BS

ENTER CIC   T/F 01740 655437
2 Chapel Terrace, Ferryhill
Durham DL17 8JL
E info@entercic.org
W www.entercic.org

ESSEX TALENT AGENCY   T/F 01268 812655
33 Basildon Drive, Laindon
Essex SS15 5RN
E info@essextalentagency.co.uk
W www.essextalentagency.co.uk

**EUROKIDS CASTING &
MODEL AGENCY**   T 01925 761083
*Contact: Jodie Keith (Senior Casting Agent). Accepts
Showreels. Children & Teenagers. Commercials. Film.
Television. Walk-On. Supporting Artists*
The Warehouse Studios, Glaziers Lane
Culcheth, Warrington, Cheshire WA3 4AQ
T 01925 761210
E jodie@eka-agency.com
W www.eka-agency.com

EXCEL AGENCY   T 01772 755343
Contact: Kay Purcell
1 Sandfield Street, Leyland
Preston, Lancashire PR25 3HJ
E xlagency@yahoo.com
W www.excelagency.co.uk

**EXPRESSIONS CASTING
AGENCY**   T 01623 424334
3 Newgate Lane, Mansfield
Nottingham NG18 2LB
E expressions-uk@btconnect.com
W www.expressionsperformingarts.co.uk

**FEA MANAGEMENT
(FERRIS ENTERTAINMENT)**   T 07801 493133
London. Belfast. Cardiff. Los Angeles. France. Spain
Number 8
132 Charing Cross Road
London WC2H 0LA
E info@ferrisentertainment.com
W www.ferrisentertainment.com

FILM CAST CORNWALL & SW   T 07811 253756
Falmouth, Cornwall,
E enquiries@filmcastcornwall.co.uk
W www.filmcastcornwall.co.uk

FIORENTINI, Anna AGENCY   T 020 7682 3677
Islington Business Design Centre, Unit 101
52 Upper Street, London N1 0QH
T 07904 962779
E rhiannon@annafiorentini.com
W www.annafiorentini.com

**FOOTSTEPS THEATRE SCHOOL
CASTING AGENCY**   T 07584 995309
Westfield Lane, Idle, Bradford BD10 8PY
E gwestman500@btinternet.com

FUSION MANAGEMENT   T 020 7834 6660
201A Victoria Street, London SW1W 5NE
T 07949 635921
E info@fusionmng.com
W www.fusionmng.com

FUSION STARS AGENCY THE   T 07716 371887
*Contact: Laura Burrows. Television. Theatre. Modelling. Film.
Voice Overs. 3-17 yrs*
Office: 'Red Cottage', Barleylands Road
Basildon, Essex SS15 4BG
E office@fusionstarsagency.co.uk
W www.fusionstarsagency.co.uk

GALLOWAYS   T 020 3770 6823
Suite 410, Henry Wood House
2 Riding House Street
London W1W 7FA
E info@gallowaysagency.com
W www.gallowaysagency.com

**GENESIS THEATRE SCHOOL
& AGENCY**   T 01536 460928
88 Hempland Close, Great Oakley
Corby, Northants NN18 8LT
T 07745 002821
E info@saracharles.com

GLOBAL7   T/F 020 7281 7679
Kemp House, 152 City Road, London EC1V 2NX
T 07956 956652
E global7castings@gmail.com
W www.global7casting.com

GOBSTOPPERS MANAGEMENT   T 01442 269543
37 St Nicholas Mount, Hemel Hempstead
Herts HP1 2BB
T 07961 372319
E gobstoppersmanagement@hotmail.co.uk

GOLDILOCKS AGENCY   T 07967 793585
T 07772 479226
E info@goldilocksagency.co.uk
W www.goldilocksagency.co.uk

GOLDMANS MANAGEMENT   T 01323 643961
3 Cranborne Avenue, Eastbourne BN20 7TS
E casting@goldmansmanagement.co.uk
W www.goldmansmanagement.co.uk

GROUNDLINGS MANAGEMENT   T 023 9273 9496
Kemp House, 152 City Road, London EC1V 2NX
E richard@groundlings.co.uk
W www.groundlings.co.uk

GSA KIDS AGENCY T 01483 684048
Contact: S. Lloyd
Guildford School of Acting, Stag Hill Campus
Guildford, Surrey GU2 7XH
E s.k.lloyd@gsa.surrey.ac.uk

GTA CASTING T 07803 001783
19 Farnell Street, Glasgow
Lanarkshire G4 9SE
E shaaron@gamta.org.uk
W www.gamta.org.uk

**HAPPY FEET
MANAGEMENT LTD** T 07912 898692
Contact: Holly Greenaway
Broadwater House, 6 London Road
Tunbridge Wells, Kent TN1 1DQ
E bookings@happyfeetmanagement.com
W www.happyfeetmanagement.com

**HARLEQUIN STUDIOS DANCE &
DRAMA SCHOOL** T 07981 925742
122A Phyllis Avenue, Peacehaven
East Sussex BN10 7RQ
E janice@harlequinstudios.co.uk

HARRIS AGENCY LTD T 01923 211644
71 The Avenue, Watford
Herts WD17 4NU
E theharrisagency@btconnect.com

HervL ARTISTES' AGENCY T 01322 352766
Children (0-20 yrs). Actors. Extras. Dancers. Models.
Singers
Admiral Park, Victory Way, Crossways Business Park
Dartford, Kent DA2 6QD
E info@hervl.com
W www.hervl.co.uk

HOBSONS KIDS T 020 8995 3628
2 Dukes Gate, Chiswick
London W4 5DX
F 020 8996 5350
E gaynor@hobsons-international.com
W www.hobsons-international.com

**HOXTON STREET
MANAGEMENT** T 020 7503 5131
Hoxton Hall, 130 Hoxton Street
London N1 6SH
E ben@hoxtonhall.co.uk
W www.hoxtonhall.co.uk

**ILUZION TALENT
MANAGEMENT** T 07850 970566
Contact: Tara Branson
Beech Lawn, Beech Grove, Mayford
Surrey GU22 0SX
E admin@iluziontalentmanagement.co.uk
W www.iluziontalentmanagement.co.uk

**INDEPENDENT THEATRE
WORKSHOP AGENCY** T 00 353 86 8227714
3-19 yrs
8 Terminus Mills, Clonskeagh Road
Ranelagh, Dublin 6
E agency@itwstudios.ie
W www.itwstudios.ie

**INSPIRATIONS SCHOOL OF
PERFORMING ARTS** T 07946 352305
18 Bryanston Road, Tilbury RM18 8DD
E info@inspirationsspa.co.uk

INSPIRE MANAGEMENT T 0115 988 1800
The Attic Studio, 3rd Floor
46-48 Carrington Street
Nottingham NG1 7FG
E admin@inspireacademy.co.uk
W www.inspireacademy.co.uk

INTER-CITY KIDS T/F 01942 321969
27 Wigan Lane, Wigan
Greater Manchester WN1 1XR
E intercitycasting@btconnect.com

**INTERSTELLAR
CASTINGS LTD** T 0161 222 4790
Contact: Katie Roberts
16A Church Street West, Radcliffe
Greater Manchester M26 2SQ
T 07467 234380
E info@interstellarcastings.co.uk
W www.interstellarcastings.co.uk

JADA MANAGEMENT T 01702 464446
16 Torrington, Shoeburyness
Southend on Sea, Essex SS3 8DD
T 07961 916292
E jadaoffice2012@gmail.com
W www.jadaschool.co.uk

JEFFREY & WHITE JUNIORS T 01462 429769
7 Paynes Park, Hitchin
Hertfordshire SG5 1EH
E info@jeffreyandwhite.co.uk
W www.jeffreyandwhite.co.uk

JERMIN, Mark MANAGEMENT T 01792 458855
Swansea Metropolitan,
University of Wales, Trinity Saint David
Mount Pleasant, Swansea SA1 6ED
E info@markjermin.co.uk
W www.markjermin.co.uk

JIGSAW ARTS MANAGEMENT T 020 8447 4530
*Representing Children & Young People from Jigsaw
Performing Arts Schools*
64-66 High Street, Barnet
Herts EN5 5SJ
E enquiries@jigsaw-arts.co.uk
W www.jigsaw-arts.co.uk

**JOHNSTON &
MATHERS MANAGEMENT** T 020 8449 4968
PO Box 3167, Barnet
Herts EN5 2WA
E johnstonmathers@aol.com
W www.johnstonandmathers.com

K KIDS T 020 7379 1616
0-16 yrs. Commercials. Film. Stage
4th Floor, 43 Aldwych, London WC2B 4DN
T 07961 572899
E mail@ktalent.co.uk
W www.ktalent.co.uk

KIDS @ JFA THE T 020 3092 1515
3rd Floor, 207 Regent Street
London W1B 3HH
E agent@thekidsatjuliefoxassociates.co.uk
W www.thekidsatjuliefoxassociates.co.uk

KIDS @ JFA THE T 01270 780880
Northern Office
Office 4, 22 Jordan Street, Liverpool L1 0AH
E agent@thekidsatjuliefox.co.uk
W www.thekidsatjuliefox.co.uk

KIDS LONDON T 020 7924 9595
67 Dulwich Road, London SE24 0NJ
F 020 7501 8711
E info@kidslondonltd.com
W www.kidslondonltd.com

KIDS MANAGEMENT T 01444 401595
Studio 35 Truggers, Handcross
Haywards Heath, West Sussex RH17 6DQ
T 07966 382766
E info@kidsmanagement.co.uk
W www.kidsmanagement.co.uk

KIDS PLUS T 07799 791586
Malcolm House, Harris Primary Academy Crystal Palace
Malcolm Road, Penge, London SE20 8RH
E geraldi.gillma@btconnect.com
W www.kidsplusagency.co.uk

KIDZ 2 DAY T 01708 747581
74 Western Road, Romford
Essex RM1 3LP
E kim@kidz2day.co.uk
W www.kidz2day.co.uk

KIDZ LTD T 0871 2180884
7 Ellerbeck Crescent, Worsley, Manchester M28 7XN
F 0871 2180843
E info@kidzltd.com
W www.kidzltd.com

KIDZ ON THE HILL ARTISTS T 07881 553480
Muswell Hill, London N10
E admin@kidzonthehill.co.uk
W www.kidzonthehill.co.uk

**KOOLKIDZ THEATRICAL
AGENCY LTD** T 07581 232615
Based in West Cornwall
St Johns Hall, Alverton Street
Penzance, Cornwall TR18 2SP
T 07580 596580
E kool-kidz@sky.com
W www.koolkidztheatricalagency.co.uk

KOSKA, Ann AGENCY T 01753 785031
Room 9, Small Process Building, Pinewood Studios,
Pinewood Road, Iver Heath, Bucks SL0 0NH
E askpinewood@mac.com
W www.annkoskaagency.com

**KRACKERS KIDS
THEATRICAL AGENCY** T/F 01708 502046
6-7 Electric Parade, Seven Kings Road
Ilford, Essex IG3 8BY
E krackerskids@hotmail.com
W www.krackerskids.co.uk

KYT AGENCY T 01227 730177
Mulberry Croft, Mulberry Hill, Chilham CT4 8AJ
T 07967 580213
E agency@kentyouththeatre.co.uk
W www.kentyouththeatre.co.uk

LAMONT CASTING AGENCY T 07736 387543
2 Harewood Avenue, Ainsdale, Merseyside PR8 2PH
E diane@lamontcasting.co.uk
W www.lamontcasting.co.uk

**LESLIE, Sasha
MANAGEMENT** T/F 020 8969 3249
In association with ALLSORTS DRAMA FOR CHILDREN
34 Crediton Road, London NW10 3DU
E sasha@allsortsdrama.com

LINTON MANAGEMENT T 0161 761 2020
3 The Rock, Bury BL9 0JP
E carol@linton.tv

**LITTLE ADULTS ACADEMY & MODELLING
AGENCY LTD** T 020 3130 0798
44 Broadway, Stratford, London E15 1XH
E harvardbenjamin7@hotmail.co.uk
W www.littleadultsagency.com

**LITTLE ALLSTARS CASTING &
MODELLING AGENCY** T 0161 702 8257
*Representing Babies, Children & Teenagers UK Wide for
Television, Film, Modelling, Stage, Corporate & Role Play*
23 Falconwood Chase, Worsley
Manchester M28 1FG
T 07584 992429
E casting@littleallstars.co.uk
W www.littleallstars.co.uk

LIVING THE DREAM TALENT AGENCY T 01727 751613
145-147 St John Street, London EC1V 4PW
T 07845 267501
E agency@livingthedreamcompany.co.uk
W www.livingthedreamcompany.co.uk

LOWE, Suzie AGENCY T 07799 684683
61 Valley Walk, Felixstowe, Suffolk IP11 7TD
E suzieloweagency@hotmail.co.uk
W www.suzieloweagency.com

LUCIA VICTORIA AGENCY MANAGEMENT LTD T 01254 207575
Children & Young Performers Casting Agency
22 Highland Drive, Chorley
Lancashire PR7 7AD
E casting@lucia-victoria.co.uk
W www.lucia-victoria.co.uk

MAD FISH MANAGEMENT T 07545 052088
1 Wellington Place, 3-15 Terminus Road
Bexhill On Sea, East Sussex TN39 3LR
T 07715 459637
E madfishmanagement@hotmail.com
W www.madfishmadfish.co.uk

MARMALADE MANAGEMENT T 01628 483808
Jam Theatre Studios, Archway Court
45A West Street, Marlow
Buckinghamshire SL7 2LS
E info@marmalademanagement.co.uk
W www.marmalademanagement.co.uk

McDONAGH, Melanie MANAGEMENT (ACADEMY OF PERFORMING ARTS & CASTING AGENCY) T 07909 831409
14 Apple Tree Way, Oswaldtwistle
Accrington, Lancashire BB5 0FB
T 01254 392560
E mcdonaghmgt@aol.com
W www.mcdonaghmanagement.co.uk

MGA MANAGEMENT & CASTING T 07595 711159
207 Balgreen Road, Edinburgh EH11 2RZ
E admin@mgamanagement.com
W www.mgamanagement.com

MIDDLEWEEK NEWTON TALENT MANAGEMENT T 020 3394 0079
3rd Floor, 95A Rivington Street
London EC2A 3AY
E agents@mntalent.co.uk
W www.mntalent.co.uk

MIM AGENCY T 0871 2377963
Clayton House, 59 Piccadilly
Manchester M1 2AQ
E info@mimagency.co.uk
W www.mimagency.co.uk

MINI MILLS @ WAM! T 07900 735566
7 Richmond Close, Princes Gate
Bishops Stortford
Hertfordshire CM23 4PG
T 07512 998007
E info@windmillartistsmanagement.co.uk
W www.windmillartistsmanagement.co.uk

MONDI ASSOCIATES LTD T 07817 133349
Contact: Michelle Sykes
Unit 3 O, Cooper House
2 Michael Road
London SW6 2AD
E info@mondiassociates.com
W www.mondiassociates.com

MOVIE MITES LONDON LTD T 020 3633 3728
Contact: Lynda Connikie
1-9 Hardwicks Square, Wandsworth
London SW18 4AW
E admin@moviemiteslondon.com
W www.moviemiteslondon.com

NFD AGENCY T 01977 681949
The Studio, 21 Low Street
South Milford LS25 5AR
E alyson@northernfilmanddrama.com
W www.northernfilmanddrama.com

NG PERSONAL MANAGEMENT T 07810 138535
6 Garston Crescent, Watford
Hertfordshire WD25 0LD
E info@ngpersonalmanagement.co.uk
W www.ngpersonalmanagement.co.uk

NOTTINGHAM ACTORS STUDIO LTD THE   **T** 0115 860 2179
The Nottingham Actors Studio
Lower Ground Floor
1 Kayes Walk, The Lace Market
Nottingham NG1 1PY
E rachael.pacey@nottinghamactorsstudio.co.uk
W www.thenottinghamactorsstudio.co.uk

O'FARRELL STAGE & THEATRE SCHOOL   **T** 020 7474 6466
Babies, Children, Teenagers & Young Adults
36 Shirley Street, Canning Town
London E16 1HU
T 07956 941497
E linda@ofarrells.wanadoo.co.uk

ORA CASTING   **T** 020 3322 9144
86-90 Paul Street, London EC2A 4NE
E info@oracasting.com
W www.oracasting.com

ORGANIC KIDZ TALENT AGENCY   **T** 020 8449 4968
Boutique Agency. 4-18 yrs
c/o JAM, PO Box 3167
Barnet EN5 2WA
E organickidzagent@aol.com
W www.organickidzagency.co.uk

PACE THEATRE COMPANY   **T** 0141 8487471
Spires Studios, School Wynd
Paisley, Renfrewshire PA1 2DA
F 0141 8426300
E linsey@pacetheatre.co.uk

PALMER, Jackie AGENCY & YOUNG PERFORMERS   **T** 01494 520978
30 Daws Hill Lane, High Wycombe
Bucks HP11 1PW
E agent@jpaassociates.co.uk
W www.jpaassociates.co.uk

PC THEATRICAL, MODEL & CASTING AGENCY   **T** 07904 549665
10 Strathmore Gardens, Edgware
Middlesex HA8 5HJ
T 020 8381 2229
E twinagy@aol.com
W www.twinagency.com

PD MANAGEMENT   **T** 020 7794 0905
17 The Heights, Frognal
London NW3 6XS
E pdmanagement1@gmail.com
W www.pdmanagement.org

PEANUTS TALENT   **T** 07932 636385
Contact: Helen Coker, Kathryn Ackley
Kingsland Church Studios, Priory Green
Newcastle Upon Tyne NE4 2DW
T 07950 932845
E helen@peanutscasting.co.uk
W www.peanutstalent.tv

PHA YOUTH   **T** 0161 273 4444
Tanzaro House, Ardwick Green North
Manchester M12 6FZ
F 0161 273 4567
E youth@pha-agency.co.uk
W www.pha-agency.co.uk

PLATFORM TALENT MANAGEMENT LTD   **T** 07926 553765
16 Shalbourne Rise
Camberley
Surrey GU15 2EJ
E ben@ptmagency.co.uk
W www.ptmagency.co.uk

POLLYANNA MANAGEMENT LTD   **T** 020 7481 1911
Raine House, Raine Street
Wapping E1W 3RL
M 07801 884837
E pollyannamanagement@gmail.com
W www.pollyannatheatre.org

PROKIDS MANAGEMENT   **T** 0151 336 7382
Based in the North West & London
32 Springcroft, Parkgate
Neston, Cheshire CH64 6SE
E mail@prokidsmanagement.co.uk
W www.prokidsmanagement.co.uk

PURESTAR KIDZ AGENCY   **T** 07886 969713
Contact: Tim Noble
7 Heather Place, Esher
Surrey KT10 8NN
E timnoble@purestarproductions.com
W www.purestarproductions.com

PWASSOCIATES   **T** 01296 733258
7 Catherine Cottages, Calvert Road
Middle Claydon, Bucks MK18 2HA
E agency@pwacademy.com
W www.pwacademy.com

QUIRKY KIDZ CREATIVE MANAGEMENT   **T** 01494 415196
The Academy, Queensmead Road
High Wycombe
Buckinghamshire HP10 9XA
E hello@quirkykidz.co.uk
W www.quirkykidz.co.uk

RA CASTING   **T** 01474 878494
RA Studios, 152A Milton Road
Gravesend, Kent DA12 2RG
E casting@robynacademy.com
W www.robynacademy.com

RBAPA AGENCY   **T** 01189 868985
43 Upper Redlands Road, Reading
Berkshire RG1 5JE
E mail@rbapaagency.com
W www.rbapaagency.co.uk

RBM YOUNG PERFORMERS   **T** 020 7976 6021
Contact: Sarah London
3rd Floor, 1 Lower Grosvenor Place
London SW1W 0EJ
E info@rbmactors.com
W rbmactors.com

RDDC MANAGEMENT AGENCY   **T** 01706 211161
52 Bridleway, Waterfoot
Rossendale, Lancashire BB4 9DS
E info@rddc.co.uk
W www.rddc.co.uk

REACT KIDS AGENCY   **T** 01926 710001
83 Dudley Road, Kenilworth
Warwickshire CV8 1GR
T 07900 921779
E admin@reactkidsagency.co.uk
W www.reactkidsagency.co.uk

REACT MANAGEMENT   **T** 01254 883692
c/o The Civic Arts Centre, Union Road
Oswaldtwistle, Lancashire BB5 3HZ
E management@reactacademy.co.uk
W www.reactacademy.co.uk

REBEL SCHOOL OF THEATRE ARTS & CASTING AGENCY LTD   **T** 01484 603736
Based in Leeds & Huddersfield
PO Box 169, Huddersfield HD8 1BE
E sue@rebelschool.co.uk
W www.rebelschool.co.uk

Mark Jermin
★★★ Management

www.markjermin.co.uk
Children and young adults from all over the UK

Audition workshops and classes in London, Manchester, Bristol and Wales.
Children with open performance licences, guaranteed to be licensed for any production and at very short notice.
Swansea Metropolitan University of Wales, Trinity Saint David, Mount Pleasant, Swansea SA1 6ED
Phone: 01792 458855   Fax: 01792 458844   Email: info@markjermin.co.uk

---

RED 24 MANAGEMENT   T 020 7404 5722
1st Floor, Kingsway House
103 Kingsway, London WC2B 6QX
E miles@red24management.com
W www.red24managment.com

RED HEAD AGENCY THE   T 07813 129466
14 Hornsby Square
Southfields Business Park
Basildon, Essex SS15 5SD
T 01268 415304
E office.theredheadagency@gmail.com
W www.the-red-head-agency.co.uk

**REDROOFS THEATRE
SCHOOL AGENCY**   T 01628 674092
26 Bath Road, Maidenhead
Berks SL6 4JT
T 07531 355835 (Holiday Times)
E sam@redroofs.co.uk
W www.redroofs.co.uk

REGAN MANAGEMENT
59 Mount Stuart Square
Cardiff Bay, Cardiff CF10 5LR
E cardiff@reganmanagement.co.uk
W www.reganmanagement.co.uk

REGAN MANAGEMENT
Barley Mow Centre, 10 Barley Mow Passage
Chiswick, London W4 4PH
E london@reganmanagement.co.uk
W www.reganmanagement.co.uk

REGAN MANAGEMENT
MediaCityUK, The Greenhouse
111 Broadway, Salford M50 2EQ
E manchester@reganmanagement.co.uk
W www.reganmanagement.co.uk

RHODES AGENCY   T 01708 747013
5 Dymoke Road, Hornchurch
Essex RM11 1AA
E rhodesarts@hotmail.com

**RIDGEWAY STUDIOS
MANAGEMENT**   T 01992 633775
Office: 106 Hawkshead Road, Potters Bar
Hertfordshire EN6 1NG
E info@ridgewaystudios.co.uk
W www.ridgewaystudios.co.uk

**RISING STARS PERFORMANCE
AGENCY**   T 07709 429354
53 Hurlingham Road
Bexleyheath, Kent DA7 5PE
T 07958 617976
E risingstars_agency@yahoo.co.uk

RKA TALENT   T 020 7287 6934
10 Greek Street, London W1D 4DH
E youth@rkatalent.com
W www.rkatalent.com

RL&P AGENCY   T 01277 812970
Contact: Rachel Clements, Laura Scott
Little Tillingham Hall Farm, Dunnings Lane
West Horndon, Essex CM13 3HE
E rlp_agency@outlook.com

ROKIT ACTORS MANAGEMENT   T 01565 654482
Contact: Victoria Gough
PO Box 408, Knutsford
Cheshire WA16 IDH
E info@rokitperformingarts.co.uk
W www.rokitperformingarts.co.uk

ROSE WOODS & AMBRIDGE   T 07974 225950
Contact: Kim Ambridge
14 Fords Grove, London N21 3DN
E rosewoods1547@gmail.com

**ROSS, David ACTING
ACADEMY THE**   T 07957 862317
8 Farrier Close, Sale
Cheshire M33 2ZL
E info@davidrossacting.com
W www.davidrossacting.com

ROYCE MANAGEMENT   T 020 8650 1096
121 Merlin Grove, Beckenham
Kent BR3 3HS
E office@roycemanagement.co.uk
W www.roycemanagement.co.uk

RS MANAGEMENT   T 020 8257 6477
186 Waltham Way, London E4 8AZ
E info@rsmagency.co.uk
W www.rsmagency.co.uk

SCALA KIDS CASTING   T 0113 250 6823
42 Rufford Avenue, Yeadon
Leeds LS19 7QR
E office@scalakids.com
W www.scalakids.com

SCALLYWAGS AGENCY LTD   T 020 7739 8820
12-18 Hoxton Street, London N1 6NG
E info@scallywags.co.uk
W www.scallywags.co.uk

SCENE II THEATRICAL AGENCY   T 01371 878020
The Arts Centre,
1 Haslers Lane
Great Dunmow, Essex CM6 1XS
E sceneiiagency@aol.com
W www.sceneii.net

SCHOOL CASTING   **T** 01325 463383
Liddiard Theatre, Polam Hall, Grange Road
Darlington, Durham DL1 5PA
F 01325 383539
E information@polamhall.com
W www.polamhall.com

SCREAM MANAGEMENT LTD   **T** 0161 850 1996
The Greenhouse, MediaCityUK
Salford, Manchester M50 2EQ
T 0161 850 1994
E kids@screammanagement.com
W www.screammanagement.com

SELECT MANAGEMENT   **T** 07855 794747
*Actors. Models. Presenters. Dancers. Children. Teenagers
& Adults*
PO Box 748, London NW4 1TT
T 07956 131494
E mail@selectmanagement.info
W www.selectmanagement.info

SEVEN AGENCY MANAGEMENT   **T** 0161 850 1057
Actors. Children. Modelling. Stage. Television
82 King Street, Manchester M2 4WQ
T 07714 252026
E guy@7casting.co.uk
W www.7casting.co.uk

SHACK ATTACK   **T** 07974 235955
1 The Withies, Leatherhead
Surrey KT22 7EY
E lucy@danceshack.co.uk

SHARMAN, Alan AGENCY   **T** 0121 212 0090
Office 6 Fournier House, 8 Tenby Street
Birmingham, West Midlands B1 3AJ
E info@alansharmanagency.com
W www.alansharmanagency.com

SHARPE ACADEMY   **T** 07500 569024
*Based in North West London. Representing Children 3-16
yrs & Adults*
107 Amersham Road, High Wycombe
Buckinghamshire HP13 5AD
E agency@sharpeacademy.co.uk
W www.sharpeacademy.co.uk

SHH TALENT AGENCY   **T** 01761 438885
Contact: Lucy Wakerell
Victoria Hall, Church Street
Radstock, Bath, Somerset BA3 3QG
E thebigshhtalentagency@gmail.com
W www.thebigshh.co.uk

SHINE MANAGEMENT   **T** 07880 721689
Flat 10, Valentine House, Church Road
Guildford, Surrey GU1 4NG
E shinetime@hotmail.co.uk
W www.shinetimeworkshops.com

SHOWDOWN MANAGEMENT   **T** 01483 893688
*Part-time Theatre School & Agency for Children, Young
Performers & Professional Adult Representation*
16 Garden Close, Shamley Green
Guildford, Surrey GU5 0UW
E info@showdowntheatrearts.co.uk
W www.showdowntheatrearts.co.uk

**SIGNATURE MODEL
MANAGEMENT**   **T** 07791 231680
Contact: Chloe Hopkins
2 Bishops Green, Dunmow CM6 1NF
E info@signaturemodels.co.uk
W www.signaturemodels.co.uk

SILVERLEE MANAGEMENT   **T** 07771 194598
Contact: Royah Hamed
E info@silverleemanagement.co.uk
W www.silverleemanagement.co.uk

SIMON & HOW ASSOCIATES   **T** 020 7739 8865
Contact: Simon Penn
12-18 Hoxton Street, London N1 6NG
E info@simonhow.com
W www.simonhow.com

**SIMON, Frances PERSONAL
MANAGEMENT**   **T** 07876 541923
45 Pottery Lane, York YO31 8SR
E frances.simon@btinternet.com
W www.francessimon.co.uk

SINGER, Sandra ASSOCIATES   **T** 01702 331616
21 Cotswold Road, Westcliff-on-Sea
Essex SS0 8AA
T 07795 144143
E sandrasingeruk@aol.com
W www.sandrasinger.com

SMARTYPANTS AGENCY   **T** 020 7434 7666
13 Berwick Street, Soho
London W1F 0PW
E office@smartypantsagency.co.uk
W www.smartypantsagency.co.uk

SMITH, Elisabeth LTD   **T** 01923 269477
8 Dawes Lane, Sarratt
Rickmansworth, Herts WD3 6BB
E models@elisabethsmith.co.uk
W www.elisabethsmith.co.uk

**SNA / THRESHOLD
THEATRE ARTS**   **T** 020 7125 0468
3rd Floor, International House
1-6 Yarmouth Place, London W1J 7BU
T 07949 601935
E steve@stevenealonassociates.co.uk

SOTE AGENCY   **T** 01273 457734
Contact: Marcus Watson
61 Lincoln Street, Brighton
East Sussex BN2 9UG
E info@soteagency.co.uk
W www.soteagency.co.uk

SPEAKE, Barbara AGENCY   **T** 020 8743 6096
East Acton Lane, London W3 7EG
E speakekids2@aol.com
W www.barbaraspeake.com

SRA AGENCY   **T** 020 7112 8739
Susan Roberts Academy
Lockhart Road, Cobham
Surrey KT11 2AX
T 07766 761267
E agency@sraagency.com

STAGE A MANAGEMENT LTD   **T** 07837 072775
*Represents Centre Stage Academy & Academy of
Performance Training Students & Selected Adult Artists*
9 Beech Grove, Midhurst
West Sussex GU29 9JA
E stageamanagement@gmail.com
W www.csa-theatreschool.co.uk

STAGE KIDS AGENCY   **T** 01707 328359
Children, Teenagers & Adults
1 Greenfield, Welwyn Garden City
Herts AL8 7HW
E stagekds@aol.com
W www.stagekids.co.uk

**STAGE 84 PERFORMING
ARTS LTD**   **T** 01274 611984
The Old Fire Station
29A Town Lane, Idle
Bradford, West Yorkshire BD10 8NT
T 07731 436094
E info@stage84.com
W www.stage84.com

ACTING KIDZ *Nurturing Young Actors & Models throughout the UK Aged 0-18*

If your child has that special something then please apply to **Acting Kidz** at: **www.ActingKidz.co.uk   T: 0845 645 8000**

STAGECOACH AGENCY.ie   T 01989 769547
Suite 2, 1st Floor Offices, Cantilupe Chambers
Cantilupe Road, Ross-on-Wye HR9 7AN
E tarquin@stagecoachagency.co.uk
W www.stagecoachagency.co.uk

STAGECOACH AGENCY UK   T 01989 769547
Suite 2, 1st Floor Offices, Cantilupe Chambers
Cantilupe Road, Ross-on-Wye HR9 7AN
E tarquin@stagecoachagency.co.uk
W www.stagecoachagency.co.uk

**STAGE ONE KIDS THEATRE
SCHOOL & AGENCY**   T/F 01992 651222
77 Queens Road, Buckhurst Hill
Essex IG9 5BW
T 07912 760504
E stageone@btinternet.com
W www.stageonekids.co.uk

**STAGEWORKS PERFORMING
ARTS SCHOOL**   T 07956 176166
PO Box 4810, Henley on Thames
Oxon RG9 9GN
T 01491 877205
E enquiries@stageworks.org.uk
W www.stageworks.org.uk

**STARDOM CASTING AGENCY &
THEATRE SCHOOL**   T 07740 091019
15 Gordon Street
Sutton in Craven BD20 7EU
E liz.stardom@btinternet.com
W www.stardom.org.uk

STARMAKER   T 0118 988 7959
17 Kendal Avenue, Shinfield
Reading, Berks RG2 9AR
E dave@starmakeruk.org
W www.starmakeruk.org

STARSTRUCK TALENT LTD   T 07762 887716
In association with Starstruck Theatre School
1 & 2 St Chads Court, School Lane
Rochdale OL16 1QU
E lisa@starstrucktalent.co.uk
W www.starstrucktalent.co.uk

**STEP ON STAGE
MANAGEMENT**   T 07973 900196
*Drama, Dance, Musical Theatre, Singing, Piano, Playwriting
& Youth Theatre for Children & Young People in
Twickenham, Hampton Hill, Richmond, St Margarets*
Mylor House, 29 Burgoyne Road
Sunbury on Thames, Middlesex TW16 7PN
E info@steponstageacademy.co.uk
W www.steponstageacademy.co.uk

STOMP! MANAGEMENT   T 020 8446 9898
62 Sellwood Drive, Barnet, Herts EN5 2RL
E stompmanagement@aol.com
W www.stompmanagement.com

STOP THINK BIG TALENT   T 07840 034553
Contact: Sophie Elliott
23 Lobden Crescent, Whitworth
Rochdale OL12 8PU
E sjelliott_822@msn.com

**STRANGE TOWN YOUNG
ACTORS AGENCY**   T 0131 629 0292
Contact: Ruth Hollyman
Out of the Blue, 36 Dalmeny Street
Edinburgh EH6 8RG
E info@strangetown.org.uk
W www.strangetown.org.uk

STUDIO 74 LTD   T 020 8295 4256
The Hall, St Augustines Avenue
Bromley, Kent BR2 8AG
E info@studio74agency.co.uk
W www.studio74dance.co.uk

**SUPER 8 STAGE &
SCREEN AGENCY**   T 01483 825332
Contact: Matthew Bearne
64 Weymede, Byfleet, Surrey KT14 7DQ
E info@super8stageandscreenacademy.com
W super8stageandscreenacademy.com

SUPERARTS AGENCY   T 07721 927714
Based in London. Blog: superartsagency.blogspot.com
E superarts@btinternet.com
W www.superartsagency.com

**TAKE2 CASTING AGENCY &
TALENT MANAGEMENT**   T 00 353 87 2563403
28 Beech Park Road, Foxrock, Dublin 18, Ireland
E pamela@take2.ie
W www.take2.ie

TAKE2 MANAGEMENT   T 0161 832 7715
Suite 5, Basil Chambers
65 High Street, Manchester M4 1FS
F 0161 839 1661
E chris@take2management.co.uk
W www.take2management.co.uk

TAKE2 MANAGEMENT   T 0113 403 2930
34 Park Cross Street, Leeds LS1 2QH
E chris@take2management.co.uk
W www.take2management.co.uk

TAKE ONE AGENCY   T 07517 313710
*Representing Children in Theatre, Television, Film.
Workshops for 5+ yrs*
17 Elm Tree Walk, Tring HP23 5EB
E info@takeoneagency.com
W www.takeoneagency.com

**TALENTED KIDS PERFORMING
ARTS SCHOOL & AGENCY**   T/F 00 353 45 485464
23 Burrow Manor, Calverstown
Kilcullen, Co. Kildare, Ireland
T 00 353 87 2480348
E talentedkids@hotmail.com
W www.talentedkidsireland.com

**TANWOOD THEATRICAL
AGENCY**   T 07775 991700
Liberatus Studios, Isis Estate
Stratton Road, Swindon SN1 2PG
E tanwood@tiscali.co.uk
W www.tanwood.co.uk

TELEVISION WORKSHOP THE   T 0115 845 0764
Nottingham Group
30 Main Street, Calverton
Notts NG14 6FQ
E ian@thetelevisionworkshop.co.uk

THIS IS YOUTH   T 020 7175 0566
Children, Teenagers & Young Adults
194B Addington Road
Selsdon
Croydon CR2 8LD
E hello@thisisyouth.com
W www.thisisyouth.com

THOMAS, Beverley AGENCY   T 01792 774847
39 Heol-Nant-Gelli, Treboeth
Swansea SA5 9DU
T 07974 822130
E beverleythomasuk@yahoo.co.uk

TICKLEDOM AGENCY   T 020 8341 7044
31 Rectory Gardens
London N8 7PJ
T 07947 139414
E agency@tickledomtheatreschool.com
W www.tickledomtheatreschool.com

TIFFIN MANAGEMENT   T 07568 566211
In association with MTPAS
High Street, Stony Stratford, Milton Keynes MK11 7AE
E agency@mtpas.co.uk
W www.tiffin-management.co.uk

TINY ANGELS   T 07914 424385
Contact: Donia Youssef
Kemp House, 152-160 City Road, London EC1V 2NX
T 07024 030277 (Lisa)
E info@tiny-angel.co.uk
W www.tiny-angel.co.uk

TK MANAGEMENT   T 07910 139326
Spires Meade, 4 Bridleways, Wendover, Bucks HP22 6DN
F 01296 623696
E tkpamanagement@aol.com

**TLA BOUTIQUE
MANAGEMENT**   T 0113 289 3433
Contact: Tonicha Lawrence
Serenissima, Church Hill
Thorner, Leeds, West Yorkshire LS14 3EG
E tonichalawrence@gmail.com
W www.tlaboutiquemanagement.com

TMG ASSOCIATES   T 020 7437 1383
*Contact: Lou Davidson.
(Now M&GKIDS @ TMG ASSOCIATES)*
4 Cavendish Square, London W1G 0PG
T 07973 818254
E tanya.greep@googlemail.com
W www.tmgkids.london

TOMORROW'S TALENT AGENCY   T 01245 690080
Contact: By e-mail only
Based in Chelmsford, Essex,
E agents@tomorrowstalent.co.uk
W www.tomorrowstalent.co.uk

TOP TALENT AGENCY LTD   T 01727 855903
*Representing Child Actors & Adult Actors. TV. Films.
Commericials. Modelling. Theatre.*
PO Box 860, St Albans, Herts AL1 9BR
F 01727 260903
E admin@toptalentagency.co.uk
W www.toptalentagency.co.uk

TOTS 'N' DARLINGS AGENCY   T 020 7118 2728
Bizzy Studios, 1st Floor Hall, 10-12 Pickford Lane
Bexleyheath, Kent DA7 4QW
E agency@totsndarlings.com
W www.totsndarlings.com

TRUE STARS ACADEMY   T 020 7619 9166
6-16 yrs
180 Piccadilly, London W1J 9HF
E queries@truestarsacademy.com
W uk.truestarsacademy.com

TUESDAYS CHILD LTD   T/F 01625 501765
Children, Teenagers & Adults
Oakfield House, Springwood Way, Macclesfield SK10 2XA
E admin@tuesdayschildagency.co.uk
W www.tuesdayschildagency.co.uk

TV TALENT   T 07886 825843
36 Armitage Close, Middleton
Manchester, Lancashire M24 4PA
E agency@tvtalentmanagement.co.uk
W www.tvtalentmanagement.co.uk

TWINS
See PC THEATRICAL, MODEL & CASTING AGENCY

**UK THEATRE SCHOOL PERFORMING
ARTS ACADEMY & UK
CASTING AGENCY**   T 0141 332 1818
*Contact: Lizanne Thomson, Sheryl Hamilton,
Danny Murphy*
4 West Regent Street, Glasgow G2 1RW
E staff@uktheatreschool.com
W www.uktheatreschool.com

UNITED AGENTS LLP   T 020 3214 0800
12-26 Lexington Street, London W1F 0LE
E info@unitedagents.co.uk   W www.unitedagents.co.uk

URBAN ANGELS   T 0845 8387773
Unit F32B, Parkhall Business Centre
40 Martell Road, London SE21 8EN
F 0845 8387774   E south@urbanangelsagency.com

URBAN ANGELS NORTH　　T 0845 5191990
Contact: Alysia Lewis
F 0845 8387774
E north@urbanangelsagency.com
W www.urbanangelsagency.com

URBAN TALENT　　T 0161 228 6866
Contact: Liz Beeley
Nemesis House, 1 Oxford Court
Bishopsgate
Manchester M2 3WQ
E liz@nmsmanagement.co.uk
W www.urbantalent.tv

VADA CASTING MANAGEMENT　　T 07796 688571
Contact: Vanessa Buckley
1 Minster Close, Greetland
Halifax, West Yorkshire HX4 8QW
E vadacastingmanagement@gmail.com
W www.vacademyofdramaticarts.com

VALLÉ THEATRICAL
AGENCY THE　　T 01992 622861
The Vallé Academy Studios
Wilton House
Delamare Road, Cheshunt
Herts EN8 9SG
F 01992 622868
E agency@valleacademy.co.uk
W www.valleacademy.co.uk

VAN RENSBURG ARTIST
MANAGEMENT (VAM)　　T 07724 937331
19 Seaview Terrace
Joppa, Edinburgh EH15 2HD
E michelle@vanartman.co.uk
W www.vanartman.co.uk

VISIONS AGENCY　　T 07857 237806
The Studio, 39A Foxbury Road
Bromley
Kent BR1 4DG
E admin@visionsagency.co.uk
W www.visionsagency.co.uk

WE ARE CHARACTERS LTD　　T 07824 444765
24 Deniston Road
Heaton Moor
Stockport, Cheshire SK4 4RF
E richard@wearecharacters.co.uk
W www.wearecharacters.co.uk

WILLIAMSON & HOLMES　　T 020 7240 0407
Twitter: @WilliamsonHolme
5th Floor, Sovereign House
212-224 Shaftesbury Avenue
London WC2H 8PR
E carolyn@williamsonandholmes.co.uk
W www.williamsonandholmes.co.uk

WINGS AGENCY　　T 01483 428998
29 Portsmouth Road
Godalming, Surrey GU7 2JU
T 07745 443448
E wingsagency@gmail.com
W www.wingsmanagement.co.uk

WIVELL, Betty ACADEMY OF
PERFORMING ARTS THE　　T 020 8764 5500
Contact: Elizabeth Reeves
52 Norbury Court Road
Norbury, London SW16 4HT
E ereeves@bettywivell.com
W www.bettywivell.com

WYSE AGENCY　　T 01223 832288
Hill House, 1 Hill Farm Road
Whittlesford, Cambs CB22 4NB
E frances.wyse@btinternet.com

YAT MANAGEMENT (YOUNG ACTORS
THEATRE MANAGEMENT)　　T 020 7278 2101
70-72 Barnsbury Road, London N1 0ES
E agent@yati.org.uk
W www.yati.org.uk

YOUNG, Sylvia AGENCY　　T 020 7723 0037
Sylvia Young Theatre School
1 Nutford Place
London W1H 5YZ
T 07779 145732
E info@sylviayoungagency.com

YOUNG ACTORS
COMPANY LTD THE　　T 07450 033628
3 Marshall Road, Cambridge CB1 7TY
E leigh@theyoungactorscompany.com
W www.theyoungactorscompany.com

YOUNG ACTORS GROUP THE　　T 01273 719226
Contact: Jane Murray-Watson
22 The Drove, Brighton
East Sussex BN1 5AF
T 07980 564849
E agency@theyoungactorsgroup.com
W www.theyoungactorsgroup.com

YOUNGBLOOD THEATRE
COMPANY　　T 07870 661243
c/o The BWH Agency Ltd
35 Soho Square
London W1D 3QX
E ybtc2000@aol.com

YOUNGSTARS THEATRE SCHOOL
& AGENCY　　T 07966 176756
Contact: Coralyn Canfor-Dumas. 4-18 yrs
4 Haydon Dell, Bushey
Herts WD23 1DD
E youngstarsagency@gmail.com
W www.youngstarsagency.co.uk

YT90　　T 01580 857257
Glassenbury Hill Farm
Glassenbury Road
Cranbrook, Kent TN17 2QF
E info@yt93.co.uk
W www.yt93.co.uk

ZADEK NOWELL
MANAGEMENT　　T 07957 144948
398 Long Lane, London N2 8JX
T 07841 753728
E zadeknowell@gmail.com
W www.zadeknowell.co.uk

ACORN ENTERTAINMENTS LTD   T 01285 644622
PO Box 64, Cirencester GL7 5YD
E info@acornents.co.uk
W www.acornents.co.uk

ARTIST PROMOTION MANAGEMENT   T 020 7224 1992
113 Great Portland Street
London W1W 6QQ
E info@harveygoldsmith.com
W www.harveygoldsmith.com

ASKONAS HOLT LTD   T 020 7400 1700
Lincoln House
300 High Holborn
London WC1V 7JH
E info@askonasholt.co.uk
W www.askonasholt.co.uk

AVALON PROMOTIONS LTD   T 020 7598 7333
4A Exmoor Street, London W10 6BD
E promotions@avalonuk.com
W www.avalonuk.com

BLOCK, Derek CONCERT   T 020 7724 2101
2D, 4-6 Canfield Place, London NW6 3BT
E dbcp@derekblock.co.uk

FLYING MUSIC   T 020 7221 7799
FM House, 110 Clarendon Road
London W11 2HR
E info@flyingmusic.co.uk
W www.flyingmusic.com

GUBBAY, Raymond LTD   T 020 7025 3750
Dickens House, 15 Tooks Court
London EC4A 1LB
E info@raymondgubbay.co.uk
W www.raymondgubbay.co.uk

HOBBS, Liz GROUP LTD   T 01636 555666
Music Factory
Jessop Way, Newark, Nottinghamshire NG24 2ER
E enquiries@lizhobbsgroup.com
W www.lizhobbsgroup.com

HOCHHAUSER, Victor   T 020 7794 0987
4 Oak Hill Way
London NW3 7LR
E admin@victorhochhauser.co.uk
W www.victorhochhauser.co.uk

IMG ARTS & ENTERTAINMENT   T 020 8233 5300
1 Burlington Way
London W4 2TH
E concerts@imgworld.com
W www.imgworld.com

McINTYRE, Phil ENTERTAINMENTS LTD   T 020 7291 9000
3rd Floor, 85 Newman Street
London W1T 3EU
E info@mcintyre-ents.com
W www.mcintyre-ents.com

MEADOW, Jeremy   T 020 7436 2244
Something for the Weekend
26 Goodge Street
London W1T 2QG
F 0870 7627882
E info@jeremymeadow.com

RBM COMEDY   T 020 7630 7733
3rd Floor
1 Lower Grosvenor Place
London SW1W 0EJ
E info@rbmcomedy.com
W www.rbmcomedy.com

ROSENTHAL, Suzanna   T 020 7436 2244
Something for the Weekend
26 Goodge Street
London W1T 2QG
E admin@sftw.info

STAGE LEISURE SERVICES & PROMOTIONS   T 01482 853555
25 St. Anthonys Close
Kingston-Upon-Hull HU6 7FE
E sls.promotions@gmx.co.uk
W www.anightwiththestars.co.uk

Is your CV up-to-date?
• • • • • • • • • Top tips for promoting yourself!

- **Keep your credits up-to-date**
  An absolute must – always take responsibility for updating your own profile, as and when you gain credits and new skills.

- **Review your skills**
  Add new skills as they are learnt; remove old skills that you can no longer complete. The more skilled you are, the more you maximise your marketability.

- **Make sure your professional training appears**
  Also, remember to update this section as you undertake further training across your career.

- **Update your photograph**
  Ensure that you are representing yourself as you would now appear at an audition.

- **Add multimedia**
  Make sure casting professionals see and hear just how good you are with video and audio clips.

www.spotlight.com

Dance Agents

Why do I need a dance agent?

As with any other agent, a dance agent will submit their clients for roles, negotiate contracts, handle paperwork and offer advice. In return for these services they will take commission, usually ranging from 10-15%. The agents listed in this section specialise in representing and promoting dancers. They will possess the relevant contacts in the industry that you need to get auditions and jobs.

How should I use these listings?

If you are a dancer getting started in the industry, looking to change your existing agent, or wishing to take on an additional agent that represents you for dance alongside your main acting agent, the following listings will supply you with up-to-date contact details for dance agencies. Every company listed is done so by written request to us. Please see the main 'Agents and Personal Managers' advice section for further guidance on choosing and approaching agents.

Should I pay an agent to join their books? Or sign a contract?

Equity (the actors' trade union) does not recommend that artists pay an agent to join their client list. Before signing a contract, you should be very clear about the terms and commitments involved. For advice on both of these issues, or if you experience any problems with a current agent, we recommend that you contact Equity www.equity.org.uk. They also produce the booklet You and your Agent which is free to all Equity members and available from their website's members' area.

What is Spotlight Dancers?

Spotlight Dancers is a specialist casting resource. Online profiles are used by dance employers throughout the UK to locate dancers and send out casting or audition information. Dancers wishing to promote themselves for job roles in commercial theatre, musicals, opera, film, television, live music, video, corporate events and many other areas of the industry should consider joining: visit www.spotlight.com/dancers for more information.

Should I join Spotlight Actors/ Actresses or Dancers?

Depending on your skills, training and experience, you may be eligible for both. If you are interested in promoting yourself both as an actor and as a dancer, then consider having two separate online profiles. If you only want to join one or the other, then you will need to consider which area of the industry you want to focus on in your career. Musical theatre experience can qualify you for either, depending on whether your training/ roles involved mainly dancing or acting. This is something you will need to think about and something you should discuss with your agent, if you sign with one.

Where can I find more information?

Please refer to our information and advice pages in the 'Dance Companies' listings for further information about the dance industry.

A UNITED PRODUCTION T/F 020 8673 0627
Choreographers, Dancers & Stylists. Twitter: @lyndonlloyd
9 Shandon Road
Clapham
London SW4 9HS
E info@united-productions.co.uk
W www.united-productions.co.uk

ABCAST T 01978 511856
5 Bowyer Street
London N1 5RR
E info@abcast.co.uk
W www.abcast.co.uk

AJK DANCE ETC T 020 7831 9192
8B Lambs Conduit Passage
Holborn, London WC1R 4RH
E info@ajkdance.com
W www.ajkdance.com

BARRETT, Becky
MANAGEMENT T 020 8840 7828
Specialising in Musical Theatre & Dance
11 Central Chambers
The Broadway
London W5 2NR
E info@beckybarrettmanagement.co.uk
W www.beckybarrettmanagement.co.uk

BODYWORK AGENCY T 01223 314461
25-29 Glisson Road
Cambridge CB1 2HA
T 07792 851972
E agency@bodyworkds.co.uk

BOSS DANCE T 0161 237 0100
Fourways House
57 Hilton Street
Manchester M1 2EJ
F 0161 236 1237
E info@bossdance.co.uk
W www.bosscasting.co.uk

BOX ARTIST MANAGEMENT
LTD - BAM T 07732 704431
Choreographers. Musical Theatre. Commercial Dancers.
Corporate Entertainment
The Attic
The Old Finsbury Town Hall
Rosebery Avenue
London EC1R 4RP
E hello@boxartistmanagement.com
W www.boxartistmanagement.com

CREATIVE KIDZ & ADULTZ T 07908 144802
235 Fox Glove House
Fulham Road
London SW6 5PQ
T 020 7381 3684
E agency@creativekidzandco.co.uk
W www.creativekidzandco.co.uk

DANCERS T 020 7637 1487
Trading as FEATURES
1 Charlotte Street
London W1T 1RD
E info@features.co.uk
W www.features.co.uk

DANCERS INC T 020 7205 2316
Twitter: @dancersincworld
INC Artists Ltd
64 Great Eastern Street
London EC2A 3QR
E miranda@international-collective.com
W www.dancersincworld.com

ELLITE MANAGEMENT T 0845 6525361
'The Dancer', 8 Peterson Road
Wakefield WF1 4EB
T 07957 631510
E enquiries@ellitemanagement.co.uk
W www.elliteproductions.co.uk

EVENT MODEL MANAGEMENT T 020 3286 3135
Dancers. Models
Riverbank House
1 Putney Bridge Approach
London SW6 3JD
T 07581 223738
E info@eventmodel.co.uk
W www.eventmodelmanagement.co.uk

FEATURES T 020 7637 1487
1 Charlotte Street
London W1T 1RD
E info@features.co.uk
W www.features.co.uk

FUSION MANAGEMENT T 020 7834 6660
201A Victoria Street
London SW1W 5NE
T 07949 635921
E info@fusionmng.com
W www.fusionmng.com

HEADNOD TALENT
AGENCY LTD T 020 3222 0035
RichMix 1st Floor West
35-47 Bethnal Green Road
London E1 6LA
E info@headnodagency.com
W www.headnodagency.com

JK DANCE PRODUCTIONS T 0161 669 4401
T 020 7871 3055
E hello@jkdance.co.uk
W www.jkdance.co.uk

KEW PERSONAL
MANAGEMENT T 07876 457402
PO Box 679
Surrey RH1 6EN
E info@kewpersonalmanagement.com
W www.kewpersonalmanagement.com

KMC AGENCIES T 0845 5193071
Garden Studios
71-75 Shelton Street
Covent Garden
London WC2H 9JQ
E london@kmcagencies.co.uk
W www.kmcagencies.co.uk

KMC AGENCIES T 0845 5193071
48 Ancoats Street
Manchester M4 5AB
E casting@kmcagencies.co.uk
W www.kmcagencies.co.uk

**LIVING THE DREAM
TALENT AGENCY** T 01727 751613
145-147 St John Street
London EC1V 4PW
T 07845 267501
E agency@livingthedreamcompany.co.uk
W www.livingthedreamcompany.co.uk

LONGRUN ARTISTES AGENCY T 07748 723228
Contact: Gina Long
71-75 Shelton Street
Covent Garden
London WC2H 9JQ
E longrunartistes@icloud.com
W www.longrunartistes.com

LOVE RUDEYE AGENCY T 020 7014 3023
Contact: Kevin Archbold
18 West Central Street
London WC1A 1JJ
E info@loverudeye.com
W www.loverudeye.com

**MARLOWES AGENCY:
TV, THEATRE & DANCE** T 020 7193 4484
HMS President
Victoria Embankment
Blackfriars
London EC4Y 0HJ
E mitch@marlowesagency.com
W www.marlowesagency.com

MITCHELL MAAS McLENNAN T 020 8301 8745
MPA Offices, 29 Thomas Street
Woolwich, London SE18 6HU
T 07540 995802
E agency@mmm2000.co.uk
W www.mmm2000.co.uk

MODELS IN MOTION UK LTD T 07789 884134
E modelsinmotionlondon@gmail.com
W www.modelsinmotionlondon.com

NEW WAVE AGENCY T 020 7609 0150
16 Globe Court
107 Tollington Road
London N7 7JH
E newwaveagency@yahoo.com
W www.newwaveagency.co.uk

PRODANCE T 020 7193 8554
Dancers. Acts. Choreographers
Suite 3A, Oriental Road
Woking, Surrey GU22 7AH
E info@prodance.co.uk
W www.prodance.co.uk

**RAZZAMATAZZ
MANAGEMENT** T/F 01342 301617
204 Holtye Road
East Grinstead RH19 3ES
T 07836 268292
E razzamatazzmanagement@btconnect.com

ROEBUCK, Gavin T 020 7370 7324
51 Earls Court Square
London SW5 9DG
E info@gavinroebuck.com
W www.gavinroebuck.com

**SCRIMGEOUR, Donald
ARTISTS AGENT** T 020 8444 6248
49 Springcroft Avenue
London N2 9JH
E vwest@dircon.co.uk

**SINGER, Sandra
ASSOCIATES** T 01702 331616
Dancers & Choreographers
21 Cotswold Road
Westcliff-on-Sea
Essex SS0 8AA
E sandrasingeruk@aol.com
W www.sandrasinger.com

S.O.S. T 020 7735 5133
Twitter: @sebholden
85 Bannerman House
Lawn Lane
London SW8 1UA
T 07740 359770
E info@sportsofseb.com
W www.sportsofseb.com

STUDIO ACCELERATE T 020 3130 4040
Accelerate Productions Ltd
374 Ley Street
Ilford IG1 4AE
T 07956 104086
E info@accelerate-productions.co.uk
W www.accelerate-productions.co.uk

SUCCESS T 020 7734 3356
Room 236, 2nd Floor
Linen Hall
162-168 Regent Street
London W1B 5TB
F 020 7494 3787
E ee@successagency.co.uk
W www.successagency.co.uk

**SUMMERS, Mark
MANAGEMENT** T 020 7229 8413
1 Beaumont Avenue
West Kensington
London W14 9LP
E louise@marksummers.com
W www.marksummers.com

TASTE OF CAIRO T 07801 413161
Bellydancers. UK & Europe
22 Gilda Crescent Road, Eccles
Manchester M30 9AG
E hello@tasteofcairo.com
W www.tasteofcairo.com

T W MANAGEMENT AGENCY T 01253 292733
66-74 The Promenade
Blackpool
Lancashire FY1 1LD
E marie.cavney@twmanagementagency.co.uk
W www.twmanagementagency.co.uk

W ATHLETIC T 020 8948 2759
34 Hill Street
Richmond-upon-Thames
London TW9 1TW
E london@wathletic.com
W www.wathletic.com

Literary Agents

Who are literary agents?

Literary agents represent writers and promote their work to publishers, commissioners and editors. Literary agents will also negotiate contracts and sales for their clients and also handle dramatic rights. In return, they will take commission usually ranging from 10-15%. Some literary agents may represent a specific genre of work whereas others cover a diverse range of writing from books and plays to television, radio and film drama.

Why do I need a literary agent?

A literary agent can help a writer become more marketable and appealing and open up a much wider net of contacts and opportunities. The chances of becoming a published author or successful screenwriter are very small, and only very few experience success. Securing an agent to represent you is a step towards this but in itself is by no means a guarantee of success.
For playwrights, some theatres welcome submissions directly, however, there are several ways that having an agent can improve your chances; they will work with a writer to get a manuscript or synopsis/pitch in perfect condition, often through extensive editorial work and collaboration. They have years of experience in identifying the right editors, publishers and commissioners who will be interested in a specific work and have invaluable insight into the current market and what type of work is being visioned years in advance. Many 'super' agencies now handle a range of clients from talent through to writers, directors and producers and so have an in-depth knowledge of the market from every perspective. Further down the line, an agent is there to guide their client's career, negotiate contracts, make foreign sales, handle rights and other similar issues.

How do I approach a literary agent?

Consult the listings and make a shortlist of the ones you wish to approach. If they have specified how they want to be contacted, whether by e-mail, post or telephone, make sure you are using this information to your advantage. Most literary agents would prefer post or e-mail rather than a phone call, as it will be your writing that sells you. Do your research and check that the agent handles the kind of writing you do. Some agents only deal with specific genres so make sure you are aware of this before contacting them. Always make sure you are addressing the specific agent and not "sir or madam" or "to whom it may concern". If a contact name is not detailed in the listing, check the website for submission guidelines or try phoning to see who you should send submissions to. Presentation is important; always check spelling and grammar, submissions should be word-processed not handwritten. Your submission should include a short covering letter, a synopsis and a self-addressed envelope with enough postage for the return of your manuscript. Note: legitimate agents do not charge reading or upfront fees.

How should I use these listings?

If you are a first-time writer looking to get published or promoted or you are thinking about changing your agent, the following listings will supply you with up-to-date contact details for many of the UK's leading literary agencies. Every agency listed is done so by written request to us. Members of the Personal Managers' Association (PMA) have indicated their membership status under their name.

Some agencies have also chosen to list other information such as relevant contact names, the fields of work they represent and their preferred method of contact from new applicants. Use this information to narrow down your search and optimise your chances of finding a suitable agent.

A & B PERSONAL MANAGEMENT LTD T 020 7794 3255
PO Box 64671, London NW3 9LH
E b.ellmain@aandb.co.uk

AGENCY (LONDON) LTD THE T 020 7727 1346
PMA Member
24 Pottery Lane, Holland Park
London W11 4LZ
F 020 7727 9037
E info@theagency.co.uk
W www.theagency.co.uk

ASPER, Pauline MANAGEMENT T/F 01424 870412
PMA Member
Jacobs Cottage, Reservoir Lane
Sedlescombe, East Sussex TN33 0PJ
E pauline.asper@virgin.net

BERLIN ASSOCIATES T 020 7836 1112
PMA Member
7 Tyers Gate, London SE1 3HX
E agents@berlinassociates.com
W www.berlinassociates.com

BLAKE FRIEDMANN T 020 7387 0842
PMA Member. Novels, Non-fiction & TV/Film Scripts
1st Floor, Selous House
5-12 Mandela Street
London NW1 0DU
E info@blakefriedmann.co.uk
W www.blakefriedmann.co.uk

BRITTEN, Nigel MANAGEMENT T 020 8778 7444
28 Woodbastwick Road
London SE26 5LH
E office@nbmanagement.com

BRODIE, Alan REPRESENTATION LTD T 020 7253 6226
PMA Member. Contact: Alan Brodie
Paddock Suite, The Courtyard
55 Charterhouse Street
London EC1M 6HA
F 020 7183 7999
E abr@alanbrodie.com
W www.alanbrodie.com

CANN, Alexandra REPRESENTATION T 01983 523312
Box 116, 4 Montpelier Street
London SW7 1EE
E alex@alexandracann.co.uk

CASAROTTO RAMSAY & ASSOCIATES LTD T 020 7287 4450
PMA Member
Waverley House
7-12 Noel Street
London W1F 8GQ
F 020 7287 9128
E info@casarotto.co.uk
W www.casarotto.co.uk

CLOWES, Jonathan LTD T 020 7722 7674
PMA/Association of Authors' Agents Member
10 Iron Bridge House
Bridge Approach
London NW1 8BD
F 0871 5283647
E admin@jonathanclowes.co.uk

COCHRANE, Elspeth PERSONAL MANAGEMENT
Existing Clients only. No New Applicants. See ASQUITH & HORNER in Agents & Personal Managers section

COHEN MAYER, Charlie ASSOCIATES T 07850 077825
Personal Managers. Talent Agency
121 Brecknock Road
Camden
London N19 5AE
E houseofsaintjude@gmail.com

CURTIS BROWN GROUP LTD T 020 7393 4400
PMA Member
5th Floor, Haymarket House
28-29 Haymarket
London SW1Y 4SP
F 020 7393 4401
E cb@curtisbrown.co.uk
W www.curtisbrown.co.uk

DAISH, Judy ASSOCIATES LTD T 020 8964 8811
PMA Member
2 St Charles Place
London W10 6EG
F 020 8964 8966
E judy@judydaish.com
W www.judydaish.com

DENCH ARNOLD AGENCY THE T 020 7437 4551
PMA Member
10 Newburgh Street
London W1F 7RN
F 020 7439 1355
E contact@dencharnold.com
W www.dencharnold.com

de WOLFE, Felix T 020 7242 5066
PMA Member
2nd Floor, 20 Old Compton Street
London W1D 4TW
F 020 7242 8119
E info@felixdewolfe.com
W www.felixdewolfe.com

FILLINGHAM, Janet ASSOCIATES T 020 8748 5594
PMA Member
52 Lowther Road, London SW13 9NU
E info@janetfillingham.com
W www.janetfillingham.com

FILM RIGHTS LTD T 020 8001 3040
11 Pandora Road, London NW6 1TS
F 020 8711 3171
E information@filmrights.ltd.uk
W www.filmrights.ltd.uk

FITCH, Laurence LTD T 020 8001 3040
11 Pandora Road, London NW6 1TS
F 020 8711 3171
E information@laurencefitch.com

FRA T 020 8255 7755
PMA Member. Formerly FUTERMAN, Rose & ASSOCIATES. AAA Member. TV/Film, Showbiz & Music Business Biographies
91 St Leonards Road
London SW14 7BL
E guy@futermanrose.co.uk
W www.futermanrose.co.uk

FRENCH, Samuel LTD T 020 7387 9373
PMA Member
52 Fitzroy Street, Fitzrovia
London W1T 5JR
F 020 7387 2161
E theatre@samuelfrench-london.co.uk
W www.samuelfrench-london.co.uk

GLASS, Eric LTD T 020 7229 9500
25 Ladbroke Crescent
Notting Hill
London W11 1PS
F 020 7229 6220
E eglassltd@aol.com

HANCOCK, Roger LTD T 020 8341 7243
44 South Grove House
South Grove, London N6 6LR
E tim@rogerhancock.com

HIGHAM, David ASSOCIATES LTD T 020 7434 5900
PMA Member
F 020 7437 1072
E dha@davidhigham.co.uk
W www.davidhigham.co.uk

HOSKINS, Valerie ASSOCIATES LTD T 020 7637 4490
PMA Member
20 Charlotte Street, London W1T 2NA
F 020 7637 4493
E vha@vhassociates.co.uk

IMAGINE TALENT T 07876 685515
E christina@imaginetalent.co.uk
W www.imaginetalent.co.uk

INDEPENDENT TALENT GROUP LTD T 020 7636 6565
PMA Member. Formerly ICM, London
40 Whitfield Street
London W1T 2RH
F 020 7323 0101
W www.independenttalent.com

JFL AGENCY LTD T 020 3137 8182
PMA Member
48 Charlotte Street
London W1T 2NS
E agents@jflagency.com
W www.jflagency.com

KASS, Michelle ASSOCIATES T 020 7439 1624
PMA Member
85 Charing Cross Road
London WC2H 0AA
F 020 7734 3394
E office@michellekass.co.uk

KENIS, Steve & CO T 020 7434 9055
PMA Member
95 Barkston Gardens
London SW5 0EU
F 020 7373 9404
E sk@sknco.com

MACFARLANE CHARD ASSOCIATES LTD T 020 7636 7750
PMA Member
33 Percy Street, London W1T 2DF
E enquiries@macfarlane-chard.co.uk
W www.macfarlane-chard.co.uk

MACNAUGHTON LORD REPRESENTATION T 020 7499 1411
PMA Member
44 South Molton Street, London W1K 5RT
E info@mlrep.com
W www.mlrep.com

MANS, Johnny PRODUCTIONS T 01992 470907
Incorporating Encore Magazine
PO Box 196, Hoddesdon
Herts EN10 7WG
E johnnymansagent@aol.com
W www.johnnymansproductions.co.uk

MARJACQ SCRIPTS LTD T 020 7935 9499
Prose. Screenplays. No Stage Plays or Musicals
Submissions: Box 412
19-21 Crawford Street
London W1H 1PJ
F 020 7935 9115
W www.marjacq.com

MARVIN, Blanche AGENCY T/F 020 7722 2313
Blanche Marvin MBE. Drama Critic for LTR. Critic's Circle Member. No Unsolicited Materials
21A St Johns Wood High Street
London NW8 7NG
E blanchemarvin17@hotmail.com

M.B.A. LITERARY & SCRIPT AGENTS LTD T 020 7387 2076
PMA Member
62 Grafton Way, London W1T 5DW
E submissions@mbalit.co.uk
W www.mbalit.co.uk

McLEAN, Bill PERSONAL MANAGEMENT LTD T 020 8789 8191
23B Deodar Road, London SW15 2NP

MEMPHIS, THADDAEUS & GOLD TALENT & LITERARY AGENCY T 07850 077825
121 Brecknock Road, Camden
London N19 5AE
E houseofsaintjude@gmail.com

MILBURN BROWNING ASSOCIATES T 020 3582 9370
PMA Member. Representing Scripted Material for Film/ Theatre/Television
The Old Truman Brewery
91 Brick Lane, London E1 6QL
F 020 3582 9377
E info@milburnbrowning.com
W www.milburnbrowning.com

MLR
See MACNAUGHTON LORD REPRESENTATION

MORRIS, William ENDEAVOR ENTERTAINMENT T 020 7534 6800
100 New Oxford Street
London WC1A 1HB
F 020 8929 8400
W www.wma.com

NARROW ROAD COMPANY THE T 020 7831 4450
PMA Member
1st Floor, 37 Great Queen Street
London WC2B 5AA
E richardireson@narrowroad.co.uk

PFD T 020 7344 1000
Drury House, 34-43 Russell Street
London WC2B 5HA
E info@pfd.co.uk
W www.peterfraserdunlop.com

ROSICA COLIN LTD T 020 7370 1080
1 Clareville Grove Mews
London SW7 5AN

SAYLE SCREEN LTD T 020 7823 3883
PMA Member. Screenwriters & Directors for Film, Stage & Television
11 Jubilee Place, London SW3 3TD
F 020 7823 3363
E info@saylescreen.com

SEIFERT, Linda
MANAGEMENT LTD T 020 3214 8293
PMA Member
Unit 315, Screenworks
22 Highbury Grove
London N5 2ER
E contact@lindaseifert.com
W www.lindaseifert.com

SHARLAND
ORGANISATION LTD T 01933 626600
The Manor House, Manor Street
Raunds, Northants NN9 6JW
E tso@btconnect.com

SHEIL LAND
ASSOCIATES LTD T 020 7405 9351
PMA Member. Literary, Film & Stage
52 Doughty Street, London WC1N 2LS
F 020 7831 2127
E info@sheilland.co.uk

STEEL, Elaine T 01273 739022
PMA Member. Writers' Agent
49 Greek Street, London W1D 4EG
E es@elainesteel.com

STEINBERG, Micheline
ASSOCIATES T 020 3214 8292
PMA Member
Suite 315, Screenworks, 22 Highbury Grove
London N5 2ER
T 07989 132112
E info@steinplays.com
W www.steinplays.com

STEVENS, Rochelle & CO T 020 7359 3900
PMA Member
2 Terretts Place, Upper Street
London N1 1QZ
F 020 7354 5729
E info@rochellestevens.com
W www.rochellestevens.com

TENNYSON AGENCY THE T 020 8543 5939
10 Cleveland Avenue, Merton Park
London SW20 9EW
E submissions@tenagy.co.uk

TYRRELL, Julia
MANAGEMENT T 020 8374 0575
PMA Member
57 Greenham Road, London N10 1LN
F 020 8374 5580
E info@jtmanagement.co.uk
W www.jtmanagement.co.uk

WARE, Cecily
LITERARY AGENTS T 020 7359 3787
PMA Member
19C John Spencer Square
London N1 2LZ
F 020 7226 9828
E info@cecilyware.com
W www.cecilyware.com

WEINBERGER, Josef LTD T 020 7580 2827
PMA Member
12-14 Mortimer Street
London W1T 3JJ
F 020 7436 9616
E general.info@jwmail.co.uk
W www.josef-weinberger.com

WESSON, Penny T 020 7722 6607
PMA Member
26 King Henry's Road
London NW3 3RP
F 020 7483 2890
E penny@pennywesson.com

WILLIAMSON, Simon
AGENCY THE (SWA) T 020 7281 1449
155 Stroud Green Road
London N4 3PZ
E info@swagency.co.uk
W www.swagency.co.uk

Presenters' Agents

How do I become a presenter?

There is no easy answer to this question. Some presenters start out as actors and move into presenting work, others may be 'experts' such as chefs, designers or sports professionals who are taken on in a presenting capacity. Others may have a background in stand-up comedy. All newsreaders are professional journalists with specialist training and experience. Often presenters work their way up through the production side of broadcasting, starting by working as a runner or researcher and then moving up to appear in front of the camera. To get this kind of production work you could contact film and television production companies, many of whom are listed in Contacts. A number of performing arts schools, colleges and academies also offer useful part-time training courses for presenters. See the 'Drama Training, Schools and Coaches' section for college/school listings.

Why do I need a presenting agent?

As with any other agent, a presenting agent will promote their clients to job opportunities, negotiate contracts on their behalf, handle paperwork and offer advice. In return for these services they take commission usually ranging from 10-15%. The listings in this section will supply you with up-to-date contact details for presenter agencies. They will possess the relevant contacts in the industry that you need to get auditions and jobs.

How should I use these listings?

Before you approach any agency looking for representation, do some research into their current client list and the areas in which they specialise. Many have websites you can visit. Once you have made a short-list of the ones you think are most appropriate, you should send them your CV with a covering letter and a good quality, recent photograph, which is a genuine likeness of you. Showreels can also be a good way of showcasing your talents, but only send these if you have checked with the agency first. Enclosing a stamped-addressed envelope with sufficient postage (SAE) will also give you a better chance of a reply. Please see the main 'Agents and Personal Managers' advice section for further guidance on choosing and approaching agents.

Should I pay an agent to join their books? Or sign a contract?

Equity (the actors' trade union) does not recommend that artists pay an agent to join their client list. Before signing any contract, you should be very clear about the terms and commitments involved. For advice on both of these issues, or if you experience any problems with a current agent, we recommend that you contact Equity www.equity.org.uk. They also produce the booklet You and your Agent which is free to all Equity members and available from their website's members' area.

What is Spotlight Presenters & Personalities?

Spotlight Presenters & Personalities is a specialist resource with profiles of over five hundred professional television and radio presenters and is a great way of promoting yourself for work. It is used by production companies, casting directors, television and radio stations, advertising agencies and publicists to browse and locate talent for future productions. Membership is available to any presenter with proven professional broadcast experience. Just starting out in your presenting career? Please see www.spotlight.com/join to join or for more information.

Should I join Spotlight Actors/Actresses or Presenters & Personalities?

Depending on your skills, training and experience, you may be eligible for both if you are interested in promoting yourself as an actor and as a presenter. You will however have to prove that you already have professional experience and/or relevant training in both areas.

CASE STUDY

Sue Sammon at Chase Personal Management has been an agent in the UK for almost 30 years looking after Models, Presenters Celebrities and more recently Actors.

So you want to be a Presenter?

Over the past 15 years with the explosion of the internet and satellite TV, many people have approached me and said 'I'd really like to be a TV presenter' but what actually makes a good presenter? They need to be able to conduct extensive research, interview, listen, react quickly to situations, have lots of energy and be able to communicate well with others. We have worked with several presenters at the beginning of their careers in different genres from Children's shows on CBBC, The Gadget Show on Channel 5, QVC, talkSPORT Radio, BskyB and many more.

"Build a picture of what sort of presenter you want to be"

I receive hundreds of showreels from wannabe presenters and very few spark my interest. Just going out into the street taping interviews with the general public won't get any agents or TV commissioners juiced. Before you start, sit down and really make notes on what subjects you are interested in, which TV shows you like and feel you could contribute to. Build a picture of what sort of presenter you want to be. Next, research a topic you are passionate about, find relevant people to interview and contact them. Don't be scared of contacting well known experts/personalities, they may speak to you if you are serious and the idea is sound. It could be something local to you, and you may offer your services for free to start with to local companies/media. If it's a certain show you would like to work on and feel you could really contribute, then make a video that looks like you are on the show (never use their logo though as this won't go down very well). Practice on your smartphone and watch yourself again and again then ask someone you know with a video camera to shoot you. Or approach a local college, as they may have a film production dept and some of the students might like to get involved. Use as many outsourced facilities as you can.

We cover the following types of presenting:

Shopping TV can be lucrative and fun, but you need to be able to talk constantly for hours on end about the products you are selling and still sound fresh at the end of the day. Live television is very demanding.

Corporate Presenting is mainly for company websites talking about their products or services and can be a good source of income. It usually requires more business like profiles wearing smart suits and working from a script with or without autocue.

Live Events can take the form of a company corporate event in conference or a public event in one of the many venues around the country or abroad. We have worked events as far away as Australia, Singapore and the USA. In this case you will need to be able to command small or large audiences and will have to have adlib skills and plenty of charisma.

Mainstream Television is where most people want to be but the competition is tough. News Channels require a journalistic qualification, though you can sometimes start in production and work your way up, whilst following a journalism course as we secured for one of our presenters on Sky Sports News. There are also more opportunities now with the increasing presence of On-line Channels as well. Your agent will have contacts and work to promote you to the relevant channels. A word of warning here, just because you secure a gig in this area, doesn't mean you have instant power to make huge demands. Listen to your agent, they are experienced in negotiating deals to maximise your income and develop your professional credibility in the business.

Finally, the role of the agent is to help develop and guide you with your goals so you need to be as clear as possible. Agents only receive income on commission from jobs done by their artists, they're highly motivated to get you work once they have taken you on their books. Your relationship with your agent is a team effort. I say to all my new artists, whether they are presenters, actors or models that activity is the key to success, get involved with your industry. Don't chase the fame or you will never be satisfied. Follow your passion and you will succeed.

**To find out more visit
www.chasepersonalmanagement.co.uk**

ABCAST　　T 01978 511856
5 Bowyer Street, London N1 5RR
E info@abcast.co.uk
W www.abcast.co.uk

APM ASSOCIATES　　T 020 8953 7377
Contact: Linda French
Elstree Studios, Shenley Road
Borehamwood WD6 1JG
T 07918 166706
E apm@apmassociates.net
W www.apmassociates.net

**A R G
(ARTISTS RIGHTS GROUP LTD)**　　T 020 7436 6400
4A Exmoor Street, London W10 6BD
F 020 7436 6700
E argall@argtalent.com
W www.argtalent.com

ARLINGTON ENTERPRISES LTD　　T 020 7580 0702
1-3 Charlotte Street, London W1T 1RD
F 020 7580 4994
E info@arlington-enterprises.co.uk
W www.arlingtonenterprises.co.uk

BARR, Becca MANAGEMENT　　T 020 3137 2980
97 Mortimer Street, London W1W 7SU
E info@beccabarrmanagement.co.uk
W www.beccabarrmanagement.co.uk

BLACKBURN MANAGEMENT　　T 020 7292 7555
Argyll House, All Saints Passage
London SW18 1EP
E presenters@blackburnmanagement.co.uk
W www.blackburnmanagement.co.uk

CAMERON, Sara MANAGEMENT
See TAKE THREE MANAGEMENT

**CHASE PERSONAL
MANAGEMENT**　　T 07929 447745 (Lisa Foulds)
3 Kew Road, Richmond, Surrey TW9 2NQ
T 07775 683955 (Sue Sammon)
E sue@chasemanagement.co.uk
W www.chasepersonalmanagement.co.uk

CHP ARTIST MANAGEMENT　　T 01844 345630
Meadowcroft Barn, Crowbrook Road, Askett
Princes Risborough
Buckinghamshire HP27 9LS
T 07976 560580
E chp.artist.management@gmail.com
W www.chproductions.org.uk

CINEL GABRAN MANAGEMENT　　T 029 2066 6600
Ty Cefn, 14-16 Rectory Road, Canton, Cardiff CF5 1QL
E info@cinelgabran.co.uk
W www.cinelgabran.co.uk

CINEL GABRAN MANAGEMENT　　T 01947 605376
Adventure House, Newholm
Whitby, North Yorkshire YO21 3QL
T 07552 168573
E mail@cinelgabran.co.uk
W www.cinelgabran.co.uk

CRAWFORDS　　T 020 8947 9999
PO Box 56662, London W13 3BH
E cr@wfords.com
W www.crawfords.tv

CURTIS BROWN　　T 020 7393 4460
Haymarket House, 28-29 Haymarket
London SW1Y 4SP
F 020 7393 4401
E presenters@curtisbrown.co.uk
W www.curtisbrown.co.uk

DAA MANAGEMENT　　T 020 7255 6123
Welbeck House, 66-67 Wells Street
London W1T 3PY
F 020 7255 6128
E info@daamanagement.co.uk
W www.daamanagement.co.uk

DAVID ANTHONY PROMOTIONS　　T 01925 632496
Twitter: @davewarwick2
PO Box 286, Warrington
Cheshire WA2 8GA
T 07836 752195
E dave@davewarwick.co.uk
W www.davewarwick.co.uk

DEVINE ARTIST MANAGEMENT　　T 0161 726 5726
Tempus Building, 9 Mirabel Street
Manchester M3 1NP
E manchester@devinemanagement.co.uk
W www.devinemanagement.co.uk

**DHM LTD
(DICK HORSEY MANAGEMENT)**　　T/F 01923 710614
Contact: Roger de Courcey
Suite 1, Cottingham House, Chorleywood Road
Rickmansworth, Herts WD3 4EP
E roger@dhmlimited.co.uk
W www.dhmlimited.co.uk

DOWNES PRESENTERS AGENCY　　T 07973 601332
E downes@presentersagency.com
W www.presentersagency.com

**EVANS, Jacque
MANAGEMENT LTD**　　T 020 8699 1202
Top Floor Suite, 14 Holmesley Road
London SE23 1PJ
F 020 8699 5192
E jacque@jemltd.demon.co.uk

EXCELLENT TALENT　　T 0845 2100111
3-8 Bolsover Street, London W1W 6AB
E marie-claire@excellenttalent.com
W www.excellenttalent.com

FLETCHER ASSOCIATES　　T 020 8361 8061
*Broadcasting Experts. Corporate Speakers. Journalists.
Historians*
Studio One, 25 Parkway
London N20 0XN
F 020 8361 8866
W www.fletcherassociates.net

**FORD-CRUSH, June PERSONAL MANAGEMENT
& REPRESENTATION**　　T 020 8742 7724
PO Box 57948, London W4 2UJ
T 07711 764160
E june@junefordcrush.com
W www.junefordcrush.com

GAY, Noel ORGANISATION　　T 020 7836 3941
19 Denmark Street, London WC2H 8NA
E info@noelgay.com
W www.noelgay.com

GLOBAL7　　T/F 020 7281 7679
Kemp House, 152 City Road
London EC1V 2NX
T 07956 956652
E global7castings@gmail.com
W www.global7casting.com

GLORIOUS MANAGEMENT　　T 020 7704 6555
Lower Ground Floor, 79 Noel Road
London N1 8HE
E lisa@glorioustalent.co.uk
W www.gloriousmanagement.com

GRANT, James MEDIA T 020 8742 4950
94 Strand On The Green, Chiswick, London W4 3NN
F 020 8742 4951
E enquiries@jamesgrant.co.uk
W www.jamesgrant.co.uk

HICKS, Jeremy
ASSOCIATES LTD T 020 7580 5741
3 Stedham Place, London WC1A 1HU
F 020 7636 3753
E info@jeremyhicks.com
W www.jeremyhicks.com

iCAN TALK LTD T 01858 466749
Palm Tree Mews, 39 Tymecrosse Gardens
Market Harborough, Leicestershire LE16 7US
T 07850 970143
E hello@icantalk.co.uk
W www.icantalk.co.uk

JGPM T 020 7440 1850
4th Floor, 75A Berwick Street, London W1F 8TG
E victoria@jgpm.co.uk
W www.jgpm.co.uk

JLA (JEREMY LEE
ASSOCIATES LTD) T 020 7907 2800
Supplies Celebrities & After Dinner Speakers
14 Berners Street, London W1T 3LJ
F 020 7907 2801
E talk@jla.co.uk
W www.jla.co.uk

JOYCE, Michael
MANAGEMENT T 020 7544 1065
Twitter: @michaeljoycetv
6th Floor, International House
223 Regent Street, London W1B 2QP
T 07817 448635
E michael@michaeljoyce.tv
W www.michaeljoycemanagement.com

KBJ MANAGEMENT LTD T 020 7054 5999
Television Presenters
22 Rathbone Street, London W1T 1LG
E general@kbjmanagement.co.uk
W www.kbjmgt.co.uk

KNIGHT, Hilary
MANAGEMENT LTD T 01604 781818
Grange Farm, Church Lane
Old, Northamptonshire NN6 9QZ
E hilary@hkmanagement.co.uk
W www.hkmanagement.co.uk

KNIGHT AYTON
MANAGEMENT T 020 7831 4400
35 Great James Street, London WC1N 3HB
E info@knightayton.co.uk
W www.knightayton.co.uk

LYTE, Seamus
MANAGEMENT LTD T 07930 391401
Contact: Seamus Lyte. By e-mail
E seamus@seamuslyte.com
W www.seamuslyte.com

M&C SAATCHI MERLIN T 020 7259 1460
36 Golden Square, London W1F 9JG
E enquiries@mcsaatchimerlin.com
W www.mcsaatchimerlin.com

MACFARLANE CHARD
ASSOCIATES LTD T 020 7636 7750
33 Percy Street, London W1T 2DF
F 020 7636 7751
E enquiries@macfarlane-chard.co.uk
W www.macfarlane-chard.co.uk

MARKS PRODUCTIONS LTD T 020 7486 2001
16 Chester Terrace, Regents Park, London NW1 4ND

MARSH, Billy ASSOCIATES LTD T 020 7598 7300
4A Exmoor Street, London W10 6BD
E isabell@billymarsh.co.uk
W www.billymarsh.co.uk

McKENNA, Deborah LTD T 020 8846 0966
Celebrity Chefs & Lifestyle Presenters only
Riverbank House, 1 Putney Bridge Approach
London SW6 3BQ
E hello@dml-uk.com
W www.dml-uk.com

MEDIA PEOPLE
(THE CELEBRITY GROUP) T 0871 2501234
12 Nottingham Place, London W1M 3FA
E info@celebrity.co.uk
W www.celebrity.co.uk

MILES, John ORGANISATION T 01275 854675
Cadbury Camp Lane, Clapton-in-Gordano
Bristol BS20 7SB
F 01275 810186
E john@johnmiles.org.uk
W www.johnmilesorganisation.org.uk

MLA TALENT T 020 7993 8337
Formerly Mike Leigh Associates
International House, 24 Holborn Viaduct
London EC1A 2BN
E mike@mlatalent.com
W www.mlatalent.com

MONDI ASSOCIATES LTD T 07817 133349
Contact: Michelle Sykes
Unit 3 O, Cooper House, 2 Michael Road
London SW6 2AD
E info@mondiassociates.com
W www.mondiassociates.com

MOON, Kate
MANAGEMENT LTD T 01604 686100
Pelham Barn, Draughton
Northampton NN6 0JQ
E kate@katemoonmanagement.com
W www.katemoonmanagement.com

MPC ENTERTAINMENT T 020 7624 1184
Contact: Michael P. Cohen (CEO)
MPC House, 15-16 Maple Mews, London NW6 5UZ
F 020 7624 4220
E info@mpce.com
W www.mpce.com

MTC (UK) LTD T 020 7935 8000
71 Gloucester Place, London W1U 8JW
F 020 7935 8066
E office@mtc-uk.com
W www.mtc-uk.com

NOEL, John MANAGEMENT T 020 7428 8400
Block B, Imperial Works
Perren Street, London NW5 3ED
E john@johnnoel.com
W www.johnnoel.com

OFF THE KERB PRODUCTIONS T 020 7490 1500
Comedy Presenters & Comedians
44 Clerkenwell Close, London EC1R 0AZ
F 020 7437 0647
E info@offthekerb.co.uk
W www.offthekerb.co.uk

PANMEDIA UK LTD T 020 8446 9662
18 Montrose Crescent
London N12 0ED
E enquiries@panmediauk.co.uk
W www.panmediauk.com

PEOPLEMATTER.TV T 020 7415 7070
Contact: Tony Fitzpatrick
40 Bowling Green Lane, Clerkenwell
London EC1R 0NE
F 020 7415 7074
E tony@peoplematter.tv
W www.peoplematter.tv

PFD T 020 7344 1000
Presenters. Public Speakers
Drury House, 34-43 Russell Street
London WC2B 5HA
E info@pfd.co.uk
W www.peterfraserdunlop.com

PV MEDIA LTD T 01905 616100
County House, St Mary Street
Worcester WR1 1HB
E md@pvmedia.co.uk

**RARE TALENT ACTORS
MANAGEMENT** T 0161 273 4444
Tanzaro House, Ardwick Green North
Manchester M12 6FZ
F 0161 273 4567
E info@raretalentactors.com
W www.raretalentactors.com

**RAZZAMATAZZ
MANAGEMENT** T/F 01342 301617
204 Holtye Road, East Grinstead
West Sussex RH19 3ES
T 07836 268292
E razzamatazzmanagement@btconnect.com

RED 24 MANAGEMENT T 020 7404 5722
R24 Offices, 1st Floor Kingsway House
103 Kingsway, London WC2B 6QX
E info@red24management.com
W www.red24management.com

RED CANYON MANAGEMENT T 07931 381696
T 07939 365578
E info@redcanyon.co.uk
W www.redcanyon.co.uk

REDWOOD TALENT T 0113 880 0822
Contact: Emma Helliwell
15 Queen Square
Leeds LS2 8AJ
T 07712 722282
E info@redwoodtalent.com
W www.redwoodtalent.com

REYNOLDS, Sandra AGENCY T 020 7387 5858
Contact: Jessie Byford
Amadeus House, 27B Floral Street
London WC2E 9DP
E jessie@sandrareynolds.co.uk
W www.sandrareynolds.co.uk

SELECT MANAGEMENT T 07855 794747
*Actors. Models. Presenters. Dancers. Children. Teenagers
& Adults*
PO Box 748, London NW4 1TT
T 07956 131494
E mail@selectmanagement.info
W www.selectmanagement.info

SINGER, Sandra ASSOCIATES T 01702 331616
21 Cotswold Road, Westcliff-on-Sea
Essex SS0 8AA
E sandrasingeruk@aol.com
W www.sandrasinger.com

SOMETHIN' ELSE T 020 7250 5500
20-26 Brunswick Place
London N1 6DZ
E info@somethinelse.com
W www.somethinelse.com

TAKE THREE MANAGEMENT T 020 7209 3777
110 Gloucester Avenue, Primrose Hill
London NW1 8HX
F 020 7209 3770
E sara@take3management.com
W www.take3management.co.uk

TALENT4 MEDIA LTD T 020 7183 4330
Studio LG6, Shepherds Building Central
Charecroft Way, London W14 0EH
F 020 7183 4331
E enquiries@talent4media.com
W www.talent4media.com

TRIPLE A MEDIA T/F 020 7637 5839
30 Great Portland Street
London W1W 8QU
E info@tripleamedia.com
W www.tripleamedia.com

TROIKA T 020 7336 7868
10A Christina Street, London EC2A 4PA
F 020 3544 2919
E casting@troikatalent.com
W www.troikatalent.com

**WANDER, Jo
MANAGEMENT LTD** T 020 7209 3777
110 Gloucester Avenue, Primrose Hill
London NW1 8HX
E jo@jowandermanagement.com
W www.jowandermanagement.com

WASSERMAN MEDIA GROUP T 020 7255 8155
6th Floor, 33 Soho Square
London W1D 3QU
E broadcasting@wmgllc.com
W www.wassermantvtalent.com

WISE BUDDAH TALENT T 020 7307 1600
74 Great Titchfield Street
London W1W 7QP
E talent@wisebuddah.com
W www.wisebuddah.com

ZWICKLER, Marlene & ASSOCIATES
1 Belgrave Crescent Lane
Edinburgh EH4 3AG
E info@mza-artists.com
W www.mza-artists.com

Voice Over Agents

How do I become a voice over artist?

The voice over business has opened up a lot more to newcomers in recent years; you don't have to be a celebrity to be booked for a role. However, it is a competitive industry, and it is important to bear in mind that only a select few are able to earn a living from voice over work. It is more likely that voice over work could become a supplement to your regular income.

In order to get work you must have a great voice and be able to put it to good use. Being able to act does not necessarily mean that you will also be able to do voice overs. Whether your particular voice will get you the job or not will ultimately depend on the client's personal choice, so your technical ability to do voice over work initially comes second in this industry. Once the client has chosen you, however, then you must be able to consistently demonstrate that you can take direction well, you don't need numerous takes to get the job finished, you have a positive attitude and you don't complain if recording goes a little over schedule.

Before you get to this stage, however, you will need a professional-sounding voicereel and, in the majority of cases, an agent.

How do I produce a voicereel?

Please see the 'Promotional Services' section for advice on creating your voicereel.

Why do I need a voice over agent?

As with any other agent, a voice over agent will promote their clients for appropriate roles, negotiate contracts on their behalf, handle paperwork and offer advice. In return for these services they take commission usually ranging from 10-15%. The agents listed in this section specialise in representing and promoting voice over artists, mostly in the commercial and corporate sectors, but also areas such as radio and animation. They will possess the relevant contacts in the industry that you need to get auditions and roles. In this industry in particular, time is money, and clients are often more likely to trust that an agent can provide someone who can get the job done in the least amount of takes

but still sounds good in every project, rather than taking on an unknown newcomer.

How do I find work in radio?

Please see the 'Radio' section of Contacts for further information and advice on this specific area of voice work.

How should I use these listings?

Whether you are completely new to the industry, looking to change your existing agent, or wishing to take on an additional agent to represent you for voice overs alongside your main acting or presenting agent, the listings in this section will supply you with up-to-date contact details for voice over agencies. Every company listed is done so by written request to us. Please see the main 'Agents and Personal Managers' advice section for further guidance on choosing and approaching agents.

Should I pay an agent to join their books? Or sign a contract?

Equity (the actors' trade union) does not recommend that artists pay an agent to join their client list. Before signing a contract, you should be very clear about the terms and commitments involved. For advice on both of these issues, or if you experience any problems with a current agent, we recommend that you contact Equity www.equity.org.uk. They also produce the booklet You and your Agent which is free to all Equity members and available from their website's members' area.

Voice Over Agents

CASE STUDY

Damn Good Voices is a bijou agency that makes a big noise. Simon Cryer is the Creative Director and Kingsley Hall the lead agent.

Who are we?

Damn Good Voices is a boutique voice over agency that caters to a range of highly skilled voice over artists, as well as a wide range of young new talent entering the business. We have strong connections with the commercial, gaming, corporate and documentary markets. It's a highly competitive industry, so you must be serious about delivering the ultimate voiceover, be willing to put in the hours and have a knack for delivering something special for clients.

What makes a great Voiceover Artist? – Training, Practice, Adaptability, A Great Agent. Practice

Like any instrument, your voice needs constant practice and tuning in order for it to be ready to be used to its full potential. You wouldn't expect to drag your granny's old zither out of the loft, blow off the dust and have it play perfectly with no tuning or TLC. Practice makes perfect!

Flexibility and adaptability are key to being any type of artist, but as a voice over artist they are of paramount importance. Last minute sessions, demanding directors and indecisive clients can leave you feeling like you've just had your head in the tumble dryer; a calm, unflappable nature is the key to surviving in an ever changing, fast paced industry.

Self-promotion is key in an industry that is getting busier by the minute. The advent of the internet and accessibility of home studios means that everyone and anyone can set up as a voice over artist – and this is where having a good voice over agent and a huge amount of talent comes in to play.

What should a voice over agent offer its talent?

There are a couple of main types of voice over agent, those that focus on celebrity talent and those that focus on a mix of highly skilled individuals with a lesser profile. The key thing is to not risk getting 'lost' within the mix of talent the agent already has on their books. Look for an agent who perhaps doesn't have a sound like yours already, and make sure to do your research before you apply for representation. Find an agent that is right for you and someone that you feel you could have a good working relationship with. It is important to remember that this is a partnership and there has to be give and take. A good agent will promote you to the right people, raise your profile in the industry and negotiate fees on your behalf, as well as advise you when it's time to walk away from a job because the fees are insultingly/damagingly low.

"Flexibility and adaptability are key to being any type of artist, but as a voice over artist they are of paramount importance. Last minute sessions, demanding directors and indecisive clients can leave you feeling like you've just had your head in the tumble dryer"

What are voice over agents looking for?

We look for talent that can bring a script to life, are able to take direction well and of course, stand out of the crowd. This business is highly competitive and only the great will survive! Trends in delivery styles change, trends in accents change and simply having a great voice is not enough. We need talent that guarantees to deliver the job as briefed in the least amount of takes, as time, is money!

We expect our talent to make themselves as available as possible for auditions, demo recordings and last minute sessions. Flexibility is a key part of the process as many sessions are turned around at very short notice… don't be surprised to get a phone call asking if you can make it to a session in the next hour.

Top Tips

1. Voice over work is very rewarding and can be over in a matter of hours, yet the fees can be relatively high for the amount of time spent on a job. But the voice over industry is highly competitive and only a small percentage earn a living purely from voice over work. You should initially see voice over work as a supplement to your regular income.

2. Voice over work opens up the opportunity to play a wider range of roles due to jobs being non-visual, thus offering you more castability as clients often don't care what you look like!

3. Many companies will go 'all out' to get voice over talent for cheap – be wary of these jobs as in the long term they can damage the voice over industry by driving down the price – certainly if you do not have an agent only take work that pays over £150 per hour (exclusive of any buyouts or usage).

4. Be flexible and patient in the studio. At the end of a three hour session a great voice over artist can hear the phrase 'Could you die again, but this time make it sound a little more orc-like?' and not go into a blind panic.

Good luck finding the right agent for you and remember to keep on keeping on!

Warning!

We receive around 30 submissions a week from a wide range of voices. It can take several days/weeks for agents to respond and engage with new voice submissions, as their focus will continue to be on bringing in work for talent currently on their books. Of course, we do have quieter spells when we can deal with submissions a little quicker! So please be patient with us.

**To find our more visit
www.damngoodvoices.com**

ADVOICE   T 020 7323 2345
40 Whitfield Street, London W1T 2RH
E info@advoice.co.uk
W www.advoice.co.uk

AHA TALENT LTD
See JONESES THE

ALPHABET AGENCY   T 020 7252 4343
Also known as Alphabet Kidz Ltd
Daisy Business Park, 19-35 Sylvan Grove
London SE15 1PD
E contact@alphabetkidz.co.uk
W www.alphabetkidz.co.uk

**AMERICAN AGENCY
VOICES THE**   T 020 7485 8883
14 Bonny Street, London NW1 9PG
E americanagency@btconnect.com
W www.americanagency.tv

**ANOTHER TONGUE
VOICES LTD**   T 020 7494 0300
The Basement, 10-11 D'Arblay Street
London W1F 8DS
F 020 7494 7080
E john@anothertongue.com
W www.anothertongue.com

ARCHANGEL VOICES LTD   T 020 8873 7095
Contact: Raphael McAuliffe
22 Portsmouth Avenue, Thames Ditton
Surrey KT7 0RT
E office@archangelvoices.co.uk
W www.archangelvoices.co.uk

ASQUITH & HORNER
*Existing Clients only. No New Applicants. See ASQUITH
& HORNER in Agents & Personal Managers*

BABBLE   T 020 7434 0002
30 Great Portland Street, London W1W 8QU
E hello@babblevoices.com
W www.babblevoices.com

**BRAIDMAN, Michelle
ASSOCIATES LTD**   T 020 7237 3523
2 Futura House, 169 Grange Road
London SE1 3BN
E info@braidman.com

CALYPSO VOICES   T 020 7734 6415
27 Poland Street, London W1F 8QW
F 020 7437 0410
E jane@calypsovoices.com
W www.calypsovoices.com

CHATTERBOX VOICES LTD   T 020 3744 3558
*Contact: Camilla Laxton, Joanna Shiokka,
Charlotte Sutton*
8 Doncaster Gardens
Middlesex UB5 4BN
E info@chatterboxvoices.co.uk
W www.chatterboxvoices.co.uk

**CONWAY VAN GELDER
GRANT LTD**   T 020 7287 1070
Twitter: @CvGG_Voices
3rd Floor, 8-12 Broadwick Street
London W1F 8HW
F 020 7287 1940
E kate@conwayvg.co.uk
W www.conwayvangeldergrant.com

CREATIVE KIDZ & ADULTZ   T 07908 144802
235 Fox Glove House, Fulham Road
London SW6 5PQ
T 020 73813684
E agency@creativekidzandco.co.uk
W www.creativekidzandco.co.uk

DAMN GOOD VOICES   T 07702 228185
Chester House, Studio 1:04
1-3 Brixton Road, London SW9 6DE
T 07809 549887
E damngoodvoices@me.com
W www.damngoodvoices.com

DEVINE VOICES LTD   T 020 7412 8919
Contact: Tezia Perret
8 Percy Street, London W1T 1DJ
E hello@devinevoices.com
W www.devinevoices.com

EARACHE VOICES   T 020 7287 2291
73 Beak Street, London W1F 9SR
F 020 7287 2288
E enquiries@earachevoices.com
W www.earachevoices.com

EXCELLENT TALENT   T 0845 2100111
118-120 Great Titchfield Street, London W1W 6SS
F 020 7637 4091
E info@excellenttalent.com
W www.excellenttalent.com

**FERRIS ENTERTAINMENT
VOICES**   T 07801 493133
London. Belfast. Cardiff. Los Angeles. France. Spain
Number 8, 132 Charing Cross Road
London WC2H 0LA
E info@ferrisentertainment.com
W www.ferrisentertainment.com

FIRST VOICE AGENCY   T 01494 730166
26 Wood Pond Close, Seer Green
Beaconsfield, Bucks HP9 2XG
E office@firstvoiceagency.com
W www.firstvoiceagency.com

FOREIGN LEGION   T 020 8450 4451
76 Park Avenue North, London NW10 1JY
E voices@foreignlegion.co.uk
W www.foreignlegion.co.uk

FOREIGN VERSIONS LTD   T 0333 123 2001
Translation
E info@foreignversions.co.uk
W www.foreignversions.com

theshowreel

London's Spoken-Word Specialists

How would you like to invest your money in a voiceover demo that actually stands you a chance of getting work?

Testimonials

Definitely the best showreels
Leigh Matty - Just Voices Agency

Professional demo reels that the industry expects
Matt Chopping - WAM Voices

Professional, sharp, well presented quality demos
Ben Romer Lee – Vocal Point

The best produced audio reels we receive
Victoria Braverman - Voicebookers.com

Professional and high quality demos
Penny Brown - Voicecall

Unfailingly produce exceptional demos every time
Vicky Crompton - Talking Heads

Great quality reels
Red 24 Management

Professional and unique showreels, 2 very important aspects for a top quality demo
Jennifer & Clair - Shining Management Ltd

Learn the skills needed on our one day voiceover workshop

Learn the "insider" secrets to starting a career in this lucrative industry.

Everyday we get calls and emails from people who want to know how to get started and they come from all walks of life not just from the "acting" side. In fact we've taught news readers, after dinner speakers, sales reps, teachers, actors, DJs, dentists, presenters, vets, lawyers, painters, biochemists and even "Brian" a Concord pilot (seriously) and have come to understand that just because people "tell" you that you've got a good sounding voice doesn't mean you should drop everything and make a demo.

A comprehensive, fun and interactive workshop.

Packed with insider information and loads of "tricks and techniques" on how to succeed in today's industry, this workshop gives you the opportunity to learn the skills and techniques used by working professionals. Small class sizes allow you plenty of time behind the "mic" and the chance to experience what it's really like to be in a commercial recording situation while being directed by one of London's most experienced Voice Producers, JP Orr.

This "heads up" will give you the headstart you need to move your voice career forward.

We know it's not possible to teach you everything there is to know about voiceovers in a single workshop, but we guarantee that having attended this session you will, with our help, be able to make an educated decision about whether voiceovers are for you.

If it is, then we will help you move forward. If it's not, then we will be honest and tell you that you would be wasting your time pursuing this line of work.

We also know that you can't get practical "hands-on" information in any one book, on the internet or at the end of a telephone. We've seen and pretty much heard it all and are willing to share our knowledge with you to help you get started. After all, you only get one chance to "get it right".

It's a serious decision you are about to make. We suggest you at least learn the basics before you spend your hard-earned money on a Voice Showreel you may end up not using.

28 years' working with London's top agents and the best voices in the business.

Our Logo goes on every demo we produce. A badge we've earned by not "just turning out" voice demos that have no chance of getting our clients work. That's why the top London agents choose us to produce their clients' voice demos.

But don't just take our word for it. Call them and ask them. Most will send you to us to "cut" your reel. Why? Because they know we offer a proven process for all our clients. A voiceover plan that works!

- Learn the skills to get started
- Put those skills into practice
- Record your Showreel
- Learn how to market your voice

Our One Day Voiceover Workshop: Special Offer Just £145.00

Our next workshop dates are now online at:

www.theshowreel.com

Please also feel free to call one of our **voice team** if you have any other questions:

020 7043 8660

The Showreel Limited

The Showreel: Soho Recording Studios, 22-24 Torrington Place, London WC1E 7HZ

SonicPondStudio

Professional, high quality, tailor made Voicereels, digitally recorded in a friendly, informal studio by an actor with 22 years' experience. Full day's unrushed recording. Consultation included. All direction and help given to make it a painless, fun process.

t: 020 7690 8561
e: martin@sonicpond.co.uk
w: www.sonicpond.co.uk

voicereels   spotlight clips   showreels   MT demos

GAY, Noel VOICES T 020 7836 3941
19 Denmark Street, London WC2H 8NA
F 020 7287 1816
E info@noelgay.com
W www.noelgay.com

GLOBAL7 T/F 020 7281 7679
Kemp House, 152 City Road
London EC1V 2NX
T 07956 956652
E global7castings@gmail.com
W www.global7casting.com

**GREAT BRITISH VOICE
COMPANY THE** T 07504 076020
339 Norristhorpe Lane, Liversedge
West Yorkshire WF15 7AZ
E info@gbvcoltd.com
W www.gbvcoltd.com

HAMILTON HODELL T 020 7636 1221
Contact: Louise Donald
20 Golden Square, London W1F 9JL
E louise@hamiltonhodell.co.uk
W www.hamiltonhodell.co.uk

HARVEY VOICES T 020 7952 4361
No Unsolicited Correspondence
49 Greek Street, London W1D 4EG
E info@harveyvoices.co.uk
W www.harveyvoices.co.uk

HOBSONS VOICES T 020 8995 3628
2 Dukes Gate, Chiswick
London W4 5DX
F 020 8996 5350
E voices@hobsons-international.com
W www.hobsons-international.com

HOPE, Sally ASSOCIATES T 020 7613 5353
108 Leonard Street, London EC2A 4XS
F 020 7613 4848
E casting@sallyhope.biz
W www.sallyhope.biz

iCAN TALK LTD T 01858 466749
Palm Tree Mews
39 Tymecrosse Gardens
Market Harborough, Leicestershire LE16 7US
E hello@icantalk.co.uk
W www.icantalk.co.uk

INTER VOICE OVER T 020 7262 6937
3rd Floor, 207 Regent Street
London W1B 3HH
E info@intervoiceover.com
W www.intervoiceover.com

J H A VOICE T 020 7580 5741
3 Stedham Place
London WC1A 1HU
F 020 7636 3753
E info@jeremyhicks.com
W www.jeremyhicks.com

JONESES THE T 020 7253 8462
74 Clerkenwell Road, London EC1M 5QA
E mail@meetthejoneses.co.uk
W www.meetthejoneses.co.uk

JUST VOICES AGENCY THE T 020 7881 2567
140 Buckingham Palace Road, London SW1W 9SA
F 020 7881 2569
E info@justvoicesagency.com
W www.justvoicesagency.com

KIDZTALK LTD T 01737 350808
Young Voices. Children. Teenagers. Twenties
F 01737 352456
E studio@kidztalk.com
W www.kidztalk.com

LEHRER, Jane VOICES T 020 7435 9118
PO Box 66334, London NW6 9QT
F 020 7435 9117
E voices@janelehrer.co.uk
W www.janelehrer.co.uk/voices.html

LIP SERVICE CASTING LTD T 020 7734 3393
Contact: By e-mail. Voice Overs only. Twitter:
@lipservicevoice
60-66 Wardour Street, London W1F 0TA
E bookings@lipservice.co.uk
W www.lipservice.co.uk

**LONDON VOICE
BOUTIQUE THE** T 020 7060 9456
Warwick House, Chapone Place, London W1D 3BF
E info@londonvoiceboutique.com
W www.londonvoiceboutique.com

LOUD & CLEAR VOICES LTD T 020 8450 7519
27 Mortimer Street, London W1T 3BL
E info@loudandclearvoices.com
W www.loudandclearvoices.com

M2M VOICES T 020 7631 1721
Specialises in Comedy
91 Brick Lane, London E1 6QL
E info@m2mvoices.com
W www.m2mvoices.com

**MARKHAM, FROGGATT
& IRWIN** T 020 7636 4412
4 Windmill Street, London W1T 2HZ
E tig@markhamfroggattirwin.com
W www.markhamfroggattandirwin.com

**MEMPHIS, THADDAEUS & GOLD TALENT &
LITERARY AGENCY** T 07850 077825
121 Brecknock Road, Camden
London N19 5AE
E houseofsaintjude@gmail.com

MONSTER VOICE T 020 7462 9950
Mappin House, 4 Winsley Street
London W1W 8HF
E mail@monstervoice.co.uk
W www.monstervoice.co.uk

MONSTER VOICE CARDIFF T 029 2034 4205
2nd Floor, 3-5 The Balcony
Castle Arcade, Cardiff CF10 1BU
E cardiff@monstervoice.co.uk
W www.monstervoice.co.uk

**MOON, Kate
MANAGEMENT LTD** T 01604 686100
Pelham Barn, Draughton
Northampton NN6 9JQ
E kate@katemoonmanagement.com
W www.katemoonmanagement.co.uk

PEMBERTON VOICES T 020 7224 9036
51 Upper Berkeley Street
London W1H 7QW
E fay@pembertonassociates.com
W www.pembertonvoices.com

QVOICE T 020 7520 9460
Adam House, 7-10 Adam Street
The Strand, London WC2N 6AA
E info@qvoice.co.uk
W www.qvoice.co.uk

**RABBIT VOCAL
MANAGEMENT LTD** T 020 7287 6466
94 Strand on the Green
London W4 3NN
E info@rabbitvocalmanagement.co.uk
W www.rabbitvocalmanagement.co.uk

RED 24 VOICES T 020 7404 5722
R24 Office, 1st Floor Kingsway House
103 Kingsway, London WC2B 6QX
E miles@red24management.com
W www.red24management.com/voices

RHUBARB VOICES T 020 8742 8683
1st Floor, 1A Devonshire Road
Chiswick, London W4 2EU
F 020 8742 8693
E enquiries@rhubarbvoices.co.uk
W www.rhubarbvoices.co.uk

SCREAM MANAGEMENT LTD T 0161 850 1996
The Greenhouse, Broadway
MediaCityUK, Salford M50 2EQ
E info@screammanagement.com
W www.screammanagement.com

SHINING MANAGEMENT LTD T 020 7734 1981
PO Box 1045, Chislehurst BR7 9AR
E info@shiningvoices.com
W www.shiningvoices.com

SUGAR POD VOICES T 020 8374 4701
Studio 8C
Chocolate Factory 1
5 Clarendon Road
Wood Green, London N22 6XJ
T 07967 673552
E info@sugarpodproductions.com
W www.sugarpodproductions.com

TALKING HEADS T 020 7292 7575
Argyll House
All Saints Passage
London SW18 1EP
E voices@talkingheadsvoices.com
W www.talkingheadsvoices.com

TERRY, Sue VOICES LTD　　T 020 7434 2040
4th Floor
35 Great Marlborough Street
London W1F 7JF
E sue@sueterryvoices.com
W www.sueterryvoices.com

TONGUE & GROOVE　　T 0161 228 2469
PO Box 173, Manchester M19 0AR
F 0161 249 3666
E info@tongueandgroove.co.uk
W www.tongueandgroove.co.uk

UNITED VOICES　　T 020 3214 0937
12-26 Lexington Street
London W1F 0LE
E voices@unitedagents.co.uk
W www.unitedvoices.tv

VOCAL POINT　　T 020 7419 0700
16 Manette Street, London W1D 4AR
E enquiries@vocalpoint.net
W www.vocalpoint.net

VOICE AGENCY THE　　T 020 7240 2345
Hudson House, 8 Tavistock Street
London WC2E 7PP
E info@thevoiceagency.co.uk
W www.thevoiceagency.co.uk

VOICE BANK LTD　　T 0161 973 8879
PO Box 825, Altrincham
Cheshire WA15 5HH
T 07931 792670
E elinors@voicebankltd.co.uk
W www.voicebankltd.co.uk

VOICE SHOP　　T 020 8742 7077
1st Floor, Thomas Place
1A Devonshire Road, London W4 2EU
F 020 8742 7011
E info@voice-shop.co.uk
W www.voice-shop.co.uk

VOICE SQUAD　　T 020 8450 4451
76 Park Avenue North, London NW10 1JY
E voices@voicesquad.com
W www.voicesquad.com

**VOICEBANK, THE IRISH
VOICE-OVER AGENCY**　　T 00 353 1 2350838
35 Thomastown Road, Dun Laoghaire
Co Dublin, Ireland
E voicebank@voicebank.ie
W www.voicebank.ie

VOICECALL　　T 020 7209 1064
67A Gondar Gardens
London NW6 1EP
T 07920 044615
E voices@voicecall-online.co.uk
W www.voicecall-online.co.uk

**VOICEOVER GALLERY
(LONDON) THE**　　T 020 7987 0951
12 Cock Lane, London EC1A 9BU
E info@thevoiceovergallery.co.uk
W www.thevoiceovergallery.co.uk

**VOICEOVER GALLERY
(MANCHESTER) THE**　　T 0161 881 8844
110 Timberwharf
32 Worsley Street
Manchester M15 4LD
E manchester@thevoiceovergallery.co.uk
W www.thevoiceovergallery.co.uk

VOICEOVERS.CO.UK　　T 020 7099 2264
PO Box 326, Plymouth
Devon PL4 9YQ
E info@voiceovers.co.uk
W www.voiceovers.co.uk

**VOICES AT THE
ARTISTS PARTNERSHIP**　　T 020 7439 1456
101 Finsbury Pavement
London EC2A 1RS
F 020 7734 6530
E email@theartistspartnership.co.uk
W www.theartistspartnership.co.uk/voices

**VSI - VOICE & SCRIPT
INTERNATIONAL**　　T 020 7692 7700
Foreign Language Specialists
132 Cleveland Street, London W1T 6AB
F 020 7692 7711
E info@vsi.tv
W www.vsi.tv

WAM VOICES　　T 020 7836 9222
The Voice Agency of Waring & McKenna
17 South Molton Street
London W1K 5QT
E info@wamvoices.com
W www.wamvoices.com

WOOTTON, Suzy VOICES　　T 01604 765872
72 Towcester Road, Far Cotton
Northampton NN4 8LQ
E suzy@suzywoottonvoices.com
W www.suzywoottonvoices.com

WORDS-OUT　　T 020 7183 0017
Hunters House
1 Redcliffe Road
London SW10 9NR
E karin@words-out.com
W www.words-out.com

YAKETY YAK　　T 020 7430 2600
Contact: Helen Galway, Jake Lawrence
3rd Floor, 14 Newburgh Street
London W1F 7RT
E hello@yaketyyak.co.uk
W www.yaketyyak.co.uk

Walk-On & Supporting Artists' Agents

Who are Walk-on & Supporting Artists?

Sometimes known as 'extras', walk-on and supporting artists appear in the background of television and film scenes in order to add a sense of realism, character or atmosphere. They do not have individual speaking roles, unless required to make background/ambient noise.

Working as a walk-on or supporting artist does not require any specific 'look', training or experience as such; however it does involve more effort than people think. Artists are often required to start very early in the morning (6am is not uncommon) and days can be long with lots of waiting around, sometimes in tough conditions on location. It is certainly not glamorous, nor is it a way to become a television or film star!

Artists must be reliable and available at very short notice, which can make it difficult to juggle with other work or family commitments. Requirements vary from production to production and, as with mainstream acting work, there are no guarantees that you will get regular work, let alone be able to earn a living as a walk-on.

How should I use these listings?

If you are serious about working as a walk-on artist, you will need to register with an agency in order to be put forward for roles. In return for finding you work, you can expect an agency to take commission usually ranging from 10-15%. The listings in this section contain contact details of many walk-on and supporting artist agencies. Some will specialise in certain areas, so make sure you research the different companies carefully to see if they are appropriate for you. Many have websites you can visit. It is also worth asking questions about how long an agency has existed, and about their recent production credits.

When approaching an agency, you should send them your CV with a covering letter and a recent photograph which is a genuine, natural likeness of you. Enclosing a stamped-addressed envelope with sufficient postage (SAE) will give you a better chance of a reply.

Should I pay an agent to join their books? Or sign a contract?

Equity (the actors' trade union) does not generally recommend that artists pay an agent to join their client list. Before signing any contract, you should be clear about the terms and commitments involved. Always speak to Equity www.equity.org.uk or BECTU www.bectu.org.uk if you have any concerns or queries. Equity also produces the booklet You and your Agent which is free to all Equity members and available from their website's members' area.

Where can I find more information?

You may find it useful to contact the Film Artists Association (FAA), a subdivision of BECTU, who provide union representation for walk-on and supporting artists. For further details visit www.bectu.org.uk/get-involved/background-artistes

2020 CASTING LTD T 020 8746 2020
2020 Hopgood Street, London W12 7JU
E info@2020casting.com
W www.2020casting.com

ABCAST T 01978 511856
5 Bowyer Street, London N1 5RR
E info@abcast.co.uk
W www.abcast.co.uk

ACADEMY EXTRAS T 01204 417403
Film. Television. Based in the North West
490 Halliwell Road, Bolton, Lancs BL1 8AN
E admin@academyextras.co.uk
W www.academyextras.co.uk

AGENCY OAKROYD T 07840 784337
Oakroyd, 89 Wheatley Lane
Ben Rhydding, Ilkley, Yorkshire LS29 8PP
E paula@agencyoakroyd.com
W www.agencyoakroyd.com

ALLSORTS AGENCY T 020 8472 3924
Waterfront Studios, 1 Dock Road, London E16 1AH
T 07950 490364
E bookings@allsortsagency.com
W www.allsortsagency.com

**ALLSTARS ACTORS
MANAGEMENT** T 0161 702 8257
23 Falconwood Chase, Worsley, Manchester M28 1FG
T 07584 992429
E extras@allstarsactors.tv
W www.allstarsactors.tv

ARTIST MANAGEMENT UK LTD T 0151 523 6222
6 Gondover Avenue, Orrell Park, Liverpool L9 8AZ
E chris@artistmanagementuk.com
W www.artistmanagementuk.com

AVENUE ARTISTES LTD T 023 8076 0930
PO Box 1573, Southampton SO16 3XS
E info@avenueartistes.com
W www.avenueartistes.com

BACKGROUND WALES T 0845 4082468
Suite 2, 1st Floor Offices, Cantilupe Chambers
Cantilupe Road, Ross-on-Wye HR9 7AN
F 0845 4082464
E tarquin@backgroundwales.co.uk
W www.backgroundwales.co.uk

BELLA CASTING AGENCY T 07456 741141
Represent Children & Adults
136 Rowson Street, Wirral CH45 2PW
E info@bellacasting.com
W www.bellacasting.com

BONNIE & BETTY LTD T 020 8301 8333
9-11 Gunnery Terrace, Royal Arsenal
London SE18 6SW
E agency@bonnieandbetty.com
W www.bonnieandbetty.com

BOSS CASTING T 0161 237 0100
Fourways House, 57 Hilton Street
Manchester M1 2EJ
F 0161 236 1237
E cath@bosscasting.co.uk
W www.bosscasting.co.uk

CAIRNS AGENCY T 0141 237 8580
Contact: Robert Brown
63 Bath Street, Glasgow G2 2SZ
E office@thecairns-agency.com
W www.thecairns-agency.com

CASTING COLLECTIVE THE T 020 8962 0099
Commercials. Film. Photographic. Television
109-111 Farringdon Road, London EC1R 3BW
E jodie@castingcollective.co.uk
W www.castingcollective.co.uk

CASTING NETWORK LTD THE T 020 8391 2979
4 Vidler Close, Chessington, Surrey KT9 2GL
E info@thecastingnetwork.co.uk
W www.thecastingnetwork.co.uk

CELEX CASTING LTD T 01332 232445
Adults & Children
PO Box 7317, Derby DE1 0GS
T 07932 066021
E anne@celex.co.uk

CENTRAL CASTING LTD T 020 8327 4244
See also KNIGHT, Ray CASTING LTD
Elstree Studios, Room 38, John Maxwell Building
Shenley Road, Borehamwood, Herts WD6 1JG
E casting@rayknight.co.uk
W www.rayknight.co.uk

COPS ON THE BOX T 07710 065851
Advisers. Walk-ons. Supporting Artists.
Twitter: @copsonthebox1
BM BOX 7301, London WC1N 3XX
E info@cotb.co.uk
W ww.cotb.co.uk

CREATIVE KIDZ & ADULTZ T 07908 144802
235 Fox Glove House, Fulham Road, London SW6 5PQ
T 020 73813684
E agency@creativekidzandco.co.uk
W www.creativekidzandco.co.uk

DAVID AGENCY THE T 020 8618 2064
26-28 Hammersmith Grove, London W6 7BA
E casting@davidagency.co.uk
W www.davidagency.co.uk

DK MODEL & CASTING T 0114 257 3480
4 Park Square, Thorncliffe Park
Chapeltown, Sheffield, South Yorkshire S35 2PH
F 0114 257 3482
E mail@dkmodels.net
W www.dkmodels.net

ELLIOTT AGENCY LTD THE T 01273 454111
17 Osborne Villas, Hove, East Sussex BN3 2RD
E elliottagency@btconnect.com
W www.elliottagency.co.uk

ETHNIKA CASTING T 0141 334 6246
14 Bowmont Gardens, Glasgow G12 9LR
T 07778 296002
E ethnikacasting@yahoo.co.uk
W www.ethnikacasting.co.uk

EUROKIDS & EKA CASTING AGENCIES T 01925 761083
Contact: Jodie Keith (Senior Casting Agent).
Accepts Showreels. Children, Teenagers & Adults up to 85 yrs. Commercials. Film. Television. Walk-on & Supporting Artists
The Warehouse Studios, Glaziers Lane
Culcheth, Warrington, Cheshire WA3 4AQ
T 01925 761210
E jodie@eka-agency.com
W www.eka-agency.com

EXTRA PEOPLE LTD T 020 3542 3685
London, Birmingham & Manchester
E team@extra-people.com W www.extra-people.com

FACE MUSIC T 01209 820796
Musicians Representation
Lambourne Farm, TR16 5HA
E facemusic@btinternet.com

FBI AGENCY T 07050 222747
Leeds & Manchester
PO Box 250, Leeds LS1 2AZ
T 07515 567309
E casting@fbi-agency.co.uk W www.fbi-agency.co.uk

FILM CAST CORNWALL & SW T 07811 253756
Falmouth, Cornwall
E enquiries@filmcastcornwall.co.uk
W www.filmcastcornwall.co.uk

FRESH AGENTS LTD   **T** 01273 711777
Actors. Presenters. Extras. Models. Child Models.
Families. Promotional Event Staff. Work in London and all
over the UK
The Dock, Wilbury Villas
Hove, East Sussex BN3 6AH
T 0845 4080998
E info@freshagents.co.uk
W www.freshagents.co.uk

FUSION MANAGEMENT   **T** 020 7834 6660
201A Victoria Street, London SW1W 5NE
T 07949 635921
E info@fusionmng.com
W www.fusionmng.com

GUYS & DOLLS CASTING   **T** 020 8906 4144
Concorde House, Grenville Place
Mill Hill, London NW7 3SA
E info@guysanddollscasting.com
W www.guysanddollscasting.com

HervL ARTISTES AGENCY   **T** 01322 352766
Admiral Park, Victory Way
Crossways Business Park
Dartford, Kent DA2 6QD
E info@hervl.com
W www.hervl.co.uk

INDUSTRY CASTING   **T** 0161 839 1551
Suite 5, Basil Chambers
65 High Street, Manchester M4 1FS
F 0161 839 1661
E lois@industrycasting.co.uk
W www.industrycasting.co.uk

IPM: IMPERIAL PERSONAL
MANAGEMENT LTD   **T** 0113 244 3222
IPM Casting. Contact: Charlotte Blackburn
The Studio, 102 Kirkstall Road
Leeds, West Yorkshire LS3 1JA
E info@ipmcasting.com
W www.ipmcasting.com

JPM EXTRAS   **T** 0191 221 2491
A Division of Janet Plater Management Ltd
D Floor, Milburn House
Dean Street, Newcastle upon Tyne NE1 1LF
E extras@jpmactors.com
W www.jpmactors.com

KNIGHT, Ray CASTING LTD   **T** 020 8327 4244
Elstree Studios, Room 38, John Maxwell Building
Shenley Road, Borehamwood, Herts WD6 1JG
E casting@rayknight.co.uk
W www.rayknight.co.uk

SÉVA
DHALIVAAL
07956 553879

KREATE LIVE MEDIA LTD   **T** 020 7401 9007
32 Southwark Bridge Road
London SE1 9EU
F 020 7401 9008
E hello@kreate.co.uk
W www.kreate.co.uk

LEMON CASTING   **T** 0161 205 2096
The Sharp Project, Thorpe Road
Newton Heath, Manchester M40 5BJ
T 07723 317489
E info@lemoncasting.co.uk

LINE OF SIGHT MILITARY
AGENCY   **T** 07701 007822
Contact: Matt Lyons
8 Northumberland Avenue
London WC2N 5BY
E matt@losproductions.co.uk
W www.losproductions.co.uk

LINTON MANAGEMENT   **T** 0161 761 2020
3 The Rock, Bury BL9 0JP
E mail@linton.tv
W www.lintonmanagement.co.uk

MAD DOG CASTING LTD   **T** 020 7269 7910
The Pavilion Building, Ealing Studios
Ealing Green, London W5 5EP
E info@maddogcasting.com
W www.maddogcasting.com

McDONAGH, Melanie MANAGEMENT
(ACADEMY OF PERFORMING ARTS
& CASTING AGENCY)   **T** 07909 831409
14 Apple Tree Way, Oswaldtwistle
Accrington, Lancashire BB5 0FB
T 01254 392560
E mcdonaghmgt@aol.com
W www.mcdonaghmanagement.co.uk

MIM AGENCY   **T** 0871 2377963
Clayton House, 59 Piccadilly
Manchester M1 2AQ
E info@mimagency.co.uk
W www.mimagency.co.uk

MINT CASTING AGENCY LTD   **T** 0161 834 7773
Suite 439-440, Royal Exchange
Manchester M2 7EP
E mark@mintcasting.tv
W www.mintcasting.tv

NEMESIS CASTING LTD   **T** 0161 228 6404
Nemesis House, 1 Oxford Court
Bishopsgate, Manchester M2 3WQ
E julie@nmsmanagement.co.uk
W www.nemesiscasting.co.uk

NIDGES CASTING AGENCY
See BOSS CASTING

ONSET EXTRAS LTD   **T** 07795 370678
Contact: Poppy Lloyd
Stockbrook House
8 King Street
Duffield, Derbyshire DE56 4EU
E poppy@onsetextras.co.uk
W www.onsetextras.co.uk

ORIENTAL CASTING
AGENCY LTD   **T** 020 8660 0101
Contact: Billie James
22 Wontford Road, Purley
Surrey CR8 4BL
E billiejames@btconnect.com

PAN ARTISTS AGENCY LTD   T 07890 715115
Cornerways, 34 Woodhouse Lane
Sale, Cheshire M33 4JX
T 07508 857943
E panartists@btconnect.com
W www.panartists.co.uk

PC THEATRICAL MODEL &
CASTING AGENCY   T 07904 549665
10 Strathmore Gardens, Edgware
Middlesex HA8 5HJ
T 020 8381 2229
E twinagy@aol.com
W www.twinagency.com

PHA CASTING   T 0161 273 4444
Tanzaro House
Ardwick Green North
Manchester M12 6FZ
F 0161 273 4567
E info@pha-agency.co.uk
W www.pha-agency.co.uk

PHOENIX CASTING AGENCY   T 0117 973 1100
PO Box 387, Bristol BS8 9HD
F 0117 973 4160
E caron@phoenixagency.biz
W www.phoenixagency.biz

POLEASE   T 05600 650524
Specialist in Police & Military Actors & Supporting
Artistes. Uniform Hire & Props also Available
1 Noake Road, Hucclecote
Gloucester GL3 3PE
T 07811 504079
E info@polease.co.uk
W www.polease.co.uk

REGENCY AGENCY   T 0113 236 0940
6 Wesley Street, Farsley
Leeds LS28 5LE
E jtiller3450@hotmail.com
W www.rogoncyagency.co.uk

RENTACROWD CASTING   T 07877 984636
11 Craigcrest Place
Condorrat G67 4GY
E alana@rentacrowd.com
W www.rentacrowd.co.uk

REYNOLDS, Sandra AGENCY LTD
(COMMERCIALS)   T 020 7387 5858
Commercials
Amadeus House
27B Floral Street
London WC2E 9DP
F 020 7387 5848
E jessie@sandrareynolds.co.uk
W www.sandrareynolds.co.uk

REYNOLDS, Sandra
AGENCY LTD (EAST ANGLIA)   T 01603 623842
Commercials
Bacon House
35 St Georges Street
Norwich NR3 1DA
E alex@sandrareynolds.co.uk
W www.sandrareynolds.co.uk

RHODES AGENCY   T 01708 747013
5 Dymoke Road
Hornchurch, Essex RM11 1AA
F 01708 730431
E rhodesarts@hotmail.com

SAINT JUDE - TALENT & LITERARY AGENCY T 07850 077825
121 Brecknock Road
London N19 5AE
E houseofsaintjude@gmail.com

SAPPHIRES MODEL & ARTIST MANAGEMENT LTD T 020 3603 9460
50 Great Portland Street
London W1W 7ND
E contact@sapphiresmodel.com
W www.sapphiresmodel.com

SCREAM MANAGEMENT LTD T 0161 850 1996
The Greenhouse
MediaCityUK
Salford, Manchester M50 2EQ
T 0161 850 1995
E info@screammanagement.com
W www.screammanagement.com

SCREENLITE AGENCY T 01932 561388
Shepperton Studios, Studios Road
Shepperton
Middlesex TW17 0QD
T 01932 592271
E enquiries@screenliteagency.co.uk
W www.screenliteagency.co.uk

SEVEN AGENCY MANAGEMENT T 0161 850 1057
Actors. Children. Modelling. Stage. Television
82 King Street, Manchester M2 4WQ
T 07714 252026
E info@7casting.co.uk
W www.7casting.co.uk

SHARMAN, Alan AGENCY T 0121 212 0090
Office 6, Fournier House
8 Tenby Street
Jewellery Quarter
Birmingham B1 3AJ
E info@alansharmanagency.com
W www.alansharmanagency.com

SLICK CASTING LTD T/F 07957 398213
Unit 23, Oaklands Avenue, London N9 7LN
T 07944 939462
E info@slickcasting.com
W www.slickcasting.com

SOLOMON ARTISTES T 020 7748 4409
30 Clarence Street, Southend-on-Sea
Essex SS1 1BD
T 01702 437118
E solomonartistes@hotmail.co.uk
W www.solomon-artistes.co.uk

SPORTS PROMOTIONS (UK) LTD T 020 8771 4700
56 Church Road, Crystal Palace, London SE19 2EZ
F 020 8771 4704
E cameron@sportspromotions.co.uk
W www.sportspromotions.co.uk

STAV'S CASTING AGENCY T 07539 810640
82 Station Crescent, Tottenham
Haringey, London N15 5BD
E stavros.louca@facebook.com
W www.stavscastingagency.com

SUMMERS, Mark MANAGEMENT T 020 7229 8413
1 Beaumont Avenue, West Kensington
London W14 9LP
E louise@marksummers.com
W www.marksummers.com

TUESDAYS CHILD LTD T/F 01625 501765
Children & Adults
Oakfield House, Springwood Way
Macclesfield SK10 2XA
E admin@tuesdayschildagency.co.uk
W www.tuesdayschildagency.co.uk

UNI-VERSAL EXTRAS T 0845 0090344
Pinewood Studios, Pinewood Road
Iver Heath, Buckinghamshire SL0 0NH
E info@universalextras.co.uk
W www.universalextras.co.uk

ALDERSHOT: West End Centre   T 01252 408040
Queens Road, Aldershot
Hants GU11 3JD
BO 01252 330040
E west.end.centre@hampshireculturaltrust.org.uk
W www.westendcentre.co.uk

BILLERICAY:
Billericay Arts Association   T 01277 659286
The Fold, 72 Laindon Road
Billericay
Essex CM12 9LD
E baathefold@yahoo.co.uk
W www.baathefold.org.uk

BINGLEY: Bingley Arts Centre   T 01274 519814
Home of Bingley Little Theatre
Main Street, Bingley
West Yorkshire BD16 2LZ
E office@bingleyartscentre.co.uk

BIRMINGHAM:
Custard Factory   T 0121 224 7777
Gibb Street, Digbeth
Birmingham B9 4AA
E info@custardfactory.co.uk
W www.custardfactory.co.uk

BOSTON: Blackfriars Theatre
& Arts Centre   T 01205 363108
Spain Lane, Boston
Lincolnshire PE21 6HP
F 01205 358855
E director@blackfriarsartscentre.co.uk
W www.blackfriarsartscentre.co.uk

BRACKNELL:
South Hill Park Arts Centre   T 01344 484858
Contact: Ron McAllister (Chief Executive)
Ringmead, Bracknell
Berkshire RG12 7PA
BO 01344 484123
E admin@southhillpark.org.uk
W www.southhillpark.org.uk

BRENTFORD: Watermans   T 020 8232 1019
40 High Street, Brentford TW8 0DS
BO 020 8232 1010
E info@watermans.org.uk
W www.watermans.org.uk

BRIDGWATER:
Bridgwater Arts Centre   T 01278 422700
11-13 Castle Street, Bridgwater
Somerset TA6 3DD
E info@bridgwaterartscentre.co.uk
W www.bridgwaterartscentre.co.uk

BRISTOL: Arnolfini   T 0117 917 2300
16 Narrow Quay, Bristol BS1 4QA
E boxoffice@arnolfini.org.uk

BUILTH WELLS:
Wyeside Arts Centre   T 01982 553668
Castle Street, Builth Wells
Powys LD2 3BN
BO 01982 552555
E boxoffice@wyeside.co.uk
W www.wyeside.co.uk

BURY: The Met   T 0161 761 7107
Contact: David Agnew (Director)
Market Street, Bury, Lancs BL9 0BW
BO 0161 761 2216
E post@themet.biz
W www.themet.biz

CANNOCK:
Prince of Wales Centre   T 01543 466453
Contact: Richard Kay (General Manager)
Church Street, Cannock
Staffs WS11 1DE
BO 01543 578762
E r.k@wllt.org

CARDIFF: Chapter   T 029 2030 4400
Market Road, Canton, Cardiff CF5 1QE
E enquiry@chapter.org
W www.chapter.org

CHIPPING NORTON:
The Theatre   T 01608 642349
*Contact: John Terry (Director), Jo Ludford
(General Manager), Emily Mosely (Casting)*
2 Spring Street, Chipping Norton
Oxon OX7 5NL
BO 01608 642350
E admin@chippingnortontheatre.com
W www.chippingnortontheatre.com

CHRISTCHURCH:
The Regent Centre   BO 01202 499199
Contact: Greg Rawlings (Manager)
51 High Street, Christchurch
Dorset BH23 1AS
E admin@regentcentre.co.uk
W www.regentcentre.co.uk

CIRENCESTER:
New Brewery Arts   T 01285 657181
Brewery Court, Cirencester
Glos GL7 1JH
E admin@newbreweryarts.org.uk
W www.newbreweryarts.org.uk

COLCHESTER:
Colchester Arts Centre   T 01206 500900
Contact: Anthony Roberts (Director)
Church Street, Colchester
Essex CO1 1NF
E info@colchesterartscentre.com
W www.colchesterartscentre.com

COVENTRY:
Warwick Arts Centre   T 024 7652 3734
Contact: Alan Rivett (Director)
University of Warwick
Coventry CV4 7AL
BO 024 7652 4524
E arts.centre@warwick.ac.uk
W www.warwickartscentre.co.uk

CUMBERNAULD:
Cumbernauld Theatre   T 01236 737235
Kildrum, Cumbernauld G67 2BN
BO 01236 732887
E info@cumbernauldtheatre.co.uk
W www.cumbernauldtheatre.co.uk

DERRY: The Playhouse   T 028 7126 8027
5-7 Artillery Street
Derry/Londonderry BT48 6RG
E info@derryplayhouse.co.uk
W www.derryplayhouse.co.uk

EDINBURGH:
Scottish Storytelling Centre   T 0131 556 9579
Contact: Reception
43-45 High Street
Edinburgh EH1 1SR
E reception@scottishstorytellingcentre.com
W www.tracscotland.org/scottish-storytelling-centre

EPSOM: Playhouse   T 01372 742226
Contact: Elaine Teague
Ashley Avenue, Epsom
Surrey KT18 5AL
BO 01372 742555
E eteague@epsom-ewell.gov.uk
W www.epsomplayhouse.co.uk

EXETER: Exeter Phoenix   T 01392 667060
Contact: Patrick Cunningham (Director)
Bradninch Place
Gandy Street
Exeter, Devon EX4 3LS
BO 01392 667080
E admin@exeterphoenix.org.uk
W www.exeterphoenix.org.uk

FAREHAM:
Ashcroft Arts Centre   T 01329 235161
Contact: Hannah Ashwell (Director/Programmer)
Osborn Road, Fareham
Hants PO16 7DX
BO 01329 223100
E ashcroft@hants.gov.uk
W www.ashcroft.org.uk

FROME: Merlin Theatre   T 01373 461360
Bath Road, Frome
Somerset BA11 2HG
BO 01373 465949
E merlintheatreoffice@gmail.com
W www.merlintheatre.co.uk

GAINSBOROUGH:
Trinity Arts Centre   T 01427 676655
Trinity Street
Gainsborough
Lincolnshire DN21 2AL
E karen.whitfield@west-lindsey.gov.uk
W www.trinityarts.co.uk

GREAT TORRINGTON:
The Plough Arts Centre   T 01805 622552
9-11 Fore Street
Great Torrington
Devon EX38 8HQ
BO 01805 624624
E mail@theploughartscentre.org.uk
W www.theploughartscentre.org.uk

GREENOCK: The Beacon   T 01475 723723
Contact: Pauline Kane
Custom House Quay
Greenock PA15 1HJ
E info@beaconartscentre.co.uk
W www.beaconartscentre.co.uk

HAVANT: Spring Arts &
Heritage Centre   BO 023 9247 2700
Contact: Sophie Fullerlove (Director)
East Street, Havant
Hants PO9 1BS
E info@thespring.co.uk
W www.thespring.co.uk

HELMSLEY:
Helmsley Arts Centre   T 01439 772112
Contact: Em Whitfield Brooks (Artistic Director)
Meeting House Court
Helmsley
York YO62 5DW
BO 01439 771700
E director@helmsleyarts.co.uk
W www.helmsleyarts.co.uk

HEMEL HEMPSTEAD:
Old Town Hall   T 01442 228090
Contact: Sara Railson (Art Team Leader)
High Street, Hemel Hempstead
Herts HP1 3AE
BO 01442 228091
E othadmin@dacorum.gov.uk
W www.oldtownhall.co.uk

HEXHAM: Queens Hall Arts   BO 01434 652477
Contact: Geof Keys (Artistic Director)
Beaumont Street
Hexham
Northumberland NE46 3LS
E boxoffice@queenshall.co.uk
W www.queenshall.co.uk

HORSHAM: The Capitol   T 01403 756080
Twitter: @capitolhorsham
North Street, Horsham
West Sussex RH12 1RG
F 01403 756092
E contact@thecapitolhorsham.com
W www.thecapitolhorsham.com

HUDDERSFIELD: Kirklees Communities &
Leisure Services   T 01484 221000
4th Floor South, Civic Centre 1
Huddersfield HD1 2YU
E arts.creativity@kirklees.gov.uk
W www.kirklees.gov.uk

INVERNESS: Eden Court   T 01463 239841
Contact: Colin Marr (Director)
Bishop's Road, Inverness IV3 5SA
BO 01463 234234
E admin@eden-court.co.uk
W www.eden-court.co.uk

ISLE OF WIGHT: Quay Arts   T 01983 822490
Sea Street, Newport Harbour
Isle of Wight PO30 5BD
E info@quayarts.org
W www.quayarts.org

JERSEY: Jersey Arts Centre   T 01534 700400
Contact: Daniel Austin (Director)
Phillips Street, St Helier
Jersey JE2 4SW
BO 01534 700444
E enquiries@artscentre.je
W www.artscentre.je

KENDAL:
Brewery Arts Centre   BO 01539 725133
Contact: Richard Foster (Chief Executive)
Highgate, Kendal
Cumbria LA9 4HE
E admin@breweryarts.co.uk
W www.breweryarts.co.uk

KING'S LYNN:
King's Lynn Arts Centre   T 01553 779095
29 King Street
King's Lynn
Norfolk PE30 1HA
BO 01553 764864
E info@kingslynnarts.co.uk
W www.kingslynnarts.co.uk

LEICESTER: Phoenix Square   T 0116 242 2803
Midland Street
Leicester LE1 1TG
BO 0116 242 2800
W www.phoenix.org.uk

LICHFIELD: Lichfield Arts   T 01543 262223
Donegal House, Bore Street
Lichfield WS13 6LU
E info@lichfieldarts.org.uk
W www.lichfieldarts.org.uk

LISKEARD: Sterts Theatre   T 01579 362382
Upton Cross, Liskeard, Cornwall PL14 5AZ
E office2@stertsarts.org
W www.sterts.co.uk

LONDON: The Albany   T 020 8692 4446
Douglas Way, Deptford
London SE8 4AG
F 020 8469 2253
E reception@thealbany.org.uk
W www.thealbany.org.uk

LONDON: The Amadeus   T 020 7286 1686
50 Shirland Road, Little Venice
London W9 2JA
E info@theamadeus.co.uk
W www.theamadeus.co.uk

LONDON: artsdepot   BO 020 8369 5454
5 Nether Street, Tally Ho Corner
North Finchley, London N12 0GA
E info@artsdepot.co.uk
W www.artsdepot.co.uk

LONDON:
Battersea Arts Centre   T 020 7223 6557
Lavender Hill, Battersea
London SW11 5TN
BO 020 7223 2223
E boxoffice@bac.org.uk
W www.bac.org.uk

LONDON: Chats Palace   T 020 8533 0227
42-44 Brooksby's Walk, Hackney
London E9 6DF
E info@chatspalace.com
W www.chatspalace.com

LONDON: The Cockpit   T/BO 020 7258 2925
Gateforth Street, London NW8 8EH
E mail@thecockpit.org.uk
W www.thecockpit.org.uk

LONDON:
The Hangar Arts Trust   T 020 3004 6173
Unit 7A, Mellish House
Harrington Way, London SE18 5NR
E info@hangarartstrust.org
W www.hangarartstrust.org

LONDON: Hoxton Hall
Arts Centre   T 020 7684 0060
Contact: Ben West (Casting Director)
130 Hoxton Street, London N1 6SH
E info@hoxtonhall.co.uk
W www.hoxtonhall.co.uk

LONDON: Institute of
Contemporary Arts   T 020 7930 0493
Contact: Matt Williams (Curator). No in-house
Productions or Castings
The Mall, London SW1Y 5AH
BO 020 7930 3647
W www.ica.org.uk

LONDON: Islington
Arts Factory   T 020 7607 0561
2 Parkhurst Road, London N7 0SF
E info@islingtonartsfactory.org
W www.islingtonartsfactory.org

LONDON: Jacksons Lane   T 020 8340 5226
269A Archway Road, London N6 5AA
BO 020 8341 4421
E admin@jacksonslane.org.uk
W www.jacksonslane.org.uk

LONDON: Menier
Chocolate Factory   T 020 7378 1712
Contact: David Babani (Artistic Director)
53 Southwark Street
London SE1 1RU
BO 020 7378 1713
E office@menierchocolatefactory.com
W www.menierchocolatefactory.com

LONDON: October Gallery   T/F 020 7242 7367
24 Old Gloucester Street, London WC1N 3AL
E press@octobergallery.co.uk
W www.octobergallery.co.uk

LONDON: Omnibus   T 020 7498 4699
1 Clapham Common Northside
London SW4 0QW
E enquiries@omnibus-clapham.org
W www.omnibus-clapham.org

LONDON: Ovalhouse   T 020 7582 0080
Contact: Rachel Briscoe & Rebecca Atkinson-Lord
(Directors of Theatre), Deborah Bestwick (Director)
52-54 Kennington Oval
London SE11 5SW
E info@ovalhouse.com
W www.ovalhouse.com

LONDON: Polish Social &
Cultural Association   T 020 8741 1940
238-246 King Street, London W6 0RF

MAIDENHEAD: Norden Farm Centre
for the Arts   T 01628 682555
Contact: Jane Corry (Chief Executive & Artistic Director)
Altwood Road, Maidenhead SL6 4PF
BO 01628 788997
E admin@nordenfarm.org
W www.nordenfarm.org

MAIDSTONE: Hazlitt Theatre   T 01622 753922
Contact: Natalie Price (General Manager)
Earl Street, Maidstone
Kent ME14 1PL
BO 01622 758611
E hazlitt.boxoffice@parkwoodtheatres.co.uk

MANCHESTER: The Lowry   BO 0843 2086000
Contact: Steve Cowton (Senior Theatre Programmer)
Pier 8, Salford Quays M50 3AZ
F 0161 876 2021
E boxofficeadmin@thelowry.com
W www.thelowry.com

MILFORD HAVEN:
Torch Theatre   T 01646 694192
Contact: Peter Doran (Artistic Director)
St Peter's Road, Milford Haven
Pembrokeshire SA73 2BU
BO 01646 695267
E info@torchtheatre.co.uk
W www.torchtheatre.co.uk

NORWICH:
Norwich Arts Centre   T 01603 660387
St Benedicts Street, Norwich, Norfolk NR2 4PG
BO 01603 660352
E pasco@norwichartscentre.co.uk
W www.norwichartscentre.co.uk

NOTTINGHAM: Nottingham
Lakeside Arts   T 0115 846 7777
University Park
Nottingham NG7 2RD
E lakeside-marketing@nottingham.ac.uk
W www.lakesidearts.org.uk

NUNEATON: Abbey Theatre   T 024 7632 7359
Contact: Tony Deeming (Chairman)
Pool Bank Street
Nuneaton
Warks CV11 5DB
BO 024 7635 4090
E admin@abbeytheatre.co.uk
W www.abbeytheatre.co.uk

POOLE: Lighthouse Poole
Centre for the Arts   T 0844 4068666
Kingland Road, Poole
Dorset BH15 1UG
W www.lighthousepoole.co.uk

RADLETT:
The Radlett Centre   T 01923 857546
1 Aldenham Avenue, Radlett
Herts WD7 8HL
F 01923 857592
E admin@radlettcentre.com
W www.radlettcentre.co.uk

ROTHERHAM:
Rotherham Civic Theatre   T 01709 823621 (T/BO)
Contact: Mark Scott (Theatre Manager)
Catherine Street
Rotherham
South Yorkshire S65 1EB
T 01709 823641 (Admin)
E theatre.tickets@rotherham.gov.uk
W www.rotherhamtheatres.co.uk

SALISBURY:
Salisbury Arts Centre   T 01722 343020
Bedwin Street
Salisbury
Wiltshire SP1 3UT
BO 01722 321744
E info@salisburyarts.co.uk
W www.salisburyartscentre.co.uk

SHREWSBURY: The Gateway
Education & Arts Centre   T 01743 355159
The Gateway
Chester Street
Shrewsbury
Shropshire SY1 1NB
E gateway.centre@shropshire.gov.uk
W www.shropshire.gov.uk

STAMFORD:
Stamford Arts Centre   T 01780 480846
Contact: Graham Burley (General Manager)
27 St Mary's Street
Stamford
Lincolnshire PE9 2DL
BO 01780 763203
E boxoffice@stamfordartscentre.com
W www.stamfordartscentre.com

STIRLING:
MacRobert Arts Centre   T 01786 467155
University of Stirling
Stirling FK9 4LA
BO 01786 466666
E info@macrobert.org
W www.macrobert.org

SWANSEA: Taliesin Arts Centre   T 01792 295238
Contact: Sybil Crouch (Head of Cultural Services)
Swansea University, Singleton Park
Swansea SA2 8PZ
BO 01792 602060
E s.e.crouch@swansea.ac.uk
W www.taliesinartscentre.co.uk

TOTNES: The Arts at
Dartington   T 01803 847000
Dartington Hall Trust, Totnes
Devon TQ9 6EN
BO 01803 847070
E arts@dartington.org
W www.dartington.org/arts

TUNBRIDGE WELLS:
Trinity Theatre   T 01892 678670
Church Road
Tunbridge Wells
Kent TN1 1JP
BO 01892 678678
E enquiries@trinitytheatre.net

ULEY: Prema Arts Centre   T 01453 860703
Contact: Gordon Scott (Director)
Bethesda Chapel
South Street, Uley
Nr Dursley, Glos GL11 5SS
E hello@prema.org.uk
W www.prema.org.uk

VALE OF GLAMORGAN:
St Donats Arts Centre   T 01446 799309
Contact: Karen Davies (Commercial Director)
St Donats Castle
The Vale of Glamorgan CF61 1WF
BO 01446 799100
E enquiries@stdonats.com

WASHINGTON:
Arts Centre Washington   T 0191 219 3455
Biddick Lane, Fatfield
Washington, Tyne & Wear NE38 8AB
E acw@sunderland.gov.uk

WELLINGBOROUGH:
The Castle   T 01933 229022
Contact: Darren Walter (Director), Phillip Money
(Theatre Administrator)
Castle Way, Wellingborough
Northants NN8 1XA
BO 01933 270007
E info@thecastle.org.uk
W www.thecastle.org.uk

WIMBORNE: Layard Theatre   T 01202 847529
Contact: Chris Thomas (Director of Drama),
Christine Haynes (Administrator)
Canford School, Canford Magna
Wimborne, Dorset BH21 3AD
BO 01202 847525
E layardtheatre@canford.com

WINDSOR: The Firestation Centre
for Arts & Culture   T 01753 866865
The Old Court, St Leonards Road
Windsor, Berks SL4 3BL
E info@firestationartscentre.com
W www.firestationartscentre.com

WREXHAM: Oriel Wrecsam   T 01978 292093
11 Chester Street
Wrexham LL13 8BE
E oriel.wrecsam@wrexham.gov.uk

C →

Casting Directors
Consultants
Costumes, Wigs & Make-Up

CDG
For information regarding membership of
the Casting Directors' Guild please see:
W www.thecdg.co.uk

Casting Directors

Who are casting directors?

Casting directors are employed by directors/
production companies to source the best
available performers for roles across television,
film, radio, theatre and commercials. They do the
groundwork and present a shortlist of artists to
the director, who often makes the final selection.
Many casting directors work on a freelance
basis, others are employed permanently by larger
organisations such as the BBC or the National
Theatre. Discovering new and emerging talent
also plays an important part in their job.

Why should I approach them?

If you are an actor looking for work, you can
promote yourself directly to casting directors by
sending them your photo and CV. They keep
actors' details on file and may consider you for
future productions. Bear in mind that you will not
be guaranteed a response as casting directors
are physically unable to reply to every one of
the vast numbers of letters they receive from
actors, but it is worth your while to explore this
opportunity to find work.

How should I approach them?

Many of the casting directors in this section have
indicated the method in which they prefer actors
to contact them for the first time. This tends to
be by post but some accept or prefer e-mails.
Some are happy to receive telephone calls, but
be aware that casting directors are very busy
and you should not continually call them with
questions or updates once you have sent your
CV. If they have not specified whether they prefer
postal or e-mail contact, you should send them
your CV, a headshot and a covering letter by post
only, as this is the traditional method of contacting
casting professionals. You should always include
a stamped-addressed envelope (SAE) big enough
to contain your 10 x 8 photo and with sufficient
postage. This will increase your chances of
getting a reply. Write your name and telephone
number on the back of your headshot in case it
gets separated from your CV.

Should I send a casting director my showreel and/or voicereel?

Some casting directors have also indicated that
they are happy for actors to send showreels and/
or voicereels along with their CVs and headshots,
but if this is not specified, we would recommend
that you leave these out of your correspondence
but highlight in your covering letter that they are
available or provide links to where they may be
able to view online showreels. If a casting director
is interested in you, they can contact you later
for these items, but they usually prefer not to sift
through hundreds of unsolicited showreels until
they have first established an interest in an actor.

How do I target my search?

It is not advisable to send a generic CV to every
casting director listed in this section. Research
the names and companies and then target your
letters accordingly. Find out what areas of the
industry each one usually casts for (some specify
this in their listing) and what productions they
have previously cast. Keep an eye on television,
film and theatre credits so you become familiar
with the casting directors used for different
productions. Some of these casting directors
have their own websites. If a casting director has
'CDG Member' after their name, it means they
are a member of the Casting Directors' Guild,
the professional organisation of casting directors
working in the UK (see www.thecdg.co.uk
for more information and their case study in
this section).

How do I write an effective CV and covering letter?

Once you have made a short-list of suitable
casting directors you should send them your
CV, your headshot, and an individually tailored
covering letter. The covering letter should
demonstrate that you have researched the
casting director and ideally you will have a
particular reason for contacting them at this
time: perhaps you can tell them about your next
showcase, or where they can see you currently
appearing. Your CV should be no longer than one
page, up-to-date and spell-checked.

Please see the 'Promotional Services' section of
Contacts for further advice on writing CVs and
covering letters.

How do I prepare for a casting/ audition?

Make sure you are fully prepared with accurate information about the audition time, venue, format and the people you will be meeting. Unless it's a last minute casting, you should always read the script in advance and try to have some opinions on it. If you are asked in advance to prepare a piece, always stick to the brief with something suitable and relevant.

On the day, allow plenty of time to get there so you are not flustered when you arrive. Try to be positive and enjoy yourself. Remember, the casting director doesn't want to spend several days auditioning - they want you to get the job! Never criticise previous productions you have worked on. And at the end of the casting, remember to take your script away unless you are asked to leave it, otherwise it can look as if you're not interested.

Please see 'Rehearsal Rooms and Casting Suites' for more detailed advice on preparing for and attending auditions.

Should I attend a casting in a house or flat?

Professional auditions are rarely held anywhere other than an official casting studio or venue. Be very wary if you are asked to go elsewhere. Trust your instincts. If something doesn't seem right to you, it probably isn't. Always take someone with you if you are in any doubt.

How do I become a casting director?

The best way to gain experience in this field is to work as a casting assistant. Vacancies are sometimes advertised in The Stage www.thestage.co.uk. Alternatively you could try sending your CV to casting directors asking for an internship or work experience. Just as we advise actors, remember to research any casting director you are considering approaching to make sure they actually work in the area you are interested in. Work experience is likely to be unpaid, but the experience and contacts you gain will be invaluable. You may find it helpful to refer to Equity's advice leaflet Low Pay/No Pay which is available to all Equity members from their website's members' area.

Casting Directors

When you read CDG after a casting director's name, you know they are a member of The Casting Directors' Guild and will therefore have a minimum of five years' experience. The current CDG Committee has the following advice for actors.

Casting directors are there to help actors and not to hinder them. We want you to do your best as that reflects back on us, and you should realise that we are only as good as the actors we submit for each role. Much of our work consists of creating a shortlist of potential actors and reducing it to a suitably sized group to present for audition. We also spend a great deal of time watching you work. Members of the CDG endeavour to cover as many performances as possible on film, television and in the theatre. There is no substitute to seeing you act.

When asked to attend an interview or audition, an actor should feel confident in asking their agent any relevant questions about the role and the project. If this is not forthcoming, arrive early and seek information from the casting director or, better still, contact them the day before. If it is only possible to speak to the casting director on the day, preferably do so before entering the audition room, rather than in front of the director or producer. The casting director will be happy to help.

Sometimes you will only receive pages for a role, but a casting director will always endeavour to give you as much information about a character as is available. When possible, read the entire play/screenplay rather than just the scenes your 'character' appears in, and ideally be able to talk about the script as a whole during the interview. Take your time when reading; preparation is worth a lot but don't be fazed if you get lost over their script. If you feel that a scene is going terribly it's ok to start again.

For most non-theatre jobs these days you will find that your meeting will be recorded. These are then shown to the various producers involved, and this is when the process can slow down. It takes time to build a company and for final casting choices to be made.

Casting is a matter of interpretation. As well as character information derived from the script, the vision of the producer, director, casting director and indeed the actor all come into play.

There are many reasons why one actor will be chosen over another, and even the best audition might not necessarily secure a part. Every aspect of the actor comes into play. Is he/ she too young or too mature? Do they work as a family? Could they be mother and son? Does the chemistry work? There is also the frustrating problem of scripts, and parts, being re-written. A character may have an entirely different physical description in a later draft. Sadly we do not have control over this.

When it comes to contacting casting directors, most are happy to receive letters, updated photos and CVs. The best correspondence for casting directors to receive is performance information. Letters should be brief and to the point, with the production name, director, venue and/ or television channel clearly stated. If you are enquiring about work be as specific as possible, e.g. "I would like to be seen for the part of … in … because …" or something similar. Dear Sir or Madam letters just don't work.

CVs should be well laid out. List most recent work first and use your spell checker. 6x4 photos are fine to send but include an SAE if you want them returned. Casting directors rarely like unsolicited DVDs and showreels: you must be aware that we do get inundated. Also bear in mind that not receiving a response to your letter does not mean it hasn't been read and filed: it is virtually impossible to reply to the volume of mail received from actors.

In our greener world it's great that Spotlight and other web media now have the facility for us to view CVs, photos and showreels online. Use the technology: it's very easy to keep your CV up-to-date online and you can change your photo, showreel or voicereel at any time of year without having to do a huge mail out to let people know.

Actors are a fundamental tool of this industry: CDG members are aware of this and aim to put actors at their ease. Audition nerves are a given but you should feel secure that the reason you are in the room is because someone wants you to get that role and not because they want to see you fail.

To find out more visit www.thecdg.co.uk

CASE STUDY

Matilda James is the Casting Director at Shakespeare's Globe.

At the Globe we cast upwards of 250 actors per year for shows in the outdoor space, in the Sam Wanamaker Playhouse under the candles, and on tour. It's predominantly classical work, but there's also new writing, music, concerts, so while everything I say here is specific to casting at the Globe, I hope it can be useful for any theatre audition.

The first thing to say is that a casting director will always want you to do well. Directors are busier and busier and their time is precious, so if you're in the room, it's because we think you can get the job.

That said, the brutal truth is that you have to get good at auditions. In all likelihood, you'll do more of those than anything else. It's also realistically the only bit of the casting process that you can have control over: there are a thousand pieces in the puzzle that you can't affect – the vagaries/constraints of cross-casting (most Globe companies do both a Shakespeare and a new play), matching to another actor in terms of type or chemistry, balancing musical ability across a company, and all these before factoring in directorial preference/style – but doing your best in the room really is in your hands.

> **"A casting director will always want you to do well. Directors are busier and busier and their time is precious, so if you're in the room, it's because we think you can get the job"**

So make sure you've prepared, and prepared well. Read the play, and read it again. We'll either specify scenes or ask for two of choice – but be familiar with all of it in case a director wants to look at something you've not prepared.

It's easy to read Shakespearean verse as poetry – beautiful lines, lyrical, evocative – but that doesn't mean we'll understand what it means as speech.

And it won't help you work out why you're saying those words, at that moment, to whom, and what you're trying to achieve by saying them. The language is your tool – to convince or recruit or dismiss or provoke or seduce, or whatever it may be – but it's active, in the moment. Unlocking the why behind every line will not only make sure you know exactly what you're saying, but also make the language feel vivid and direct and alive.

> **"The brutal truth is that you have to get good at auditions. In all likelihood, you'll do more of those than anything else. It's also realistically the only bit of the casting process that you can have control over"**

That will help you feel freer in the meeting to respond to direction. The director will want to see how you can sensitively adjust your performance in response to notes. Auditions are normally 15-20 minutes long, so you might not have long to re-work things, so take the notes with speed and grace, but be confident in asking to restart a scene if you feel it's going awry.

We'll always aim to get you the materials as far in advance as possible. If you've been given the material late, then it's my responsibility to tell the director you've not had long with it. Trust that I will: don't go in and apologise, because it will make you look unprepared and could wrong-foot you from the start.

Don't be afraid of asking questions in advance: do you need to be off-book? Own accent or RP? Should you direct your reading at us or imagine there's someone else there? Those questions are ones I'm often asked, so some brief answers (Globe specific):

- Being off-book is brilliant. But it should liberate, not limit you. It will never count against you to have the book there: more important is making sure you are fully on top of the thoughts and not unnerved by a memory test.

Casting Directors

- If an accent isn't specified, I would always prefer to hear it in your own voice – the greater sense we have of you as a person in the meeting, the greater affiliation we can see with the character. Hearing regional accents, or actually just your own natural inflections, help to make it more real, more honest.

- At the Globe, you can see every member of the audience all the time, and can talk to a specific someone at the back of the yard as easily as to the actor sharing the stage with you. It's a space that manages to be both epic and intimate at the same time. So direct it to us. There's a clarity, an openness and an immediacy that plays well when you do.

There's no secret to a good audition, just some traps to avoid and some things to remember. Don't bring props. Don't spend ages shifting chairs around. Do your research and be on time. Make justifiable choices about the character, and feel comfortable letting them go if you're asked to. Don't be intimidated if the director asks you questions: there's no pressure to be dazzling, just ready and present and true. Everyone in the room just wants to meet you, get to know you. Go in and come out positive, with your work done. That way, whatever happens, it won't have been a wasted opportunity.

To find out more about The Globe visit www.shakespearesglobe.com

1505　　　　　T 020 7112 8750
20 Bedford Street, London WC2E 9HP
E hello@weare1505.co.uk
W www.weare1505.co.uk

A C A CASTING　　　T/F 020 7384 2635
Contact: Catherine Arton
London
E catherine@acacasting.com

ACTING-UP.COM CASTING　T 07434 843070
Based in Liverpool & London
PO Box 2732, Liverpool L2 3PF
E casting@acting-up.com
W www.acting-up.com

ADAMSON-PARKER, Jo　T 07787 311270
Contact: By e-mail. Accepts Showreels
E jo@northerndrama.co.uk

AILION, Pippa　　　T 020 7738 7556
CDG Member
Unit 67B, Eurolink Business Centre
49 Effra Road, London SW2 1BZ
E enquiries@pippaailioncasting.co.uk

ALL DIRECTIONS OF LONDON
Contact: By Post only
7 Rupert Court, Off Wardour Street, London W1D 6EB

ALLISTON & CO.　　　T 020 3390 3456
Contact: Richard Alliston
Suite 2, 3rd Floor, 207 Regent Street
London W1B 3HH
E casting@allistonandco.com
W www.allistonandco.com

ANDERSON, Jane
*CDG Member. Contact: By e-mail. Accepts Links to
Online Showreels only. Film. Television. Based between
Manchester/London*
E casting@janeandersononline.com
W www.janeandersononline.com

ANDREW, Dorothy CASTING　T 0161 344 2709
CDG Member
E dorothyandrewcasting@gmail.com

APL CASTING　　　T 020 8655 7653
Contact: Paul Leno
3B Nettlefold Place, West Norwood, London SE27 0JW
E info@apltheatre.com
W www.apltheatre.com

**ARMITAGE, Charlotte
CASTING**　　　　T 07506 129997
16 East Park Road, Spofforth
Harrogate HG3 1BH
E charlotte@cacasting.co.uk
W www.cacasting.co.uk

ARNELL, Jane
Flat 2, 39 St Peters Square
London W6 9NN
E janearnellcasting@gmail.com

ARNOLD, Jim　　　T 020 7738 7556
CDG Member. Contact: By e-mail only
c/o Pippa Ailion Casting
E jim@pippaailioncasting.co.uk

ARTHUR, Camilla CASTING　T 07557 220636
*Contact: By e-mail. Commercials. Film. Modelling.
Street Casting & Fashion*
20B Warrington Crescent
London W9 1EL
E camilla@camillaarthurcasting.com
W www.camillaarthurcasting.com

ASHTON HINKINSON CASTING　T 020 7580 6101
Unit 15, Panther House
38 Mount Pleasant
London WC1X 0AN
E casting@ahcasting.com
W www.ashtonhinkinson.com

BAIG, Shaheen CASTING　T 020 7240 4278
E info@shaheenbaigcasting.com
W www.shaheenbaigcasting.com

BARNES, Derek　　　T 020 8228 7096
CDG Member
BBC DRAMA SERIES CASTING
BBC Elstree, Room N208
Neptune House, Clarendon Road
Borehamwood, Herts WD6 1JF

BARNETT, Briony　　T 020 7836 3751
CDG Member
11 Goodwins Court
London WC2N 4LL

BEACH CASTING LTD　　T 020 7836 6477
Contact: Brendan McNamara
405 Strand, London WC2R 0NE
E brendan@beach-casting.com
W www.beach-casting.com

Casting Directors

BEASTALL, Lesley CASTING T 020 7727 6496
Contact: Lesley Beastall
41E Elgin Crescent, London W11 2JD
E casting@lbcasting.co.uk
W www.lesleybeastallcasting.com

BECKLEY, Rowland T 020 8228 7130
BBC DRAMA SERIES CASTING
BBC Elstree, Room N208
Neptune House, Clarendon Road
Borehamwood, Herts WD6 1JF

BERKERY CASTING T 020 7112 7566
Contact: James Berkery
2 Hurst Courst, Station Road
Sidcup DA15 7AN
E info@berkerycasting.com
W www.berkerycasting.com

BERTRAND, Leila CASTING T/F 020 8964 0683
CDG Member
E leila@leilabcasting.com
W www.leilabcasting.com

BEVAN, Lucy T 020 8567 6655
CDG Member
Ealing Studios, Ealing Green
London W5 5EP

BEWICK, Maureen T 020 8450 1604
104A Dartmouth Road, London NW2 4HB

BIRD, Sarah T 020 7371 3248
CDG Member
PO Box 32658, London W14 0XA

BIRKETT, Hannah CASTING T 020 7871 2969
Contact: By e-mail
26 York Street, London W1 6PZ
E hannah@hbcasting.com

BLIGH, Nicky
CDG Member
E nicky@nickyblighcasting.com

BRACKE, Siobhan T 020 8891 5686
CDG Member. Contact: By Post
Basement Flat, 22A The Barons
St Margaret's TW1 2AP

BUCKINGHAM, Jo T 07753 605491
CDG Member
E jo@jobuckinghamcasting.co.uk
W www.jobuckinghamcasting.co.uk

CANDID CASTING T 020 7490 8882
Unit 2G Woodstock Studios
36 Woodstock Grove, London W12 8LE
E mail@candidcasting.co.uk
W www.candidcasting.co.uk

CANNON, John T 020 8228 7322
CDG Member
BBC DRAMA SERIES CASTING
BBC Elstree, Room N208, Neptune House
Clarendon Road, Borehamwood, Herts WD6 1JF

CANNON DUDLEY & ASSOCIATES T 020 7433 3393
Contact: Carol Dudley (CDG Member). Film. Stage. Television
F 020 7813 2048
E cdacasting@blueyonder.co.uk

CARROLL, Anji T 07957 253769
CDG Member. Contact: By e-mail. Stage. Film. Television. Commercials
E casting@anjicarroll.tv

CASTING ANGELS THE
Based in London & Paris
Suite 4, 14 College Road
Bromley, Kent BR1 3NS

CASTING COMPANY (UK) THE
Contact: Michelle Guish
E casting@michguish.com

CASTING COUCH THE T 07932 785807
Contact: Moira Townsend. No CVs/Photos by Post
213 Trowbridge Road, Bradford on Avon
Wiltshire BA15 1EU
E moira@charactersstageschool.com

CASTING FOX THE T 01628 771084
Contact: By e-mail only
E assistant@thecastingfox.co.uk

CATLIFF, Suzy
CDG Member. Co-author of The Casting Handbook
E soosecat@mac.com
W www.suzycatliff.co.uk

CHAND, Urvashi T 020 8208 3861
CDG Member
Chand Casting, 69 Teignmouth Road
London NW2 4EA
T 07980 213050
E urvashi@chandcasting.com
W www.chandcasting.com

CHARD, Alison T 020 7223 9125
CDG Member
23 Groveside Court
4 Lombard Road
Battersea, London SW11 3RQ
E chardcasting@gmail.com

CHARKHAM CASTING T 07956 456630
Contact: Beth Charkham
Suite 361, 14 Tottenham Court Road
London W1T 1JY
E charkhamcasting@btconnect.com

CHATTAN, Sapphira CASTING T 07436 803496
91 Stocking Park Road
Lightmoor Village
Telford, Shropshire TF4 3QZ
E casting@sapphirachattan.com
W www.sapphirachattan.com

CHILI CASTING LTD T 0845 6457000
112-114 North Acton Road
London NW10 6QH
E chilicastinglondon@gmail.com
W www.chilicasting.co.uk

CLARK, Andrea T 020 7381 9933
Adults & Children. Commercials. Film. Stage. Television
E andrea@aclarkcasting.com
W www.aclarkcasting.com

CLAYPOLE, Sam CASTING
PO Box 123, Darlington
Durham DL3 7WA
E contact@samclaypolecasting.com
W www.samclaypolecasting.com

CLAYTON, Rosalie   **T** 020 3605 6338
CDG Member
E office@rosalieclayton.com

CLOUTER, Lou CASTING   **T** 07905 146271
79 Empress Avenue, Aldersbrook
London E12 5SA
E lou@loucloutercasting.com
W www.loucloutercasting.com

**COCHRANE, Kharmel
CASTING LTD**   **T** 07885 384196
23 St Michael's Street, London W2 1QU
E kharmel@kharmelcochrane.co.uk
W www.kharmelcochrane.com

COLLYER-BRISTOW, Ellie   **T** 07986 607075
E ellie@collyerbristowcasting.com

CORDORAY, Lin
109 Haliburton Road, St Margarets
Twickenham TW1 1PE

COTTON, Irene   **T** 020 8299 2787
CDG Member
25 Druce Road, Dulwich Village
London SE21 7DW
T 020 8299 1595
E irenecotton@btinternet.com

CRAMPSIE, Julia   **T** 020 8228 7170
CDG Member. Casting Executive
BBC DRAMA SERIES CASTING
BBC Elstree, Room N208
Neptune House, Clarendon Road
Borehamwood, Herts WD6 1JF

**CRAWFORD, Kahleen
CASTING**   **T** 0141 425 1725
CDG Member
Film City Glasgow, Govan Town Hall
401 Govan Road, Glasgow G51 2QJ
E casting@kahleencrawford.com
W www.kahleencrawford.com

**CROCODILE CASTING
COMPANY THE**   **T** 020 8203 7009
Contact: Claire Toeman, Tracie Saban. By e-mail only
E croccast@aol.com
W www.crocodilecasting.com

CROSS, Louise   **T** 020 8341 2200
CDG Member
128A North View Road, London N8 7LP
E louisecross@mac.com

CROWE, Sarah CASTING   **T** 020 7286 5080
75 Amberley Road, London W9 2JL
F 020 7286 5030
E info@sarahcrowecasting.co.uk

CROWLEY, Suzanne
CDG Member. See CROWLEY POOLE CASTING

CROWLEY POOLE CASTING   **T** 020 7379 5965
*Contact: Suzanne Crowley (CDG Member), Gilly Poole
(CDG Member)*
11 Goodwins Court
London WC2N 4LL
E email@crowleypoole.co.uk

CURTIS, Sophie   **T** 07786 838588
E casting@sophiecurtis.net

THE CASTING
DIRECTORS' GUILD
OF GREAT BRITAIN
& IRELAND

The professional organisation for
Casting Directors of film, television,
theatre and commercials in the UK.

Setting the benchmark of professionalism
in the industry since 1995. Visit our site to
find over 150 affiliated Casting Directors.

www.thecdg.co.uk
Email: info@thecdg.co.uk

DAVIES, Jane CASTING　T 020 8715 1036
Contact: Jane Davies (CDG Member), John Connor
(CDG Member). By e-mail only. Film. Television. Comedy
E info@janedaviescasting.co.uk

DAVIS, Leo (Miss)
See JUST CASTING

DAVY, Gary　T 020 7253 3633
CDG Member. Film. Television
17 Remington Street (Off City Road)
Angel
London N1 8DH
E casting@garydavy.com

DAWES, Gabrielle　T 020 7435 3645
CDG Member
PO Box 52493
London NW3 9DZ
E gdawescasting@tiscali.co.uk

DAWES, Stephanie　T 07802 566642
CDG Member
13 Nevern Square
London SW5 9NW
E stephaniedawes5@gmail.com

DE FREITAS, Paul
CDG Member
E info@pauldefreitas.com

DEITCH, Jane ASSOCIATES　T 07711 856789
2 High Street, Wilden
Bedford MK44 2PB
E jane@janedeitch.co.uk

DICKENS, Laura　T 07958 665468
CDG Member
197 Malpas Road, London SE4 1BH
E dickenscasting@aol.com

DONMAR WAREHOUSE　T 020 7240 4882
Contact: Alastair Coomer (Casting Director).
CDG Member
41 Earlham Street
Covent Garden
London WC2H 9LX
E casting@donmarwarehouse.com
W www.donmarwarehouse.com

DONNELLY, Laura CASTING　T 07917 414014
CV & Showreel on request. Film. Stage. Television
E laura@lauradonnellycasting.com
W www.lauradonnellycasting.com

DOWD, Kate　T 020 7828 8071
CDG Member
3rd Floor, 18 Buckingham Palace Road
London SW1W 0QP

DOWLING, Shakyra CASTING　T 07958 391198
Twitter: @shakyradowling
74A Crescent Road, London W22 7RZ
E me@shakyradowlingcasting.com
W www.shakyradowlingcasting.com

DUDLEY, Carol
CDG Member. See CANNON DUDLEY & ASSOCIATES

DUFF, Julia　T 020 7836 5557
CDG Member
11 Goodwins Court, London WC2N 4LL
E info@juliaduff.co.uk

DUFF, Maureen　T 020 7586 0532
CDG Member
PO Box 47340
London NW3 4TY
E info@maureenduffcasting.com

DUFFY, Jennifer　T 07949 137554
CDG Member
Based in London
E casting@jennyduffy.co.uk

EAST, Irene CASTING　T 020 8876 5686
CDG Member. Contact: By Post. Film. Stage
40 Brookwood Avenue
Barnes
London SW13 0LR
E irneast@aol.com

EDWARDS, Daniel CASTING　T 020 7835 5616
CDG Member
E daniel@danieledwardscasting.com

EJ CASTING　T 07891 632946
E info@ejcastingonline.com
W www.ejcastingonline.com

EMMERSON, Chloe
Contact: By e-mail
E c@chloeemmerson.com

ERDELY, Kristina CASTING　T 07970 071605
E casting@kristinaerdely.com
W www.kristinaerdely.com

EVANS, Camilla CASTING
CDG Member
E camilla@camillaevans.com
W www.thecdg.co.uk

EVANS, Richard　T 020 8994 6304
CDG Member
10 Shirley Road
London W4 1DD
E contact@evanscasting.co.uk
W www.evanscasting.co.uk

EYE CASTING THE　T 020 7377 2700
Top Floor, 92 Commercial Street
Off Puma Court, London E1 6LZ
W www.theeyecasting.com

FEARNLEY, Ali CASTING　T 020 7613 7320
6A Stamford Works
3 Gillett Square N16 8JH
T 07764 945614
E cast@alifearnley.com

FIGGIS, Susie　T 020 7482 2200
19 Spencer Rise
London NW5 1AR

FILDES, Bunny CASTING　T 020 7935 1254
CDG Member
56 Wigmore Street, London W1

FOREMAN, Giles CASTING
& COACHING　T 020 7437 3175
Contact: Lindsay Richardson
Studio Soho, 2A Royalty Mews
22-25 Dean Street
London W1D 3AR
E contact@foremancasting.com
W www.foremancasting.com

SHEILA BURNETT
P H O T O G R A P H Y

Damian Lewis

Caroline Quentin

Kitty Lovett

Michael Absalom

020 7289 3058 | 07974 731391
www.sheilaburnett-headshots.com
Student Rates

FOX, Celestia T 020 8742 2319
73 St Elmo Road, London W12 9DZ
E celestiafox@me.com

FRANKUM, Marc T 020 8691 2911
CDG Member
PO Box 45293
London SE10 1BF
E marc@marcfrankum.com

FRECK, Rachel T/F 020 8673 2455
CDG Member
E casting@rachelfreck.com

FREE RANGE CASTING T 07854 794007
Contact: Sandy Tedford. Based in London
E sandy@freerangecasting.com
W www.freerangecasting.com

FRISBY, Jane CASTING T 020 8340 7835
Contact: By e-mail. Accepts Showreels Online.
Commercials. Corporates. Feature Films
51 Ridge Road, London N8 9LJ
E janefrisby@hotmail.co.uk

FRUITCAKE T 020 7993 5165
Contact: Thomas Adams, Andrew Mann
Studio 125, 77 Beak Street
London W1F 9DB
T 020 7993 6042
E casting@fruitcakelondon.com
W www.fruitcakelondon.com

FUNNELL, Caroline T 020 7326 4417
CDG Member
25 Rattray Road, London SW2 1AZ

GIBBONS, Martin CASTING T 07976 912776
Unit 17, Wesley Enterprise Centre
Royce Road, Manchester M15 5BP
E info@martingibbons.com
W www.martingibbons.com

GILLHAM, Tracey CASTING T 01932 562112
Contact: Tracey Gillham (CDG Member),
Michelle Cavanagh (Casting Assistant)
Suite 929 Old House, Shepperton Studios
Studios Road, Shepperton
Middlesex TW17 0QD
E tracey@traceygillhamcasting.co.uk

GILLON, Tamara CASTING T 020 8766 0099
26 Carson Road, London SE21 8HU
F 020 8265 6330
E tamara@tamaragillon.com
W www.tamaragillon.com

GLOBAL7 T/F 020 7281 7679
Kemp House, 152 City Road
London EC1V 2NX
T 07956 956652
E global7castings@gmail.com
W www.global7casting.com

GOLD, Nina T 020 8960 6099
CDG Member
117 Chevening Road, London NW6 6DU
F 020 8968 6777
E info@ninagold.co.uk

GOOCH, Miranda CASTING T 020 8962 9578
Contact: By Post/e-mail. Accepts Showreels/Voicereels.
Film. Stage. Television
102 Leighton Gardens
London NW10 3PR
F 020 8962 9579
E mirandagooch@gmail.com

GREEN, Jill CASTING T 020 7632 4747
CDG Member
Wellington House, 1st Floor
125 Strand, London WC2R 0AP
T 020 7632 4748
E office@jillgreencasting.org
W www.jillgreencasting.org

GREENE, Francesca CASTING T 020 8450 5577
37 Keyes Road, London NW2 3XB
E francescagreene@btinternet.com
W www.francescagreenecasting.com

GRINDROD, David
ASSOCIATES LTD T 020 7437 2506
Contact: David Grindrod (CDG Member), Stephen
Crockett (CDG Member), Will Burton (CDG Member)
4th Floor, The Palace Theatre
Shaftesbury Avenue
London W1D 5AY
E dga@grindrodcasting.co.uk

GROSVENOR, Angela T 020 8244 5665
CDG Member
66 Woodland Road, London SE19 1PA
E angela.grosvenor@virgin.net

GUISH, Michelle
See CASTING COMPANY (UK) THE

HAMMOND, Louis T 020 7610 1579
CDG Member
E louis@louishammond.co.uk

HAMMOND COX
CASTING T 020 7734 3335 (Office)
Contact: Michael Cox (CDG Member), Thom Hammond
2nd Floor, 1 Noel Street, Soho
London W1F 8GA
T 07834 362691 (Michael)
E office@hammondcoxcasting.com
W www.hammondcoxcasting.com

HAMPSON, Janet CASTING T 07931 513223
CDG Member. Based in Manchester
E janet@janethampson.co.uk
W www.janethampson.co.uk

HANCOCK, Gemma
CDG Member. Contact: By e-mail
E gemma@hancockstevenson.com

HARKIN, Julie CASTING T 020 7336 0433
CDG Member
17 Remington Street, Angel, London N1 8DH
E info@julieharkincasting.com

HAWES, Jo T 01628 773048
CDG Member. Children's Casting & Administration.
Theatre. Film. Television
21 Westfield Road, Maidenhead
Berkshire SL6 5AU
T 07824 337222
E joanne.hawes2013@gmail.com
W www.johawes.com

HAWSER, Gillian CASTING T 020 7731 5988
CDG/CSA Member. Contact: Gillian Hawser
24 Cloncurry Street, London SW6 6DS
F 020 7731 0738
E gillianhawser@btinternet.com

HB CASTING T 020 7871 2969
London
T 07957 114175
E hannah@hbcasting.com
W www.hbcasting.com

Chili Casting

LONDON'S PREMIER CASTING AGENTS

- ★ Contact us for advice or help with your project
- ★ We can secure all talent from supporting to lead roles
- ★ Competitive rates! We work within your budget
- ★ We can even help you find your crew; from runners to directors

Contact: ChiliCastingLondon@gmail.com   www.ChiliCasting.co.uk   **Tel: 0845 645 7000**

HB CASTING   T 0161 241 7786
Manchester
T 07957 114175
E hannah@hbcasting.com
W www.hbcasting.com

HILL, Serena   T 00 61 2 92501727
Sydney Theatre Company
Pier 4, Hickson Road
Walsh Bay, NSW 2000, Australia
E shill@sydneytheatre.com.au

HINTON, Maddy CASTING   T 020 8940 5535
270C Kew Road, TW9 3EE
E casting@maddyhinton.com
W www.maddyhinton.com

HOLM, Lissy
See JUST CASTING

HOOTKINS, Polly   T 020 7692 1184
CDG Member. Contact: By e-mail
T 07545 784294
E phootkins@clara.net

HORAN & HINES   T 020 7267 5261
Contact: Julia Horan (CDG Member)
26 Falkland Road, London NW5 2PX
E julia@horanandhines.com

HORAN & HINES   T 020 7267 5261
Contact: Lotte Hines
26 Falkland Road, London NW5 2PX
E lotte@horanandhines.com

HOWE, Gary CASTING   T 029 2045 3883
34 Orbit Street, Roath, Cardiff
South Wales CF24 0JX
E garyhowecasting@talktalk.net

HUBBARD, Amy CASTING   T 020 3567 1210
Contact: Amy Hubbard (CDG Member), Simon Cox
Great Western Studios, Studio 209
65 Alfred Road, London W2 5EU
E amyhubbardcasting@gmail.com

HUBBARD, Dan CASTING LTD   T 020 7292 4970
Contact: Dan Hubbard (CDG Member)
6 Ganton Street, London W1F 7QW
E dan@hubbardcasting.com

HUBBARD CASTING   T 020 7292 4975
Contact: Ros Hubbard (CDG Member),
John Hubbard (CDG Member). No Showreels
6 Ganton Street, London W1F 7QW
E martin@hubbardcasting.com

HUGHES, Sarah   T 020 8291 0304
CDG Member
E sarahhughescasting@gmail.com
W www.sarahhughescasting.co.uk

HUGHES, Sylvia   T 07770 520007
Casting Suite, The Deanwater
Wilmslow Road, Woodford
Cheshire SK7 1RJ
T 07594 272229
E sylviahughes007@gmail.com

IN HOUSE CASTING   T 07921 843508
Flat 2 St James Heights
191 Burrage Road
London SE18 7HH
E info@inhousecasting.com
W www.inhouseagency.co.uk

JAFFA, Janis CASTING   T 020 8740 1629
CDG Member
E janis@janisjaffacasting.co.uk

JAY, Jina CASTING   T 020 8607 8887
CDG Member
Office 2, Sound Centre
Twickenham Film Studios
The Barons, St Margarets
Twickenham, Middlesex TW1 2AW

JELOWICKI, Ilenka   T 07909 542294
8 Muswell Avenue, London N10 2EG
E ilenkajelowicki@hotmail.com
W www.inkcasting.co.uk

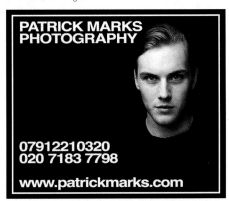

JENKINS, Lucy
CDG Member. See JENKINS McSHANE CASTING

JENKINS, Victor
CDG Member. See VHJ CASTING

JENKINS McSHANE CASTING   T 020 8943 5328
Contact: Lucy Jenkins (CDG Member)
74 High Street, Hampton Wick
Kingston upon Thames KT1 4DQ
E lucy@jenkinsmcshanecasting.com

JENKINS McSHANE CASTING   T 020 8693 7411
Contact: Sooki McShane (CDG Member)
86A Underhill Road, London SE22 0QU
E sooki@jenkinsmcshanecasting.com

JENNER, Rebecca   T 07903 347958
Studio 3, 549 Barlow Moor Road
Manchester M21 8AN
E casting@rebeccajenner.com
W www.rebeccajenner.com

JN PRODUCTION & CASTING   T 020 7324 2630
Contact: Paul Hunt, Tina Newland
27 Cowper Street, London EC2A 4AP
E paul@jncasting.com

JOHN, Priscilla CASTING LTD   T 020 8741 4212
CDG Member
PO Box 22477, London W6 0GT

JOHNSON, Alex CASTING   T 020 7229 8779
Contact: By e-mail. Accepts Showreels. Children.
Commercials. Film. Stage. Television
1 Clarendon Cross, London W11 4AP
E alex@alexjohnsoncasting.com

JOHNSON, Marilyn   T 07876 031086
CDG Member
Apartment 58, The Ink Building
130-136 Barlby Road, London WC2N 4LL
E casting@marilynjohnsoncasting.com

JONES, Sue
CDG Member
E info@suejones.net

JUST CASTING   T 020 7229 3471
Contact: Leo Davis, Lissy Holm
20th Century Theatre, 291 Westbourne Grove
London W11 2QA
E info@justcasting.net

KATE & LOU CASTING   T 020 7323 1952
Contact: Kate Evans, Lou Smernicki
Twitter: @kateandloucast
The Basement, Museum House
25 Museum Street, London WC1A 1JT
T 07976 252531
E cast@kateandloucasting.com
W www.kateandloucasting.com

KENNEDY, Anna CASTING LTD   T 020 8677 6710
8 Rydal Road, London SW16 1QN
T 07973 119269
E anna@kennedycasting.com

KEOGH, Beverley
CASTING LTD   T 0161 273 4400
Contact: Beverley Keogh. CDG Member
29 Ardwick Green North, Ardwick Green
Manchester M12 6DL
F 0161 273 4401
E drama@beverleykeogh.tv

KESTER, Gaby
E casting@gabykester.com

KHANDO CASTING   T 020 3463 8492
1 Marlborough Court
London W1F 7EE
E casting@khandoentertainment.com
W www.khandoentertainment.com

KING, Belinda
CREATIVE PRODUCTIONS   T 01604 720041
Providing the world's luxury cruise lines with the finest
show at sea
BK Studios, 157 Clarence Avenue
Northamptonshire NN2 6NY
E casting@belindaking.com

KING, Cassandra CASTING   T 07813 320673
73 Victor Road
Teddington TW11 8SP
E cassyking@yahoo.co.uk

KINNEAR, Kirsty   T 020 8354 7388
E kinnearcast@virginmedia.com

KLIMEK, Nana CASTING   T 020 3222 0035
RichMix 1st Floor West
35-47 Bethnal Green Road
London E1 6LA
E casting@nanaklimek.com
W www.nanaklimek.com

KNIGHT-SMITH, Jerry   T 0161 615 6761
CDG Member
c/o Royal Exchange Theatre Company
St Ann's Square
Manchester M2 7DH

KOREL, Suzy   T 07973 506793
CDG Member
E suzy@korel.org

KRUGER, Beatrice   T 00 39 06 92956808
FBI CASTING S.r.l.
17 via della Scala
00153 Roma, Italy
F 00 39 06 23328203
E beatrice.kruger@fbicasting.it
W https://pro-labs.imdb.com/name/nm0472561

KYLE, Greg   T 020 8876 6763
71B North Worple Way, Mortlake
London SW14 8PR
T 07967 744056
E kylecasting@btinternet.com

LARCA LTD   T 07779 321954
Welsh Language/English. Commercials. Film. Stage.
Television
59 Mount Stuart Square, Cardiff Bay
Cardiff CF10 5LR
E assistant@larca.co.uk
W www.larca.co.uk

LEUNG, Sarah
E sarah@sarahleungcasting.co.uk

LEVENE, Jon   T 020 7792 8501
T 07977 570899
E jonlevene@mac.com
W www.jonlevenecasting.co.uk

LINDSAY-STEWART, Karen   T 020 7439 0544
CDG Member
E asst@klscasting.co.uk

SPOTLIGHT
The home of casting

Spotlight Database & Website

Browse over 60,000 performers' CVs with photos, showreels, voicereels and contact details

Use Spotlight's award-winning search engine to find exactly the right performer for the part

E-mail casting calls to hundreds of UK agents and performers

Spotlight Rooms & Studios

Hold your auditions in the heart of central London

www.spotlight.com/spaces
020 7440 5030

www.spotlight.com
020 7437 7631
casting@spotlight.com

LOVE CASTING T 07722 668815
Contact: Chris Maloney. All Media Nationwide Casting
Service. TV. Film. Commercials. Radio. Music Videos
E lovecasting@email.com

LUNN, Maggie T 020 7226 8334
CDG Member
T 07973 785645
E maggie@maggielunn.co.uk

MAD DOG CASTING LTD T 020 7269 7910
Contact: By Post/e-mail. Accepts Showreels/Voicereels.
Real People. Street Casting
The Pavilion Building, Ealing Studios
Ealing Green, London W5 5EP
E info@maddogcasting.com
W www.maddogcasting.com

MAGSON, Kay T 0113 236 0251
CDG Member. Contact: By e-mail. Stage
PO Box 175, Pudsey, Leeds LS28 7WY
E kay.magson@btinternet.com

MARCH, Heather CASTING T 020 3056 8862
Contact: By e-mail. Commercials. Idents. Photographic
32 Threadneedle Street, London EC2R 8AY
E hello@heathermarchcasting.com
W www.heathermarchcasting.com

McDAID-WREN, Ri
Contact: By e-mail
Based in London
E ri@ri-mcd.com

McLEOD, Carolyn CASTING T 07946 476425
Contact: By e-mail only. Commercials. Film. Television
1st Floor, 193 Wardour Street, London W1F 8ZF
E info@cmcasting.co.uk
W www.cmcasting.co.uk

McLEOD, Thea T 07941 541314
E mcleodcasting@hotmail.com

McMURRICH, Chrissie T 020 8568 0137
CDG Member. Contact: By Post. Accepts Showreels
16 Spring Vale Avenue, Brentford, Middlesex TW8 9QH

McSHANE, Sooki
CDG Member. See JENKINS McSHANE CASTING

McSWAN, Laura T 020 8228 7319
BBC DRAMA SERIES CASTING
BBC Elstree, Room N208
Neptune House, Clarendon Road
Borehamwood, Herts WD6 1JF

McWILLIAMS, Debbie T 020 7207 7322
CDG Member
T 07903 509007
E debbie@castingconsultancy.com

MEULENBERG, Thea T 00 31 20 6265846
Keizersgracht 116, 1015 CW Amsterdam
The Netherlands
E info@theameulenberg.com
W www.theameulenberg.com

MILLER, Hannah
CDG Member. See ROYAL SHAKESPEARE COMPANY

MOISELLE, Frank T 00 353 1 2802857
7 Corrig Avenue, Dun Laoghaire
Co. Dublin, Ireland

MOISELLE, Nuala T 00 353 1 2802857
7 Corrig Avenue, Dun Laoghaire
Co. Dublin, Ireland

MOORE, Stephen T 020 8241 6713
CDG Member
E stephen@stephenmoorecasting.co.uk
W www.stephenmoorecasting.co.uk

MORGAN, Andy CASTING LTD T 020 8674 5375
Contact: Andy Morgan. CDG Member
E office@andymorgan.org

MORLEY, Adam T 07855 133836
The Lodge, Wentworth Hall, The Ridgeway
Mill Hill, London NW7 1RJ
E adam.e.morley@gmail.com

MORRISON, Melika T/F 020 7381 1571
Contact: By Post. Accepts Showreels. Film. Radio.
Television
12A Rosebank, Holyport Road
London SW6 6LG

MOUNTJOY, Lee CASTING T 0161 850 1656
(Manchester)
T 020 7112 8353 (London)
E info@leemountjoy.com
W www.leemountjoy.com

MURDER MY DARLINGS T 020 7386 0560
Contact: Sue Pocklington
Based in London
E office@murdermydarlings.com
W www.murdermydarlings.com

MURPHY, Sabrina CASTING T 07956 450755
E casting@sabrinamurphy.co.uk
W www.murphycharpentier.co.uk

NATIONAL THEATRE
CASTING DEPARTMENT T 020 7452 3336
Contact: Wendy Spon, Head of Casting (CDG Member),
Charlotte Bevan, Casting Associate (CDG Member),
Juliet Horsley, Casting Associate (CDG Member),
Jacob Sparrow, Casting Assistant. By Post
Upper Ground, South Bank
London SE1 9PX
F 020 7452 3340
W www.nationaltheatre.org.uk

NEEDLEMAN, Sue T 020 8959 1550
CDG Member
19 Stanhope Gardens, London NW7 2JD

NORCLIFFE, Belinda T 020 8992 1333
Contact: Belinda Norcliffe (CDG Member), Matt Selby,
Heidi Lawry
23 Brougham Road, London W3 6JD
T 020 8992 8643
E belinda@bncasting.co.uk

NORTH, Sophie T 020 3372 4878
Branbridges House, Branbridges Road
East Peckham, Kent TN12 5HD
T 07956 516606
E sophie@sophienorthcasting.com

O'BRIEN, Debbie T 01462 742919
72 High Street, Ashwell
Nr Baldock, Herts SG7 5NS
F 01462 743110
E info@debbieobrien.net

O'CONNOR, Orla　　　T 0131 553 0559
CDG Member
The Out of the Blue Drill Hall, 36 Dalmeny Street
Edinburgh EH6 8RG
E info@orlaoconnorcasting.co.uk
W www.orlaoconnorcasting.co.uk

O'DONNELL, Rory　　　T 07940 073165
E rory@raindance.co.uk

PALMER, Helena
CDG Member. See ROYAL SHAKESPEARE COMPANY

PARRISS, Susie CASTING　　　T 020 8543 3326
CDG Member
PO Box 40, Morden SM4 4WJ

PEREIRA HIND, Simone　　　T 07973 818885
CDG Member. Formerly Simone Ireland
Space Club, 37 Castle Terrace
Edinburgh EH1 2EL
E simonepereirahind@gmail.com
W www.simonepereirahind.com

PETTS, Tree CASTING　　　T 020 8458 8898
125 Hendon Way, London NW2 2NA
T 07966 283252
E casting@treepetts.co.uk
W www.treepettscasting.com

PLANTIN, Kate　　　T 01932 782350
CDG Member
4 Riverside, Lower Hampton Road
Sunbury on Thames TW16 5PW
E kate@kateplantin.com
W www.kateplantin.com

POERSCOUT-EDGERTON, Reg　　T 020 3397 3149
CSA Member
Ground Floor, 4 Windmill Street
London W1T 2HZ
E casting@4windmillstreet.com

POOLE, Gilly
CDG Member. See CROWLEY POOLE CASTING

PROCTOR, Carl　　　T 020 7681 0034
CDG Member
15B Bury Place, London WC1A 2JB
T 07956 283340
E carlproctorcasting@gmail.com
W www.carlproctorcasting.com

PRYOR, Andy　　　T 020 7492 1726
CDG Member
31-35 Kirby Street, London EC1N 8TE

PURO CASTING　　　T 020 7193 8799
F 07006 056678
E office@purocasting.com
W www.purocasting.com

RADCLIFFE, Gennie　　　T 0161 952 0580
CDG Member
ITV PLC, Trafford Wharf Road
Trafford, Manchester M17 1FZ

**RANCH CASTING
COMPANY THE**　　　T 020 8374 6072
Contact: By e-mail/Telephone. Commercials. Corporate.
Idents. Photographic Campaigns. Pop Promos
E info@theranchcasting.co.uk
W www.theranchcasting.co.uk

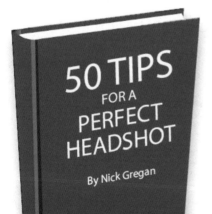

REICH, Liora   T 020 8444 1686
25 Manor Park Road, London N2 0SN
E casting@liorareich.fsnet.co.uk

RENNIE, Nadine   T 020 7478 0104
CDG Member
Soho Theatre, 21 Dean Street
London W1D 3NE
E nadine@sohotheatre.com

REVOLVER CASTING LTD   T 07958 922829
70 Sylvia Court, Cavendish Street
London N1 7PG
E waynesearcher@mac.com
W www.revolvercasting.com

REYNOLDS, Gillian CASTING   T 028 9091 8218
Scottish Provident Building
7 Donegall Square West
Belfast, County Antrim BT1 6JH
E gillreynoldscasting@gmail.com
W www.gillianreynoldscasting.com

**REYNOLDS, Gillian
CASTING**   T 00 353 87 2619718
17 Shamrock Street, Broadstone
Dublin 7
E gillreynoldscasting@gmail.com
W www.gillianreynoldscasting.com

REYNOLDS, Gillian CASTING   T 0872 619718
25 Saint Kevin's Parade, Portobello
Dublin 8
E gillreynoldscasting@gmail.com
W www.gillianreynoldscasting.com

REYNOLDS, Simone   T 020 8672 5443
CDG Member
60 Hebdon Road, London SW17 7NN
E simonemreynolds@gmail.com

RHODES JAMES, Kate   T 020 8943 3265
CDG Member
KRJ Casting Ltd
E office@krjcasting.com

RICHTER CASTING   T 020 3131 0128
Contact: Illsa Richter
86-90 Paul Street, London EC2A 4NE
E ilisarichter@live.co.uk

RIPLEY, Jane   T 020 8340 5123
E jane@janeripleycasting.co.uk

ROBERTS, Barbara   T 07811 568925
CDG Member. Children
E barbara@robertscasting.com

ROBERTSON, Sasha CASTING   T 020 8993 8118
Contact: Sasha Robertson (CDG Member)
35 Allison Road, London W3 6HZ
E casting@sasharobertson.com
W www.sasharobertson.com

RONANE, Jessica CASTING   T 020 8607 0836
CDG Member
12 Richmond Lodge, Twickenham Studios
The Barons, Twickenham TW1 2AW
E jessica@jessicaronane.com

ROSE, Dionne
DRB Pictures, 86-90 Paul Street, London EC2A 4NE
E castings@drbpictures.co.uk

ROWAN, Amy CASTING   T 00 353 1 2140514
PO Box 10247, Blackrock
Co. Dublin, Ireland

ROWE, Annie CASTING   T 020 8354 2699
98 St Albans Avenue, London W4 5JR
W www.annierowe-casting.com

**ROYAL SHAKESPEARE
COMPANY**   T 020 7845 0530
*Contact: Hannah Miller, Head of Casting (CDG Member),
Helena Palmer (CDG Member), Annelie Powell, Matthew
Dewsbury, Alex Campbell*
Casting Department, 1 Earlham Street
London WC2H 9LL
E suggestions@rsc.org.uk
W www.rsc.org.uk

**RUBIN, Shaila EUROPEAN
CASTING SERVICE**   T 00 39 06 72901906
Cinecitta Studios Via Tuscolana 1055, 00173 Roma
Teatro 6/7 Stanza 8, Italy
E sernass@gmail.com

RUTHERFORD, Neil   T 07960 891911
Neil Rutherford Casting
E neil@neilrutherford.com
W www.neilrutherford.com

SCHILLER, Ginny   T 020 8806 5383
CDG Member
9 Clapton Terrace, London E5 9BW
E ginny@ginnyschiller.co.uk

SCHOFIELD, Gilly
CDG Member
E gillyschofield1@btinternet.com

SCOTT, Laura   T 020 7978 6336
CDG Member
56 Rowena Crescent, London SW11 2PT
E laurascottcasting@mac.com

SEARBY, Alice   T 020 7727 5600
2nd Floor, 138 Portobello Road
London W11 2DZ
E alice.searby@mac.com

SEARCHERS THE   T 07958 922829
70 Sylvia Court, Cavendish Street
London N1 7PG
E waynesearcher@mac.com

SEECOOMAR, Nadira   T 020 8892 8478
CDG Member
E nadira.seecoomar@gmail.com

SELECT CASTING LTD   T 07855 794747
PO Box 748, London NW4 1TT
T 07956 131494
E info@selectcasting.co.uk
W www.selectcasting.co.uk

SHAW, David   T 0161 273 4400
CDG Member
29 Ardwick Green North, Ardwick Green
Manchester M12 6DL

SHAW, Phil   T 020 8715 8943
Contact: By Post. Commercials. Film. Stage. Television
Suite 476, 2 Old Brompton Road
South Kensington, London SW7 3DQ
E philshawcasting@gmail.com

SHEPHERD, Debbie CASTING　T 020 7240 0400
Suite 16, 63 St Martin's Lane
London WC2N 4JS
E debbie@debbieshepherd.com

SID PRODUCTIONS LTD　T 01932 863194
Susan Head (Director)
T 07766 761267
E casting@sidproductions.co.uk
W www.sidproductions.co.uk

SILVEY, Denise　T 07711 245848
St Martin's Theatre, West Street
London WC2H 9NZ
E ds@denisesilvey.com
W www.denisesilvey.com

SIMPSON, Georgia　T 028 9147 0800
CDG Member
E georgia@georgiasimpsoncasting.com
W www.georgiasimpsoncasting.com

SINGER, Sandra ASSOCIATES　T 01702 331616
Contact: By e-mail
21 Cotswold Road, Westcliff-on-Sea
Essex SS0 8AA
E sandrasingeruk@aol.com
W www.sandrasinger.com

SMITH, Michelle CASTING LTD　T 0161 439 6825
*Contact: Michelle Smith (CDG Member). Television. Film.
Animation. Commercials. Corporate*
220 Church Lane, Stockport SK7 1PQ
E enquiries@michellesmithcasting.co.uk
W www.michellesmithcasting.co.uk

SMITH, Suzanne　T 020 7278 0045
CDG Member
99 Leighton Road, Kentish Town
London NW5 2RB
E zan@dircon.co.uk

SNAPE, Janine CASTING
CDG Member
c/o Melbourne Theatre Company, Australia
E j.snape@mtc.com.au

SPORTSCASTINGS.COM　T 07973 863263
Contact: Penny Burrows
3 Thornlaw Road
London SE27 0SH
E info@sportsmodels.com
W www.sportsmodels.com

STAFFORD, Aaron　T 020 8372 0611
Freelance. Commercials. Film. Television
14 Park Avenue, Enfield
Greater London EN1 2HP
E aaron.stafford@blueyonder.co.uk

STAFFORD, Emma CASTING　T 0161 833 4263
E jade@emmastafford.tv
W www.emmastafford.tv

STAFFORD, Helen　T 020 8360 6329
14 Park Avenue, Enfield
Greater London EN1 2HP
E helenstaffordcasting@gmail.com

STARK CASTING　T 020 8800 0060
T 07956 150689
E anna@starkcasting.com
W www.starkcasting.com

STERNE, Robert　T 020 8960 6099
CDG Member
Nina Gold Casting, 117 Chevening Road
London NW6 6DU
E robert@ninagold.co.uk

STEVENS, Gail　T 020 7600 0061
CDG Member. Gail Stevens Casting
84-85 Long Lane, London EC1A 9ET
E office@gailstevenscasting.com

**STEVENS MILLEFIORINI,
Danny**　T 00 39 389 4352200
Via Sillaro 14, Cerveteri
Rome 00052, Italy
T 00 39 348 268015
E dannystevens62@gmail.com

STOLL, Liz　T 020 8228 8285
BBC DRAMA SERIES CASTING
BBC Elstree, Room N208
Neptune House, Clarendon Road
Borehamwood, Herts WD6 1JF

STRONGE, Carla　T 028 9045 7727
296 Albertbridge Road, Belfast
Antrim BT5 4GX
E info@carlastrongecasting.com
W www.carlastrongecasting.com

STYRING, Faye　T 020 7157 3000
ITV, The Television Centre
Leeds LS3 1JS
E faye.styring@itv.com

SUMMERS, Mark CASTING　T 020 7229 8413
Twitter: @marksummerscast
1 Beaumont Avenue
West Kensington
London W14 9LP
E mark@marksummers.com
W www.marksummers.com

SYSON GRAINGER CASTING　T 020 7287 5327
*Contact: Lucinda Syson (CDG/CSA Member), Elaine
Grainger (CDG Member)*
Rooms 7-8, 2nd Floor
83-84 Berwick Street, London W1F 8TS
F 020 7287 3629
E office@sysongraingercasting.com

TABAK, Amanda
CDG Member. See CANDID CASTING

THOMAS, Hazel PRODUCTIONS   T 07948 211083
Flat 6, Highwood Manor
21 Constitution Hill
Ipswich, Suffolk IP1 3RG
E htproductions@live.co.uk
W www.hazel-thomas.wix.com/htproductions

TOPPING, Nicci   T 07802 684256
Panther House
Studio 4, East Block
38 Mount Pleasant
London WC1X 0AN
E general@toppscasting.co.uk
W www.toppscasting.co.uk

TOPPING, Nicci   T 07802 684256
10 Haddon Road, Chorlton
Manchester M21 7QU
E general@toppscasting.co.uk
W www.toppscasting.co.uk

TOPPING, Nicci   T 07802 684256
The Media Centre
7 Northumberland Street
West Yorkshire HD1 1RL
T 01484 511988
E general@toppscasting.co.uk
W www.toppscasting.co.uk

TREVELLICK, Jill   T 020 8340 2734
CDG Member
92 Priory Road, London N8 7EY
E jill@jilltrevellick.com

TREVIS, Sarah   T 020 8354 2398
CDG Member

VALENTINE HENDRY, Kelly
CDG Member. See VHJ CASTING

VAUGHAN, Sally   T 020 7735 6539
CDG Member
2 Kennington Park Place
London SE11 4AS
E svaughan12@btinternet.com

VHJ CASTING   T 020 7255 6146
Contact: Kelly Valentine Hendry (CDG Member), Victor
Jenkins (CDG Member)
Welbeck House
66-67 Wells Street
London W1T 3PY
E assistant@vhjcasting.com
W www.vhjcasting.com

VOSSER, Anne CASTING   T 01252 404716
156 Lower Farnham Road
Aldershot
Hampshire GU12 4EL
T 07968 868712
E anne@vosser-casting.co.uk
W www.vosser-casting.co.uk

WEIR, Fiona   T 020 7727 5600
CDG Member
2nd Floor, 138 Portobello Road
London W11 2DZ

WEST, June
CDG Member
E info@junewestcasting.com
W www.junewestcasting.com

WESTERN, Matt   T 07740 702077
E matt@mattwestern.co.uk
W www.mattwestern.co.uk

WHALE, Toby   T 020 8993 2821
CDG Member
80 Shakespeare Road, London W3 6SN
F 020 8993 8096
E toby@whalecasting.com
W www.whalecasting.com

WICKSTEED, Rose   T 020 7249 8386
CSA Member
Based in London,
E casting@rosewicksteed.com
W www.rosewicksteed.com

WILDMANHALL CASTING   T 020 7373 2036
Contact: Vicky Wildman, Buffy Hall
1 Child's Place, London SW5 9RX
E wildmanhall@mac.com

WILLIAMS-PARKER, Rachelle   T 020 8228 7109
BBC DRAMA SERIES CASTING
BBC Elstree, Room N208
Neptune House, Clarendon Road
Borehamwood, Herts WD6 1JF

WILLIS, Catherine   T 020 7255 6131
CDG Member. Contact: By e-mail
Wellbeck House, 66-67 Wells Street
London W1T 3PY
E catherine@cwcasting.co.uk

WRIGHT, Rebecca   T 020 3371 1531
CDG Member
E office@rebeccawrightcasting.com
W www.rebeccawrightcasting.com

YOUNGSTAR CASTING   T 023 8047 7717
Children & Teenagers only
Head Office, 1st Floor, Unit 3
Mitchell Point, Ensign Way
Hamble, Southampton SO31 4RF
E info@youngstar.tv
W www.youngstar.tv

**ZIMMERMANN, Jeremy
CASTING**   T 020 7478 5161
2nd Floor, 41 Maiden Lane
London WC2E 7LJ
E info@zimmermanncasting.com

THE KNIGHTS OF MIDDLE ENGLAND

The Knights of Middle England are a professional Jousting Stunt Team providing a range of services for the Theatre, Film & TV industry and are the UK's leading Jousting School.

We offer: • Trained Horses & Riders for the TV & Film Industry • Medieval Knights Sword Fighting
• 5 Day Intensive Horse Riding Course for Actors
• Learn Stunt Riding, Jousting & Horseback Archery with our Tailor Made Courses or Experience Days

Based in the heart of the Midlands in Warwick, Warwickshire. Direct Trains – Euston to Coventry – 1hr only / London Marylebone to Warwick – 1hr 15 mins – pick up available
e: info@knightsofmiddleengland.co.uk   **t:** 00 44 (0)1926 400401   **www.knightsofmiddleengland.com**

A1 ANIMALS   T/F 0844 3351733
Farm & Domestic Animals
70 Frobisher Road, Bilton
Rugby
Warwickshire CV22 7HU
T 07860 416545
E a1animals@btinternet.com
W www.a1animals.co.uk

A-Z ANIMALS LTD   T 01372 377111
The Bell House, Bell Lane
Fetcham, Surrey KT22 9ND
T 07836 721288
E info@a-zanimals.co.uk
W www.a-zanimals.co.uk

ABAS ANIMAL HIRE   T 07971 861684
136 Court Road, Orpington
Kent BR6 0PZ
E lorraine@animal-hire.co.uk
W www.animal-hire.co.uk

ACADEMY OF PERFORMANCE COMBAT THE   T 07928 324706
197 Church Road
Northolt UB5 5BE
E info@theapc.org.uk
W www.theapc.org.uk

ACTING AUDITION SUCCESS   T 020 8731 6686
Audition Coaching for Drama UK Schools. Camera Technique. Career Advice
53 West Heath Court, London NW11 7RG
E philiproschactor@gmail.com
W www.actingauditionsuccess.co.uk

ACTORS' ADVISORY SERVICE   T 020 8287 2839
Provides Advice to Actors, Agents, Photographers etc
29 Talbot Road, Twickenham
Middlesex TW2 6SJ

ACTOR'S ONE-STOP SHOP THE   T 020 8279 8073
Showreels Edited & Filmed
2B Dale View Crescent, Chingford
London E4 6PQ
T 07894 152651
E info@actorsonestopshop.com
W www.actorsonestopshop.com

ADVOCATE AGENCY ID - THE BRANDING SERVICE FOR ACTORS   T 01279 850618
F 01279 850625
E id@advocate.agency
W www.advocate.agency

AGENTFILE   T 07050 683662
Software for Agents
E admin@agentfile.com
W www.agentfile.com

AKA   T 020 7836 4747
Advertising. Design. Digital. Marketing. Promotions. Sales & Ticketing
1st Floor, 115-117 Shaftesbury Avenue
Cambridge Circus
London WC2H 8AF
F 020 7836 8787
E aka@akauk.com
W www.akauk.com

ALTERNATIVE ANIMALS   T 07956 564715
Contact: Trevor Smith. Animatronics. Taxidermy
11 Hillside Gardens
High Wycombe
Bucks HP13 7LQ
F 07770 666088
E animalswork1@yahoo.co.uk
W www.animalswork.co.uk

ANIMAL ACTING   T 01253 853953
Animals. Horse-drawn Vehicles. Props. Stunts
33 Broadhurst Road, Thornton-Cleveleys
Lancashire FY5 3HR
T 07831 800567
E information@animalacting.com
W www.animalacting.com

ANIMAL ACTORS   T 07710 348777
Animals. Birds. Reptiles
95 Ditchling Road
Brighton, Sussex BN1 4ST

ANIMAL AMBASSADORS   T 01993 778847
Contact: Kay Weston. Animal Consultant & Trainer/ Animal Agent
The Glades, 119 Brize Norton Road
Minster Lovell
Oxon OX29 0SH
T 07831 558594
E kay@animalambassadors.co.uk
W www.animalambassadors.co.uk

ANIMALS GALORE LTD **T** 01342 842400
Trained animals with professional, qualified handlers.
Film, Television, Commercials, Advertising, Pop Videos,
Theatre, Events etc
208 Smallfield Road, Horley, Surrey RH6 9LS
T 07850 870884
E info@animals-galore.co.uk
W www.animals-galore.co.uk

ASSOCIATED STUDIOS THE **T** 020 7385 2038
The Hub @ St Alban's Fulham, 2 Margravine Road
London W6 8HJ
E info@associatedstudios.co.uk
W www.associatedstudios.co.uk

AUDIO DESCRIPTION
For Blind & Visually Impaired Audiences. West End
& on Tour
E info@theatredescription.com

**AUTOMOBILE
ASSOCIATION (THE AA)** **T** 01256 492640
Fanum House, Basing View
Basingstoke RG21 4EA

BAILEY, Bernice **T** 01306 741310
Tutor & Chaperone
Spur Lacey, Camilla Drive
Westhumble, Surrey RH5 6BU
E bpbailey_uk@yahoo.co.uk

**BAM! BAIRD ARTISTS MANAGEMENT
CONSULTING** **T/F** 001 705 424 6507
Specialising in US & Canadian Visas, Work Permits,
Withholding, Taxes etc
7132 County Road #21, PO Box 597
Alliston, Ontario, Canada L9R 1V7
E robert@bairdartists.com
W www.bairdartists.com

BARTERCARD **T** 0800 8406333
Churchill House, 1 London Road
Slough, Berkshire SL3 7FJ
E info@uk.bartercard.com
W www.bartercard.co.uk

BIG PICTURE **T** 020 7371 4455
Contact: Jayne Thorburn (Field Marketing)
13 Netherwood Road, London W14 0BL
E humanresources@ebigpicture.co.uk
W www.ebigpicture.co.uk

BLACK, Liam A. THEATRICAL **T** 01383 610711
Illusion, Special Effects & Magic Designer for Television,
Theatre & Film
12 Downfield, Cowdenbeath, Fife KY4 9JE
E liamablacktheatrical@gmail.com

**BRITISH ASSOCIATION OF
DRAMATHERAPISTS** **T/F** 01242 235515
Waverley, Battledown Approach
Cheltenham, Glos GL52 6RE
E info@badth.org.uk
W www.badth.org.uk

**BYFORD, Simon PRODUCTION
MANAGEMENT SERVICES** **T** 01273 623972
Production & Event Management
22 Freshfield Place, Brighton, East Sussex BN2 0BN
T 07885 474455
E simon@simonbyfordpms.com
W www.simonbyfordpms.com

BYRNE, John **T** 020 7117 2603
One-to-one Advice from The Stage's Career Adviser
E info@newwondermanagement.co.uk
W www.performingcareers.com

**CAP PRODUCTION
SOLUTIONS LTD** **T** 07973 432576
Technical Production Services
116 Wigmore Road, Carshalton
Surrey SM5 1RQ
E leigh@leighporter.com

CASTLE MAGICAL SERVICES **T/F** 01904 709500
Contact: Michael Shepherd. Magical Effect Consultants
Broompark, 131 Tadcaster Road
Dringhouses, York YO24 1QJ
E admin@castlemagicalservices.co.uk

**CAULKETT, Robin
Dip SM MIIRSM** **T** 07970 442003
Abseiling. Rope Work
3 Churchill Way, Mitchell Dean
Glos GL17 0AZ
E robincaulkett@talktalk.net

**CELEBRITIES
WORLDWIDE LTD** **T** 020 7637 4178
Celebrity Contacts & Booking
E claire@celebritiesworldwide.com
W www.celebritiesworldwide.com

CELEBRITY REPTILES **T/F** 020 8659 0877
11 Tramway Close, London SE20 7DF
E info@celebrityreptiles.co.uk
W www.celebrityreptiles.co.uk

CHAPERONE **T/F** 020 8650 8997
For Children in Performing Arts
31 Whitecroft Way, Beckenham
Kent BR3 3AQ
T 07930 353381
E elaineboyle@msn.com

CHAPERONE **T/F** 020 8933 0076
Licensed Chaperone for Children in the Entertainment
Industry including Film, Television & Theatre
T 07989 702950
E robmeyer4@aol.com

CHAPERONEAGENCY **T** 07960 075928
E chaperoneagency@hotmail.co.uk
W www.chaperoneagency.com

CHAPERONES & TUTORS LTD **T** 07535 337423
Covering the whole of the UK to Film, Television & Stage.
Offices based in the Midlands & London
E arlene@chaperonesandtutors.co.uk
W www.chaperonesandtutors.co.uk

CHARCOALBLUE LLP **T** 020 7928 0000
17 Short Street, London SE1 8LJ
E studio@charcoalblue.com
W www.charcoalblue.com

CHEESEMAN, Virginia **T** 01628 522632
Entomological Supplier
21 Willow Close
Flackwell Heath
High Wycombe, Bucks HP10 9LH
T 07971 838724
E virginia@virginiacheeseman.co.uk
W www.virginiacheeseman.co.uk

CHEKHOV, Michael
CENTRE UK **T** 020 8696 7372
Information Centre for the Work of Michael Chekhov
in the UK including Biographies, Academic Contacts,
International Links, Training Links & other Information
E info@michaelchekhov.org.uk
W www.michaelchekhov.org.uk

CHILDCHAPERONE.CO.UK **T** 07956 427442
Contact: Denise Smith. Licensed Chaperone. Stage,
Television & Film Industry
E denisesmith916@btinternet.com
W www.childchaperone.co.uk

CLASS - MEDIA LAW LLB, LPC **T** 07597 378995
25 Falkner Square, Liverpool L8 7NZ
E clundon@googlemail.com

COBO MEDIA **T/F** 020 8699 8655
Performing Arts, Entertainment & Leisure Marketing
43A Garthorne Road
London SE23 1EP
E admin@cobomedia.com
W www.cobomedia.com

COLCLOUGH, John **T** 020 8873 1763
Practical Independent Guidance for Actors & Actresses
E info@johncolclough.com
W www.johncolclough.com

COMBAT INTERNATIONAL **T** 01877 331166
St Kessogs, Ancaster Square
Callender FK17 8ED
E info@clanranald.org
W www.clanranald.org

COPS ON THE BOX **T** 020 8650 9828
Twitter: @copsonthebox1
BM BOX 7301, London WC1N 3XX
T 07710 065851
E info@cotb.co.uk
W www.cotb.co.uk

COTSWOLD FARM PARK **T** 01451 850307
Rare Breed Farm Animals
Guiting Power, Cheltenham
Gloucestershire GL54 5UG
F 01451 850423
E info@cotswoldfarmpark.co.uk

CREATIVE MAGIC DIRECTOR **T** 01727 838656
Contact: Tony Middleton
67 De Tany Court, St Albans
Herts AL1 1TX
T 07738 971077
E anthonyjjmiddleton@gmail.com
W www.middletonenterprisesuk.com

CREATURE FEATURE **T/F** 01387 860648
Animal Agent
Gubhill Farm, Ae, Dumfries
Scotland DG1 1RL
T 07770 774866
E david@creaturefeature.co.uk
W www.creaturefeature.co.uk

CROFTS, Andrew **T/F** 01403 864518
Book Writing Services
Westlands Grange, West Grinstead
Horsham, West Sussex RH13 8LZ
E croftsa@aol.com
W www.andrewcrofts.com

DALLA VECCHIA, Sara **T** 07877 404743
Italian Teacher
13 Fauconberg Road
London W4 3JZ
E saraitaliantuition@gmail.com

DHALIVAAL, Séva **T** 07956 553879
Supporting Artist

DOLBADARN FILM HORSES **T/F** 01286 870277
Dolbadarn Hotel, High Street
Llanberis, Gwynedd
North Wales LL55 4SU
T 07710 461341
E info@filmhorses.co.uk
W www.filmhorses.co.uk

DR VOICE **T** 07850 697807
Vocal Coaching
3 Mills Studios, London E3 3DU
E drvoice@drvoice.tv
W www.drvoice.tv

DUDLEY, Yvonne
LRPS ARAD FISTD **T** 020 8989 1528
Stories for Films & Television
55 Cambridge Park
Wanstead, London E11 2PR
T 07870 372637

EARLE, Kenneth
PERSONAL MANAGEMENT **T** 020 7274 1219
214 Brixton Road, London SW9 6AP
T 07711 270698
E kennethearle@agents-uk.com
W www.kennethearlepersonalmanagement.com

ENTERTAINMENT
MANCHESTER **T** 07454 961577
Theatre Reviewers of Amateur and Professional Theatre
in Manchester
86 Cotefield Road, Manchester M22 1UG
E info@entertainmentmcr.co.uk
W www.entertainmentmcr.co.uk

ES GLOBAL LTD **T** 020 7055 7200
Creative Solutions for Music, Sporting, Corporate &
Hospitality Events
3 Vyner Street, London E2 9DG
E info@esglobalsolutions.com
W www.esglobalsolutions.com

FACADE **T/F** 020 8699 8655
Creation & Production of Musicals
43A Garthorne Road
London SE23 1EP
E facade@cobomedia.com

FERRARI, Maggie **T** 01798 344356
26 Orchard Close, Petworth
West Sussex GU28 0SA
T 07986 045724
E margaret.ferrari@btinternet.com

FERRIS ENTERTAINMENT
MUSIC **T** 07801 493133
Music for Film & Television. London. Cardiff. Belfast.
Los Angeles. France. Spain
Number 8, 132 Charing Cross Road
London WC2H 0LA
E info@ferrisentertainment.com
W www.ferrisentertainment.com

FIGHT CHOREOGRAPHER & ACTION DIRECTOR
T 07975 757558

Contact: Nic Main (Professional Actor, Film Fighting Choreographer)
Based in the South East,
E nicmain1@hotmail.com
W www.nicmain.com

FILM & TV HORSES
T/F 01753 864464

Crown Farm
Eton Wick Road
Eton, Windsor SL4 6PG
T 07831 629662
E filmhorses@yahoo.co.uk
W www.filmhorses.com

FLAMES MARTIAL ARTS ACADEMY
T 07950 396389

Contact: Adam Richards
Unit 2, 128 Milton Road Business Park
Gravesend, Kent DA12 2PG
E stunts@adamrichardsstunts.co.uk
W www.adamrichardsfightdirector.com

GET STUFFED
T 020 7226 1364

Taxidermy
105 Essex Road, London N1 2SL
T 07831 260062
E taxidermy@thegetstuffed.co.uk
W www.thegetstuffed.co.uk

GHOSTWRITER/AUTHOR/ SCRIPTWRITER
T 01227 721071

Contact: John Parker
Dove Cottage, The Street
Ickham CT3 1QP
T 07702 999920
E ghostwriterforyourbook@ymail.com
W www.ghostwriteruk.info

GILMOUR Rev/Prof/Dr Glenn Msc.D IMM SHsc.D Dip.Coun. BCMA.Reg
T 0114 321 6500

Fully Qualified/International Medium & Clairvoyant. Healer/Counsellor. Holistic Therapist. Consultant Paranormal/Metaphysics/Occult for Radio & Television
45 Studfield Road, Sheffield S6 4ST
E drglenngilmour@yahoo.com
W www.drglenngilmour.com

GLOBAL ACCESS WORLD-WIDE ENTERTAINMENT VISAS
T 001 323 936 7100

5670 Wilshire Boulevard, Suite 1970
Los Angeles 90036, USA
F 001 323 936 7197
E info@globalaxs.net
W www.globalaxs.net

GOLDIELLE PROMOTIONS
T 07977 936826

Event Management & Entertainment
68 Lynton Drive, Hillside
Southport, Merseyside PR8 4QQ
T 01704 566604
E goldielle@yahoo.co.uk
W www.goldiellepromotions.com

GRADY, Chris ORGANISATION
T 07713 643971

Coaching, Mentoring & Personal Performance Training
Gothic House, High Road
Great Finborough
Suffolk IP14 3AQ
E chris@chrisgrady.org
W www.chrisgrady.org

GRAY, Robin COMMENTARIES
T 01420 23347

Equestrian Equipment. Horse Race Commentaries. Voice Overs
Comptons, Isington
Alton, Hants GU34 4PL
T 07831 828424
E comptons1@hotmail.co.uk

HANDS UP PUPPETS
T 07909 824630

Contact: Marcus Clarke
7 Cavendish Vale, Nottingham NG5 4DS
E enquiries@handsuppuppets.com
W www.handsuppuppets.com

HARLEY PRODUCTIONS
T 020 8202 8863

78 York Street, London W1H 1DP
T 020 7486 2986
E harleyprods@aol.com

HAYES, Susan
T 07721 927714

Choreographer, Show Consultant & Director of Superarts Agency & Academy of Performing Arts. Based in London
E superarts@btinternet.com

HERITAGE RAILWAY ASSOCIATION
T 01993 883384

10 Hurdeswell, Long Hanborough
Witney, Oxfordshire OX29 8DH
E john.crane@hra.gb.com
W www.heritagerailways.com

HILTON HORSES
T 07958 292222

Contact: Samantha Jones
478 London Road, Ashford
Middlesex TW15 3AD
E samantha@hilton-horses.com
W www.hilton-horses.com

iTREND RESEARCH LTD
T 07977 425518

Contact: Andrew Jenkins. Audience Research. Audience Surveys. Focus Groups
8-9 Hertford Street, London W1J 7RJ
E andrew@itrendresearch.com
W www.itrendresearch.com

JMA
T 020 7263 9867

Marketing. Media
8 Heathville Road, London N19 3AJ
E jma@janemorganassociates.com

JOE PUBLIC
T 020 7831 7077

Specialist Consultancy & Campaign Management
The Dutch House, 307-308 High Holborn
London WC1V 7LL
E mail@joepublicmarketing.com
W www.joepublicmarketing.com

JOHNSON, Gareth LTD
T 01239 891368

Producing & Management for Theatre
1st Floor, 19 Garrick Street
London WC2E 9AX
T 07770 225227
E gjltd@mac.com
W www.garethjohnsonltd.com

JOHNSON, Gareth LTD
T 01239 891368

Producing & Management for Theatre
Plas Hafren, Eglwyswrw
Crymych, Pembrokeshire SA41 3UL
T 07770 225227
E gjltd@mac.com
W www.garethjohnsonltd.com

Consultants

JORDAN, Richard PRODUCTIONS T 020 7243 9001
Festivals. General Management. Production Consultancy. UK & International Productions
Mews Studios, 16 Vernon Yard
London W11 2DX
F 020 7313 9667
E info@richardjordanproductions.com

JOSEPH'S AMAZING CAMELS T 01608 661367
The Old Farmhouse, White House Farm
Idlicote, Warwickshire CV36 5DN
E josephandrebecca@jacamels.co.uk
W www.jacamels.co.uk

KEAN LANYON LTD T 020 7697 8453
Contact: Sharon Kean, Iain Lanyon. PR & Web/ Graphic Consultants
United House, North Road
Islington, London N7 9DP
T 07973 843133
E sharon@keanlanyon.com
W www.keanlanyon.com

KELLER, Don T 020 8800 4882
Marketing Consultancy. Project Management
65 Glenwood Road, Harringay
London N15 3JS
E info@donkeller.co.uk

KIEVE, Paul T 07939 252526
Magical Effects for Film & Stage
2 St Philip's Road, London E8 3BP
E mail@stageillusion.com
W www.stageillusion.com

KNIGHTS OF ARKLEY THE T/F 01269 861001
Medieval Jousting Displays, Armour for Film, Television, Corporate & Private Functions
Glyn Sylen Farm, Five Roads
Llanelli SA15 5BJ
E penny@knightsofarkley.fsnet.co.uk
W www.knightsofarkley.com

KNIGHTS OF MIDDLE ENGLAND THE T 01926 400401
Horses & Riders for Film, Opera & Television
Warwick International School of Riding, Guys Cliffe
Coventry Road, Warwick CV34 5YD
E info@knightsofmiddleengland.co.uk
W www.knightsofmiddleengland.com

LAMBOLLE, Robert T 020 8455 4564
Script Evaluation & Editing
618B Finchley Road, London NW11 7RR
E lambhorn@gmail.com

LAWINSPORT.COM T 020 3286 8003
Contact: Sean Cottrell (CEO). International Sports Law Publication Providing High Quality Daily Sports Law & Business Information, Topical Articles of Legal Opinion, Blogs & Videos by those working in the field. Information about Sports Law Firms, Books, Conferences & Courses
E sean.cottrell@lawinsport.com
W www.lawinsport.com

LEAN, David Lawson T 01932 230273
Chaperone Service for Children in Entertainment
72 Shaw Drive, Walton-on-Thames
Surrey KT12 2LS
E dlawsonlean@gmail.com
W www.davidlawsonlean.com

LEEP MARKETING & PR T 07973 558895
Marketing. Press. Publicity
5 Hurdwick Place, London NW1 2JE
E philip@leep.biz

LEO MEDIA & ENTERTAINMENT GROUP THE T 00 37 7 93258797
In Association with Argentum of Monaco. Executive Production. Film, Television & Literary Consultancy. Legal Work
PO Box 68006, London NW4 9FW
E info@leomediagroup.com
W www.argentum.mc

LES AMIS D'ONNO T 01835 869757
Performing Horses, Stunt Riders & Performing Dogs for Film & Television
Lanton Hill Farm, Jedburgh TD8 6SY
E lesamisdonno@btinternet.com
W www.lesamisdonno.com

LINE OF SIGHT PRODUCTIONS T 07701 007822
Military, Fire Service & Police Technical Advisers backed by Help for Heroes
8 Northumberland Avenue, London WC2N 5BY
E matt@losproductions.co.uk
W www.losproductions.co.uk

LOCATION TUTORS NATIONWIDE T 020 7978 8898
Fully Qualified & Experienced Teachers Working with Children on Film Sets & Covering all Key Stages of National Curriculum
16 Poplar Walk, Herne Hill, London SE24 0BU
T 07806 887471
E locationtutorsnationwide@gmail.com
W www.locationtutors.co.uk

LONDON COMPUTER DOCTOR T 020 7652 4296
Computer Support
66 Heath Road, Clapham, London SW8 3BD
E joe@londoncomputerdoctor.com
W www.londoncomputerdoctor.com

LONDON LITERARY PUB CRAWL COMPANY THE T 020 8090 5082
Promotes the Art & Literature of London through Tours & Infodramas
2nd Floor, 12 Fouberts Place
Carnaby Street, London W1F 7PA
T 07435 362424
E tours@mavericktheatre.co.uk
W www.londonliterarypubcrawl.com

LOVE, Billie HISTORICAL PHOTOGRAPHS T 01983 812572
Picture Research. Formerly 'Amanda' Theatrical Portraiture
3 Winton Street, Ryde, Isle of Wight PO33 2BX
E billielove@tiscali.co.uk

LUXFACTOR GROUP (UK) THE T 0845 3700589
Corporate Consultancy, Media Relations, Entertainment Management, Broadcast, Social Media & Film Production, Client & Event Management.
Twitter: @luxfactor
Fleet Place, 12 Nelson Drive
Petersfield, Hampshire GU31 4SJ
F 0845 3700588
E info@luxfactor.co.uk
W www.luxfactor.co.uk

MAGICIANS.CO.UK　　T 0845 0062442
Entertainers & Illusion Consultants
Burnhill House, 50 Burnhill Road
Beckenham BR3 3LA
F 0845 0062443
E mail@magicians.co.uk

MAGICIANS IN LONDON　　T 07973 512845
Contact: Mike Alan. Magician and Magical Adviser for the BBC
The House of Magic
45 Bedford Street
London WC2E 9HA
E mikealan25@yahoo.com
W www.magiciansinlondon.co.uk

MAIN, Nic　　T 07975 757558
Experienced Stage, Television & Film Action/Fight Director/Actor
62 Kingsway, Blackwater
Camberley, Surrey GU17 0JB
E nicmain1@hotmail.com
W www.nicmain.com

MALAGUEIRA, Fatima THEATRICAL AGENT CONSULTANT　　T 07775 708460
For Actors, Agents & PR Companies
30 Granta Terrace, Great Shelford
Cambridge CB22 5DJ
E fatima.malagueira@gmail.com
W www.roomtobreathe.uk.com

MAYS, Lorraine　　T 01494 771029
Face Painting & Entertainment Trainer
Park View, Stanley Avenue
Chesham, Bucks HP5 2JF
T 07778 106552
E lorrainebmays@aol.com

McKENNA, Deborah LTD　　T 020 8846 0966
Celebrity Chefs & Lifestyle Presenters only
Riverbank House
1 Putney Bridge Approach
London SW6 3BQ
E hello@dml-uk.com
W www.dml-uk.com

MEDIA LEGAL　　T 01732 460592
Jurisconsults
Town House, 5 Mill Pond Close
Sevenoaks, Kent TN14 5AW

MILDENBERG, Vanessa　　T 07796 264828
Director. Movement Director. Choreographer. 'Across the Board'
Flat 6, Cameford Court
New Park Road, London SW2 4LH
E vanessamildenberg@me.com
W www.vanessamildenberg.com

MILITARY ADVISORY & INSTRUCTION SPECIALISTS　　T 01904 491198
Contact: Johnny Lee Harris. Advice on Weapons, Drill, Period to Present. Ex-Army Instructor. Health & Safety. IOSH. Military Bugler & Drummer. Actor. PSV Licence. Own Scarlets (Scarlet Uniform), Bugle & Drum. Chieftain Tank Driver & Gunner. Horse Rider
38 Knapton Close, Strensall
York YO32 5ZF
T 07855 648886
E johnmusic1@hotmail.com

MILLENNIUM BUGS　　T 07770 666088
Live Insects
28 Greaves Road, High Wycombe
Bucks HP13 7JU
T 07956 566252
E animalswork1@yahoo.co.uk
W www.animalworld.org.uk

MINIMAL RISK　　T 01432 379950
Security Risk Consultancy & Former Military Recruitment
Rural Enterprise Centre, Rotherwas
Hereford HR2 6FE
E enquiries@minimalrisk.co.uk
W www.minimalrisk.co.uk

MINISTRY OF FUN THE　　T 020 7708 6116
Entertainment. Promotions. PR Marketing Campaigns
Unit A&B, 22 Amelia Street
London SE17 3BZ
E ministry@ministryoffun.net
W www.ministryoffun.net

MUSIC SOLUTIONS LTD　　T 020 7866 8160
Garden Studios, 71-75 Shelton Street
London WC2H 9JQ
E mail@musicsolutionsltd.com

NORDIC NOMAD TRAINING / BUSINESS ADVICE　　T 07980 619165
Workshops, Courses, Books & One-to-One Advice Sessions on 'Making a Living' & 'Running a Successful Arts Business' for Actors, Dancers & Performers
E tanja@nordicnomad.com
W www.nordicnomad.com

OATWAY, Christopher　　T 07873 485265
Social Media, Editing Scripts. Twitter: @djchrisoatway
495 Altrincham Road, Baguley Hall
Manchester M23 1AR
E christopherjoatway@gmail.com

ORANGE TREE STUDIO LTD & RICHARD PARDY MUSIC SERVICES　　T 07768 146200
Saxophone, Woodwinds, Brass Section & Bands for Hire (Live or in Studio). Original Music/Composition & Production
31A New Road, Croxley Green
Herts WD3 3EJ
E richard@orangetreestudio.com
W www.redhornz.co.uk

PA & ADMIN SUPPORT SERVICES　　T 07939 954575
Contact: Louise Carmichael. Professional PA. Admin Services including CV Formatting
3 Clough Mill, Walsden
West Yorkshire, England OL14 7QX
E louisecarmichaelpa@gmail.com

PENROSE, Scott　　T 07767 336882
Magic & Illusion Effects for Film, Stage & Television
17 Berkeley Drive, Billericay
Essex CM12 0YP
E mail@stagemagician.com
W www.stagemagician.com

PSYCHOLOGY GROUP THE　　T 0870 6092445
Assessments. Counselling. Expert Opinion. Presentation. Psychotherapy
F 0845 2805243
E info@psychologygroup.co.uk
W www.psychologygroup.co.uk

PUKKA PRESENTING   T 020 8455 1385
Training in Television Presenting & Presentation Techniques
Appletree Cottage, 51 Erskine Hill
London NW11 6EY
E kathryn@pukkapresenting.co.uk
W www.pukkapresenting.co.uk

PUPPET CENTRE   T 020 7228 5335
Development & Advocacy Agency for Puppetry & Related Animated Theatre
BAC, Lavender Hill
London SW11 5TN
E pct@puppetcentre.org.uk
W www.puppetcentre.org.uk

PUPPETS - MAGICAL MART   T/F 020 8300 3579
Magic, Ventriloquism & Punch & Judy Consultant
42 Christchurch Road, Sidcup
Kent DA15 7HQ
W www.johnstylesentertainer.co.uk

RAINBOW BIGBOTTOM   T 01494 771029
Children's Warm-up Artist for Stage & Television. Agent: Mark Starr, Keyhold Management
Park View, Stanley Avenue
Chesham, Bucks HP5 2JF
W www.topbearproductions.co.uk

RB HEALTH & SAFETY SOLUTIONS LTD   T 0845 2571489
Specialists in Theatre & Production Health & Safety Audits, Consultancy, Risk Assessments & Training
Blacklands Business Centre, 15 Fearon Road
Hastings, East Sussex TN40 1DA
E richard@rbhealthandsafety.co.uk
W www.rbhealthandsafety.co.uk

REACH TO THE SKY   T 0843 2892503
Contact: Dr J. Success Life Coach
Brook Street, Mayfair, London W1K 4HR
T 07961 911027
E drj@reachtothesky.com
W www.reachtothesky.com

RICHARDS, Adam   T 07950 396389
Fight Director
Unit 2, 128 Milton Road Business Park
Gravesend, Kent DA12 2PG
E stunts@adamrichardsstunts.co.uk
W www.adamrichardsfightdirector.com

RIPLEY-DUGGAN PARTNERSHIP THE   T 020 7436 1392
Tour Booking
26 Goodge Street, London W1T 2QG
E info@ripleyduggan.com

ROBERTSON, Bronwyn   T 01789 550380
Contact: Bronwyn Robertson (Experienced PA). Admin Support
T 07815 192135
E bronwyn@theartsva.com
W www.theartsva.com

ROCKWOOD ANIMALS ON FILM   T 029 2088 5420
Lewis Terrace, Llanbradach
Caerphilly CF83 3JZ
T 07973 930983
E martin@rockwoodanimals.com
W www.rockwoodanimals.com

ROSCH, Philip   T 020 8731 6686
Audition Coaching for Drama UK Schools. Camera Technique. Career Advice
53 West Heath Court
London NW11 7RG
E philiproschactor@gmail.com
W www.actingauditionsuccess.co.uk

SCHOOL OF NATIONAL EQUITATION LTD   T 01509 852366
Contact: Sam Humphrey
Bunny Hill Top, Costock
Loughborough, Leicestershire LE12 6XN
T 07977 930083
E sam@bunnyhill.co.uk
W www.bunnyhill.co.uk

SHADEÈ, Magus Lynius: RITUAL FORMAN, INVOCATIONS   T 07740 043156
Direct Voice Communication. Materialisations. Psychic. Occult Investigator. Consultant
Suite 213, 91 Western Road
Brighton BN1 2NW
E maguslyniusshadee@hotmail.com
W www.occultcentre.com

SHAW, Phil CASTING & CONSULTANCY   T 07702 124935
One-to-one Career Marketing Advice for Actors from a Bespoke Consultancy & Mentoring Service
Suite 476, 2 Old Brompton Road
South Kensington, London SW7 3DQ
E philshawcasting@gmail.com

SINCLAIR, Andy   T 07831 196675
Mime
E andynebular@hotmail.com
W www.andyjsinclair.co.uk

SPORTS PROMOTIONS (UK) LTD   T 020 8771 4700
Production Advisers. Safety. Sport. Stunts
56 Church Road
Crystal Palace
London SE19 2EZ
F 020 8771 4704
E cameron@sportspromotions.co.uk
W www.sportspromotions.co.uk

STAGE CRICKET CLUB   T 020 7402 7543
Cricketers & Cricket Grounds
41 Hanover Steps, St George's Fields
London W2 2YG
E brianjfilm@aol.com
W www.stagecc.co.uk

STAGECOACH AGENCY CHAPERONES   T 01989 769547
Suite 2, 1st Floor Offices
Cantilupe Chambers
Cantilupe Road, Ross-on-Wye HR9 7AN
E tarquin@stagecoachagency.co.uk
W www.stagecoachagency.co.uk

STREET DEFENCE   T 07919 350290
Fight Choreographer. Advanced Screen Combatant. Conditioning Specialist
6 Clive Close, Potters Bar
Hertfordshire EN6 2AE
E streetdefence@hotmail.co.uk
W www.streetdefenceuk.com

STUNT ACTION SPECIALISTS (S.A.S.)   **T** 01273 230214
Corporate & Television Stunt Work
110 Trafalgar Road, Portslade
East Sussex BN41 1GS
E mail@stuntactionspecialists.co.uk
W www.stuntactionspecialists.co.uk

STUNT DOGS & ANIMALS   **T/F** 01869 338546
3 The Chestnuts, Clifton
Deddington, Oxon OX15 0PE
E gill@stuntdogs.net

TALENT SCOUT THE   **T** 01924 464049
Referral Service. Agents & Managers
19 Edge Road, Thornhill
Dewsbury, West Yorkshire WF12 0QA
E connect@thetalentscout.org

THEATRE PROJECTS CONSULTANTS   **T** 020 7482 4224
Creative Advice on Perfomance Spaces
4 Apollo Studios, Charlton Kings Road
London NW5 2SW
F 020 7284 0636
E uk@theatreprojects.com
W www.theatreprojects.com

THERAPEDIA LONDON BRIGHTON   **T** 07941 300871
Contact: Dr Grey Madison. Chartered Psychologist (BPS)
93 Gloucester Place, London W1U 6JQ
E info@gregmadison.net
W www.gregmadison.net

TODD, Carole   **T** 07775 566275
Director. Choreographer. Show Doctor. Consultancy for Acts Development & Audition Advice
E ctdirector@gmail.com

TOP NOTCH NANNIES   **T** 020 7824 8209
142 Buckingham Palace Road
London SW1W 9TR
T 020 7881 0893
E jean@topnotchnannies.com
W www.topnotchnannies.com

TUTORS ON LOCATION   **T** 0800 0488864
Holly House, Village Road
Christleton, Chester, Cheshire CH3 7AS
E enquiries@tutorsonlocation.co.uk
W www.tutorsonlocation.co.uk

TWINS FX THE   **T** 0845 0523683
Special Effects for Film, Stage & Television Productions
T 07971 589186
E info@thetwinsfx.com
W www.thetwinsfx.com

URBAN PAWS UK   **T** 07784 517847
Contact: Layla Flaherty (Company Director). Supplies Dogs for Advertising & Film & Television Projects
Merseyside, Claughton CH43 8ST
E info@urbanpawsuk.com
W www.urbanpawsuk.com

VERNON, Doremy   **T/F** 020 8767 6944
Archivist. Author 'Tiller Girls'. Dance Routines Tiller Girl Style
16 Ouseley Road, London SW12 8EF
E mrs.worthington@hotmail.co.uk

VOCALEYES   **T** 020 7375 1043
Audio Description "Describing The Arts"
1st Floor, 54 Commercial Street
London E1 6LT
E enquiries@vocaleyes.co.uk
W www.vocaleyes.co.uk

WELBOURNE, Jacqueline   **T** 07977 247287
Choreographer. Circus Trainer. Consultant
43 Kingsway Avenue, Kingswood
Bristol BS15 8AN
E jackie.welbourne@gmail.com

WHITE DOVES COMPANY LTD THE   **T** 020 8508 1414
Provision of up to 300 Doves for Release
Suite 210 Sterling House
Langston Road
Loughton, Essex IG10 3TS
F 020 8502 2461
E thewhitedovecompany@yahoo.co.uk
W www.thewhitedovecompany.co.uk

WHITE, Leonard   **T** 01273 514473
Director. Stage & Television Credits
Highlands, 40 Hill Crest Road
Newhaven, East Sussex BN9 9EG
E leoguy.white@virgin.net

WILD FANGS   **T** 07969 434050
Animals for all Media Work, Specialising in Reptiles & Snakes. Twitter: @WildFangsUK
E wildfangs@outlook.com
W www.wildfangsuk.wordpress.com

WINDOW, S. PHOTOS   **T** 07455 011639
Archival Documentation of Performance, Practice, Design & Architecture
269 Southborough Lane
Bromley, Kent BR2 8AT
E info@swindowphotos.com
W www.swindowphotos.com

WISE MONKEY FINANCIAL COACHING   **T** 01273 691223
Contact: Simonne Gnessen
14 Eastern Terrace Mews
Brighton BN2 1EP
E simonne@financial-coaching.co.uk
W www.financial-coaching.co.uk

WOLF SPECIALISTS THE   **T** 0118 971 3330
The UK Wolf Conservation Trust
UK Wolf Centre
Butlers Farm, Beenham
Berks RG7 5NT
E ukwct@ukwolf.org
W www.ukwolf.org

YOUNGBLOOD   **T** 020 7193 3207
Fight Co-ordinators & Directors
E info@youngblood.co.uk
W www.youngblood.co.uk

YOUR GOLF DAY   **T** 0845 1309517
Event Management & Promotions. Specialising in Golf Days
Roche Hill, Bury Road
Rochdale OL11 5EU
E jennifer@yourgolfday.co.uk
W www.yourgolfday.co.uk

Costumes, Wigs & Make-Up

CASE STUDY

Sally Stone is the Costume Hire Manager at West Yorkshire Playhouse Costume Hire - Transformation is our Business.

West Yorkshire Playhouse Costume Hire engulfs the second floor of an old mill building, very close to the theatre itself. The store is home to over two decades of costumes straight from the WYP stages and offers them all for professional or public hire. I lead a dedicated team of volunteers who, on any given day, could be working with customers from theatre, film, television, marketing and production companies to amateur dramatics societies, education and the most stunning and individual weddings and fancy dress parties across the country. My team's enthusiasm for the tens of thousands of items in their care means each costume goes on to play a part in more weird and wonderful stories than the producer, costumer designer or actor who wore it could ever have anticipated, long after the curtain has dropped.

"The question we get asked most often at Costume Hire is 'How do you get any work done?' From the moment a member of the public, or seasoned professional, enters Costume Hire they're immersed in a world of possibilities, you can see it all over their faces, it is wonderment and the sudden energy to try everything on at once - it is hard to resist, even for us. It certainly makes outlining a day in the life of Costume Hire an almost impossible task.

"It's an intense process and forms a connection between costume and Costume Designer that never ends"

With each and every customer, regardless of background, we start at the end…what do you want to end up with? Who is the character? What is the theme? This is where our team of volunteers come into their own. Acting as adviser and stylist we help customers identify what they need, where to look and how to tailor their choices to their budgets. It's 11am on a Saturday morning and in comes a panic stricken lady with her reluctant husband trailing behind her. "We have party to go to tonight and I'd like to go as a saloon girl". Her husband is much less specific, "I hate dressing up…" he says with a roll of the eye. Rest assured – get that man in a frock coat and before long he is sporting thigh high boots, a tricorn and swinging his cutlass shouting "ahoy there me hearties". Transformation is our business and it's magical to see it unfold before your eyes.

But, as with any production our costumes are from, there is always more than one storyline ongoing at Costume Hire. As our Saloon Girl and Pirate return to their original identities we have a student taking pictures for a college project, the cast of an amateur dramatics group busy having a costume fitting and a Theatre in Education company arriving to collect their regular fortnightly order, all whilst I am on the phone arranging a one-to-one, out of hours appointment, with the costume designer working on the BBC drama, The Great Train Robbery.

But how did these costumes first come to life? This is down to the expertise of the West Yorkshire Playhouse wardrobe department, who create or source every facet of a character's costume. It's an intense process and forms a connection between costume and Costume Designer that never ends, the department is always on hand to advise and share their skills in maintaining and repairing the costumes in our care. Costume Hire also exists as a living archive for the Wardrobe Department, meaning the whole team are very familiar faces and can often be seen to-ing and fro-ing between the two buildings pushing shopping trollies laden with Costume Hire stock. The 1980's section was recently raided by the team when costuming our production of Little Voice, 70% of the show was costumed from our stock.

Costume Hire also has close relationships with other departments at West Yorkshire Playhouse, such as the costume-based workshops we deliver to schools through the Arts Development team and our mobile Photo-Booth Dress-Up experience, which has supported Marketing Department activities within the theatre and raised awareness of Costume Hire at external events and private parties.

In my role as Costume Hire Manager it is my responsibility to foster all of the relationships between colleagues, volunteers and our customers, to orchestrate the care and maintenance of our vast costume stock (doing more loads of washing than one human should ever have to do in one life time!) and ensuring I build a profit that is then fed back into the theatre and helps fund future productions and further costume making. Costume Hire is a vital cog in the machine that is West Yorkshire Playhouse and, I like to think, perhaps the best dressed one!"

To find our more visit www.wyp.org.uk/about-us/what-we-do/costume-hire

ACADEMY COSTUMES LTD
T 020 7620 0771
50 Rushworth Street
London SE1 0RB
E info@academycostumes.com
W www.academycostumes.com

ADMIRAL COSTUMES
T 01908 372504
Contact: Ruth Hewitt
86 Westbrook End
Newton Longville
Milton Keynes, Bucks MK17 0BX
E info@admiralcostumes.co.uk
W www.admiralcostumes.co.uk

ALL-SEWN-UP
T/F 01422 843407
Specialise in accurate, practical & reproductions of historical costumes
3 Brunswick Street
Hebden Bridge
West Yorkshire HX7 6AJ
E nwheeler_allsewnup@hotmail.com
W www.allsewnup.org.uk

ANELLO & DAVIDE
T 020 7938 2255
Bespoke Handmade Shoes
15 St Albans Grove, London W8 5BP
E enquiries@handmadeshoes.co.uk
W www.handmadeshoes.co.uk

ANGELS
T 020 7836 5678
Fancy Dress. Revue
119 Shaftesbury Avenue
London WC2H 8AE
F 020 7240 9527
E fun@fancydress.com
W www.fancydress.com

ANGELS THE COSTUMIERS
T 020 8202 2244
1 Garrick Road
London NW9 6AA
F 020 8202 1820
E angels@angels.uk.com
W www.angels.uk.com

ANTOINETTE COSTUME HIRE
T 020 3490 8060
Events. Film. Stage
Rear of 184-190 Farnaby Road
Bromley, Kent BR2 0BB
E antoinettehire@aol.com
W www.costumehirelondon.com

ARMS & ARCHERY
T 01920 460335
Armour. Banners. Chainmail. Medieval Tents. Warrior Costumes. Weaponry
Thrift Lane, Off London Road
Ware, Herts SG12 9QS
E armsandarchery@btconnect.com

ATTLE COSTUMIERS LTD
T 01932 341600
Contact: Jamie Attle. Costume Services for Theatre, Film & Television for hire, bespoke and alterations. Specialist in costumes for Pantomime
Unit 5, Trade City
Avro Way
Brooklands, Weybridge
Surrey KT13 0YF
E info@attlecostumiers.com
W www.attlecostumiers.com

BAHADLY, R.
T 01625 615878
Hair & Make-up Artist. Hair Extensions. Bald Caps. Ageing & Casualty. Available for Test Shots
47 Ploughmans Way
Macclesfield
Cheshire SK10 2UN
T 07973 553073
E rosienico@hotmail.co.uk

BALLETPRO LTD,
THE GRISHKO DISTRIBUTORS
T 01223 861425
Importer & Distributor of Dance Shoes & Dancewear
The Old Sunday School, Chapel Street
Waterbeach, Cambridge CB25 9HR
F 01223 280388
E info@grishko.co.uk
W www.grishko.co.uk

BELLIN HANSEN, Sophie
COSTUME SUPERVISOR
MAKER
T 07726 181148
Specialist in Dance & Physical Disciplines
E sophie.bellinhansen@hotmail.com
W www.sophiebellin.eu

BERTRAND, Henry
T 020 7424 7000
London Stockhouse for Silk
52 Holmes Road, London NW5 3AB
F 020 7424 7001
E dberke@henrybertrand.co.uk
W www.henrybertrand.co.uk

BIRMINGHAM COSTUME HIRE
T 0121 622 3158
Suites 209-210, Jubilee Centre
130 Pershore Street
Birmingham B5 6ND
F 0121 622 2758
E info@birminghamcostumehire.co.uk
W www.facebook.com/BirminghamCostume

BLAIR, Julia
T 07917 877742
Make-up Artist. Film. Photographic. Stage. Television
6A Boston Parade
London W7 2DG
E julia0blair@gmail.com
W www.juliablair.co.uk

BRADLEY-HILL, Justine
T 07962 177733
Bespoke Milliner
The Studio, 29 Green Lane
Addingham, Ilkley
West Yorkshire LS29 0JH
E info@justinebradley-hill.co.uk
W www.justinebradley-hill.co.uk

BRIGGS, Ron DESIGN
T 020 8444 8801
Theatrical Tailors. Costume Design & Making. Bespoke Embroidery. Rhinestone Application
1 Bedford Mews
London N2 9DF
E costumes@ronbriggs.com
W www.ronbriggs.com

BURGESS, Romy
T 07731 633865
Hair & Theatrical Make-up Artist
Flat 2, Rochester Mansions
Hove BN3 2HA
E romy_932@hotmail.com

BURLINGTONS BOUTIQUE T 020 3617 6111
Hairdressers, Make-up, Photography Studio
14 John Princes Street, London W1G 0JS
E reception@burlingtonsboutique.com
W www.burlingtonsboutique.com

CALICO FABRICS T 07986 385434
*Suppliers of Unbleached Calico Fabrics for Stage,
Costumes, Backdrops plus Cotton, Silks, Linens,
Jersey, Tweeds, Velvets including Liberty Prints & James
Hare Silks*
E amir@calicofabrics.co.uk
W www.calicofabrics.co.uk

CAPEZIO LONDON T 020 7379 6042
Dance Products
33 Endell Street, London WC2H 9BA
E capeziolondon@capezio.com
W www.capezioeurope.com

CHRISANNE LTD T 020 8640 5921
Specialist Fabrics & Accessories for Dance & Stage
110-112 Morden Road, Mitcham, Surrey CR4 4XB
F 020 8640 2106
E sales@chrisanne.com
W www.chrisanne.com

CLANRANALD COSTUME T 01877 331166
St Kessogs, Ancaster Square, Callander FK17 8ED
E info@clanranald.org
W www.clanranald.org

CLASSIQUE DANCE SHOP T 023 9223 3334
3-5 Stakes Hill Road, Waterlooville
Hampshire PO7 7JB
E audreyhersey@gmail.com
W www.classiquedance.co.uk

COLTMAN, Mike
See COSTUME CONSTRUCTION LTD

COOK, Sheila TEXTILES T 020 7603 3003
Vintage Textiles, Costumes & Accessories for Sale/Hire
26 Addison Place, London W11 4RJ
E sheilacook@sheilacook.co.uk
W www.sheilacook.co.uk

COSPROP LTD T 020 7561 7300
Accessories. Costumes
469-475 Holloway Road, London N7 6LE
F 020 7561 7310
E enquiries@cosprop.com
W www.cosprop.com

COSTUME BOUTIQUE T 020 7193 6877
Costume Hire for Events & Parties
Unit 26, Acklam Workspace, 10 Acklam Road
London W10 5QZ
T 020 8960 3636
E enquiries@costumeboutique.co.uk
W www.costumeboutique.co.uk

**COSTUME
CONSTRUCTION LTD** T/F 01242 581847
Costumes. Masks. Props. Puppets
Unit 1 Crooks Industrial Estate, Croft Street
Cheltenham GL53 0ED
E mike@costumeconstruction.co.uk
W www.costumeconstruction.co.uk

COSTUME CREATIONS T 01902 738282
10 Olinthus Avenue
Wolverhampton WV11 3DE
E yourcostume@googlemail.com
W www.costumecreations.co.uk

COSTUME SOLUTIONS T 020 7603 9035
Costume Stylist
43 Rowan Road
London W6 7DT
E sequinedslippers@hotmail.com

COSTUME STORE LTD THE T 01273 479727
Costume Accessories
3 Upper Stalls, Iford
Lewes
East Sussex BN7 3EJ
F 01273 477191
E enquiries@thecostumestore.co.uk
W www.thecostumestore.co.uk

COSTUME STUDIO LTD T 020 7275 9614
Costumes. Wigs
Montgomery House
159-161 Balls Pond Road
London N1 4BG
T/F 020 7923 9065
E costume.studio@btconnect.com
W www.costumestudio.co.uk

**COUTURE BEADING &
EMBELLISHMENT** T 020 8925 2714
108 Hiltongrove Business Centre
Hatherley Mews
Walthamstow
London E17 4QP
T 07866 939401
E enquiries@couturebeading.com
W www.couturebeading.com

**CRAZY CLOTHES
CONNECTION** T 020 7221 3989
*Vintage Clothing, Shoes & Accessories. Male & Female.
1920s-1980s. Sale or Hire. Open Fridays/Saturdays
11.30-6.30 only*
134 Lancaster Road
Ladbroke Grove
London W11 1QU
W www.crazy-clothes.co.uk

COSTUME-MAKERS FOR STAGE & SCREEN

tel: 020 8444 8801
RON BRIGGS DESIGN
1 Bedford Mews, London N2 9DF
e.mail: costumes@ronbriggs.com
www.ronbriggs.com

DANCIA INTERNATIONAL
T 020 7831 9483
The Dancer's Shop
168 Drury Lane
London WC2B 5QA
E london@dancia.co.uk
W www.dancia.co.uk/london

DAVIES, Bryan Philip
COSTUMES
T 01323 304391
Lavish Pantomime. Musical Shows. Opera
25 Glynleigh Drive, Polegate
East Sussex BN26 6LU
T 07931 249097
E bryan@bpdcostumes.co.uk
W www.bpdcostumes.co.uk

DELAMAR ACADEMY
T/F 020 8579 9511
Make-up Training
Ealing Studios, Building D, 2nd Floor
Ealing Green, London W5 5EP
E info@delamaracademy.co.uk
W www.delamaracademy.co.uk

DESIGN & ALTER
T 020 7498 4360
Alteration. Re-Styling. Made to Measure
14 Ingate Place, Battersea
London SW8 3NS
E info@designandalter.com
W www.designandalter.com

DR. BOO
T 020 8693 4823
Independent Cosmetic Make-up Studio/Treatment Rooms
22 North Cross Road
East Dulwich
London SE22 9EU
E boogirls@hotmail.co.uk
W www.drboo.co.uk

EASTON, Derek
T/F 01273 588262
Wigs For Film, Stage & Television
1 Dorothy Avenue, Peacehaven
East Sussex BN10 8LP
T 07768 166733
E wigs@derekeastonwigs.co.uk
W www.derekeastonwigs.co.uk

EDA ROSE MILLINERY
T 01491 837174
Ladies' Hats. Design & Manufacture
Lalique, Mongewell
Wallingford, Oxon OX10 8BP
F 01491 835909
E edarose.lawson@btconnect.com

EIA MILLINERY DESIGN /
EIAHATART
T 001 773 206 9330
By Appointment
1620 West Nelson Street
Chicago
Illinois 60657-3027, USA
E info@eiahatart.com

EVOLUTION SETS &
COSTUMES LTD
T 01304 615333
Set & Costume Hire
Langdon Abbey, West Langdon
Dover, Kent CT15 5HJ
F 01304 615353
E dorcas@evolution-productions.co.uk

FOTONICA
T 07840 550097
Contact: Sheree Tams. Design for Set, Costumes, Props & Installations for Stage, Dancer, Opera, Film etc
233 Russell Court, Woburn Place
London WC1H 0ND
E sheree.tams@gmail.com
W www.shereetams.com

FOXTROT COSTUMES &
PROPS LTD
T 020 8964 3555
Armoury Services. Costume & Prop Hire. Firearms
3B Brassie Avenue, East Acton
London W3 7DE
E info@foxtrot-productions.co.uk
W www.foxtrot-productions.co.uk

FREED OF LONDON
T 020 7240 0432
Dance Shoes. Dancewear
94 St Martin's Lane
London WC2N 4AT
F 020 7240 3061
E shop@freed.co.uk
W www.freedoflondon.com

FUNN LTD
T 0870 8743866
Silk, Cotton & Wool Stockings. Opaque Opera Tights. 40's Rayon Stockings (over the Knee, Stay-ups)
26 Arunside (off Blackbridge Lane)
Horsham
West Sussex RH12 1SJ
F 0870 8794450
E funnsales@gmail.com

GAMBA THEATRICAL
See THEATRE SHOES LTD

GAV NICOLA
THEATRICAL SHOES
T 07961 974278
T 00 34 673803783
E gavnicola@yahoo.com
W www.theatricalshoes.com

GILLHAM, Felicite
T 01761 437142
Wig Makers for Film, Opera & Stage
Gallis Ash, Kilmersdon
Near Bath, Somerset BA3 5SZ
T 07802 955908
E felicite@gillywigs.co.uk

GROUNDLINGS
COSTUME HIRE
T 023 9273 9496
Over 11,000 Period & Modern Costumes
42 Kent Street, Portsmouth
Hampshire PO1 3BS
E wardrobe@groundlings.co.uk
W www.groundlings.co.uk

GROVE, Sue DESIGNS
T 023 8078 6849
Costume Designers & Makers. Historical Specialist
12 Ampthill Road, Shirley
Southampton, Hants SO15 8LP
E sue.grove1@tiscali.co.uk

HAIRAISERS
T 020 8965 2500
Hair Extensions. Wigs
9-11 Sunbeam Road, Park Royal
London NW10 6JP
F 020 8963 1600
E info@hairaisers.com
W www.hairaisersshop.com

HAND & LOCK   T 020 7580 7488
Bespoke Embroidery for Costumes, Fashion & Interiors
86 Margaret Street, London W1W 8TE
F 020 7580 7499
E enquiries@handembroidery.com
W www.handembroidery.com

HANSEN, Kasper   T 07847 316196
Set & Costume Designer for Theatre & Dance
T 00 00 4551954050
E contact@kasper-hansen.com
W www.kasper-hansen.com

HARVEYS OF HOVE   T 01273 430323
Military Specialists. Theatrical Costumes
110 Trafalgar Road, Portslade, Sussex BN41 1GS
E harveys.costume@ntlworld.com
W www.harveysofhove.co.uk

HENRY, Lewis LTD   T 020 7636 6683
Dress Makers
111-113 Great Portland Street, London W1W 6QQ
E info@lewishenrydesigns.com

HERON, Cassie
MAKE-UP ARTIST   T 07540 348139
Make-up Artist SFX, Hair Styling. Based in Liverpool
E cassie_14@msn.com

HIREARCHY   T 01202 394465
Classic & Contemporary Costume
45-47 Palmerston Road, Boscombe
Bournemouth, Dorset BH1 4HW
E hirearchy1@gmail.com
W www.hirearchy.co.uk

HISTORY IN THE MAKING   T 023 9225 3175
*Historically Correct Costumes & Armour for Film,
Television & Theatre*
4A Aysgarth Road, Waterlooville, Hampshire PO7 7UG
E info@history-making.com
W www.history-making.com

HODIN, Annabel   T 020 7431 8761
Costume Designer & Stylist. Personal Shopper
12 Eton Avenue, London NW3 3EH
T 07836 754079
E annabelhodin@aol.com

HOPKINS, Trisha   T 01704 873055
6 Willow Grove, Formby L37 3NX
T 07957 368598
E trisha_hopkins@hotmail.co.uk

JULIETTE DESIGNS   T 020 7263 7878
Diamante Jewellery Manufacturers
90 Yerbury Road, London N19 4RS
F 020 7281 7326
E juliettedesigns@hotmail.com
W www.stagejewellery.com

KATIE'S WIGS   T 07900 250853
Wig Supplier & Maker
4 Round Hill Road, Leeds LS28 8BJ
E katie.hunt@katieswigs.com

KIDD, Ella J.   T 01603 304445
*Bespoke Millinery, Wigs & Head-dresses for Film, Stage
& Television*
W www.ellajkidd.co.uk

KRYOLAN UK   T 020 7240 3111
*Professional Make-up for the Film, Theatre & Television
Industries*
22 Tavistock Street, London WC2E 7PY
F 020 7379 3410
E info-uk@kryolan.com
W www.uk.kryolan.com

**LARGER THAN LIFE
STAGEWEAR**   T 020 8466 9010
Theatrical Costumes for Hire
Unit E36 Big Yellow Store, Farwig Lane
Bromley, Kent BR1 3RB
T 07802 717714
E info@largerthanlifestagewear.co.uk
W www.largerthanlifestagewear.co.uk

LG CREATIVE   T 07590 237289
*Contact: Lauren Gregory. Make-up Artist. SFX.
Prosthetics*
15C Healey Street, London NW1 8SR
E lauren@lg-creative.com
W www.lg-creative.com

**MADDERMARKET THEATRE
COSTUME HIRE**   T 01603 626292
Costume & Wig Hire. Period Clothing
St John's Alley, Norwich NR2 1DR
F 01603 661357
E office@maddermarket.org
W www.maddermarket.co.uk

**MAKE-UP
LONDON ACADEMY**   T 020 7272 9848
12 Brecknock Road, London N7 0DD
E info@makeuplondonacademy.com
W www.makeuplondonacademy.com

MARINHO, Margarida   T 07973 216468
*Make-up Artist & Hair Stylist for Film, Television,
Advertising, Editorial & SFX*
E magui@magui.co.uk
W www.mm-mua.co.uk

MASCOTS UK & HIRE LTD   T 01525 405889
*Professional Character Mascot Costumes available to
Hire & Buy*
20 Dunstable Street, Ampthill
Beds MK45 2JT
E sales@mascotuk.com
W www.mascotuk.com

MASTER CLEANERS THE   T 020 7431 3725
*Dry Cleaning of Theatrical Costumes &
Antique Garments*
189 Haverstock Hill, London NW3 4QG
E info@themastercleaners.com
W www.themastercleaners.com

McCORMACK, Mitsuki
*Media Make-up Artist. Make-up, Hair Styling, SFX &
Airbrush*
Based in London
W www.mitsukimccormack.wix.com/mitsuki-mccormack-

McGAHERN, Becky   T 07771 800172
Hair & Make-up Artist
26A Wadley Road, London E11 1JF
E becky@beckymcgahern.com
W www.beckymcgahern.com

MEANANDGREEN.COM T 0845 8991133
British Army Surplus & Military Fashion from around the world
87 Darlington Street, Wolverhampton WV1 4EX
E custserv@meanandgreen.com
W www.meanandgreen.com

MORRIS, Heather T 020 8771 7170
Hair Replacement. Wigs
Fortyseven, 47A Westow Street
Crystal Palace, London SE19 3RW
W www.fortysevenhair.co.uk

NATIONAL THEATRE T 020 7820 1358 (Props)
Costume, Furniture & Props Hire
Chichester House, Kennington Park Estate
1-3 Brixton Road, London SW9 6DE
T 020 7452 3970 (Costume)
E costume_hire@nationaltheatre.org.uk

ONE REPRESENTS LTD T 020 7467 1400
Photographers, Stylists, Creatives, Make-up, Hair
3rd Floor, 66-68 Margaret Street
London W1W 8SR
F 020 7467 1401
E info@onerepresents.com
W www.onerepresents.com

ORIGINAL KNITWEAR T 01726 844807
Contact: Gina Pinnick. Knitwear for Theatre, Film, Television & Advertising includes Stretch Fake Fur
Avalon, Tregoney Hill
Mevagissey, Cornwall PL26 6RG
T 07957 376855
E okcina@btinternet.com
W www.originalknitwear.co.uk

PACE, Terri MAKE-UP ARTIST T 07939 698999
Photographic Beauty. Special Effects. Theatre. Face Painting. Tutoring
E info@terripace.com
W www.terripace.com

PAINTED LADY THE T 07895 820041
Make-up Consultant & Trainer
581 London Road, Stoke on Trent, Staffordshire ST4 5AZ
E ashaleeblueeyes@hotmail.co.uk

PALMER, Johnny T 07961 308885
Wardrobe Manager, Wig & Make-up Artist
4A Queen Square, Glasgow
Lanarkshire G41 2AZ
E jonboyjohnny@yahoo.co.uk

PATEY (LONDON) LTD T 020 8291 4820
The Hat Workshop, Connaught Business Park
Malham Road, London SE23 1AH
F 020 8291 6275
E trevor@pateyhats.com
W www.pateyhats.com

PERIOD COSTUME SHOP T 07975 928857
E lady@periodcostumeshop.co.uk
W www.periodcostumeshop.co.uk

PHA CREATIVES T 0161 273 4444
Hair & Make-up Artists
Tanzaro House, Ardwick Green North
Manchester M12 6FZ
E info@pha-agency.co.uk
W www.pha-agency.co.uk

PINK POINTES DANCEWEAR T/F 01708 438584
1A Suttons Lane, Hornchurch
Essex RM12 6RD
E pink.pointes@btconnect.com
W www.pinkpointes.co.uk

PORSELLI T 0845 0170817
Dancewear, Uniforms, Shoes, Accessories
4 Frensham Road
Sweet Briar Industrial Estate
Norwich NR3 2BT
F 01603 406676
E porselliuk@aol.com
W www.dancewear.co.uk

RAINBOW PRODUCTIONS LTD T 020 8254 5300
Manufacture & Handling of Costume Characters
Unit 3, Green Lea Park
Prince George's Road
London SW19 2JD
F 020 8254 5306
E info@rainbowproductions.co.uk
W www.rainbowproductions.co.uk

REPLICA WAREHOUSE T/F 01477 534075
Costumiers. Props
200 Main Road, Goostrey
Cheshire CW4 8PD
E lesleyedwards@replicawarehouse.co.uk
W www.replicawarehouse.co.uk

ROBBINS, Sheila T 01865 735524
Wig Hire
Broombarn, 7 Ivy Cottages
Hinksey Hill, Oxford OX1 5BQ

ROYAL EXCHANGE THEATRE COSTUME HIRE T/F 0161 819 6660
Period Costumes & Accessories
47-53 Swan Street, Manchester M4 5JY
E costume.hire@royalexchange.co.uk
W www.royalexchange.co.uk

ROYER, Hugo INTERNATIONAL LTD T 01252 878811
Hair & Wig Materials
10 Lakeside Business Park, Swan Lane
Sandhurst, Berkshire GU47 9DN
F 01252 878852
E enquiries@royer.co.uk
W www.hugoroyer.com

RSC COSTUME HIRE T 01789 205920
28 Timothy's Bridge Road
Stratford Enterprise Park
Stratford-upon-Avon
Warwickshire CV37 9UY
E costume.hire@rsc.org.uk

RUMBLE, Jane T 020 8904 6462
Masks, Millinery & Helmets Made to Order
121 Elmstead Avenue, Wembley
Middlesex HA9 8NT

SAGUARO, Jen T 07773 385703
Costume, Drape & Fabric Commissions
35 Southey Street
Bristol BS2 9RE
E jrsaguaro@googlemail.com

SEXTON, Sallyann
T 01923 211644
Hair & Make-up Designer
c/o The Harris Agency Ltd
71 The Avenue
Watford, Herts WD17 4NU
T 07973 802842
E theharrisagency@btconnect.com

SINGER, Sandra ASSOCIATES
T 01702 331616
Fashion Stylists for Stage & Television. Costume/ Designer
21 Cotswold Road
Westcliff-on-Sea
Essex SS0 8AA
E sandrasingeruk@aol.com
W www.sandrasinger.com

SLEIMAN, Hilary
T 020 8555 6176
Specialist & Period Knitwear
72 Godwin Road
London E7 0LG
T 07940 555663
E hilarysleiman1@gmail.com

SOFT PROPS
T 020 7587 1116
Costume & Model Makers
92 Fentiman Road, London SW8 1LA
F 020 7207 0062
E jackie@softprops.co.uk

STAGEWORKS WORLDWIDE PRODUCTIONS
T 01253 342426
Largest Costume Wardrobe in the North
525 Ocean Boulevard
Blackpool FY4 1EZ
F 01253 342702
E simone.bolajuzon@stageworkswwp.com
W www.stageworkswwp.com

STEVENS, Anita
T 07713 132456
Make-up Artist, Airbrush Artist & Hair Stylist. Fashion, Television & Film
Blackheath, London SE3 0SN
E anita@anitastevens.com
W www.anitastevens.com

STRIBLING, Joan
T 07791 758480
Film. Television. Stage Designer. Hair. Make-up. Prosthetics. Fine Art. Music. BBC background. BAFTA Craft, RTS & Design & Arts Director's Awards
Based in London / West Country,
E joanstribling@hotmail.com
W www.joanstribling.co.uk

SWINFIELD, Rosemarie
T 07976 965520
Rosie's Make-up Box. Make-up Design & Training
E rosiesmake-up@uw.club.net
W www.rosemarieswinfield.com

TALK TO THE HAND PUPPETS
T 020 7627 1052
Custom Puppets for Film, Stage & Television
Studio 27B
Spaces Business Centre
15-17 Ingate Place
London SW8 3NS
T 07855 421454
E iestynmevans@hotmail.com
W www.talktothehandpuppets.com

THEATRE SHOES LTD
T 020 8884 4484
Trading as GAMBA Theatrical
Unit 1A, Lee Valley Trading Estate
Rivermead Road, London N18 3QW
F 020 8529 7995
E info@theatreshoes.com

THEATRICAL SHOEMAKERS LTD
T 020 8884 4484
Footwear
Unit 1A, Lee Valley Trading Estate
Rivermead Road
London N18 3QW
E info@theatreshoes.com
W www.shoemaking.co.uk

TRYFONOS, Mary MASKS
T 020 7502 7883
Designer & Maker of Masks & Costume Properties
59 Shaftesbury Road
London N19 4QW
T 07764 587433
E marytryfonos@aol.com

WEST YORKSHIRE FABRICS LTD
T/F 0113 225 6550
Barathea. Crepe. Linen. Stretch Fabrics. Suiting. Venetian. Cut Lengths
Unit 5 Milestone Court
Stanningley
Leeds LS28 6HE
E neil@wyfabrics.com

WEST YORKSHIRE PLAYHOUSE
T 0113 213 7242
Costume Hire
6 St Peter's Building
St Peter's Square
Leeds, West Yorkshire LS2 8AH
E sally.stone@wyp.org.uk
W www.wyp.org.uk/about-us/what-we-do/costume-hire

WIG ROOM LTD THE
T 01256 415737
22 Coronation Road, Basingstoke
Hants RG21 4HA
E darren@wigroom.co.uk

WIG SPECIALITIES LTD
T 020 7724 0020
Handmade Wigs, Facial Hair & Wig Hire
77 Ashmill Street
London NW1 6RA
F 020 7724 0069
E wigspecialities@btconnect.com
W www.wigspecialities.co.uk

WIGS BY TRACEY BRIDGE
T 01453 765329
21A Dudbridge Meadow, Dudbridge
Stroud, Gloucestershire GL5 3NH
T 07505 529039
E wigsbytraceybridge@yahoo.com
W www.wigsbytraceybridge.com

WIGS, MAKE-UP & COSTUME SPECIALIST
T 07516 323000
12 Waterford Lane, Witney
Oxfordshire OX28 1GB
E rachellisajones@hotmail.co.uk

WILLIAMS, Emma
T 07710 130345
Costume Designer & Stylist. Film, Stage & Television
E ewuk@mac.com

D →

DRAMA UK
For information about Drama UK
please see:
W www.dramauk.co.uk

CDET
For information
regarding membership
of the Council for Dance
Education and Training
please see:
W www.cdet.org.uk

Dance Companies

How do I become a professional dancer?

Full-time vocational training can start from as young as ten years old. A good starting point for researching the different schools and courses available is CDET (Council for Dance Education & Training) www.cdet.org.uk. There are many dance colleges offering professional training accredited by CDET, and nearly three hundred university courses which include some form of dance training. It is estimated that over one thousand dancers graduate from vocational training schools or university courses every year, so it is a highly competitive career. Therefore anyone wanting to be a professional dancer must obtain as many years of training and experience as possible, plus go to see plenty of performances spanning different types and genres of dance. If you require further information on vocational dance schools, applying to accredited dance courses, auditions and funding, contact CDET's information line 'Answers for Dancers' on 020 7240 5703.

What are dance companies?

There are more than two hundred dance companies in the UK, spanning a variety of dance styles including ballet, contemporary, hip hop and African. A dance company will either be resident in a venue, be a touring company, or a combination of both. Many have websites which you can visit for full information. Most dance companies employ ensemble dancers on short to medium contracts, who may then work on a number of different productions for the same company over a number of months. In addition, the company will also employ principal/leading dancers on a role-by-role basis.

What are dance organisations?

There are numerous organisations which exist to support professional dancers; covering important areas including health and safety, career development, networking and legal and financial aspects. Other organisations (e.g. regional/ national dance agencies) exist to promote dance within the wider community.

I have already trained to be a dancer. Why do I need further training?

Dance training should not cease as soon as you get your first job or complete a course. Throughout your career you should continuously strive to maintain your fitness levels, enhance and develop your existing skills and keep learning new ones in order to retain a competitive edge. You must also be prepared to continuously learn new dance styles and routines for specific roles. Ongoing training and classes can help you stay fit and active, and if you go through a period of unemployment you can keep your mind and body occupied, ready to take on your next job.

How should I use these listings?

The following listings will supply you with up-to-date contact details for a wide range of dance companies and organisations, followed by listings for dance training and professional classes. Members of CDET have indicated their membership status under their name. Always research schools and classes thoroughly, obtaining copies of prospectuses where available. Most vocational schools offer two and three year full-time training programmes, many also offer excellent degree programmes. Foundation courses offer a sound introduction to the profession, but they can never replace a full-time vocational course. Many schools, studios and organisations also offer part-time/evening classes which offer a general understanding of dance and complementary technique or the opportunity to refresh specific dance skills; they will not, however, enable a student to become a professional dancer.

How else can I find work as a dancer?

Dance also plays a role in commercial theatre, musicals, opera, film, television, live music and video, corporate events and many other industries. Dancers may also want to be represented by an agent. Agents have many more contacts within the industry than an individual dancer can have and can offer advice and negotiate contracts on your behalf as well as submit you for jobs. A number of specialist dance agencies are listed in the 'Agents: Dance' section.

Dance Companies

What other careers are available in dance?

Opportunities also exist to work as a teacher, choreographer, technician or manager. For information about teaching, contact CDET. Dance UK (www.danceuk.org) is a good source for information for anyone considering working in a supporting role within the industry.

What should I do to avoid injury?

An injury is more likely to occur if you are inflexible and unprepared for sudden physical exertion. The last thing you want to do is to pick up an injury, however minor, and be prevented from working, so continuous training during both employment and unemployment will help you to minimise the risk of an injury during a performance or rehearsal. If you do sustain an injury you will want to make sure it does not get any worse by getting treatment with a specialist. The British Association for Performing Arts Medicine (BAPAM) provides specialist health support for performers, free health assessment clinics and a directory of performing arts health practitioners and specialists. Visit www.bapam.org.uk for more information.

I'm not a professional dancer but I enjoy dancing. Why should I use these listings?

People don't just dance to perform, teach or advise within the industry. Dance can be pursued for fun, recreation, social reasons and for health. Training and professional advice should still be pursued to ensure that you do not injure yourself while dancing and prevent yourself from working. You can also use the 'Dance Training & Professional Classes' listings to find suitable dance lessons in your area, which you could attend to make friends, keep fit and stay occupied.

Where can I find more information?

For further advice about the dance industry, you could try contacting CDET (www.cdet.org.uk) for training information, Dance UK (www.danceuk.org) regarding the importance and needs of dance and dancers, or BAPAM (www.bapam.org.uk) for health issues.

You may want to get involved with MOVE IT! – the UK's biggest dance exhibition which takes place every year in the spring. For more information visit www.moveitdance.co.uk. If you are looking for a dance agent to promote you to job opportunities, please see the 'Agents: Dance' section of Contacts.

CASE STUDY

Joanne Lyons is the general manager at Candoco Dance Company; the contemporary dance company of disabled and non-disabled dancers, founded in 1991.

We produce excellent and profound experiences for audiences and participants that excite, challenge and broaden perceptions of art and ability, and place people and collaboration at the heart of our work. Achieving excellence through inclusive practice.

Candoco works hard to promote 'inclusive practice' in the mainstream dance sector and the arts at large, i.e. making the arts accessible for all. We believe that including people in all their diversity makes for excellent, interesting and groundbreaking dance.

"The more open you are to seeking out different people to work with and to learning from them, the more exciting your creative processes will be"

Of course the artistic product has to be of the highest level in order to make the biggest impact and help change people's perceptions of 'who can dance'. That is why Candoco is always seeking out the best people we can work with and those who clearly have bags of potential to develop.
Here are our top tips for dancers, choreographers or others involved in dance, to improve your game and get yourself in the door.

1. Get training and experience
Candoco knows that vocational training, in particular, is very hard to access for some (e.g. disabled people). That is why we, as a company, consider auditionees and collaborators not only on the basis of their dance training, but also on the basis of their natural performance skills and comparable dance experience.
Whatever training or experience you are able to access, use it all to gain a deep knowledge of your own body and how it moves. This will give you confidence in your own movement style, ensuring you have a strong basis from which to develop.

2. Explore
Gain a good breadth of experience by exposing yourself to different opportunities and by challenging yourself to regularly step out of your comfort zone. Repertory companies, in particular, work with a range of choreographers who may use a variety of creative approaches. Therefore, the more versatile a dancer you are and the broader your skillset the better. A good approach is to attend open classes with different companies, especially those you have little connection with (e.g. if you're a contemporary dancer, go do some hip hop).

3. Collaborate
The vast majority of dance companies consist of more than one dancer and it is inevitable that you will work within many different teams in many different contexts during your career, whether you are a dancer, choreographer or other artistic collaborator. The more open you are to seeking out different people to work with and to learning from them, the more exciting your creative processes will be and the richer the eventual artistic product.

4. Build relationships
Amidst the immense competition of the dance sector, building relationships is one way to get noticed with companies and collaborators you are interested in working with. For example, attend workshops or a summer school with a company you like the look of. Chat with their dancers and find out about their methodology. Make yourself known to the artistic director and show them how keen you are. Engage with them online and go to see their shows. Invite them to your shows and ask for feedback.

5. Submit excellent applications
Finally, audition applicants often fall at the very first hurdle with poor applications. Here are some practical tips for your application:

- Read the application guidelines thoroughly and follow them, e.g. if the guidelines say "CVs not accepted", don't submit your CV.

- Have someone else proofread your application documents for typos and inconsistent formatting. These documents are what you sell yourself with, so make sure they make sense and are free of mistakes. The tone should be friendly but formal – remember you are a professional.

- Include, in your cover letter or personal statement, why it is you are applying for this position and this company. You need to set yourself apart from the other applicants, so the clearer you are on your reasons for applying the stronger the application.

To be kept informed of training opportunities with Candoco, visit www.candoco.co.uk/mailing-list/ To find out more email info@candoco.co.uk or "like" us on Facebook

**AKADEMI SOUTH
ASIAN DANCE UK**　　T 020 7691 3210
Hampstead Town Hall
213 Haverstock Hill, London NW3 4QP
E info@akademi.co.uk
W www.akademi.co.uk

ANJALI DANCE COMPANY　　T 01295 251909
The Mill Arts Centre
Spiceball Park
Banbury, Oxfordshire OX16 5QE
E info@anjali.co.uk
W www.anjali.co.uk

BALLET CYMRU　　T 01633 892927
E dariusjames@welshballet.co.uk
W www.welshballet.co.uk

BALLETBOYZ　　T 020 8549 8814
52A Canbury Park Road
Kingston-Upon-Thames, Surrey KT2 6JX
E info@balletboyz.com
W www.balletboyz.com

**BALLROOM, LONDON
THEATRE OF**　　T 020 8722 8798
Contact: Paul Harris® (Artistic Director)
24 Montana Gardens
Sutton, Surrey SM1 4FP
E office@paulharris.uk.com
W www.londontheatreofballroom.com

**BIRMINGHAM
ROYAL BALLET**　　T 0121 245 3500
Thorp Street, Birmingham B5 4AU
F 0121 245 3570
E brbinfo@brb.org.uk
W www.brb.org.uk

CANDOCO DANCE COMPANY　　T 020 7704 6845
2T Leroy House, 436 Essex Road
London N1 3QP
F 020 7704 1645
E info@candoco.co.uk
W www.candoco.co.uk

COMPANY OF CRANKS　　T 07963 617981
1st Floor, 62 Northfield House
London SE15 6TN
E mimetic16@yahoo.com
W www.mimeworks.com

**CREATIVE KIDZ STAGE SCHOOL
& PERFORMANCE TEAM**　　T 07908 144802
Samuel Lewis Trust Community Centre, Vanston Place
Fulham, London SW6 1AS
T 020 7381 3684
E info@creativekidzandco.co.uk
W www.creativekidzandco.co.uk

DAVIES, Siobhan DANCE　　T 020 7091 9650
*Investigative Contemporary Arts Organisation, Applying
Choreography across a Wide Range of Creative Disciplines*
Siobhan Davies Studios, 85 St George's Road
London SE1 6ER
E info@siobhandavies.com
W www.siobhandavies.com

DV8 PHYSICAL THEATRE　　T 020 7655 0977
Artsadmin, Toynbee Studios
28 Commercial Street
London E1 6AB
F 020 7247 5103
E dv8@artsadmin.co.uk
W www.dv8.co.uk

ENGLISH NATIONAL BALLET LTD T 020 7581 1245
Markova House, 39 Jay Mews
London SW7 2ES
F 020 7225 0827
E info@ballet.org.uk
W www.ballet.org.uk

ENGLISH YOUTH BALLET T 01689 856747
Appledowne, The Hillside
Orpington, Kent BR6 7SD
T 07732 383600
E misslewis@englishyouthballet.co.uk
W www.englishyouthballet.co.uk

GREEN CANDLE DANCE COMPANY T 020 7739 7722
Oxford House, Derbyshire Street
Bethnal GreeN, London E2 6HG
E info@greencandledance.com
W www.greencandledance.com

IJAD DANCE COMPANY T 07930 378639
33 Allison Road, London NW10 2DD
E hello@ijaddancecompany.com
W www.ijaddancecompany.com

JEYASINGH, Shobana DANCE COMPANY T 020 7697 4444
Omnibus Office 113, 39-41 North Road
London N7 9DP
E admin@shobanajeyasingh.co.uk
W www.shobanajeyasingh.co.uk

KHAN, Akram COMPANY T 020 7354 4333
Screenworks, Unti 311
22 Highbury Grove
London N5 2ER
E office@akramkhancompany.net
W www.akramkhancompany.net

KOSH THE T/F 020 7263 7419
Physical Theatre
59 Stapleton Hall Road, London N4 3QF
E info@thekosh.com

LUDUS DANCE T 01524 35936
Assembly Rooms, King Street, Lancaster LA1 1RE
F 01524 847744
E info@ludusdance.org
W www.ludusdance.org

NEW ADVENTURES T 020 7713 6766
Sadler's Wells, Rosebery Avenue
London EC1R 4TN
E info@new-adventures.net
W www.new-adventures.net

NORTHERN BALLET T 0113 220 8000
2 St Cecilia Street, Quarry Hill, Leeds LS2 7PA
F 0113 220 8001
E info@northernballet.com
W www.northernballet.com

PAVILION DANCE SOUTH WEST T 01202 203630
Westover Road, Bournemouth BH1 2BU
E info@pdsw.org.uk
W www.pdsw.org.uk

PHOENIX DANCE THEATRE T 0113 236 8130
2 St Cecilia Street, Quarry Hill
Leeds LS2 7PA
E info@phoenixdancetheatre.co.uk
W www.phoenixdancetheatre.co.uk

PLACE THE T 020 7121 1000
17 Duke's Road, London WC1H 9PY
F 020 7121 1142
E info@theplace.org.uk
W www.theplace.org.uk

PMB PRESENTATIONS LTD T 020 7368 3337
Vicarage House
58-60 Kensington Church Street, London W8 4DB
E info@pmbpresentations.co.uk
W www.pmbpresentations.co.uk

RAMBERT T 020 8630 0600
99 Upper Ground, London SE1 9PP
F 020 8747 8323
E info@rambert.org.uk
W www.rambert.org.uk

ROYAL BALLET THE T 020 7240 1200
Royal Opera House, Covent Garden
London WC2E 9DD
E lettie.heywood@roh.org.uk
W www.roh.org.uk

SCOTTISH BALLET T 0141 331 2931
Tramway, 25 Albert Drive, Glasgow G41 2PE
W www.scottishballet.co.uk

SCOTTISH DANCE THEATRE T 01382 342600
Dundee Repertory Theatre, Tay Square
Dundee DD1 1PB
F 01382 228609
E sdt@scottishdancetheatre.com
W www.scottishdancetheatre.com

SPLITZ THEATRE ARTZ T 01638 577095
Walnut Tree House, 1A New Road
Exning, Newmarket, Suffolk CB8 7JP
E clare@splitz-ta.net
W www.splitz-ta.net

SPRINGS DANCE COMPANY T 07775 628442
65 John Kennedy Court, Newington Green Road
London N1 4RT
E info@springsdancecompany.org.uk
W www.springsdancecompany.org.uk

UNION DANCE T 020 7836 7837
Top Floor, 6 Charing Cross Road, London WC2H 0HG
E corrine.bougaard@uniondance.co.uk
W www.uniondance.co.uk

ZIKZIRA PHYSICAL THEATRE T 020 3674 4432
46 Highlever Road, London W10 6PT
E zz@zikzira.com
W www.zikzira.com

Dance Organisations

ACCELERATE PRODUCTIONS LTD   T 020 3130 4040
Studio Accelerate, 374 Ley Street
Ilford IG1 4AE
E info@accelerate-productions.co.uk
W www.accelerate-productions.co.uk

AKADEMI SOUTH ASIAN DANCE UK   T 020 7691 3210
Hampstead Town Hall
213 Haverstock Hill
London NW3 4QP
E info@akademi.co.uk
W www.akademi.co.uk

ALLIED DANCING ASSOCIATION   T 0151 724 1829
137 Greenhill Road, Mossley Hill
Liverpool L18 7HQ
E carolparryada@yahoo.co.uk

ASSOCIATION OF DANCE OF THE AFRICAN DIASPORA   T 020 7841 7357
Unit A402A, The Biscuit Factory
100 Clements Road, London SE16 4DG
F 020 7833 2363
E info@adad.org.uk
W www.adad.org.uk

AWARENESS THROUGH DANCE   T 0844 2412987
*Using dance to impact social change. Volunteering
opportunities for dancers around the world*
141 Cambridge Street, London SW1V 4QA
E info@awarenessthroughdance.org
W www.awarenessthroughdance.org

BENESH INSTITUTE THE   T 020 7326 8031
36 Battersea Square, London SW11 3RA
E beneshinstitute@rad.org.uk
W www.benesh.org

BRITISH ARTS THE   T 01708 756263
12 Deveron Way, Rise Park
Romford RM1 4UL
E sally.chennelle1@ntlworld.com
W www.britisharts.org

BRITISH ASSOCIATION OF TEACHERS OF DANCING   T 0141 427 3699
Pavilion, 8 Upper Level
Watermark Business Park
315 Govan Road, Glasgow G51 2SE
E enquiries@batd.co.uk
W www.batd.co.uk

BRITISH BALLET ORGANIZATION   T 020 8748 1241
Dance Examining Society. Teacher Training
E info@bbo.org.uk
W www.bbo.org.uk

BRITISH THEATRE DANCE ASSOCIATION   T 0845 1662179
Garden Street, Leicester LE1 3UA
F 0116 251 4781
E info@btda.org.uk
W www.btda.org.uk

CHISENHALE DANCE SPACE   T 020 8981 6617
64-84 Chisenhale Road, Bow
London E3 5QZ
E mail@chisenhaledancespace.co.uk
W www.chisenhaledancespace.co.uk

COUNCIL FOR DANCE EDUCATION & TRAINING (CDET)   T 020 7240 5703
Old Brewer's Yard, 17-19 Neal Street
Covent Garden
London WC2H 9UY
F 020 7240 2547
E info@cdet.org.uk
W www.cdet.org.uk

CRE8 & INNOV8 CIC   T 020 3714 3393
Contact: David Stinson
64B Regents Studios
8 Andrews Road
London E8 4QN
E info@i-path.biz
W www.cre8andinnov8.com

DANCE4   T 0115 941 0773
Twitter: @dance_4
College Street Centre, College Street
Nottingham NG1 5AQ
E info@dance4.co.uk
W www.dance4.co.uk

DANCE BASE NATIONAL CENTRE FOR DANCE   T 0131 225 5525
Twitter: @DanceBase
14-16 Grassmarket, Edinburgh EH1 2JU
E dance@dancebase.co.uk
W www.dancebase.co.uk

DANCE HOUSE   T 0141 552 2442
The Briggait, 141 Bridgegate
Glasgow G1 5HZ
E info@dancehouse.org
W www.dancehouse.org

DANCE IN DEVON   T 01803 868116
Dartington Space, Dartington Hall
Totnes, Devon TQ9 6EN
E info@danceindevon.org.uk
W www.danceindevon.org.uk

DANCEEAST   T 01473 295230
Jerwood DanceHouse
Foundry Lane
Ipswich IP4 1DW
E info@danceeast.co.uk
W www.danceeast.co.uk

DANCE MANCHESTER   T 0161 232 7179
Z-arts, Stretford Road
Hulme, Manchester M15 5ZA
E info@dancemanchester.org.uk
W www.dancemanchester.org.uk

DANCERS' CAREER DEVELOPMENT   T 020 7831 1449
Twitter: @dcd_dancers
Plouviez House, 19-20 Hatton Place
London EC1N 8RU
E admin@thedcd.org.uk
W www.thedcd.org.uk

DANCE UK   T 020 7713 0730
*Including the Healthier Dancer Programme & The National
Institute of Dance Medicine & Science*
Unit A402A, The Biscuit Factory
Drummond Road, London SE16 4DG
F 020 7833 2363
E info@danceuk.org
W www.danceuk.org

DANCE UMBRELLA　　T 020 7407 1200
Somerset House, West Wing
Strand, London WC2R 1LA
F 020 7378 8405
E mail@danceumbrella.co.uk
W www.danceumbrella.co.uk

DANCEXCHANGE　　T 0121 689 3170
National Dance Agency
Birmingham Hippodrome, Thorp Street
Birmingham B5 4TB
E info@dancexchange.org.uk
W www.dancexchange.org.uk

DAVIES, Siobhan DANCE　　T 020 7091 9650
*Studio & Events Hires. Professional Development for
Dance Artists*
Siobhan Davies Studios
85 St George's Road, London SE1 6ER
F 020 7091 9669
E info@siobhandavies.com
W www.siobhandavies.com

EAST LONDON DANCE　　T 020 8279 1050
Stratford Circus, Theatre Square, London E15 1BX
E office@eastlondondance.org
W www.eastlondondance.org

EVERYBODY DANCE　　T 07870 429528
*Contact: Rachel Freeman. Aerial & Community Dance for
Disabled & Non-disabled Artists of All Ages*
Longlands Barn, Whitbourne
Worcester, Worcestershire WR6 5SG
E rfeverybodydance@gmail.com

GREENWICH DANCE　　T 020 8293 9741
The Borough Hall, Royal Hill
London SE10 8RE
E info@greenwichdance.org.uk
W www.greenwichdance.org.uk

**IDTA (INTERNATIONAL DANCE
TEACHERS' ASSOCIATION)**　　T 01273 685652
International House, 76 Bennett Road
Brighton, East Sussex BN2 5JL
F 01273 674388
E info@idta.co.uk
W www.idta.co.uk

**IMPERIAL SOCIETY OF
TEACHERS OF DANCING**　　T 020 7377 1577
*Examination Board & Educational Charity offering Dance
Teacher Qualifications*
22-26 Paul Street, London EC2A 4QE
F 020 7655 8869
E marketing@istd.org
W www.istd.org

**LANGUAGE OF
DANCE CENTRE**　　T 020 7749 1131
Oxford House, Derbyshire Street, London E2 6HG
E info@lodc.org
W www.lodc.org

**LONDON CONTEMPORARY
DANCE SCHOOL**　　T 020 7121 1111
The Place, 17 Duke's Road, London WC1H 9PY
F 020 7121 1142
E lcds@theplace.org.uk
W www.lcds.ac.uk

LUDUS DANCE　T 01524 35936
The Assembly Rooms, King Street
Lancaster LA1 1RE
E info@ludusdance.org
W www.ludusdance.org

MDI　T 0151 708 8810
National Dance Agency
24 Hope Street, Liverpool L1 9BX
E info@mdi.org.uk
W www.mdi.org.uk

**NATIONAL RESOURCE
CENTRE FOR DANCE**　T 01483 689316
University of Surrey
Guildford GU2 7XH
F 01483 689500
E nrcd@surrey.ac.uk
W www.surrey.ac.uk/nrcd

**PAVILION DANCE
SOUTH WEST**　T 01202 203630
Pavilion Theatre, Westover Road
Bournemouth BH1 2BU
E info@pdsw.org.uk
W www.pdsw.org.uk

PEOPLE DANCING　T 0116 253 3453
LCB Depot, 31 Rutland Street
Leicester LE1 1RE
F 0116 261 6801
E info@communitydance.org.uk
W www.communitydance.org.uk

PLACE THE　T 020 7121 1000
17 Duke's Road, London WC1H 9PY
F 020 7121 1142
E info@theplace.org.uk
W www.theplace.org.uk

**PROFESSIONAL TEACHERS
OF DANCING**　T 01935 848547
Contact: Jo Pillinger
The Studios, Morcombelake, Dorset DT6 6DY
E ptdenquiries@msn.com
W www.professionalteachersofdancing.co.uk

SOUTH EAST DANCE　T 01273 696844
*National Development Organisation for Dance in South
East England*
28 Kensington Street, Brighton BN1 4AJ
F 01273 697212
E sed@southeastdance.org.uk
W www.southeastdance.org.uk

SWINDON DANCE　T 01793 601700
National Dance Agency
Town Hall Studios, Regent Circus, Swindon SN1 1QF
E info@swindondance.org.uk
W www.swindondance.org.uk

YORKSHIRE DANCE　T 0113 243 9867
Dance Development Agency
3 St Peters Buildings, St Peters Square
Leeds LS9 8AH
E admin@yorkshiredance.com
W www.yorkshiredance.com

Paul Harris®
Choreographer
2014 - 2015

Choreography and Coaching in Period and Contemporary Social Dance

TV: The Great Fire | Call The Midwife
Film: Far From The Madding Crowd (starring Carey Mulligan)

www.paulharris.uk.com | office@paulharris.uk.com | Swing Waltz Pavane Salsa Tango Quadrille Charleston Schottische

---

ACADEMY FOR THEATRE ARTS THE　　　T 01782 660818
1 Vale View, Porthill
Newcastle under Lyme, Staffordshire ST5 0AF
E no1theacademy@aol.com
W www.jillclewes.co.uk

AIRCRAFT CIRCUS LTD　　　T 020 8317 8401
Circus Training & Performance
Unit 7A, Mellish House
Harrington Way, London SE18 5NR
E info@aircraftcircus.com
W www.aircraftcircus.com

ARTS EDUCATIONAL SCHOOLS LONDON　　　T 020 8987 6666
Cone Ripman House, 14 Bath Road
Chiswick, London W4 1LY
E receptionist@artsed.co.uk
W www.artsed.co.uk

ATENEO DELLA DANZA　　　T 00 39 0577 222774
Professional Training Centre
Via dei Pispini 39/45, Siena 53100
Tuscany, Italy
E info@ateneodelladanza.it
W www.ateneodelladanza.it

AVIV DANCE STUDIOS　　　T/F 01923 250000
Watford Boys Grammar School
Rickmansworth Road
Watford WD18 7JF
E info@avivdance.com
W www.avivdance.com

BALLROOM, LONDON THEATRE OF　　　T 020 8722 8798
Artistic Director: Paul Harris® (Mentor "Faking It")
24 Montana Gardens, Sutton
Surrey SM1 4FP
E office@paulharris.uk.com
W www.londontheatreofballroom.com

BHAVAN - HOME OF INDIAN ARTS THE　　　T 020 7381 3086
Training in Indian Classical Music, Dance, Languages & Yoga
4A Castletown Road, London W14 9HE
E info@bhavan.net
W www.bhavan.net

BIG ACT THE　　　T 0117 239 1274
Contact: Martin Williams
14-16 Wilson Place, Bristol BS2 9HJ
E info@thebigact.com
W www.thebigact.com

BIRD COLLEGE DANCE MUSIC & THEATRE PERFORMANCE　　　T 020 8300 6004
CDET Member. Professional Training in Dance & Musical Theatre. HE & FE Programmes
Alma Road, Sidcup, Kent DA14 4EO
F 020 8308 1370
E performance@birdcollege.co.uk
W www.birdcollege.co.uk

BODENS PERFORMING ARTS　　　T 020 8447 0909
Contact: Adam Boden. Acting Workshops. Audition Technique. Dancing. Improvisation. Singing. Part-time. Performing Arts Classes
Bodens Performing Arts
99 East Barnet Road, New Barnet, Herts EN4 8RF
E info@bodens.co.uk
W www.bodens.co.uk

CAMBRIDGE PERFORMING ARTS AT BODYWORK COMPANY DANCE STUDIOS　　　T 01223 314461
CDET Member
Bodywork Company Dance Studios
25-29 Glisson Road, Cambridge CB1 2HA
E admin@bodyworkds.co.uk
W www.bodywork-dance.co.uk

CANDOCO DANCE COMPANY　　　T 020 7704 6845
Company of Disabled & Non-Disabled Dancers
2T Leroy House, 436 Essex Road, London N1 3QP
E info@candoco.co.uk
W www.candoco.co.uk

CENTRAL SCHOOL OF BALLET　　　T 020 7837 6332
Full Time Vocational Training. Open Classes Beginner/ Professional Level
10 Herbal Hill, Clerkenwell Road, London EC1R 5EG
F 020 7833 5571
E info@csbschool.co.uk
W www.centralschoolofballet.co.uk

CENTRE PERFORMING ARTS COLLEGE THE　　　T 01634 848009
CDET Member
681 Maidstone Road, Rochester, Kent ME1 3QJ
E dance@thecentrepac.com
W www.thecentrepac.com

CLASSIQUE SCHOOL OF DANCE　　　T 02392 233334
Ballet. Contemporary. Jazz. Modern. Tap. Stage (2 yrs-Adult). Drama. Singing
3-5 Stakes Hill Road
Waterlooville, Hampshire PO7 7JB
E classique_enquiries@yahoo.co.uk
W www.classiquedance.co.uk

COLLECTIVE DANCE & DRAMA　　　T/F 020 8428 0037
The Studio, Rectory Lane
Rickmansworth, Herts WD3 1FD
E info@collectivedance.co.uk
W www.collectivedance.co.uk

CONTI, Italia ACADEMY OF THEATRE ARTS　　　T 020 7608 0044
CDET Member. Drama UK Member. Courses: Performing Arts Diploma, 3 yr. Performing Arts with Teacher Training, 3 yr. Intensive Performing Arts, Acting, 1 yr. Foundation Performing Arts, 1 yr. BA (Hons) Acting, 3 yr. Foundation Acting, 1 yr. Singing, 1 yr. Theatre Arts School (academic yrs 7-11)
Italia Conti House, 23 Goswell Road, London EC1M 7AJ
E admin@italiaconti.co.uk
W www.italiaconti.com

COUNCIL FOR DANCE EDUCATION & TRAINING (CDET) T 020 7240 5703
Old Brewer's Yard, 17-19 Neal Street
Covent Garden, London WC2H 9UY
F 020 7240 2547
E info@cdet.org.uk
W www.cdet.org.uk

CPA STUDIOS T 01708 766007
CDET Member
The Studios, 219B North Street
Romford, Essex RM1 4QA
E collegeadmin@cpastudios.co.uk
W www.cpastudios.co.uk

D&B SCHOOL OF PERFORMING ARTS & D&B THEATRE SCHOOL T 020 8698 8880
CDET Member
Central Studios, 470 Bromley Road
Bromley, Kent BR1 4PQ
E info@dandbperformingarts.co.uk
W www.dandbperformingarts.co.uk

DANCE BASE NATIONAL CENTRE FOR DANCE T 0131 225 5525
14-16 Grassmarket, Edinburgh EH1 2JU
E dance@dancebase.co.uk
W www.dancebase.co.uk

DANCE HOUSE T 0141 552 2442
The Briggait, 141 Bridgegate
Glasgow G1 5HZ
E info@dancehouse.org
W www.dancehouse.org

DANCE LONDON T 08442 412987
141 Cambridge Street, London SW1V 4QA
E info@dance-london.com
W www.dance-london.com

DANCE RESEARCH COMMITTEE - IMPERIAL SOCIETY OF TEACHERS OF DANCING T 01233 712469
Training in Historical Dance
c/o Ludwell House, Charing
Kent TN27 0LS
F 01233 712768
E n.gainesarmitage@tiscali.co.uk
W www.istd.org

DANCE STUDIO LEEDS LTD THE T 0113 242 1550
Mill 6, 1st Floor, Mabgate Mills
LeedsWest Yorkshire LS9 7DZ
E katie@thedancestudioleeds.com
W www.thedancestudioleeds.com

DANCE STUDIO THE T 020 8360 5700
Evening & Weekend Classes (3-18 yrs)
843-845 Green Lanes, Winchmore Hill
London N21 2RX
E thedancestudio@btconnect.com
W www.thedancestudio.co.uk

DANCEWORKS T 020 7629 6183
Also Fitness, Yoga & Martial Arts Classes
16 Balderton Street, London W1K 6TN
E info@danceworks.net
W www.danceworks.net

DAPA T 01254 699221
Dance. Drama. Music. Singing. All Ages & Abilities
The Wharf Studios
Eanam Wharf
Blackburn, Lancashire BB1 5BY
E info@dapacentre.co.uk
W www.dapa.info

DAVIES, Siobhan STUDIOS T 020 7091 9650
Daily Professional Classes. Open Dance & Body Conditioning Classes for Wider Community
85 St George's Road, London SE1 6ER
F 020 7091 9669
E info@siobhandavies.com
W www.siobhandavies.com

DIRECTIONS THEATRE ARTS CHESTERFIELD LTD T/F 01246 854455
1A-2A Sheffield Road, Chesterfield, Derbyshire S41 7LL
E julie.cox5@btconnect.com
W www.directionstheatrearts.org

D M ACADEMY T 01274 585317
The Studios, Briggate
Shipley, Bradford, West Yorks BD17 7BT
E info@dmacademy.co.uk
W www.dmacademy.co.uk

DUFFILL, Drusilla THEATRE SCHOOL T 01444 232672
Suite F, KBF House, 55 Victoria Road
Burgess Hill, West Sussex RH15 9LH
E drusilladschool@btinternet.com
W www.drusilladuffilltheatreschool.co.uk

EAST LONDON DANCE T 020 8279 1050
Stratford Circus, Theatre Square, London E15 1BX
E office@eastlondondance.org
W www.eastlondondance.org

ELMHURST SCHOOL FOR DANCE T 0121 472 6655
CDET Member
249 Bristol Road, Edgbaston
Birmingham B5 7UH
F 0121 472 6654
E enquiries@elmhurstdance.co.uk
W www.elmhurstdance.co.uk

ENGLISH NATIONAL BALLET SCHOOL T 020 7376 7076
CDET Member
Carlyle Building, Hortensia Road
London SW10 0QS
F 020 7376 3404
E info@enbschool.org.uk
W www.enbschool.org.uk

EXPRESSIONS ACADEMY OF PERFORMING ARTS T 01623 424334
CDET Member
3 Newgate Lane, Mansfield
Nottingham NG18 2LB
E expressions-uk@btconnect.com
W www.expressionsperformingarts.co.uk

GEORGIE SCHOOL OF THEATRE ARTS T/F 01484 606994
101 Lane Head Road, Shepley
Huddersfield, West Yorkshire HD8 8DB
E ken.george1001@gmail.com

GREASEPAINT ANONYMOUS T 020 8360 9785
Flat 13, Oak Lodge, 50 Eversley Park Road
London N21 1JL
T 07930 421216
E info@greasepaintanonymous.co.uk
W www.greasepaintanonymous.co.uk

HAMMOND SCHOOL THE T 01244 305350
CDET Member
Hoole Bank, Mannings Lane, Chester CH2 4ES
F 01244 305351
E info@thehammondschool.co.uk
W www.thehammondschool.co.uk

HARRIS, Paul T 07958 784462
Contact: Paul Harris®. Choreography. Movement for Actors. Tuition in Period & Contemporary Social Dance
24 Montana Gardens, Sutton
Surrey SM1 4FP
E office@paulharris.uk.com
W www.paulharris.uk.com

ISLINGTON ARTS FACTORY T 020 7607 0561
2 Parkhurst Road, London N7 0SF
E info@islingtonartsfactory.org
W www.islingtonartsfactory.org

KS DANCE LTD T 01925 837693
CDET Member
9A Centre 21, Bridge Lane
Woolston, Warrington, Cheshire WA1 4AW
E admin@ksd-online.co.uk
W www.ksd-online.co.uk

LAINE THEATRE ARTS T 01372 724648
CDET Member
The Studios, East Street
Epsom, Surrey KT17 1HH
F 01372 723775
E webmaster@laine-theatre-arts.co.uk
W www.laine-theatre-arts.co.uk

**LIVERPOOL INSTITUTE
FOR PERFORMING ARTS** T 0151 330 3000
CDET Member
Mount Street, Liverpool L1 9HF
E admissions@lipa.ac.uk
W www.lipa.ac.uk

LIVERPOOL THEATRE SCHOOL T 0151 728 7800
CDET Member. Musical Theatre & Professional Classes
19 Aigburth Road, Liverpool, Merseyside L17 4JR
T 07515 282877
E info@liverpooltheatreschool.co.uk
W www.liverpooltheatreschool.co.uk

**LONDON CONTEMPORARY
DANCE SCHOOL** T 020 7121 1111
Full-time Vocational Training at Degree & Postgraduate Level
The Place, 17 Duke's Road, London WC1H 9PY
F 020 7121 1145
E lcds@theplace.org.uk
W www.lcds.ac.uk

**LONDON DANCE
PROGRAMME** T 0844 2412987
77 Blackfriars Road, Number 2, London SE1 8HA
E info@londondanceprogramme.com
W www.londondanceprogramme.com

**LONDON SCHOOL
OF CAPOEIRA** T 020 7281 2020
Unit 1-2 Leeds Place, Tollington Park
London N4 3RF
E info@londonschoolofcapoeira.com
W www.londonschoolofcapoeira.com

LONDON STUDIO CENTRE T 020 7837 7741
CDET Member
Artsdepot, 5 Nether Street
Tally Ho Corner, North Finchley, London N12 0GA
E info@londonstudiocentre.org
W www.londonstudiocentre.org

**MANN, Stella COLLEGE OF
PERFORMING ARTS LTD** T 01234 213331
CDET Member. Professional Training Course for Performers & Teachers
10 Linden Road, Bedford, Bedfordshire MK40 2DA
E stellamanncollege@hotmail.com
W www.stellamanncollege.co.uk

**MGA ACADEMY OF
PERFORMING ARTS THE** T 0131 466 9392
207 Balgreen Road, Edinburgh EH11 2RZ
E info@themgaacademy.com
W www.themgaacademy.com

MIALKOWSKI, Andrzej T 01604 239755
Choreographer. Teacher. IDTA Member. Ballroom. Latin American. Street. Zumba. Ballet
Step By Step Dance School, 24 Henry Street
Northampton, Northamptonshire NN1 4JE
T 07849 331430
E info@danceschool-stepbystep.com
W www.danceschool-stepbystep.com

**MIDLANDS ACADEMY OF
DANCE & DRAMA** T/F 0115 911 0401
CDET Member & Trinity Validated
Century House, Building B
428 Carlton Hill, Nottingham NG4 1QA
E admin@maddcollege.supanet.com
W www.maddcollege.co.uk

**MILLENNIUM PERFORMING
ARTS LTD** T 020 8301 8744
CDET Member
29 Thomas Street, Woolwich, London SE18 6HU
E info@md2000.co.uk
W www.md2000.co.uk

**NEW LONDON PERFORMING
ARTS CENTRE** T 020 8444 4544
Performing Arts Classes (3-19 yrs). Dance Teacher Training ISTD, DDI & DDE. All Dance Styles. GCSE Course. A-Levels. RAD & ISTD Exams
76 St James Lane, Muswell Hill, London N10 3RD
E info@nlpac.co.uk
W www.nlpac.co.uk

**NORTHERN ACADEMY OF
PERFORMING ARTS** T 01482 310690
Anlaby Road, Hull HU1 2PD
F 01482 212280
E napa@northernacadem.org.uk
W www.northernacademy.org.uk

NORTHERN BALLET SCHOOL T 0161 237 1406
CDET Member
The Dancehouse, 10 Oxford Road
Manchester M1 5QA
F 0161 237 1408
E enquiries@northernballetschool.co.uk
W www.northernballetschool.co.uk

**NORTHERN SCHOOL OF
CONTEMPORARY DANCE** T 0113 219 3000
98 Chapeltown Road, Leeds LS7 4BH
E info@nscd.ac.uk
W www.nscd.ac.uk

PERFORMERS COLLEGE T 01375 672053
CDET Member
Southend Road, Corringham
Essex SS17 8JT
E lesley@performerscollege.co.uk
W www.performerscollege.co.uk

PINEAPPLE DANCE STUDIOS T 020 7836 4004
7 Langley Street, London WC2H 9JA
F 020 7836 0803
W www.pineapple.uk.com

PLACE THE T 020 7121 1000
17 Duke's Road, London WC1H 9PY
F 020 7121 1142
E info@theplace.org.uk
W www.theplace.org.uk

PROFESSIONAL TEACHERS OF DANCING   T 01935 848547
Contact: Jo Pillinger
The Studios, Morcombelake, Dorset DT6 6DY
T 07552 667378
E ptdenquiries@msn.com
W www.professionalteachersofdancing.co.uk

RAMBERT SCHOOL OF BALLET & CONTEMPORARY DANCE   T 020 8892 9960
Clifton Lodge, St Margaret's Drive
Twickenham, Middlesex TW1 1QN
F 020 8892 8090
E info@rambertschool.org.uk
W www.rambertschool.org.uk

RETINA DANCE COMPANY   T 0115 947 6202
Weekly Classes. Training. Workshops. Residencies
College Street Centre, College Street
Nottingham NG1 5AQ
E retinadance@uk.com
W www.retinadance.uk.com

RIDGEWAY STUDIOS PERFORMING ARTS CENTRE   T 01992 633775
Cheshunt & Cuffley Studios
Office: 106 Hawkshead Road, Potters Bar
Hertfordshire EN6 1NG
E info@ridgewaystudios.co.uk
W www.ridgewaystudios.co.uk

RIVERSIDE REFLECTIONS BATON TWIRLING TEAM   T/F 01322 410003
34 Knowle Avenue, Bexleyheath, Kent DA7 5LX
T 07958 617976
E clare@riversidereflections.co.uk
W www.riversidereflections.co.uk

ROEBUCK, Gavin   T 020 7370 7324
Classical Ballet
51 Earls Court Square, London SW5 9DG
E info@gavinroebuck.com

ROJO Y NEGRO TANGO   T 020 8520 2726
Argentine Tango Academy
Union Tavern - Upstairs, 52 Lloyd Baker Street
Farringdon, Kings Cross, London WC1X 9AA
T 07748 648322
E info@rojoynegroclub.com
W www.rojoynegroclub.com

ROYAL ACADEMY OF DANCE   T 020 7326 8000
36 Battersea Square, London SW11 3RA
F 020 7924 3129
E info@rad.org.uk
W www.rad.org.uk

SAFREY ACADEMY OF PERFORMING ARTS   T 07956 920813
*Dance. Drama. Singing. Classes at: South London
Liberal Synagogue, 1 Prentis Road
Streatham, London SW16 1ZW*
Correspondence only: S.A.P.A, 10 St Julians Close
London SW16 2RY
E info@safreyarts.co.uk
W www.safreyarts.co.uk

SLP COLLEGE   T 0113 286 8136
CDET Member
5 Chapel Lane, Leeds LS25 1AG
E info@slpcollege.cc.uk
W www.slpcollege.co.uk

STARMAKERZ THEATRE SCHOOL   T 07771 595171
Oxted School, Bluehouse Lane
Oxted, Surrey RH8 0AB
E vicky@starmakerz.co.uk
W www.starmakerz.co.uk

TIFFANY THEATRE COLLEGE   T 01702 710069
969-973 London Road, Leigh on Sea
Essex SS9 3LB
E info@tiffanytheatrecollege.com
W www.tiffanytheatrecollege.com

TRING PARK SCHOOL FOR THE PERFORMING ARTS   T 01442 824255
CDET Member
Tring Park, Tring
Hertfordshire HP23 5LX
E info@tringpark.com
W www.tringpark.com

TRINITY LABAN CONSERVATOIRE OF MUSIC & DANCE   T 020 8305 9400
Creekside, London SE8 3DZ
F 020 8691 8400
W www.trinitylaban.ac.uk

URDANG ACADEMY   T 020 7713 7710
CDET Member
The Old Finsbury Town Hall, Rosebery Avenue
London EC1R 4RP
F 020 7278 6727
E info@theurdangacademy.com
W www.theurdang.london

VALLÉ ACADEMY OF PERFORMING ARTS   T 01992 622862
The Vallé Academy Studios
Wilton House
Delamare Road, Cheshunt
Herts EN8 9SG
F 01992 622868
E enquiries@valleacademy.co.uk
W www.valleacademy.co.uk

WAINWRIGHT, Benjamin   T 07950 811327
Choreography. Teaching
11 Laburnum Avenue, Sunnyside
Rotherham, South Yorkshire S66 3PR
E b-wainwright@live.co.uk

WIVELL, Betty ACADEMY OF PERFORMING ARTS THE   T 020 8764 5500
Ballet. Jazz. Modern. Tap. Drama. Singing
52 Norbury Court Road, Norbury
London SW16 4HT
E ereeves@bettywivell.com
W www.bettywivell.com

YOUNG ACTORS THEATRE   T 020 7278 2101
70-72 Barnsbury Road, Islington
London N1 0ES
E info@yati.org.uk
W www.yati.org.uk

YOUNG, Sylvia THEATRE SCHOOL   T 020 7258 2330
1 Nutford Place, London W1H 5YZ
F 020 7724 8371
E syoung@syts.co.uk
W www.syts.co.uk

ALRA (ACADEMY OF LIVE & RECORDED ARTS)　T 020 8870 6475
Studio 24-25
The Royal Victoria Patriotic Building
John Archer Way
London SW18 3SX
E info@alra.co.uk
W www.alra.co.uk

ARTS EDUCATIONAL SCHOOLS LONDON　T 020 8987 6666
14 Bath Road
London W4 1LY
E receptionist@artsed.co.uk
W www.artsed.co.uk

BIRMINGHAM SCHOOL OF ACTING　T 0121 331 7220
Birmingham City University
Millennium Point
Curzon Street
Birmingham B4 7XG
F 0121 331 7221
E info@bsa.bcu.ac.uk
W www.bcu.ac.uk/bsa

BRISTOL OLD VIC THEATRE SCHOOL　T 0117 973 3535
1-2 Downside Road, Clifton
Bristol BS8 2XF
E enquiries@oldvic.ac.uk
W www.oldvic.ac.uk

CONTI, Italia ACADEMY　T 020 7733 3210
Avondale, 72 Landor Road
London SW9 9PH
E acting@italiaconti.co.uk
W www.italiaconti-acting.co.uk

DRAMA CENTRE LONDON　T 020 7514 7936
Central Saint Martins College of Arts & Design
Granary Building
1 Granary Square
London N1C 4AA
T 020 7514 9363
E drama@arts.ac.uk
W www.arts.ac.uk/csm/drama-centre-london

DRAMA STUDIO LONDON　T 020 8579 3897
Grange Court
1 Grange Road
London W5 5QN
F 020 8566 2035
E admin@dramastudiolondon.co.uk
W www.dramastudiolondon.co.uk

EAST 15 ACTING SCHOOL　T 020 8508 5983
Hatfields, Rectory Lane
Loughton IG10 3RY
E east15@essex.ac.uk
W www.east15.ac.uk

GSA, GUILDFORD SCHOOL OF ACTING　T 01483 684040
University of Surrey
Stag Hill Campus
Guildford, Surrey GU2 7XH
E gsaenquiries@gsa.surrey.ac.uk
W www.gsauk.org

GUILDHALL SCHOOL OF MUSIC & DRAMA　T 020 7628 2571
Silk Street, Barbican
London EC2Y 8DT
E info@gsmd.ac.uk
W www.gsmd.ac.uk

LAMDA　T 020 8834 0500
155 Talgarth Road, London W14 9DA
F 020 8834 0501
E enquiries@lamda.org.uk
W www.lamda.org.uk

LIVERPOOL INSTITUTE FOR PERFORMING ARTS THE　T 0151 330 3000
Mount Street
Liverpool L1 9HF
E reception@lipa.ac.uk
W www.lipa.ac.uk

MANCHESTER SCHOOL OF THEATRE AT MANCHESTER METROPOLITAN UNIVERSITY　T 0161 247 1305
Mabel Tylecote Building
Cavendish Street
Manchester M15 6BG
E theatre@mmu.ac.uk
W www.theatre.mmu.ac.uk

MOUNTVIEW ACADEMY OF THEATRE ARTS　T 020 8881 2201
Ralph Richardson Memorial Studios
Kingfisher Place
Clarendon Road
London N22 6XF
F 020 8829 0034
E enquiries@mountview.org.uk
W www.mountview.org.uk

OXFORD SCHOOL OF DRAMA THE　T 01993 812883
Sansomes Farm Studios
Woodstock
Oxford OX20 1ER
F 01993 811220
E info@oxforddrama.ac.uk
W www.oxforddrama.ac.uk

ROSE BRUFORD COLLEGE　T 020 8308 2600
Lamorbey Park
Burnt Oak Lane
Sidcup, Kent DA15 9DF
F 020 8308 0542
E enquiries@bruford.ac.uk
W www.bruford.ac.uk

ROYAL ACADEMY OF DRAMATIC ART　T 020 7636 7076
62-64 Gower Street
London WC1E 6ED
E enquiries@rada.ac.uk
W www.rada.ac.uk

ROYAL CENTRAL SCHOOL OF SPEECH & DRAMA THE　T 020 7722 8183
Eton Avenue, Swiss Cottage
London NW3 3HY
E enquiries@cssd.ac.uk
W www.cssd.ac.uk

Drama Training

Why do I need drama training?

The entertainment industry is an extremely competitive one, with thousands of performers competing for a small number of jobs. In such a crowded market, professional training will increase an actor's chances of success, and professionally trained artists are also more likely to get representation. Drama training can begin at any age and should continue throughout an actor's career.

I have already trained to be an actor. Why do I need further training?

Drama training should not cease as soon as you graduate or get your first job. Throughout your career you should strive to enhance your existing skills and keep up-to-date with the techniques new actors are being taught, even straight after drama school, in order to retain a competitive edge. You must also be prepared to learn new skills for specific roles if required. Ongoing drama training and classes can help you stay fit and active, and if you go through a period of unemployment you can keep your mind and body occupied, ready to take on your next job.

What kind of training is available?

For the under 18s, stage schools provide specialist training in acting, singing and dancing. They offer a variety of full and part-time courses. After 18, students can attend drama school. The standard route is to take a three-year, full-time course, in the same way you would take a university degree. Some schools also offer one or two-year courses.

What is Drama UK?

Drama UK comprises Britain's leading drama schools. It exists in order to strengthen the voice of the member schools, to set and maintain the highest standards of training within the vocational drama sector, and to make it easier for prospective students to understand the range of courses on offer and the application process. The member schools listed in the section 'Drama Schools: Drama UK' offer courses in Acting, Musical Theatre, Directing and Technical Theatre training. For more information you can visit their website www.dramauk.co.uk

How should I use these listings?

The following listings provide up-to-date contact details for a wide range of performance courses, classes and coaches. Every company listed is done so by written request to us. Some companies have provided contact names, areas of specialisation and a selection of courses on offer.

I want to apply to join a full-time drama course. Where do I start?

Your first step should be to research as many different courses as possible. Have a look on each school's website and request a prospectus. Ask around to find out where other people have trained or are training now and who they recommend. You would be advised to begin your search by considering Drama UK courses. Please refer to the Drama UK Guide to Professional Training in Drama & Technical Theatre for a description of each school, its policy and the courses it offers together with information about funding, available from www.dramauk.co.uk

What types of courses are available?

Drama training courses generally involve three-year degree or diploma courses, or one-year postgraduate courses if you have already attended university or can demonstrate a certain amount of previous experience. Alternatively, short-term or part-time foundation courses are available, which can serve as an introduction to acting but are not a substitute for a full-time drama course.

When should I apply?

Deadlines for applications to drama courses vary between schools so make sure you check each school's individual deadlines. Most courses start in September. If the school you are considering requires you to apply via UCAS, you must submit your application between mid-September 2015 and 15th January 2016 to guarantee that your application will be considered for a course beginning in 2016. You can apply after that until 30th June, but the school is then under no obligation to consider your application.

See www.ucas.ac.uk/students/applying/whentoapply or contact the individual school for more details.

Drama Training

What funding is available to me?

Drama courses are unavoidably expensive. Most students have to fund their own course fees and other expenses, whether from savings, part-time work or a student loan. However, if you are from a low-income household you may qualify for a maintenance grant from the government to cover some of the costs. Some Drama UK accredited courses offer a limited number of students Dance and Drama Awards (DaDA) scholarships, introduced to increase access to dance, drama and stage management training for talented students. These scholarships include help with both course fees and living expenses. Find out what each school offers in terms of potential financial support before applying.

Another possibility is to raise funds from a charity, trust or foundation. As with applying to agents and casting professionals for representation and work, do your research first and target your letters to explain how your needs meet each organisation's objectives, rather than sending a generalised letter to everyone. You are much more likely to be considered if you demonstrate that you know the background of the organisation and what they can offer performers.

How can my child become an actor?

If your child is interested in becoming an actor, they should try to get as much practical experience as possible. They could also join a stage school or sign with an agent. Contact details for stage schools can be found among the listings in this section. Please also see the 'Agents: Children & Teenagers' section for more information.

What about other forms of training?

Building on your initial acting course is essential for both new and more experienced actors. There are so many new skills you can learn – you could take stage fighting classes, hire a vocal coach, attend singing and dance lessons and many more. These will enhance your CV and will give you a competitive edge. It is also extremely useful to take occasional 'refresher' courses on audition skills, different acting techniques and so on in various forms such as one-to-one lessons, one-off workshops or evening classes, to make sure you are not rusty when your next audition comes along.

Where can I find more information?

The Actors Centre runs over 1700 classes and workshops a year to encourage performers to develop their talent throughout their career in a supportive environment. They also run introductory classes for people who are interested in becoming actors but currently have no training or experience. Visit their website www.actorscentre.co.uk for more information.

The Actors' Guild (TAG) offers on-going professional development for actors in the UK, through actor-led workshops and services. See www.actorsguild.co.uk for more information.

You may also want to refer to the 'Dance Training & Professional Classes' section for listings which will help you to add additional skills to your CV as well as keep fit. If you are interested in a career behind rather than in front of the camera or stage, please see the Drama UK Guide to Careers Backstage, available from www.dramauk.co.uk

Rosalind Eleazar

Photo: Wolf Marloh

Rosalind trained at the London Academy of Music and Dramatic Art (LAMDA) on the two year Foundation Degree for Professional Acting Course. She was the winner of the Spotlight Prize at the Showcase in 2015.

I had already studied Spanish and Mandarin at University, so I wanted to choose a course that was shorter than three years but still had the 100% practical element that most three year courses have. So the LAMDA two year course seemed perfect for me and I was lucky enough to gain a place.

Drama school is very intense to say the least! I remember my first term being one of the most difficult times of my life. Drama training requires you to take huge risks, fall on your face, and be exceptionally vulnerable, open and trusting which really took its toll on me. However, after getting through this testing time (which most people have at some point during their training) you realise how worth every penny training is.

The highlight of my training was spending two years with my year group. It's incredible how close you become. As cheesy as it sounds, this group of people will be there to support you when you fall and celebrate when you succeed. Literally the friendships you make are priceless.

Some advice I could give, is to treat your fellow classmates with kindness. There will come a time when you need them to be by your side, so look after each other. Take as many risks as you possibly can (easier said than done, I know) but looking back on my time, when I learnt the most is when I failed. Try not to be defensive, teachers are only trying to make us the best we can be and because we can be highly sensitive people (obviously, we are actors!), sometimes we take things too personally. When it comes to getting agents etc. in your final year, know that things happen for people at different times and try not to compare yourself to anyone else. Good luck!

Edward Bluemel

Photo: Craig Sugden

Edward trained at the Royal Welsh College of Music and Drama. He was awarded the highly commended actor award at the Spotlight Prize at the Showcase in 2015.

Who knows why any of us decide to become actors. All we are told as we go through countless school plays, youth theatre classes and a weird amount of homemade videos of us doing news reading (possibly this one was just me?) is that it is a mistake - that we will fail and be miserable and poor and maybe become drama teachers if we are lucky. Now do we do it because we can't resist sinking our teeth into a nice, juicy text? Possibly. Is it because we just 'love to make an audience feel something'? Perhaps. Or is it because we are actually a bunch of thinly veiled egotists who are all massive show offs? Let's face it, probably.

But there is something else. A need. No one goes 'I'd love to be a doctor but actually I think I'm more likely to have success as an actor so I'll do that'. This profession is never a second choice. All of us do this because we HAVE to do it. To us there is no other way. We are actors, we have made our decision to be actors and we will try and try and try until we succeed/run out of food.

Now in drama school, people understand this and you are surrounded by individuals in the same position as you. Day in, day out you train with these people and you make each other better. My classmates at school were an inspiration to me on a daily basis and together we improved as a year and more importantly, as an ensemble.

My journey to drama school was fairly regular and I was lucky with the support I received. I went to a school which did an annual Shakespeare and a bi-annual musical. I even had the opportunity to co-write, direct and star in a play at the Edinburgh Fringe which received a total of seven stars. To then help get into drama school I went to The Actor's Workshop in Bristol which expertly prepared me for drama school auditions and sure enough I got in.

My training has easily been the most challenging and enjoyable experience of my life. I now feel prepared and ready to take on this profession face first and if you're mad enough, you should do it too so we can prove all the nay-sayers wrong and all those obscure family friends who said 'well remember me when you're in Hollywood! right.'

Drama Training

CASE STUDY

Edinburgh born and bred, Jo Cameron Brown studied at the Royal Scottish Academy of Drama, before her 25 odd years in acting, and then as a post-graduate in voice and dialect studies at Central.

She now combines a successful acting career in television (from Outlander, The Singing Detective to soaps) and theatre (from the NTS & Glasgow Citizens to the RNT and West End) with a busy time coaching actors including: Sean Bean, Jamie Bell, Helena Bonham Carter, Jessica Chastain, Lindsay Duncan, Joseph Fiennes, Ciaran Hinds, Jude Law, Damian Lewis, James McAvoy, Neve McIntosh, Art Malik, Emily Mortimer, Samantha Morton, Sophia Myles, Mark Steele, Tilda Swinton and Michelle Yeoh.

"The way we sound tells the story of who we are" Once upon a time, I was asked to write a book... I got as far as this title! But for me this little phrase of mine says it all. And it is why researching, developing, finding, a character's voice is so exciting. It leads to true discovery.

I love both strands of my career with an equal passion, one feeds the other, and provides a challenging and thrilling perspective on the often surprisingly practical alchemy of our art.

People say you can't teach anybody to act...that may be so, but what you most definitely can do is develop your skill, learn your technique, build your confidence, polish your craft, and have lots of fun doing it. If it is at all possible, drama school training is indispensable; a glorious time with so much to be discovered and developed outside of the pressures which are undoubtedly one of the negative aspects of our thrilling industry. And it is so important after your formal training, to keep in touch, to keep involved, to keep working on that special unique product that is you!

As an actress with over 30 years' experience in all media, I grew to understand how helpful and exciting it was to work with a personal coach when developing a character. And now as a qualified, experienced and recognised dialect and voice coach, I can offer that personal one-to-one service and feedback. We can become very isolated as performers, in a state of uncertainty and indecision. A coach like myself can offer research and source material, a sounding board, a grounding, specific technical guidance, a bespoke, enjoyable time, And a special Equity rate!

"We are in charge! We quite literally, call the shots!"

Let's look at one of the practical challenges facing us currently: the self tape audition. There are pros and cons in this development. The main disadvantage is that the actor is denied that chance to make a connection, to ask questions, to make a mark personally. But let's be honest, how often do we blow that chance, precisely because nerves get the better of us, we rush and gabble, and as the minutes go interminably on, are overcome by that nagging, insistent little complaint of self-criticism - 'you're losing this, you're blowing it' and rather than being able to turn things around, you shut down, and spend the next few days in the depths of despair! Going over it again and again, giving ourselves the hardest time, couldah, wouldah, shoudah!

"If you think of yourself as the answer to their problem, immediately you have placed yourself in a positive dynamic"

But it doesn't have to be that way, so now let us look at the positive of a self tape: We are in charge! We quite literally, call the shots! But how to approach it? Presuming you have been given a reasonable timescale, some background and the sides, although sometimes scripts are so protected, this may not happen till the last minute, (but there are still strategies we can employ). Now... Contact your coach, and work out some dates, according to the timescale and availability. Then together we can investigate the text, talk about who this person is, where they hail from, what this project requires, and most importantly, and this is crucial, how you can solve the casting dilemma. If you think of yourself as the answer to their problem, immediately you have placed yourself in a positive dynamic, in a productive frame of mind and relationship with that camera, and through that camera, with the people who need their problem solved. Then we have some fun rehearsing, making choices, almost work-shopping the text, so that it is learned through the manner that is most meaningful, practical discovery. Of course my particular fascination is, how do they sound? And the different characteristics, physicalities, and resonances of different dialects can offer a wonderful fresh perspective to help make those words leap off the page, sounding authentic and valid. I always work first from character, and find appropriate vocal connections...much more meaningful than a phonetic transcription and a list of vowel changes. I can provide these if we need them, but these sessions are always about what works for you, and will always come back to - Who is this person? And why? What are they like? Let's find a voice that chimes with that.

And then we record. Whether you go for a professional technical set-up, which will have further cost implications, or do it on your trusty iPhone, let's get started. We can do as many takes as necessary, un-pressurised by the thought of those 10 other hopefuls, all of whom looked much more suitable in the casting director's waiting room. I do not profess to have expert camera knowledge, but I do know what works on camera, and how to make your self tape work best for you so that you have impact. And I know for a fact that many parts have been cast from iPhone selfies, so get practising! If you can afford a step up technically then I am sure that helps, but the main point is to be able to connect personally - to engage and interest the watcher - eye contact and a brief introduction, and then to project the very, very best of yourself, as near as to how you would do it on your take, that perfect take, and in a way that lets the watcher relax, feeling confident you have answered their problem of "who could play this?"

And if it doesn't work out, then you can hold your head up, feeling good about your contribution, in the knowledge that you may not have been exactly right for that part, but a good contribution in front of those who may employ us, is never wasted.

Above all, it is essential to retain enthusiasm, and to remain interested, curious and open, and crucially to keep having fun; on-going classes and workshops with practitioners with current industry experience help keep you in touch with that original joyful enthusiasm.

**To find our more visit
www.jocameronbrown.com**

A B ACADEMY
THEATRE SCHOOL　　　　**T/F** 0161 429 7413
Full range of training in Acting, Technical Theatre &
Young People's Activities
Act Out Ltd, 22 Greek Street
Stockport, Cheshire SK3 8AB
E ab22actout@aol.com

ABBI ACTING MA BA Hons
Accredited Drama School Tutor & Actress. One-to-one
Sessions in Auditioning, Speech & Voice, Corporate
Presentation, Public Speaking, Shakespeare & Text,
Relaxation
Based in North London
E stephanie.schonfield@googlemail.com

ABOMELI TUTORING
Contact: Charles Abomeli BA LLAM. Development
Coach. Stage & Screen Acting Technique
E charlesabm@aol.co.uk
W www.charlesabomeli.com

ACADEMY ARTS
THEATRE SCHOOL & AGENCY　　**T** 01245 422595
6A The Green, Writtle
Chelmsford, Essex CM1 3DU
E info@academyarts.co.uk
W www.academyarts.co.uk

ACADEMY OF
CREATIVE TRAINING　　　**T** 01273 818266
Contact: Janette Eddisford. Actor Training in Brighton,
Hove & Eastbourne
8-10 Rock Place, Brighton
East Sussex BN2 1PF
T 07740 468338
E info@actbrighton.org
W www.actbrighton.org

ACADEMY OF PERFORMANCE
COMBAT　　　　　　　**T** 07928 324706
197 Church Road, Northolt
Middlesex UB5 5BE
E info@theapc.org.uk
W www.theapc.org.uk

ACADEMY OF PERFORMANCE TRAINING
(APT THE DRAMA SCHOOL)
Courses: Professional Acting Diploma, 2 yrs. Television &
Film Acting, 1yr. Drama School Preparation, 1 yr
Guildford, Surrey
W www.aptraining.co.uk

ACCENT @ THE RICHER VOICE　**T** 07967 352551
Contact: Richard Ryder. Accent Specialist
9 Kamen House, 17-21 Magdalen Street
London Bridge, London SE1 2RH
E richard@therichervoice.com
W www.therichervoice.com

ACCENT KIT APP　　　　　**T** 07967 352551
Free to download on iPhone & Android
9 Kamen House, 17-21 Magdalen Street
London SE1 2RH
E theaccentkit@gmail.com
W www.theaccentkit.com

ACKERLEY STUDIOS OF SPEECH, DRAMA &
PUBLIC SPEAKING　　　　**T** 0151 724 3449
Est. 1919. Contact: Margaret Parsons
16 Fawley Road, Allerton
Liverpool L18 9TF
E johnmutch@talktalk.net

ACT 2 CAM　　　　　　　**T** 0191 270 4255
Screen Acting Academy
Sudio B3, Linskill Centre
Linskill Terrace, North Shields
Tyne & Wear NE30 2AY
E info@act2cam.com
W www.act2cam.com

ACT 2 DRAMA SCHOOL　　　**T** 07939 144355
Performing Arts School (5-18 yrs)
105 Richmond Avenue, Highams Park
London E4 9RR
E management@act2drama.co.uk
W www.act2drama.co.uk

ACT & VOICE　　　**T** 07850 910237 (Dee)
Contact: Dee Mardi, Andrew Alton-Read. Drama
& Performance Classes (5-16 yrs). Drama School
Preparation, Coaching in Acting & Singing for
Children & Adults
Based in Chelmsford, Essex
T 07854 536817 (Andrew)
E enquiries@actandvoice.co.uk
W www.actandvoice.co.uk

ACT NOW! PERFORMING
ARTS ACADEMY　　　　　**T** 07920 855410
Performing Arts Training (4-21 yrs). Part-time
Trestle Arts Base, Russett Drive
St Albans, Hertfordshire AL4 0JQ
E actnowperformingarts@mac.com
W www.actnowperformingartsschool.co.uk

ACT ONE DRAMA STUDIO　　**T** 07904 339024
Acting Classes & Workshops
PO Box 4776, Sheffield S11 0EX
E info@actonedramastudio.co.uk
W www.actonedramastudio.co.uk

ACT UP　　　　　　　　　**T** 020 8767 7659
Acting Classes for Everyone. Acting Workshops. Audition
Technique. Pre-Drama School (18+ yrs). Casting &
Production. Agency
The Office, 93 Chasefield Road
London SW17 8LW
E info@act-up.co.uk
W www.act-up.co.uk

ACTING AUDITION SUCCESS　**T** 020 8731 6686
Contact: Philip Rosch. Audition Coaching for Drama UK
Schools. Audition Technique. Drama School Preparation.
Improvisation. Private Acting Classes
53 West Heath Court, London NW11 7RG
E philiproschactor@gmail.com
W www.actingauditionsuccess.co.uk

ACTION LAB　　　　　　　**T** 020 8810 0412
Contact: Miranda French, Peter Irving. Part-time Acting
Courses & Private Coaching. Based in London &
West Dorset
34 Northcote Avenue, London W5 3UT
T 07979 623987
E miranda@mirandafrench.com

ACTORS CENTRE THE　　　**T** 020 7632 8001
Career and Casting Advice. Voice. Accent/Dialect
Coaching. Acting for Camera. Audition Technique.
Television Presenting. Voice Overs. Showreels.
Shakespeare. The Meisner Technique. Performance
Workshops
1A Tower Street, London WC2H 9NP
E reception@actorscentre.co.uk
W www.actorscentre.co.uk

ACTORS COMPANY LA THE
Based in Hollywood & London
916A North Formosa Avenue, West Hollywood
Los Angeles, CA 90046, USA
E info@theactorscompanyla.co.uk
W www.theactorscompanyla.co.uk

ACTORS STUDIO   T 01753 650951
*Acting Workshops. Audition Technique. Improvisation.
Screen Acting Technique. Private Acting Classes. Stage
School for Children*
Main Admin, Pinewood Studios, Pinewood Road
Iver Heath, Bucks SL0 0NH
E info@actorsstudio.co.uk
W www.actorsstudio.co.uk

ACTORS' SURGERY THE   T 07956 344255
*Contact: Katie Morgan (BA Hons, PG Dip, PGCE). Acting
Classes for Adults in London taught by Professional
Actress/Coach. Group & one-to-one Coaching Available.
Audition Preparation. Drama School Entry. Improvisation.
Meisner Technique. Working the Text. Confidence
Building. General Skills. Coaching/Consulting for Plays,
Television, Films*
E theactorssurgery@gmail.com
W www.theactorssurgery.com

ACTOR'S TEMPLE THE   T 020 3004 4537
*Professional Actors offering Training & Support to
Fellow Actors*
13-14 Warren Street, London W1T 5LG
E bookings@actorstemple.com
W www.actorstemple.com

ACTORS' THEATRE SCHOOL   T 020 8450 0371
Foundation Course
32 Exeter Road, London NW2 4SB
E info@theactorstheatreschool.co.uk
W www.theactorstheatreschool.co.uk

ACTORS TRAINING STUDIO   T 07710 172477
*Part-time, Evening & Weekend Acting Workshops &
Short Courses in London*
c/o The Red Hedgehog, 255-257 Archway
Highgate, London N6 5BS
E workshops@actorstrainingstudio.co.uk
W www.actorstrainingstudio.co.uk

ACTS   T 020 8360 0352
Ayres-Clark Theatre School
c/o 12 Gatward Close, Winchmore Hill
London N21 1AS
E actsn21@talktalk.net

ALEXANDER, Helen   T 020 8543 4085
Audition Technique. Drama School Entry
14 Chestnut Road, Raynes Park
London SW20 8EB
E helen-alexander@outlook.com

ALL EXPRESSIONS
THEATRE SCHOOL   T 020 8274 1320
218 Staines Road, Twickenham
Middlesex TW2 5AP
E maggie@allexpressions.co.uk
W www.allexpressions.co.uk

ALLSORTS - DRAMA   T/F 020 8969 3249
*Part-time Courses & Drama Training (3-18 yrs). Based in
Kensington, Notting Hill, Hampstead, Fulham & Putney*
34 Crediton Road, London NW10 3DU
E info@allsortsdrama.com
W www.allsortsdrama.com

John Colclough Advisory
Practical independent guidance for actors and actresses

www.johncolclough.com | t: 020 8873 1763 | e: info@johncolclough.com

---

ALLSTARS ACTORS MANAGEMENT DRAMA SCHOOL FOR CHILDREN   T 07584 992429
Based in Manchester,
E drama@littleallstars.co.uk
W www.littleallstars.co.uk

ALRA (ACADEMY OF LIVE & RECORDED ARTS)
See DRAMA SCHOOLS: DRAMA UK

ALTON-READ, Andrew   T 07854 536817
Coaching in Acting & Singing
E andrewaltonread@gmail.com

AMERICAN ACCENTS AND DIALECTS   T 07981 398207
Contact: Kara Tsiaperas. American Voice Coach
1 Conyers Close, Woodford Green, Essex IG8 9PX
E kara@usaaccents.co.uk
W www.usaaccents.co.uk

AMERICAN DIALECT COACHING & RP   T 07956 602508
Contact: Anne Wittman. Private Coaching in American Dialects & RP. All USA Dialects Covered. Accent Correction for Foreign Speakers. Acting Coaching & Audition Preparation
Based in London N8
E wittmananne@yahoo.com
W www.spokenstates.com

AMERICAN MUSICAL THEATRE ACADEMY OF LONDON   T 020 7253 3118
Musical Theatre Courses
Europa House, 13-17 Ironmonger Row
London EC1V 3QG
E info@americanacademy.co.uk
W www.americanacademy.co.uk

AMERICAN VOICES   T 07875 148755
Contact: Lynn Bains. Acting Teacher & Director. American Accent/Dialect Coach
20 Craighall Crescent, Edinburgh EH6 4RZ
E mail@lynnbains.com

AND ALL THAT JAZZ   T 020 8993 2111
Contact: Eileen Hughes. Accompanist. Vocal Coaching
163 Gunnersbury Lane, Acton Town
London W3 8LJ

ARABESQUE SCHOOL OF PERFORMING ARTS   T/F 01243 531144
Quarry Lane, Chichester PO19 8NY
E arabesqueschool@aol.com
W www.arabesqueschool.com

ARDEN SCHOOL OF THEATRE THE   T 0161 920 4890
BA (Hons) Acting for Live & Recorded Media. BA (Hons) Musical Theatre. HNC Acting for Camera. FdA Theatre & Performance. FdA Dance & Performance
The Manchester College, Nicholls Campus
Ardwick, Manchester M12 6BA
E enquiries@themanchestercollege.ac.uk
W www.themanchestercollege.ac.uk

ARTEMIS STUDIOS   T 01344 429403
Performing Arts School
South Hill Park Mansion, Ringmead
Bracknell RG12 7PA
E info@artemis-studios.co.uk
W www.artemis-studios.co.uk

ARTS1 SCHOOL OF PERFORMANCE   T 01908 604756
Classes in Acting, Singing & Dance. RAD, ISTD, LAMDA. CDET Recognised School
The Box Studios, Sunrise Parkway
Linford Wood, Milton Keynes MK14 6LS
E info@arts1.co.uk
W www.arts1.co.uk

ARTS EDUCATIONAL SCHOOLS LONDON
See DRAMA SCHOOLS: DRAMA UK

ARTS UNIVERSITY BOURNEMOUTH THE   T 01202 533011
7 Fern Barrow, Wallisdown
Poole, Dorset BH12 5HH
E hello@aub.ac.uk
W www.aub.ac.uk

ASCENDANCE THEATRE ARTS   T 07812 773893
Contact: Sophie Herrmann
12 John Bachelor Way, Penarth Marina
Glamorgan CF64 1SD
E agency@ascendancetheatrearts.co.uk
W www.ascendancetheatrearts.co.uk

ASHCROFT ACADEMY OF DRAMATIC ART THE   T/F 0844 8005328
Dance ISTD. Drama LAMDA. Singing (4-18 yrs)
Harris Primary Academy Crystal Palace, Malcolm Road
Penge, London SE20 8RH
T 07799 791586
E info@ashcroftacademy.com
W www.ashcroftacademy.com

ASHFORD, Clare BSc PGCE LLAM ALAM (Recital) ALAM (Acting)   T 020 8660 9609
20 The Chase, Coulsdon
Surrey CR5 2EG
E clareashford@rocketmail.com

ASSOCIATED STUDIOS THE   T 020 7385 2038
Contact: Hannah Taylor, Yvonne l'Anson. Professional Development & Training
The Hub @ St Alban's Fulham, 2 Margravine Road
London W6 8HJ
E info@associatedstudios.co.uk
W www.associatedstudios.co.uk

AUDITION COACH   T 0161 969 1444
Contact: Martin Harris. Acting Workshops. Audition Techniques. Group Evening Classes. Private Acting Classes
32 Baxter Road, Sale, Manchester M33 3AL
T 07788 723570
E martin@auditioncoach.co.uk
W www.auditioncoach.co.uk

ROYCE SPARKS

Recognised and certified by world experts as a teacher of the Meisner Technique, with launched training intensives in the United States, Canada and Europe.

Offering classes and coaching in the next generation of Meisner Training, including material targeted for screen, Shakespeare, physical theatre, process development and more. Private coaching available for auditions and stage/screen.

Yearly training intensive:

The London Acting Experience, July/August 2016, with a daily core training in the Meisner Technique and movement, as well as guest workshops from industry experts and professionals. Previous guests have included: Terence Stamp, Michael Attenborough, Complicite, Frantic Assembly, Larry Silverberg, Ross Mullan, Nickolas Grace, Brigid Panet and more! A different charity is selected each year as a beneficiary recipient.

'This idea of excellent professional training for actors, combined with an awareness of the world's needs and how to meet them, is a rare but much needed presence in the arts. Royce Sparks and his London Acting Experience program is doing just this very thing, and it's a gem.'

Robert Westenberg: Tony-nominee, Original Broadway Cast *Into the Woods*

Complicite, Gerard Julien /AFP/Getty Images

roycesparks.com

@Royce_Sparks
facebook.com/groups/meisnerinternational/

AUDITION DOCTOR
T 020 7357 8237
Bespoke Acting Classes
1 Gloucester Court, Swan Street, London SE1 1DQ
T 07764 193806
E tilly@auditiondoctor.co.uk
W www.auditiondoctor.co.uk

AUDITIONS: THE COMPLETE GUIDE
E enquiries@auditionsthecompleteguide.com
W www.auditionsthecompleteguide.com

AUTHENTIC PERFORMANCE ACADEMY
T 01865 521168
Contact: Melissa D'Amico. Stage School (5-20 yrs)
74 Banbury Road, Oxford
Oxfordshire OX2 6JR
E admin@authenticperformanceacademy.com
W www.authenticperformanceacademy.com

AVERY-CLARK, Kenneth
T 020 7253 3118
Musical Theatre. Voice Coach
Europa House,° 13-17 Ironmonger Row
London EC1V 3QG
T 07734 509810
E ken@americanacademy.co.uk

BATE, Richard MA (Theatre)
LGSM (TD) PGCE (FE) Equity
T 07720 865774
*Audition Technique. Vocal & Acting Training. Drama
School Entry*
45A Derngate, Derngate Mews
Northampton, Northamptonshire NN1 1UE
E rich.bate@yahoo.co.uk

BATES, Esme
T 01235 201517
*BA Hons Royal Central School of Speech & Drama.
Experienced Speech & Drama Youth Director. ESL/SEN
inclusive. Writer of Female, Male, Hawking or Dalek?
Poetry-Speaking Vol. 1 & Moving Movie Monologues*
Oxford Blue, 8 East Street
Didcot, Oxfordshire OX11 8EJ
T 07941 700941
E batesesme@gmail.com
W www.esmebates.weebly.com

BATTERSEA ARTS CENTRE (BAC)
T 020 7326 8210
*Young People's Theatre Workshops & Performance
Projects (12-25 yrs)*
Lavender Hill, London SW11 5TN
F 020 7978 5207
E homegrown@bac.org.uk
W www.bac.org.uk

BENCH, Paul MEd LGSM ALAM FRSA LJBA (Hons) PGCE ACP (Lings) (Hons) MASC (Ph) MIFA (Reg)
T/F 01743 233164
*Audition Technique. Corporate Vocal Presentation.
LAMDA Exams, Grades to Diploma Level. Private Acting
Classes. Public Speaking. Stress Management.
Vocal Coaching*
1 Whitehall Terrace, Shrewsbury
Shropshire SY2 5AA
E pfbench@aol.com
W www.paulbench.co.uk

BIG ACT THE
T 0117 239 1274
Range of courses for Children, Young People & Students
14-16 Wilson Place, Bristol BS2 9HJ
E info@thebigact.com
W www.thebigact.com

BIG LITTLE THEATRE SCHOOL
T 01202 434499
*Acting Examination & Audition Prep (LAMDA). All Grades
up to Grade 8 Gold. Early Years Drama & Dance.
Performance in Education Workshops. Professional
Development Programme. RAD Ballet, Tap & Modern,
Performance Dance & Tap. Singing Technique Classes
& Private Lessons. Musical Theatre Classes. Summer
Schools. Themed Holiday Workshops. Youth Theatre
Companies. Senior Musical Projects*
Garnet House, 2A Harvey Road
Bournemouth, Dorset BH5 2AD
E info@biglittle.biz
W www.biglittle.biz

BIG TALENT SCHOOL & AGENCY THE
T 029 2046 4506
Contact: Shelley Barrett-Norton
59 Mount Stuart Square, Cardiff CF10 5LR
T 07886 020923
E info@thebigtalent.co.uk
W www.thebigtalent.co.uk

BIRD COLLEGE
T 020 8300 6004
Professional Dance & Musical Theatre College
Alma Road, Sidcup
Kent DA14 4ED
F 020 8308 1370
E performance@birdcollege.co.uk
W www.birdcollege.co.uk

BIRMINGHAM SCHOOL OF ACTING
See DRAMA SCHOOLS: DRAMA UK

BIRMINGHAM THEATRE SCHOOL THE
T 0121 440 1665
The Old Fire Station
285-287 Moseley Road
Highgate, Birmingham B12 0DX
E info@birminghamtheatreschool.co.uk
W www.birminghamtheatreschool.com

BLACKSTONE, Sarah VOICE COACHING
T 07804 048541
Voice, Accent & Singing Coach
E info@sbvoiceworks.com
W www.sbvoiceworks.com

BODENS COLLEGE OF PERFORMING ARTS
T 020 8447 0909
*Contact: Adam Boden. Full-time college (16-19 yrs).
Level 3 BTEC & Trinity Diploma*
99 East Barnet Road, New Barnet
Herts EN4 8RF
E adam@bodens.co.uk
W www.performingartscollege.co.uk

the actors centre

Patrons: David Harewood MBE, Joely Richardson, Rafe Spall

where actors work... and play.

The UK's leading organisation which supports actors throughout their careers.

f 🐦 **/TheActorsCentre   actorscentre.co.uk**
1a Tower Street, London, WC2H 9NP
020 7240 3940

Supported by:

BODENS PERFORMING ARTS   T 020 8447 0909
Contact: Adam Boden. Acting Workshops. Audition Technique. Dancing. Improvisation. Part-time Performing Arts Classes. Singing
Bodens Performing Arts
99 East Barnet Road
New Barnet, Herts EN4 8RF
E info@bodens.co.uk
W www.bodens.co.uk

BOWES, Sara   T 07830 375389
Child Acting Coach for Film & Commercials
25 Holmes Avenue, Hove BN3 7LA
E saracrowe77@gmail.com

BOYD, Beth   T 020 8398 6768
Private Acting Coach
10 Prospect Road, Long Ditton
Surbiton, Surrey KT6 5PY

BRADSHAW, Irene   T 020 7794 5721
Private Coach. Voice & Audition Preparation
Flat F, Welbeck Mansions
Inglewood Road
West Hampstead, London NW6 1QX
T 07949 552915
E irene@irenebradshaw.fsnet.co.uk
W www.voice-power-works.co.uk

**BRAITHWAITE'S
ACROBATIC SCHOOL**   T 020 8954 5638
8 Brookshill Avenue, Harrow Weald
Middlesex HA3 6RZ

BRAL SCHOOL OF ACTING   T 07852 348144
Training is based on Coordination Technique, developed by Grzegorz Bral & other Song of the Goat Theatre Practitioners
The Leadenhall Building
Level 30, 122 Leadenhall Street
London EC3V 4AB
E alicia@bralschool.com
W wwwbralschool.com

BRANSTON, Dale   T 020 8696 9958
Singing Teacher. Singing Audition Preparation. Repertoire
Ground Floor Flat
16 Fernwood Avenue
Streatham, London SW16 1RD
T 07767 261713
E branpickle@yahoo.co.uk

**BREAK A LEG
MANAGEMENT LTD**   T/F 020 7250 0662
Workshops run by Professional Teachers & Directors
The City College, University House, Room 33
55 East Road, London N1 6AH
E agency@breakalegman.com
W www.breakalegman.com

**BRIDGE THEATRE
TRAINING COMPANY THE**   T 020 7424 0860
Contact: Mark Akrill. Drama School (over 18 yrs). Acting. Dance. Film, Television & Radio Technique. Improvisation. Movement. Professional Studies. Singing. Stage Combat. Voice. Courses: Professional Acting Course, 2 yr, full-time, Diploma. Postgraduate Professional Acting Course (over 21 yrs), 1 yr, full-time, Diploma
90 Kingsway, Tally Ho Corner
North Finchley, London N12 0EX
E admin@thebridge-ttc.org
W www.thebridge-ttc.org

BRISTOL OLD VIC THEATRE SCHOOL
See DRAMA SCHOOLS: DRAMA UK

**BRIT SCHOOL FOR PERFORMING
ARTS & TECHNOLOGY THE**   T 020 8665 5242
60 The Crescent, Croydon CR0 2HN
F 020 8665 8676
E admin@brit.croydon.sch.uk
W www.brit.croydon.sch.uk

**BRITISH ACTION
ACADEMY LTD**   T 0844 4146007
Screen Action Training
Shieling House, 30 Invincible Road
Farnborough, Hampshire GU14 7QU
E info@britishactionacademy.com
W www.britishactionacademy.com

**BRITISH AMERICAN
DRAMA ACADEMY**   T 020 7487 0730
14 Gloucester Gate, Regent's Park
London NW1 4HG
E info@badaonline.com
W www.badaonline.com

CAMERON BROWN, Jo PGDVS
Dialect. Dialogue. Voice Coaching for Film, Stage, Television & Auditions
E jocameronbrown@hotmail.com
W www.jocameronbrown.com

HOLLY WILSON LLAM.

Actor Teacher-London Drama Schools
Voice / Speech & Drama / Audition coaching / Private tuition

T: 020 8878 0015   e: hbwilson@fastmail.co.uk

CAMPBELL, Jon   T 07854 697971
Acting Classes
36 Fentiman Road, London SW8 1LF
E jon@joncampbellacting.co.uk
W www.joncampbellacting.co.uk

CAMPBELL, Ross
ARCM Dip RCM (Perf)   T 01252 510223
Professor, Royal Academy of Music. Head of Singing
& Music, GSA, 2004-2011. Director & Head of Musical
Theatre, Musical Theatre Ireland. Private Teaching
Studios in London & Surrey
17 Oldwood Chase, Farnborough
Hants GU14 0QS
T 07956 465165
E rosscampbell@ntlworld.com
W www.rosscampbell.biz

CANNON, Dee   T 07586 313390
Freelance Acting Coach in Film, Television & Theatre.
Author of "In-Depth Acting"
Flat 9, 2A Regina Road
London N4 3QH
E dee@deecannon.com
W www.deecannon.com

CAPO FERRO
FIGHT ENSEMBLE   T 07791 875902
Contact: Paul Casson-Yardley. Acting Workshops.
Drama School (over 18 yrs). Improvisation. Private Acting
Classes. Stage School for Children. Courses: Basic
Introduction to Stage Fighting, Fight Choreography,
Stage Combat Past & Present, Stage Combat with
Weapons & Props. All Abilities. All Courses Day/Half Day
168 Richmond Road, Sheffield, Yorkshire S13 8TG
E capo.ferro.ensemble@gmail.com

CELEBRATION THEATRE
COMPANY FOR THE YOUNG   T 020 8994 8886
Contact: Neville Wortman. Drama School (over 18 yrs).
Drama School Preparation & 13-15 yrs LAMDA Bronze,
Silver & Gold Medals. Private Acting Classes. Summer
School. Vocal Coaching. Courses: Audition & Interview
Techniques, 'Shakespeare Today', Speaking in Public,
'The Confident Voice', 10 week Saturday Classes
School of Economic Science Building, Studio 11-13
Mandeville Place, London W1U 3AJ
T 07976 805976
E neville@speakwell.co.uk
W www.speakwell.co.uk

PAMELA SCHERMANN
DIRECTOR
THEATRE, OPERA, MUSICAL

ONE-TO-ONE COACHING

IN NEWLY REFURBISHED, PRIVATE
REHEARSAL STUDIO. CONVENIENTLY
LOCATED IN EAST LONDON.

★ AUDITION AND DRAMA SCHOOL
  PREPARATION
★ ACTING FOR OPERA SINGERS
★ CHARACTER ANALYSIS / WORK
★ SHOWCASE PERFORMANCES

www.pamelaschermann.com
info@pamelaschermann.com

CENTRAL LONDON
DRAMA COACHING
T 07950 720868

Audition Technique. Text Analysis. Vocal Presentation Skills. Trinity Examinations. CRB Checked
Based in WC1,
E euniceroberts1@gmail.com

CENTRE FOR SOLO
PERFORMANCE
T 07952 960424

Workshops, Events & Opportunities for those interested in Creating Original Solo Performance Work
Conway Hall, 25 Red Lion Square
London WC1R 4RL
E luke@centreforsoloperformance.com
W www.centreforsoloperformance.com

CENTRE STAGE
ACADEMY THEATRE SCHOOL
T 07773 416593

Weekend Theatre School in Midhurst & Chichester (5-20 yrs)
9 Beech Grove, Midhurst & Haslemere
West Sussex GU29 9JA
E brett.east@hotmail.com
W www.csatheatreschool.co.uk

CENTRE STAGE SCHOOL
OF PERFORMING ARTS
T 020 8886 4264

Students (4-18 yrs). Based in North London
The Croft, 7 Cannon Road
Southgate, London N14 7HE
F 020 8886 7555
E carole@centrestageuk.com
W www.centrestageuk.com

CENTRE STAGE
THEATRE ACADEMY
T 01689 330557

Performing Arts Training for Children. Five Branches across South London/Kent
91 Eldred Drive, Orpington
Kent BR5 4PE
E info@centrestagetheatreacademy.com
W www.centrestagetheatreacademy.com

CENTRESTAGE SCHOOL
OF PERFORMING ARTS
T 020 7328 0788

Drama School Auditions. Private Coaching for Professionals
Centrestage House
117 Canfield Gardens
London NW6 3DY
E vickiwoolf@centrestageschool.co.uk
W www.centrestageschool.co.uk

CHARD, Verona
LRAM Dip RAM
T 07985 440902

Private Pupils Welcome. British & International Vocal Academy Founder. Visiting Singing Tutor at Royal Central School of Speech & Drama. Vocal Expert X Factor, Poland, 2012. Coach of Award-winning Jazz Singers & West End Leads. Vocal Producer for Record Labels
Ealing House, 33 Hanger Lane
London W5 3HJ
E verona@veronachard.com
W www.musicalballoonband.com

CHARRINGTON, Tim
T 020 7987 3028

Dialect/Accent Coaching
54 Topmast Point, Strafford Street
London E14 8SN
T 07967 418236
E tim.charrington@gmail.com
W www.timcharrington.co.uk

CHASE, Stephan
PRODUCTIONS LTD
T 020 8878 9112

Private Coach for Acting, Auditions, Public Speaking & Script Work. Originator of Managing Authentic Presence. Founder of Rhubarb Voice Agency
The Studio, 22 York Avenue
London SW14 7LG
E stephan@stephanchase.com
W www.stephanchase.com

CHEKHOV, Michael
STUDIO LONDON
T 020 8696 7372

Contact: Graham Dixon. Monthly Acting Workshops. Private Acting Classes. Summer School. Vocal Coaching. Skype Sessions
Admin: 48 Vectis Road
London SW17 9RG
E info@michaelchekhovstudio.org.uk
W www.michaelchekhovstudio.org.uk

CHERRY PIE
PERFORMANCE
T 07939 422081

Workshops for Actors, Performers, Presenters & Professionals
20 Coronation Court, Croston
Lancs PR26 9HF
E enquiries@cherrypieperformance.co.uk
W www.cherrypieperformance.co.uk

CHRISKA STAGE SCHOOL
T 01928 739166

37-39 Whitby Road, Ellesmere Port
Cheshire L64 8AA
E chrisbooth41@hotmail.com
W www.chriska.co.uk

CHRYSTEL ARTS
THEATRE SCHOOL
T 01494 785589

Part-time Classes for Children, Teenagers & Young Adults in Dance, Drama & Musical Theatre. ISTD & LAMDA Examinations
Edgware Parish Hall
Rectory Lane
Edgware, Middlesex HA8 7LG
T 020 8952 6010
E chrystelarts@waitrose.com

CHURCHER, Mel MA
T 07778 773019

Acting & Vocal Coach
E melchurcher@hotmail.com
W www.melchurcher.com

CIRCOMEDIA
T/F 0117 947 7288

Centre for Contemporary Circus & Physical Performance
Britannia Road, Kingswood
Bristol BS15 8DB
E info@circomedia.com
W www.circomedia.com

CITY LIT
T 020 7492 2542

Accredited & Non-Accredited part-time & full-time Day & Evening Courses. Acting Workshops. Shakespeare, Stanislavski, Meisner Audition Techniques. Screen & Radio Acting/Presenting. Camera Training. Dancing. Dialect/Accent Coaching. Directing. Elocution Coaching. Improvisation. Presenting. Professional Preparation. Agent & Casting Directors Masterclasses. Public Speaking. Clowning. Stand-up Comedy. Singing. Story Telling. Stage & Fighting for Film. CL Rep Company
1-10 Keeley Street
Covent Garden, London WC2B 4BA
E drama@citylit.ac.uk
W www.citylit.ac.uk/dramaschool

CLANRANALD TRUST:
COMBAT INTERNATIONAL   **T** 01877 331136
Educational organisation dedicated to promoting
increased awareness of Scottish Culture & Heritage
St Kessogs, Ancaster Square
Callander FK17 8ED
E info@clanranald.org
W www.clanranald.org

CLEMENTS, Anne
MA LGSM FRSA   **T** 07963 818845
Audition Technique. Role Exploration. Dialect/Accent/
Voice Coaching. Drama School Advice & Preparation.
Close to Hampstead Tube NW3
E woodlandcreature10@hotmail.com

COLDIRON, M. J.   **T** 07941 920498
Audition Preparation & Presentation Skills. Private
Coaching
54 Millfields Road, London E5 0SB
E jiggs@blueyonder.co.uk

COLGAN, Valerie   **T** 020 7267 2153
Audition Technique. Voice Production
The Green, 17 Herbert Street, London NW5 4HA

COMBAT ACTOR SCHOOL   **T** 07950 024561
6A Rushock Trading Estate
Droitwich Road, Droitwich
Worcestershire WR9 0NR
E info@combatactorschool.co.uk
W www.combatactorschool.co.uk

COMBER, Sharrone
BA (Hons) MAVS (CSSD) PGCE   **T** 07752 029422
Audition & Monologue Speech Technique for Drama &
Performing Arts School Entry. Vocal Coach Specialist.
Dialect & Accent Coaching. Elocution. Presentation
Skills. Private Acting Classes. Public Speaking
E sharronecomber@hotmail.com

COMPLETE WORKS THE   **T** 020 7377 0280
The Old Truman Brewery
91 Brick Lane
London E1 6QL
E info@tcw.org.uk
W www.tcw.org.uk

CONTI, Italia ACADEMY
See DRAMA SCHOOLS: DRAMA UK

CONTI, Italia ACADEMY OF THEATRE ARTS T 020 7608 0044
Courses: Performing Arts Diploma, 3 yr. Professional Dance Diploma, 3 yr. Performing Arts with Teacher Training, 3 yr. Intensive Performing Arts, 1 yr. Foundation Performing Arts, 1 yr. BA (Hons) Acting, 3 yr. Foundation Acting, 1 yr. Singing, 1 yr. Theatre Arts School (Academic yrs 7-11)
Italia Conti House, 23 Goswell Road
London EC1M 7AJ
F 020 7253 1430
E admin@italiaconti.co.uk
W www.italiaconti.com

CORNER, Clive AGSM LRAM T 01305 860267
Qualified Teacher. Audition Training. Private Coaching
'The Belenes', 60 Wakeham
Portland DT5 1HN
E cornerassociates@aol.com

COURT THEATRE TRAINING COMPANY T/F 020 7739 6868
The Courtyard Theatre
Bowling Green Walk
40 Pitfield Street, London N1 6EU
E info@courttheatre.org.uk
W www.courttheatretraining.org.uk

COX, Gregory BA Joint Hons T 07931 370135
Bristol Old Vic Graduate with 35 Years' Experience (including West End & NT). Audition Coaching. Drama Coaching. Sight Reading Skills. Voice Work
Based in South West London,
E gregoryedcox@hotmail.com

CPA STUDIOS T 01708 766007
3 yr Professional Musical Theatre Diploma Course
The Studios
219B North Street
Romford, Essex RM1 4QA
F 01708 766077
E collegeadmin@cpastudios.co.uk
W www.cpastudios.co.uk

CREATIVE PERFORMANCE LTD T 020 8908 0502
Touring Storytelling. Shows & Mobile Workshops in Circus Skills (Plate Spinning, Juggling, Mini Cycling, Ribbon Twirling, Parachute Games). Drama, Dance & Singing for Nurseries, Libraries, Schools, Youth Clubs & Play Schemes. Google+: creativeperformance1
Pembroke Road, North Wembley
Middlesex HA9 7PD
E creative.performance@yahoo.co.uk

CROSKIN, Phil T 07837 712323
RADA Trained. Presentation Skills. Adding Value to Public Profiles. Auditions
E philcroskin@fastmail.fm

CROWE, Ben T 07952 784911
Accent, Acting & Audition Tuition
25 Holmes Avenue
Hove BN3 7LA
E bencrowe@hotmail.co.uk

CYGNET THEATRE T 01392 277189
Professional Actor Training
Friars Gate, Exeter
Devon EX2 4AZ
E info@cygnettheatre.co.uk
W www.cygnettheatre.co.uk

D&B SCHOOL OF PERFORMING ARTS & D&B THEATRE SCHOOL T 020 8698 8880
Central Studios, 470 Bromley Road
Bromley BR1 4PQ
E info@dandbperformingarts.co.uk
W www.dandbperformingarts.co.uk

DAVIDSON, Clare T 020 8348 0132
Coach & Theatre Director
30 Highgate West Hill, London N6 6NP
E davidson_clare@hotmail.com
W www.claredavidson.co.uk

DEBUT SCHOOL OF PERFORMING ARTS T 01274 618288
12 Tenterfields House, Meadow Road
Apperley Bridge, Bradford BD10 0LQ
E jacqui.debut@btinternet.com
W www.debuttheatreschool.co.uk

DE COURCY, Bridget T 020 8883 8397
Singing Teacher
19 Muswell Road, London N10
E singinglessons@bridgetdecourcy.co.uk

De FLOREZ, Jane LGSM PG Dip T 020 7602 0741
Singing. Acting for Singers. Audition Technique. Drama School Audition Preparation. Language Tutoring. Music Theory for Singers. Public Speaking. Speech & Drama Tuition. Singing. Vocal Coaching. Courses: Musical Theatre, 1 yr, part-time. Classical/Opera Singing, 2 yrs, part-time. General Singing & Music Theory, 1 yr, part-time. Choir Preparation, 6 months, part-time
Kensington, London W14 9AS
E janedeflorez@gmail.com
W www.singingteacherlondon.com

DFL GROUP THE T 01494 762130
Contact: Coral Ash. Audition technique and drama training for drama school entrance
164 Amersham Way, Little Chalfont
Buckinghamshire HP6 6SG
E dfldramaforlife@tiscali.co.uk

DIGNAN, Tess MA T 07528 576915
Audition, Text & Voice Coach
004 Oregon Building, Deals Gateway
Lewisham SE13 7RR
E tess.dignan@gmail.com

DIRECTIONS THEATRE ARTS (CHESTERFIELD) LTD T/F 01246 854455
Musical Theatre School
Studios: 1A-2A Sheffield Road, Chesterfield
Derby S41 7LL
T 07973 768144
E julie.cox5@btconnect.com
W www.directionstheatrearts.org

DOGGETT, Antonia T 07814 155090
Courses: Cold Reading, 3 weeks, part-time. Shakespeare, 6 weeks, part-time. Advanced LAMDA Grades/Drama School Audition Preparation, 6 weeks, part-time. Acting Techniques, 6 weeks, part-time. Acting Workshops. Audition Technique, Drama Scool Preparation. Private Acting Classes, Public Speaking, Vocal Coaching. Accent Softening
Conway Hall, 25 Red Lion Square
London WC1R 4RL
E antoniadoggettcontact@gmail.com
W www.antoniadoggett.co.uk

DORSET SCHOOL OF ACTING THE   T 01202 922675
Courses: 1 yr Diploma in Acting & Musical Theatre, 1 yr, full-time. Trinity ATCL Level 4 Qualification. 2 yr Accelerated Diploma in Acting & Musical Theatre, 2 yr, full-time. Trinity LTCL Level 6 Qualification. Adult Acting Courses in Film/Screen & Stage, part-time. Youth Theatre Programmes, part-time. Acting Classes. Musical Theatre Classes. Audition Technique. Dancing. Drama School Preparation. Improvisation. Singing. Summer Schools. Vocal Coaching. Acting Coaching.
c/o Lighthouse
21 Kingland Road
Poole, Dorset BH15 1UG
E admin@dorsetschoolofacting.co.uk
W www.dorsetschoolofacting.co.uk

DOVER YOUTH THEATRE   T 07703 207878
Contact: Marie Kelly, Nadine Lawson
8 Harold Street, Dover
Kent CT16 1SF
F 01304 202544
E doveryouththeatre@hotmail.com
W www.doveryouththeatre.co.uk

DRAMA ASSOCIATION OF WALES   T 029 2045 2200
Workshops for Amateur Actors & Directors
Splott Library, Singleton Road
Splott, Cardiff CF24 2ET
E office@dramawales.org.uk

DRAMA CENTRE LONDON
See DRAMA SCHOOLS: DRAMA UK

DRAMA DIRECT LTD   T 01373 471486
Contact: Mark McGann. Screen Acting Workshops. Stage Acting Classes
56 Alexandra Road, Frome
Somerset BA11 1LX
E mark@dramadirect.net
W www.dramadirectblog.com

DRAMA FOR KIDS   T 07973 513619
Speech & Drama Lessons for Children
22 Aughantarragh Road, Armagh
County Armagh BT60 4QG
E info@dramaforkids.org.uk
W www.dramaforkids.org.uk

DRAMA STUDIO EDINBURGH THE
T 0131 453 3284
Children's Weekly Drama Workshops
19 Belmont Road
Edinburgh EH14 5DZ
E info@thedramastudio.com
W www.thedramastudio.com

DRAMA STUDIO LONDON
See DRAMA SCHOOLS: DRAMA UK

DULIEU, John
T 020 8696 9958
Acting Coach. Audition & Role Preparation
16 Fernwood Avenue, Streatham
London SW16 1RD
T 07803 289599
E john_dulieu@yahoo.com

DURRENT, Peter
T 01787 248263
Audition & Rehearsal Pianist. Vocal Coach
10 Old Station Close, Lavenham
Sudbury, Suffolk CO10 9FA
E tunefuldurrent@gmail.com

DYSON, Kate LRAM
T 01273 607490
Audition Technique Coaching. Drama
39 Arundel Street, Kemptown BN2 5TH
T 07812 949875
E katedyson222@icloud.com

E(IN)MOTION
T 07766 062910
Contact: Tiziana Silvestre. Physical Theatre, Movement
Coaching & Fitness for Performers & Productions on
Stage & Set.
Based in London E3 4JJ
E tiziana.silvestre.Einm@gmail.com

EARNSHAW, Susi THEATRE SCHOOL
T 020 8441 5010
*Full-time Stage School (11-18 yrs). GCSEs & Vocational
Qualifications. Saturday Theatre School (5-16 yrs).
After School & Holiday Courses*
The Bull Theatre
68 High Street
Barnet, Herts EN5 5SJ
E info@sets.org.uk
W www.susiearnshaw.co.uk

EAST 15 ACTING SCHOOL
See DRAMA SCHOOLS: DRAMA UK

EASTON, Lydia
T 07977 511621
Singing Teacher
4 Courland Grove, London SW8 2PX
E lydzeaston@yahoo.com

ÉCOLE INTERNATIONALE DE THÉÂTRE JACQUES LECOQ
T 00 33 1 47704478
*Acting Workshops. Drama School (over 21 yrs). Mime.
Movement & Creative Theatre. Play Writing*
57 rue du Faubourg Saint-Denis
75010 Paris
France **F** 00 33 1 45234014
E contact@ecole-jacqueslecoq.com
W www.ecole-jacqueslecoq.com

EDINBURGH LIGHTING & SOUND SCHOOL (ELSS)
T 07590 015957
c/o Black Light
West Shore Trading Estate
West Shore Road, Edinburgh EH5 1QF
E contact@edinburghlightingandsoundschool.co.uk
W www.edinburghlightingandsoundschool.co.uk

EDUCATION IN STAGE & THEATRE ARTS (E.S.T.A.)
T 020 8741 2843
16 British Grove, Chiswick, London W4 2NL
F 020 8746 3219
E esta@charkham.net
W www.estatheatreschool.com

EEDLE, Ben
T 07587 526286
*Voice Coaching. Audition Preparation. Monologue
Stucturing*
273 Camberwell New Road, London SE5 0TF
E ben@theenglishbears.com
W www.theenglishbears.com

EXPRESSIONS ACADEMY OF PERFORMING ARTS
T 01623 424334
3 Newgate Lane, Mansfield
Nottingham NG18 2LB
E expressions-uk@btconnect.com
W www.expressionsperformingarts.co.uk

FAIRBROTHER, Victoria MA CSSD LAMDA Dip
T 07877 228990
*Audition Technique. Improvisation. Private Acting
Classes. Public Speaking. Vocal Coaching*
15A Devonport Road, Shepherd's Bush
London W12 8NZ
E victoriafairbrother1@hotmail.com

FAIRCLOUGH, Amanda STAGE & FILM SCHOOL
T 07929 823110
Children 4-18 yrs
Horwich Resource Centre, Beaumont Road
Horwich, Bolton, Lancashire BL6 7BG
E info@stageandfilmschool.co.uk
W www.stageandfilmschool.co.uk

FAITH, Gordon BA IPA Dip.REM.Sp LRAM
T 020 7328 0446
Speech & Voice
1 Wavel Mews, Priory Road
West Hampstead, London NW6 3AB
E gordon.faith@tiscali.co.uk
W www.gordonfaith.co.uk

FERRIS, Anna Theresa
T 01258 881098
*MA Voice Studies, Royal Central School of Speech &
Drama. Voice & Text Coach working in Dorset, Somerset
& Wiltshire*
E atcferris@gmail.com

FERRIS ENTERTAINMENT PERFORMING ARTS
T 07801 493133
*Acting Classes. London. Belfast. Cardiff. Los Angeles.
France. Spain*
Number 8, 132 Charing Cross Road
London WC2H 0LA
E info@ferrisentertainment.com
W www.ferrisentertainment.com

FINBURGH, Nina
T 020 7435 9484
*Cold & Prepared Readings Specialist. Masterclasses &
Individuals. (Equity Members only)*
1 Buckingham Mansions, West End Lane
London NW6 1LR
E ninafinburgh@aol.com

FOOTSTEPS THEATRE SCHOOL & AGENCY
T/F 07554 761307
Dance, Drama & Singing Training
Westfield Lane, Bradford
West Yorkshire BD10 8PY
E gwestman500@btinternet.com

FORD, Carole Ann ADVS　　T 020 8815 1832
Acting Coach. Communication Skills
Based in N10,
E emko2000@aol.com

FOURTH MONKEY　　T 020 7281 0360
Actor Training Programmes, 1 & 2 yr, full-time. Repertory
& Ensemble Focused Training
97-101 Seven Sisters Road, London N7 7QP
E office@fourthmonkey.co.uk
W www.fourthmonkey.co.uk

FRANKLIN, Michael
Meisner Technique
Correspondence: c/o Spotlight, 7 Leicester Place
London WC2H 7RJ
E info@acteach.info

FRANKLYN, Susan　　T 07780 742891
Audition Speeches. Confidence. Interview Technique.
Presentation. Sight Reading
E susan.franklyn1@btinternet.com

FURNESS, Simon　　T 07702 619665
Actor Training. Audition Preparation & Technique
c/o The Actors' Temple, 13-14 Warren Street
London W1T 5LG
E simonfurness@googlemail.com

GFCA (GILES FOREMAN
CENTRE FOR ACTING)　　T 020 7437 3175
4-term Postgraduate-Level Intensive Acting & Acting/
Directing/Writing Diploma (PGIP). 4-term Actor-Director
Postgraduate-Level Intensive Diploma (PGIAD). 3-term
Foundation ATCL Diploma. Part-time courses: 12-week
Acting, all levels inc Professionals, 10-week Movement,
Voice, Improvisation, Meisner, On-Camera. Malmgren/
Laban Analysis. Short Courses: International Acting
Masterclasses & Workshops all year, Summer Schools,
Audition Technique. Private Acting Coaching. Twitter: @
gilesForeman1
Studio Soho, 2A Royalty Mews, (entrance by Quo Vadis)
22-25 Dean Street, London W1D 3AR
E info@gilesforeman.com
W www.gilesforeman.com

GILLETT, Prue
ACTOR TRAINING　　T 07786 512841
One-to-one tuition & Meisner training in small groups
with qualified Acting coach based in Altrincham, South
Manchester & Leek, North Staffordshire. Courses
arranged elsewhere on request
E coaching@pruegillett.com
W www.pruegillett.com/coaching

GMA TELEVISION
PRESENTER TRAINING　　T 01628 673078
Presenting for Television, Radio, Live Events. Autocue.
Improvisation. Scriptwriting. Talkback. Vocal Coaching
86 Beverley Gardens, Maidenhead
Berks SL6 6SW
T 07769 598625
E geoff@gma-training.co.uk
W www.gma-training.co.uk

GRAYSON, John　　T 07702 188031
Audition Coaching. Vocal Technique. Improvisation
Skills. Also Coaching for Public Speaking. Experienced
Classical & Musical Theatre Performer. Singing Lessons.
Vocal Coaching
2 Jubilee Road, St Johns
Worcester WR2 4LY
E jgbizzybee@btinternet.com

GREASEPAINT ANONYMOUS   T 020 8360 9785
Youth Theatre & Training Company. Part-time Theatre Workshops run weekly through School Term Time. Holiday Courses at Easter & Summer. Acting Workshops. Dancing. Singing (4-30 yrs)
Flat 13 Oak Lodge
50 Eversley Park Road
London N21 1JL
T 07930 421216
E info@greasepaintanonymous.co.uk

GROUNDLINGS THEATRE   T 023 9273 9496
Drama School Training for Young People & Adults
42 Kent Street, Portsmouth
Hampshire PO1 3BT
E richard@groundlings.co.uk
W www.groundlings.co.uk

GRYFF, Stefan   T 020 7723 8181
Screen Acting Coach

GSA, GUILDFORD SCHOOL OF ACTING
See DRAMA SCHOOLS: DRAMA UK

GUILDHALL SCHOOL OF MUSIC & DRAMA
See DRAMA SCHOOLS: DRAMA UK

HABER, Margie   T 001 310 854 0462
On-camera Audition Technique Training in Los Angeles
971 N. La Cienega Boulevard, #207
Los Angeles, CA 90069, USA
F 001 310 854 0870
E info@margiehaber.com
W www.margiehaber.com

HANCOCK, Allison LLAM   T/F 020 8891 1073
Acting. Audition Coach. Dramatic Art. Elocution. Speech Correction. Voice
38 Eve Road, Isleworth
Middlesex TW7 7HS
E allisonhancock@blueyonder.co.uk

HARRIS, Sharon NCSD LRAM LAM STSD IPA Dip DA (London Univ)   T 01923 211644
Speech & Drama Specialist Teacher. Private Acting Coach for Screen & Stage. Training for RADA, LAMDA & ESB Exams. Audition Technique. Drama School & National Youth Theatre Audition Preparation
71 The Avenue, Watford
Herts WD17 4NU
T 07956 388716
E theharrisagency@btconnect.com

HARRISON RUTHERFORD, Lucie MA Voice Studies, BA (Hons) Drama   T 07773 798440
Voice Tutor & Acting Coach
Based in Richmond upon Thames,
E lurutherford@gmail.com
W www.lucieharrison.co.uk

HASS, Leontine
Vocal Coach. CEO/Founding Principal of Associated Studios
E leontine@associatedstudios.co.uk
W www.leontinehass.com

HAWES, Jo   T 01628 773048
Masterclasses in The Art of Auditioning for Children. From 7 yrs upwards
21 Westfield Road, Maidenhead
Berkshire SL6 5AU
E joanne.hawes2013@gmail.com
W johawes.com

HESTER, John LLCM (TD)   T 020 8224 9580
Member of The Society of Teachers of Speech & Drama. Acting Courses for all Ages. Acting Workshops. Audition Technique. Dialect/Accent Coaching. Drama School Auditions (over 18 yrs). Elocution Coaching. Private Acting Classes. Public Speaking. Stage School for Children. Vocal Coaching
105 Stoneleigh Park Road, Epsom
Surrey KT19 0RF
E hjohnhester@aol.com

HETHERINGTON, Caro   T 07723 620728
Voice & Dialect Coach
7 Dodcott Barns, Burleydam
Whitchurch, Cheshire SY13 4BQ
E carolinehetherington@gmail.com
W www.carohetherington.co.uk

HIGGS, Jessica   T 020 7701 8477
Voice
34 Mary Datchelor House
2D Camberwell Grove
London SE5 8FB
T 07940 193631
E juhiggs@aol.com

HOFFMANN-GILL, Daniel   T 07946 433903
Acting & Audition Tuition
E danielhg@gmail.com

HOOKER, Jennifer Jane   T 07725 977146
Private Acting Coach. Audition Technique. Private Acting Classes. Public Speaking. Approved to teach Susan Batson Tecnique. Based in North West London - Nearest tube Marylebone
E jj@jjhooker.com
W www.jjhooker.com

HOOPLA IMPRO   T 07976 975348
Contact: Steve Roe. Acting Workshops. Improvisation. Public Speaking. Comedy. Courses: Beginners Improvisation, 8 weeks, part-time. Performance Improvisation, 8 weeks, part-time. Stand-up Comedy, 8 weeks, part-time. Sketch Comedy, 8 weeks, part-time. All levels of experience, beginners welcome. Various venues around London.
E hooplaimpro@gmail.com
W www.hooplaimpro.com

HOPE STREET LTD   T 0151 708 8007
Professional Development Opportunities for Emerging & Established Artists
13A Hope Street
Liverpool L1 9BQ
E peter@hope-street.org
W www.hope-street.org

HOPKINS, Abigail   T 07847 420882
Audition & Acting Coach
E creativeacting@hotmail.co.uk

HOUSEMAN, Barbara   T 07767 843737
Ex-RSC Voice Dept. Author 'Finding Your Voice' & 'Tackling Text'. Voice. Text. Acting. Confidence
E barbarahouseman@hotmail.com
W www.barbarahouseman.com

HOWARD, Ashley BA MA   T 07821 213752
Voice Coach
5 St John's Street, Aylesbury
Bucks HP20 1BS
E ashleynormanhoward@me.com
W www.ashleyhoward.me

HUDSON, Mark T 0161 238 8900
Film & Television Acting & Dialect Coach
14-32 Hewitt Street, Manchester M15 4GB
E actorclass@aol.com

HUGHES, Dewi T 07836 545717
Voice. Text. Accents. Auditions
Flat 1, 4 Fielding Road
London W14 0LL
E dewi.hughes@gmail.com

HUGHES-D'AETH, Charlie T 07811 010963
RSC Text & Voice Coach. Acting & Audition Technique.
Presentation Skills. Public Speaking. Vocal Coaching
E chdaeth@aol.com

IDENTITY SCHOOL OF ACTING T 020 7502 4672
160-170 Cannon Street Road, London E1 2LH
E studentadmin@identitydramaschool.com
W www.identitydramaschool.com

IMPULSE COMPANY THE T/F 07525 264173
Meisner-Based Core Training
E info@impulsecompany.co.uk
W www.impulsecompany.co.uk

INDEPENDENT THEATRE
WORKSHOP THE T 00 353 1 2600831
Theatre School & Agency for Children & Teenagers
8 Terminus Mills, Clonskeagh
Dublin 6, Ireland
E office@itwstudios.ie
W www.itwstudios.ie

INTERACT T 07961 982198
Contact: Lauren Bigby (LGSM). Acting Workshops.
Audition Technique. Elocution Coaching. Private Acting
Classes. Public Speaking
18 Knightbridge Walk, Billericay
Essex CM12 0HP
E renbigby@hotmail.com

INTERNATIONAL PERFORMING
ARTS & THEATRE LTD T 020 3714 3393
Accredited Awarding Body. Programmes in Dance,
Singing, Acting & Musical Theatre
HQ, Fearon Hall
Loughborough
Leicestershire LE11 1PL
E info@i-path.biz
W www.i-path.biz

INTERNATIONAL SCHOOL
OF SCREEN ACTING T 020 8709 8719
Courses: 1 yr Advanced, full-time. 2 yr, full-time. Drama
School (over 18 yrs)
3 Mills Studios
The Old Lab
Three Mill Lane, London E3 3DU
E office@screenacting.co.uk
W www.screenacting.co.uk

J VOX VOCAL ACADEMY T 07546 100745
Contact: Jay Henry. The Voice, BBC Vocal Coach. Vocal
Training & Audition Preparation for Television & Reality
Shows. Microphone Technique
Dunbar, Latimer Road
Barnet EN5 5NF
T 07854 596916
E info@jvox.co.uk
W www.jvoxacademy.com

JACK, Andrew T 07740 980184
Dialect Coach
The Boathouse, Timsway
Staines-Upon-Thames, Middlesex TW18 3JY
W www.andrewjack.com

JACK, Paula T 07836 615839
Dialect Coach. Language Specialist
E dialect.guru@mac.com
W www.paulajack.com

JAM ACADEMY THE T 01628 483808
Performance & Production Training & Qualifications
Jam Theatre Company, 45A West Street
Marlow, Bucks SL7 3NH
E info@thejamacademy.co.uk
W www.thejamacademy.co.uk

JAMES, Linda
RAM Dip Ed IPD LRAM T 020 8568 2390
Dialect & Speech Coach
25 Clifden Road, Brentford
Middlesex TW8 0PB

JAQUARELLO, Roland BA T 020 8567 5988
Audition Technique. Drama School Entrance.
Radio Coaching
11 Chestnut Grove, London W5 4JT
T 07808 742307
E rolandjaquarello@gmail.com
W www.rolandjaquarello.com

JARVIS, Nathan T 07970 963282
Singing Teacher. Audition Preparation & Technique
158C Croydon Road, Penge
London SE20 7YZ
E nathanjarvis81@hotmail.com
W www.nathancjarvis.co.uk

JG DANCE LTD T 01491 572000
Dance Academy & Theatre College
Melody House, 198 Grey's Road
Henley-on-Thames, Oxon RG9 1QU
E info@jgdance.co.uk
W www.jgdance.co.uk

JIGSAW PERFORMING
ARTS SCHOOLS T 020 8447 4530
64-66 High Street, Barnet, Herts EN5 5SJ
F 020 8447 4531
E enquiries@jigsaw-arts.co.uk
W www.jigsaw-arts.co.uk

JINGLES, Jo T 01494 778989
Music, Singing & Movement
1 Boismore Road, Chesham, Bucks HP5 1SH
E headoffice@jojingles.co.uk
W www.jojingles.com

JK'S PERFORMANCE
ACADEMY T 01685 882525
Contact: Julia Kelleher
6 Waterloo Street, Cwmbach
Aberdare, Rhondda Cynon Taff CF44 0ED
T 07852 901616
E info@jksperformanceacademy.co.uk
W www.jksperformanceacademy.co.uk

JOHNSON, David DRAMA T 07969 183481
Acting Tutor
PO Box 618, Oldham
Greater Manchester OL1 9GU
E johnsondrama@googlemail.com
W www.davidjohnsondrama.co.uk

K-BIS THEATRE SCHOOL T 01273 566739
Clermont Hall
Cumberland Road
Brighton, East Sussex BN1 6SL
E k-bis@live.co.uk
W www.kbistheatreschool.co.uk

KADHIM, Najwa T 07977 603483
Arabic Language & Dialect Specialist. Arabic Native
Speaker
7 Cotman Close, Westleigh Avenue
London SW15 6RG
E najwakadhim@gmail.com

KENT YOUTH THEATRE
STAGE & SCREEN ACADEMY T 01227 730177
Contact: Richard Andrews. Weekly Classes plus Stage
& Screen Productions. From 3 yrs upwards. KYT Agency
for Professional Work
Office: Mulberry Croft, Mulberry Hill
Chilham CT4 8AJ
T 07967 580213
E richard@kentyouththeatre.co.uk
W www.kentyouththeatre.co.uk

KERR, Louise T 020 8509 2767
Voice Coach
20A Rectory Road, London E17 3BQ
T 07780 708102
E louise@resonancevoice.com
W www.resonancevoice.com

KIDZ ON THE HILL
PERFORMING ARTS SCHOOL T 07881 553480
Weekly Classes in Ballet, Street Dance, Acting, Singing.
Free Trials
Pages Lane, Muswell Hill
London, Haringey N10 1PP
E admin@kidzonthehill.co.uk
W www.kidzonthehill.co.uk

KINGSTON JUNIOR
DRAMA COMPANY T 01932 230273
Youth Theatre (10-14 yrs)
72 Shaw Drive, Walton-on-Thames
Surrey KT12 2LS
E kingstonjdc@aol.com
W www.davidlawsonlean.com

KIRKLEES COLLEGE T 01484 437047
Courses in Acting, Dance & Musical Theatre (BTEC)
Highfields Annexe, New North Road
Huddersfield HD1 5LS
E info@kirkleescollege.ac.uk

KNYVETTE, Sally T 020 7385 2216
Drama Tuition. Specialising in Drama School Entrance.
Particular Focus on Shakespeare. Audition Speech
Preparation for Theatre, Film & Television (includes filmed
playback). References available. West Brompton nearest
Tube. 74 & 430 Buses to the Door
239 Lillie Road, Fulham
London SW6 7LN
T 07958 972425
E salkny@gmail.com
W www.sallyknyvette.co.uk

KOGAN ACADEMY OF
DRAMATIC ARTS T 020 7272 0027
9-15 Elthorne Road, London N19 4AJ
F 020 7272 0026
E info@scienceofacting.com
W www.scienceofacting.com

KRIMPAS, Titania T 07957 303958
One-to-one Tuition, all Levels. Tailored to Suit
Experienced Actors & Beginners
36 Deronda Road
London SE24 9BG
E titaniakrimpas@gmail.com

KSA PERFORMING ARTS T 020 8090 5801
Training in all aspects of Musical Theatre & Acting
Beckenham Halls
4 Bromley Road
Beckenham BR3 5JE
E info@ksapa.org.uk
W www.ksapa.co.uk

LAINE THEATRE ARTS T 01372 724648
Training College for Performing Arts
The Studios, East Street
Epsom, Surrey KT17 1HH
F 01372 723775
E info@laine-theatre-arts.co.uk
W www.laine-theatre-arts.co.uk

LAMDA
See DRAMA SCHOOLS: DRAMA UK

LAMONT DRAMA SCHOOL
& CASTING AGENCY T 07736 387543
Contact: Diane Lamont. Acting Skills. Audition
Technique. Coaching. Part-time Lessons
2 Harewood Avenue, Ainsdale
Merseyside PR8 2PH
E diane@lamontcasting.co.uk
W www.lamontcasting.co.uk

LAURIE, Rona T 020 7262 4909
Audition Coach. Public Speaking. Voice & Speech
Technique
Flat 1, 21 New Quebec Street
London W1H 7SA

LEAN, David Lawson
BA Hons PGCE T 01932 230273
Acting Tuition for Children. LAMDA Exams. Licensed
Chaperone
72 Shaw Drive, Walton-on-Thames
Surrey KT12 2LS
E dlawsonlean@gmail.com
W www.davidlawsonlean.com

LEE, Steven T 07771 665582
Performance Pianist & Piano Teacher
80 Kimberley Road
Southbourne
Bournemouth, Dorset BH6 5BY
E stevenleepianist@yahoo.com

LEE THEATRE SCHOOL THE T 01268 793090
Office: 48 Brook Road, Benfleet
Essex SS7 5JF
T 07875 164375
E poultonlee.theatre@gmail.com
W www.poultonlee.com

LEVENTON, Patricia BA Hons T 020 7624 5661
Audition & Dialect Coach. RP, Irish, American etc. Sight
Reading. Drama School Entry
113 Broadhurst Gardens
West Hampstead
London NW6 3BJ
T 07703 341062
E patricia@lites2000.com

LHK YOUTH THEATRE
COMPANY T 01744 808907
Training for 6-18 yrs in the North West
20 Maltby Close
St Helens WA9 5GJ
E info@lhkproductions.co.uk
W www.lhkyouththeatre.co.uk

LIPTON, Rick T 07961 445247
Dialect/Accent Coaching
14 Lock Road
Richmond
Surrey TW10 7LH
E info@ricklipton.com
W www.ricklipton.com

LIR, NATIONAL ACADEMY OF DRAMATIC ART THE T 00 353 1 896 2559
Trinity Technology and Enterprise Campus
Pearse Street, Dublin 2
E info@thelir.ie
W www.thelir.ie

LITTLE ACTORS THEATRE CLUB LIVERPOOL T 0151 336 4302
Community Stage School for Children. Dance.
Drama. Singing
c/o 9 Carlton Close, Parkgate
Neston, Cheshire CH64 6TD
E mail@littleactorstheatre.com
W www.littleactorstheatre.com

LITTLE ACTORS THEATRE CLUB NESTON T 0151 336 4302
Dance, Drama & Singing Training (2-11 yrs)
9 Carlton Close, Parkgate
Neston, Cheshire CH64 6TD
E mail@littleactorstheatre.com
W www.littleactorstheatre.com

LITTLE ALLSTARS CASTING DRAMA SCHOOL T 0161 702 8257
Children & Young Performers
T 07584 992429
E drama@littleallstars.co.uk
W www.littleallstars.co.uk

LITTLE SHAKESPEARE THEATRE SCHOOL T 07724 937331
Classes, Workshops, Shakespearean Performances &
Training for Young Actors led by Professional Actors
19 Seaview Terrace, Edinburgh, Joppa EH15 2HD
E michelle@littleshakespearetheatreschool.co.uk
W www.littleshakespearetheatreschool.co.uk

LIVERPOOL INSTITUTE FOR PERFORMING ARTS THE
See DRAMA SCHOOLS: DRAMA UK

LLOYD, Gabrielle T 020 8946 4042
Audition Technique. Drama School Entrance. LAMDA
Exams. Private Acting Classes. Public Speaking.
Vocal Coaching
Based in South West London,
E gubilloyd@hotmail.com

LOCATION TUTORS NATIONWIDE T 020 7978 8898
Fully Qualified & Experienced Teachers Working with
Children on Film Sets & Covering all Key Stages of
National Curriculum
16 Poplar Walk, Herne Hill, London SE24 0BU
T 07806 887471 (Text Messages)
E locationtutorsnationwide@gmail.com
W www.locationtutors.co.uk

LONDON ACTORS WORKSHOP T 07748 846294
Workshop Studio based in Endell Street, Covent Garden
Enquiries: 29B Battersea Rise, London SW11 1HG
E info@londonactorsworkshop.co.uk
W www.londonactorsworkshop.co.uk

LONDON INTERNATIONAL SCHOOL OF PERFORMING ARTS T 020 8215 3390
Bridge House, 3 Mills Studios
Three Mill Lane, London E3 3DU
F 020 8215 3392
E welcome@lispa.co.uk
W www.lispa.co.uk

LONDON LANGUAGE TRAINING T 07941 468639
English Language Coaching for Overseas Actors Looking
to Improve Fluency, Pronunciation & Intonation. All
Courses Taught by English Language Teacher, Trainer &
Author Luke Vyner
E luke@londonlanguagetraining.co.uk
W www.londonlanguagetraining.co.uk

LONDON REPERTORY COMPANY ACADEMY T/F 020 7258 1944
PO Box 59385
London NW8 1HL
E academy@londonrepertorycompany.com
W www.londonrepertorycompany.com

LONDON SCHOOL OF DRAMATIC ART T 020 7581 6100
Foundation & Advanced Diplomas in Acting (full & part-
time). Drama School (over 18 yrs). Short
Summer Courses
4 Bute Street, South Kensington
London SW7 3EX
E enquiries@lsda-acting.com
W www.lsda-acting.com

LONDON SCHOOL OF MUSICAL THEATRE T 020 7407 4455
Price Studios, 110 York Road, London SW11 3RD
E info@lsmt.co.uk

LONDON STUDIO CENTRE T 020 7837 7741
Courses in Theatre Dance, 3 yrs, full-time, BA. Saturday
Classes & Summer Courses
artsdepot, 5 Nether Street
Tally Ho Corner, North Finchley
London N12 0GA
E info@londonstudiocentre.org
W www.londonstudiocentre.org

LONG OVERDUE THEATRE SCHOOL THE T 0845 8382994
Drama, Dance & Singing for Children
16 Butterfield Drive, Amesbury
Wiltshire SP4 7SJ
E stefpearmain@hotmail.com
W www.tlots.co.uk

LONGMORE, Wyllie T 0161 264 0089
Acting Techniques. Voice & Speech. Presentation Skills
Based in Manchester
E info@wyllielongmore.co.uk
W www.wyllielongmore.co.uk

MACKINNON, Alison T 07973 562132
Accent. Audition Preparation. Presentation. Voice
Based in London SE6,
E alimac810@gmail.com

MAD RED THEATRE SCHOOL AT THE MADDERMARKET THEATRE, NORWICH T 01603 628600
Contact: Jen Dewsbury. Courses: Youth Theatre (ages
2-19 yrs), 1 term, part-time. Adult Evening Classes, 1
term, part-time. Open Stagers (55+ yrs), 1 term, part-
time. Youth Summer School, 1 week Intensive, full-time.
Acting Workshops. Drama School (over 18 yrs). Drama
School Preparation. Private Acting Classes. Stage
School for Children
Maddermarket Theatre, St John's Alley
Norwich NR2 1DR
F 01603 661357
E jenny.dewsbury@maddermarket.org
W www.mad-red.co.uk

MANCHESTER SCHOOL OF ACTING　　T/F 0161 238 8900
14-32 Hewitt Street
Manchester M15 4GB
E info@manchesterschoolofacting.co.uk
W www.manchesterschoolofacting.co.uk

MANCHESTER SCHOOL OF THEATRE AT MANCHESTER METROPOLITAN UNIVERSITY
See DRAMA SCHOOLS: DRAMA UK

MARLOW, Chris　　T 07792 309992
Voice & Speech Teacher
RDDC, 52 Bridleway, Waterfoot
Rossendale, Lancashire BB4 9DS
E christopher.marlow@btinternet.com
W www.rddc.co.uk

MARLOW, Jean LGSM　　T 020 8450 0371
32 Exeter Road
London NW2 4SB

MARPLE DRAMA　　T 07874 216681
Drama Workshops & Acting Classes for Children & Adults
7 Ridge Road, Marple
Cheshire SK6 7HL
E enquiries@marpledrama.com
W www.marpledrama.com

MARTIN, Mandi SINGING TECHNIQUE　　T 020 8950 7525
Previously at London Studio Centre, Bodywork & Millennium Performing Arts. Currently Available for Private Lessons
T 07811 758656
E mandi.martin@sky.com

MASTERS PERFORMING ARTS COLLEGE LTD　　T 01268 777351
Performing Arts Course
Arterial Road, Rayleigh
Essex SS6 7UQ
E info@mastersperformingarts.co.uk

McCARTHY, Sara　　T 07876 298613
Vocal & Performance Training
9 Tennyson Road, Stoke
Coventry, West Midlands CV2 5HX
E sara@saramccarthy.co.uk
W www.saramccarthy.co.uk

McDAID, Marj　　T 07815 993203
Voice Coach
1 Chesholm Road, Stoke Newington
London N16 0DP
E marjmcdaid@hotmail.com
W www.voicings.co.uk

McDONAGH, Melanie MANAGEMENT (ACADEMY OF PERFORMING ARTS & CASTING AGENCY)　　T 07909 831409
14 Apple Tree Way, Oswaldtwistle
Accrington, Lancashire BB5 0FB
T 01254 392560
E mcdonaghmgt@aol.com
W www.mcdonaghmanagement.co.uk

McKEAND, Ian　　T 07768 960530
Audition Technique. Drama School Entry
Based in Lincoln,
E ian.mckeand@ntlworld.com
W http://homepage.ntlworld.com/ian.mckeand1

McKELLAN, Martin　　**T** 07425 204070
Acting Workshops. Dialect/Accent Coaching. Private
Acting Classes. Vocal Coaching
Covent Garden, London WC2H 9PA
E dialectandvoice@yahoo.co.uk

MELADRAMA　　**T** 07789 004062
Contact: Melanie Ash. Acting School & Agency
E melanie@meladrama.co.uk
W www.meladrama.co.uk

MELAINEY, John
THE CASTING COACH　　**T** 07952 232255
Casting Technique. Sight Reading. Coaching. Audition
Coaching. Audition on Camera Service
49 Herbert Road, Wimbledon
London SW19 3SQ
E john@johnmelainey.com
W www.121auditioncoach.com

MELBOURNE ACTING STUDIO:
LONDON　　**T** 07752 948351
Contact: Bruce Alexander. Group & Private Acting
Classes for Beginners & Professional Actors
University House, 55 East Road
London N1 6AH
E info@melbourneactingstudio.com
W www.melbourneactingstudio.co.uk

MELLECK, Lydia　　**T** 020 7794 8845
Pianist & Coach for Auditions & Repertoire, RADA,
Mountview. Accompanist. Singing for Beginners.
Vocal Coaching. Workshops
10 Burgess Park Mansions, London NW6 1DP
E lyd.muse@yahoo.co.uk

MGA ACADEMY OF
PERFORMING ARTS THE　　**T** 0131 466 9392
207 Balgreen Road, Edinburgh EH11 2RZ
E info@themgaacademy.com
W www.themgaacademy.com

MICHAELJOHN'S
ACTING ACADEMY　　**T** 020 3463 8492
In association with Khando Entertainment. Contact:
Ajay Nayyar. Acting Studio. 4 hours classes twice a week
E info@khandoentertainment.com

MICHEL, Hilary ARCM　　**T** 020 8343 7243
Singing Teacher & Vocal Coach. Audition Songs.
Accompanist. Piano, Recorder & Theory Teacher
21 Southway, Totteridge, London N20 8EB
T 07775 780182
E hilarymich@optimamail.co.uk

MILLER, Robin　　**T** 07957 627677
Audition Coaching. Dialect/Accent Coaching
Based in St Margarets/Twickenham,
E robinjenni@hotmail.com

MORE DRAMATIC
THEATRE COMPANY　　**T** 07869 130735
Acting, Dancing & Musical Theatre Classes
37 Carthall Road, Coleraine BT51 3LP
E info@moredrama.co.uk
W www.moredrama.co.uk

MORLEY COLLEGE　　**T** 020 7450 1889
Courses: Actor Training, Performance Skills, Making
Theatre & Personal Development
61 Westminster Bridge Road, London SE1 7HT
E drama@morleycollege.ac.uk
W www.morleycollege.ac.uk

MORRISON, Elspeth　　**T** 07790 919870
Accent & Dialect Coach
E elsp.morrison@talk21.com

MORRISON, J Stuart MA Voice Studies
(RCSSD) FVCM (TD)
(Hons) FIfL FRSA　　**T** 020 3651 2100
Voice, Speech & Acting Coach
24 Deans Walk
Coulsdon
Surrey CR5 1HR
T 07825 618596
E stuartvoicecoach@yahoo.co.uk
W www.voiceandspeechtrainer.com

MOUNTVIEW ACADEMY OF THEATRE ARTS
See DRAMA SCHOOLS: DRAMA UK

MTA THE　　**T** 020 8885 6543
2 yr professional Musical Theatre Training
Bernie Grant Arts Centre
Town Hall Approach
Tottenham Green, London N15 4RX
T 07904 987493
E info@themta.co.uk
W www.themta.co.uk

MURRAY, Barbara
LGSM LALAM　　**T** 01923 823182
129 Northwood Way, Northwood
Middlesex HA6 1RF
E barbarahalliwell@gmail.com

MUSICAL KIDZ
COMPANY THE　　**T** 07989 353673
Spires Meade, 4 Bridleways
Wendover, Bucks HP22 6DN
F 01296 623696
E themusicalkidz@aol.com
W www.themusicalkidz.co.uk

MUSICAL THEATRE AUDITIONS
Information, Tips & Resources for Musical Theatre
Auditions
Based in London
E hello@musicaltheatreauditions.info
W www.musicaltheatreauditions.info

NATHENSON, Zoë　　**T** 07956 833850
Audition Technique. Film Acting. Sight Reading. Group
Classes. Self Tapes
E zoe.act@btinternet.com
W www.zoenathenson.com

NEO - NUNCHAKU EXERCISE
ORGANISATION　　**T** 020 8337 6181
Fight Scene Staging, Planning & Training. Training in the
use of Nunchaku vs Nunchaku & Other Weapons. Venue
based in Kingston, London
Mail to: 202 Bridgewood Road
Worcester Park
Sutton, Surrey KT4 8XU
E neo@neo-nunchaku.co.uk
W www.neo-nunchaku.co.uk

NEW COLLEGE, LANARKSHIRE
MOTHERWELL CAMPUS　　**T** 01698 232323
Courses: Acting. Musical Theatre. HNC/D, BA Hons
1 Enterprise Way
Motherwell ML1 2TX
E information@newcollegelanarkshiremotherwellcampus.co.uk
W www.nclan.ac.uk

NEW LONDON PERFORMING ARTS CENTRE   T 020 8444 4544
Courses in Performing Arts (3-19 yrs). Dance. Drama. Singing. Instruments. GCSE/A-Level Courses, LAMDA, ISTD & RAD. Holiday Workshops. Specialist Professional Preparation Classes
76 St James Lane, Muswell Hill
London N10 3RD
E info@nlpac.co.uk
W www.nlpac.co.uk

NEWNHAM, Caryll   T 01255 670973
Singing Teacher
69 Old Road, Frinton
Essex CO13 9BX
T 07976 635745
E caryllnewnham@gmail.com

**NOBLE, Penny
PSYCHOTHERAPY**   T 07506 579895
Character-Centred Counselling & Training. Character Development. Performance Support. Safe Emotion Memory Work. Script Work. Self-esteem & Confidence
8 Shaftesbury Gardens, Victoria Road
North Acton, London NW10 6LJ
E pennynobletherapy@googlemail.com
W www.pennynoblepsychotherapy.com

**NORTHERN:
DRAMA ACTING SCHOOL**   T 07787 311270
Led by Jo Adamson-Parker
c/o The Carriageworks Theatre, Leeds LS1
E ndas@northerndrama.co.uk

**NORTHERN ACADEMY
OF PERFORMING ARTS**   T 01482 310690
Drama, Dance & Musical Theatre Training 3-19 yrs. Community classes all ages
Anlaby Road, Hull HU1 2PD
F 01482 212280
E napa@northernacademy.org.uk
W www.northernacademy.org.uk

NORTHERN FILM & DRAMA   T 01977 681949
Acting Workshops. Television Audition Technique. Drama School. On Location Filming. Film & Television Training. Improvisation. Private Acting Classes. Stage School for Children
The Studio, 21 Low Street
South Milford
Leeds LS25 5AR
E info@northernfilmanddrama.com
W www.northernfilmanddrama.com

NPAS @ THE STUDIOS   T/F 00 353 1 8944660
Classes in Dance, Drama, Musical Theatre & Ballet
NPAS The Factory, 35A Darrow Street
Dublin 4, Ireland
E info@npas.ie
W www.npas.ie

O.J. SONUS   T 020 8963 0702
Voice Over Workshops. Voicereel Production with Professional Coaching Available
14-15 Main Drive, East Lane Business Park
Wembley HA9 7NA
T 07929 859401
E info@ojsonus.com
W www.ojsonus.com

**OLLERENSHAW, Maggie
BA (Hons) Dip Ed**   T 020 7286 1126
Acting Workshops. Audition Technique. Career Guidance. Private Acting. Television & Theatre Coaching
151D Shirland Road, London W9 2EP
T 07860 492699
E maggieoll@aol.com

OLSON, Lise   T 0121 331 7220
Acting through Song. American Accents. Vocal Coaching. Working with Text
c/o Birmingham School of Acting
Millennium Point
Curzon Street, Birmingham B4 7XG
E lise.olson@bcu.ac.uk

OMOBONI, Lino T/F 020 8741 2038
Private Acting Classes
182 Riverside Gardens, London W6 9LQ
T 07525 187468
E bluewand@btinternet.com

OPEN VOICE T 07704 704930
*Contact: Catherine Owen. Auditions. Consultancy.
Personal Presentations*
9 Bellsmains, Gorebridge, Near Edinburgh EH23 4QD
E catherineowenopenvoice@gmail.com

ORAM, Daron T 07905 332497
*Voice, Text & Accent Coach. Teaches on the Actor
Training & Voice Teacher Training Courses at the Royal
Central School of Speech & Drama. Also Coached for
the RSC, West End & National Tours. A Designated
Linklater Voice Teacher*
E darono@yahoo.com

OSBORNE HUGHES, John T 020 8653 7735
*Acting Coach. London/Los Angeles. Acting
Workshops. Audition Technique. Drama School
(over 18s). Private Acting Classes. Public Speaking.
Courses: Introduction to Acting, part-time.
Advanced Acting Technique*
Miracle Tree Productions, 51 Church Road
London SE19 2TE
T 07801 950916
E info@miracletreeproductions.com
W www.spiritualpsychologyofacting.com

OSCARS THEATRE ACADEMY T 01484 545519
Contact: Paula Danholm
Oscars Management, Spring Bank House
1 Spring Bank, New North Road, Huddersfield
West Yorkshire HD1 5NR
E management@oscarsacademy.co.uk

OXFORD SCHOOL OF DRAMA THE
See DRAMA SCHOOLS: DRAMA UK

**PALMER, Jackie STAGE
SCHOOL** T 01494 510597
30 Daws Hill Lane, High Wycombe, Bucks HP11 1PW
F 01494 510479
E info@jackiepalmerstageschool.co.uk
W www.jpaassociates.co.uk

PARKES, Frances MA AGSM T/F 020 8542 2777
*Contact: Frances Parkes, Sarah Upson. Dialect/Accent
Coaching & Script Coach. Interview Skills for Castings.
Presenting. Private Acting Classes. Public Speaking.
Speak English Clearly Programme for Actors with English
as a Second Language*
Suite 5, 3rd Floor, 1 Harley Street, London W1G 9QD
T 01782 827222 (Upson Edwards)
E frances@maxyourvoice.com
W www.maxyourvoice.com

**PERFORMANCE FACTORY
STAGE SCHOOL THE** T 01792 701570
The Performance Factory Wales Ltd, Kemys Way
Swansea Enterprise Park SA6 8QF
E info@theperformancefactorywales.com
W www.theperformancefactorywales.com

**PERFORMANCE
PREPARATION ACADEMY (PPA)** T 01483 459080
Unit 5, Riverside Business Centre, Walnut Tree Close
Guildford, Surrey GU1 4UG
E enquiries@ppacademy.co.uk
W www.ppacademy.co.uk

PERFORMERS COLLEGE T 01375 672053
Contact: Brian Rogers, Susan Stephens
Southend Road, Corringham, Essex SS17 8JT
F 01375 672353
E lesley@performerscollege.co.uk
W www.performerscollege.co.uk

**PERFORMERS
THEATRE SCHOOL** T 0151 708 4000
*Classes in Drama, Dance & Singing. Stage School for
Children. Holiday & Summer Schools*
22 Hope Street, Liverpool L1 9BY
E info@performerstheatre.co.uk
W www.performerstheatre.co.uk

PHOENIX ASSOCIATES T 020 3714 3393
*Associate Courses in Ballet & Musical Theatre for ages
7-21. Courses run on Sundays*
HQ, Fearon Hall, Loughborough, Leics LE11 1PL
E info@i-path.biz
W www.phoenix-associate.co.uk

**PHYSICAL THEATRE &
MOVEMENT COACHING** T 07840 205199
Glenville Grove, London SE8 4BJ
E fbpratauk@gmail.com
W fernandaprata.com

**POLLAND, Charlotte Anne DipRSL DipLCM
ALCM (Mus) ALCM (Hons)** T 07806 604737
*Singing, Acting & Music Theory Coach. Skype Coaching
& Accredited Exams available*
Suite 7, Ibstock Business Centre, 57 High Street
Ibstock, Leicestershire LE67 6LH
E enquiries@charlotteannepolland.co.uk
W www.charlotteannepolland.co.uk

**POLLYANNA
TRAINING THEATRE** T 020 7481 1911
Children's Theatre School 2-18 yrs
Raine House, Raine Street, London E1W 3RL
T 07801 884837
E pollyannamanagement@gmail.com
W www.pollyannatheatre.org

POOR SCHOOL T 020 7837 6030
242 Pentonville Road, London N1 9JY
E acting@thepoorschool.com
W www.thepoorschool.com

**POPPIES YOUTH THEATRE
& AGENCY** T 07795 370678
Stockbrook House, 8 King Street
Duffield, Derbyshire DE56 4EU
E poppies09@live.com
W www.poppies-yta.co.uk

PRICE, Janis R. T 07977 630829
Voice & Text Coach
E janis@janisprice.fsnet.co.uk

**QUEEN MARGARET
UNIVERSITY, EDINBURGH** T 0131 474 0000
Queen Margaret University Drive, Musselburgh
East Lothian EH21 6UU
F 0131 474 0001
E admissions@qmu.ac.uk
W www.qmu.ac.uk

**QUESTORS THEATRE
EALING THE** T 020 8567 0011
12 Mattock Lane, London W5 5BQ
E academy@questors.org.uk
W www.questors.org.uk

ISSA INTERNATIONAL SCHOOL OF SCREEN ACTING
A Drama School dedicated to training Actors for Screen

WWW.SCREENACTING.CO.UK

3 Mills Studios, London E3 3DU

office@screenacting.co.uk

020 8709 8719

RAPIERSHARP (STAGE & SCREEN COMBAT)   T 07710 763735
Performance Combat & Fight Directing Services for Stage, Film & Television. Specialised Weapons & Unarmed Combat Training leading to British Academy of Dramatic Combat (BADC) qualifications. Training & Workshops for all Levels. Consultancy & Weapon Hire
E rapiersharp@hotmail.com
W www.rapiersharp.com

RAZZAMATAZ THEATRE SCHOOLS   T 01228 550129
2nd Floor, Atlas Works, Nelson Street
Denton Holme, Carlisle CA2 5NB
E franchise@razzamataz.co.uk
W www.razzamataz.co.uk

RC-ANNIE LTD   T 020 8123 5936
Fight Directing Services. Stage & Screen Combat Training. Theatrical Blood & Weaponry Supplies
E info@rc-annie.com
W www.rc-annie.com

REACT ACADEMY OF THEATRE ARTS   T 01254 883692
Specialist Training in Drama, Musical Theatre, Dance & Music Production
c/o The Civic Arts Centre, Union Road
Oswaldtwistle, Lancashire BB5 3HZ
E info@reactacademy.co.uk
W www.reactacademy.co.uk

REALLY YOUTHFUL THEATRE COMPANY THE   T 07909 083939
Audition Technique. LAMDA/Trinity Guildhall. Arts Award. Private Acting Classes (Children & Adults). Stage School for Children. Summer School
LAMP, Riverside, Adelaide Road
Leamington Spa CV32 5AH
E info@rytc.co.uk
W www.rytc.co.uk

REBEL SCHOOL OF THEATRE ARTS & CASTING AGENCY LTD   T 01484 603736
Based in Leeds & Huddersfield
PO Box 169, Huddersfield HD8 1BE
T 07808 803637
E sue@rebelschool.co.uk   W www.rebelschool.co.uk

REDROOFS THEATRE SCHOOL   T 01628 674092
26 Bath Road, Maidenhead, Berkshire SL6 4JT
T 07531 355835
E sam@redroofs.co.uk   W www.redroofs.co.uk

REP COLLEGE THE   T 0118 942 1144
Intensive Repertory Theatre Actor Training
17 St Mary's Avenue, Purley on Thames
Berks RG8 8BJ
E tudor@repcollege.co.uk
W www.repcollege.co.uk

RICHMOND DRAMA SCHOOL   T 020 8891 5907 ext 4018
Acting Workshops. Audition Technique. Drama School (over 18 yrs). Drama School Preparation. Public Speaking. Courses: 1 yr Foundation. Access to HE Drama
Richmond Adult & Community College
Parkshot, Richmond, Surrey TW9 2RE
E info@racc.ac.uk
W www.richmonddramaschool.com

RIDGEWAY STUDIOS PERFORMING ARTS COLLEGE   T 01992 633775
Office: 106 Hawkshead Road, Potters Bar
Hertfordshire EN6 1NG
E info@ridgewaystudios.co.uk
W www.ridgewaystudios.co.uk

RISING STARS DRAMA SCHOOL   T 0845 2570127
Contact: Jessica Andrews. Acting Workshops. Audition Technique. Filming Techniques. Films Made. Improvisation. LAMDA Examinations
10 Orchard Way, Measham, Derbyshire DE12 7JZ
E info@risingstarsdramaschool.co.uk
W www.risingstarsdramaschool.co.uk

ROKEY, Farshid　　T 07583 300127
Private Coaching for Screen & Theatre Auditions
27 Cromwell Grove, London W6 7RQ
E rokey-91@hotmail.com

ROSCH, Philip　　T 020 8731 6686
Contact: Philip Rosch. Audition Coaching for Drama UK
Schools. Audition Technique. Drama School Preparation.
Improvisation. Private Acting Classes
53 West Heath Court, London NW11 7RG
E philiproschactor@gmail.com
W www.actingauditionsuccess.co.uk

ROSE BRUFORD COLLEGE
See DRAMA SCHOOLS: DRAMA UK

ROSS, David
ACTING ACADEMY THE　　T 07957 862317
Contact: David Ross. Acting Workshops. Audition
Technique. Dialect/Accent Coaching. Drama School
Preparation. Improvisation. Stage School for Children.
Vocal Coaching
8 Farrier Close, Sale, Cheshire M33 2ZL
E info@davidrossacting.com
W www.davidrossacting.com

ROSSENDALE DANCE &
DRAMA CENTRE　　T 01706 211161
Contact: Chris Marlow. LAMDA LCM TCL Grade &
Diploma Courses & Exams. Acting Workshops. Audition
Technique. Dancing. Dialect/Accent Coaching. Drama
School (over 18 yrs). Elocution. Improvisation. Private
Acting Classes. Public Speaking. Stage School for
Children. Vocal Coaching
52 Bridleway, Waterfoot,Rossendale, Lancs BB4 9DS
E rddc@btinternet.com

ROYAL ACADEMY OF DRAMATIC ART
See DRAMA SCHOOLS: DRAMA UK

ROYAL ACADEMY OF MUSIC　　T 020 7873 7483
Musical Theatre Department
Marylebone Road, London NW1 5HT
E mth@ram.ac.uk
W www.ram.ac.uk/mth

ROYAL CENTRAL SCHOOL OF SPEECH &
DRAMA THE
See DRAMA SCHOOLS: DRAMA UK

ROYAL CONSERVATOIRE
OF SCOTLAND　　T 0141 332 4101
100 Renfrew Street, Glasgow G2 3DB
E registry@rcs.ac.uk
W www.rcs.ac.uk

ROYAL WELSH COLLEGE OF
MUSIC & DRAMA　　T 029 2039 1361
Drama Department, Castle Grounds
Cathays Park, Cardiff CF10 3ER
E admissions@rwcmd.ac.uk
W www.rwcmd.ac.uk

RUMBELOW, Sam　　T 020 7622 9742
Acting & Method Acting Coach. Classes held at
Brick Lane E1
84 Union Road, London SW4 6JU
E main@methodacting.co.uk
W www.methodacting.co.uk

SADDLEWORTH
DRAMA CENTRE　　T 0161 624 5378
Manor House, Oldham Road
Springhead, Oldham OL4 4QJ
E judesdrama@yahoo.co.uk
W www.judesdrama.co.uk

SALES, Stephanie　　T 020 8995 9127
Professional Acting Coach
61 Brookfield Road, Chiswick
London W4 1DF
E steph@stephaniesales.co.uk
W www.stephaniesales.co.uk/dramacoaching

SAMPSON PILATES　　T 01328 712116
Pilates Teacher Training (Active IQ Level 3 - Cert).
Physical Coaching. Specialing in Physical Rehabilitation
7A Park Road, Holkham
Wells-next-the-Sea, Norfolk NR23 1RG
E info@sampsonpilates.com
W www.sampsonpilates.com

SAMUELS, Marianne　　T 07974 203001
Voice, Accents, Text & Public Speaking
Based in Nottingham,
E marianne@voice-ms.com
W www.voice-ms.com

SCALA SCHOOL OF
PERFORMING ARTS　　T 0113 250 6823
Children & Young Performers. Drama Workshops.
Training for Musical Theatre, Dance, Voice Training &
Group Singing. Stage School & Casting Agency
for Children
Office: 42 Rufford Avenue, Yeadon
Leeds LS19 7QR
E office@scalakids.com
W www.scalakids.com

SCARESCOTLAND　　T 07983 249443
Contact: Stevie Douglas, Chris Campbell. Train & provide
actors who wish to work in the scare industry genre
39 Clyde Place, Glasgow, South Lanarkshire G72 7QU
E hello@scarescotland.co.uk
W www.scarescotland.co.uk

SCHER, Anna THEATRE THE　　T 07535 144899
Improvisation based classes open to all actors
of all levels
Saint Silas Church Pentonville
Penton Street, London N1 9UL
E info@nicknightmanagement.com
W www.annaschertheatre.com

SCHERMANN, Pamela　　T 07528 779822
Director. Auditions & Drama School Preparation. Acting
for Opera Singers. Showcases
Flat 15 Opus Studios, 214 Plaistow Road
London E13 0AQ
E info@pamelaschermann.com
W www.pamelaschermann.com

SCHOOL OF
THEATRE EXCELLENCE　　T 07739 904318
Contact: Chris Sheils. Performing Arts Training (6-18 yrs)
61 Lincoln Street, Brighton BN2 9UG
E chris@sotebrighton.co.uk
W www.sotebrighton.co.uk

SELF TAPING: THE ACTOR'S GUIDE
Illustrated ebook. Advice & Resources for Self Taping
E info@selftaping.com
W www.selftaping.com

SEMARK, Rebecca
LLAM, LaLAM　　T 07956 850330
Elocution. Voice & Vocal Coaching. Audition Technique.
Drama School Preparation. LAMDA Exams. Private
Acting Classes & Public Speaking for Children & Adults.
Stage School Entry for Children including Singing
Based in Epping, Essex,
E rebecca@semark.biz
W www.semark.biz

SHAPES IN MOTION   T 07802 709933
Contact: Sarah Perry. Movement & Acting Coaching.
Workshops. Laban. Yoga & Yoga Therapy
Based in London,
E sarah@shapesinmotion.com
W www.shapesinmotion.com

SHAW, Phil   T 020 8715 8943
Actors' Consultancy Service. Industry Career
Coach/Mentor. Acting. Voice. Audition Coaching.
Drama School Preparation
Suite 476, 2 Old Brompton Road
South Kensington, London SW7 3DQ
E philshawcasting@gmail.com

SHENEL, Helena   T 020 7724 8793
Singing Teacher
205 John Aird Court
London W2 1UX

**SHINE TIME MUSICAL THEATRE
& ACTING**   T 07880 721689
Contact: Laura Green. Audition Technique. Dancing.
Drama School Preparation. Improvisation. LAMDA Acting
Solo Examinations. Musical Theatre & Acting Holiday
Workshops. Private Acting Classes. Singing. Stage
School for Children. Vocal Coaching
Flat 10, Valentine House, Church Road
Guildford, Surrey GU1 4NG
E shinetime@hotmail.co.uk
W www.shinetimeworkshops.com

SHOWSONG ACCOMPANIST   T 020 8993 2111
163 Gunnersbury Lane, London W3 8LJ

SIMMONS, Ros MA   T 020 8347 8089
Accents/Dialects. Voice. Auditions. Presentations
The Real Speaking Company
120 Hillfield Avenue
Crouch End, London N8 7DN
T 07957 320572
E info@realspeaking.co.uk
W www.realspeaking.co.uk

SINGER, Sandra ASSOCIATES   T 01702 331616
LAMDA & ISTD Exams. Acting Workshops. Audition
Technique. Dancing. Dialect/Accent Coaching. Part-time
Drama School (over 18 yrs). Improvisation. Private Acting
Classes. Singing. Stage School for Children. Vocal
Coaching
21 Cotswold Road, Westcliff-on-Sea
Essex SS0 8AA
E sandrasingeruk@aol.com
W www.sandrasinger.com

SINGER STAGE SCHOOL   T 01702 331616
Part-time Vocational Stage School & Summer School.
6-21 yrs. Acting Workshops. Audition Technique.
Dancing. Dialect/Accent Coaching for Entry to Drama
School (over 18 yrs). Improvisation. ISTD. Private Acting
Classes. LAMDA. Singing. Stage School for Children.
Member of National Youth Theatre
Office: 21 Cotswold Road, Westcliff-on-Sea
Essex SS0 8AA
E sandrasingeruk@aol.com   W www.sandrasinger.com

SLP COLLEGE   T 0113 286 8136
5 Chapel Lane, Garforth
Leeds, West Yorkshire LS25 1AG
F 0113 287 4487
E info@slpcollege.co.uk   W www.slpcollege.co.uk

SO-MEDIA　　　　　　T 020 8789 7495
Professional Showreel Services & Training
7 Knight House, 22 Scott Avenue
Putney SW15 3PB
E info@so-media.co.uk
W www.so-media.co.uk

**SOCIETY OF TEACHERS OF
SPEECH & DRAMA THE**　　T 01623 627636
Registered Office: 73 Berry Hill Road
Mansfield, Notts NG18 4RU
E ann.k.jones@btinternet.com
W www.stsd.org.uk

**SONNETS THEATRE
ARTS SCHOOL**　　　　　T 0845 0038910
Thorneycombe, Vernham Dean
Andover, Hampshire SP11 0JY
E sonnetsagency@hotmail.co.uk
W www.sonnets-tas.co.uk

SPEAK EASILY　　　　T 020 3174 1316
Voice, Text & Accent Coaches
E morwenna.rowe@speak-easily.com
W www.speak-easily.com

**SPEAKE, Barbara
STAGE SCHOOL & AGENCY**　T 020 8743 1306
Full-time Drama School. Coaches. Part-time School.
Theatrical Agency. Rehearsal & Casting Studio
East Acton Lane, London W3 7EG
F 020 8743 2746
E enquiries@barbaraspeake.com
W www.barbaraspeake.com

**SPEED, Anne-Marie Hon ARAM MA (Voice
Studies) CSSD ADVS BA**　T 07957 272554
Vanguard Estill Practitioner. Accents. Auditions.
Coaching. Vocal Technique for Speaking & Singing
E info@thevoiceexplained.com
W www.thevoiceexplained.com

**SPIRITUAL PSYCHOLOGY
OF ACTING THE**　　　　T 020 8653 7735
Contact: John Osborne Hughes. Acting Workshops.
Audition Technique. Drama School Preparation.
Private Acting Classes. Courses: Introduction
to Acting, 2 days (weekend), part-time. Creative
Visualisation, 1 day
51 Church Road, London SE19 2TE
E info@spiritualpsychologyofacting.com
W www.spiritualpsychologyofacting.com

SPLITZ THEATRE ARTZ　T 01638 577095
Dance & Theatre School
1A New Road, Exning
Suffolk CB8 7JP
E clare@splitz-ta.net
W www.splitz-ta.net

SPONTANEITY SHOP THE　T 020 7788 4080
Improvisation, Comedy & Drama Workshops & Courses
85-87 Bayham Street
London NW1 0AG
E info@the-spontaneity-shop.com
W www.the-spontaneity-shop.com

SPYMONKEY　　　　　T 07766 712757
The Old Market
11A Upper Market Street
Hove BN3 1AS
E education@spymonkey.co.uk
W www.spymonkey.co.uk

STAGE2 YOUTH THEATRE　T 07961 018841
Saturdays. Twitter: @Stage2YT
Millennium Point, Curzon Street
Birmingham B4 7XG
E info@stage2.org
W www.stage2.org

STAGE2 YOUTH THEATRE　T 07961 018841
Administration: 12 Valentine Road, Kings Heath
Birmingham, West Midlands B14 7AN
E info@stage2.org
W www.stage2.org

**STAGE 84
PERFORMING ARTS LTD**　T 01274 611984
Evening & Weekend Classes & Summer Schools
The Old Fire Station, 29A Town Lane, Idle
Bradford, West Yorkshire BD10 8NT
T 07731 436094
E info@stage84.com
W www.stage84.com

STAGECOACH THEATRE ARTS　T 01932 254333
The Courthouse, Elm Grove
Walton-on-Thames, Surrey KT12 1LZ
F 01932 222894
E mail@stagecoach.co.uk
W www.stagecoach.co.uk

STAGEFIGHT & ECSPC　　T 07813 308672
School of Performance Combat
138 Wilden Lane, Stourport-on-Severn
Worcestershire DY13 9LP
E info@stagefight.co.uk
W www.stagefight.co.uk

STARLIGHT STAGE SCHOOL　T 07581 368677
Holly Road, Thornton Cleveleys
Lancashire FY5 4HH
E charlotte_starlight@hotmail.com
W www.starlight-stageschool.co.uk

STARS PERFORMING ARTS　T 07840 616287
Contact: Su Tucker. Performing Arts Classes for Children
& Graded Performance Exams
120A Hartopp Road, Leicester
Leicestershire LE2 1WF
E su@starsperformingarts.com
W www.starsperformingarts.com

**STARSTRUCK
PERFORMING ARTS**　　　T 07734 964648
Contact: Samantha Smith. Performing Arts Classes
(3-20 yrs)
85 Hewson Road, Lincoln
Lincolnshire LN1 1RZ
E sam@starstruckacademy.co.uk
W www.starstruckacademy.co.uk

**STEP ON STAGE ACADEMY
OF PERFORMING ARTS**　　T 07973 900196
Contact: Emma-Louise Tinniswood. Stage School
for Children. Acting Workshops & Audition Coaching.
Musical Theatre Courses & Workshops. Acting for Stage
& Screen. Dancing. Singing. Summer School. School
Workshops & Teacher INSET. Courses: GCSE Drama,
1 yr, part-time. LAMDA, 1 term-1 yr, part-time. Acting.
Musical Theatre. Audition Technique. Film Acting. Stage
Make-up. Stage Combat
29 Burgoyne Road, Sunbury-on-Thames
Middlesex TW16 7PN
E info@steponstageacademy.co.uk
W www.steponstageacademy.co.uk

city lit

exceptional, affordable, vocational training

Approximately 500 part-time courses for adults available ranging from beginners to professionals.

Call the Drama, dance and speech department on **020 7492 2542** or e-mail: **drama@citylit.ac.uk**

Request a course guide at:
www.citylit.ac.uk

- Professional Acting Diploma (2 year)
- Foundation and Access Acting courses
- Acting and Dance classes
- Agent and Casting Directors Master-classes
- Method and Meisner classes
- TV Presenting, Radio, Voice-over and Screen Acting
- Story-telling, Stand-up Comedy, Performing Magic
- Weekend workshops
- Technical Theatre Skills (Foundation and Rep Company Crew)
- Stage fighting - Beginners and Advanced classes
- Musical Theatre etc.

drama | uk
recognised

STEPHENSON, Sarah
GMusRNCM PGDip RNCM   T 07581 716233
Vocal Coach. Piano Accompanist. Master Teacher of Estill Voice Training. Based in London/East Sussex
E s.stephenson@ntlworld.com

STINSON, David
THEATRE SCHOOL   T 020 3714 3393
Professional Training in Dance, Singing & Acting. Holiday & Summer School programmes. Chain of schools nationwide
HQ, Fearon Hall
Rectory Road
Loughborough, Leics LE11 1PL
E info@i-path.biz
W www.davidstinsontheatreschool.com

STIRLING ACADEMY   T 01204 848333
Contact: Glen Mortimer. Acting Workshops. Audition Techniques. Audition Training for Camera. Drama School. Improvisation. Private Acting Classes. Showreels
490 Halliwell Road, Bolton
Lancashire BL1 8AN
F 0844 4128689
E admin@stirlingacademy.co.uk
W www.stirlingacademy.co.uk

STOCKTON RIVERSIDE
COLLEGE   T 01642 865400
Further Education & Training
Harvard Avenue, Thornaby
Stockton TS17 6FB
W www.stockton.ac.uk

STOMP! THE SCHOOL OF
PERFORMING ARTS   T 020 8446 9898
Stage School for Children. Street Dance. Acting & Singing Classes (5-19 yrs). Weekends. Mill Hill Area
62 Sellwood Drive, Barnet
Herts EN5 2RL
E stompschoolnw7@aol.com
W www.stompschool.com

STREET DEFENCE   T 07919 350290
Fight Choreographer. Advanced Screen Combatant. Conditioning Specialist
6 Clive Close
Potters Bar
Hertfordshire EN6 2AE
E streetdefence@hotmail.co.uk
W www.streetdefenceuk.com

STREETON, Jane   T 07968 788857
Singing Teacher, RADA. Author of 'Singing on Stage: An Actor's Guide'
24 Richmond Road, Leytonstone
London E11 4BA
E janestreetonsop@aol.com
W www.singingonstage.co.uk

STUDIOS THE   T 07710 968642
School of Performing Arts
Taplow & Hitcham Hall
Institute Road
Taplow, Maidenhead SL6 0NS
E studiosschool@hotmail.com
W www.thestudiosschoolofperformingarts.co.uk

SUPERSTARS IN THE MAKING   T 07531 814820
Performing Arts Academy
St John's Hall, Beryl Road
Barry CF62 8DN
E director@superstarsinthemaking.com
W www.superstarsinthemaking.com

TALENTED KIDS PERFORMING ARTS SCHOOL
& MVW TALENT AGENCY   T/F 00 353 45 485464
Contact: Maureen V. Ward. Agency. Acting Workshops. Audition Technique. Dance. Drama School (over 18 yrs). Elocution. Improvisation. Modelling. Musical Theatre. Singing. Stage School for Children. Vocal Coaching
23 Burrow Manor
Calverstown
Kilcullen, Co. Kildare, Ireland
T 00 353 87 2480348
E talentedkids@hotmail.com
W www.talentedkidsireland.com

THAT'S A WRAP ACTING SCHOOL FOR
CHILDREN & TEENAGERS   T 01753 650951
Acting Workshops. Audition Technique. Improvisation
Actors Studio, Admin Building, Pinewood Studios
Pinewood Road, Iver Heath, Bucks SL0 0NH
E info@actorsstudio.co.uk
W www.actorsstudio.co.uk

THEATRETRAIN   T 01327 300498
Performing Arts for 6 18 yrs. Annual Large Scale Productions. Open to All. No Experience Required
Orchard Studio, PO Box 42
Hitchin, Herts SG4 8ES
E admin@theatretrain.co.uk
W www.theatretrain.co.uk

THREE4ALL
THEATRE COMPANY   T 01227 276217
Drama Training
57 Millstrood Road
Whitstable
Kent CT5 1QF
E alison.mead49@gmail.com

TIP TOE STAGE SCHOOL   T 07940 521864
Dance, Drama, Singing & Performing Arts Training,
part-time
For correspondence only:
65 North Road, South Ockendon
Essex RM15 6QH
E julie@tiptoestageschool.co.uk
W www.tiptoestageschool.co.uk

TO BE OR NOT TO BE   T 07958 996227
Contact: Anthony Barnett. LAMDA Exams. Showreels.
Theatre/Audition Pieces. Television/Film Acting
Technique
40 Gayton Road, King's Lynn
Norfolk PE30 4EL
E tony@tobeornottobe.org.uk
W www.showreels.org.uk

TODD, Paul   T 020 7229 9776
Singing. Audition Technique. Acting. Percussion.
Improvisation. Vocal Coaching. Any age, any level
3 Rosehart Mews
London W11 3JN
T 07813 985092
E paultodd@talk21.com

TOMORROW'S TALENT   T 01245 690080
Theatre School & Agency for Young Performers.
Courses: Foundation Course in Acting & Musical
Theatre, 1 yr
Based in Chelmsford, Essex
E mail@tomorrowstalent.co.uk
W www.tomorrowstalent.co.uk

TOP HAT STAGE &
SCREEN SCHOOL   T/F 01727 812666
Contact: Warren Bacci. Acting Workshops. Dancing.
Singing. Stage School for Children. Courses: School
Term Weekends, part-time. Summer Holidays, part-time.
Youth Theatre, Weeknights, part-time. Schools in Potters
Bar, Harpenden, Wheathampstead, Welwyn, Stevenage,
St Albans & Harpenden & Surrey
PO Box 860, St Albans
Herts AL1 9BR
E info@tophatstageschool.co.uk
W www.tophatstageschool.co.uk

TRING PARK SCHOOL
FOR THE PERFORMING ARTS   T 01442 824255
Contact: Adelia Wood-Smith. Courses: Dance, 3 yrs,
full-time. Qualification: Diploma in Dance. Drama, 2 yrs,
full-time. Musical Theatre, 2 yrs, full-time. Commercial
Music, 2 yrs, full-time. Audition Technique. Drama
School Preparation. Improvisation. Singing. Summer
School. Vocal Coaching
Tring Park, Tring
Hertfordshire HP23 5LX
E info@tringpark.com
W www.tringpark.com

TROLLOPE, Ann   T 07943 816276
Voice/Acting Coach
Solihull, West Midlands
E ann-t@uwclub.net

TROTTER, William
BA MA PGDVS   T/F 020 8459 7594
Voice, Speech & Text for Actors on Stage & Screen
25 Thanet Lodge, Mapesbury Road
London NW2 4JA
T 07946 586719
E william.trotter@ukspeech.co.uk
W www.ukspeech.co.uk

TUCKER, John   T 07903 269409
Voice Coach
503 Mountjoy House, Barbican
London EC2Y 8BP
E mail@john-tucker.com
W www.john-tucker.com

TWICKENHAM
THEATRE WORKSHOP   T 020 8898 5882
Katie Abbott LTCL
29 Campbell Road, Twickenham
Middlesex TW2 5BY
E frabbt@aol.com

UKTHEATRESCHOOL
CHARITABLE TRUST   T 0141 332 1818
Contact: Lizanne Lambie Thomson. Accredited
performing arts training 4-18 yrs
4 West Regent Street, Glasgow G2 1RW
E staff@uktheatreschool.com
W www.uktheatreschool.com

VADA CASTING
MANAGEMENT   T 07796 688571
Contact: Vanessa Buckley
1 Minster Close, Greetland
Halifax, West Yorkshire HX4 8QW
E vadacastingmanagement@gmail.com
W www.vacademyofdramaticarts.com

VALLÉ ACADEMY OF
PERFORMING ARTS   T 01992 622862
The Vallé Academy Studios, Wilton House
Delamare Road, Cheshunt, Herts EN8 9SG
F 01992 622868
E enquiries@valleacademy.co.uk
W www.valleacademy.co.uk

VERNON ACTING METHOD   T 0161 773 7670
Screen Acting
20 Ruskin Road, Manchester M25 9GL
E info@vernonactingmethod.co.uk
W www.vernonactingmethod.co.uk

VERRALL, Charles   T 020 7833 1971
Acting & Public Speaking Coach, Writer & Director
19 Matilda Street, London N1 0LA
E info@charlesverrall.com
W www.learntoact.co.uk

VIVIAN, Michael   T 020 8876 2073
Acting Workshops. Audition Technique. Improvisation.
Private Acting Classes. Public Speaking
15 Meredyth Road, Barnes, London SW13 0DS
T 07958 903911
E vivcalling@aol.com

VOCAL CONFIDENCE
Contact: Alix Longman. Voice & Acting Technique.
All Vocal Problems Attended. Audition Preparation
Presentation. Accent & Dialect Coaching. Skype
sessions available for overseas clients
E alix@vocalconfidence.com
W www.vocalconfidence.com

GORDON FAITH B.A., IPA., Dip.R.E.M. Sp., L.R.A.M.
SPEECH AND VOICE TEACHER

- Ex BBC Repertory   • All Speech Work Undertaken

020-7328 0446   www.gordonfaith.co.uk   1 Wavel Mews, Priory Rd. London NW6 3AB

VOICE & DIALECT COACH   T 07723 620728
Contact: Caroline Hetherington
7 Dodcott Barns, Burleydam, Whitchurch SY13 4BQ
E voice@carohetherington.co.uk
W www.carohetherington.co.uk

**VOICE MASTER
INTERNATIONAL**   T 020 8455 1666
*Creators of the Hudson Voice Technique: Unique
Technique for Voiceovers, Actors & Autocue*
88 Erskine Hill, London NW11 6HR
T 07921 210400
E info@voicemaster.co.uk
W www.voicemaster.co.uk

VOICEATWORK   T 07973 871479
Voice Coach
5 Anhalt Road, London SW11 4NZ
E kateterris@voiceatwork.co.uk
W www.voiceatwork.co.uk

VOICES & PERFORMANCE   T 07712 624083
*Contact: Julia Gaunt ALCM TD-Musical Theatre. Audition
Technique. Corporate Training. Community Workshops.
Courses: Singing for Musical Theatre, 1-2 days. Voice
Care, 1 day*
E joolsmusicbiz@aol.com
W www.joolsmusicbiz.com

VOICES LONDON   T 07774 445637
*Contact: Ann Leberman. Estill Certified Master Teacher.
Technical Singing Coach*
E ann@voicesvocal.co.uk
W www.voicesvocal.co.uk

VOXTRAINING LTD   T 020 7434 4404
Demo CDs. Voice Over Training
20 Old Compton Street, London W1D 4TW
E info@voxtraining.com
W www.voxtraining.com

WALLACE, Elaine BA   T 07856 098334
Voice
249 Goldhurst Terrace, London NW6 3EP
E im@voicebiz.biz

WALSH, Anne   T 07932 440043
Accents. Dialect. Speech. RP. Accent-softening
The Pronunciation Rooms, The Garden Studios
71-75 Shelton Street, London WC2H 9JQ
E anne@confidentlyspeaking.co.uk
W www.confidentlyspeaking.co.uk

WALSH, Genevieve   T 020 7627 0024
Acting Tuition. Audition Coaching
37 Kelvedon House, Guildford Road
Stockwell, London SW8 2DN
T 07801 948864

WALTZER, Jack   T 07949 136862
Professional Acting Workshops
E elif@jackwaltzer.com
W www.jackwaltzer.com

**WEAKLIAM, Brendan PGDipMusPerf
BMusPerf Dip ABRSM**   T 07724 558955
Singing Teacher. Voice Coach
20 Kingsdown Road, Leytonstone, London E11 3LP
E brendanweakliam@gmail.com

WEBB, Bruce   T 01508 518703
Audition Technique. Singing
Abbots Manor, Kirby Cane
Bungay, Suffolk NR35 2HP

WELBOURNE, Jacqueline   T 07977 247287
Choreographer. Circus Trainer. Consultant
43 Kingsway Avenue, Kingswood
Bristol BS15 8AN
E jackie.welbourne@gmail.com

WERKKIT   T 07830 120536
*Intensive Training Programmes for International Students
in Performing & Creative Arts*
2/21 Culmington Road, Ealing
London W13 9NJ
E info@werkkit.com
W www.werkkit.com

**WESTMINSTER
KINGSWAY COLLEGE**   T 0870 0609800
Performing Arts, Musical Theatre & Music
King's Cross Centre, 211 Gray's Inn Road
London WC1X 8RA
E courseinfo@westking.ac.uk
W www.westking.ac.uk

**WHITE, Susan BA TEFL LGSM MA Voice
Studies Distinction**   T 020 7244 0402
*Creative Development of Connection to Creative
Impulse. How to engage & release truthfully your
presence, energy, vocal vibrations. One-to-one/groups:
Deep, effective, experimental coaching of core creativity*
E susan@per-sona.com
W www.per-sona.com

**WILDCATS THEATRE SCHOOL
& POST-16 ACADEMY**   T 01780 762000
*Contact: Emma Hancock. Courses: Performing Arts -
Musical Theatre & Dance, 2 yrs, full-time. Qualification:
BTEC Level 3. Performing Arts - Performance, 2 yrs,
full-time. Qualification: HND. Stage School for Children.
Summer School*
Castle House, St Peter's Hill
Stamford PE9 2PE
E admin@wildcats-uk.com
W www.wildcatstheatreschool.co.uk

WILDER, Andrea   T 07919 202401
Theatre for Education & Training
23 Cambrian Drive
Colwyn Bay
Conwy LL28 4SL
F 07092 249314
E andreawilder@fastmail.fm
W www.catspawtheatre.com

WILSON, Holly   T 020 8878 0015
3 Worple Street, Mortlake
London SW14 8HE
E hbwilson@fastmail.co.uk

WIMBUSH, Martin Dip GSMD   T 020 8877 0086
*Audition Technique. Drama School Entry. Elocution.
Public Speaking. Vocal Coaching*
Flat 4, 289 Trinity Road
Wandsworth Common, London SW18 3SN
T 07930 677623
E martinwimbush@btinternet.com
W www.martinwimbush.com

WINDLEY, Joe   T 07867 780856
*Accent, Speech, Voice, Text & Presentation Skills for
Film, Stage & Television*
Based in London SW13
E joe.windley@gmail.com

WINDSOR, Judith Ph. D   T 01782 827222
American Accents/Dialects
Woodbine, Victoria Road
Deal, Kent CT14 7AS
E sarah.upson@voicecoach.tv

**WOOD, Tessa Teach Cert
AGSM CSSD PGDVS**   T 020 8896 2659
Voice Coach
43 Woodhurst Road, London W3 6SS
T 07957 207808
E tessaroswood@aol.com

**WOODHOUSE, Alan
AGSM ADVS**   T 07748 904227
*Acting Coach. Acting Workshops. Audition Technique.
Drama School Preparation. Elocution. Private Acting
Classes. Public Speaking. Vocal Coaching*
33 Burton Road, Kingston upon Thames
Surrey KT2 5TG
E alanwoodhouse50@hotmail.com
W www.woodhouse-voice.co.uk

WORTMAN, Neville   T 07976 805976
Speech Coach. Voice Training
School of Economic Science Building
11 Mandeville Place, London W1U 3AJ
E neville@speakwell.co.uk
W www.speakwell.co.uk

WYNN, Madeleine   T 01394 450265
*Audition Technique. Acting & Directing Coach. Drama
School Entry. LAMDA Exams. Acting Classes. Public
Speaking. LAMDA Teacher Training*
40 Barrie House
Hawksley Court
Albion Road, London N16 0TX
E madeleinewynn@toucansurf.com
W www.plainspeaking.co.uk

**YORKSHIRE ACADEMY OF FILM &
TELEVISION ACTING**   T 07512 921934
Contact: Charlotte Armitage
16 East Park Road, Spofforth
Harrogate, North Yorkshire HG3 1BH
E info@yafta.co.uk
W www.yafta.co.uk

**YOUNG, Sylvia
THEATRE SCHOOL**   T 020 7258 2330
*Full-time Academic & Vocational Training (10-16 yrs).
Part-time Singing, Dance & Drama Classes (4-18 yrs).
Holiday Courses & Experience Days (7-18 yrs). Adult
Classes. Nearest Tube Marble Arch, Edgware Road &
Baker Street*
1 Nutford Place
London W1H 5YZ
E info@sylviayoungtheatreschool.co.uk
W www.syts.co.uk

YOUNG ACTORS THEATRE   T 020 7278 2101
Drama Classes, Workshops & Productions
70-72 Barnsbury Road, London N1 0ES
E info@yati.org.uk
W www.yati.org.uk

**YOUNGSTARS THEATRE SCHOOL
& AGENCY**   T 020 8950 5782
*Contact: Coralyn Canfor-Dumas. Part-time Children's
Theatre School (4-18 yrs). Commercials. Dance. Drama.
Film. Singing. Stage. Television. Voice Overs*
4 Haydon Dell, Bushey
Herts WD23 1DD
T 07966 176756
E youngstarsagency@gmail.com
W www.youngstarsagency.co.uk

**YOUNGSTAR TELEVISION &
FILM ACTING SCHOOLS**   T 023 8047 7717
Part-time TV Acting Schools across the UK (8-20 yrs)
Head Office, 1st Floor
Unit 3, Mitchell Point
Ensign Way, Hamble
Southampton SO31 4RF
E info@youngstar.tv
W www.youngstar.tv

YOURVOICECOACH   T 01273 204779
*Contact: Dee Forrest (Associate Voice Tutor, School
of Acting/Surrey University). Accents/Dialects, Vocal
Technique, Vocal Power, Articulation (Elocution). Text
Delivery. Sightreading. Confidence Building/NLP. Public
Speaking. Vocal Coaching. London & Brighton Studios.
Skype Coaching Available*
20 Landseer Road
Hove BN3 7AF
T 07957 211065
E yourvoicecoach@hotmail.co.uk
W www.yourvoicecoach.co.uk

F →

ALDEBURGH FESTIVAL OF MUSIC & THE ARTS   T 01728 687100
10-26 June 2016
Aldeburgh Music, Snape Maltings Concert Hall
Snape, Suffolk IP17 1SP
BO 01728 687110
E enquiries@aldeburgh.co.uk   **W** www.aldeburgh.co.uk

BATH INTERNATIONAL MUSIC FESTIVAL   T 01225 462231
20-31 May 2016
Bath Festivals, Abbey Chambers
Kingston Buildings, Bath BA1 1NT
BO 01225 463362
E info@bathfestivals.org.uk   **W** www.bathfestivals.org.uk

BATH LITERATURE FESTIVAL   T 01225 462231
26 February-6 March 2016
Bath Festivals, Abbey Chambers
Kingston Buildings, Bath BA1 1NT
BO 01225 463362
E info@bathfestivals.org.uk   **W** www.bathfestivals.org.uk

BRIGHTON DOME & BRIGHTON FESTIVAL   T 01273 700747
7-29 May 2016
12A Pavilion Buildings, Castle Square, Brighton BN1 1EE
BO 01273 709709
E info@brightonfestival.org   **W** www.brightonfestival.org

BRIGHTON FRINGE   T 01273 764900
6 May-5 June 2016
5 Palace Place, Brighton BN1 1EF
E participantservices@brightonfringe.org
W www.brightonfringe.org

BUXTON FESTIVAL   T 01298 70395
8-24 July 2016
3 The Square, Buxton, Derbyshire SK17 6AZ
BO 0845 1272190
E info@buxtonfestival.co.uk   **W** www.buxtonfestival.co.uk

DANCE UMBRELLA   T 020 7257 9380
October 2016
Somerset House, West Wing, Strand, London WC2R 1LA
E mail@danceumbrella.co.uk
W www.danceumbrella.co.uk

DUBLIN THEATRE FESTIVAL   T 00 353 1 677 8439
25 September-16 October 2016
44 East Essex Street, Temple Bar, Dublin 2, Ireland
F 00 353 1 633 5918
E info@dublintheatrefestival.com
W www.dublintheatrefestival.com

EDINBURGH FESTIVAL FRINGE   T 0131 226 0026
7-31 August 2016
Edinburgh Festival Fringe Society Ltd
180 High Street, Edinburgh EH1 1QS
BO 0131 226 0000
E admin@edfringe.com   **W** www.edfringe.com

EDINBURGH INTERNATIONAL FESTIVAL   BO 0131 473 2000
5-29 August 2016
The Hub, Castlehill, Edinburgh EH1 2NE
E boxoffice@eif.co.uk   **W** www.eif.co.uk

HARROGATE INTERNATIONAL FESTIVAL   T 01423 562303
July 2016
32 Cheltenham Parade, Harrogate
North Yorkshire HG1 1DB
F 01423 521264
E info@harrogate-festival.org.uk
W www.harrogateinternationalfestival.com

HENLEY FRINGE & FILM (TRUST) THE   T 07742 059762
July 2016
Aston Farm House, Remenham Lane
Henley on Thames, Oxon RG9 3DE
E info@henleyfringe.org   **W** www.henleyfringe.org

INTERNATIONAL PLAYWRITING FESTIVAL   T 020 7580 1000
Annual Competition for New Plays. Established 1986.
Entries Accepted from September. Selected Plays are
Showcased in Festival Weekend each Summer
E intplayfest@outlook.com
W www.internationalplaywritingfestival.com

KING'S LYNN FESTIVAL   T 01553 767557
17-30 July 2016
Suite 2, 3rd Floor, Bishops Lynn House
18 Tuesday Market Place
King's Lynn, Norfolk PE30 1JW
BO 01553 764864 (open from mid April)
E info@kingslynnfestival.org.uk
W www.kingslynnfestival.org.uk

LIFT   T 020 7968 6800
Bi-Annual Festival. June 2016
3rd Floor, Institute of Contemporary Arts
12 Carlton House Terrace, London SW1Y 5AH
E kate@liftfestival.com   **W** www.liftfestival.com

LONDON SKETCH COMEDY FESTIVAL   T 07782 244248
May 2016
20-22 Wenlock Road, London N1 7GU
E admin@londonsketchfest.com
W www.londonsketchfest.com

MOVE IT 2016   T 020 7288 6447
18-20 March 2016
ExCel London, Royal Victoria Dock
1 Western Gateway, London E16 1XL
E info@moveitdance.co.uk
W www.moveitdance.co.uk

NATIONAL STUDENT DRAMA FESTIVAL (NSDF)   T 020 7036 9027
19-25 March 2016
Registered Office:, 49 South Molton Street
London W1K 5LH
E info@nsdf.org.uk   **W** www.nsdf.org.uk

PERFORM 2015   T 020 7288 6625
18-20 March 2016
London ExCel, 1 Western Gateway, London E16 1XL
E info@performshow.co.uk   **W** www.performshow.co.uk

TELEGRAPH BATH CHILDREN'S LITERATURE FESTIVAL THE   T 01225 462231
30 September-9 October 2016
Bath Festivals, Abbey Chambers
Kingston Buildings, Bath BA1 1NT
BO 01225 463362
E info@bathfestivals.org.uk
W www.bathfestivals.org.uk

ULSTER BANK BELFAST FESTIVAL AT QUEEN'S   T 028 9097 1034
9 October-1 November 2016
Lanyon North, Belfast BT7 1NN
BO 028 9097 1197
E belfastfestival@qub.ac.uk
W www.belfastfestival.com

WEST END LIVE   T 020 7641 3297
June 2016
E westendlive@westminster.gov.uk
W www.westendlive.co.uk

Festivals

What do I need to know about the listed festivals?

The festivals listed in this section are all dedicated to creative and performing arts. Festivals are an opportunity for like-minded people to gather together to appreciate and learn from both well-established and new and up-and-coming acts and performers.

Why should I get involved?

Being a spectator at a festival is a chance to see others in action and to see a variety of shows that are not necessarily mainstream. This is an opportunity to see talent in its rawest form, which is exactly why casting directors often attend drama festivals: they may spot someone who is just what they are looking for, who would otherwise have gone unnoticed in a pile of CVs.

Taking part in festivals will be something else to add to your CV and will help develop your skills. This not only means performance skills but social skills as well: you will meet hundreds of new faces with the same passion for their work as you, so this is a great opportunity to make friends and useful contacts in the industry.

What do I need to bear in mind?

Before committing to performing at a festival, there are a number of issues to take into consideration. You will usually be unpaid and you will have to set aside enough money to fund the time spent rehearsing for and performing at the festival, not to mention travel, accommodation and food expenses. Not only that, you must also consider that you will be putting yourself out of the running for any paid work offered to you during this time. Make sure you let your agent know the dates you will be unavailable for work. You may find it helpful to refer to Equity's Low Pay/No Pay advice leaflet, which is available to all Equity members from their website's members' area.

You may be required to not just perform but help out with any odd jobs involved with your show, such as setting up the stage and handing out flyers. If you are considering taking your own show to a festival, you will have to think well in advance about entrance fees, choosing and hiring a suitable venue, publicising your show, casting if necessary, finding technicians, buying or hiring props, costumes, sets and so on. You must weigh up the financial outlays and potential headaches with the learning and networking opportunities that come with being involved in festivals.

How can I get involved?

If you are a performer at a festival, casting professionals could be there looking for you! Let them know that you will be performing and where and when. Send them a covering letter giving details and enclose your CV and headshot if you have not already done so in previous correspondence. You could do the same with agents if you are currently searching for new representation.

Spotlight members performing at the Edinburgh Festival Fringe can access a number of free services including a Spotlight VIP area, a series of career advice seminars, one-to-one advice sessions with a Spotlight expert and free Wi-Fi. For full information or to book tickets for seminars please visit www.edfringe.com from June onwards and enter 'Spotlight' in the show/performer field.

Most festivals have websites which you can browse for further information on what to expect and how to get involved. Even if you simply go as a spectator to a festival, you will learn a lot and will have the opportunity to network. If you are performing in or organising a show, make sure you know exactly what you are letting yourself in for and make the most of your time there!

Festivals

CASE STUDY

Paul G Raymond & Luke Manning make up the comedy duo In Cahoots. Their Edinburgh '15 show In Cahoots: Two White Guys was at the Pleasance Courtyard. Paul tells us of their festival experience.

During my time at University, I got as involved as possible with the Edinburgh Fringe, going to the festival in student plays of varying degrees of quality every summer. When not doing these shows, I spent lots of time drinking, and watching comedy. It was the perfect training ground; performing shows for an hour every day, and then wandering Edinburgh's pubs-turned-comedy-venues drinking Brewdog out of plastic cups and letting my little comedy brain get drunk on both niche Scottish cider and an array of live, fresh, Fringe shows. I was inspired!

In 2013 we took our first Edinburgh show to the festival, and followed it up in 2014. And then in 2015 we adapted another show.

Edinburgh is a great place to cut your teeth doing what you love, to hone your craft whilst also getting to see the masters at work. You're going to learn a lot about yourself and your work from a month of performing in a high pressure environment.

"Keep reworking your show during the festival. Tighten bits up and try different things out"

If you're taking your own show to Edinburgh, we recommend starting with one of the many free festivals at the Fringe. There's far less financial risk, as well as a slightly more open minded audience, meaning less pressure on you, which in turn allows you to be the beautiful artist you know you are. Test out your show at a venue local to you, and pack it out with friends and family and get them to heap praise on the good bits and gently tell you which bits weren't quite as strong. The Camden Fringe is also a great place to put on a show, as well as a strong alternative to going to Edinburgh for the whole month if you can't afford the high amount of

rent people charge. Rent can sometimes be a thousand pounds a month for a room. Sadly, this is fairly average. There are, however, bargains to be found, or rather, made. Team up with other performers and get a massive house and pack it with performers (the legal amount, we know what you're like), trawl through Gumtree for a spare room in a local's flat, or just save up and shell out for an eight hundred quid room in a flat with a couple of friends, and subsidise costs by flyering for other peoples shows when you're up there. This is why the Free Fringe is so important – their costs are so low that you can go up with just over a grand, and potentially even make some of that back, or break even. Charmingly encourage donations at the end of your show, and they'll be generous even if the show was rough around the edges. Brilliant acts such as Imran Yusuf started out doing free shows.

If you're starting out, don't shell out on PR or producers – do it yourself. By doing it yourself you will understand the mechanics of how these things work, and it will stand you in good stead for when you eventually do employ people to do this for you.

Keep reworking your show during the festival. Tighten bits up and try different things out, so by the end of the Fringe you've got a really strong piece of work that you can be really proud of.

Flyer for your show. You're going to sell your product better than anyone else.

Talk to people. Reviewers wear funny lanyards, get chatting to them and hand them a flyer.

Look after yourself up there. Stock up on Manuka honey, it flies off the shelves in the local shops. See as much as you can. Enjoy it. Take nights off drinking. I know it's delicious and takes the pain of a two-star review away, but just do it.

Bring a rain mac. And an umbrella. 'Why both?' You ask. Edinburgh, that's why.

To find our more visit http://incahootscomedy.wix.com/incahoots

Danielle Phillips

Photo: Nick James

Danielle is studying in her final year at London Academy of Music & Dramatic Arts.

It started back at home in Doncaster. I always found it infinitely more fun playing my favourite Disney characters or mimicking adults than being myself, plus it helped to get me out of trouble… sometimes! I auditioned for the National Youth Theatre when I was 15 and met Matt Stevens-Woodhead – Artistic Director of FYSA Theatre Company – it was truly a chance meeting and one of those 'happens for a reason' things. (Thanks Mr. Fate!) Three years later Matt offered me an audition for 'The 56' and the rest is history.

We were ecstatic when we found out the show had been selected for NSDF. It is a vital organisation to the arts; a hub for young talent putting on their work. It's where the industry's next generation resides. I urge everyone to leap at the opportunity if it's offered to you, make the work you want to make, make the connections you want to make, and most importantly have a laugh. Because if we don't have fun then what's the point choosing such a financially unstable career. We must do it for the love right?

What then? We were elated to take 'The 56' on a UK national tour and then back up to Edinburgh again for the summer and premier our new FYSA production 'E15' at Gilded Balloon, and through this process we have developed strong relationships with the figureheads of the E15 housing movement. I was lucky enough to march on the front line of the anti Austerity march with the Focus E15 mothers in May, and likewise with 'The 56' honoured to perform at Bradford City football club for the survivors of the fire and their families. These projects for me have been about people and their communities and representing their unheard voices. We are looking forward to developing both productions with the support of Battersea Arts Centre. I feel like I have expanded my understanding of the many ways in which theatre can inform, educate and even mobilise.

In short, smile, start a conversation and occasionally buy in the first round - it could work in your favour.

Vincenzo Monachello

Photo: Tirion Eilir Haf Jenkins

Vincenzo graduated in 2015 with a BA in Philosophy from University College London.

My NSDF experience could not have been more worthwhile and rewarding. I had heard such wonderful things about the festival from students who had previously been, and it did not fail to live up to and exceed my expectations. First of all, our company were able to revive our show in a space which had been expertly transformed from a sports hall into a fully functional theatre. We also had the opportunity to attend a variety of workshops as well as network with theatre professionals. I have made some wonderful contacts through having been to NSDF; people who genuinely supported our show and gave us some brilliant feedback.

The show I was a part of was a musical called 'Parade' by Jason Robert Brown. The story, which is based on real-life events, centred around Leo Frank, a Jewish man accused of killing a young girl who worked in his factory. Our company was made up of extremely talented individuals, and the show was directed, musically directed, choreographed and produced with such professionalism and expertise. Fortunately at UCL, shows are produced to an incredible standard, and I have thoroughly enjoyed being a member of the Drama and Musical Theatre societies during my time there.

I think an important piece of advice for aspiring performers, is to be as proactive as possible when it comes to finding auditions and maintaining contact with people who care about your success. Since the festival, I have been able to secure some exciting auditions for future projects, as well as keep in contact with the unbelievably supportive judges of this year's festival. I headed to the Edinburgh Fringe (festivals really are the way forward!) with a new writing play, and hope to audition for a postgraduate course in acting in a year's time.

ACTOR'S ONE-STOP SHOP THE   T 020 8279 8073
Showreels- Edited & Filmed
2B Daleview Crescent
London E4 6PQ
T 07894 152651
E info@actorsonestopshop.com
W www.actorsonestopshop.com

ALBANY THE   T 020 8692 4446
Douglas Way, London SE8 4AG
F 020 8469 2253
E hires@thealbany.org.uk
W www.thealbany.org.uk

ARRI RENTAL   T 01895 457100
3 Highbridge, Oxford Road
Uxbridge, Middlesex UB8 1LX
F 01895 457101
E info@arrirental.com
W www.arrirental.com

CENTRELINE VIDEO LTD   T 0118 941 0033
138 Westwood Road
Tilehurst
Reading RG31 6LL
W www.centrelinevideo.co.uk

CHANNEL 2020 LTD   T 0844 8402020
Phoenix Square
4 Midland Street
Leicester, LE1 1TG
E info@channel2020.co.uk
W www.channel2020.co.uk

CHANNEL 2020 LTD   T 0844 8402020
3rd Floor, 28 Marshalsea Road
London SE1 1HF
E info@channel2020.co.uk
W www.channel2020.co.uk

CRYSTAL MEDIA   T 0131 240 0988
2 Melville Street
Edinburgh EH3 7NS
F 0131 240 0989
E hello@crystal-media.co.uk
W www.crystal-media.co.uk

DARKSIDE STUDIOS LTD   T 01634 723838
Contact: Tony Fisher
40 Holborn Viaduct
London EC1N 2PB
E info@darksidestudios.uk
W www.darksidestudios.uk

D. C. WILLIAMS Henry VIDEO PRODUCTIONS
Shoot, Direct & Edit Professional Videos. Visit website for contact details
W www.hdcw.co.uk

DELUXE 142   T 020 7878 0000
Post-production Facilities
Film House
142 Wardour Street
London W1F 8DD
W www.deluxe142.co.uk

EXECUTIVE AUDIO VISUAL   T 020 7723 4488
DVD Editing & Duplication Service. Photography Services
E chris.jarvis60@gmail.com

GREENPARK PRODUCTIONS LTD   T 01566 782107
Film & Video Archives
Illand, Launceston
Cornwall PL15 7LS
E info@greenparkimages.co.uk
W www.greenparkimages.co.uk

HARLEQUIN PRODUCTIONS   T 020 8653 2333
15-17 Church Road
London SE19 2TF
E neill@harlequinproductions.co.uk
W www.harlequinproductions.co.uk

HARVEY HOUSE FILMS LTD   T 07968 830536
Animation. Full Pre/Post-production. Graphics. Showreels
The Mission Hall
Cunnington Street
London W4 5ER
E chris@harveyhousefilms.co.uk
W www.harveyhousefilms.co.uk

HELIJIB   T 07906 820287
Contact: Mark Berry
Gypps Cottage, Barrow Lane
Tunbridge Wells, Kent TN3 0BP
E info@helijib.co.uk
W www.helijib.co.uk

HIREACAMERA.COM   T 01435 873028
Equipment Hire. Video & Photography. Accessories. Lenses
Unit 5, Wellbrook Farm
Berkeley Road, Mayfield
East Sussex TN20 6EH
F 01435 874841
E enquiries@hireacamera.com
W www.hireacamera.com

IVORY TOWER ENT   T 01753 657174
Contact: Jim Groom
Pinewood Studios
Room 123 N Block
Pinewood Road, Iver Heath
Buckinghamshire SL0 0NH
E info@ivorytoweruk.com
W www.ivorytoweruk.com

MPC (THE MOVING PICTURE COMPANY)   T 020 7434 3100
Post-production
127 Wardour Street
London W1F 0NL
F 020 7287 5187
E mailbox@moving-picture.com
W www.moving-picture.com

ONSIGHT LTD   T 020 7637 0888
Film Equipment Rental
Shepperton Studios
Middlesex TW17 0QD
E hello@onsight.co.uk
W www.onsight.co.uk

PANAVISION UK   T 020 8839 7333
The Metropolitan Centre
Bristol Road
Greenford, Middlesex UB6 8GD
F 020 8839 7300
W www.panavision.co.uk

PLACE THE   **T** 020 7121 1000
17 Duke's Road
London WC1H 9PY
F 020 7121 1142
E info@theplace.org.uk
W www.theplace.org.uk

**PRO-LINK RADIO
SYSTEMS LTD**   **T** 01527 577788
Walkie Talkie & Communications Hire & Sales
84 Wynall Lane, Stourbridge
West Midlands DY9 9AQ
F 01527 577757
E admin@prolink-radio.com
W www.prolink-radio.com

RICH TV   **T** 0161 635 6207
Bridge House, 42 Newbridge Lane
Stockport, Cheshire SK1 2NA
E sales@richtv.co.uk
W www.richtv.co.uk

SALON LTD   **T** 020 8963 0530
Editing Equipment Hire. Post-production
D12 Genesis Business Park, Whitby Avenue
London NW10 7SE
E hire@salonrentals.com
W www.salonrentals.com

SOUNDHOUSE LTD THE   **T** 0161 832 7299
MediaCityUK, Blue
Manchester M50 2HQ
E mike@thesoundhouse.com
W www.thesoundhouse.tv

TEN80MEDIA   **T** 07814 406251
Studio: 517 Foleshill Road, Coventry
West Midlands CV6 5AU
E info@ten80media.com
W www.ten80media.com

VIDEO INN PRODUCTION   **T** 01604 864868
AV Equipment Hire. Conferences & Events
Glebe Farm, Wooton Road
Quinton, Northampton NN7 2EE
E enquiries@videoinn.co.uk
W www.videoinn.co.uk

**VSI - VOICE & SCRIPT
INTERNATIONAL**   **T** 020 7692 7700
*Dubbing. DVD Encoding & Authoring Facilities. Editing.
Subtitling. Voice Overs*
132 Cleveland Street, London W1T 6AB
F 020 7692 7711
E info@vsi.tv
W www.vsi.tv

W6 STUDIO   **T** 020 7385 2272
*Editing Facilities. Music Videos. Photography. Showreels.
Video Production*
359 Lillie Road, Fulham, London SW6 7PA
T 07836 357629
E kazkam@hotmail.co.uk
W www.w6studio.co.uk

**WARNER BROTHERS
DE LANE LEA**   **T** 020 7432 3800
Film & TV Sound Dubbing & Editing Suite
75 Dean Street, London W1D 3PU
E reception@wbdelanelea.com
W www.wbsound.com/london

1066 PRODUCTIONS LTD
34 Pine Hill, Epsom, Surrey KT18 7BG
E admin@1066productions.com
W www.1066productions.com

247 TELEVISION   T 01753 650000
Pinewood Studios, Pinewood Road
Iver Heath, Bucks SL0 0NH
F 01865 890504
E 247@247television.com
W www.247television.com

2PRODUCTION   T 020 8440 4848
*Creative Production Co. Voice Over Demos. Professional
Direction & Production. Corporate Films. Music
Production*
E paul@2production.com
W www.2production.com

30 BIRD PRODUCTIONS   T 07970 960995
Cambridge Junction, Clifton Way
Cambridge CB1 7GX
E info@30bird.org
W www.30bird.org

ACADEMY   T 020 7395 4155
16 West Central Street, London WC1A 1JJ
F 020 7240 0355
E reception@academyfilms.com
W www.academyfilms.com

AGILE FILMS   T 020 7000 2882
Unit 1, 68-72 Redchurch Street
London E2 7DP
E info@agilefilms.com
W www.agilefilms.com

ALGORITHM-GROUP   T 07549 892062
Film, Television & Animation. Manchester & Los Angeles
13 The Highgrove, Bolton
Lancashire BL1 5PX
E andy@algorithm-group.com
W www.algorithm-group.com

**AN ACQUIRED TASTE
TV CORP**   T 020 8686 1188
51 Croham Road, South Croydon CR2 7HD
F 020 8686 5928
E cbennetttv@gmail.com

ASF PRODUCTIONS LTD   T 07770 277637
*Contact: Alan Spencer, Malcolm Bubb. Commercials.
Corporate Videos. Documentaries. Feature Films. Films*
38 Clunbury Court, Manor Street
Berkhamsted, Herts HP4 2FF
E info@asfproductions.co.uk

**ASHFORD ENTERTAINMENT
CORPORATION LTD THE**   T 020 8660 9609
*Contact: Frazer Ashford. By e-mail. Documentaries.
Drama. Feature Films. Films. Television*
20 The Chase, Coulsdon, Surrey CR5 2EG
E info@ashford-entertainment.co.uk
W www.ashford-entertainment.co.uk

ASSOCIATED PRESS   T 020 7482 7400
The Interchange, Oval Road
Camden Lock, London NW1 7DZ

AVALON TELEVISION LTD   T 020 7598 8000
4A Exmoor Street, London W10 6BD
F 020 7598 7281
W www.avalonuk.com

BAILEY, Catherine LTD   T 020 7483 3330
110 Gloucester Avenue, Primrose Hill, London NW1 8JA
E cbl@cbltd.net
W www.cbltd.net

BBC WORLDWIDE LTD   T 020 8433 2000
Media Centre, Media Village
201 Wood Lane W12 7TQ
W www.bbcworldwide.com

BEST PICTURE FILMS LTD   T 01745 294835
Contact: Gemma Haughton
34 Ffordd Idwal, Prestatyn
Denbighshire LL19 7JG
E info@bestpicturefilm.co.uk
W www.bestpicturefilm.co.uk

BROADSIDE FILMS   T 07581 670525
*Independent Film Company run by & for Under 21s.
Dedicated to making a wide range of films through young
& new talent. Competitions for Film Makers predominantly
for Over 18s. Opportunities for Under 18s include: Script
Writing, Production, Acting, Post Production etc.*
13 Pleasant View, Llanelli SA15 4LF
E broadsidefilms@hotmail.com

BRUNSWICK FILMS LTD   T 020 8960 0066
Formula One Motor Racing Archive
26 Macroom Road, Maida Vale
London W9 3HY
F 020 8960 4997
E info@brunswickstudios.co.uk
W www.brunswickfilms.com

BRYANT WHITTLE LTD   T 020 8311 8752
49 Federation Road, Abbey Wood
London SE2 0JT
E amanda@bryantwhittle.com
W www.bryantwhittle.com

CARDINAL BROADCAST   T 01753 639210
Room 114, N Block, Pinewood Studios
Iver Heath, Bucks SL0 0NH
W www.mentalhealthtv.co.uk

**CENTRE SCREEN
PRODUCTIONS**   T 0161 832 7151
Eastgate, Castle Street
Castlefield, Manchester M3 4LZ
F 0161 832 8934
E info@centrescreen.co.uk
W www.centrescreen.co.uk

CHANNEL 2020 LTD   T 0844 8402020
Phoenix Square, 4 Midland Street
Leicester LE1 1TG
E info@channel2020.co.uk
W www.channel2020.co.uk

CHANNEL X LTD   T 0845 9002940
4 Candover Street, London W1W 7DJ
E info@channelx.co.uk
W www.channelx.co.uk

CLEVER BOY MEDIA LTD   T 01753 650951
Pinewood Studios
Pinewood Road
Iver Heath, Bucks SL0 0NH
E tim@cleverboymedia.com
W www.cleverboymedia.com

COLLINGWOOD & CO   T 020 8993 3666
10-14 Crown Street, Acton
London W3 8SB
F 020 8993 9595
E info@collingwoodandco.co.uk
W www.collingwoodandco.co.uk

COMMUNICATOR LTD   T 01763 852635
76 Station Road, Steeple Morden
Royston, Herts SG8 0NS
E info@communicator.ltd.uk

COMPLETE WORKS THE T 020 7377 0280
The Old Truman Brewery, 91 Brick Lane
London E1 6QL
F 020 7247 7405
E info@tcw.org.uk
W www.tcw.org.uk

COMTEC LTD T 0844 8805238
5 Ravensfield Gardens, Stoneleigh
Surrey KT19 0ST
E info@comtecav.co.uk
W www.comtecav.co.uk

COURTYARD PRODUCTIONS T 01732 700324
Film & Television Post Production
Little Postlings Farmhouse, Four Elms
Kent TN8 6NA
E courtyard@mac.com

CPL PRODUCTIONS LTD T 020 7240 8101
38 Long Acre, London WC2E 9JT
F 020 7836 9633
E info@cplproductions.co.uk
W www.cplproductions.co.uk

**CREATIVE
PARTNERSHIP THE** T 020 7439 7762
115-117 Shaftesbury Avenue
London WC2H 8AF
F 020 7437 1467
W www.thecreativepartnership.co.uk

CROFT TELEVISION T 01628 668735
*Contact: Nick Devonshire. By e-mail. Commercials.
Corporate Videos. Live Events*
Croft House, Progress Business Centre
Whittle Parkway
Slough, Berkshire SL1 6DQ
F 01628 668791
E nick@croft-tv.com
W www.croft-tv.com

CUPSOGUE PICTURES T 020 3411 2058
81 Brook Street, Raunds NN9 6LL
E enquiries@cupsoguepictures.com
W www.cupsoguepictures.com

DANCETIME LTD T/F 020 8742 0507
1 The Orchard, Chiswick, London W4 1JZ
E berry@tabletopproductions.com
W www.tabletopproductions.com

**DARLOW SMITHSON
PRODUCTIONS LTD** T 020 7482 7027
1st Floor, Shepherds Building Central, Charecroft Way
Shepherd's Bush, London W14 0EE
E mail@dsp.tv
W www.dsp.tv

DELUXE 142 T 020 7878 0000
Film House, 142 Wardour Street
London W1F 8DD
W www.deluxe142.co.uk

DISNEY, Walt COMPANY THE T 020 8222 1000
3 Queen Caroline Street, Hammersmith
London W6 9PE
F 020 8222 2795
W www.disney.co.uk

**DISTANT OBJECT
PRODUCTIONS LTD** T 01635 281760
*Video Production. Corporate. Documentary.
Internet Broadcasting*
11 Lime Tree Mews, 2 Lime Walk
Headington, Oxford OX3 7DZ
E production@distantobject.com
W www.distantobject.com

DLT ENTERTAINMENT UK LTD T 020 7631 1184
10 Bedford Square, London WC1B 3RA
F 020 7636 4571
W www.dltentertainment.com

DOLPHIN CASTING T 020 3697 7121
14-16 Dowgate Hill, London EC4R 2SU
E dolphincasting522@gma .com

DRAMATIS PERSONAE LTD T 020 7834 9300
Contact: Nathan Silver, Nicolas Kent
19 Regency Street, London SW1P 4BY
E ns@nathansilver.com

DRB PICTURES
86-90 Paul Street, London EC2A 4NE
E info@andorapictures.co.uk

**DREADNOUGHT
PRODUCTIONS LTD** T 01708 222938
10 Dee Close, Upminster
Essex RM14 1QD
E terence@terencemustoo.com
W www.terencemustoo.com

**DREAMING WILL
INITIATIVE THE** T/F 020 7793 9755
PO Box 38155, London SE17 3XP
E londonswo@hotmail.com
W www.lswproductions.co.uk

ECOSSE FILMS LTD T 020 7371 0290
Brigade House, 8 Parsons Green
London SW6 4TN
F 020 7736 3436
E info@ecossefilms.com
W www.ecossefilms.com

**EDGE PICTURE
COMPANY LTD THE** T 020 7836 6262
20-22 Shelton Street, London WC2H 9JJ
F 020 7836 6949
E ask.us@edgepicture.com
W www.edgepicture.com

**EFFINGEE
PRODUCTIONS LTD** T 07946 586939
Contact: Lesley Kiernan. By e-mail. Television
E info@effingee.com
W www.effingee.com

ENDEMOL UK PLC T 0870 3331700
*Including Endemol UK Productions, Initial, Remarkable
& Zeppotron*
Shepherds Building Central, Charecroft Way
Shepherd's Bush, London W14 0EE
F 0870 3331800
E info@endemoluk.com
W www.endemoluk.com

ENGINE CREATIVE T 01604 453177
The Church Rooms, Agnes Road
Northampton, Northants NN2 6EU
E wecancreate@enginecreative.co.uk
W www.enginecreative.co.uk

**ENLIGHTENMENT
INTERACTIVE** T 01695 727555
East End House, 24 Ennerdale
Skelmersdale WN8 6AJ
W www.trainingmultimedia.co.uk

EON PRODUCTIONS LTD T 020 7493 7953
Eon House, 138 Piccadilly, London W1J 7NR
F 020 7408 1236

EXTRA DIGIT LTD
PO Box 71676, London NW3 9TX
W www.extradigit.com

EYE FILM & TELEVISION T 0845 6211133
Epic Studios
112-114 Magdalen Street
Norwich NR3 1JD
E production@eyefilmandtv.co.uk
W www.eyefilmandtv.co.uk

**FARNHAM FILM
COMPANY THE** T 01252 710313
34 Burnt Hill Road, Lower Bourne
Farnham GU10 3LZ
E info@farnhamfilm.com
W www.farnhamfilm.com

FEELGOOD FICTION LTD T 020 8746 2535
Union House
65 Shepherds Bush Green
London W12 8TX
E feelgood@feelgoodfiction.co.uk
W www.feelgoodfiction.co.uk

FENIXX PRODUCTIONS T 07837 338990
*Music Video Specialists. Commercial Production
Company & Creative Team*
E us.fenixx@gmail.com
W www.fenixx.tv

**FERRIS ENTERTAINMENT
FILMS** T 07801 493133
London. Belfast. Cardiff. Los Angeles. France. Spain
Number 8, 132 Charing Cross Road
London WC2H 0LA
E info@ferrisentertainment.com
W www.ferrisentertainment.tv

**FESTIVAL FILM &
TELEVISION LTD** T 020 8297 9999
Festival House, Tranquil Passage
London SE3 0BJ
F 020 8297 1155
E info@festivalfilm.com
W www.festivalfilm.com

FIFTY ONE PRODUCTIONS T 01639 648672
Contact: Cheryl Ingram
Office NA 059A, Centerprise
Dwr-y-Felin Road, Neath
West Glamorgan SA10 7RF
F 07092 987858
E info@fiftyoneproductions.co
W www.fiftyoneproductions.co

FILMS OF RECORD LTD T 020 7428 3100
6 Anglers Lane, Kentish Town
London NW5 3DG
F 020 7284 0626
W www.filmsofrecord.com

**FLOOD, Mark
ANIMATIONS LTD** T 07535 028566
40 Wellington Street, Glasgow G2 6HJ
E mccanimations@hotmail.co.uk

FLYING TIGER PRODUCTIONS T 01458 830491
Contact: Tasha Collins
The Old Clinic, 10 St John's Square
Glastonbury, Somerset BA6 9LJ
E info@flyingtigerproductions.co.uk
W www.flyingtigerproductions.co.uk

**FOCUS PRODUCTIONS
PUBLICATIONS** T 01789 298948
58 Shelley Road, Stratford-upon-Avon
Warwickshire CV37 7JS
F 01789 294845
E maddern@focuspublishers.co.uk
W www.focusproductions.co.uk

**FREMANTLEMEDIA /
FREMANTLEMEDIA UK** T 020 7691 6000
1 Stephen Street, London W1T 1AL
W www.fremantlemedia.com

GALA PRODUCTIONS LTD T 020 8741 4200
25 Stamford Brook Road, London W6 0XJ
E info@galaproductions.co.uk
W www.galaproductions.co.uk

GALLEON FILMS LTD T 020 8310 7276
Head Office: 50 Openshaw Road, London SE2 0TE
E alice@galleontheatre.co.uk
W www.galleontheatre.co.uk

GAY, Noel TELEVISION LTD T 07738 124362
PO Box 4613, Ascot
Berks SL5 5BU
E charles.armitage@virgin.net

GHA GROUP T 020 7439 8705
33 Newman Street, London W1T 1PY
F 020 7636 4448
E info@ghagroup.co.uk
W www.ghagroup.co.uk

GOLDHAWK ESSENTIAL T 020 7439 7113
Radio Productions
20 Great Chapel Street, London W1F 8FW
E lucinda@essentialmusic.co.uk

**GRANT NAYLOR
PRODUCTIONS LTD** T 01932 592175
David Lean Building, Shepperton Studios
Studios Road, Shepperton, Middlesex TW17 0QD
E enquiries@grantnaylor.co.uk

GREAT GUNS LTD T 020 7692 4444
43-45 Camden Road, London NW1 9LR
F 020 7692 4422
E reception@greatguns.com
W www.greatguns.com

GUERILLA FILMS LTD T 020 8758 1716
35 Thornbury Road, Isleworth, Middlesex TW7 4LQ
E david@guerilla-films.com
W www.guerilla-films.com

**HAMMERWOOD FILM
PRODUCERS** T 01273 277333
110 Trafalgar Road, Portslade, Sussex BN41 1GS
E filmangels@freenetname.co.uk
W www.filmangel.co.uk

HANDS UP PRODUCTIONS LTD T 07909 824630
7 Cavendish Vale, Sherwood, Nottingham NG5 4DS
E marcus@handsuppuppets.com
W www.handsuppuppets.com

**HARRISON, Stephen FILM &
PRODUCTION SERVICES** T 07970 723097
42 Pembroke, Bracknell, Berkshire RG12 7RD
E spharrison@me.com
W www.stephenharrison.me.uk

HARTSWOOD FILMS T 020 3668 3060
3A Paradise Road, Richmond, Surrey TW9 1RX
F 020 3668 3050
W www.hartswoodfilms.co.uk

HEAD, Sally PRODUCTIONS T 020 8994 8650
60 Strand on the Green, London W4 3PE
E sally@sallyheadproductions.com

HEADSTRONG PICTURES T 020 7239 1010
85 Gray's Inn Road, London WC1X 8TX
F 020 7239 1011
E mail@walltowall.co.uk
W www.shedproductions.com

HEAVY ENTERTAINMENT LTD T 020 7494 1000
111 Wardour Street, London W1F 0UH
F 020 7494 1100
E info@heavy-entertainment.com
W www.heavy-entertainment.com

**HERMES ENTERTAINMENT
INC LTD (HE)** T 07875 628299
*Contact: Modeste Jean-Marc (Producer/Distributor).
Production & Distribution. Specialising in Motion Picture
Industry based in Paris/London/Hollywood*
72/6 Grove Lane, Camberwell Green, London SE5 8TW
F 020 7703 7927
E modeste500@gmail.com

HIT ENTERTAINMENT LTD T 020 7554 2500
5th Floor, Maple House
149 Tottenham Court Road, London W1T 7NF
F 020 7388 9321
E creative@hitentertainment.com
W www.hitentertainment.com

**HOLMES ASSOCIATES &
OPEN ROAD FILMS** T 020 7813 4333
The Studio, 37 Redington Road, London NW3 7QY
E holmesassociates@blueyonder.co.uk

HOWARD, Danny T 01625 875170
Director. Television, Video & Online Web Production
AmbitActivate Ltd, 52 Shrigley Road
Poynton, Cheshire SK12 1TF
E danny@ambitactivate.co.uk
W www.ambitactivate.co.uk

HUNGRY MAN LTD T 020 7239 4550
1-2 Herbal Hill, London EC1R 5EF
F 020 7239 4589
E ukreception@hungryman.com
W www.hungryman.com

HURRICANE FILMS LTD T 0151 707 9700
13 Hope Street, Liverpool L1 9BQ
E info@hurricanefilms.co.uk
W www.hurricanefilms.net

ICE PRODUCTIONS LTD T 0121 288 4864
The Mail Box, Lonsdale House
52 Blucher Street, Birmingham B1 1QU
E admin@ice-productions.com
W www.ice-productions.com

ICON FILMS LTD T 0117 910 2030
3rd Floor College House
32-36 College Green, Bristol BS1 5SP
F 0117 910 2031
W www.iconfilms.co.uk

IMAGE PRODUCTIONS T 07729 304795
Makes Films with Children for Children
PO Box 133, Bourne, Lincolnshire PE10 9QJ
E info@imageproductions.co.uk
W www.imageproductions.co.uk

**IMPERIAL FILM
PRODUCTIONS LTD** T 01273 301151
Contact: Franz von Habsburg FBKS
16 Tudor Close, Dean Court Road
Rottingdean, East Sussex BN2 7DF
T 07739 329747
E franz@imperialfilmproductions.com
W www.imperialfilmproductions.com

**INGLENOOK
PRODUCTIONS LTD** T 07518 049767
Victoria Warehouse, Trafford Wharf Road
Manchester M17 1AB
E hello@inglenookproductions.com
W www.inglenookproductions.com

IRREGULAR FEATURES LTD T 07771 665382
11 Keslake Road, London NW6 6DJ
E mforstater@msn.com

J. I. PRODUCTIONS T 07732 476409
90 Hainault Avenue, Giffard Park
Milton Keynes, Bucks MK14 5PE
E jasonimpey@live.com
W www.jiproductions.co.uk

JACKSON, Brian FILMS LTD T 020 7402 7543
39-41 Hanover Steps, St George's Fields
Albion Street, London W2 2YG
W www.brianjacksonfilms.com

JMP-MEDIA T 07947 241821
Corporate Videos. Television
18 Westmead, Princes Risborough
Buckinghamshire HP27 9HR
E carolyn@jmp-media.tv
W www.jmp-media.tv

JMS GROUP LTD THE T 01603 811855
Park Farm Studios, Hethersett
Norwich, Norfolk NR9 3DL
F 01603 812255
E info@jms-group.com
W www.jms-group.com

JUNCTION 15 PRODUCTIONS T 01782 562531
EMMY Award Winners. Corporate. Television
Unit 10, Rosevale Road
Parkhouse Estate
Newcastle under Lyme ST5 7EF
E info@junction15.com
W www.junction15.com

KHANDO ENTERTAINMENT T 020 3463 8492
Contact: By e-mail (for Script Submissions)
1 Marlborough Court, London W1F 7EE
E production@khandoentertainment.com

KNOWLES, Dave FILMS T 023 8084 2190
*Contact: Jenny Knowles. Corporate, Training & Project
Documentary Video Productions*
34 Ashleigh Close, Hythe SO45 3QP
E mail@dkfilms.co.uk
W www.dkfilms.co.uk

**KUEN TAO FILM
PRODUCTION** T 07950 396389
Contact: Adam Richards
30 Dombey Close, Higham
Rochester, Kent ME3 7AE
E kuentao88@gmail.com
W www.adamrichardsfightdirector.com

**LANDSEER
PRODUCTIONS LTD** T 020 7794 2523
27 Arkwright Road, London NW3 6BJ
E kchoward1@mac.com
W www.landseerfilms.com

**LIGHT AGENCY &
PRODUCTIONS LTD** T 020 8090 0006
*Contact: Lucy Misch. By Post/e-mail/Telephone.
Commercials. Corporate Videos. Documentaries.
Music Videos. Television. Showreel Editing. Software
Development*
27 Mospey Crescent, Epsom, Surrey KT17 4NA
E production@lightproductions.tv
W www.lightproductions.tv

LIME PICTURES T 0151 722 9122
Campus Manor, Childwall
Abbey Road, Liverpool L16 0JP
F 0151 722 6839

MALLINSON TELEVISION PRODUCTIONS   T 0141 332 0589
Commercials
29 Lynedoch Street, Glasgow G3 6EF
F 0141 332 6190
E reception@mtp.co.uk

MANIC MEDIA GROUP UK & EUROPE THE   T 020 8411 0888
Contact: Ian Zachary Whittingham
77 Brick Lane, Shoreditch
London E1 6QL
E sayhello@themanicmediagroup.com
W www.manicmediagroup.eu

MANS, Johnny PRODUCTIONS   T 01992 470907
Incorporating Encore Magazine
PO Box 196, Hoddesdon, Herts EN10 7WG
T 07974 755997
E johnnymansagent@aol.com
W www.johnnymansproductions.co.uk

MANSFIELD, Mike PRODUCTIONS   T 020 8947 6884
4 Ellerton Road, London SW20 0EP
E mikemantv@aol.com

MARTIN, William PRODUCTIONS   T 01865 390258
The Studio, Tubney Warren Barns
Tubney, Oxfordshire OX13 5QJ
F 01865 390148
E info@wmpcreative.com
W www.wmpcreative.com

MAVERICK MOTION LTD   T 020 7460 1371
46 Highlever Road, London W10 6PT
E mm@maverickmotion.com
W www.maverickmotion.com

MAVERICK TELEVISION   T 0121 771 1812
Progress Works, Heath Mill Lane
Birmingham B9 4AL
F 0121 771 1550
E mail@mavericktv.co.uk
W www.mavericktv.co.uk

MBP TV   T 01403 741620
Saucelands Barn, Coolham
Horsham, West Sussex RH13 8QG
F 01403 741647
E info@mbptv.com
W www.mbptv.com

McINTYRE, Phil TELEVISION LTD   T 020 7291 9000
3rd Floor, 85 Newman Street, London W1T 3EU
F 020 7291 9001
E info@mcintyre-ents.com
W www.mcintyre-ents.com

MEMPHIS & GOLD FILMS   T 07850 077825
121 Brecknock Road, Camden
London N19 5AE
E houseofsaintjude@gmail.com

MENTORN MEDIA   T 020 7258 6800
77 Fulham Palace Road, London W6 8JA
F 020 7258 6888
E reception@mentorn.tv

MET FILM PRODUCTION   T 020 8280 9110
Ealing Studios, Ealing Green
London W5 5EP
F 020 8280 9111
E reception@metfilm.co.uk
W www.metfilm.co.uk

MINAMONFILM   T 020 8674 3957
Contact: Min Clifford. By e-mail/Telephone. Corporate Videos. Documentaries. Drama. Films. Online Promotions
117 Downton Avenue, London SW2 3TX
E studio@minamonfilm.co.uk
W www.minamonfilm.co.uk

MINI PRODUCTIONS LTD   T 07989 471660
Contact: Bicky Henriques. International Film/TV Entertainment Production Company. Feature/Short Films. TV Shows. Music Videos. Promotional Videos. TV Commercials. Theatre Shows. Weddings/Events. All Services Available Internationally. Suits all budgets.
Berkeley Square House, Berkeley Square
Mayfair, London W1J 6BD
E miniproductions@bickyhenriques.com
W www.bickyhenriques.com

MISTRAL FILMS LTD   T 020 7284 2300
31 Oval Road, London NW1 7EA
E info@mistralfilm.co.uk

MUMMU LTD   T 020 7012 1673
Independent Studio Creating Animated, Filmed & Illustrated Content
Unit 1.1, 128 Hoxton Street, London N1 6SH
E info@mummu.co.uk
W www.mummu.co.uk

MURPHY, Patricia FILMS LTD   T 020 7267 0007
Office 133, 33 Parkway, Camden, London NW1 7PN
E office@patriciamurphy.co.uk

MY SPIRIT PRODUCTIONS LTD   T 01634 323376
Paranormal & Psychic Radio & Television Production
Maidstone TV Studios, Vinters Park
Maidstone ME14 5NZ
E info@myspiritradio.com
W www.myspiritradio.com

NEAL STREET PRODUCTIONS LTD   T 020 7240 8890
1st Floor, 26-28 Neal Street, London WC2H 9QQ
E post@nealstreetproductions.com
W www.nealstreetproductions.com

NEW MOON TELEVISION   T 020 7479 7010
10-11 Archer Street, London W1D 7AZ
F 020 7479 7011
E production@new-moon.co.uk
W www.new-moon.co.uk

NEW PLANET FILMS LTD   T 020 8426 1090
PO Box 640, Pinner HA5 9JB
E info@newplanetfilms.com
W www.newplanetfilms.com

NEXUS PRODUCTIONS LTD   T 020 7749 7500
Animation, Mixed Media, Live Action & Interactive Production for Commercials, Broadcast, Pop Promos & Title Sequences
25 Chart Street, London N1 6FA
F 020 7749 7501
E info@nexusproductions.com
W www.nexusproductions.com

NFD PRODUCTIONS LTD   T/F 01977 681949
Contact: By Post/e-mail/Telephone. Children's Entertainment. Commercials. Corporate Videos. Drama. Films. Television. Short Films. Showreels.
Twitter: @platform2c
The Studio, 21 Low Street
South Milford, Leeds, Yorkshire LS25 5AR
T 07966 473455
E contact@nfdproductions.com
W www.nfdproductions.com

NOMADIC FILMS T 020 7221 7775
Features. Documentaries. Music Videos. Commercials.
Corporate Promos
15 Poland Street, London W1F 8QE
E info@nomadicfilms.com
W www.nomadicfilms.com

OMNI PRODUCTIONS LTD T 0117 954 7170
14-16 Wilson Place, Bristol BS2 9HJ
E info@omniproductions.co.uk
W www.omniproductions.co.uk

ON SCREEN
PRODUCTIONS LTD T 01291 636300
Ashbourne House, 33 Bridge Street
Chepstow, Monmouthshire NP16 5GA
F 01291 636301
E action@onscreenproductions.com
W www.onscreenproductions.com

OPEN SHUTTER
PRODUCTIONS LTD T 01753 841309
Contact: John Bruce. Drama. Documentaries. Films.
Television
100 Kings Road, Windsor
Berkshire SL4 2AP
T 07753 618875
E openshutterproductions@googlemail.com

OVC MEDIA LTD T 020 7402 9111
Contact: Eliot M. Cohen. By e-mail. Animation.
Documentaries. Drama. Feature Films. Films. Television
88 Berkeley Court, Baker Street
London NW1 5ND
F 020 7723 3064
E eliot@ovcmedia.com
W www.ovcmedia.com

P4FILMS T 07831 342634
Film & Video for Television, Commercials & Corporate
Cheltenham Film Studios
Hatherley Lane, Cheltenham
Gloucestershire GL51 6PN
E info@p4films.com
W www.p4films.com

PARK VILLAGE LTD T 020 7387 8077
1 Park Village East
London NW1 7PX
E info@parkvillage.co.uk

PASSION PICTURES LTD T 020 7323 9933
Animation. Documentary. Television
1st Floor-4th Floor
33-34 Rathbone Place
London W1T 1JN
F 020 7323 9030
E info@passion-pictures.com

PATHE PICTURES LTD T 020 7323 5151
4th Floor, 6 Ramillies Street
London W1F 7TY
F 020 7631 3568
W www.pathe.co.uk

PICTURE BOX FILMS LTD
8 Warwick Road
Kingston Upon Thames
Surrey KT1 4DW
E stevendrew40@hotmail.com

PICTURE PALACE FILMS LTD T 020 7586 8763
13 Egbert Street, London NW1 8LJ
F 020 7586 9048
E info@picturepalace.com
W www.picturepalace.com

PIER PRODUCTIONS LTD T 01273 691401
8 St Georges Place
Brighton BN1 4GB
E info@pierproductionsltc.co.uk

PINBALL LONDON T 0845 2733893
The Workshop, Harley Lane
East Sussex TN21 8AG
E info@pinballonline.co.uk
W www.pinballonline.co.uk

PINEWOOD PICTURES T 020 7637 2612
3rd Floor, 12 Great Portland Street
London W1W 8QN
F 020 7636 5481

PODCAST COMPANY THE T 0844 5041226
101 Wardour Street
London W1F 0UG
E info@thepodcastcompany.co.uk
W www.thepodcastcompany.co.uk

PODCAST COMPANY THE T 0844 5041226
3 The Avenue, London N3 2LB
E info@thepodcastcompany.co.uk
W www.thepodcastcompany.co.uk

POSITIVE IMAGE LTD T 01753 842248
25 Victoria Street, Windsor
Berkshire SL4 1HE
E theoffice@positiveimage.co.uk

POTBOILER
PRODUCTIONS LTD T 020 7734 7372
9 Greek Street, London W1D 4DQ
F 020 7287 5228
E info@potboiler.co.uk
W www.potboiler.co.uk

POZZITIVE TELEVISION LTD T 020 7255 1112
1st Floor, 25 Newman Street
London W1T 1PN
E pozzitive@pozzitive.co.uk
W www.pozzitive.co.uk

PRETTY CLEVER PICTURES T 01730 817899
Hurst Cottage, Old Budgington Lane
Hollist Lane, Eastbourne
Midhurst, West Sussex GU29 0QN
T 07836 616981
E pcpics@globalnet.co.uk

PRODUCERS THE T 020 7636 4226
111 Priory Road, London NW6 3NN
E info@theproducersfilms.co.uk
W www.theproducersfilms.co.uk

QUADRILLION T 01628 487522
17 Balvernie Grove
London SW18 5RR
E enqs@quadrillion.tv
W www.quadrillion.tv

RARELY PURE,
NEVER SIMPLE T 07809 142048
Showreels
145-147 St John's Street
Clerkenwell
London EC1V 4PW
E info@rarelypureneversimple.com
W www.rarelypureneversimple.com

RAW TALENT COMPANY THE T 0131 510 0133
Contact: Helen Raw. Film Production & Actor Training
Workshops
E helen@therawtalentcompany.co.uk
W www.therawtalentcompany.co.uk

READ, Rodney T 020 8891 2875
45 Richmond Road, Twickenham
Middlesex TW1 3AW
T 07956 321550
E rodney_read@hotmail.co.uk
W www.rodney-read.com

**RECORDED PICTURE
COMPANY LTD** T 020 7636 2251
24 Hanway Street, London W1T 1UH
F 020 7636 2261
E rpc@recordedpicture.com

RED KITE ANIMATION T 0131 554 0060
89 Giles Street, Edinburgh EH6 6BZ
E info@redkite-animation.com
W www.redkite-animation.com

RED ROSE CHAIN T 01473 603388
Gippeswyk Hall, Gippeswyk Avenue
Ipswich, Suffolk IP2 9AF
E info@redrosechain.com
W www.redrosechain.com

REDRUSH TALENT T 07803 594961
22 Burnsall Street, London SW3 3ST
E janice@redrushtalent.com
W www.redrushtalent.com

REDWEATHER PRODUCTIONS T 0117 916 6456
Brunswick Court, Brunswick Square
Bristol BS2 8PE
E production@redweather.co.uk
W www.redweather.co.uk

RENIERMEDIA T 01462 892669
Television & Film Production & Consulting
11 The Twitchell, Baldock SG7 6DN
E renierv@aol.com
W www.reniermedia.com

REPLAY FILM & NEW MEDIA T 020 7637 0473
*Contact: Danny Scollard. Animation. Corporate Videos.
Documentaries. Drama. E-Learning. Live Events. Script
Writing. Web Design*
Museum House, 25 Museum Street
London WC1A 1JT
E sales@replayfilms.co.uk
W www.replayfilms.co.uk

REUTERS LTD T 020 7250 1122
The Thomson Reuters Building
30 South Collonade
Canary Wharf, London E14 5EP

RIVERSIDE TV STUDIOS T 020 8237 1123
65 Aspenlea Road, London W6 8LH
F 020 8237 1121
E info@riversidetv.co.uk
W www.riversidetv.co.uk

ROEBUCK PRODUCTIONS T 01937 835900
Commer House, Station Road
Tadcaster, North Yorkshire LS24 9JF
F 01937 835901
E john@roebuckproductions.com
W www.roebuckproductions.com

RSA FILMS T 020 7437 7426
42-44 Beak Street, London W1F 9RH
F 020 7734 4978
W www.rsafilms.com

SANDS FILMS STUDIOS T 020 7231 2209
82 St Marychurch Street, London SE16 4HZ
F 020 7231 2119
E info@sandsfilms.co.uk
W www.sandsfilms.co.uk

SCALA PRODUCTIONS LTD T 020 7916 4771
249 Gray's Inn Road
London WC1X 8QZ
E scalaprods@aol.com

SCREEN FIRST LTD T 01248 716973
Cil-y-Coed, Llansadwrn
Menai Bridge, Anglesey LL59 5SE
E paul.madden@virgin.net

SEPTEMBER FILMS LTD T 020 8563 9393
Glen House, 22 Glenthorne Road
Hammersmith, London W6 0NG
F 020 8741 7214
E info@septemberfilms.com

SEVENTH ART PRODUCTIONS T 01273 777678
63 Ship Street, Brighton BN1 1AE
E info@seventh-art.com
W www.seventh-art.com

SHELL FILM & VIDEO UNIT T 020 7934 3318
Shell Centre, York Road, London SE1 7NA
E jane.poynor@shell.com

SHOOGLY PEG PRODUCTIONS T 01382 782665
Contact: Helen Raw
c/o Park Avenue, Dundee, Tayside DD4 6PL
E casting@shooglypegproductions.com
W www.shooglypegproductions.com

SIGHTLINE T 01483 813311
*Video & Interactive Media. Full Creative & Technical
Production Resources for Producing Videos (Promotion,
Training, Employee Communications), e-Learning,
Interactive Presentations*
Based in Guildford
F 01483 813317
E keith@sightline.co.uk
W www.sightline.co.uk

SILK SOUND T 020 7434 3461
Commercials. Corporate Videos. Documentaries
13 Berwick Street, London W1F 0PW
F 020 7494 1748
E bookings@silk.co.uk
W www.silk.co.uk

SINDIBAD FILMS LTD T 020 7259 2707
Tower House, 226 Cromwell Road
London SW5 0SW
E info@sindibad.co.uk
W www.sindibad.co.uk

SITCOM SOLDIERS LTD T 07712 669097
*Specialising in Commercials, Music Videos & Digital
Content across a Global Platform*
Windy Yetts, Windy Harbour Lane
Bromley Cross, Bolton BL7 9AP
E info@sitcomsoldiers.com
W www.sitcomsoldiers.com

SNEEZING TREE FILMS T 020 7436 8036
1st Floor, 37 Great Portland Street, London W1W 8QH
E firstname@sneezingtree.com
W www.sneezingtree.com

**SNOWBALL
PRODUCTIONS LTD** T 07412 833383
E emily@snowballproductions.co.uk
W www.snowballproductions.co.uk

**SOLOMON THEATRE
COMPANY LTD** T 01725 518760
Penny Black, High Street, Damerham
Nr Fordingbridge, Hampshire SP6 3EU
E office@solomontheatre.co.uk
W www.solomontheatre.co.uk

SONY PICTURES   T 020 7533 1000
25 Golden Square, London W1F 9LU
F 020 7533 1015

SPACE CITY PRODUCTIONS   T 020 7371 4000
77-79 Blythe Road, London W14 0HP
F 020 7371 4001
E info@spacecity.co.uk
W www.spacecity.co.uk

**SPEAKEASY
PRODUCTIONS LTD**   T 01738 828524
Wildwood House, Stanley
Perth PH1 4NH
F 01738 828419
E info@speak.co.uk
W www.speak.co.uk

SPECIFIC FILMS LTD   T 020 7580 7476
33 Percy Street, London W1T 2DF
F 020 7636 6886
E info@specificfilms.com

SPIRAL PRODUCTIONS LTD   T 020 7428 9948
Unit 17-18, The Dove Centre
109 Bartholomew Road
London NW5 2BJ
F 020 7485 1845
E info@spiral.co.uk
W www.spiral.co.uk

STANDFAST FILMS   T 020 8466 5580
The Studio, 14 College Road
Bromley, Kent BR1 3NS

STANTON MEDIA   T 01296 489539
6 Kendal Close, Aylesbury
Bucks HP21 7HR
E info@stantonmedia.com
W www.stantonmedia.com

**STONE PRODUCTIONS
CREATIVE LTD**   T 01255 822172
Lakeside Studio, 62 Mill Street
St Osyth, Essex CO16 8EW
F 01255 822160
E kevin@stone-productions.co.uk
W www.stone-productions.co.uk

STUDIO AKA   T 020 7434 3581
Animation
30 Berwick Street, London W1F 8RH
F 020 7437 2309
E nikki@studioaka.co.uk
W www.studioaka.co.uk

TABARD PRODUCTIONS LTD   T 07860 364222
*Contact: John Herbert. By e-mail. Corporate Videos.
Documentaries*
4 Bloomsbury Place
London WC1A 2QA
F 01367 252294
E johnherbert@tabard.co.uk
W www.tabardproductions.com

TABLE TOP PRODUCTIONS   T 020 8994 1269
*Contact: Alvin Rakoff. By e-mail. Feature Films.
Television. Theatre*
1 The Orchard, Bedford Park
Chiswick, London W4 1JZ
T/F 020 8742 0507
E alvin@alvinrakoff.com

TAKE 3 PRODUCTIONS LTD   T 020 7354 5577
(Part of The Sequel Group)
79 Essex Road, London N1 2SF
E richard.smith@sequelgroup.co.uk
W www.take3.co.uk

TAKE FIVE PRODUCTIONS   T 020 7287 2120
37 Beak Street, London W1F 9RZ
F 020 7287 3035
E info@takefivestudio.com
W www.takefivestudio.com

TALKBACKTHAMES   T 020 7861 8000
20-21 Newman Street, London W1T 1PG
F 020 7861 8001
W www.fremantlemedia.com

TANDEM CREATIVE   T 01442 261576
Corporate Videos, Time Lapse & Documentaries
17C Alexandra Road, Hemel Hempstead
Herts HP2 5BS
E info@tandem.tv
W www.tandem.tv

THEATRE WORKSHOP   T 0131 555 3854
Film. Theatre
Out of the Blue Drill Hall 36 Dalmeny Street
Edinburgh EH6 8RG
W www.theatre-workshop.com

THEOTHER COMPANY LTD   T 020 8858 6999
*Contact: Sarah Boote. By e-mail. Drama.
Documentaries. Music Videos. Corporate Videos*
30 Glenluce Road, Blackheath
London SE3 7SB
E contact@theothercompany.co.uk
W www.theothercompany.co.uk

THIN MAN FILMS   T 020 7734 7372
9 Greek Street, London W1D 4DQ
F 020 7287 5228
E info@thinman.co.uk

**TIGER ASPECT
PRODUCTIONS**   T 020 7434 6700
Shepherds Building Central
Charecroft Way
London W14 0EE
F 020 8222 4700
E general@tigeraspect.co.uk
W www.tigeraspect.co.uk

TOP BANANA   T 01562 700404
The Studio, Broome
Stourbridge, West Midlands DY9 0HA
F 01562 700930
E enquiries@top-b.com
W www.top-b.com

TOPICAL TELEVISION LTD   T 023 8071 2233
61 Devonshire Road
Southampton SO15 2GR
F 023 8033 9835
E post@topical.co.uk

TRAFALGAR 1 LTD   T 020 7722 7789
*Contact: Hasan Shah. By Post/e-mail. Documentaries.
Feature Films. Films. Music Videos. Television*
153 Burnham Towers, Fellows Road
London NW3 3JN
E t1ltd@blueyonder.co.uk

TUALEN PICTURES   T 020 7193 7995
95 Old Woolwich Road, Greenwich
London SE10 9PP
E production@tualen.com
W www.tualen.com

**TV PRODUCTION
PARTNERSHIP LTD**   T 01264 861440
4 Fullerton Manor, Fullerton
Hants SP11 7LA
E dbj@tvpp.tv
W www.tvpp.tv

Film, Radio, Television & Video Production Companies

TV STUDIO THE T 020 8677 7143
85 Lewin Road
London SW16 6JX
E info@thetvstudio.co.uk
W www.thetvstudio.co.uk

TWOFOUR T 01752 727400
Corporate Videos. Documentaries. Live Events.
Television
Twofour Studios, Estover
Plymouth PL6 7RG
F 01752 727450
E enquiry@twofour.co.uk
W www.twofour.co.uk

**TYBURN
ENTERTAINMENT LTD** T 01494 670335
2 Chapel Court
London SE1 1HH
F 01494 678775
E tyburngeneral@btconnect.com

**TYBURN FILM
PRODUCTIONS LTD** T 01494 670335
2 Chapel Court, London SE1 1HH
F 01494 678775
E tyburngeneral@btconnect.com

VECTOR PRODUCTIONS T 0844 8019770
Corporate Videos, Television & Film Production
Moulton Park Industrial Estate
Northampton NN3 6AQ
E production@vectortv.co.uk
W www.vectortv.co.uk

VERA PRODUCTIONS LTD T 020 7292 1480
26 Bloomsbury Street
London WC1B 3QJ
F 020 7292 1481
E info@vera.co.uk

VIDEO ENTERPRISES T 01494 534144
Contact: Maurice Fleisher. Corporate Videos.
Documentaries. Live Events. Television
12 Barbers Wood Road
High Wycombe
Bucks HP12 4EP
T 07831 875216
E videoenterprises@ntlworld.com
W www.videoenterprises.co.uk

VIDEOTEL PRODUCTIONS T 020 7299 1800
Corporate Videos
84 Newman Street, London W1T 3EU
F 020 7299 1818
E mail@videotel.com
W www.videotel.com

**VSI - VOICE &
SCRIPT INTERNATIONAL** T 020 7692 7700
132 Cleveland Street, London W1T 6AB
E info@vsi.tv
W www.vsi.tv

W3KTS LTD T 01904 647822
10 Portland Street, York YO31 7EH
T 0845 8727949
E info@w3kts.com

W6 STUDIO T 020 7385 2272
Editing Facilities. Music Video. Photography.
Video Production
359 Lillie Road, Fulham
London SW6 7PA
T 07836 357629
E kazkam@hotmail.co.uk
W www.w6studio.co.uk

WALKING FORWARD MEDIA T 01480 496309
29 Hampton Close, Fenstanton
Cambridgeshire, PE28 9HB
E info@walkingforward.co.uk
W www.walkingforward.co.uk

WALKOVERS VIDEO LTD T 01249 750428
Facilities. Production
Kington Langley, Chippenham
North Wiltshire SN15 5NU
T 07831 828022
E walkoversvideo@btinternet.com

WALSH BROS LTD T/F 020 8858 6870
Contact: By e-mail. Animation. Documentaries. Drama.
Feature Films. Films. Television
29 Trafalgar Grove, Greenwich
London SE10 9TB
E info@walshbros.co.uk
W www.walshbros.co.uk

**WARNER BROS
PRODUCTIONS LTD** T 020 3427 7777
Warner Suite (Bldg. 242)
Warner Bros Studios Leavesden
Warner Drive, Leavesden, Herts WD25 7LP

**WARNER SISTERS
PRODUCTIONS LTD** T 020 8567 6655
Ealing Studios, Ealing Green
London W5 5EP
E ws@warnercini.com

WEST DIGITAL T 020 8743 5100
Broadcast Post-production
59 Goldhawk Road
London W12 8EG
F 020 8743 2345
E lucie@westdigital.co.uk

WHITEHALL FILMS T 020 8785 3737
6 Embankment, Putney
London SW15 1LB
F 020 8788 2340
E whitehallfilms@gmail.com

WORKING TITLE FILMS LTD T 020 7307 3000
26 Aybrook Street
London W1U 4AN
W www.workingtitlefilms.com

WORLD PRODUCTIONS LTD T 020 3002 3113
101 Finsbury Pavement
London EC2A 1RS
E enquiries@world-productions.com
W www.world-productions.com

WORLD WIDE PICTURES T 020 7613 6580
103 The Timber Yard
Drysdale Street
London N1 6ND
E info@worldwidepictures.tv
W www.worldwidepictures.tv

WORTHWHILE MOVIES LTD T 001 416 469 0459
Providing the Services of Bruce Pittman as Film Director
191 Logan Avenue, Toronto
Ontario, Canada M4M 2NT
E bruce.pittman@sympatico.ca

YA I NO PRODUCTIONS T 07914 614667
Lowfield House, Anlaby
East Riding of Yorkshire HU10 7BA
E info@yainoproductions.com
W www.yainoproductions.com

ZEPHYR FILMS LTD T 020 7794 0011
E info@zephyrfilms.co.uk

Film & Television Schools

What are film and television schools?

The schools listed in this section offer various courses to those who wish to become part of the behind-camera world of the entertainment industry. These courses include filmmaking, producing, screenwriting and animation, to name a few. Students taking these courses usually have to produce a number of short films in order to graduate. The following advice has been divided into two sections: for potential students and for actors.

Advice for filmmakers/writers:

Why should I take a course?

The schools listed here offer courses which enable a budding filmmaker or scriptwriter to develop their skills with practical training. These courses are designed to prepare you for a career in a competitive industry. They also provide you with an opportunity to begin networking and making contacts with industry professionals.

How should I use these listings?

Research a number of schools carefully before applying to any courses. Have a look at the websites of the schools listed first to get an idea of the types of courses on offer, what is expected from students, and the individual values of each school. Request a prospectus from the school if they do not have full details online. Word of mouth recommendations are invaluable if you know anyone who has attended or taught at a school. You need to decide what type of course suits you – don't just sign up for the first one you read about. See what is available and give yourself time to think about the various options.

Advice for actors:

Why should I get involved?

Student films can offer new performers the chance to develop skills and experience in front of a camera; learning scripts, working with other actors and working with crew members. Making new contacts and learning how to get on with those you are working with, whether in front of or behind camera, is a vital part of getting along in the acting community.

In addition, you are likely to receive a certain amount of exposure from the film. The student filmmaker may show it to teachers, other students, other actors, and most importantly directors when applying for jobs, and you would normally be given your own copy of the film which you can show to agents or casting directors if requested, or use a clip of it in your showreel.

For more experienced actors, working on a student film can offer the opportunity to hone existing skills and keep involved within the industry. It can also be useful to observe new actors and keep up-to-date with new training ideas and techniques.

How do I get involved?

It may be helpful to see if the schools' websites have any advice for actors interested in being considered for parts in student films and suggesting how they should make contact. If there is no advice of this kind, it would be worth either phoning or e-mailing to ask if the school or its students would consider actors previously unknown to them. If this is the case, ask who CVs and headshots should be sent to, and whether they would like to see a showreel or voicereel (for animation courses).

If you are asked to play a role in a student film, make sure you are not going to a student's home and that someone knows where you are going and when. Equity also recommends that actors request a contract when working on any film; you could receive payment retrospectively if the film becomes a success. You may find it helpful to refer to Equity's Low Pay/No Pay advice leaflet which is available to all Equity members from their website's members' area, and to check if your employer has signed the Equity Film School Agreement, which will ensure you will receive the minimum wage.

Should I use a clip of a student film on my showreel?

Casting directors would generally prefer to see some form of showreel than none at all. If you do not have anything else you can show that has been professionally broadcast, or do not have the money to get a showreel made from scratch, then a student film is an acceptable alternative. See the 'Promotional Services' section for more information on showreels.

Where can I find more information?

Students and actors may want to visit Shooting People's website www.shootingpeople.org for further advice and daily e-mail bulletins of student/ short film and TV castings. Filmmakers can upload their films to the site for others to view.

BRADFORD - WHISTLING WOODS INTERNATIONAL FILM SCHOOL   T 01274 43087
Contact: Trevor Griffiths
Bradford College, Great Horton Road
Bradford, Yorkshire BD7 1AY
E t.griffiths@bradfordcollege.ac.uk
W www.bradfordfilmschool.com

BRIGHTON FILM SCHOOL   T 01273 602070
Head of School: Gary Barber. HNC & HND in Filmmaking.
Diploma in Cinematography & Directing. Short Courses in
Filmmaking & Screenwriting
84-86 London Road
Brighton BN1 4DF
E info@brightonfilmschool.co.uk
W www.brightonfilmschool.co.uk

LEEDS BECKETT UNIVERSITY   T 0113 812 8053
Courses: Filmmaking, MA & BA (Hons). Animation,
BA (Hons)
Northern Film School
Leeds Beckett University
Electric Press, 1 Millennium Square
Leeds LS2 3AD
F 0113 812 8080
E aetenquiries@leedsmet.ac.uk
W www.leedsbeckett.ac.uk

LONDON ACADEMY OF MEDIA FILM & TELEVISION   T 020 7138 2909
1 Lancing Street, London NW1 1NA
E study@londonacademy.co.uk
W www.media-courses.com

LONDON COLLEGE OF COMMUNICATION   T 020 7514 6569
Film & Video Course
Elephant & Castle, London SE1 6SB
F 020 7514 6843
E info@lcc.arts.ac.uk
W www.arts.ac.uk/lcc

LONDON FILM ACADEMY   T 020 7386 7711
The Old Church, 52A Walham Grove
London SW6 1QR
E info@londonfilmacademy.com
W www.londonfilmacademy.com

LONDON FILM SCHOOL THE   T 020 7836 9642
Courses: Filmmaking, 2 yr, MA. Screenwriting, 1 yr, MA.
International Film Business, 1 yr, MA (in association with
University of Exeter). PhD Film by Practice. Specialised
Professional Short Courses & Workshops
24 Shelton Street, London WC2H 9UB
F 020 7497 3718
E info@lfs.org.uk
W www.lfs.org.uk

LONDON SCHOOL OF FILM, MEDIA & PERFORMANCE   T 020 7487 7505
Regent's University, Inner Circle
Regent's Park, London NW1 4NS
F 020 7487 7425
E lsfmp@regents.ac.uk
W www.regents.ac.uk/lsfmp

MIDDLESEX UNIVERSITY   T 020 8411 5555
Television Production Course
School of Media & Performing Arts
Hendon Campus
The Burroughs, Hendon
London NW4 4BT
E b.glynn@mdx.ac.uk
W www.mdx.ac.uk

NATIONAL FILM & TELEVISION SCHOOL   T 01494 671234
MA & Diploma Courses in the Key Filmmaking Disciplines.
Short Courses for Freelancers
Beaconsfield Studios, Station Road
Beaconsfield, Bucks HP9 1LG
F 01494 674042
E info@nfts.co.uk
W www.nfts.co.uk

NATIONAL YOUTH FILM ACADEMY   T 0845 3096239
For Young Actors & Film-makers aged 16-25
Arch 1, Hymers Court
Brandling Street
Gateshed, Newcastle NE8 2BA
E info@nyfa.org.uk
W www.nyfa.org.uk

NORTHERN FILM SCHOOL   T 0113 812 8000
Leeds Beckett University
Electric Press
1 Millennium Square
Leeds LS2 3AD
E northernfilmschool@leedsbeckett.ac.uk
W www.northernfilmschool.co.uk

RAINDANCE FILM PARTNERSHIP LLP   T 020 7930 3412
Short Courses. 1 yr Postgraduate Degrees
10 Craven Street
London WC2N 5PE
E info@raindance.co.uk
W www.raindance.org

UNIVERSITY FOR THE CREATIVE ARTS   T 01252 892883
Pre-degree, Undergraduate & Postgraduate Degrees in
Creative Arts Courses
Falkner Road, Farnham
Surrey GU9 7DS
E enquiries@ucreative.ac.uk
W www.ucreative.ac.uk

UNIVERSITY OF WESTMINSTER SCHOOL OF MEDIA ARTS & DESIGN   T 020 7911 5000
Undergraduate Courses: Film & Television Production.
Contemporary Media Practice. Postgraduate Courses:
Theory, Culture & Industry
Admissions & Enquiries:
Watford Road
Northwick Park
Harrow, Middlesex HA1 3TP
W www.westminster.ac.uk/film

3 MILLS STUDIOS T 020 7363 3336
Three Mill Lane, London E3 3DU
F 0871 5944028
E info@3mills.com
W www.3mills.com

ANIMAL PROMOTIONS LTD T 07778 156513
White Rocks Farm, Underriver
Sevenoaks, Kent TN15 0SL
F 01732 763767
E happyhoundschool@yahoo.co.uk
W www.whiterocksfarm.co.uk

ARDMORE STUDIOS LTD T 00 353 1 2862971
Herbert Road, Bray
Co. Wicklow, Ireland
E film@ardmore.ie
W www.ardmore.ie

BACKSTAGE CENTRE THE T 020 3668 5753
25m x 35m Sound Stage
100 Tonne Rigging, 1000kVA
High House Production Park
Vellacott Close
Purfleet, Essex RM19 1RJ
E info@thebackstagecentre.com
W www.thebackstagecentre.com

BEACON PRODUCTIONS T 001 330 415 5120
Contact: Len Brown
2827 Sickels Circle S.E.
Massillon, OH, USA 44646
E len@beaconproductions.com
W www.beaconproductions.com

CLAPHAM ROAD STUDIOS T 020 7582 9664
Animation. Live Action
161 Clapham Road, London SW9 0PU
W www.claphamroadstudios.co.uk

EALING STUDIOS T 020 8567 6655
Ealing Green, London W5 5EP
E assistant.lucybevan@mac.com
W www.ealingstudios.com

ELSTREE STUDIOS T 020 8953 1600
Shenley Road, Borehamwood
Hertfordshire WD6 1JG
F 020 8905 1135
E info@elstreestudios.co.uk
W www.elstreestudios.co.uk

LONDON STUDIOS THE T 020 7157 5555
London Television Centre
Upper Ground
London SE1 9LT
F 020 7157 5757
E sales@londonstudios.co.uk
W www.londonstudios.co.uk

PINEWOOD STUDIOS T 01753 651700
Pinewood Road, Iver Heath
Buckinghamshire SL0 0NH
W www.pinewoodgroup.com

REUTERS TELEVISION T 020 7250 1122
The Thomson Reuters Building
30 South Colonnade
Canary Wharf, London E14 5EP

RIVERSIDE STUDIOS T 020 8237 1000
65 Aspenlea Road
London W6 8LH
F 020 8237 1001
E reception@riversidestudios.co.uk
W www.riversidestudios.co.uk

SANDS FILMS STUDIOS T 020 7231 2209
82 St Marychurch Street
London SE16 4HZ
F 020 7231 2119
E info@sandsfilms.co.uk
W www.sandsfilms.co.uk

SHEPPERTON STUDIOS T 01932 562611
Studios Road, Shepperton
Middlesex TW17 0QD
W www.pinewoodgroup.com

SILVER ROAD STUDIOS T 020 8746 2000
Green Screen Studios. Filming & Photographic Studios.
Conference/Function Room. Cinema/Screening Room.
Casting Room. Make-up Rooms. Voice Overs. Editing.
In-house Equipment Hire. Maintenance. Free Parking
E info@silverroadstudios.co.uk
W www.silverroadstudios.co.uk

TWICKENHAM STUDIOS LTD T 020 8607 8888
The Barons
Twickenham TW1 2AW
E sales@twickenhamstudios.com
W www.twickenhamstudios.com

G

Good Digs Guide

Compiled by Janice Cramer
and David Banks

This is a list of digs recommended by
those who have used them.

To keep the list accurate please send
recommendations for inclusion to:

Good Digs Guide
Spotlight, 7 Leicester Place
London WC2H 7RJ
E contacts@spotlight.com

If you are a digs owner wishing
to be listed, your application must
include 2 recommendations from
performers who have stayed
in your accommodation.

ABERDEEN: Milne, Mrs A. T 01224 638951
5 Sunnyside Walk
Aberdeen AB24 3NZ

ABERYSTWYTH:
Vegetarian Penrhiw T 07837 712323
Farmhouse near Aberystwyth providing Accommodation
& Vegetarian Breakfasts
Penrhiw, Llanafan
Aberystwyth, Dyfed SY23 4BA
E penrhiw@fastmail.fm
W www.vegetarianpenrhiw.com

AYR: Dunn, Sheila T 01292 284531
The Dunn-Thing Guest House, 13 Park Circus
Ayr KA7 2DJ

BATH: Tapley, Jane T 01225 446561
Camden Lodgings
3 Upper Camden Place
Bath BA1 5HX
E peter@tapley.ws

BIRMINGHAM: Hurst, Mr P. T 0121 449 8220
41 King Edward Road, Moseley
Birmingham B13 8HR
T 07976 726809
E phurst1com@aol.com

BIRMINGHAM:
Mountain, Marlene P. T 0121 454 5900
268 Monument Road, Edgbaston
Birmingham B16 8XF

BIRMINGHAM:
Wilson, Mrs Yolande T 0121 440 5182
17 Yew Tree Road, Edgbaston
Birmingham B15 2LX
T 07706 032201
E yolandewilson17@gmail.com

BLACKPOOL: Lees, Jean T 01253 621059
Ascot Flats, 6 Hull Road
Central Blackpool FY1 4QB

BLACKPOOL:
Somerset Apartments T/F 01253 346743
22 Barton Avenue, Blackpool FY1 6AP
E somersetapartments@tiscali.co.uk
W www.blackpool-somerset-apartments.co.uk

BLACKPOOL:
Waller, Veronica & Bob T 01253 627003
The Brooklyn Hotel, 7 Wilton Parade
Blackpool FY1 2HE
E brooklynhotel@live.co.uk
W www.brooklynblackpool.com

BOLTON: Duckworth, Paul T 07762 545129
19 Burnham Avenue, Bolton BL1 6BD
E pauljohnathan@msn.com

BOURNEMOUTH: Sitton, Martin T 01202 293318
Flat 2, 9 St Winifreds Road
Meyrick Park, Bournemouth BH2 6NX
E martinbmouth@hotmail.co.uk

BRADFORD: Smith, Theresa T 01274 778568
8 Moorhead Terrace, Shipley
Bradford BD18 4LA
E theresaannesmith@hotmail.com

BRIGHTON: Benedict, Peter T 07752 810122
19 Madeira Place, Brighton BN2 1TN
E peter@peterdanielbenedict.co.uk
W www.madeiraplace.co.uk

BRIGHTON: Chance, Michael
& Drinkel, Keith T 01273 779585
6 Railway Street, Brighton BN1 3PF
T 07876 223359
E mchance@lineone.net

BRIGHTON: Dyson, Kate T 01273 607490
1 Double Room
39 Arundel Street, Kemptown BN2 5TH
T 07812 949875
E katedyson222@icloud.com

BRISTOL: Ham, Phil & Jacqui T 0117 902 5213
Double room. Walking distance from Bristol town centre
78 Stackpool Road, Southville
Bristol BS3 1NN
T 07956 962422
E jacquic@tiptopmusic.com

BURY ST EDMUNDS:
Bird, Mrs S. T 01284 754492
30 Crown Street, Bury St Edmunds
Suffolk IP33 1QU
E josandsue@homebird2.plus.com

BURY ST EDMUNDS:
Harrington-Spier, Sue T 01284 768986
39 Well Street, Bury St Edmunds
Suffolk IP33 1EQ
E sue.harringtonspier@gmail.com

BUXTON: Kitchen, Mrs G. T 01298 26555
Silverlands Holiday Apartments
c/o 156 Brown Edge Road
Buxton, Derbyshire SK17 7AF
T 01298 79381
E swiftcaterequip2@aol.com

CAMBRIDGE: Dunn, Anne T 01954 210291
The Dovecot, 1 St Catherine's Hall
Coton, Cambridge CB23 7GU
T 07774 131797
E dunn@annecollet.fsnet.co.uk

CANTERBURY: Ellen, Nikki T 01227 720464
Crockshard Farmhouse, Wingham
Canterbury CT3 1NY
E crockshard_bnb@yahoo.com
W www.crockshard.com

CANTERBURY: Waugh, Gilda T 07730 040602
Two Bedrooms. 15 min walk from Central Canterbury.
Park & Ride 5 mins walk
185 Wincheap, Canterbury CT1 1TG

CARDIFF: Blade, Mrs Anne T 029 2022 5860
25 Romilly Road, Canton
Cardiff CF5 1FH

CARDIFF: Kelly, Sheila T 029 2039 5078
166 Llandaff Road, Canton
Cardiff CF11 9PX
T 07875 134381
E mgsmkelly1@gmail.com

CARDIFF: Kennedy, Rosie T 07746 946118
Duffryn Mawr Farm House, Pendoylan
Vale of Glamorgan
E rosie@duffrynmawrcottages.com
W www.duffrynmawrcottages.co.uk

CARDIFF: Lewis, Nigel T 029 2049 4008
66 Donald Street, Roath, Cardiff CF24 4TR
T 07813 069822
E nigel.lewis66@btinternet.com

CARDIFF:
Ty Rosa Boutique B&B   **T** 029 2022 1964
118 Clive Street, Cardiff CF11 7JE
F 029 2002 7930
E info@tyrosa.com
W www.tyrosa.com/theatre-digs

CHESTERFIELD: Cook, Chris   **T** 01246 202631
27 Tennyson Avenue, Chesterfield
Derbyshire S40 4SN
T 07969 989558
E chris_cook@talk21.com

CHESTERFIELD:
Foston, Mr & Mrs   **T** 01246 235412
Anis Louise Guest House, 34 Clarence Road
Chesterfield S40 1LN
E anislouise@gmail.com
W www.anislouiseguesthouse.co.uk

COVENTRY:
Snelson, Paddy & Bob   **T** 01926 852850
Banner Hill Farmhouse, Rouncil Lane
Kenilworth CV8 1NN

DARLINGTON: Bird, Mrs   **T** 01748 822771
Gilling Old Mill, Gilling West
Richmond, N Yorks DL10 5JD
E admin@yorkshiredales-cottages.com

DARLINGTON: George Hotel   **T** 01325 374576
Piercebridge
Darlington DL2 3SW
E george@bulldogmail.co.uk
W www.george-ontees.co.uk

DERBY: Boddy, Susan   **T** 01332 701384
St Wilfrids, Church Lane
Barrow-upon-Trent, Derbyshire DE73 7HB

DERBY: Coxon, Mary   **T** 01332 347460
Short Term Accommodation. Theatricals only
1 Overdale Road, Derby DE23 6AU
T 07850 082943
E marycoxon@hotmail.co.uk

EASTBOURNE: Allen, Peter   **T** 07712 439289
16 Enys Road, Eastbourne BN21 2DN
E peterscallen@gmail.com

EAST LONDON: Horn, Cryn   **T** 020 8470 4868
Peaceful house in East London. Good transport links & in easy reach of Theatre Royal Stratford East & Three Mills Film Studios. Wifi available. Shared bathroom & kitchen. Vegetarian household. No smoking. Room 1: Small double room. Room 2: Single room.
27 Donald Road, Upton Park
London E13 0QF
T 07958 107620
E crynhorn@easynet.co.uk

EDINBURGH:
ACS Properties-Edinburgh Digs   **T** 01620 826880
Contact: Ashley Smith, Carole Smith. Short Term Letting in Edinburgh
Office: 7 St Lawrence, Haddington
East Lothian EH41 3RL
T 07581 100777
E ashley@acs-properties.com
W www.acs-properties.com

EDINBURGH:
Glen Miller, Edna   **T** 0131 556 4131
£90 per person, per week
25 Bellevue Road, Edinburgh EH7 4DL

EDINBURGH: Tyrrell, Helen   **T** 0131 229 7219
Two single rooms in large, bright flat overlooking city-centre park. 10 mins walk from several Edinburgh theatres. Wi-fi. Full access to kitchen & sitting room. Charges: £100 per week, £18 per day (including breakfast) Reductions for students
9 Lonsdale Terrace, Edinburgh EH3 9HN
T 07929 960510
E hkmtyrrell@gmail.com

GLASGOW: Baird, David W.   **T** 0141 423 1340
6 Beaton Road, Maxwell Park
Glasgow G41 4LA
T 07842 195597
E b050557@yahoo.com

GLASGOW:
Leslie-Carter, Simon   **T** 01475 732204
52 Charlotte Street, Glasgow G1 5DW
T 07814 891351
E slc@52charlottestreet.co.uk
W www.52charlottestreet.co.uk

INVERNESS: Blair, Mrs   **T** 01463 232878
McDonald House, 1 Ardross Terrace
Inverness IV3 5NQ
E f.blair@homecall.co.uk

IPSWICH: Ball, Bunty   **T** 01473 256653
56 Henley Road, Ipswich IP1 3SA
E bunty.ball.t21@btinternet.com

IPSWICH: Bennett, Liz   **T** 01473 623343
Gayfers, Playford
Ipswich IP6 9DR
E lizzieb@clara.co.uk

IVY HOUSE, MALVERN   **T** 07956 035987
111 Graham Road, Great Malvern
Worcestershire WR14 2JP
E wilfred@legion.plus.com

LEEDS: Cannon, Rosey
& Sanders, Karen   **T** 07969 832955
14 Toronto Place, Chapel Allerton
Leeds LS7 4LJ
T 07538 989471
E cannon.rosey42@googlemail.com

LINCOLN: Carnell, Andrew   **T** 01522 569892
Tennyson Court Cottages, 3 Tennyson Street
Lincoln LN1 1LZ
E andrew@tennyson-court.co.uk
W www.tennyson-court.co.uk

LIVERPOOL: Maloney, Anne   **T** 0151 734 4839
16 Sandown Lane, Wavertree
Liverpool L15 8HY
T 07977 595040

LLANDUDNO:
Blanchard, Mr D. & Mrs A.   **T** 01492 877822
Oasis Hotel, 4 Neville Crescent
Central Promenade, Llandudno LL30 1AT
E oasishotel4@btconnect.com

LONDON: Cavanah, Anne Marie   **T** 07939 220299
Forest Hill, London SE23 2SL
E anmariecavanah@aol.com

LONDON: Home Rentals B&B   **T** 020 8840 1071
Agency
7 Park Place, Ealing
London W5 5NQ
E home_rentals@btinternet.com

LONDON: Kempton, Victoria   T 020 8888 5595
66 Morley Avenue
London N22 6NG
T 07946 344697
E vjkempton@onetel.com

LONDON: Mesure, Nicholas   T 020 8853 4337
16 St Alfege Passage, Greenwich
London SE10 9JS
T 07941 043841
E info@st-alfeges.co.uk

LONDON: Montagu, Beverley   T 020 7263 3883
13 Hanley Road
London N4 3DU
E beverley@montagus.org

LONDON: Rothner, Stephanie   T 020 8446 1604
44 Grove Road, North Finchley
London N12 9DY
T 07956 406446

LONDON: Walsh, Genevieve   T 020 7627 0024
37 Kelvedon House, Guildford Road
Stockwell, London SW8 2DN
T 07801 948864

LONDON: Warren, Mrs Sally   T 020 8994 0560
28 Prebend Gardens, Chiswick
London W4 1TW

LONDON: Wilson, Sylvia   T 07758 265351
1 Marlborough Mansions
39 Bromells Road
Clapham SW4 0BA
E sylvia.wilson155@gmail.com

LONDON: Wood, Hilary   T 020 8331 6639
59 Prince John Road, Eltham
London SE9 6QB
F 07092 315384
E rainbowtheatrelondoneast@yahoo.co.uk

MALVERN: McLeod, Mr & Mrs   T 01684 574994
Sidney House
40 Worcester Road
Malvern WR14 4AA
E info@sidneyhouse.co.uk
W www.sidneyhouse.co.uk

MANCHESTER:
Dyson, Mrs Edwina   T 0161 434 5410
33 Danesmoor Road
West Didsbury
Manchester M20 3JT
T 07947 197755
E edwinadyson@hotmail.com

MANCHESTER:
Heaton, Miriam   T 0161 773 4490
58 Tamworth Avenue, Whitefield
Manchester M45 6UA

MANCHESTER: Higgins, Mark   T 07872 819636
New build less than 1 mile from Lowry or Opera House.
Pictures available on request. Parking Available
72 Camp Street, Manchester M7 1LG
T 0161 879 4712
E icenlemon30@hotmail.com

MANCHESTER:
Jones, Miss P. M.   T 0161 766 9243
'Forget-me-not Cottages', 12&14 Livsey Street
Whitefield, Manchester M45 6AE
E patricia@whitefieldcottages.co.uk

MANCHESTER:
Prichard, Fiona   T 0161 434 4877
45 Bamford Road, Didsbury
Manchester M20 2QP
T 07771 965651
E fionaprichard@hotmail.com

MANCHESTER: Twist, Susan   T 0161 225 1591
45 Osborne Road
Levenshulme
Manchester M19 2DU
T 07957 886940
E sue.twist@o2.co.uk

MANSFIELD: Ward, Judith   T 01623 431359
4 Bedrooms. 3 minutes from Palace Mansfield Theatre.
Near Town Centre. Parking available
16 Watson Avenue, Mansfield
Nottinghamshire NG18 2BS
T 07742 589133
E judithaward@hotmail.com

MILFORD HAVEN:
Henricksen, Bruce & Diana   T 01646 695983
Belhaven House Hotel (near Torch Theatre)
28-29 Hamilton Terrace
Milford Haven SA73 3JJ
T 07436 582854
E brucehenricksen@mac.com
W www.westwaleshotel.com

NEWCASTLE UPON TYNE:
Rosebery Hotel   T 0191 281 3363
Contact: The Manager
2 Rosebery Crescent, Jesmond
Newcastle upon Tyne NE2 1ET
W www.roseberyhotel.com

NEWCASTLE UPON TYNE:
Theatre Digs Newcastle   T 0191 226 1345
73 Moorside North
Newcastle upon Tyne NE4 9DU
E pclarerowntree@yahoo.co.uk
W www.theatredigsnewcastle.co.uk

NEWPORT: Price, Mrs Dinah   T 01633 420216
Great House, Isca Road
Old Village, Caerleon
Gwent NP18 1QG
E dinahprice123@btinternet.com
W www.greathousebb.co.uk

NORWICH:
Busch, Julia Cornaby   T 01603 612833
8 Chester Street
Norwich NR2 2AY
T 07920 133250
E juliacbusch@aol.com

NOTTINGHAM: Davis, Mrs B.   T 0115 947 4179
3 Tattershall Drive, The Park
Nottingham NG7 1BX
E bjgdavis@gmail.com

NOTTINGHAM: Offord, Mrs   T 0115 947 6924
5 Tattershall Drive, The Park
Nottingham NG7 1BX

NOTTINGHAM: Santos, Mrs S.   T 0115 966 3018
Eastwood Farm, Hagg Lane
Epperstone, Nottingham NG14 6AX
T 07931 101911
E info@eastwoodfarm.co.uk
W www.eastwoodfarm.co.uk

**NOTTINGHAM: Seymour Road Studios
Bed & Breakfast**   T 07946 208211
42 Seymour Road, West Bridgford
Nottingham NG2 5EF
E fran@seymourroadstudios.co.uk
W www.seymourroadstudios.co.uk

OXFORD: Petty, Susan   T 01993 703035
Self-catering Cottages. Sleeps 4-10. 12 miles from Oxford
Witney, Oxfordshire
E ianpetty@btinternet.com

PETERBOROUGH: Smith, J.   T 01733 211847
Fen-Acre, 20 Barber Drove North
Crowland, Peterborough PE6 0BE
T 07759 661896
E julie@fen-acreholidaylet.com
W www.fen-acreholidaylet.com

PLYMOUTH: Ball, Fleur   T 01752 670967
3 Hoe Gardens, Plymouth PL1 2JD
E fleurball@blueyonder.co.uk

PLYMOUTH: Carson, Mr & Mrs   T 01752 872124
Beech Cottages, Parsonage Road
Newton Ferrers, Nr Plymouth PL8 1AX
T 07791 108146
E beechcottages@aol.com

**PLYMOUTH:
Humphreys, John & Sandra**   T 01752 220176
Free Wi-fi
Lyttleton House, 4 Crescent Avenue
Plymouth PL1 3AN

PLYMOUTH: Mead, Teresa   T 01752 664046
Ashgrove House, 218 Citadel Road
The Hoe, Plymouth PL1 3BB
E ashgroveho@aol.com

**PLYMOUTH:
Spencer, Hugh & Eloise**   T 01752 664066
10 Grand Parade, Plymouth PL1 3DF
T 07966 412839
E hugh.spencer@hotmail.com

POOLE: Saunders, Mrs   T 01202 741637
1 Harbour Shallows, 15 Whitecliff Road
Poole BH14 8DU
E saunders.221@btinternet.com

**PORTSMOUTH: Dave & Gerald's
Theatrical Digs**   T 023 9275 3359
*10 mins from King's Theatre & 20 mins from New
Theatre Royal*
26 Wimborne Road, Southsea
Portsmouth, Hants PO4 8DE
E d.yetman@btinternet.com

PORTSMOUNTH: Goss, Diana   T 07770 453693
10 Duncan Road, Southsea
Portsmouth PO5 2QU
E dgoss20817@aol.com
W www.notmagnum.co.uk

SALISBURY: Brumfitt, Ms S.   T 01722 334877
26 Victoria Road, Salisbury, Wilts SP1 3NG
E slbrumfitt@gmail.com

**SCARBOROUGH:
Holly Croft B&B**   T 01723 375376
28 Station Road, Scalby
Scarborough, North Yorkshire YO13 0QA
E christine.goodall@tesco.net
W www.holly-croft.co.uk

SHEFFIELD: Slack, Penny   T 0114 234 0382
Rivelin Glen Quarry, Rivelin Valley Road
Sheffield S6 5SE
E penelopeslack@icloud.com
W www.quarryhouse.org.uk

SHOREHAM: Cleveland, Carol   T 01273 567954
Near Brighton
1 Oxen Court, Oxen Avenue
Shoreham-by-Sea BN43 5AS
T 07973 363939
E info@carolcleveland.com

**STOKE-ON-TRENT:
Bank End Farm**   T 07956 854949
Hammond Avenue, Brown Edge
Stoke-on-Trent, Staffs ST6 8QU
E bankendholidaycottage@gmail.com

**STOKE-ON-TRENT:
Hindmoor, Mrs**   T 01782 264244
Self-catering and B&B
Verdon Guest House
44 Charles Street
Hanley, Stoke-on-Trent ST1 3JY
E debbietams@ymail.com
W www.stokeaccommodation.com

**STRATFORD-UPON-AVON:
Caterham House**   T 01789 267309
58-59 Rother Street
Stratford-upon-Avon CV37 6LT
E caterhamhousehotel@btconnect.com

TAUNTON: Parker, Sue   T 01278 458580
Admirals Rest, 5 Taunton Road
Bridgwater TA6 3LW
E info@admiralsrest.co.uk

TAUNTON: Read, Mary   T 01823 334148
Pyreland Farm, Cheddon Road
Taunton, Somerset TA2 7QX

**WINCHESTER:
South Winchester Lodges**   T 01962 820490
The Green, South Winchester Golf Club
Winchester, Hampshire SO22 5SW

**WOLVERHAMPTON:
Riggs, Peter A.**   T 01902 846081
'Bethesda', 56 Chapel Lane
Codsall, Nr Wolverhampton WV8 2EJ
T 07930 967809
E peterriggs53@gmail.com

WOLVERHAMPTON: York Hotel   T 01902 758211
138 Tettenhall Road, Wolverhampton
West Midlands WV6 0BQ
E frontdesk@theyorkhotel.com
W www.theyorkhotel.com

WORTHING: Symonds, Mrs Val   T 01903 201557
23 Shakespeare Road
Worthing BN11 4AR
T 07951 183252

YORK: Blacklock, Tom   T 01904 620487
155 Lowther Street, York YO31 7LZ
E thomas.blacklock@btinternet.com

YORK: Harrand, Greg   T 01904 637404
Hedley House Hotel & Apts
3 Bootham Terrace
York YO30 7DH
E greg@hedleyhouse.com

H →

Health & Wellbeing

Please note: Readers should take care to research any company or individual before agreeing to treatment or services listed in this section.

Health & Wellbeing

CASE STUDY

Amelie Leroy trained as a physiotherapist in Switzerland and has worked for several years in various hospitals and private sports clinics. She is registered with HCPC and a member of Chartered Society of Physiotherapy.

My heart has always been in theatre and a few years ago, I decided to train as an actor at a drama school in London. This led me to work as a performer on various theatre productions in the UK, from devising to physical theatre and ensemble productions. These shows included dance, Laban, martial arts as well as puppetry and mask work. Still working within the arts, I now specialise in treating fellow performers, dancers and sports people.

The need of each individual varies greatly, from rehabilitation of injuries and pain problems to optimising movement patterns (e.g. aerials, puppetry etc.).

I currently work as a freelance physiotherapist with 'Complete Physio', on theatre productions and on an individual basis. Here are some insights I gained through my work as a performer and physiotherapist.

"It normally takes about three months to learn and reprogram a new habit"

Habits, patterns and routines

To make our lives easier, our brain and body is built up of movement patterns and behavioural habits. This makes us more efficient as we don't have to consider every small movement or be conscious of every single decision. However, these habits can become something that is holding us back and it is wise to review them once in a while. Are they healthy? Do they support us in reaching our acting and life goals? It normally takes about three months to learn and reprogram a new habit. This means for example that if you take up running or working out at the

gym, the first three months will be the hardest. Hang in there until this new habit is stored in your brain as the new norm. Routines can also help to reduce mental resistance.

I tend to use the same stretch routine after every work out, which means that my body gets used to the sequence and will know what to expect next.

Balance

It is all about getting the balance right between the different systems we work on. Important ones are:

- conditioning / cardiovascular training (cardio)
- strengthening
- neuromuscular proprioception / balance
- new skill sets / movement patterns
- stretching

For example; it wouldn't make sense to train in cardio (running, swimming, cycling) more often than strengthening. This could result in newly formed muscles being burnt like fat. For this exact reason, I often recommend to strengthen three times a week, if you intend to run twice a week (although this is slightly different for marathon runners). The body is highly economic, whatever it feels is not needed on a regular basis, it will reduce or remove again.

Different effects on body and mind

There are multiple benefits of cardio, but to mention a few; it releases 'feel good' hormones, which will help ease fatigue and enforces a positive outlook on life. Additionally, it improves lung capacity, which will have an effect on your speech (think of those lengthy Shakespearean monologues). It also enhances your immune system and reduces your susceptibility to colds and the flu. Muscle strengthening in turn has the effect of preventing injuries, as one of their functions is to protect joints, ligaments and bones. It also helps to improve posture and mental resilience. Hip muscle stretching is very important to centre your voice and is again a main player on posture as well.

New skill sets, movement patterns and overcoming fears

Gaining new skills not only adds a further selling point to your CV, it also opens up your body and mind to trying out new things. When preparing as a physical theatre performer, I had to face my fear of heights in aerials and my nervousness in handstand and tumbling. I found that facing my fears has improved my mental disposition in taking more and bolder risks. I certainly take this new found courage into the audition room.

Overtraining

Resting is as important as training. It is indeed possible to over-train, when you don't allow the body to replenish and recover.

Typical signs of over-training are a decline in improvement (e.g. of strength, flexibility, speed) and constant dull muscle pain (longer than 72 hours after work out) etc. The probability of injuries during this time is increased. It is recommended to have one to two days rest per week, when you just laze around!

Different options

There are many different opportunities for getting fitter and expanding your skill set. One option is to barter your skills. Many actors have multiple talents and I have known performers swap accent classes for personal trainer sessions or therapy treatments for instrument classes. You only need to find a cheap room to rent and sometimes a park will do just as well. 'The Gym' group is also a cheap gym option (around £20 per month), which lets you use their branches all over the UK. It also offered me the luxury of having a shower in Edinburgh city centre during the Fringe Festival. It also makes sense to see a therapist or personal trainer, who can evaluate your current condition and give suggestions on things to work on and future goals. Start with an action plan and take it from there step by step.

For further enquiries, contact Amelie at a@amelie-leroy.com

Health & Wellbeing

How should I use these listings?

You will find a variety of companies in this section which could help you enhance your health and wellbeing physically and mentally. They include personal fitness and lifestyle coaches, counsellors, exercise classes and beauty consultants amongst others. Even if you feel you have your career and lifestyle under control, you may still find the following advice helpful:

Your health is vital to your career as a performer. From a business perspective, your body is part of your promotional package and it needs to be maintained. Try to keep fit and eat healthily to enhance both your outward appearance and your inner confidence. You need to ensure that if you are suddenly called for an audition you look suitable for and feel positive about the part you are auditioning for.

Keeping fit also helps you to minimise the risk of an injury. An injury is more likely to occur if you are inflexible and unprepared for sudden physical exertion. If you do pick up an injury or an illness you will want to make sure it does not get any worse by getting treatment with a specialist. Mental health is just as important. If you suffer from a psychological problem such as stage fright, an addiction or depression, you should make sure that you address and deal with the issues involved. You may need to see a counsellor or a life coach for guidance and support.

If you are unemployed, it can be difficult to retain a positive mindset. The best thing you can do is to keep yourself occupied. Think about taking on part-time work outside of acting (see the 'Non-Acting Jobs' section), exercise by jogging or running, or joining a dance or drama class to keep you active and well connected.

Spotlight 10k Challenge

Spotlight was delighted to host our 2015 10k Challenge in Regent's Park in aid of charity Acting for Others (www.actingforothers.co.uk). We had a large amount of runners and volunteers take part in the event on Sunday 13th September. Acting for Others offers financial and emotional assistance and support to those in the entertainment profession who have fallen on hard times. Here's to the next challenge!

BAPAM

Free, Specialist Medical Support for Performers, Teachers and Production Crew.

You already know how tough working in the performing arts can be but did you know that there is an organisation dedicated to keeping you healthy and working at your best, who give free specialist advice to help you overcome work-related illness or injury?

The British Association for Performing Arts Medicine (BAPAM) is a unique medical charity providing clinical advice from healthcare practitioners who understand the demands of a performing arts career. BAPAM clinicians include GPs, rheumatology and orthopaedic consultants, physiotherapists, osteopaths and psychologists. Expert medical assessments are offered free of charge (a voluntary donation is welcomed).

Common health concerns BAPAM can advise you about include voice problems, performance anxiety, stress, and physical injuries caused or exacerbated by accidents, playing musical instruments, awkward or heavy costumes, props and equipment, and workplace conditions.

If you need further treatment or help, BAPAM can liaise with appropriate support and therapeutic services including NHS professionals, specialist practitioners registered on the BAPAM Directory of Performing Arts Medicine Practitioners, and other health and welfare organisations in the performing arts community. In their London clinic BAPAM provide facilities and support to healthcare practitioners which enables them to offer some reduced cost treatments.

Many health problems can be prevented through good practice. BAPAM's freely available health resources cover topics including warm up exercises, safe technique, posture, diet, lifestyle and psychological self-care. Training events and workshops for performers, educators and employers can also be arranged.

Call 020 7404 8444 Monday to Friday 9am to 5pm or visit www.bapam.org.uk

1ST SUCCESS   T 01628 780470
Empowerment, Confidence & Stress Therapies.
Challenge Blocks, Anxieties, Stresses & Fears
The Amber Zone, 13 St Mark's Crescent
Maidenhead, Berks SL6 5DA
E joanna@1stsuccess.com
W www.1stsuccess.com

1STSUCCESS.COM   T 07898 230000
Hypnotherapy
13 St Marks Crescent, Maidenhead
Berkshire, Berks SL6 5DA
E joanna@1stsuccess.com
W www.1stsuccess.com

ALEXANDER ALLIANCE   T 01727 843633
Alexander Technique. Audition & Voice Coaching
3 Hazelwood Drive, St Albans, Herts
E bev.keech@ntlworld.com
W www.alextech.co.uk

ALEXANDER TECHNIQUE   T 020 7731 1061
Contact: Jackie Coote MSTAT
27 Britannia Road, London SW6 2HJ
E jackiecoote@alexandertec.co.uk
W www.alexandertec.co.uk

ALKALI   T 020 8788 8588
Cosmetic Dentistry. Straightening. Whitening
226A Upper Richmond Road, Putney
London SW15 6TG
E hello@alkaliaesthetics.co.uk
W www.alkaliaesthetics.co.uk

AURA DENTAL SPA   T 020 7722 0040
Cosmetic Dentistry. Invisible Braces & Teeth Whitening,
50% Discount
5 Queens Terrace, London NW8 6DX
E info@auradentalspa.com
W www.auradentalspa.com

BEYONDYOGA   T 07837 355362
Holistic Bespoke Yoga in the Familial Lineage of
Krishnamacharya
Apartment 307, 3 Eastfields Avenue, London SW18 1GN
E tissie@biawellbeing.com
W www.biawellbeing.com

BLOOMSBURY ALEXANDER CENTRE THE   T 020 7404 5348
Alexander Technique
Bristol House, 80A Southampton Row
London WC1B 4BB
T 07884 015954
E enquiries@alexcentre.com
W www.alexcentre.com

BODYWISE YOGA & NATURAL HEALTH   T 020 3116 2098
21 Old Ford Road, London E2 9RL
E info@bodywisehealth.org
W www.bodywisehealth.org

BOXMOOR HOUSE DENTAL PRACTICE   T 01442 253253
451 London Road
Hemel Hempstead HP3 9BE
F 01442 244454
E reception@boxmoordental.com

BREATHE FITNESS PERSONAL TRAINING   T 07840 180094
Twitter: @BreatheFitPT
19 Woolcombes Court, London SE16 5RQ
E anthony@breathefitness.uk.com
W www.breathefitness.uk.com

BURT, Andrew   T 020 8992 5992
Counselling
74 Mill Hill Road, London W3 8JU
E burt.counsel@tiscali.co.uk
W www.andrewburtcounselling.co.uk

COACHING FOR LEADERS LTD   T 0845 1701300
Executive Coaching. Management & Team Development
& Training
90 Long Acre, Covent Garden
London WC2E 9RZ
E coaching@coachingforleaders.co.uk
W www.coachingforleaders.co.uk

COGNITIVE BEHAVIOURAL THERAPY (CBT)
Based in West & North London
E info@therapycbt.co.uk
W www.therapycbt.co.uk

COLLEGE PRACTICE THE T 020 7267 6445
Massage. Osteopathy. Pilates. Podiatry. Sports Therapy
60 Highgate Road, London NW5 1PA
E thecollegepracticeuk@gmail.com
W www.thecollegepractice.com

**CONSTRUCTIVE TEACHING
CENTRE LTD** T 020 7727 7222
Alexander Technique Teacher Training
13 The Boulevard, Imperial Wharf
Fulham, London SW6 2UB
E constructiveteachingcentre@gmail.com
W www.constructiveteachingcentre.com

CORTEEN, Paola MSTAT T 020 8886 1728
Alexander Technique
10B Eversley Park Road, London N21 1JU
E pmcorteen@yahoo.co.uk

COURTENAY, Julian T 07973 139376
NLP Hypnotherapy
104 Huntingdon Road, London N2 9DU
E juliancourtenay1@gmail.com

CRAIGENTINNY DENTAL CARE T 0131 669 2114
57 Duddingston Crescent, Milton Road
Edinburgh EH15 3AY
E office@craigentinny.co.uk
W www.craigentinny.co.uk

CROWE, Sara T 07830 375389
*Holistic Massage. Pregnancy Treatment. Reflexology. Gel
Nails. Waxing. 20% discount for Spotlight Card holders*
Holmes Avenue, Hove BN3 7LB
E saracrowe77@gmail.com

CRYNYOGA T 020 8470 4868
*Gentle Yoga with a Therapeutic Focus. Yoga Nidra. Deep
relaxation & healing. Classes & 1-2-1 available.*
Plaistow, East London E13 0QF
E crynhorn@easynet.co.uk
W www.crynyoga.co.uk

DAVIES, Siobhan STUDIOS T 020 7091 9650
Complementary Therapies
Treatment Room, 85 St George's Road
London SE1 6ER
F 020 7091 9669
E info@siobhandavies.com
W www.siobhandavies.com

**EDGE OF THE WORLD
HYPNOTHERAPY & NLP** T 07875 720623
*Contact: Graham Howes. ASHPH GHR Registered.
GHSC Regulated. Gastric Band/Weight Loss
Hypnotherapy. Specialist Help for Performers: Anxiety,
Audition/Stage Fright, Problems with Line Learning,
Stress. Quit Smoking. Trauma. Fear. Phobia. Panic*
Based in Central London, Essex/Suffolk Skype.
E grahamahowes@me.com
W www.hypnotherapy-colchester-ipswich.com/wp/171-2/

**EDWARDS, Simon MCAHypDABCH MHS MHA
MAPHP SQHP** T 020 7467 8498
*Hypnotherapy for Professionals in Film, Stage
& Television*
10 Harley Street, London W1G 9PF
T 07889 333680
E simonedwardsharleystreet@gmail.com
W www.simonedwards.com

ELITE SPORTS SKILLS
*Personal Training. Sports Coaching. Level 4 in
Fitness & Coaching*
E esskills@hotmail.com
W www.elitesportsskills.com

ENLIGHTENEDSELFINTEREST.COM T 07910 157064
56 Bloomsbury Street, London WC1B 3QT
E maggie@enlightenedselfinterest.com

EVOLVE WELLNESS CENTRE T 020 7581 4090
10 Kendrick Mews, South Kensington
London SW7 3HG
E info@evolvewellnesscentre.com
W www.evolvewellnesscentre.com

**EXPERIENTIAL FOCUSING
THERAPY SESSIONS** T 07941 300871
Contact: Dr Greg Madison
93-95 Gloucester Place, London W1
E info@gregmadison.net
W www.gregmadison.net

**EXPERIENTIAL FOCUSING
THERAPY SESSIONS** T 07941 300871
Contact: Dr Greg Madison
40 Wilbury Road, Brighton BN1
E info@gregmadison.net
W www.gregmadison.net

**EXPLORINGU COUNSELLING,
CENTRE FOR WELL-BEING** T 01787 829141
*Practices in Colchester, Sudbury Suffolk, Harold Wood,
Saffron Walden*
54 Station Road, Sudbury
Suffolk CO10 2SP
T 07841 979450
E info@exploringucounselling.co.uk
W www.exploringucounselling.co.uk

EXPLORING U COUNSELLING T 01787 829141
Dealing with Stress, Addictions & Lack of Confidence
The Old Press Rooms
54 Station Road
Sudbury, Suffolk CO10 2SP
E info@exploringucounselling.co.uk
W www.exploringucounselling.co.uk

FABULOUS IMPACT T 07958 984195
*Confidence & Positive Focus Coaching for
Performers. NLP*
E nicci@nicciroscoe.com
W www.nicciroscoe.com

**FAITH, Gordon BA MCHC
(UK) Dip.REM.Sp** T 020 7328 0446
*Focusing. Hypnotherapy. Obstacles to Performing.
Positive Affirmation*
1 Wavel Mews, Priory Road
West Hampstead, London NW6 3AB
E gordon.faith@tiscali.co.uk
W www.hypnotherapy.gordonfaith.co.uk

FIT 4 THE PART T 020 8311 9676
*Contact: Jon Trevor (Showbiz Personal Trainer). Health &
Fitness. Stage & Screen. Production Services. Television
Expert, over 100 hours Live Television Experience.
Production Services. Based in London*
E info@fit4thepart.com
W www.fit4thepart.com

FITNESS COACH THE T 020 7300 1414
Contact: Jamie Baird
Agua at The Sanderson, 50 Berners Street
London W1T 3NG
T 07970 782476
E jamie@thefitnesscoach.com

**HAMMOND, John B.
Ed (Hons) ICHFST** T/F 01277 632830
Fitness Consultancy. Sports & Relaxation Massage
4 Glencree, Billericay, Essex CM11 1EB
T 07703 185198
E johnhammond69@googlemail.com

HARLEY HEARING CENTRE T 020 7935 5468
*Hearing Protection. Invisible Hearing Aids. Tinnitus
Maskers*
119 Harley Street, London W1G 6AN
E info@hearing-aiddevices.co.uk

HARLEY STREET VOICE CENTRE THE   T 020 7224 2350
The Harley Street ENT Clinic
109 Harley Street
London W1G 6AN
F 020 7935 7701
E info@harleystreetent.com
W www.harleystreetent.com

HAYWARD, Sarah   T 07834 608833
Reflexology, Reiki
Wanstead, London E11
E eyelovelight2012@gmail.com
W www.eyelovelight.co.uk

HYL ENERGISER   T 07768 321092
10 Little Newport Street, London WC2H 7JJ
E info@hylenergiser.com
W www.hylenergiser.com

JOSHI CLINIC THE   T 020 7487 5456
Holistic Healthcare
57 Wimpole Street, London W1G 8YW
E reception@joshiclinic.co.uk
W www.joshiclinic.co.uk

LAURA J YOGA   T 07531 287713
Yoga Classes & Private Sessions Specifically Designed for Actors' Needs to Get Stronger, More Flexible & Gain Better Posture
110 Swaby Road, London SW18 3QZ
E laurajyoga@gmail.com
W www.laurajyoga.com

LIFE PRACTICE UK LTD   T/F 01462 431112
Specialists in Coaching, Mentoring, NLP & Hypnotherapy
Suite 1, 107 Bancroft, Hitchin
Herts SG5 1NB
E info@lifepractice.co.uk
W www.lifepractice.co.uk

LLEWELLYN, Samantha   T 07702 116594
Counsellor/Psychotherapist for individuals with drug & alcohol addiction
Beauchamp Lodge, 2 Warwick Crescent
Maida Vale, London W2 5NE
E samllewellyn@me.com

MAGIC KEY PARTNERSHIP THE   T 0844 3320234
Contact: Lyn Burgess. Media Life Coach
151A Moffat Road, Thornton Heath, Surrey CR7 8PZ
E lyn@magickey.co.uk
W www.magickey.co.uk

MARTONE, Sergio LAMDA(Dip) CBH(Dip) LREPHP MNCH   T 07742 148418
Cognitive Behavioural Hypnotherapist. Specialises in Anxiety with Auditions & Line Learning
14 Netherhall Gardens, Hampstead
London NW3 5TQ

MATRIX ENERGY FIELD THERAPY   T 01304 379466
Accredited Healer
Deal Castle House, 31 Victoria Road
Deal, Kent CT14 7AS
T 07762 821828
E donnie@lovingorganization.org

McCALLION, Anna   T 020 7602 5599
Alexander Technique. Voice
Flat 2, 11 Sinclair Gardens, London W14 0AU
E hildegarde007@yahoo.com

MELVEL TRAINING   T 07870 789482
Bespoke Drug & Alcohol Awareness Training, Talks, Seminars & E-Learning
34 Mickledon Close, Nottingham NG2 1LE
E mel@melveltraining.co.uk
W www.melveltraining.co.uk

MIESSENCE
Organic Natural Skincare. Wholefood Superfood Nutritionals
4 Little Dimocks, London SW12 9JH
E oxana.nico@gmail.com
W www.naturalhealthbeauty.miessence.com

NOBLE, Penny PSYCHOTHERAPY   T 07506 579895
8 Shaftesbury Gardens, Victoria Road
North Acton, London NW10 3LJ
E pennynobletherapy@googemail.com
W www.pennynoblepsychotherapy.com

NORTON IMPLANTS LTD   T 020 7486 9229
Implant/Reconstructive Dentistry
104 Harley Street, London W1G 7JD
F 020 7486 9119
E linda@nortonimplants.com
W www.nortonimplants.com

NUTRITIONAL THERAPY FOR PERFORMERS   T 07962 978763
Contact: Vanessa May BSc CNHC NTC & BANT Reg
18 Oaklands Road, Ealing, London W7 2DR
E vanessa@wellbeingandnutrition.co.uk
W www.wellbeingandnutrition.co.uk

ODYSSEY FITNESS   T 07527 571443
Berwick-upon-Tweed, TD15 1PX
E info@odysseyfitness.co.uk

OGUNLARU, Rasheed   T 020 7207 1082
Life & Business Coach
The Coaching Studio, 233A Mayall Road
London SE24 0PS
E rasheed@rasaru.com
W www.rasaru.com

PAMPERING WORLD
Author. Speaker. Youth Workshop Facilitator. Twitter: pamperingworld
E thanks4connecting@gmail.com
W www.pamperingworld.com

PEAK PERFORMANCE COACHING   T 01628 633509
Contact: Tina Reibl (EA, Consultant Hypnotherapist) NLP. Hypnosis. Success Strategies
The Bridge Clinic, Maidenhead, Berkshire SL6 8DG
E tina.reibl@gmail.com
W www.maidenhead-hypnotherapy.co.uk

PHYSIOTHERAPY AMELIE LEROY   T 07775 831600
141-145 Kentish Town Road, London NW1 8PB
E a@amelie-leroy.com

POLAND, Ken
DENTAL STUDIOS　　　　**T** 020 7935 6919
Film & Stage Dentistry
1 Devonshire Place, London W1G 6HH
F 020 7486 3952
E robpoland@btconnect.com

PSYCHOTHERAPY &
MEDICAL HYPNOSIS　　　**T** 07956 217266
Contact: Karen Mann DCH DHP. Including Performance
Improvement, Guilt, Anger, Trauma & Sleep Issues.
Telephone Sessions Available. Also in Hampstead
10 Harley Street
London W1G 9PF
E emailkarenmann@googlemail.com
W www.karenmann.co.uk

REACH TO THE SKY　　　**T** 0843 2892503
Contact: Dr J. Success Life Coach
Brook Street, Mayfair
London W1K 4HR
T 07961 911027
E drj@reachtothesky.com
W www.reachtothesky.com

ROBERTS, Dan　　　　**T** 020 7989 0338
Personal Training. Nutrition, Yoga & Martial Arts.
Specialising in the Physical Coniditioning of Professional
Athletes, Dancers, Models & Actors (Stage & Screen).
Based in West London. Twitter: @TeamDanRoberts
E hello@danrobertsgroup.com
W www.thedanrobertsgroup.com

ROGERS, Helen
HYPNOTHERAPY　　　　**T** 07915 093588
Lower Ground Floor
5 College Fields, Bristol BS8 3HP
E helen@helenrogers.co.uk
W www.helenrogers.co.uk

SERENDIPITY　　　　**T** 07809 458270
Remedial Sports Massage Therapist
Based in North West,
E mail@serendipity-spa.co.uk
W www.serendipity-spa.co.uk

SEYRI, Kayvan
MSc CSCS*D CES　　　**T** 07881 554636
Athletic Performance Specialist. Master Personal Trainer
E info@ultimatefitpro.com
W www.ultimatefitpro.com

SHAPES IN MOTION　　　**T** 07802 709933
Contact: Sarah Perry. Movement Coaching. Yin, Viniyoga
& Children's Yoga
Based in London
E yoga@shapeinmotion.com
W www.shapeinmotion.com

SHENAS, Dr DENTAL CLINIC　**T** 020 7589 2319
51 Cadogan Gardens
Sloane Square
Chelsea, London SW3 2TH
E info@shenasdental.co.uk
W www.shenasdental.co.uk

SMILE NW DENTAL PRACTICE　**T** 020 8458 2333
Contact: Dr Veronica Morris. Cosmetic & General Dentist
17 Hallswelle Parade, Finchley Road
Temple Fortune, London NW11 0DL
F 020 8458 5681
E enquiries@smile-nw.co.uk
W www.smile-nw.co.uk

SMILE SOLUTIONS　　　**T** 020 7449 1760
Dental Practice
24 Englands Lane, London NW3 4TG
F 020 7449 1769
E enquiries@smile-solutions.info
W www.smile-solutions.info

STAT (THE SOCIETY OF TEACHERS OF THE
ALEXANDER TECHNIQUE)　**T** 020 8808 2135
Unit W48, Grove Business Centre
560-568 High Road, London N17 9TA
F 020 8885 6524
E enquiries@stat.org.uk
W www.stat.org.uk

STEP 'N' FLEX-
ZUMBA CLASSES　　　**T** 07801 741892
Zumba® Fitness Classes across South West London.
Oval, Vauxhall & Kennington. Class only £5.
10% discount for all Spotlight members
E sarahfrench123@hotmail.com
W www.sarahfrench.zumba.com

STRANGE, Victoria　　　**T** 07854 052602
4 Richmond Road, Westoning, Bedfordshire MK45 5JZ
E veceighty@hotmail.com

STREET DEFENCE　　　**T** 07919 350290
Fight Choreographer/Advanced Screen Combatant &
Celebrity Personal Trainer
6 Clive Close, Potters Bar, Hertfordshire EN6 2AE
E streetdefence@hotmail.co.uk
W www.streetdefenceuk.com

TOPOLSKI, Suzy　　　**T** 07702 476843
Life & Performance Coaching
69 Randolph Avenue, Little Venice, London W9 1DW
E suzytopolski@aol.com

VIE MEDIC SERVICES LTD　**T** 07581 144538
Contact: Paul Holmes. Professional First Aid & Medical
Services. Quality First Aid Courses
West House, West Street
Wath-upon-Dearne, South Yorkshire S63 7QX
E enquiries@viemedic.co.uk
W www.viemedic.co.uk

VITAL TOUCH (UK) LTD THE　**T** 07976 263691
Workplace Massage, Workshops & Therapies
50 Greenham Road, Muswell Hill, London N10 1LP
E suzi@thevitaltouch.com
W www.thevitaltouch.com

WALK-IN BACKRUB　　**T/F** 020 7436 9875
On-site Massage Company
14 Neals Yard, London WC2H 9DP
E info@walkinbackrub.co.uk
W www.walkinbackrub.co.uk

WALSH, Gavin
PERSONAL TRAINING　　**T** 07782 248687
22 Stirling Court, Tavistock Street, London WC2E 7NU
E gavin@gavinwalsh.co.uk
W www.gavinwalsh.co.uk

WELLBEING　　　　　**T** 07957 333921
Contact: Leigh Jones. Personal Training. Tai Chi. Yoga
22 Galloway Close, Broxbourne, Herts EN10 6BU
E williamleighjones@hotmail.com

WELLBEING WAY　　　**T** 07905 504418
E japaneseyoga@btinternet.com
W www.shiatsuhealth.com

WOODFORD HOUSE
DENTAL PRACTICE　　　**T** 020 8504 2704
162 High Road, Woodford Green, Essex IG8 9EF
E info@improveyoursmile.co.uk
W www.improveyoursmile.co.uk

WORSLEY, Victoria　　　**T** 07711 088765
Feldenkrais Practitioner. Addresses Habits of Moving &
Breathing which Limit Range of Movement, Cause Pain
or Affect the Voice
32 Clovelly Road, London N8 7RH
E v.worsley@virgin.net
W www.feldenkraisworks.co.uk

N →

Non-Acting Jobs

42ND STREET RECRUITMENT T 020 7734 4422
Linen Hall, 162-168 Regent Street
London W1B 5TD
E info@42ndstreetrecruitment.com
W www.42ndstreetrecruitment.com

ARTISAN PEOPLE T 020 7813 2121
Temporary Non-acting Positions available in Museums &
Retail Promotions in London
Tudor House, 35 Gresse Street
London W1T 1QY
F 020 7813 1414
E simon@artisanpeople.com

AT YOUR SERVICE
EVENT STAFFING LTD T 020 7610 8610
Temporary Event Staff
Unit 6, The Talina Centre
Bagley's Lane, Fulham, London SW6 2BW
F 020 7610 8611
E pippa@ays.co.uk
W www.ays.co.uk/apply

ATTITUDE EVENTS T 020 7953 7935
Event Consultation & Staffing
412 Coppergate House, 16 Brune Street
London E1 7NJ
E nikki@attitude-events.com
W www.attitude-events.com

BREEZE PEOPLE T 023 8001 5000
Promotional Staffing Agency
38 Bedford Place
Southampton SO15 2DG
E peepz@breezepeople.co.uk
W www.breezepeople.co.uk/staff

CENTRAL EMPLOYMENT
AGENCY T 0191 232 4816
34-36 St Mary's Place
Newcastle upon Tyne NE1 7PQ
F 0191 261 2203
E enquiries@centralemployment.co.uk
W www.centralemployment.co.uk

COVENT GARDEN BUREAU T 020 7734 3374
Recruitment Consultants
5-6 Argyll Street, London W1F 7TE
E cv@coventgardenbureau.co.uk
W www.coventgardenbureau.co.uk

FISHER, Judy ASSOCIATES T 020 7437 2277
Media & Arts Recruitment Specialists
7 Swallow Street, London W1B 4DE
E cv@judyfisher.co.uk
W www.judyfisher.co.uk

FOUR SEASONS
RECRUITMENT T 020 8237 8900
Recruitment Company. Beauty. Fashion. Retail
The Triangle, 5-17 Hammersmith Grove
London W6 0LG
F 020 8237 8999
E info@fsrl.co.uk
W www.fsrl.co.uk

HANDLE RECRUITMENT T 020 7569 9999
Recruitment for Arts, Media, Entertainment &
Inspirational Brands
7 Portman Mews South, London W1H 6AY
E david.bishop@handle.co.uk
W www.handle.co.uk

JAM STAFFING LTD T 020 7237 2228
Events Company. Part-time Flexible Bar & Waiting Work at
London Events
Unit 104, The Light Box
111 Power Road, London W4 5PY
E jeremy@jamstaffing.com
W www.jamstaffing.com

JB HOSPITALITY T 020 7713 8772
Suppliers of Temporary Staff to the Catering & Hospitality
Industry
104-110 Judd Street, London WC1H 9PU
E enquiries@jbhospitality.co.uk
W www.jbhospitality.co.uk

JFL SEARCH & SELECTION T 020 7009 3500
Recruitment Consultants
27 Beak Street, London W1F 9RU
F 020 7734 6501
E info@jflrecruit.com
W www.jflrecruit.com

LEISUREJOBS T 020 7622 8500
Temporary, Promotional & Permanent Positions within
Leisure
Cloisters House, 8 Battersea Park Road
London SW8 4BG
E info@leisurejobs.com
W www.leisurejobs.com

LUMLEYS HOSPITALITY
& CATERING T 020 7630 0545
Private & Corporate Hospitality, Catering & Events
Grosvenor Gardens House
35-37 Grosvenor Gardens
London SW1W 0BS
E admin@greycoatlumleys.co.uk
W www.greycoatlumleys.co.uk

MORTIMER, Angela T 020 7287 7788
Recruitment Specialists for Perm & Temp PAs & Support
Staff in the UK & Europe
37-38 Golden Square, London W1F 9LA
E info@angelamortimer.com
W www.angelamortimer.com

OFF TO WORK T 020 7386 4497
Non-acting Employment. Promotional Work at Events
across the UK
36-37 King Street, Kings House
London EC2V 8BB
E abbie.pullman@offtowork.co.uk
W www.offtowork.co.uk

RSVP T 020 7536 3563
Telemarketing/Agency
Northern & Shell Tower, 4 Selsdon Way
London E14 9GL
E jobs@rsvp.co.uk
W www.rsvp.co.uk/careers

SENSE STAFFING T 020 7034 2000
Promotional Staffing for Experiential Marketing
1st Floor, 100 Oxford Street
London W1D 1LN
E staff@senselondon.com
W www.senselondon.com

SMITH, Amanda
RECRUITMENT LTD T 020 7681 6180
Recruitment of Temporary, Permanent & Contract Office
Support Staff
88 Kingsway, Holborn, London WC2B 6AA
E info@as-recruitment.co.uk

STUCKFORSTAFF.CO.UK T 0844 5869595
Promotions, Field Marketing & Brand Experience
446-450 Kingstanding Road
Birmingham B44 9SA
E info@stuckforstaff.com
W www.stuckforstaff.co.uk

TRIBE MARKETING LTD T 020 7702 3600
Experiential Marketing & Promotional Staffing Agency
The Wool House, 74 Back Church Lane
Whitechapel, London E1 1LX
E talent@tribemarketing.co.uk
W www.tribemarketing.co.uk

O →

Opera Companies
Organisations

**CAPITAL ARTS
CHILDREN'S CHOIR** T 020 8449 2342
Contact: Kathleen Shanks (Music Director)
Rehearsal Venue, Dragon Hall
17 Stukeley Street, Covent Garden WC2B 5LT
T 07855 232414
E capitalarts@btconnect.com
W www.capitalarts.org.uk

CO-OPERA CO T 020 8699 8650
Touring Productions. Education. Training. Workshops
5 Metro Business Centre
Kangley Bridge Road
London SE26 5BW
E admin@co-opera-co.org
W www.co-opera-co.org

ENGLISH NATIONAL OPERA T 020 7836 0111
London Coliseum, St Martin's Lane
London WC2N 4ES
F 020 7845 9277
W www.eno.org

ENGLISH TOURING OPERA T 020 7833 2555
3rd Floor, 63 Charterhouse Street
London EC1M 6HJ
E admin@englishtouringopera.org.uk
W www.englishtouringopera.org.uk

GARSINGTON OPERA T 01865 368201
The Old Garage, The Green
Great Milton, Oxford OX44 7NP
F 01865 961545
W www.garsingtonopera.org

GLYNDEBOURNE T 01273 812321
Lewes, East Sussex BN8 5UU
E info@glyndebourne.com
W www.glyndebourne.com

GRANGE PARK OPERA T 01962 737360
Sutton Manor Farm, Bishop's Sutton
Alresford SO24 0AA
E info@grangeparkopera.co.uk
W www.grangeparkopera.co.uk

GUBBAY, Raymond LTD T 020 7025 3750
Dickens House, 15 Tooks Court
London EC4A 1LB
F 020 7025 3751
E info@raymondgubbay.co.uk
W www.raymondgubbay.co.uk

KENTISH OPERA T 01732 700993
Contact: Sally Langford
Lakefields Farmhouse, Ide Hill Road
Bough Beech, Kent TN8 7PW
E sl.sweald@fsmail.net
W www.kentishopera.com

LONDON CANTAMUSICA T 020 8449 2342
*Young Professionals' Choir for Opera, Recordings
& Concerts*
Rehearsal Venue, Dragon Hall
17 Stukeley Street
Covent Garden WC2B 5LT
T 07885 232414
E capitalarts@btconnect.com
W www.capitalarts.org.uk

**LONDON CHILDREN'S
OPERA COMPANY** T/F 020 8449 2342
*Rehearsals at Dragon Hall, Covent Garden.
Students aged 8-16*
T 07885 232414
E capitalarts@btconnect.com
W www.capitalarts.org.uk

MUSIC THEATRE LONDON T 07831 243942
c/o Capriol Films, The Coach House
35 High Street, Holt
Norfolk NR25 6BN
T 01263 712600
E tony.britten@capriolfilms.co.uk
W www.capriolfilms.co.uk

OPERA CAPITAL ARTS T 020 8449 2342
*Rehearsals held at Dragon Hall, Covent Garden
WC2B 5LT*
Head Office, Capital Arts Studio
Wyllyotts Theatre, Darkes Lane
Potters Bar, Hertfordshire EN6 2HN
T 07885 232414
E capitalarts@btconnect.com
W www.capitalarts.org.uk

OPERA DELLA LUNA T 01869 325131
7 Cotmore House, Fringford
Bicester, Oxfordshire OX27 8RQ
E enquiries@operadellaluna.org
W www.operadellaluna.org

OPERA NORTH T 0113 243 9999
Grand Theatre
46 New Briggate
Leeds LS1 6NU
F 0113 244 0418
E info@operanorth.co.uk
W www.operanorth.co.uk

OPERAUK LTD T 020 7628 0025
Charity
177 Andrewes House, Barbican
London EC2Y 8BA
E rboss4@aol.com
W www.operauk.co.uk

**PEGASUS OPERA
COMPANY LTD** T/F 020 7501 9501
The Brix, St Matthew's
Brixton Hill, London SW2 1JF
E admin@pegopera.org
W www.pegasus-opera.net

PIMLICO OPERA T 01962 737360
Sutton Manor Farm
Bishop's Sutton
Alresford SO24 0AA
E info@pimlicoopera.co.uk
W www.pimlicoopera.co.uk

PMB PRESENTATIONS LTD T 020 7368 3337
Vicarage House
58-60 Kensington Church Street
London W8 4DB
E info@pmbpresentations.co.uk
W www.pmbpresentations.co.uk

ROYAL OPERA THE T 020 7240 1200
Royal Opera House, Bow Street
Covent Garden, London WC2E 9DD
W www.roh.org.uk

SCOTTISH OPERA T 0141 248 4567
39 Elmbank Crescent
Glasgow G2 4PT
E information@scottishopera.org.uk
W www.scottishopera.org.uk

WELSH NATIONAL OPERA T 029 2063 5000
Wales Millennium Centre, Bute Place
Cardiff CF10 5AL
F 029 2063 5099
E marketing@wno.org.uk
W www.wno.org.uk

ABTT (ASSOCIATION OF BRITISH THEATRE TECHNICIANS)   **T** 020 7242 9200
4th Floor, 55 Farringdon Road
London EC1M 3JB
F 020 7242 9303
E office@abtt.org.uk
W www.abtt.org.uk

ACADEMY OF PERFORMANCE COMBAT THE   **T** 07928 324706
Teaching Body of Stage Combat
197 Church Road, Northolt
Middlesex UB5 5BE
E info@theapc.org.uk
W www.theapc.org.uk

ACTORS' BENEVOLENT FUND   **T** 020 7836 6378
6 Adam Street, London WC2N 6AD
F 020 7836 8978
E office@abf.org.uk
W www.actorsbenevolentfund.co.uk

ACTORS CENTRE (LONDON) THE   **T** 020 7632 8001
Charity. Over 1700 Workshops & Courses per year for Professional Actors. Advice & Information. Introductory Courses
1A Tower Street, London WC2H 9NP
E reception@actorscentre.co.uk
W www.actorscentre.co.uk

ACTORS' CHILDREN'S TRUST   **T** 020 7636 7868
Provides Grants & Support for Actors' Children
58 Bloomsbury Street, London WC1B 3QT
E robert@tactactors.org
W www.tactactors.org

ACTORS' GUILD OF GREAT BRITAIN (TAG)   **T** 020 7112 8458
Non-profit. Workshops. Networking. Bursaries. Support
TAG Hub at Spotlight, 2nd Floor
7 Leicester Place
London WC2H 7RJ
E mail@actorsguild.co.uk
W www.actorsguild.co.uk

ADVERTISING ASSOCIATION   **T** 020 7340 1100
7th Floor North, Artillery House
11-19 Artillery Row
London SW1P 1RT
F 020 7222 1504
E aa@adassoc.org.uk
W www.adassoc.org.uk

AGENTS' ASSOCIATION (GREAT BRITAIN)   **T** 020 7834 0515
54 Keyes House, Dolphin Square
London SW1V 3NA
E association@agents-uk.com
W www.agents-uk.com

ARTS & BUSINESS   **T** 020 7566 8650
137 Shepherdess Walk, London N1 7RQ
E info@bitc.org.uk
W www.bitc.org.uk

ARTS CENTRE GROUP   **T** 0845 4581881
c/o Paintings in Hospitals
51 Southwark Street
London SE1 1RU
T 020 7407 1881
E info@artscentregroup.org.uk
W www.artscentregroup.org.uk

ARTS COUNCIL ENGLAND   T 0845 3006200
T 020 7973 6564 (Textphone)
W www.artscouncil.org.uk

**ARTS COUNCIL OF
NORTHERN IRELAND**   T 028 9038 5200
MacNeice House, 77 Malone Road
Belfast BT9 6AQ
F 028 9066 1715
E info@artscouncil-ni.org
W www.artscouncil-ni.org

ARTS COUNCIL OF WALES   T 0845 8734900
Bute Place, Cardiff CF10 5AL
F 029 2044 1400
E information@artswales.org.uk
W www.artscouncilofwales.org.uk

ARTS COUNCIL OF WALES   T 0845 8734900
The Mount, 18 Queen Street
Carmarthen SA31 1JT
F 01267 233084
E information@artscouncilofwales.org.uk
W www.artscouncilofwales.org.uk

ARTS COUNCIL OF WALES   T 01492 533440
36 Prince's Drive, Colwyn Bay
Conwy LL29 8LA
F 01492 533677
E information@artscouncilofwales.org.uk
W www.artscouncilofwales.org.uk

ASSOCIATED STUDIOS THE   T 020 7385 2038
The Hub @ St Alban's Fulham
2 Margravine Road
London W6 8HJ
E info@associatedstudios.co.uk
W www.associatedstudios.co.uk

**ASSOCIATION OF
LIGHTING DESIGNERS**   T 07817 060189
PO Box 955, Southsea PO1 9NF
E office@ald.org.uk
W www.ald.org.uk

**ASSOCIATION OF
MODEL AGENTS**   T 020 7422 0699
11-29 Fashion Street, London E1 6PX
E amainfo@btinternet.com
W www.associationofmodelagents.org

**BASCA - BRITISH ACADEMY OF
SONGWRITERS, COMPOSERS
& AUTHORS**   T 020 7636 2929
2nd Floor, 2 Pancras Square
London N1C 4AG
E info@basca.org.uk
W www.basca.org.uk

BFI SOUTH BANK   T 020 7928 3232
Belvedere Road, South Bank
London SE1 8XT
W www.bfi.org.uk

**BRITISH ACADEMY OF FILM &
TELEVISION ARTS (BAFTA)**   T 020 7734 0022
195 Piccadilly, London W1J 9LN
E info@bafta.org
W www.bafta.org

**BRITISH ACADEMY OF FILM & TELEVISION
ARTS LOS ANGELES**   T 001 323 658 6590
8469 Melrose Avenue, West Hollywood
CA 90069, USA
E office@baftala.org
W www.bafta.org/losangeles

**BRITISH ACADEMY OF STAGE
& SCREEN COMBAT**   T 07837 966559
Kemp House, 152 City Road
London EC1V 2NX
E info@bassc.org
W www.bassc.org

**BRITISH ASSOCIATION FOR PERFORMING
ARTS MEDICINE (BAPAM)**   T 020 7404 5888
Charity
4th Floor, Totara Park House
34-36 Gray's Inn Road, London WC1X 8HR
E clinic@bapam.org.uk
W www.bapam.org.uk

**BRITISH ASSOCIATION OF
DRAMATHERAPISTS THE**   T 01242 235515
Waverley, Battledown Approach
Cheltenham, Glos GL52 6RE
E enquiries@badth.org.uk
W www.badth.org.uk

**BRITISH BOARD OF
FILM CLASSIFICATION**   T 020 7440 1570
3 Soho Square, London W1D 3HD
F 020 7287 0141
E feedback@bbfc.co.uk
W www.bbfc.co.uk

BRITISH COUNCIL   T 0161 957 7755
Arts Group
10 Spring Gardens, London SW1A 2BN
E arts@britishcouncil.org
W www.britishcouncil.org/arts

**BRITISH EQUITY
COLLECTING SOCIETY**   T 020 7670 0360
1st Floor, Guild House
Upper St Martin's Lane, London WC2H 9EG
E becs@equity.org.uk
W www.equitycollecting.org.uk

BRITISH FILM INSTITUTE   T 020 7255 1444
21 Stephen Street, London W1T 1LN
F 020 7436 0165
W www.bfi.org.uk

**BRITISH LIBRARY
SOUND ARCHIVE**   T 020 7412 7831
96 Euston Road, London NW1 2DB
F 020 7412 7691
E sound-archive@bl.uk
W www.bl.uk/soundarchive

**BRITISH MUSIC HALL
SOCIETY**   T 01727 768878
Contact: Daphne Masterton (Secretary). Charity
45 Mayflower Road, Park Street
St Albans, Herts AL2 2QN
E geoff.bowden1@btinternet.com
W www.britishmusichallsociety.com

**CATHOLIC ASSOCIATION
OF PERFORMING ARTS**   T 020 7240 1221
Contact: Ms Molly Steele (Hon Secretary). By Post (SAE)
1 Maiden Lane
London WC2E 7NB
E secretary@caapa.org.uk
W www.caapa.org.uk

CIDA CO   T 0113 373 1754
The Creative & Innovation Company
Munro House, Duke Street
Leeds LS9 8AG
E info@cida.org
W www.cidaco.org

sport
music
dance
drama
childcare
uniform
trips
equipment
clothing
university

help for actors' children

Are you:
- a professional actor?
- parent of a child under 21?
- worried about money?

TACT helps children who are ill or have special needs, families in financial crisis, or where a parent is unwell or cannot work.

Confidential and friendly.

TACT
The Actors' Children's Trust
020 7636 7868
www.tactactors.org
registered charity 206809

CINEMA & TELEVISION BENEVOLENT FUND (CTBF)
T 020 7437 6567
22 Golden Square, London W1F 9AD
F 020 7437 7186
E charity@ctbf.co.uk
W www.ctbf.co.uk

CLUB FOR ACTS & ACTORS
T 020 7836 3172
Incorporating Concert Artistes Association
20 Bedford Street, London WC2E 9HP
E office@thecaa.org
W www.thecaa.co.uk

COMPANY OF CRANKS
T 07963 617981
1st Floor, 62 Northfield House
Frensham Street, London SE15 6TN
E mimetic16@yahoo.com
W www.mimeworks.com

COUNCIL FOR DANCE EDUCATION & TRAINING (CDET)
T 020 7240 5703
Old Brewer's Yard, 17-19 Neal Street
London WC2H 9UY
F 020 7240 2547
E info@cdet.org.uk
W www.cdet.org.uk

CREATIVE SCOTLAND
T 0330 333 2000
(Switchboard)
Waverley Gate, 2-4 Waterloo Place
Edinburgh EH1 3EG
T 0845 603 6000 (Enquiries)
E enquiries@creativescotland.com
W www.creativescotland.com

CRITICS' CIRCLE THE
T 020 7732 9636
Contact: Rick Jones
17 Rosenthal Road, London SE6 2BX
T 07891 120072
E rnbjones@btinternet.com
W www.criticscircle.org.uk

DANCE HOUSE
T 0141 552 2442
The Briggait, 141 Bridgegate, Glasgow G1 5HZ
E info@dancehouse.org
W www.dancehouse.org

DANCE UK
T 020 7713 0730
Including the Healthier Dancer Programme, the National Institute for Dance Medicine & Science & 'The UK Choreographers' Directory'. Professional body & charity, providing advice, information & support
Unit A402A, The Biscuit Factory
100 Clements Road, London SE16 4DG
F 020 7833 2363
E info@danceuk.org
W www.danceuk.org

DENVILLE HALL
T 01923 825843
Provides Residential, Nursing & Dementia Care to Actors & other Theatrical Professions
62 Ducks Hill Road, Northwood
Middlesex HA6 2SB
E office@denvillehall.org.uk
W www.denvillehall.org.uk

DIRECTORS UK
T 020 7240 0009
8-10 Dryden Street, London WC2E 9NA
E info@directors.uk.com
W www.directors.uk.com

DON'T PLAY ME PAY ME CAMPAIGN
Campaigning for a Greater Representation of Disabled Talent in the Entertainment Industry
E peoplenotpunchlines@gmail.com
W www.dontplaymepayme.com

D'OYLY CARTE OPERA COMPANY
T 0844 6060007
Unit N302
Westminster Business Square
1-45 Durham Street, London SE11 5JH
F 020 7820 0240
E ian@doylycarte.org.uk
W www.doylycarte.org.uk

DRAMA ASSOCIATION OF WALES
T 029 2045 2200
Voice of Amateur Theatre
Splott Library, Singleton Road
Splott, Cardiff CF24 2ET
E chair@dramawales.org.uk
W www.dramawales.org.uk

DRAMA UK
T 020 3393 6141
Drama UK supports the supply of a talented and appropriately trained workforce. We provide a unique link between the theatre, media and broadcast industries and drama training providers in the UK. We offer help and advice to drama students of all ages and award quality kite mark to the very best drama training available. Our website includes course listings from a wide range of training providers and articles from industry experts on a variety of drama related topics
Woburn House, 20 Tavistock Square
London WC1H 9HB
E info@dramauk.co.uk
W www.dramauk.co.uk

DRAMATURGS' NETWORK
Supports Theatre Makers, Dramaturgs, Literary Managers & Educational Professionals Involved in Dramaturgical Practice. Twitter: @dramaturgs_net
c/o Tinderbox Theatre Company
72 High Street
Belfast BT1 2BE
E info@dramaturgy.co.uk
W www.dramaturgy.co.uk

ENGLISH FOLK DANCE & SONG SOCIETY
T 020 7485 2206
Cecil Sharp House, 2 Regent's Park Road
London NW1 7AY
F 020 7284 0534
E info@efdss.org
W www.efdss.org

EQUITY CHARITABLE TRUST
T 020 7831 1926
Plouviez House
19-20 Hatton Place
London EC1N 8RU
E info@equitycharitabletrust.org.uk

FENS CELEBRITY BULLETIN
T 01273 666351
Tower Point, 44 North Road
Brighton, East Sussex BN1 1YR
E enquiries@celebrity-bulletin.co.uk

FILM LONDON
T 020 7613 7676
Suite 6.10, The Tea Building
56 Shoreditch High Street
London E1 6JJ
F 020 7613 7677
E info@filmlondon.org.uk
W www.filmlondon.org.uk

GLASGOW FILM OFFICE
T 0141 287 0424
Free Advice & Liaison Support for all Productions
231 George Street
Glasgow G1 1RX
F 0141 287 0311
E info@glasgowfilm.com

GRAND ORDER OF WATER RATS   T 020 7278 3248
328 Gray's Inn Road, London WC1X 8BZ
E info@gowr.net
W www.gowr.net

GROUP LINE   T 020 7420 9700
Group Bookings for London Theatre
37 Long Acre, Covent Garden
London WC2E 9JT
E enquiries@groupline.com
W www.groupline.com

INDEPENDENT THEATRE COUNCIL (ITC)   T 020 7403 1727
Professional Body offering Advice, Information, Support & Political Representation
The Albany, Douglas Way
London SE8 4AG
E admin@itc-arts.org
W www.itc-arts.org

INGMAR SAUER NETWORKS   T 00 31 6 16242010
Mathenesserdijk 288b
3026 GP Rotterdam
The Netherlands
E info@ingmarsauernetworks.com
W www.ingmarsauernetworks.com

INTERNATIONAL CENTRE FOR VOICE
The Royal Central School of Speech & Drama
Eton Avenue
London NW3 3HY
E icv@cssd.ac.uk
W www.icvoice.co.uk

IRVING SOCIETY THE
Contact: Megan Hunter
E theirvingsociety@gmail.com
W www.theirvingsociety.org.uk

LONDON SCHOOL OF CAPOEIRA   T 020 7281 2020
Units 1 & 2 Leeds Place
Tollington Park
London N4 3RF
E info@londonschoolofcapoeira.com
W www.londonschoolofcapoeira.com

LONDON SHAKESPEARE WORKOUT   T/F 020 7793 9755
PO Box 31855, London SE17 3XP
E londonswo@hotmail.com
W www.lswproductions.co.uk

NATIONAL ASSOCIATION OF YOUTH THEATRES (NAYT)   T 07804 254651
Contact: Henry Raby. Founded in 1982, NAYT works with over 1,000 Groups & Individuals to Support the Development of Youth Theatre Activity through Information & Support Services, Advocacy, Training, Participation & Partnerships
c/o Riding Lights Theatre
Friargate Theatre, Lower Friargate, York YO1 9SL
E info@nayt.org.uk
W www.nayt.org.uk

NATIONAL RESOURCE CENTRE FOR DANCE   T 01483 689316
University of Surrey, Guildford, Surrey GU2 7XH
F 01483 689500
E nrcd@surrey.ac.uk
W www.surrey.ac.uk/nrcd

NODA (NATIONAL OPERATIC & DRAMATIC ASSOCIATION)   T 01733 374790
Charity. Providing Advice, Information & Support. Largest Umbrella Body for Amateur Theatre in the UK offering Advice & Assistance on all aspects of Amateur Theatre plus Workshops, Summer School and Social Events
15 The Metro Centre, Woodston, Peterborough PE2 7UH
F 01733 237286
E info@noda.org.uk
W www.noda.org.uk

OFCOM   T 0300 1233000
Ofcom Media Office, Riverside House
2A Southwark Bridge Road, London SE1 9HA
E contact@ofcom.org.uk   W www.ofcom.org.uk

PACT   T 020 7380 8230
Trade Association for Independent Television, Feature Film & New Media Production Companies
3rd Floor, Fitzrovia House
153-157 Cleveland Street, London W1T 6QW
E info@pact.co.uk   W www.pact.co.uk

PRS FOR MUSIC   T 020 7580 5544
2 Pancras Square, London N1C 4AG
F 020 3741 4455
W www.prsformusic.com

RICHARDSON, Ralph & Meriel FOUNDATION   T 020 3755 5438
Charity. Contact: Brian Eages
c/o Howard Kennedy, 1 London Bridge
London SE1 9BG
E manager@sirralphrichardson.org.uk
W www.sirralphrichardson.org.uk

ROYAL TELEVISION SOCIETY T 020 7822 2810
3 Dorset Rise, London EC4Y 8EN
F 020 7822 2811
E info@rts.org.uk
W www.rts.org.uk

ROYAL THEATRICAL FUND T 020 7836 3322
*Provides Financial Assistance for Members of the
Entertainment Profession of all Ages & their Dependants
plus Help for those who have Experienced Illness,
Accident, Bereavement or other Personal Misfortune,
including Grants, Advice & Friendship*
11 Garrick Street, London WC2E 9AR
E admin@trtf.com
W www.trtf.com

SAMPAD SOUTH ASIAN ARTS T 0121 446 3260
*Promotes the Appreciation & Practice of South
Asian Arts*
c/o Mac Birmingham
Cannon Hill Park, Birmingham B12 9QH
E info@sampad.org.uk
W www.sampad.org.uk

SOCIETY OF AUTHORS T 020 7373 6642
*Trade Union for Professional Writers. Providing Advice,
Funding, Information & Support*
84 Drayton Gardens, London SW10 9SB
E info@societyofauthors.org
W www.societyofauthors.org

**SOCIETY OF BRITISH
THEATRE DESIGNERS** T 029 2039 1346
Professional Body. Charity. Providing Advice & Information
Theatre Design Department
Royal Welsh College of Music & Drama
Castle Grounds, Cathays Park, Cardiff CF10 3ER
E admin@theatredesign.org.uk
W www.theatredesign.org.uk

**SOCIETY OF LONDON
THEATRE THE (SOLT)** T 020 7557 6700
32 Rose Street, London WC2E 9ET
F 020 7557 6799
E enquiries@soltukt.co.uk

**SOCIETY OF TEACHERS OF
SPEECH & DRAMA THE** T 01623 627636
Registered Office: 73 Berry Hill Road, Mansfield
Nottinghamshire NG18 4RU
E ann.k.jones@btinternet.com
W www.stsd.org.uk

**SOCIETY OF
THEATRE CONSULTANTS** T 020 8455 4640
Contact: Michael Holden (Chairman)
27 Old Gloucester Street, London WC1N 3AX
E info@theatreconsultants.org.uk
W www.theatreconsultants.org.uk

STAGE CRICKET CLUB T 020 7402 7543
41 Hanover Steps, St George's Fields, London W2 2YG
E brianjfilm@aol.com   W www.stagecc.co.uk

STAGE GOLFING SOCIETY T 020 8940 8861
Sudbrook Park, Sudbrook Lane
Richmond, Surrey TW10 7AS
E sgs@richmondgolfclub.co.uk

**STAGE MANAGEMENT
ASSOCIATION** T 020 7403 7999
*Supporting Excellence in Performance. Advice,
Information & Support; Representation & Advocacy for
& about Stage Management. Offers Help Finding Work,
Information, Training & Networking Opportunities for
SMA Members*
89 Borough High Street, London SE1 1NL
E admin@stagemanagementassociation.co.uk
W www.stagemanagementassociation.co.uk

STAGE ONE T 020 7557 6737
Operating Name of The Theatre Investment Fund Ltd
32 Rose Street
London WC2E 9ET
E enquiries@stageone.uk.com
W www.stageone.uk.com

**TECHNICAL THEATRE
AWARDS** T 020 3514 3630
*Awards to Highlight Outstanding Achievement in the
Technical Theatre Industry*
c/o Production Resource Group
Sussex House, 143 Long Acre
London WC2E 9AD
E chat@technicaltheatreawards.com
W www.technicaltheatreawards.com

THEATRE CHAPLAINCY UK T 07501 829491
St Paul's Church, Bedford Street
Covent Garden
London WC2E 9ED
E info@theatrechaplaincyuk.com

**THEATRE MAD (MAKE A
DIFFERENCE TRUST)** T 020 3583 5758
*Fighting HIV & AIDS One Stage At A Time. Contact:
David Pendlebury (Charity Director). Raises funds for HIV
& AIDS projects that raise awareness & provide care,
support & education in the UK & Sub-Saharan Africa, &
supports members of the Entertainment Industry through
times of hardship. UK Charity Registration No. 1124014*
c/o Theatre Delicatessen
1st Floor, 119 Farringdon Road
London EC1R 3DA
E office@madtrust.org.uk
W www.madtrust.org.uk

THEATRES TRUST THE T 020 7836 8591
*Contact: Kate Carmichael (Resources Adviser). National
Advisory Public Body for Theatres, Protecting Theatres for
Everyone. Statutory Consultee, Charity. Provides Advice,
Support & Information, Resources & Small Capital Grants.
Twitter: @TheatresTrust*
22 Charing Cross Road
London WC2H 0QL
F 020 7836 3302
E info@theatrestrust.org.uk
W www.theatrestrust.org.uk

THEATRICAL GUILD THE T 020 7240 6062
The Charity for Backstage & Front of House
11 Garrick Street
London WC2E 9AR
E admin@ttg.org.uk
W www.ttg.org.uk

TYA - UK CENTRE OF ASSITEJ T 0121 245 2092
*International Association of Theatre for Children & Young
People. Network for Makers & Promoters of Professional
Theatre for Young Audiences*
c/o Birmingham Repertory Theatre
Centenary Square
Broad Street
Birmingham B1 2EP
E secretary@tya.uk.org
W www.tya-uk.org

**UK CHOREOGRAPHERS'
DIRECTORY THE**
See DANCE UK

UK CINEMA ASSOCIATION T 020 7734 9551
3 Soho Square
London W1D 3HD
F 020 7734 6147
E info@cinemauk.org.uk
W www.cinemauk.org.uk

UK THEATRE   T 020 7557 6700
The UK's leading membership organisation for theatre & the performing arts
32 Rose Street, London WC2E 9ET
F 020 7557 6799
E enquiries@soltukt.co.uk
W www.uktheatre.org

UK THEATRE CLUBS   T 020 8459 3972
54 Swallow Drive
London NW10 8TG
E uktheatreclubs@aol.com

UNITED KINGDOM COPYRIGHT BUREAU   T 01273 277333
110 Trafalgar Road
Portslade
East Sussex BN41 1GS
E info@copyrightbureau.co.uk
W www.copyrightbureau.co.uk

UNIVERSITY OF BRISTOL THEATRE COLLECTION   T 0117 331 5086
Incorporating the Mander & Mitcheson Theatre Collection
Vandyck Building
Cantocks Close
Bristol BS8 1UP
E theatre-collection@bristol.ac.uk

VARIETY & LIGHT ENTERTAINMENT COUNCIL (VLEC)   T 020 7834 0515
54 Keyes House, Dolphin Square, London SW1V 3NA
E association@agents-uk.com
W www.vlec.org.uk

VARIETY, THE CHILDREN'S CHARITY   T 020 7428 8100
Variety Club House
93 Bayham Street
London NW1 0AG
F 020 7428 8111
E info@variety.org.uk
W www.variety.org.uk

WILLIAMS, Tim AWARDS   T 020 7793 9755
In Memory of LSW's Late Musical Director. Seeking to Support Excellence in the Composition of Theatrical Song
PO Box 31855
London SE17 3XP
E londonswo@hotmail.com
W www.lswproductions.co.uk

WOMEN IN FILM & TELEVISION (UK)   T 020 7287 1400
WFTV is the Premier Membership Organisation for Women working in Creative Media in the UK and part of an International Network of over 10,000 Women Worldwide. Provides Advice, Information, Social Membership & Support
E info@wftv.org.uk
W www.wftv.org.uk

YOUTH MUSIC THEATRE UK (YMT)   T 020 8563 7725
Lyric Hammersmith
Lyric Square
King Street, London W6 0QL
E mail@ymtuk.org
W www.youthmusictheatreuk.org

P →

Photographers: Advertisers Only
Promotional Services:
CVs, Showreels, Websites etc
Properties & Trades
Publications: Print & Online
Publicity & Press Representatives

Each photographer listed in this section
has taken an advertisement in this edition.
See the Advertisers' Index to view each
advertisement.

Photographers

How do I find a photographer?

Having a good quality, up-to-date promotional headshot is crucial for every performer. Make sure you choose your photographer very carefully: do some research and try to look at different examples. Photographers' adverts run throughout this edition, featuring many sample shots, although to get a real feel for their work you should also try to see their portfolio or website, since this will give a more accurate impression of the quality of their photography.

If you live in or around London, please feel free to visit the Spotlight offices and look through over sixty photographers' portfolios available for you to browse, many of them from photographers listed in this edition. Our offices are open Monday - Friday, 10.00am - 5.30pm at 7 Leicester Place, London WC2H 7RJ (nearest tube is Leicester Square).

What should I expect from the photo shoot?

When it comes to your photo shoot, bear in mind that a casting director, agent or production company will want to see a photo of the 'real' you. Keep your appearance as neutral as possible so that they can imagine you in many different roles, rather than type-casting yourself from the outset and limiting your opportunities.

Your eyes are your most important feature, so make sure they are visible: face the camera straight-on and try not to smile too much because it makes them harder to see. Wear something simple and avoid jewellery, hats, scarves, glasses or props, since these will all add character. Do not wear clothes that detract from your face such as polo necks, big collars, busy patterns or logos. Always keep your hands out of the shot.

Also consider the background: some photographers like to do outdoor shots. A contrast between background and hair colour works well, whereas dark backgrounds work less well with dark hair, and the same goes for light hair on light backgrounds.

Which photograph should I choose?

When you get your contact sheet or digital proofs back from the photographer, make sure you choose a photo that looks like you – not how you would like to look. If you are unsure, ask friends or your agent for an honest opinion. Remember, you will be asked to attend meetings and auditions on the basis of your photograph, so if you turn up looking completely different you will be wasting everyone's time.

Due to copyright legislation, you must always credit the photographer when using the photo.

How should I submit my photo to Spotlight and to casting professionals?

All photographs submitted to Spotlight must be of the highest possible quality, otherwise casting professionals will not see you in the best possible light. When sending a digital image by e-mail or disk, we have certain technical specifications which can be found on our website. We would recommend that you follow similar guidelines when sending your headshot directly to casting professionals.

What are Spotlight portfolio photographs?

Every Spotlight performer can add extra photographs to their online profile which gives you the opportunity to show yourself in a range of different shots and/or roles. Members can upload up to 15 digital photos to their online profile free of charge.

Although you are allowed a maximum of 15 photos on your profile, it doesn't necessarily mean that this is advisable. 2-3 well chosen photos can make for a stronger profile than 15 poor quality ones, so be selective.

To find out more visit www.spotlight.com/artists/ multimedia/photoguidelines

Photographers

CASE STUDY

Ric Bacon has been an actor for 20 years and a professional photographer for 17. He is known for taking bold, engaging images that represent actors honestly.

Your headshot is the single most important element of your publicity. It's your shop window, your first point of contact with the industry. You want it to work for you, not against you.

"Rather than making you stand out, focusing on being attractive makes you disappear into a sea of 'nice'"

It must be an accurate and authentic representation of the real you. The person that is going to walk through the door at a casting. Our egos drive us to look as good as possible but it is unlikely that you will do yourself any favours by trying to look as attractive as possible. There is an endless amount of pretty/handsome in Spotlight and after looking through a few profiles it all begins to blend into one. Rather than making you stand out, focusing on being attractive makes you disappear into a sea of 'nice'. It is the uniqueness of you, warts and all, that is your strongest selling point. It's those little quirks that make you different that also make you compelling. The bump in the nose, the fuzzy eyebrows, the cleft chin, the scars, the deep set eyes, the big ears etc. If you attempt to 'iron out the creases' you will quite possibly be destroying the qualities that were most likely to get you noticed.

There used to be a consensus of opinion that it is best to have a neutral headshot, to remain versatile and therefore stand more chance of being considered for many different roles. This may have been true in the past but with the advent of Spotlight's multiple image gallery, actors now have more freedom to demonstrate subtle differences in their casting range.

Several conversations with casting directors have also confirmed that neutral shots are not what is desired in todays oversaturated market. Too often neutral can translate into bland and lifeless.

A casting director does not want to see lifeless, they want the opposite, they want to see an image full of life. Whether it's the joyous sparkle of joie de vivre or the glint in the eye of a mischievous rogue, they want a clue, something that they can recognise. Because if they can see it then hopefully a producer, director and ultimately an audience will also see it. Show the casting director something of what makes you who you are.

"The bump in the nose, the fuzzy eyebrows, the cleft chin, the scars, the deep set eyes, the big ears etc. If you attempt to 'iron out the creases' you will quite possibly be destroying the qualities that were most likely to get you noticed"

A nice but lifeless image just isn't going to inspire people to want to meet you.

It is also the case however, that casting directors do not want to see images that are so specific in their 'look' they can't possibly imagine you in any other way. So remember, it's a hint, a glint, a little nudge in a certain direction that is what's needed, not an overt performance. Subtlety is the word.

It is essential that you know who you are and what you're selling. How do you come across to the world? What is your most likely casting? Your path of least resistance into the marketplace? A good photographer will take this as a starting point and push you around in different directions. Lighter and warmer, darker and edgier, higher and lower status etc.

The Shoot

Arrive in a good mood, on time, fully prepared, with a spring in your step, a song in your heart and ready to play.

Before you start, tell the photographer about any specific shots that you (or your agent) think you specifically need. Once the shoot begins it is time to let go. Trust that you have made the right choices and then let the photographer take over. Let them direct and motivate you. Give up any sense of control. Don't think about what you look like, just have fun and enjoy the process. Skip, dance, sing, or do your best Zoolander impersonation. Do whatever comes to mind and wherever the mood takes you. Do not censor yourself, your thoughts or your behaviour. The time for censorship comes later when you're choosing your final images.

Choosing your final images can be hard. The ego kicks in again and you will want to use the images where you look the most attractive. Get help from others. Remove the ego.

"A nice but lifeless image just isn't going to inspire people to want to meet you"

Final words of advice

Choose a photographer who specialises in headshots, not simply portraits. Avoid any photographers that make actors look 'nice'.

Headshothunter.co.uk is a useful tool for comparing prices and packages.

Only put an image on your Spotlight gallery if it reveals something about you that isn't present in any of your other images. Two images that are similar in mood, style, or emotion make both look weaker. You can always use other images you like on your personal website or social media. My ideal number of images to show all aspects of an actor's casting range would be three. Less if possible. Never more than five. One good image is better than 10 mediocre ones.

If you don't have the best headshot possible then why not? You need to do something about it.

Vive la Différence!

To find out more visit www.ricbacon.com

AM LONDON
W www.am-london.com

ANKER, Matt   T 07835 241835
W www.mattanker.com

ANNAND, Simon   T 07884 446776
W www.simonannand.com

BARTLETT, Pete   T 07971 653994
E info@petebartlett.com
W www.petebartlett.com

BISHOP, Brandon   T 07931 383830
T 020 7275 7468
W www.brandonbishopphotography.com

BLAKE, Tony   T 07908 468725
W www.tonyblakephoto.co.uk

BURKE, Dom
E info@domburke.com
W www.domburke.com

BURNETT, Sheila   T 07974 731391
T 020 7289 3058
W www.sheilaburnett-headshots.com

ESTEVAN, Luke
E luke@lukeestevan.co.uk
W www.lukeestevan.co.uk

GIBB, Adrian   T 07971 063395
T 020 7639 6215
E adriangibb@gmail.com
W www.adriangibb.co.uk

GREGAN, Nick   T 07774 421878
T 020 8533 3003
E info@nickgregan.com
W www.nickgregan.com

HULL, Anna   T 07778 399419
E info@annahullphotography.com
W www.annahullphotography.com

LATIMER, Carole
W www.carolelatimer.com

LAWTON, Steve   T 07973 307487
W www.stevelawton.com

MACKAY, David   T 07545 657649
E david@davidmackay.photography
W www.davidmackay.photography

M.A.D. PHOTOGRAPHY   T 07949 581909
T 01707 708553
E info@mad-photography.co.uk
W www.mad-photography.co.uk

MARKS, Patrick   T 07912 210320
T 020 7183 7798
W www.patrickmarks.com

MOSTOFI, Kamal   T 07850 219183
E headshots@kamalmostofi.com
W www.head-shot.photography

P.M.N.A. PHOTOGRAPHY   T 07786 832124
E pmna101@yahoo.co.uk
W www.pmnaphotography.com

PROCTOR, Carl   T 07956 283340
E carlproctorphotos@gmail.com
W www.carlproctorphotography.com

SAYER, Howard   T 020 8123 0251
E howard@howardsayer.com
W ww.howardsayer.co.uk

SCOTT, Karen   T 07958 975950
E info@karenscottphotography.com
W www.karenscottphotography.com

SHAKESPEARE LANE,
Catherine   T 020 7226 7694
W www.csl-art.co.uk

STRAW, Ashley   T 07803 686552
E ash@ashleystraw.com

ULLATHORNE, Steve   T 07961 380969
W www.steveullathorne.com

WADE, Philip   T 07956 599691
T 020 7226 3088
E pix@philipwade.com
W www.philipwade.com

WALTON, Teresa   T 07770 855807
E photos@teresawalton.com
W www.teresawaltonphotos.com

WEBSTER, Caroline   T 07867 653019
W www.carolinewebster.co.uk

SHOWREELS ○ ● ◐ ○ ● ○ ● ○

TAKE FIVE STUDIO

**Showreel editing | Showreel filming
Headshots | Self-Taping Auditions**

37 Beak Street, London W1F 9RZ
tel: +44 (0)20 7287 2120
email: richard@takefivestudio.com
www.takefivestudio.com

10X8PRINTS.COM T 07773 108108
32 High Street, Laurencekirk AB30 1AB
E snappingsam@mac.com
W www.10x8prints.com

2PRODUCTION T 020 8440 4848
*Professional Management Voice Over Recordings
& Direction*
E info@2production.com
W www.2production.com

A1 VOX LTD T 020 7434 4404
*Audio Clips. Demo CDs. ISDN Links. Spoken Word
Audio. Soundpicture Work & Foley*
20 Old Compton Street, London W1D 4TW
E info@a1vox.com
W www.a1vox.com

ABBEY ROAD STUDIOS T 020 7266 7000
3 Abbey Road, St John's Wood
London NW8 9AY
F 020 7266 7250
E bookings@abbeyroad.com
W www.abbeyroad.com

ABSOLUTE WORKS LTD T 01525 385400
Film, Television & Creative Solutions
Danson House, Manor Farm Lane
Ledburn, Bucks LU7 0UG
T 07778 934307
E nigelmpark@gmail.com
W www.absoluteworks.com

ACTOR SHOWREELS T 07853 637965
Showreel Service
97B Central Hill, London SE19 1BY
E post@actorshowreels.co.uk
W www.actorshowreels.co.uk

ACTORS CENTRE T 020 7240 3940
1A Tower Street, London WC2H 9NP
E film@actorscentre.co.uk
W www.actorscentre.co.uk

ACTOR'S ONE-STOP SHOP THE T 07894 152651
Showreels, CVs & Websites for Performing Artists
2B Dale View Crescent, London E4 6PQ
E info@actorsone-stopshop.com
W www.actorsone-stopshop.com

ACTORSHOP.CO.UK T 07970 381944
Showreels. Voicereels. Websites
E info@actorshop.co.uk
W www.actorshop.co.uk

**AIR-EDEL RECORDING
STUDIOS LTD** T 020 7486 6466
18 Rodmarton Street, London W1U 8BJ
F 020 7224 0344
E tom.bullen@air-edel.co.uk
W www.air-edelstudios.co.uk

AN ACTOR'S LIFE FOR ME T 07855 342161
Showreels. Voicereels & CVs
722B High Road, North Finchley
London N12 9QD
E anactorslifeforme@hotmail.com
W www.anactorslifeforme.com

**ANGEL RECORDING
STUDIOS LTD** T 020 7354 2525
311 Upper Street, London N1 2TU
F 020 7226 9624
E bookings@angelstudio.co.uk

**ANT FARM STUDIOS
VOICE OVERS** T 07905 691353
Southend Farm, Southend Lane
Waltham Abbey EN9 3SE
E antfarmstudio@yahoo.co.uk
W www.antfarmstudios.co.uk

APPLE VIDEO FACILITIES T 01204 847974
The Studio, 821 Chorley Old Road
Bolton, Lancs BL1 5SL
F 01204 495020
E info@applevideo.co.uk
W www.applevideo.co.uk

ARTSPHERE CREATIVE T 0121 433 4511
Web Developement, Print & Branding, Music Production
46 Glenmore Drive, Birmingham
West Midlands B38 8YR
E webservices@artspherecreative.uk
W www.artspherecreative.uk

BESPOKE REELS T 020 7580 3773
Contact: Charlie Lort-Phillips. Twitter: @charlielortp
3rd Floor, 83 Charlotte Street, London W1T 4PR
T 07538 259748
E charlie@bespokereels.com
W www.bespokereels.com

BLUE CHECKBOX LTD T 0843 2894414
Website Design
13 Portman House, 136 High Road
London N22 6DF
E contact@bluecheckbox.com
W www.bluecheckbox.com

Promotional Services

What are promotional services?

This section contains listings for companies who provide practical services to help performers promote themselves. You might need to improve or create your CV; record a showreel or voicereel; design your own website; duplicate CDs; or print photographic repros, CVs or Z-cards: all essential ways to create a good impression with those that count in the industry.

Why do I need to promote myself?

Performers need to invest in marketing and promotion as much as any other self-employed business-person. Even if you have trained at a leading drama school, have a well-known agent, or have just finished work on a popular television series, you should never sit back and wait for the phone to ring or for the next job opportunity just to knock on your door. In such a competitive industry, successful performers are usually the ones who market themselves pro-actively and treat their careers as a 'business'.

Having up-to-date and well-produced promotional material makes a performer look professional and serious about their career: and hence a desirable person for a director or agent to work with.

Why is my CV important?

Poor presentation, punctuation and grammar create a bad first impression and you risk your CV being dismissed before it is even read. Make sure that you continually update your CV – you don't want it to look as if you haven't been working recently when you have, and you don't want to miss out on an audition because you haven't included skills you have put time and effort into achieving. Your CV should be kept to a maximum of one page and printed on good quality paper.

Why do I need a covering letter?

Always include a covering letter to introduce your CV and persuade casting professionals that it is worth reading. Remember that they receive hundreds each week. Keep your writing concise and be professional at all times. We also recommend that your letter has some kind of focus: perhaps you can tell them about your next showcase, or where they can see you currently appearing on stage. Ideally this should be addressed to an individual, not "Dear Sir or Madam" or "To Whom it May Concern".

Why is my headshot important?

Your CV should feature, or be accompanied by, a recent headshot which is an accurate and current likeness. See the 'Photographers' section for more information about promotional photography. You may need to print copies of your headshot through a repro company, some of whom are listed in this section.

Why do I need a voicereel?

If you are interested in voice over and/or radio work, you will need a professional-sounding voicereel to show agents, casting directors and potential employers what your voice is capable of. For commercial and corporate voice over work this should be no more than two minutes long with a number of short clips demonstrating your range, but showcase the strengths of your natural voice as much as possible. It should contain a mixture of commercials and narrations.

A radio voicereel should be around eight minutes long, with four clips no longer than two minutes each, and read in your natural voice. To achieve a good balance of material, one clip should be 'classical', one 'contemporary', one 'comic' and one a poem. This is designed to give an overview of your suitability to various areas of radio work.

Record your voicereel in a professional studio to ensure a high-quality result, otherwise you are unlikely to be considered in this competitive industry. For further information please see the 'Agents: Voice Over' and 'Radio' sections.

Why do I need a showreel?

Some casting directors will only consider a performer for an audition if they have first seen them demonstrating their skills in a showreel. A CV and headshot give some indication of your potential, but can only provide a basic summary.

What should I do if I don't currently have anything on film?

Showreels are expensive to produce if you don't currently have any broadcasted material to use, but it is advisable to get one professionally recorded and edited if at all possible. Showreels help you to promote yourself, but a casting director may be put off by a poor quality one. You might want to consider a Spotlight Monologue as a temporary alternative to a full showreel.

How long should my showreel be?

We would recommend no more than three or four minutes. Casting professionals receive thousands of CVs and showreels and do not have time to watch every actor for ten minutes each. This is why we suggest you do not send your showreel out with your CV, but instead mention in your covering letter that one is available.

What should I use in my showreel?

Rather than one long excerpt, it is more beneficial to demonstrate your versatility with a number of different clips. Focus on your strongest characters to enable the casting director to picture you in the roles you play best.

The first 30 seconds are the most important in your showreel, and may be the only part a busy casting director or agent has time to look at. You may wish to start with a headshot of yourself so that they know who to watch out for in the following scenes. Avoid noisy musical/uptempo soundtracks where possible and cut straight to the action.

The focus should be on you, not on the other actors, so close-up shots ought to be included. You should be speaking most if not all of the time. A visual contrast is good, whether this means filming in a different location or setting, or changing your outfit. You should avoid well-known scripts in order to prevent drawing comparisons between yourself and previous successful interpretations.

How should I use the listing in this section?

If you are looking for a company to help you with any of these promotional items, browse through this section carefully and get quotes from a number of places to compare. If you are a Spotlight member, some companies offer a discount on their services. Always ask to see samples of a company's work and ask friends in the industry for their own recommendations.

Promotional Services

CASE STUDY

David Hodge has been involved with voice overs for almost 40 years. As a founding director of Silk Sound, he has worked on a wide range of media as both an engineer and voice director, including a number of award winning projects. A period of management followed at Saunders & Gordon studios and later at the renowned Hobsons voice agency.

David continues to give talks and run workshops at accredited drama schools, and also offers a personal voicereel service. In 2014 Oberon Books published *The Voiceover Book ... Don't Eat Toast*, a guide to this fascinating craft, which was co-written with Stephen Kemble.

Rushing into making a showreel is a mistake. Time spent in research and a little self knowledge will pay dividends.

Start by getting to know your voice, specifically as others hear it.

The more you know about its strengths and limitations, the better result you'll achieve when you finally arrive in the studio. Spend time recording and playing back your voice. Then, using just a few words, begin to describe it; serious, cheeky, warm, friendly, funny, serious, sultry, assured etc. Ask friends and family how they hear it. You may be surprised by their answers!

Read aloud for 10-15 minutes every day. This will improve your vocal energy and sight reading skills.

Listen carefully to a broad range of media output. By doing this you'll begin to appreciate how voices interact with the product or programme; you'll become familiar with the variety of 'read' styles and some of the conventions. It will help you identify the type of scripts you feel suit you.

"Making a showreel is an investment in the business of being a voiceover artist"

Agents and clients alike will assess you by it. So it's important to spend time and energy getting the best result possible. Quality should never be compromised.

Visit agency websites and get a feel for what's needed and the standard of production that's expected. You'll notice that most reels feature a short montage of commercial clips, advertising traditionally being the most popular and more lucrative area of work. As you gain experience, you may want to create other showreels such as narration, character, audio-books and more.

"Make sure you're clear about what you'll get for their fee"

There are a growing number of 'specialist' showreel companies, and many post-production engineers make them in their own time. Listen to examples of their work and meet with them to discuss what you hope to achieve. It's important that you choose someone with experience to direct you. Of course, a personal recommendation is invaluable.

Make sure you're clear about what you'll get for their fee. How much recording time will you have? Will a variety of scripts be provided? Will there be at least one opportunity to make small amendments to the finished reel if necessary? How will the tracks be supplied etc.

A common mistake is to think that your voice is suited to every script and every type of product.

Pick scripts suited to your vocal range and age. Aim to include a typical sales read, a straight/ serious piece and something featuring a character (to demonstrate acting skills). If you have a regional accent then you may also want to demonstrate a more neutral accent. Throughout this process though, remain true to yourself. For example, if you don't particularly relate to humorous material then avoid comic scripts.

This is a mistake. It's the equivalent of having a headshot taken wearing a mask! The majority of work demands a natural, authentic voice, so having the most representative example at the outset gives the listener the strongest experience. Hearing your voice through a phone or any other kind of 'filter' is of no value, and avoid being overly ambitious. The majority of voice work is straight, so save your accents and character voices for a separate reel.

"Too often voice overs begin their showreels with material they think everyone wants to hear, rather than their natural voice"

Showreels should always be of a high standard with music and sound effects added to give a professional and authentic feel. However, these should not intrude, it's your voice everyone wants to hear.

When you're ready to submit your reel, treat each voice agency as a separate entity. Never send a blanket email. Look to see if they accept submissions and how they prefer them delivered. Agents are generally swamped so be patient, most will reply in time, but prompting them for a response or feedback will not be welcome.

Good luck!

For more information contact David at hodgeman53@ btinternet.com

BLUEPRINT PHOTOGRAPHIC   T 07479 538648
Contact: Daniel Erman
4 Baxendale, Whetstone, London N20 0EG
E blueprintphotographic@hotmail.com
W www.blueprintphotographic.com

CASTING COACH THE   T 07952 232255
Records & Uploads Password Protected Self-tape
Castings
49 Herbert Road, Wimbledon
London SW19 3SQ
E john@johnmelainey.com
W www.auditiononcamera.co.uk

**CASTLEFARM
SHOWREEL SERVICES**   T 020 3011 5462
Contact: Arnaud Pitois, Rebecca Gethings
2nd Floor, 3 Percy Street, London W1T 1DE
E contact@castlefarm.tv
W www.castlefarm.tv

CHANNEL 2020 LTD   T 0844 8402020
Phoenix Square, 4 Midland Street
Leicester LE1 1TG
E info@channel2020.co.uk
W www.channel2020.co.uk

CHANNEL 2020 LTD   T 0844 8402020
3rd Floor, 28 Marshalsea Road, London SE1 1HF
E info@channel2020.co.uk
W www.channel2020.co.uk

**CHASE, Stephan
PRODUCTIONS LTD**   T 020 8878 9112
Producer of Voice Overs & Showreels. Founder of
Rhubarb Voiceover Agency
The Studio, 22 York Avenue, London SW14 7LG
E stephan@stephanchase.com
W www.stephanchase.com

CONSIDER CREATIVE   T 020 3397 3816
Integrated Creative Agency. Print. Digital.
Advertising & Branding
1st Floor, The Italian Building, 41 Dockhead
London SE1 2BS
E ben@considercreative.co.uk
W www.considercreative.co.uk

CONSIDER THIS UK LTD   T 01895 619900
Design. Marketing. Print. Web
Brook House, 54A Cowley Mill Road
Uxbridge, Middlesex UB8 2QE
F 01895 251048
E develop@considerthisuk.com
W www.considerthisuk.com

**COURTWOOD
PHOTOGRAPHIC LTD**   T 01736 741222
Photographic Reproduction
Profile Prints, Unit 2, Rospeath Industrial Estate
Penzance, Cornwall TR20 8DU
E images@courtwood.co.uk
W www.courtwood.co.uk

CRE8 LIFESTYLE CENTRE   T 020 8533 1691
80 Eastway, Hackney Wick, London E9 5JH
E shellyann@cre8lifestyle.org.uk
W www.cre8lifestyle.org.uk

CreateAV (UK) LTD   T 01992 789759
Unit 14, Studio House, Delamare Road
Cheshunt EN8 9SH
F 01992 625180
E connect@createav.com
W www.createav.com

CROWE, Ben   T 07952 784911
Voice Clip Recording
25 Holmes Avenue, Hove BN3 7LB
E bencrowe@hotmail.co.uk

**CRYING OUT LOUD
PRODUCTIONS**   T 07809 549887 (Simon)
Contact: Simon Cryer, Marina Caldarone. Voice Over
Demo Specialists. Voice Training & Studio Hire
1:04 Chester House, 1-3 Brixton Road
London SW9 6DE
T 07946 533108 (Marina)
E simon@cryingoutloud.co.uk
W www.cryingoutloud.co.uk

CRYSTAL MEDIA   T 0131 240 0988
2 Melville Street, Edinburgh EN3 7NS
F 0131 240 0989
E hello@crystal-media.co.uk
W www.crystal-media.co.uk

CUTGLASS PRODUCTIONS   T 01929 400758
Contact: Phill Corran. Voice Showreel Production
Tides, Brittwell Drive
West Lulworth, Dorset BH20 5RS
T 07966 280033
E phil@cutglassproductions.com
W www.cutglassproductions.com

DELUXE 142   T 020 7878 0000
Film House, 142 Wardour Street
London W1F 8DD
W www.deluxe142.co.uk

DENBRY REPROS LTD   T 01442 242411
Photographic Reproduction
57 High Street, Hemel Hempstead, Herts HP1 3AF
E info@denbryrepros.com
W www.denbryrepros.com

DESIGNBYFLY   T 07854 072044
Contact: Gary Wright. Graphic, Digital & Website Design
3 Woodside Cottages, Hartfield Road
Forest Row, East Sussex RH18 5LU
E me@designbyfly.co.uk
W www.designbyfly.co.uk

DV2BROADCAST   T 0161 736 5300
3 Carolina Way, Salford M50 2ZY
E info@dv2broadcast.co.uk
W www.dv2broadcast.co.uk

ELMS STUDIOS   T 020 3556 1515
Contact: Phil Lawrence. Composing/Scoring for
Film & Television
10 Empress Avenue, London E12 5ES
T 07956 275554
E phillawrence@elmsstudios.com
W www.elmsstudios.co.uk

ESQUIRE SHOWREELS   T 07540 566569
19 Hillside Close, Knaphill, Woking, Surrey GU21 2HR
E simsjamie@icloud.com
W www.jamie-sims.com

ESSENTIAL MUSIC   T 020 7439 7113
20 Great Chapel Street, London W1F 8FW
E david@essentialmusic.co.uk

eSTAGE LTD   T 020 3514 3630
Website Design, Marketing
71-75 Shelton Street, Covent Garden
London WC2H 9JG
E chat@estage.net
W www.estage.net

EXECUTIVE AUDIO VISUAL   T/F 020 7723 4488
DVD Duplication Service. Showreels for Actors & Presenters
E chris.jarvis60@gmail.com

FLIXELS LTD   T 020 7193 8171
1 Bermondsey Square
London SE1 3UN
E info@flixels.co.uk
W www.flixels.co.uk

GINGER SHOWREELS   T 020 8442 4017
Flat 7, 117 Cazenove Road
London N16 6AX
E info@gingershowreels.com
W www.gingershowreels.com

GYROSCOPE STUDIOS   T 00 46 86 459223
Contact: Frank Sanderson
Hökmossevägen 34
SE12642 Hägersten
Sweden
E frank@gyroscope-studios.com
W www.gyroscope-studios.com

HARVEY HOUSE FILMS LTD   T 07968 830536
Animation. Showreels. Video Production
The Mission Hall, Cummington Street
London W4 5ER
E chris@harveyhousefilms.co.uk
W www.harveyhousefilms.co.uk

HEAVY ENTERTAINMENT LTD   T 020 7494 1000
Video, Web, Audio, Apps
111 Wardour Street, London W1F 0UH
F 020 7494 1100
E info@heavy-entertainment.com
W www.heavy-entertainment.com

HODGE, David   T 07860 466302
Bespoke Voicereels. Based in South West London
E hodgeman53@btinternet.com
W www.davidhodge.co.uk

HOTQS CREATIVE   T 07903 017819
Animation. Graphics. Showreels. Websites
E info@hotqs.uk
W www.hotqs.uk

HOTREELS   T 020 7952 4362
Voice & Showreels
E info@hotreels.co.uk
W www.hotreels.co.uk

IMAGE PHOTOGRAPHIC   T 020 7602 1190
Online Only
E digital@imagephotographic.com
W www.imagephotographic.com

JEN X FILMS
Showreels
56 Wood Lane, Ugli Campus
London W12 7SB
E info@jenxfilms.com
W www.jenxfilms.com

JMS GROUP LTD THE   T 01603 811855
Park Farm Studios, Norwich Road
Hethersett, Norfolk NR9 3DL
F 01603 812255
E info@jms-group.com
W www.jms-group.com

KEAN LANYON LTD   T 020 7697 8453
Press Representation, Branding, Web, Print & Front of House design
United House, North Road
Islington, London N7 9DP
E contact@keanlanyon.com
W www.keanlanyon.com

McANDREW, Shane   T 07941 640124
Professional Video Editing Services
2 Croft Cottage, Thrigby Road
Great Yarmouth, Norfolk NR29 3DP
E shane.j.mcandrew@gmail.com
W www.shanemcandrew.co.uk

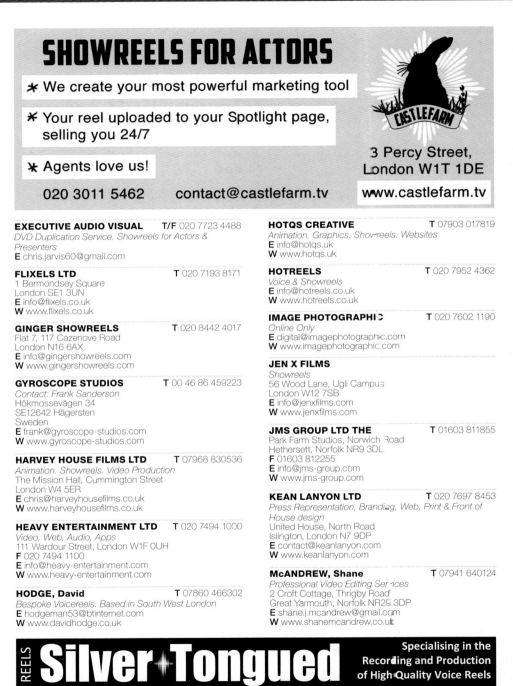

MINAMONFILM T 020 8674 3957
Specialist in Showreels
117 Downton Avenue
London SW2 3TX
E studio@minamonfilm.co.uk
W www.minamonfilm.co.uk

**MOF STUDIOS
(MINISTRY OF FUN)** T 020 7708 6116
22 Amelia Street, London SE17 3BZ
E studio@ministryoffun.net
W www.mofstudios.net

MOO.COM T 020 7392 2780
Online Printers. Business Cards
32-38 Scrutton Street
London EC2A 4RQ
W www.moo.com

**MOTIVATION
SOUND STUDIOS** T 020 7328 8305
35A Broadhurst Gardens
London NW6 3QT
F 020 7624 4879
E info@motivationsound.co.uk
W www.motivationsound.co.uk

MUSIC IN MOTION LTD T 07813 070961
Based in London
E neil@neilmyers.com
W www.neilmyers.com

O.J. SONUS T 020 8963 0702
*Recording Studio. Voice Over Recording. Voicereel
Production. Voice Over Workshops. Professional
Coaching Available*
14-15 Main Drive
East Lane Business Park
Wembley HA9 7NA
T 07929 859401
E info@ojsonus.com
W www.ojsonus.com

OLD, Dominic T 07970 101135
Web Designer
TB-111, Telegraph Buildings
2nd Floor Studios & Arts
Studio TW27, Harrington Way
London SE18 5NR
E contactme@dominicold.com
W www.dominicold.com

OLYMPIC RECORDS STUDIO T 07956 951090
58 Selhurst New Road
South Norwood
London SE25 5PU
E olympicrecords@tiscali.co.uk
W www.olympicrecordsuk.com

PINPOINT T 020 8963 0702
*Specialised Voice Over Studio. Voice Over Recording.
Voicereel Production. Voice Over Workshops.
Professional Coaching Available*
14-15 Main Drive
East Lane Business Park
Wembley HA9 7NA
T 07929 859401
E info@voice-overstudio.co.uk
W www.voice-overstudio.co.uk

PRESENTER STUDIO THE T 020 8677 7143
85 Lewin Road
London SW16 6JX
E info@presenterstudio.com
W www.presenterstudio.com

PROFILE PRINTS T 01736 741222
Photographic Reproduction
Unit 2, Plot 1A
Rospeath Industrial Estate
Crowlas, Cornwall TR20 8DU
E sales@courtwood.co.uk
W www.courtwood.co.uk

PURE LEMON T 07572 969423
6 Millan Court
Lumphanan
Aberdeenshire AB31 4QF
E music@lemondesign.net
W www.lemondesign.net

RE:AL T 01622 200123
Print. Creative. Marketing. Digital
Unit 2, Tovil Green Business Park
Maidstone, Kent ME15 6TA
E info@realprintandmedia.com
W www.realprintandmedia.com

RED FACILITIES T 0131 555 2288
61 Timber Bush, Leith
Edinburgh EH6 6QH
F 0131 555 0088
E doit@redfacilities.com
W www.redfacilities.com

**REEL DEAL
SHOWREEL CO THE** T 020 8647 1235
6 Charlotte Road
Wallington, Surrey SM6 9AX
E info@thereel-deal.co.uk
W www.thereel-deal.co.uk

REEL GEEKS.COM THE T 07951 757024
Showreel Editing for Actors
Based in West Kensington, London,
E thereelgeeks@hotmail.com
W www.thereelgeeks.com

REPLAY FILM & NEW MEDIA T 020 7637 0473
Showreels & Performance Recording
Museum House
25 Museum Street
London WC1A 1JT
E sales@replayfilms.co.uk
W www.replayfilms.co.uk

**ROUND ISLAND SHOWREELS
& VOICEREELS** T 07939 540458
Contact: Ben Warren, Guy Michaels
T 07973 445328
E mail@roundisland.net
W www.roundisland.net

SEARCH THE ARTS T 01895 619900
*Online Search Directory for Contacts & Events
within the Arts*
Brook House
54A Cowley Mill Road
Uxbridge UB8 2QE
F 01895 251048
E develop@considerthisuk.com
W www.considerthisuk.com

SETTLE THE SCORE T 07853 643346
E toby@settlethescore.co.uk
W www.settlethescore.co.uk

SHOE STRING FILMING T 07955 736926
Specialises in Shooting & Editing Showreels
E showreels@shoestringfilming.com
W www.shoestringfilming.com

SHOTS & REELS   T 07825 639006
Showreels
Based in Dalston, London. E8 2LH,
E sam@shotsandreels.com
W www.shotsandreels.com

SHOWREEL LTD THE   T 020 7043 8660 (Bookings)
Voice Over Demo Services. Training & Workshops
Soho Recording Studios, The Heals Building
22-24 Torrington Place, London WC1E 7HJ
E info@theshowreel.com
W www.theshowreel.com

SHOWREELS 4 U   T 01923 352385
Actors Showreels Filmed & Edited in HD. Voicereels.
Based near Elstree
15 Pippin Close, Shenley
Radlett, Herts WD7 9EU
E showreels4u@hotmail.com
W www.showreels4u.blogspot.com

SHOWREELZ   T 020 8994 7927
28 Eastbury Grove, Chiswick
London W4 2JZ
T 07885 253477
E brad@showreelz.com
W www.showreelz.com

SILVER~TONGUED PRODUCTIONS   T 020 8309 0659
Specialising in the Recording & Production of Voicereels
E contactus@silver-tongued.co.uk
W www.silver-tongued.co.uk

SILVERTIP FILMS LTD   T 01483 407533
Actor Showreel Production. Edits Existing Material.
Shoots New Material
8 Quadrum Park, Old Portsmouth Road
Guildford, Surrey GU3 1LU
E info@silvertipfilms.co.uk
W www.silvertipfilms.co.uk

SKATTA LTD   T 07472 321113
Skatta Studios, BBC Lighthouse
London W12 7TQ
E info@skatta.tv
W www.skatta.tv

SLICK SHOWREELS   T 020 7099 8269
Imperial House, 15-19 Kingsway WC2B 6UN
T 07798 504253
E info@slickshowreels.co.uk
W www.slickshowreels.co.uk

SMALL SCREEN SHOWREELS   T 020 8816 8896
Showreel Editing for Actors
Based in London
E info@smallscreenshowreels.co.uk
W www.smallscreenshowreels.co.uk

SOHO SHOWREELS   T 0844 5040731
101 Wardour Street
London W1F 0UG
E info@sohoshowreels.co.uk
W www.sohoshowreels.co.uk

SONICPOND STUDIO   T 020 7690 8561
Specialising in Voicereels. MT Demos. Showreels
70 Mildmay Grove South
Islington
London N1 4PJ
E info@sonicpond.co.uk
W www.sonicpond.co.uk

SOUND   T 01275 879799
Coach-house
28 Wellington Terrace
Clevedon
North Somerset BS21 7PT
E kenwheeler@mac.com
W www.soundat7.com

SOUND HOUSE LTD THE   T 0161 832 7299
MediaCityUK, Blue
Salford, Manchester M50 2HQ
F 0161 832 7266
E mail@thesoundhouse.tv
W www.thesoundhouse.tv

SOUND MARKETING   T 01225 701600
Strattons House
Strattons Walk
Melksham, Wiltshire SN12 6JL
F 01225 701601
E nicki@soundm.com
W www.soundm.com

STAGES CAPTURE THE MOMENT   T 020 7193 8519
Showreels
30 Byewaters
Croxley Green
Watford, Herts WD18 8WJ
T 07786 813812
E info@stagescapturethemoment.com
W www.stagescapturethemoment.com

STIRLING SHOWREEL SERVICE   T 01204 848333
490 Halliwell Road, Bolton
Lancashire BL1 8AN
E admin@stirlingmanagement.co.uk
W www.stirlingmanagement.co.uk

STRAY DOG CAFE PRODUCTIONS LTD   T 07455 011639
Digital Producing: Audio, Video, Photography, Websites & Social Media
269 Southborough Lane
Bromley, Kent BR2 8AT
E corinne@straydogcafeproductions.com
W www.straydogcafeproductions.com

STUDIO 359   T 07791 516859
Websites, Headshots & Showreels
21 Emmanuel Road
London SW12 0PB
E hello@studio359.co.uk
W www.studio359.co.uk

SUGAR LENS PRODUCTIONS LTD   T 07952 907168
Showreels
10 Foreland Close, Christchurch, Dorset BH23 2TQ
E info@sugarlensproductions.com
W www.sugarlensproductions.com

SUGAR POD PRODUCTIONS   T 020 8374 4701
Voice Showreels & Production Studio
Studio 8C, Chocolate Factory 1
5 Clarendon Road
Wood Green, London N22 6XJ
T 07967 673552
E info@sugarpodproductions.com
W www.sugarpodproductions.com

SYNCREDIBLE AGENCY   T 020 7117 6776
Marketing
26-28 Hammersmith Grove
London W6 7BA
E contact@syncredible.com
W www.syncredible.com

TAKE FIVE CASTING STUDIO   T 020 7287 2120
Showreels
37 Beak Street, London W1F 9RZ
F 020 7287 3035
E info@takefivestudio.com
W www.takefivestudio.com

TOUCHWOOD AUDIO PRODUCTIONS   T 0113 278 7180
6 Hyde Park Terrace, Leeds
West Yorkshire LS6 1BJ
T 07745 377772
E bruce@touchwoodaudio.com
W www.touchwoodaudio.com

TV PRESENTER TRAINING - ASPIRE   T 0800 0305471
3 Mills Studios, Three Mill Lane
London E3 3DU
E info@aspirepresenting.com
W www.aspirepresenting.com

TWITCH FILMS   T 020 7266 0946
Showreels
22 Grove End Gardens
18 Abbey Road
London NW8 9LL
E post@twitchfilms.co.uk
W www.twitchfilms.co.uk

UNIVERSAL SOUND (JUST PLAY LTD)   T 01494 723400
Old Farm Lane, London Road East
Amersham, Buckinghamshire HP7 9DH
E foley@universalsound.co.uk
W www.universalsound.co.uk

VISUALEYES   T 020 8875 8811
Photographic Reproduction
1st Floor, Riverside Business Centre
Bendon Valley, London SW18 4UQ
E imaging@visualeyes.co.uk
W www.visualeyes.co.uk

VOICE MASTER INTERNATIONAL   T 020 8455 1666
Earn Money from Home. The Only Qualification for Voice Overs
88 Erskine Hill, London NW11 6HR
T 07921 210400
E stevehudson@voicemaster.co.uk
W www.voicemaster.co.uk

VOICEREELS.CO.UK   T 07989 602880
Based in London SW16,
E rob@voicereels.co.uk
W www.voicereels.co.uk

VSI - VOICE & SCRIPT INTERNATIONAL   T 020 7692 7700
Foreign Language Specialists. Casting. Dubbing. Editing. Recording Studios. Subtitling. Translation
132 Cleveland Street
London W1T 6AB
F 020 7692 7711
E info@vsi.tv
W www.vsi.tv

WARNER BROS DE LANE LEA SOUND   T 020 7432 3800
Post-production. Re-recording Studios
75 Dean Street, London W1D 3PU
F 020 7494 3755
E reception@wbdelanelea.com
W www.wbsound.com/london

WE THEATRE   T 020 3327 3877
Flyer, Poster, Programme & Website Design for Fringe Theatre
239 Lewisham Way
London SE4 1XF
E info@wetheatre.co.uk
W www.wetheatre.co.uk

WEBVID.CO.UK   T 020 8133 1728
Contact: Neil Bentley (Heart, Capital, Galaxy), James, Vince. Web & Video Production Company. Bespoke Website Design & Video Filming/Editing
Based in South London
E hello@webvid.co.uk
W www.webvid.co.uk

WORLDWIDE PICTURES LTD   T 020 7613 6580
103 The Timber Yard
Drivedale Street
London N1 6ND
E info@worldwidepictures.tv
W www.worldwidepictures.tv

WORTH VALLEY WEB   T 07944 023597
Showreel Editing, VHS to DVD Conversion & Websites
103/105 Lidget, Oakworth
Keighley, West Yorkshire BD22 7HN
E info@worthvalleyweb.co.uk
W www.worthvalleyweb.co.uk

10 OUT OF 10 PRODUCTIONS LTD   **T** 020 8659 2558
Lighting & Sound. Design. Hire. Installation. Sales
5 Metro Business Centre
Kangley Bridge Road
London SE26 5BW
E sales@10outof10.co.uk
W www.10outof10.co.uk

147RESEARCH   **T** 01665 714777
Sources Anything Needed for Period or Modern Productions
Manderville, Amble Morpeth NE65 0SB
T 07778 002147
E jenniferdalton@147research.com
W www.147research.com

3D CREATIONS LTD   **T** 01493 652055
Production Design. Prop Makers. Scenery Contractors. Scenic Artists
Berth 33, Malthouse Lane
Gorleston, Norfolk NR31 0GW
F 01493 443124
E info@3dcreations.co.uk
W www.3dcreations.co.uk

ACROBAT PRODUCTIONS LTD   **T** 01442 843377
Acrobatic & Aerial Performers & Consultants
4 Bridgewater Court, Little Gaddesden
Berkhamsted, Herts HP4 1PX
T 07771 907030
E roger@acrobatproductions.com
W www.acrobatproductions.com

ACTION 99 CARS LTD   **T** 01923 266373
Westwick Road Farm, Westwick Row
Hemel Hempstead HP2 4UB
E david@nineninecars.com
W www.nineninecars.com

ADAMS ENGRAVING   **T** 01483 725792
Unit G1A, The Mayford Centre
Mayford Green
Woking GU22 0PP
E adamsengraving@pncl.co.uk
W www.adamsengraving.co.uk

AF WILTSHIRE (DUNSFOLD) LTD   **T** 01483 200516
Agricultural Vehicle Engineers, Repairs etc
The Agricultural Centre, Alfold Road
Dunsfold, Surrey GU8 4NP
F 01483 200491
E team@afwiltshire.co.uk

AIRBOURNE SYSTEMS INTERNATIONAL   **T** 01245 268772
All Skydiving Requirements Arranged. Parachute Hire (Period & Modern)
8 Burns Crescent, Chelmsford
Essex CM2 0TS

ALCHEMICAL LABORATORIES ETC   **T** 01636 707836
Medieval Science & Technology Recreated for Museums & Films
2 Stapleford Lane, Coddington
Newark, Nottinghamshire NG24 2QZ
E alchemyjack@gmail.com
W www.jackgreene.co.uk

ALCOHOL-FREE SHOP THE   **T** 0800 2448024
Alcohol-free Drinks for Television & Film Sets
Units 1 & 2 Manchester Industrial Park
Newton Heath
Manchester M40 5AX
E info@alcoholfree.co.uk
W www.alcoholfree.co.uk

ALL STARS AMERICAN LIMOS   **T** 07747 130685
30 Henley Meadows
Tenterden TN30 6EN
E limohire@live.co.uk
W www.limo-hire-sussex-ken .co.uk

ANELLO & DAVIDE   **T** 020 7938 2255
Bespoke Handmade Shoes
15 St Albans Grove, London W8 5BP
E enquiries@handmadeshoes.co.uk
W www.handmadeshoes.co.uk

ANNUAL CLOWNS DIRECTORY.COM   **T** 01268 745791
Contact: Salvo The Clown
13 Second Avenue, Kingsleigh Park
Thundersley, Essex SS7 3QD
E salvo@annualclownsdirectory.com
W www.annualclownsdirectory.com

AQUATECH SURVEY LTD   **T** 01452 740559
Camera Boats
2 Cobbies Rock, Epney
Gloucestershire GL2 7LN
F 01452 741958
E office@aquatech-uk.com
W www.aquatech-uk.com

ARMS & ARCHERY   **T** 01920 460335
Armour. Chainmail. Longbows. Tents. Weaponry. X-bows
Thrift Lane, Off London Road
Ware, Herts SG12 9QS
E armsandarchery@btconnect.com

ART *
Art Consultant. Supplier of Paintings & Sculpture
E info@art8star.co.uk
W www.art8star.co.uk

ART DIRECTORS & TRIP PHOTO LIBRARY   **T** 020 8642 3593
Digital Scans & Colour Slides (All Subjects,
57 Burdon Lane, Cheam
Surrey SM2 7BY
F 020 8395 7230
E images@artdirectors.co.uk
W www.artdirectors.co.uk

ASH, Riky   **T** 01476 407383
Equity Registered Stuntman/Stunt Co-ordinator
T 07850 471227
E stuntmanriky@fallingforyou.tv
W www.fallingforyou.tv

AWESOME UPHOLSTERY   **T** 01480 461195
Member of The Guild of Master Craftsmen
Unit 7, Monsal Works
Somersham Road
St Ives, Cambridgeshire PE27 3LY
E info@awesome.eu.com
W www.awesome.eu.com

BAPTY (2000) LTD　　T 020 8574 7700
Dressing, Props, Weapons etc
1A Witley Gardens, Norwood Green
Southall, Middlesex UB2 4ES
F 020 8571 5700
E team@bapty.co.uk
W www.bapty.co.uk

BEAT ABOUT THE BUSH LTD　　T 020 8960 2087
Musical Instrument Hire
Unit 23, Enterprise Way, Triangle Business Centre
Salter Street (Off Hythe Road), London NW10 6UG
T 07973 265793
E info@beataboutthebush.com
W www.beataboutthebush.com

**BIANCHI AVIATION
FILM SERVICES**　　T 01494 449810
Historic & Other Aircraft
Wycombe Air Park, Booker Marlow
Buckinghamshire SL7 3DP
F 01494 461236
E info@bianchiaviation.com
W www.bianchiaviation.com

BIG BREAK CARDS　　T 01386 438952
*Theatrical Greetings Cards for First Nights, featuring
Hamlet the Pig, drawn by Harry Venning, as seen in The
Stage. Made by Actors for Actors*
E info@bigbreakcards.co.uk
W www.bigbreakcards.co.uk

BLUE MILL LTD　　T 0116 248 8130
Dyers. Finishers
84 Halstead Street, Leicester LE5 3RD
E info@bluemill.co.uk
W www.bluemill.co.uk

BLUEBELL RAILWAY PLC　　T 01825 720800
*Period Stations. Pullman Coaches. Steam Locomotives.
Extensive Film Experience*
Sheffield Park Station, East Sussex TN22 3QL
F 01825 720804
E info@bluebell-railway.co.uk
W www.bluebell-railway.com

**BOLDGATE COMMERCIAL
SERVICES LTD**　　T 01895 236666
Unit 12, Brook Business Centre, Cowley Mill Road
Uxbridge, Middlesex UB8 2FX
F 01895 237962
E info@boldgate.co.uk
W www.boldgate.co.uk

**BOUNCY CASTLES BY
P. A. LEISURE**　　T 01282 453939
Specialists in Amusements & Fairground Equipment
Delph House, Park Bridge Road
Towneley Park, Burnley, Lancs BB10 4SD
T 07968 399053
E info@paleisure.co.uk
W www.paleisure.co.uk

BRISTOL (UK) LTD　　T 01923 779333
Scenic Paint & StageFloor Duo Suppliers. VFX Solutions
Unit 1, Sutherland Court
Tolpits Lane, Watford WD18 9SP
F 01923 779666
E tech.sales@bristolpaint.com
W www.bristolpaint.com

BRODIE & MIDDLETON LTD　　T 020 7836 3289
Theatrical Suppliers. Glitter, Paints, Powders etc
30-31 Store Street
London WC1E 7QE
F 020 7636 8733
E info@brodies.net
W www.brodies.net

**BURTON EXECUTIVE
CARS LTD**　　T 07792 013117
Unit 3 Farmers Court
16-17 High Street, Tutbury
Burton on Trent, Staffordshire DE13 9LP
E enquiries@burtonexecutivecars.co.uk
W www.burtonexecutivecars.co.uk

CANDLE MAKERS SUPPLIES　　T 020 7602 1812
Rear of 102-104 Shepherds Bush Road
(Entrance in Batoum Gardens)
London W6 7PD
E candles@candlemakers.co.uk
W www.candlemakers.co.uk

CARLINE-DSM　　T 01293 430430
14 Massetts Road, Horley
West Sussex RH6 7DE
F 01293 430432
E bookings@carlinedsm.co.uk
W www.albioncarsgatwick.co.uk

CHRISANNE LTD　　T 020 8640 5921
Specialist Fabrics & Accessories for Theatre & Dance
Chrisanne House
110-112 Morden Road
Mitcham, Surrey CR4 4XB
F 020 8640 2106
E sales@chrisanne.com
W www.chrisanne.com

CIRCUS PROMOTIONS　　T 01892 537964
Circus Hire. Entertainers. Big Tops etc
Hey Presto House
36 St Lukes Road
Tunbridge Wells, Kent TN4 9JH
T 07973 512845
E mikealan25@yahoo.com
W www.heyprestoentertainments.co.uk

CLASSIC CAR AGENCY THE　　T 01306 735398
Advertising. Film. Promotional. Publicity
The G&A Building, Sendall's Yard
Crawley Road, Horsham
West Sussex RH12 4HG
T 07788 977655
E theclassiccaragency@btopenworld.com
W www.theclassiccaragency.com

CLASSIC CAR HIRE　　T 020 8398 8304
Over 30 Classic & Vintage Vehicles
Unit 2 Hampton Court Estate
Summer Road
Thames Ditton KT7 0RG
E info@classic-hire.com
W www.classic-hire.com

CLASSIC OMNIBUS　　T 01303 248999
Vintage Open-Top Buses & Coaches
44 Welson Road, Folkestone
Kent CT20 2NP
W www.opentopbus.co.uk

COBO MEDIA T/F 020 8699 8655
Performing Arts, Entertainment & Leisure Marketing
43A Garthorne Road, London SE23 1EP
E admin@cobomedia.com
W www.cobomedia.com

COMPTON, Mike & Rosi T 020 8680 4364
Costumes. Models. Props
11 Woodstock Road, Croydon
Surrey CR0 1JS
T 07900 258646
E mikeandrosicompton@btopenworld.com

CONCEPT ENGINEERING LTD T 01628 825555
Smoke, Fog, Snow etc
7 Woodlands Business Park
Woodlands Park Avenue
Maidenhead, Berkshire SL6 3UA
F 01628 826261
E info@conceptsmoke.com
W www.conceptsmoke.com

COOK, Sheila TEXTILES T 020 7603 3003
Textiles, Costumes & Accessories for Hire/Sale
26 Addison Place, London W11 4RJ
E sheilacook@sheilacook.co.uk
W www.sheilacook.co.uk

COPS ON THE BOX T 020 8650 9828
Twitter: @copsonthebox1
BM BOX 7301, London WC1N 3XX
T 07710 065851
E info@cotb.co.uk
W www.cotb.co.uk

**COSTUMES &
SHOWS UNLIMITED** T 01253 827092
*Costume Rental & Design. Ice Rink Rental. Show
Production*
Crammond, Hillylaid Road
Thornton-Cleveleys
Lancs FY5 4EG
T 07881 970398
E iceshowpro@aol.com

CROFTS, Andrew T/F 01403 864518
Book Writing Services
Westlands Grange
West Grinstead, Horsham
West Sussex RH13 8LZ
E croftsa@aol.com
W www.andrewcrofts.com

**CUE ACTION
POOL PROMOTIONS** T 07881 828077
Advice for UK & US Pool, Snooker, Trick Shots
4 Hillview Close
Rowhedge
Colchester, Essex CO5 7HT
E sales@cueaction.com
W www.stevedaking.com

DESIGN PROJECTS T 01883 730262
Perrysfield Farm
Broadham Green
Old Oxted, Surrey RH8 9PG
T 07712 490004
W www.designprojects.co.uk

**DEVEREUX
DEVELOPMENTS LTD** T 01642 560854
Haulage. Removals. Trucking
Daimler Drive, Cowpen Industrial Estate
Billingham, Cleveland TS23 4JD
F 01642 566664
E mikebell@britdev.com

**DORANS PROPMAKERS /
SET BUILDERS** T/F 01335 300064
53 Derby Road, Ashbourne
Derbyshire DE6 1BH
E info@doransprops.com
W www.doransprops.com

DRAMA T'S T 07587 094808
*Branded Merchandise for Stage Professionals (T-shirts/
Hoodies etc)*
Based in London
E dramatictees@gmail.com
W www.dramats.com

DURRENT, Peter T 01787 248263
*Audition & Rehearsal Pianist. Cocktail Pianist.
Composer. Vocalist*
10 Old Station Close, Lavenham
Sudbury, Suffolk CO10 9FA
E tunefuldurrent@gmail.com

EAT TO THE BEAT T 01494 790702
Production & Location Caterers
Global Infusion Court, Nashleigh Hill
Chesham, Bucks HP5 3FE
F 01494 790701
E hello@eattothebeat.com
W www.globalinfusiongroup.com

ELECTRO SIGNS LTD T 020 8521 8066
97 Vallentin Road, London E17 3JJ
F 020 8520 8127
E info@electrosigns.co.uk

ESCORT GUNLEATHER T 01268 792769
Custom Leathercraft
602 High Road, Benfleet
Essex SS7 5RW
E info@escortgunleather.com
W www.escortgunleather.com

**EYE 4 DESIGN
UPHOLSTERY LTD** T 01775 680109
*Reupholstery, Bespoke Upholstery, Antique Restoration,
Television, Theatre & Set Work*
154 Station Road, Surfleet
Spalding, Lincolnshire PE11 4DG
E enquiries@eye4designupholstery.co.uk
W www.eye4designupholstery.co.uk

FACADE T/F 020 8699 8655
Musical Production Services
43A Garthorne Road, London SE23 1EP
E facade@cobomedia.com

**FELLOWES, Mark
TRANSPORT SERVICES** T 020 7386 7005
Transport. Sound & Lighting
59 Sherbrooke Road
London SW6 7QL
T 07850 332818
W www.fellowesproductions.com

FILM MEDICAL SERVICES T 020 8961 3222
Units 5 & 7, Commercial Way
Park Royal, London NW10 7XF
F 020 8961 7427
E info@filmmedical.co.uk
W www.filmmedical.co.uk

FINAL CREATION T 01530 249100
Unit 19, The Loft Studio
Hill Lane Industrial Estate
Markfield, Leicestershire LE67 9PN
F 01530 249400
E gemma@finalcreation.co.uk
W www.finalcreation.co.uk

FIREBRAND T/F 01546 870310
Real Flame Torches. Hire & Sales
Leac Na Ban, Tayvallich
By Lochgilphead, Argyll PA31 8PF
W www.studiobarnargyll.co.uk

FLAME RETARDING T 01621 818477
Grove Farm, Grove Farm Road
Tolleshunt Major, Maldon
Essex CM9 8LR
F 07092 036931
E email@flameretarding.co.uk
W www.flameretarding.co.uk

FLAMENCO PRODUCTIONS T 01905 424083
Entertainers
Sevilla 4 Cormorant Rise
Lower Wick, Worcester WR2 4BA
E delphineflamenco@tiscali.co.uk

FLINTS T 020 7703 9786
Specialist Theatre Hardware & Paints
Queen's Row, London SE17 2PX
E sales@flints.co.uk
W www.flints.co.uk

FLYING BY FOY T 020 8236 0234
Flying Effects for Stage, Television, Corporate Events etc
Unit 4, Borehamwood Enterprise Centre
Theobald Street
Borehamwood, Herts WD6 4RQ
F 020 8236 0235
E enquiries@flyingbyfoy.co.uk
W www.flyingbyfoy.co.uk

FROST, John NEWSPAPERS
Historical Newspaper Archives
E andrew@johnfrostnewspapers.com
W www.johnfrostnewspapers.com

GARRATT, Jonathan FRSA T 01747 858697
*Suppliers of Traditional & Unusual Garden Pots &
Installations. Glazed Tableware*
Jolliffe's Cottage, Stour Row
Shaftesbury SP7 0QW
E jonathan.garratt@talk21.com
W www.studiopottery.co.uk

**GAV NICOLA
THEATRICAL SHOES** T 07961 974278
T 00 34 673803783
E gavnicola@yahoo.com
W www.theatricalshoes.com

GET STUFFED T 020 7226 1364
Taxidermy
105 Essex Road, London N1 2SL
T 07831 260062
E taxidermy@thegetstuffed.co.uk
W www.thegetstuffed.co.uk

**GHOSTWRITER /
AUTHOR / SCRIPTWRITER** T 01227 721071
Contact: John Parker
Dove Cottage, The Street
Ickham CT3 1QP
T 07702 999920
E ghostwriterforyourbook@ymail.com
W www.ghostwriteruk.info

GIG...FYI T 01494 790700
Corporate Hospitality Caterers
Global Infusion Court
Nashleigh Hill, CheshamBucks HP5 3HE
F 01494 790701
E hello@gigfyi.com
W www.gigfyi.com

GORGEOUS GOURMETS LTD T 020 8944 7771
Furniture & Catering Equipment Hire
Gresham Way, Wimbledon SW19 8ED
E hire@gorgeoushire.co.uk
W www.gorgeoushire.co.uk

GOULD, Gillian ANTIQUES T 020 8455 1747
Scientific & Marine Antiques & Collectables
38 Denman Drive South, London NW11 6RH
T 07831 150060
E gillgould@dealwith.com
W www.gilliangouldantiques.co.uk

GRADAV HIRE & SALES LTD T 020 8324 2100
Lighting & Sound Hire/Sales
ELP Powerhouse, Elstree Film Studio
Shenley Road, Borehamwood, Herts WD6 1JG
F 020 8324 2933
E graham.t@elp.tv

GRAND HIRE T 020 7281 9555
Short & Long Term Piano Hire
465 Hornsey Road, London N19 4DR
F 020 7263 0154
E piano@grandhire.co.uk
W www.grandhire.co.uk

GRAY, Robin COMMENTARIES T 01420 23347
Voice Overs. Hunting Attire. Racing Colours. Saddles
Comptons, Isington, Alton, Hampshire GU34 4PL
T 07831 828424
E comptons1@hotmail.co.uk

GREENPROPS
Prop Suppliers. Artificial Flowers, Fruit, Raffia Grass, Foliage, Trees etc
E trevor@greenprops.org
W www.greenprops.org

**GREENSOURCE
SOLUTIONS LTD** T 0845 3100200
Providers of Mobile Phone Props. Supplies & Recycles Printer Consumables
14 Kingsland Trading Estate
St Phillips Road, Bristol BS2 0JZ
F 0117 304 2391
E props@greensource.co.uk
W www.greensource.co.uk

HANDS UP PUPPETS T 07909 824630
7 Cavendish Vale, Nottingham
Nottinghamshire NG5 4DS
E marcus@handsuppuppets.com
W www.handsuppuppets.com

**HARLEQUIN FLOORS
(BRITISH HARLEQUIN PLC)** T 01892 514888
Floors for Dance, Display, Entertainment & the Performing Arts
Festival House, Chapman Way
Tunbridge Wells, Kent TN2 3EF
T 0800 289932
E enquiries@harlequinfloors.com
W uk.harlequinfloors.com/en

HERON & DRIVER T 020 7394 8688
Scenic Furniture & Prop Makers
Unit 7, Dockley Road Industrial Estate
Rotherhithe, London SE16 3SF
E mail@herondriver.co.uk
W www.herondriver.co.uk

HI-FLI T 0161 278 9352
Flying Effects
18 Greencourt Drive
Manchester M38 0BZ
E mikefrost@hi-fli.co.uk

**HISTORICAL INTERPRETER
& ROLE PLAYING** T 020 8866 2997
Contact: Donald Clarke
80 Warden Avenue, Rayners Lane
Harrow, Middlesex HA2 9LW
T 07811 606285
E info@historicalinterpretations.co.uk
W www.historicalinterpretations.co.uk

**HISTORY IN THE
MAKING LTD** T 023 9225 3175
Weapon & Costume Hire
4A Aysgarth Road
Waterlooville, Hampshire PO7 7UG
E info@history-making.com
W www.history-making.com

**HOME JAMES
CHAUFFEUR SERVICE** T 0121 356 5088
Moor Lane, Witton
Birmingham B6 7HH
E enquiries@homejamescars.com
W www.homejamescars.com

HOMESITE ESTATE AGENTS T 020 7243 3535
16 Lambton Place, London W11 2SH
F 020 7243 5794
E info@homesite.co.uk
W www.homesite.co.uk

HOWARD, Rex DRAPES T 020 8955 6940
Trading Division of Hawthorns
Unit F, Western Trading Estate
London NW10 7LU
E hire@hawthorns.uk.com

IMPACT T 020 8601 3527
Private & Contract Hire of Coaches
7-9 Wadsworth Perivale, London UB6 7JD
F 020 8840 4880
E info@impactgroup.co.uk
W www.impactgroup.co.uk

IMPACT MARKETING T 020 7729 5978
Print Distribution & Display
Tuscany Wharf, 4B Orsman Road
London N1 5QJ
F 020 7729 5994
E contactus@impactideas.co.uk
W www.impactideas.co.uk

IMPACT PERCUSSION   **T** 020 8299 6700
Percussion Instruments for Sale
Unit 7, Goose Green Trading Estate
47 East Dulwich Road, London SE22 9BN
F 020 8299 6704
E sales@impactpercussion.com

JAPAN PROMOTIONS   **T/F** 020 7278 4099
Japanese Culture Agency
200 Russell Court
3 Woburn Place, London WC1H 0ND
E info@japan-promotions.co.uk
W www.japan-promotions.co.uk

JULIETTE DESIGNS   **T** 020 7263 7878
Diamante Jewellery Manufacturer: Necklaces,
Crowns etc
90 Yerbury Road, London N19 4RS
F 020 7281 7326
E juliettedesigns@hotmail.com
W www.stagejewellery.com

KEIGHLEY & WORTH
VALLEY LIGHT RAILWAY LTD   **T** 01535 645214
Crew. Props. Carriages, Engines & Stations
The Railway Station, Haworth, Keighley
West Yorkshire BD22 8NJ
F 01535 647317
E admin@kwvr.co.uk
W www.kwvr.co.uk

KENSINGTON EYE CENTRE   **T** 020 7937 8282
Opticians. Special Eye Effects
37 Kensington Church Street, London W8 4LL
E kensingtoneyecentre@gmail.com
W www.kensingtoneyecentre.com

KIRBY'S AFX LTD   **T/F** 020 8723 8552
8 Greenford Avenue, Hanwell, London W7 3QP
T 07958 285608
E mail@afxuk.com
W www.afxuk.com

KNEBWORTH HOUSE
GARDENS & PARK   **T** 01438 812661
Knebworth, Herts SG3 6PY
E info@knebworthhouse.com
W www.knebworthhouse.com

LAREDO, Alex   **T** 01306 889423
Expert with Ropes, Bullwhips, Shooting & Riding
29 Lincoln Road, Dorking, Surrey RH4 1TE
T 07745 798118
E sarah.paige@btinternet.com

LAREDO WILD WEST TOWN   **T** 01580 891790
Wild West Entertainment
1 Bower Walk, Staplehurst, Tonbridge, Kent TN12 0LU
T 07947 652771
E colin.winter123@btinternet.com
W www.laredo.org.uk

LEES-NEWSOME LTD   **T** 0845 0708005
Manufacturers of Flame Retardant Fabrics
Ashley Works, Unit 2, Rule Business Park
Grimshaw Lane, Middleton
Manchester M24 2AE
F 0845 0708006
E info@leesnewsome.co.uk
W www.leesnewsome.co.uk

LEIGHTON HALL   **T** 01524 734474
Historic House
Carnforth, Lancashire LA5 9ST
F 01524 720357
E info@leightonhall.co.uk
W www.leightonhall.co.uk

LEVRANT, Stephen - HERITAGE
ARCHITECTURE LTD   **T** 020 8748 5501
Architects. Historic Building Consultants
62 British Grove, Chiswick
London W4 2NL
E info@heritagearchitecture.co.uk

LIGHT ARMOURIES   **T** 07761 219755
Hand-made Latex & Foam Weapons, Shields, Props
& Armour
Unit 16, Chase Farm
Vicarage Lane West
North Weald, Essex CM16 6AL
E mikel42@hotmail.com
W www.lightarmoury.co.uk

LIMELIGHT
ENTERTAINMENT   **T** 020 8853 9570
Theatre Merchandise
Unit 13, The io Centre, The Royal Arsenal
Seymour Street, London SE18 6SX
F 020 8853 9579
E enquiries@thelimelightgroup.co.uk

LONDON MUSEUM OF
WATER & STEAM THE   **T** 020 8568 4757
Green Dragon Lane, Brentford
Middlesex TW8 0EN
F 020 8569 9978
E museum@waterandsteam.org.uk
W www.waterandsteam.org.uk

LONDON QUALITY
DRY CLEANERS LTD   **T** 020 7935 7316
Dry Cleaners. Dyers. Launderers. Costumes &
Stage Curtains
222 Baker Street, London NW1 5RT

LONO DRINKS   **T** 0800 8250035
Units 1 & 2, Manchester Industrial Estate
Holt Street, Newton Heath
Manchester M40 5AX
E info@lono.co.uk
W www.lono.co.uk

LOS KAOS   **T** 01291 680074
Animatronics. Puppetry. Street Theatre
Quay House, Quayside
Brockweir, Gloucestershire NP16 7NQ
E kaos@loskaos.co.uk
W www.loskaos.co.uk

LUCKINGS   **T** 020 8332 2000
Stage Hands. Storage. Transporters
Boston House, 69-75 Boston Manor Road
Brentford, Middlesex TW8 9JJ
F 020 8332 3000
E info@luckings.co.uk
W www.luckings.co.uk

LUCKINGS SCREEN
SERVICES   **T** 020 8332 2000
Artists' Trailers/Splits/2-3 Ways
Boston House, 69-75 Boston Manor Road
Brentford, Middlesex TW8 9JJ
F 020 8332 3000
E info@luckings.co.uk
W www.luckings.co.uk

LYON EQUIPMENT   **T** 01539 626250
Petzl & Beal Rope Access Equipment (PPE) for Industrial
& Theatrical Work
Junction 38, M6, Tebay
Cumbria CA10 3SS
F 01539 624040
E workandrescue@lyon.co.uk
W www.lyon.co.uk

M A C   T 0161 969 8311
Sound Hire
1-2 Attenburys Park, Park Road
Altrincham, Cheshire WA14 5QE
F 0161 962 9423
E hire@macsound.co.uk
W www.macsound.co.uk

MACKIE, Sally LOCATIONS   T 01608 652001
Location Finding & Management
Lavender Cottage, Evenlode
Moreton-in-Marsh
Gloucestershire GL56 0NN
T 07860 533355
E sally@mackie.biz
W www.sallymackie-locations.com

MAGICAL MART   T/F 020 8300 3579
*Magic. Punch & Judy. Ventriloquists' Dolls. Hire &
Advising. Callers by Appointment*
42 Christchurch Road
Sidcup, Kent DA15 7HQ
W www.johnstylesentertainer.co.uk

**MAINSTREAM
LEISURE GROUP**   T 020 3044 2923
Riverboat/Canal Boat Hire
Trident Court, 1 Oakcroft Road
Chessington, Surrey KT9 1BD
F 020 3044 2926
E info@mainstreamleisure.co.uk
W www.mainstreamleisure.co.uk

MARCUS HALL PROPS   T 020 7252 6291
Contact: Chris Marcus, Jonathan Hall
Unit 2BC Vanguard Court
36-38 Peckham Road
London SE5 8QT
E chris@marcushallprops.com
W www.marcushallprops.com

MARKSON PIANOS   T 020 7935 8682
8 Chester Court, Albany Street
London NW1 4BU
F 020 7224 0957
E info@marksonpianos.com
W www.marksonpianos.com

**McDONAGH, Melanie
MANAGMENT**   T 07908 225278
*TV Horse-drawn Cinderella Carriage. As seen in
'Marriage and Mayhem', 'Britain's Got Talent', 'Don't Tell
the Bride', 'Sweet Sixteen (UK)', 'This Morning' & 'Four
Weddings'. Used at Charity Events including Unicef
Cinderella Ball*
T 07909 831409
E info@famouscinderellacarriage.co.uk
W www.mcdonaghmanagement.co.uk

McNEILL, Brian   T 01706 812291
Vintage Truck & Coaches
Hawk Mount, Kebs Road
Todmorden, Lancashire OL14 8SB
E autotrans@uk2.net
W www.rollingpast.com

MIDNIGHT ELECTRONICS   T 0191 224 0088
Sound Hire
Off Quay Building, Foundry Lane
Newcastle upon Tyne NE6 1LH
E info@midnightelectronics.co.uk
W www.midnightelectronics.co.uk

**MILITARY, MODELS &
MINIATURES**   T 020 7700 7036
Model Figures
38A Horsell Road, London N5 1XP
F 020 7700 4624
E pevans113@btinternet.com

MOBILE MENAGERIE UK   T 07784 382410
Contact: Michael Fordham, Emma Lock
93 Wroxhams Gardens, Potters Bar
Hertfordshire EN6 3DN
E michael@michaelmobilemenagerie.co.uk
W www.wild2you.co.uk

MODDED MOTORS AGENCY   T 07989 128131
Suppliers of Modified Cars
Unit 7, 51 Radlett Road
Frogmore, St Albans AL2 2JE
E contact@moddedmotorsagency.com
W www.moddedmotorsagency.com

MODELBOX   T 01837 810923
Computer Aided Design. Design Services
41C Market Street, Hatherleigh, Devon EX20 3JP
E info@modelbox.co.uk
W www.modelboxplans.com

**MOORFIELDS
PHOTOGRAPHIC LTD**   T 0151 236 1611
2 Old Hall Street, Liverpool L3 9RQ
E info@moorfieldsphoto.com
W www.moorfieldsphoto.com

MORGAN, Dennis
Cinematographer
Cornwall
E info@dennismorgan.co.uk

MORTON, G. & L.   T 01430 860185
Farming. Horses
Hashome Carr, Holme-on-Spalding Moor
Yorkshire YO43 4BD
E janet_morton@hotmail.com

MOTORHOUSE HIRE LTD   T 020 7495 1618
Contact: Michael Geary. Action Vehicles
Park Farm, Warfield
Berkshire RG42 5RH
E michael@motorhousehire.co.uk

MR SHIZ
Mural Artist & Props Maker
Clapham, London SW4 6HR
E info@mrshiz.com
W www.mrshiz.com

NEWMAN HIRE COMPANY   T 020 8743 0741
Lighting Hire
16 The Vale, Acton, London W3 7SB
E info@newmanhire.co.uk

NORTHERN LIGHT T 0131 622 9100
Assembly Street, Leith, Edinburgh EH6 7RG
E info@northernlight.co.uk
W www.northernlight.co.uk

NOSTALGIA AMUSEMENTS T 01923 863230
Contact: Brian Davey
Scotchells, Apse Heath
Newport Road, Sandown PO36 9PG
T 07973 506869
E bdavey@globalnet.co.uk
W www.nostalgia-hire.co.uk

**NOTTINGHAM JOUSTING ASSOCIATION
SCHOOL OF NATIONAL
EQUITATION LTD** T 01509 852366
*Jousting & Medieval Tournaments. Horses & Riders for
Films & Television*
Bunny Hill Top, Costock
Loughborough, Leicestershire LE12 6XN
E info@bunnyhill.co.uk
W www.bunnyhill.co.uk

OCEAN LEISURE T 020 7930 5050
*Scuba Diving. Watersports Retail. Underwater & Extreme
Camera Specialists*
11-14 Northumberland Avenue, London WC2N 5AQ
F 020 7930 3032
E info@oceanleisure.co.uk
W www.oceanleisure.co.uk

OFFSTAGE BOOKS T 020 8444 4717
BlackGull Bookshop, 121 High Road, London N2 8AG
E offstagebooks@gmail.com

PAPERFLOW PLC T 020 8331 2000
Office Equipment. Stationery
Unit 6, Meridian Trading Estate
20 Bugsbys Way, Charlton, London SE7 7SJ
F 020 8331 2001
E sales@paperflowgroup.com

PAPERPROPMAKER T 07545 281486
*Paper Props Created for Stage, Film & Television. Letters,
Notebooks, Paper Ephemera etc. Handwritten or Printed.
Any Style or Period Reproduced*
Based in London,
E sianwillis@live.co.uk

PATERSON, Helen T 020 7730 6428
Typing Services
40 Whitelands House, London SW3 4QY
E pater@waitrose.com

**PERIOD PETROL PUMP
COLLECTION** T 01379 643978
c/o Diss Ironworks, 7 St Nicholas Street
Diss, Norfolk IP22 4LB
E info@dissironworks.co.uk
W www.periodpetrolpumps.co.uk

PHOSPHENE T 01449 770011
Lighting & Sound. Design. Hire. Sales
Milton Road South, Stowmarket, Suffolk IP14 1EZ
E phosphene@btconnect.com
W www.phosphene.co.uk

PINK POINTES DANCEWEAR T/F 01708 438584
1A Suttons Lane, Hornchurch, Essex RM12 6RD
E pink.pointes@btconnect.com

PLUNGE PRODUCTIONS T 01273 421819
Prop Making. Set Building
Unit 3, Bestwood Works
Drove Road, Brighton BN41 2PA
E info@plungeproductions.com
W www.plungeproductions.com

PLUSFILM LTD T 01489 895559
Action Vehicle Hire & SFX Vehicles Designed & Built
T 07885 619783
E stephen.lamonby@gmail.com
W www.plusfilm.com

**POLAND, Anna: SCULPTOR &
MODELMAKER** T 023 8040 5166
Sculpture, Models, Puppets, Masks etc
Salterns, Old Bursledon
Southampton, Hampshire SO31 8DH
E polandanna@hotmail.com

**POLLEX PROPS /
FIREBRAND** T/F 01546 870310
Prop Makers
Leac Na Ban, Tayvallich
Lochgilphead, Argyll PA31 8PF
E firebrand.props@btinternet.com

PRINTMEDIA GROUP
E info@printmediagroup.eu
W www.printmediagroup.eu

PROBLOOD T/F 01728 723865
11 Mount Pleasant, Framlingham
Suffolk IP13 9HQ

**PROFESSOR PATTEN'S
PUNCH & JUDY** T 01707 873262
Hire & Performances. Advice on Traditional Show
14 The Crest, Goffs Oak
Hertfordshire EN7 5NP
E dennis@dennispatten.co.uk
W www.dennispatten.co.uk

PROP FARM LTD T 01909 723100
Contact: Pat Ward
Grange Farm, Elmton
Nr Creswell, North Derbyshire S80 4LX
F 01909 721465
E pat@propfarm.co.uk

PROP STUDIOS LTD T 01444 250088
Unit 3 Old Kiln Works, Ditchling
Common Industrial Estate, Hassocks BN6 8SG
F 01444 250089
E info@propstudios.co.uk
W www.propstudios.co.uk

**PUNCH & JUDY PUPPETS
& BOOTHS** T/F 020 8300 3579
Hire & Advisory Service. Callers by Appointment
42 Christchurch Road, Sidcup, Kent DA15 7HQ
W www.johnstylesentertainer.co.uk

**RAINBOW
PRODUCTIONS LTD** T 020 8254 5300
*Creation & Appearances of Costume Characters.
Stage Shows*
Unit 3, Greenlea Park
Prince George's Road, London SW19 2JD
F 020 8254 5306
E info@rainbowproductions.co.uk
W www.rainbowproductions.co.uk

RE:AL T 01622 200123
Print. Creative. Marketing. Digital
Unit 2, Tovil Green Business Park
Maidstone, Kent ME15 6TA
E info@realprintandmedia.com
W www.realprintandmedia.com

RENT-A-CLOWN T/F 020 7608 0312
Contact: Mattie Faint
37 Sekforde Street, Clerkenwell, London EC1R 0HA
E mattiefaint@gmail.com

REPLAY FILM & NEW MEDIA   T 020 7637 0473
Showreels. Television Facilities Hire
Museum House, 25 Museum Street
London WC1A 1JT
E sales@replayfilms.co.uk
W www.replayfilms.co.uk

ROBERTS, Chris INTERIORS   T 07956 512074
*Specialist Painters & Decorators. Classic & Modern
Decorating*
117 Colebrook Lane, Loughton IG10 2HP
E procopi@hotmail.com

ROOTSTEIN, Adel LTD   T 020 7381 1447
Mannequin Manufacturer
9 Beaumont Avenue, London W14 9LP
F 020 7386 9594
W www.rootstein.com

RORKIES BUS   T 07846 022119
*London Routemaster Bus Available for Film Work,
Advertising & Private Hire*
Flat 4, 26 Devonshire Gardens
Margate, Kent CT9 3AE
E rorke.steve@yahoo.co.uk
W www.rorkiesbus.co.uk

**ROYAL HORTICULTURAL
HALLS THE**   T 0845 3704606
*Film Location: Art Deco & Edwardian Buildings.
Conferences. Events. Exhibitions. Fashion Shows*
80 Vincent Square, London SW1P 2PE
E horthalls@rhs.org.uk
W www.rhhonline.co.uk

RUDKIN DESIGN   T 01327 301770
*Design Consultants. Advertising, Brochures,
Corporate etc*
10 Cottesbrooke Park, Heartlands Business Park
Daventry, Northamptonshire NN11 8YL
E arudkin@rudkindesign.co.uk
W www.rudkindesign.co.uk

RUMBLE, Jane   T 020 8904 6462
Props to Order. No Hire
121 Elmstead Avenue, Wembley
Middlesex HA9 8NT

SABAH   T 001 954 566 6219 (Office)
*UK Stylist/Designer/Coordinator. Now Based in Ft.
Lauderdale, Florida. Specialising in Fashion, Wardrobe
& Props*
2841 N. Ocean Boulevard Apt 501
Fort Lauderdale, Florida 33308, USA
T 001 954 383 2179 (Mobile)
E sabah561@aol.com

SALVO THE CLOWN   T 01268 745791
13 Second Avenue, Kingsleigh Park
Thundersley, Essex SS7 3QD
E salvo@annualclownsdirectory.com
W www.annualclownsdirectory.com

SAPEX SCRIPTS   T 020 8236 1600
The Maxwell Building, Elstree Film Studios
Shenley Road, Borehamwood, Herts WD6 1JG
F 020 8324 2771
E scripts@sapex.co.uk
W www.sapex.co.uk

**SCHULTZ & WIREMU FABRIC
EFFECTS LTD**   T/F 020 8469 0151
Distressing. Dyeing. Printing
Unit 6, Titan Business Estate, Finch Street
London SE8 5QA
E swfabricfx@mail.com
W www.schultz-wiremufabricfx.co.uk

SCRIPTRIGHT   T 020 8354 0580
*Contact: S.C. Hill. Script & Manuscript Typing Services.
Script Reading & Assessment Services. Copy Editing etc*
22 Carthew Road
London W6 0DX
E samc.hill@virgin.net

SCRIPTS BY ARGYLE   T 07905 293319
*Play, Film & Book Typing/Editing in Professional Layout.
London Collection of Manuscript on Request*
43 Clappers Lane, Fulking
West Sussex BN5 9ND
E argyle.associates@me.com

**SHIRLEY LEAF &
PETAL COMPANY**   T/F 01424 427793
Flower Makers Museum & Manufacturers
58A High Street, Old Town
Hastings, East Sussex TN34 3EN

SHOWFILE   T 07582 513623
*Contact: Enzo Roff. Stock images for Video Projection.
Web based*
E enzo@showfile.com
W www.showfile.com

SIDE EFFECTS   T 020 7587 1116
FX. Models. Props
92 Fentiman Road, London SW8 1LA
F 020 7207 0062
E sfx@lineone.net

SNOW BUSINESS   T/F 01453 840077
World Leaders in Snow & Winter Effects
The Snow Mill, Bridge Road
Ebley, Stroud, Gloucestershire GL5 4TR
E snow@snowbusiness.com
W www.snowbusiness.com

SOFT PROPS   T 020 7587 1116
Modelmakers
92 Fentiman Road, London SW8 1LA
F 020 7207 0062
E jackie@softprops.co.uk

**STANSTED AIRPORT
TAXIS & CHAUFFEURS**   T 0845 6436705
55 Croasdaile Road
Stansted Airport
Essex CM24 8DW
E enquiries@stanstedtaxiservice.co.uk
W www.stanstedtaxiservice.co.uk

**STEELDECK RENTALS /
SALES LTD**   T 020 7833 2031
Modular Staging. Stage Equipment Hire
Unit 58, T Marchant Trading Estate
42-72 Verney Road
London SE16 3DH
F 020 7232 1780
E rentals@steeldeck.co.uk
W www.steeldeck.co.uk

**STOKE BRUERNE BOAT
COMPANY LTD**   T 07966 503609
Passenger Boat Operator
Wharf Cottage, Stoke Bruerne
Northants NN12 7SE
W www.stokebruerneboats.co.uk

SUPERHIRE PROPS LTD   T 020 8453 3900
Prop Hire Specialist. Victorian to Present Day
55 Chase Road
London NW10 6LU
F 020 8965 8107
E dawn@superhire.com
W www.superhire.com

TAYLOR, Charlotte   T 020 8876 9085
Stylist/Set Decorator
18 Eleanor Grove, Barnes, London SW13 0JN
T 07836 708904
E charlottetaylor.info@gmail.com

**THAMES LUXURY
CHARTERS LTD**   T 020 7357 7751
Eagle Wharf, 53 Lafone Street, London SE1 2LX
F 020 7378 1359
E sales@thamesluxurycharters.co.uk
W www.thamesluxurycharters.co.uk

THEATRESEARCH LTD   T 01423 780497
Theatre Consultants
Dacre Hall, Dacre
North Yorkshire HG3 4ET
F 01423 781957
E office@theatresearch.co.uk
W www.theatresearch.co.uk

**THEATRICAL
SHOEMAKERS LTD**   T 020 8884 4484
Footwear
Unit 1A, Lee Valley Trading Estate
Rivermead Road, London N18 3QW
E info@theatreshoes.com
W www.shoemaking.co.uk

THEME TRADERS LTD   T 020 8452 8518
Props. Prop Hire. Party Planners. Productions
The Stadium, Oaklands Road
London NW2 6DL
F 020 8450 7322
E mailroom@themetraders.com
W www.themetraders.com

TOP SHOW   T/F 01904 750022
Props. Scenery. Conference Specialists
North Lane, Huntington, Yorks YO32 9SU

TRANSCRIPTS   T 07973 200197
*Conferences. Interviews. Post-production Scripts.
Proofreading. Videos. Working Formats: Digital,
CD/DVD, Tapes*
E lucy@transcripts.demon.co.uk

TRYFONOS, Mary MASKS   T 020 7502 7883
Mask, Headdress & Puppet Specialist
59 Shaftesbury Road
London N19 4QW
T 07764 587433
E marytryfonos@aol.com

TURN ON LIGHTING   T/F 020 7359 7616
Antique Lighting c1850-1950
11 Camden Passage, London N1 8EA
E info@turnonlighting.co.uk
W www.turnonlighting.co.uk

**UK SAME DAY
DELIVERY SERVICE**   T 07785 717179
Contact: Philip Collings
18 Billingshurst Road, Broadbridge Heath
Horsham, West Sussex RH12 3LW
F 01403 266059
E philcollings60@hotmail.com

UPSTAGE COMMUNICATIONS   T 020 7403 6510
Live Communications Agency
Studio A, 7 Maidstone Buildings Mews
72-76 Borough High Street
London SE1 1GD
F 020 7403 6511
E amee@upstagecommunications.com
W www.upstagecommunications.com

**VENTRILOQUIST
DOLLS HOME**   T/F 020 8300 3579
Hire & Helpful Hints. Callers by Appointment
42 Christchurch Road, Sidcup
Kent DA15 7HQ
W www.johnstylesentertainer.co.uk

VENTRILOQUIST DUMMY HIRE   T 01707 873262
Contact: Dennis Patten. Hire & Advice
14 The Crest, Goffs Oak
Herts EN7 5NP
E dennis@dennispatten.co.uk
W www.dennispatten.co.uk

VINMAG ARCHIVE LTD   T 020 8533 7588
84-90 Digby Road, London E9 6HX
E pictures@vinmagarchive.com
W www.vintagemagazinecompany.co.uk

VINTAGE CARRIAGES TRUST   T 01535 680425
*Owners of the Museum of Rail Travel at Ingrow
Railway Centre*
Keighley, West Yorkshire BD21 5AX
F 01535 610796
E admin@vintagecarriagetrust.org
W www.vintagecarriagetrust.org

VOCALEYES   T 020 7375 1043
Audio Description "Describing the Arts"
1st Floor, 54 Commercial Street
London E1 6LT
F 020 7247 5622
E enquiries@vocaleyes.co.uk
W www.vocaleyes.co.uk

WALKING YOUR DOG   T 01322 634807
Dog Walking & Pet Services for South East London
T 07867 502333
E info@walkingyourdog.net
W www.walkingyourdog.net

**WEBBER, Peter
RITZ STUDIOS**   T 020 8870 1335
Music Equipment Hire. Rehearsal Studios
Courtyard Studios, The Bridge
Esmond Street, London SW15 2LP
E ben@peterwebberhire.com
W www.ritzstudios.com

**WESTED LEATHERS
COMPANY**   T 01322 660654
Suede & Leather Suppliers/Manufacturers
Little Wested House, Wested Lane
Swanley, Kent BR8 8EF
E wested@wested.com

WESTWARD, Lynn BLINDS   T 020 8742 8333
Window Blind Specialist
458 Chiswick High Road
London W4 5TT
F 020 8742 8444
E info@lynnwestward.com
W www.lynnwestward.com

WHITE ROOM STUDIO   T 020 8674 8151
Unit 03, 45 Morrish Road
London SW2 4EE
E info@whiteroomstudio.co.uk
W www.whiteroomstudio.co.uk

WORBEY, Darryl STUDIOS   T 020 7639 8090
Specialist Puppet Design & Construction
Ground Floor, 33 York Grove
London SE15 2NY
T 07815 671564
E info@darrylworbeystudios.com

**ACTIONS: THE ACTORS'
THESAURUS** T 020 8749 4953
By Marina Caldarone & Maggie Lloyd-Williams
Nick Hern Books, The Glasshouse
49A Goldhawk Road, London W12 8QP
F 020 8735 0250
E info@nickhernbooks.co.uk
W www.nickhernbooks.co.uk

**ACTORS & PERFORMERS
YEARBOOK** T 020 7631 5600
Methuen Drama, Bloomsbury Publishing Plc
50 Bedford Square, London WC1B 3DP
F 020 7631 5800
E actorsyb@bloomsbury.com
W www.actorsandperformers.com

AMATEUR STAGE MAGAZINE T 020 7096 1603
3rd Floor, 207 Regent Street, London W1B 3HH
F 020 7681 3867
E editor@amateurstagemagazine.co.uk
W www.amateurstagemagazine.co.uk

**ANNUAIRE DU CINEMA
BELLEFAYE** T 00 33 1 42335252
*French Actors' Directory, Production, Technicians & all
Technical Industries & Suppliers*
30 rue Saint Marc, 75002 Paris, France
F 00 33 1 42963303
E contact@bellefaye.com
W www.bellefaye.com

ARTISTES & AGENTS T 020 7224 9666
Richmond House Publishing Co Ltd, Suite D2
4-6 Canfield Place, London NW6 3BT
E sales@rhpco.co.uk
W www.rhpco.co.uk

AUDITIONS: THE COMPLETE GUIDE
E info@auditionsthecompleteguide.com
W www.auditionsthecompleteguide.com

AUDITIONS UNDRESSED T 020 7839 4888
By Dan Bowling
c/o Global Artists, 23 Haymarket, London SW1Y 4DG
E michaelgarrett@globalartists.co.uk

AURORA METRO PRESS (1989) T 020 3261 0000
*Biography, Drama, Fiction, Humour, Reference &
International Literature in English Translation*
67 Grove Avenue, Twickenham TW1 4HX
E info@aurorametro.com
W www.aurorametro.com

BEAT MAGAZINE T 01753 866865
Arts & Culture Magazine
c/o Firestation Centre for Arts & Culture, The Old Court
St Leonards Road, Windsor, Berks SL4 3BL
E editor@beatmagazine.co.uk
W www.beatmagazine.co.uk

**BRITISH PERFORMING
ARTS YEARBOOK** T 020 7333 1723
Rhinegold Publishing, Rhinegold House
20 Rugby Street, London WC1N 3QZ
E bpay@rhinegold.co.uk
W www.rhinegold.co.uk

BRITISH THEATRE.COM T 020 7096 1603
3rd Floor, 207 Regent Street
London W1B 3HH
F 020 7681 3867
E sales@3foldmedia.co.uk
W www.britishtheatre.com

**BRITISH THEATRE
DIRECTORY** T 020 7224 9666
Richmond House Publishing Co Ltd
Suite D2, 4-6 Canfield Place, London NW6 3BT
E sales@rhpco.co.uk
W www.rhpco.co.uk

BROADCAST T 020 3033 2872
Media Business Insight Ltd
Zetland House, 5-25 Scrutton Street
London EC2A 4HJ
T 01604 828706 (Subscriptions)
E customerservices@subscribe.broadcastnow.co.uk
W www.broadcastnow.co.uk

BROADWAY BABY T 020 3327 3872
*Reviewer at Edinburgh & Brighton Fringe & also in
London. Print & Online Reviews*
239 Lewisham Way, London SE4 1XF
E pressreleases@broadwaybaby.com
W www.broadwaybaby.com

CASTCALL T 01582 456213
Casting Information Services. Incorporating Castfax
106 Wilsden Avenue, Luton LU1 5HR
E admin@castcall.co.uk
W www.castcall.co.uk

CASTNET LTD T 020 8420 4209
*Jobs Information, Casting & Personal Websites for UK
Actors & Casting*
20 Sparrows Herne, Bushey, Herts WD23 1FU
E admin@castnet.co.uk
W www.castnet.co.uk

CASTWEB T 020 7720 9002
7 St Luke's Avenue, London SW4 7LG
E info@castweb.co.uk
W www.castweb.co.uk

CELEBRITY BULLETIN THE T 01273 666351
FENS Information, Tower Point
44 North Road, Brighton BN1 1YR
E enquiries@celebrity-bulletin.co.uk

CONFERENCE & INCENTIVE TRAVEL MAGAZINE T 020 8267 4285
Teddington Studios, Broom Road
Teddington, Middlesex TW11 9BE
E cit@haymarket.com
W www.citmagazine.com

CREATIVE REVIEW HANDBOOK T 020 7970 6455
Centaur Media Plc, 79 Wells Street, London W1T 3QN
W www.creativereview.co.uk

DRAMACLASSES.BIZ T 01923 721109
Directory of Drama & Performing Arts Schools
44 Nightingale Road, Rickmansworth
Hertfordshire WD3 7DB
E hello@dramaclasses.biz
W www.dramaclasses.biz

EQUITY MAGAZINE T 020 7670 0211
Guild House, Upper St Martin's Lane, London WC2H 9EG
F 020 7379 7001
E ppemberton@equity.org.uk
W www.equity.org.uk

FORESIGHT-NEWS T 020 7970 4293
The Profile Group, Centaur Media Plc
Wells Point, London W1T 3QN
E info@foresightnews.com
W www.foresightnews.com

FOURTHWALL MAGAZINE T 020 7096 1603
Incorporating The Drama Student Magazine
3rd Floor, 207 Regent Street, London W1B 3HH
E editor@fourthwallmagazine.co.uk
W www.fourthwallmagazine.co.uk

HERN, Nick BOOKS T 020 8749 4953
Theatre Publishers. Performing Rights Agents
The Glasshouse, 49A Goldhawk Road, London W12 8QP
F 020 8735 0250
E info@nickhernbooks.co.uk
W www.nickhernbooks.co.uk

JASPER PUBLISHING T 01604 590315
155 Harlestone Road, Northampton NN5 7AQ
F 01604 591077
E sales@jasperpublishing.com
W www.jasperpublishing.com

KAY'S UK & EUROPEAN PRODUCTION MANUALS T 020 8960 6900
Pinewood Studios, Pinewood Road
Iver Heath, Bucks SL0 0NH
E info@kays.co.uk
W www.kays.co.uk

KFTV T 020 7549 2596
Formerly KEMPS
Wilmington Publishing & Information Ltd
6-14 Underwood Street, London N1 7JQ
E skeegan@wilmington.co.uk
W www.kftv.com

KNOWLEDGE THE
6-14 Underwood Street, London N1 7JQ
E knowledge@wilmington.co.uk
W www.theknowledgeonline.com

METHUEN DRAMA T 020 7631 5600
Bloomsbury Publishing
50 Bedford Square, London WC1B 3DP
F 020 7631 5800
E methuendrama@bloomsbury.com/drama
W www.bloomsbury.com/drama

MOVIE MEMORIES MAGAZINE (Est. 1990)
3 Issues per yr. Devoted to Films & Stars (1930s to 1960s)
10 Russet Close, Scunthorpe
N Lincs DN15 8YJ
E crob.mvm@ntlworld.com

OBERON BOOKS LTD T 020 7607 3637
521 Caledonian Road, London N7 9RH
F 020 7607 3629
E info@oberonbooks.com
W www.oberonbooks.com

OFFICIAL LONDON SEATING PLAN GUIDE THE T 020 7224 9666
Richmond House Publishing Co Ltd, Suite D2
4-6 Canfield Place, London NW6 3BT
E sales@rhpco.co.uk
W www.rhpco.co.uk

OFFICIALTHEATRE.COM T 020 7183 7183
35 Kingsland Road, Shoreditch
London E2 8AA
E rebecca@officialtheatre.com

PA ENTERTAINMENT T 0870 1203200
292 Vauxhall Bridge Road, Victoria
London SW1V 1AE
F 0870 1203201
E jane.kew@pressassociation.com
W www.pressassociation.com

PACKED TO THE RAFTERS T 020 7096 1603
Silvermoon Publications, 3rd Foor
207 Regent Street, London W1B 3HH
E doug@silvermoonpublishing.co.uk
W www.packedrafterspr.co.uk

PINTER & MARTIN LTD T 020 7737 6868
6 Effra Parade, Brixton, London SW2 1PS
E info@pinterandmartin.com
W www.pinterandmartin.com

PLAYERS DIRECTORY T 001 310 247 3058
Casting Directory Published in January & July. Hard Copy & eBook. Contains Actor Photos, Representation, Resume & Demo Reels. Published since 1937
2210 W. Olive Avenue, Suite 320
Burbank, California 91506, USA
E info@playersdirectory.com
W www.playersdirectory.com

PLAYS INTERNATIONAL T 020 7720 1950
33A Lurline Gardens, London SW11 4DD
E info@playsinternational.org
W www.playsinternational.org.uk

PRESENTERS CLUB THE T 07782 224207
Presenter Promotions
123 Corporation Road, Gillingham, Kent ME7 1RG
E info@presenterpromotions.co.uk
W www.presenterpromotions.co.uk

RADIO TIMES T 020 7150 5800
Formerly Published by BBC Magazines
Immediate Media, Vineyard House
44 Brook Green, Hammersmith, London W6 7BT
E rteditor@radiotimes.com
W www.radiotimes.com

RICHMOND HOUSE PUBLISHING COMPANY LTD T 020 7224 9666
Suite D2, 4-6 Canfield Place
London NW6 3BT
E sales@rhpco.co.uk
W www.rhpco.co.uk

ROUTLEDGE PUBLISHING T 020 7017 6000
2 Park Square, Milton Park
Abington, Oxon OX14 4RN
F 020 7017 6699
E book.orders@tandf.co.uk
W www.routledge.com

SCREEN INTERNATIONAL
MBI, Zetland House
5-25 Scrutton Street, London EC2A 4HJ
W www.screendaily.com

SELF TAPING: THE ACTOR'S GUIDE
Illustrated ebook. Advice & Resources for Self Taping
E info@selftaping.com
W www.selftaping.com

SHOWBIZ FRIENDS
Social Networking Website for Professional Showbiz People
W www.showbizfriends.com

SHOWCASE　　　　　　T 01892 530460
Annual Handbook for the Worldwide Music Production Industry
The Warehouse, 1 Draper Street
Southborough, Tunbridge Wells
Kent TN4 0PG
E james@showcase-music.com
W www.showcase-music.com

SHOWCAST　　　　　　T 00 61 2 46552820
PO Box 7035, Mount Annan
NSW 2567 Australia
E danelle@showcast.com.au
W www.showcast.com.au

SHOWDIGS.CO.UK
E amy.vs@showdigs.co.uk
W www.showdigs.co.uk

SIGHT & SOUND　　　　T 020 7255 1444
British Film Institute, 21 Stephen Street
London W1T 1LN
E s&s@bfi.org.uk
W www.bfi.org.uk/sightandsound

**SO YOU WANT TO BE
AN ACTOR?**　　　　　　T 020 8749 4953
By Timothy West & Prunella Scales
Nick Hern Books, The Glasshouse
49A Goldhawk Road, London W12 8QP
F 020 8735 0250
E info@nickhernbooks.co.uk
W www.nickhernbooks.co.uk

**SO YOU WANT TO BE
A THEATRE DIRECTOR?**　　T 020 8749 4953
By Stephen Unwin
Nick Hern Books, The Glasshouse
49A Goldhawk Road, London W12 8QP
F 020 8735 0250
E info@nickhernbooks.co.uk
W www.nickhernbooks.co.uk

**SO YOU WANT TO BE
A THEATRE PRODUCER?**　　T 020 8749 4953
By James Seabright
Nick Hern Books
The Glasshouse
49A Goldhawk Road, London W12 8QP
F 020 8735 0250
E info@nickhernbooks.co.uk
W www.nickhernbooks.co.uk

**SO YOU WANT TO BE
A TV PRESENTER?**　　　　T 020 8749 4953
By Kathryn Wolfe
Nick Hern Books, The Glasshouse
49A Goldhawk Road, London W12 8QP
F 020 8735 0250
E info@nickhernbooks.co.uk
W www.nickhernbooks.co.uk

**SO YOU WANT TO BE
IN MUSICALS?**　　　　　T 020 8749 4953
By Ruthie Henshall with Daniel Bowling
Nick Hern Books, The Glasshouse
49A Goldhawk Road, London W12 8QP
F 020 8735 0250
E info@nickhernbooks.co.uk
W www.nickhernbooks.co.uk

**SO YOU WANT TO DO
A SOLO SHOW?**　　　　T 020 8749 4953
By Gareth Armstrong
Nick Hern Books, The Glasshouse
49A Goldhawk Road, London W12 8QP
F 020 8735 0250
E info@nickhernbooks.co.uk
W www.nickhernbooks.co.uk

**SO YOU WANT TO WORK
IN THEATRE?**　　　　　T 020 8749 4953
By Susan Elkin
Nick Hern Books, The Glasshouse
49A Goldhawk Road, London W12 8QP
F 020 8735 0250
E info@nickhernbooks.co.uk
W www.nickhernbooks.co.uk

**SOCIETY OF LONDON
THEATRE THE (SOLT)**　　T 020 7557 6700
Latest News & London Theatre Listings
32 Rose Street, London WC2E 9ET
E enquiries@soltukt.co.uk
W www.officiallondontheatre.co.uk

SPOTLIGHT　　　　　　T 020 7437 7631
Twitter: @SpotlightUK
7 Leicester Place, London WC2H 7RJ
E questions@spotlight.com
W www.spotlight.com

**STAGE MEDIA
COMPANY LTD**　　　　　T 020 7939 8483
47 Bermondsey Street, London SE1 3XT
F 020 7939 8479
E editor@thestage.co.uk
W www.thestage.co.uk

**TEACHING DRAMA
MAGAZINE**　　　　　　T 07785 613149
Rhinegold Publishing, 20 Rugby Street
London WC1N 3QZ
E teaching.drama@rhinegold.co.uk
W www.teaching-drama.co.uk

TELEVISUAL MEDIA UK LTD　T 020 3008 5750
Based in London
F 020 3008 5784
E advertising@televisual.com
W www.televisual.com

TIME OUT GROUP LTD　　T 020 7813 3000
4th Floor, 125 Shaftesbury Avenue
London WC2H 8AD
F 020 7813 6001
W www.timeout.com

TV TIMES　　　　　　T 020 3148 5615
IPC Media, Blue Fin Building
110 Southwark Street, London SE1 0SU
F 020 3148 8175

WHATSONSTAGE LTD　　T 020 7317 9100
16 Carlisle Street, London W1D 3BT
E feedback@whatsonstage.com
W www.whatsonstage.com

WHITE BOOK THE　　　T 020 8971 8282
Mash Media Group Ltd
4th Floor, Sterling House
6-10 St Georges Road, London SW19 4DP
E spascal@mashmedia.net
W www.whitebook.co.uk

YAMAHA MUSIC LONDON　T 020 7432 4400
Sheet Music. Musical Instruments. Guitars. Keyboards. Pianos
152-160 Wardour Street, London W1F 8YA
F 020 7432 4410
E enquiries@yamahamusiclondon.com
W www.yamahamusiclondon.com

ANTONY BARLOW ASSOCIATES **T** 020 8401 1108
Publicity & Promotion for Musicians (Concerts & CDs),
Dance & Theatre Companies
Flat 4, 15 Brambledown Road
Wallington, Surrey SM6 0TH
T 07711 929170
E artspublicity@hotmail.com

ARTHUR LEONE PR **T** 020 7836 7660
Suite 5, 17 Shorts Gardens
London WC2H 9AT
E anna@arthurleone.com
W www.arthurleone.com

AVALON PROMOTIONS **T** 020 7598 8000
Arts. Marketing. PR
4A Exmoor Street, London W10 6BD
F 020 7598 7388
E info@avalonuk.com
W www.avalonuk.com

CHESTON, Judith PUBLICITY **T** 01608 661198
30 Telegraph Street, Shipston-on-Stour
Warwickshire CV36 4DA
E judith@judithchestonpublicity.com

CLARKE, Duncan PR **T** 01904 345247
Twitter: @duncancpr
24 Severus Street, York, North Yorkshire YO24 4NL
E duncanclarkepr@live.co.uk
W www.duncanclarkepr.wordpress.com

CLOUT COMMUNICATIONS LTD **T** 020 8362 0803
15 Carlton Road, London N11 3EX
E enquiries@cloutcom.co.uk
W www.cloutcom.co.uk

ELSON, Howard PROMOTIONS **T** 01494 784760
Management. Marketing. PR. Theatre Tour Publicity
& Promotion
16 Penn Avenue, Chesham
Buckinghamshire HP5 2HS
T 07768 196310
E howardelson@btinternet.com

EMPICA LTD **T** 01275 394400
1 Lyons Court, Long Ashton Business Park
Yanley Lane, Bristol BS41 9LB
F 01275 393933
E info@empica.com
W www.empica.com

FLICK MORRIS PR **T** 07917 875625
Specialist Comedy & Theatre Publicist
3 Boarwood House, 3 Meadfarm Close
Romford RM3 9FJ
E flick@flickmorrispr.com
W www.flickmorrispr.com

GAYNOR, Avril ASSOCIATES **T** 07958 623013
126 Brudenell Road
London SW17 8DE
E gaynorama@aol.com

GOODMAN, Deborah PUBLICITY (DGPR) **T** 020 8959 9980
25 Glenmere Avenue
London NW7 2LT
E publicity@dgpr.co.uk
W www.dgpr.co.uk

GRIFFIN, Alison ASSOCIATES **T** 07768 964935
4th Floor, St Martin's House
St Martin's Lane, London WC2N 4JS
E alison@alisongriffin.co.uk

GUNG HO **T** 0121 604 6366
Contact: Paul Phedon
Unit 9, 133-137 Newhall Street
Birmingham B3 1SF
E paul@gunghoco.com
W www.gunghoco.com

HYMAN, Sue ASSOCIATES LTD **T** 020 7379 8420
Publicity. Theatre. Film. Entertainment
St Martin's House, 59 St Martin's Lane
London WC2N 4JS
T 07976 514449
E sue.hyman@btconnect.com
W www.suehyman.com

JMA **T** 020 7263 9867
Marketing. Media
8 Heathville Road, London N19 3AJ
E jma@janemorganassociates.com

JM PR
Contact: Jerome Morrow
1A Exeter Road, London NW2 4SJ
E mail@jm-pr.co.uk

JR-PR **T** 07968 009764
Contact: John Roberts
14 Hardy Close, Great Sutton
Cheshire CH66 2QH
E john@jr-pr.co.uk
W www.jr-pr.co.uk

KEAN LANYON LTD **T** 020 7697 8453
Contact: Sharon Kean
United House, North Road
Islington, London N7 9DP
T 07973 843133
E sharon@keanlanyon.com
W www.keanlanyon.com

KELLER, Don **T** 020 8800 4882
Don Keller Arts Marketing
65 Glenwood Road, Harringay
London N15 3JS
E info@donkeller.co.uk

LEEP MARKETING & PR **T** 07973 558895
Marketing. Press. Publicity
5 Hurdwick Place, London NW1 2JE
E philip@leep.biz

LONDON FLAIR PR **T** 020 3371 7945
Entertainment Specialists for Actors & Celebrities.
Film. Television
6th Floor, International House
223 Regents Street, London W1B 2QD
E cls@londonflairpr.com
W www.londonflairpm.com

MATTHEWS, Liz PR **T** 020 7253 1639
The Smokehouse
Smokehouse Yard
44-46 St John Street
London EC1M 4DF
E liz@lizmatthewspr.com
W www.lizmatthewspr.com

MAYER, Anne PR **T** 020 3659 8482
82 Mortimer Road, London N1 4LH
T 07764 192842
E annemayer@btopenworld.com

McAULEY ARTS MARKETING LTD / MAKESTHREE **T** 020 7021 0927
25 Short Street, London SE1 8LJ
E sam@makesthree.org
W www.makesthree.org

MITCHELL, Jackie   **T** 01372 465041
*JM Communications. PR, Editorial, Writing & Event
Management Services to Companies & Charities in
Surrey, London & over the UK*
4 Sims Cottages, The Green
Claygate, Surrey KT10 0JH
F 01372 471073
E jackie@jackiem.com
W www.jackiem.com

MOBIUS   **T** 020 3195 6269
2nd Floor, 34-35 Great Sutton Street
Clerkenwell, London EC1V 0DX
E info@mobiusindustries.com
W www.mobiusindustries.com

NELKIN, Chloe CONSULTING   **T** 07764 273219
Boutique PR agency for Theatre, Art & Opera
Suite 2, 52-54 Broadwick Street
London W1F 7AH
E info@chloenelkinconsulting.com
W www.chloenelkinconsulting.com

**NELSON BOSTOCK
GROUP LTD**   **T** 020 7229 4400
Creston House
10 Great Pulteney Street
London W1F 9NB
F 020 7727 2025
E info@nelsonbostock.com
W www.nelsonbostock.com

OATWAY, Christopher   **T** 07873 485265
495 Altrincham Road, Baguley Hall
Manchester M23 1AR
E christopherjoatway@gmail.com

PREMIER   **T** 020 7292 8330
*Intergrated Creative Communications Agency for
Entertainment, Arts & Culture*
2-4 Bucknall Street, London WC2H 8LA
E hello@premiercomms.com
W www.premiercomms.com

**PUBLIC EYE
COMMUNICATIONS LTD**   **T** 020 7351 1555
Suite 313, Plaza
535 Kings Road, London SW10 0SZ
F 020 7351 1010
E assistant@publiceye.co.uk

**PURPLE REIGN
PUBLIC RELATIONS**   **T** 07809 110982
Pill Box Studios, 115 Coventry Road
London E2 6GG
E monique@purplereignpr.co.uk
W www.purplereignpr.co.uk

**RICHMOND TOWERS
COMMUNICATIONS LTD**   **T** 020 7388 7421
The Tapestry Building, 51-52 Frith Street
Soho, London W1D 4SH
F 020 7388 7761
W www.rt-com.com

RKM COMMUNICATIONS LTD   **T** 020 3130 7090
Based in London & Los Angeles
14-15 Manette Street, London W1D 4AP
E info@rkmcom.com
W www.rkmcom.com

**SABOBE GROUP LTD/
MUMSRU**   **T** 07826 760885
Public Relations. Talent Management. Creative Services
3rd Floor, 207 Regent Street
London W1B 3HH
E sandra@sabobe.com
W www.sabobe.com

**SHIPPEN, Martin
MARKETING & MEDIA**   **T** 020 8968 1943
88 Purves Road
London NW10 5TB
T 07956 879165
E m.shippen@virgin.net

SILVEY, Denise   **T** 07711 245848
St Martin's Theatre, West Street
London WC2N 9NH
E ds@denisesilvey.com
W www.denisesilvey.com

SKPR THEATRE PUBLICITY   **T** 07966 578607
*Theatre & Dance PR Consultant. London, Edinburgh &
National Touring*
1 Heath Hall Lodge
French Hill
Thursley, Godalming
Surrey GU8 6NQ
E sheridan@sheridanskitchen.com

SNELL, Helen LTD   **T** 020 7240 5537
1st Floor, 62 Shaftesbury Avenue
London W1D 6LT
F 020 7240 2947
E info@helensnell.com

**SOCIETY OF LONDON
THEATRE (SOLT)**   **T** 020 7557 6727
*Contact: Anthony McNeill (Press & Corporate
Communications Manager)*
32 Rose Street, London WC2E 9ET
E anthony@soltuk.co.uk

STAFFORD, Abi   **T** 07954 371083
Freelance Journalist & Photographer
289 Birmingham Road, Birmingham
West Midlands B72 1ED
E abistafford@hotmail.com

TARGET LIVE LTD   **T** 020 3372 0950
Design. Marketing. Media. Press
45-51 Whitfield Street, London W1T 4HD
E info@target-live.co.uk
W www.target-live.co.uk

**TAYLOR HERRING
PUBLIC RELATIONS**   **T** 020 8206 5151
11 Westway Centre
69 St Marks Road
London W10 6JG
E tl@taylorherring.com
W www.taylorherring.com

TRE-VETT, Eddie   **T** 01425 475544
Brink House, Avon Castle
Ringwood, Hampshire BH24 2BL
E etv@tvmanagements.co.uk

TREVIS, Maria MARKETING   **T** 07814 304443
Associate of the Chartered Institute of Marketing
28 Ardler Road, Caversham
Reading, Berkshire RG4 5AE
E mtrevis@hotmail.com

**WILLIAMS, Tei PRESS &
ARTS MARKETING**   **T** 01869 337940
Post Office Cottage, Clifton
Oxon OX15 0PD
T 07957 664716
E artsmarketing@btconnect.com

**WINGHAM, Maureen PRESS &
PUBLIC RELATIONS**   **T** 01449 771200
69 Bury Street, Stowmarket
Suffolk IP14 1HD
E maureen.wingham@mwmedia.uk.com

R →

Radio
- BBC Local
- Independent

Rehearsal Rooms & Casting Suites

Role Play Companies / Theatre Skills in Business

Radio

Why should I work in radio?

To make a smooth transition from stage or camera to radio acting, everything that would otherwise be conveyed through body language and facial expressions must all be focused into the tone and pitch of the actor's voice.

If you have only ever considered visual acting work before, pursuing radio work would certainly enable you to expand your horizons and add additional skills to your CV. It is an opportunity to work in a different way and meet new requirements. Rehearsal and recording time is reduced in radio, which may allow you to pursue visual and radio acting alongside each other. Time constraints can be a pressure, and you have to get used to working without props (just sound effects), but this 'back to basics' existence is appealing to a lot of actors.

How can I become a radio presenter?

Presenting work in any medium comes under a different category as this is not classed as acting. It is a skill in its own right. Please refer to the 'Agents: Presenters' section for more information.

Do I need a voicereel?

This has to be your first and most important step into getting work as a radio actor. Your CV is not enough to get you a job without a professional sounding voicereel. Voice over work in commercial and corporate sectors requires a different type of reel. Please see the 'Promotional Services' section for more detailed voicereel advice in either area.

Do I need an agent?

It is not strictly necessary to have an agent for radio work. The BBC is by far the main producer of radio drama and welcomes applications directly from actors, but some independent radio stations prefer using agents to put actors forward. It might be worth doing some research on your local radio stations and finding out their preferred method of contact and making a decision from there. If you are looking for a new agent and are interested in radio work as well as straight acting work, find out whether they deal with this area of the industry before signing up. If you only want to pursue radio and/or voice over work, or are looking for a specialist agent in addition to your main agent, please see the 'Agents: Voice Over' section for further advice and listings.

How do I find work in radio?

You can send your CV and voicereel directly out to producers of radio drama, but make sure you target your search. Listen to radio plays and make a note of any producers whose work you particularly liked. This may also help you to identify what types of dramas you feel your voice would be most suited to.

Once you have done your research and made a shortlist, send your voicereel with a personalised letter. Mention the plays you liked and explain that you feel he or she will be able to use your voice in productions like these. This method is likely to be much more effective than sending out a generic covering letter en masse, and will make you stand out.

You don't need to send a headshot with your CV, but you could incorporate your photo in the body of your CV. It would be a good idea to have your name and contact details professionally printed onto your voicereel CD in case it becomes separated from your CV – see 'Promotional Services' for listings of companies that can do this for you.

Radio

CASE STUDY

Bettrys Jones was one of two winners of the Norman Beaton fellowship in 2014. She studied English and Drama at Royal Holloway University before training at The Poor School. She has been working as an actress since 2003 but had never done any radio until the competition.

I'd never done any radio before I entered the competition. I'd always really wanted the experience but never had any clue how to get into it. I was doing a play at the Sherman Theatre in Cardiff and they suggested I might like to enter. So despite feeling daunted because of my lack of knowledge and experience, I decided to give it a go.

"Don't be discouraged if you see them with their eyes closed or with their heads bowed. They're just trying to focus purely on your voice without being distracted by what your face is doing"

The competition involves a lot of preparation and a lot of holding your nerve. There are three stages to it: the heats, the semi-finals and the final. They all require you to have three monologues in each stage, so it's best to get reading as soon as you can to find the best pieces. Ask your friends and get them to listen to you doing them.

There is a time limit for each piece too so time yourself reading before you go in so you know you're within your time limit and don't rush whilst in the room. Don't panic when the green light goes on (which signals you to begin) and don't forget to breathe. My nerves go straight to my voice and being alone in that studio with the judges looking on can get to you, so try to breathe and remember they want you to do well. Don't be discouraged if you see them with their eyes closed or with their heads bowed. They're just trying to focus purely on your voice without being distracted by what your face is

doing. Also it's best not to fret too much about not having a perfect microphone technique. It's more important to make sure that your pieces do you justice, that you can embody a character convincingly that people are compelled to listen to using only your voice. The final is high pressure as it's a whole day of monologues, duologues and group work. But it is also a lot of fun being heaped together with the other 11 finalists and there is a sense of camaraderie and support, despite it being a competition. The key is to try and enjoy yourself.

"No two weeks are the same at the rep. It is the most exhilarating and enjoyable way to spend your time. The sheer volume and variety of work you get to do and the amount of times you are thrown in at the deep end is also both a bonus and terrifying. The experience is invaluable and it's a mini training ground you're unlikely to get in many other places"

The beginning of the contract: On your first day (as with most people's first days) you'll likely be thinking 'argh, I don't know anything, they made a mistake, what am I doing here!?'. Brilliantly part of winning the competition is to get a week long induction into the life and workings of the radio rep. You get tutorials and workshops in microphone technique, comedy, Shakespeare, writing radio drama and also what a typical day of recording a drama in the studio involves. By the end of the week you'll have absorbed as much as there is to absorb about all things radio. It will be the most intense week of the contract but a solid foundation to take you into the weeks ahead.

Life at the rep: No two weeks are the same at the rep. It is the most exhilarating and enjoyable way to spend your time. The sheer volume and variety of work you get to do and the amount of times you are thrown in at the deep end is also both a bonus and terrifying. The experience is invaluable and it's a mini training ground you're unlikely to get in many other places. You will average two plays a week so there is a lot of reading and preparation to do before each play. There is no time for rehearsal, so you have to make quick, clear choices before you go into the read-through. This makes the producer's job much easier. The process is a quick one which means you have to rely mostly on instinct. But you have to also be able to change your performance in a whip stitch if the producer saw it slightly differently. It helps if you have an arsenal of accents to call on. You may be asked to learn and do new accents you may never have attempted before. It's not just radio drama you'll be asked to do but readings for review shows and re-voicing for interviews and documentaries. The people you get to meet and work with will also be some of the most delightful and generous you will meet. You will find yourself becoming quicker with your decisions about characters. You'll leave the rep feeling bolder and more confident as an actor.

The freedom you get from being able to play characters that don't entirely depend on what you look like is a massive luxury. Suddenly you're not so typecast. You're able to truly play around and explore. In my opinion, there is not one ounce of you that will regret it.

To find out more about the Norman Beaton fellowship visit http://www. bbc.co.uk/soundstart/nbf.shtml

BBC RADIO BRISTOL　　　T 0117 974 1111
Contact: Tim Pemberton (Managing Editor)
Bristol Broadcasting House, Whiteladies Road
Bristol BS8 2LR
E radio.bristol@bbc.co.uk
W www.bbc.co.uk/bristol

BBC RADIO CAMBRIDGESHIRE　　　T 01223 259696
Contact: Dave Harvey (Managing Editor)
Cambridge Business Park, Cowley Road
Cambridge CB4 0WZ
E cambs@bbc.co.uk
W www.bbc.co.uk/cambridgeshire

BBC RADIO CORNWALL　　　T 01872 275421
Contact: Pauline Causey (Managing Editor)
Phoenix Wharf, Truro, Cornwall TR1 1UA
F 01872 240679
W www.bbc.co.uk/radiocornwall

BBC COVENTRY & WARWICKSHIRE　　　T 024 7653 9222
Contact: Rupert Upshon (News Desk Editor)
Priory Place, Coventry CV1 5SQ
F 024 7655 2000
E coventry.warwickshire@bbc.co.uk
W www.bbc.co.uk/coventry

BBC RADIO CUMBRIA　　　T 01228 592444
Contact: Mark Elliot (Managing Editor)
Annetwell Street, Carlisle, Cumbria CA3 8BB
F 01228 511195
E radio.cumbria@bbc.co.uk
W www.bbc.co.uk/radiocumbria

BBC RADIO DERBY　　　T 01332 361111
Contact: Simon Cornes (Editor)
56 St Helen's Street, Derby DE1 3HY
E radio.derby@bbc.co.uk
W www.bbc.co.uk/derby

BBC RADIO DEVON　　　T 01752 260323
Contact: Mark Grinnell (Managing Editor)
PO Box 1034, Plymouth PL3 5BD
F 01752 234595
E radio.devon@bbc.co.uk
W www.bbc.co.uk/devon

BBC ESSEX　　　T 01245 616000
Contact: Gerald Main (Managing Editor)
PO Box 765, Chelmsford, Essex CM2 9AB
F 01245 616025
E essex@bbc.co.uk
W www.bbc.co.uk/essex

BBC RADIO GLOUCESTERSHIRE　　　T 01452 308585
Contact: Mark Hurrell (Managing Editor)
London Road, Gloucester GL1 1SW
E radio.gloucestershire@bbc.co.uk
W www.bbc.co.uk/gloucestershire

BBC GUERNSEY　　　T 01481 200600
Contact: Sarah Solstley (Managing Editor), Kay Langlois (Assistant Editor), David Earl, Jim Cathcart, Ben Chapple (Senior Broadcast Journalists)
Broadcasting House, Bulwer Avenue
St Sampsons, Guernsey GY2 4LA
F 01481 200361
E bbcguernsey@bbc.co.uk
W www.bbc.co.uk/guernsey

BBC HEREFORD & WORCESTER　　　T 01905 748485
Contact: Jeremy Pollock (Managing Editor)
Hylton Road
Worcester WR2 5WW
E bbchw@bbc.co.uk
W www.bbc.co.uk/herefordandworcester

BBC RADIO HUMBERSIDE　　　T 01482 323232
Contact: Simon Pattern (Managing Editor)
Queens Court, Queens Gardens
Hull HU1 3RH
F 01482 226409
E radio.humberside@bbc.co.uk
W www.bbc.co.uk/humberside

BBC RADIO JERSEY　　　T 01534 870000
Contact: Jon Gripton (Editor), Matthew Price (Assistant Editor)
18 & 21 Parade Road, St Helier
Jersey JE2 3PL
F 01534 732569
E radiojersey@bbc.co.uk
W www.bbc.co.uk/jersey

BBC RADIO KENT　　　T 01892 670000
Contact: Gordon Davidson (Managing Editor)
The Great Hall
Mount Pleasant Road
Tunbridge Wells, Kent TN1 1QQ
E radio.kent@bbc.co.uk
W www.bbc.co.uk/kent

BBC RADIO LANCASHIRE　　　T 01254 262411
Contact: John Clayton (Editor)
20-26 Darwen Street, Blackburn
Lancashire BB2 2EA
E radio.lancashire@bbc.co.uk
W www.bbc.co.uk/lancashire

BBC RADIO LEEDS　　　T 0113 224 7300
Contact: Rozina Breen (Managing Editor)
BBC Yorkshire, 2 St Peter's Square
Leeds LS9 8AH
F 0113 224 7316
E radioleeds@bbc.co.uk
W www.bbc.co.uk/leeds

BBC RADIO LEICESTER　　　T 0116 251 6688
Contact: Jane Hill (Managing Editor)
9 St Nicholas Place
Leicester LE1 5LB
F 0116 251 1463
E radio.leicesternews@bbc.co.uk
W www.bbc.co.uk/radioleicester

BBC RADIO LINCOLNSHIRE　　　T 01522 511411
Contact: Charlie Partridge (Managing Editor)
Newport, Lincoln LN1 3XY
F 01522 511058
E radio.lincolnshire@bbc.co.uk
W www.bbc.co.uk/lincolnshire

BBC LONDON 94.9 FM　　　T 020 7224 2000 (Live Studio)
Contact: David Robey (Managing Editor)
Egton House, Portland Place
London W1A 1AA
T 020 8743 8000 (Switchboard)
E yourlondon@bbc.co.uk
W www.bbc.co.uk/london

BBC RADIO MANCHESTER   **T** 0161 335 6000
Contact: John Ryan (Managing Editor)
MediaCityUK
Salford M50 2EQ
W www.bbc.co.uk/manchester

BBC RADIO MERSEYSIDE   **T** 0151 708 5500
Contact: Sue Owen (Managing Editor)
PO Box 95.8
Liverpool L69 1ZJ
E radio.merseyside@bbc.co.uk
W www.bbc.co.uk/liverpool

BBC NEWCASTLE   **T** 0191 232 4141
Contact: Andrew Robson (Managing Editor)
Broadcasting Centre
Barrack Road
Newcastle upon Tyne NE99 1RN
F 0191 221 0796
E bbcnewcastle.news@bbc.co.uk
W www.bbc.co.uk/tyne

BBC RADIO NORFOLK   **T** 01603 617411
Contact: David Clayton (Managing Editor)
The Forum
Millennium Plain
Norwich NR2 1BH
E norfolk@bbc.co.uk
W www.bbc.co.uk/norfolk

BBC NORTHAMPTON   **T** 01604 239100
Contact: Jess Rudkin (Manager)
Broadcasting House
Abington Street
Northampton NN1 2BH
F 01604 230709
E northampton@bbc.co.uk
W www.bbc.co.uk/northampton

BBC RADIO NOTTINGHAM   **T** 0115 955 0500
Contact: Mike Bettison (Editor)
London Road, Nottingham NG2 4UU
F 0115 902 1984
E radio.nottingham@bbc.co.uk
W www.bbc.co.uk/nottingham

BBC RADIO SHEFFIELD   **T** 0114 267 5440
Contact: Martyn Weston (Managing Editor)
54 Shoreham Street, Sheffield S1 4RS
E radio.sheffield@bbc.co.uk
W www.bbc.co.uk/sheffield

BBC RADIO SHROPSHIRE   **T** 01743 248484
Contact: Tim Beech (Editor), Tim Page (Senior Broadcast Journalist, News)
2-4 Boscobel Drive, Shrewsbury
Shropshire SY1 3TT
F 01743 271702
E radio.shropshire@bbc.co.uk
W www.bbc.co.uk/shropshire

BBC RADIO SOLENT   **T** 023 8063 1311
Contact: Chris Carnegy (Managing Editor)
Broadcasting House
10 Havelock Road
Southampton SO14 7PW
F 023 8033 9648
E radio.solent@bbc.co.uk
W www.bbc.co.uk/solent

BBC RADIO STOKE   **T** 01782 208080
Contact: Gary Andrews (Managing Editor)
Cheapside, Hanley
Stoke-on-Trent
Staffordshire ST1 1JJ
F 01782 289115
E radio.stoke@bbc.co.uk
W www.bbc.co.uk/radiostoke

BBC RADIO SUFFOLK   **T** 01473 250000
Contact: Peter Cook (Editor)
Broadcasting House
St Matthews Street
Ipswich IP1 3EP
F 01473 210887
E radiosuffolk@bbc.co.uk
W www.bbc.co.uk/suffolk

BBC SURREY   **T** 01273 320400
Contact: Sara David (Managing Editor)
Broadcasting Centre
Guildford
Surrey GU2 7AP
F 01483 304952
E sussex@bbc.co.uk
W www.bbc.co.uk/surrey

BBC SUSSEX   **T** 01273 320400
Contact: Sara David (Managing Editor)
40-42 Queen's Road
Brighton BN1 3YB
F 01483 304952
E sussex@bbc.co.uk
W www.bbc.co.uk/sussex

BBC TEES   **T** 01642 225211
Contact: Dan Thorpe (Managing Editor)
Broadcasting House, Newport Road
Middlesbrough TS1 5DG
F 01642 211356
E tees.studios@bbc.co.uk
W www.bbc.co.uk/tees

BBC THREE COUNTIES RADIO   **T** 01582 637400
Contact: Laura Moss (Managing Editor)
1 Hastings Street
Luton LU1 5XL
F 01582 401467
E 3cr@bbc.co.uk
W www.bbc.co.uk/threecounties

BBC WEST MIDLANDS   **T** 0121 567 6767
The Mailbox, Birmingham B1 1FF
E midlandstoday@bbc.co.uk
W www.bbc.co.uk/westmidlands

BBC WILTSHIRE   **T** 01793 513626
Contact: Tony Worgan (Managing Editor)
Broadcasting House, 56-58 Prospect Place
Swindon SN1 3RW
E wiltshire@bbc.co.uk
W www.bbc.co.uk/wiltshire

BBC RADIO YORK   **T** 01904 641351
Contact: Managing Editor
20 Bootham Row, York YO30 7BF
E radio.york@bbc.co.uk
W www.bbc.co.uk/york

ABERDEEN: Northsound Radio   **T** 01224 337000
Abbotswell Road, West Tullos
Aberdeen AB12 3AJ
F 01224 4000003
E news@northsound.co.uk
W www.northsound1.com

AYR: West Sound Radio   **T** 01292 283662
Incorporating West Sound 1035 AM & West 96.7 FM
Radio House
54A Holmston Road
Ayr KA7 3BE
E carolyn.mcallister@westsound.co.uk
W www.westsound.co.uk

BELFAST:
City Beat 96.7 FM & 102.5 FM   **T** 028 9023 4967
2nd Floor, Arena Building
85 Ormeau Road, Belfast BT7 1SH
F 028 9089 0101
E info@citybeat.co.uk
W www.citybeat.co.uk

BELFAST: Cool FM   **T** 028 9181 7181
Kiltonga Industrial Estate
Newtownards
Co Down BT23 4ES
E info@coolfm.co.uk
W www.coolfm.co.uk

BELFAST: Downtown Radio   **T** 028 9181 5555
Kiltonga Industrial Estate
Newtownards
Co Down BT23 4ES
E info@downtown.co.uk
W www.downtown.co.uk

BIRMINGHAM:
Free Radio 96.4   **T** 0121 566 5200
9 Brindleyplace
4 Oozells Square
Birmingham B1 2DJ
F 0121 566 5239
W www.freeradio.co.uk

BORDERS THE:
Radio Borders   **T** 01896 759444
Tweedside Park
Galashiels TD1 3TD
F 0845 3457080
E info@radioborders.com
W www.radioborders.com

BRADFORD:
Sunrise Radio Yorkshire   **T** 01274 735043
55 Leeds Road
Bradford BD1 5AF
F 01274 728534
E info@sunriseradio.fm
W www.sunriseradio.fm

BRADFORD, HUDDERSFIELD, HALIFAX, KEIGHLEY & DEWSBURY:
Pulse & Pulse 2   **T** 01274 203040
Forster Square, Bradford BD1 5NE
E general@pulse.co.uk
W www.pulse2.net

CAMBRIDGESHIRE & PETERBOROUGH: Heart   **T** 01223 623800
Enterprise House
Vision Park, Chivers Way
Histon, Cambridge CB24 9ZR
E cambridgeshire.news@heart.co.uk
W www.heart.co.uk

CARDIFF & NEWPORT:
Capital FM & Gold FM
W www.capitalfm.com

CHESTER, NORTH WALES & WIRRAL: Heart   **T** 01978 752202
Contact: Paul Holmes (Programme Controller)
The Studios, Mold Road
Wrexham LL11 4AF
E northwestwales.news@heart.co.uk
W www.heart.co.uk

DUMFRIES: West Sound FM   **T** 01387 250999
Unit 40, The Loreburn Centre
High Street
Dumfries DG1 2BD
F 01387 265629
W www.westsoundradio.com

DUNDEE & PERTH:
Radio Tay 2   **T** 01382 200800
6 North Isla Street
Dundee DD3 7JQ
E tayam@radiotay.co.uk
W www.radiotay.co.uk

EAST MIDLANDS:
Capital East Midlands   **T** 0115 873 1500
Incorporating Ram FM, Leicester Sound & Trent FM
Chapel Quarter
Maid Marian Way
Nottingham NG1 6HQ
W www.capitalfm.com

EDINBURGH: Radio Forth   **T** 0131 556 9255
Forth House, Forth Street
Edinburgh EH1 3LE
E info@radioforth.com
W www.radioforth.com

EXETER & TORBAY: Heart   **T** 01392 354200
Hawthorn House
Exeter Business Park
Exeter EX1 3QS
F 01392 354209
W www.heart.co.uk

FALKIRK: Central FM   **T** 01324 611164
The Studio, 9 Munroe Road
Springkerse Industrial Estate
Sterling FK7 7UU
F 01324 611168
W www.centralfm.co.uk

GLASGOW: Radio Clyde Ltd   **T** 0141 565 2200
3 South Avenue
Clydebank Business Park
Glasgow G81 2RX
W www.clyde1.com

GLASGOW: Radio Clyde 2　T 0141 565 2200
3 South Avenue, Clydebank Business Park
Glasgow G81 2RX
W www.clyde2.com

**GLOUCESTER &
CHELTENHAM: Heart 102.4**　T 01452 572400
The Eastgate Shopping Centre
Gloucester GL1 1SS
W www.heart.co.uk/gloucestershire

**GUILDFORD:
96.4 Eagle Radio**　T 01483 300964
Eagle Radio Ltd
Dolphin House, 3 North Street
Guildford, Surrey GU1 4AA
E onair@964eagle.co.uk
W www.964eagle.co.uk

**HEREFORD &
WORCESTER: Free Radio**　T 01905 545500
1st Floor, Kirkham House
John Comyn Drive
Worcester WR3 7NS
W www.freeradio.co.uk

HOME COUNTIES: Heart　T 01604 795600
*Bedford, Beds, Bucks, Herts, Milton Keynes &
Northamptonshire*
4th Floor, CBXII
382-428 Midsummer Boulevard
Milton Keynes MK9 2EA
E fourcounties.news@heart.co.uk
W www.heart.co.uk

**INVERNESS:
Moray Firth Radio**　T 01463 224433
PO Box 271, Scorguie Place
Inverness IV3 8UJ
E mfr@mfr.co.uk
W www.mfr.co.uk

**ISLE OF WIGHT:
Isle of Wight Radio**　T 01983 822557
Dodnor Park, Newport
Isle of Wight PO30 5XE
F 01983 822109
E studio@iwradio.co.uk
W www.iwradio.co.uk

KENT: Heart　T 01227 772004
Radio House
John Wilson Business Park
Whitstable, Kent CT5 3QX
E news.kent@heart.co.uk
W www.heart.co.uk/kent

LIVERPOOL: Radio City　T 0151 472 6800
St John's Beacon
1 Houghton Street
Liverpool L1 1RL
W www.radiocity.co.uk

LONDON: Absolute Radio　T 020 7434 1215
1 Golden Square
London W1F 9DJ
W www.absoluteradio.co.uk

**LONDON: Capital, Heart, Smooth,
Classic FM, LBC, XFM, Gold**　T 020 7766 6000
Global Radio
30 Leicester Square
London WC2H 7LA
W www.thisisglobal.com

**LONDON:
Independent Radio News**　T 020 7182 8591
Mappin House
4 Winsley Street
London W1W 8HF
E irn@bskyb.com
W www.irn.co.uk

**LONDON:
London Greek Radio**　T 020 8349 6950
437 High Road
Finchley
London N12 0AP
E info@lgr.co.uk
W www.lgr.co.uk

LONDON: Magic 105.4 FM　T 020 7182 8233
Mappin House
4 Winsley Street
London W1W 8HF
W www.magic.co.uk

LONDON: Smooth Radio　T 0161 886 8800
26-27 Castlereagh Street
London W1H 5DL
E info@smoothradio.co.uk
W www.smoothradio.co.uk

**MANCHESTER:
Key 103 FM & Magic 1152**　T 0161 288 5000
Piccadilly Radio Ltd
Castle Quay
Castle Field
Manchester M15 4PR
F 0161 288 5151
W www.key103.co.uk

**MANCHESTER:
Wythenshawe FM**　T 0161 499 7982
Forum Learning Room G24
Forum Centre, Forum Square
Wythenshawe
Manchester M22 5RX
E jk@wfmradio.org
W www.wfmradio.org

**NORFOLK & SUFFOLK:
Heart FM**　T 01603 630621
St Georges Plain
47-49 Colegate
Norwich NR3 1DB
W www.heart.co.uk

**NORTHAMPTONSHIRE:
Connect FM 97.2, 106.8 FM
107.4 FM & DAB**　T 01536 513664
55 Headlands
Kettering
Northampton NN15 7EU
W www.connectfm.com

OXFORD & BANBURY: Heart T 01865 871000
The Chase, Calcot, Reading RG31 7RB
W www.heart.co.uk

PLYMOUTH & DEVON:
Heart South West T 01752 275600
Hawthorn House, Exeter Business Park EX1 3QS
W www.heart.co.uk

PORTSMOUTH & SOUTHAMPTON:
Capital South Coast T 01489 589911
Global Radio
Radio House, Whittle Avenue, Segensworth West
Fareham, Hampshire PO15 5SX
W www.capitalfm.com

PORTSMOUTH &
SOUTHAMPTON: Heart T 01489 589911
Global Radio
Radio House, Whittle Avenue, Segensworth West
Fareham, Hampshire PO15 5SX
W www.heart.co.uk

SOUTH MANCHESTER &
CHESHIRE: Imagine 104.9 FM T 0161 476 7340
Waterloo Place, Watson Square
Stockport, Cheshire SK1 3AZ
E studio@imaginefm.net
W www.imaginefm.net

STOKE-ON-TRENT &
STAFFORD: Signal Radio T 01782 441300
Stoke Road, Stoke-on-Trent, Staffordshire ST4 2SR
E info@signalradio.com
W www.signal1.co.uk

SUSSEX: Heart T 01273 430111
Radio House, Franklin Road
Portslade, East Sussex BN41 1AS
F 01273 316909
W www.heart.co.uk

SWANSEA: The Wave 96.4 FM T 01792 511964
Victoria Road, Gowerton, Swansea SA4 3AB
W www.thewave.co.uk

TEESSIDE: TFM Radio T 01642 888222
55 Degrees North, Pilgrim Street, Newcastle NE1 6BF
W www.tfmradio.com

TEESSIDE: TFM 2 T 01642 888222
55 Degrees North, Pilgrim Street, Newcastle NE1 6BF
W www.tfm2.co.uk

THAMES VALLEY: Heart T 0118 945 4400
The Chase, Calcot, Reading RG31 7RB
E thamesvalley.news@heart.co.uk
W www.heart.co.uk

TYNE & WEAR, NORTHUMBERLAND
& DURHAM: Metro Radio T 0191 230 6100
55 Degrees North, Pilgrim Street
Newcastle upon Tyne NE1 6BF
W www.metroradio.co.uk

TYNE & WEAR, NORTHUMBERLAND &
DURHAM: Metro 2 T 0191 230 6100
55 Degrees North, Pilgrim Street
Newcastle upon Tyne NE1 6BF
W www.metro2.co.uk

WEST COUNTRY: Heart T 0117 984 3200
1 Passage Street, Bristol BS2 0JF
F 0117 984 3229
W www.heart.co.uk

WOLVERHAMPTON & BLACK COUNTRY /
SHREWSBURY & TELFORD:
Free Radio T 0121-566 5200
9 Brindley Place, 4 Oozells Square, Birmingham B1 2DJ
W www.freeradio.co.uk

YORKSHIRE: Hallam FM, Hallam 2,
Hallam 3 T 0114 209 1000
Radio House, 900 Herries Road
Hillsborough, Sheffield S6 1RH
W www.hallamfm.co.uk

YORKSHIRE: Seaside Radio T 07583 100370
Community Radio for Southern Holderness
Shores Centre, 29-31 Seaside Road
Withernsea, East Yorkshire HU19 2DL
E justin@seasideradio.co.uk
W www.seasideradio.co.uk

YORKSHIRE & LINCOLNSHIRE:
Viking 96.9 FM & Viking 2 T 01482 325141
Commercial Road, Hull HU1 2SG
W www.vikingfm.co.uk

Rehearsal Rooms & Casting Suites

How should I prepare for an audition?

When you are called to a casting you should make sure you are fully prepared with accurate information about the audition time, venue and format. Research the casting director too: look on his/her website and pay attention to media news. What productions have they worked on previously? What do they seem to look for and expect from the actors they cast?

For most auditions you will be given a script to learn, but you could be provided with a brief in advance and asked to find something suitable yourself. It would be advisable to have about five or six pieces ready to choose from that demonstrate your range before you are even called to a casting. You should select two relevant but contrasting pieces of about two to three minutes each for your audition, with the others as backups. If you can, read the whole play in addition to your speech.

It is generally best not to use 'popular' or very well-known pieces and instead to use original modern speeches, as this prevents the likelihood of the casting director comparing you, perhaps unfavourably, with anyone else. Having said this, however, you should still rehearse at least one Shakespeare piece. To find suitable speeches you should read widely for inspiration, or you could search online. If you are still struggling, think about who your favourite playwrights are and find out if they have written anything that is not too well-known.

What should I expect when I arrive at the audition?

Arrive early for your audition, but be prepared to wait! Time slots are allocated but auditions can overrun for various reasons. Be presentable and think about how your character might choose to dress, but overall you will feel more comfortable and confident if you don't differ too much from what you would normally wear. Don't come in costume unless specifically asked.

When you enter the audition room, you may have just the casting director in the room, or you could be confronted with a panel including the director and/or producer, and an editor and cameraman if you are being filmed. Don't let this disconcert you.

Nerves are to be expected, but try to be positive and enjoy yourself. Remember, the casting director doesn't want to spend several days auditioning – they want you to get the job!

Take a few moments to work out where you should stand and where everything is. Don't ask too many questions as this can be irritating but you could ask whether to address your monologue to the casting director/camera, or whether to speak into the 'middle distance'. Make sure that your face, and in particular your eyes, can be seen as much as possible.

Once you have performed your monologue, pause and wait for the casting director to speak to you. Don't ask if they want to see a second speech. If they want another one, and if there's time, they will ask you. You may be asked your opinion on the speech so be prepared with possible answers. Never criticise previous productions you have worked on. At the end of the casting, remember to take your script away unless you are asked to leave it, otherwise it can look as if you're not interested.

Auditions are never a waste of time, even if you don't get the part. You may have performed well but you might not have been quite right for that particular role. Every audition is great practice and experience, and the casting director may very well keep you in mind for future productions.

Should I attend a casting in a house or flat?

Professional auditions are rarely held anywhere other than an official casting studio or venue. Be very wary if you are asked to go elsewhere. Trust your instincts. If something doesn't seem right to you, it probably isn't. Always take someone with you if you are in any doubt.

Rehearsal Spaces for hire

Two new, purpose built studios for hire just 15 minutes by tube from the West End. Suitable for dance, musicals, large scale rehearsals, meetings or intimate one on one work.

For full details visit our website:
www.losttheatre.co.uk
or call us on 020 7622 9208

Tube: Stockwell (Victoria & Northern Lines)
Vauxhall (Northern & Overground lines)

3 MILLS STUDIOS　　　T 020 7363 3336
Three Mill Lane
London E3 3DU
F 0871 5944028
E info@3mills.com
W www.3mills.com

ABACUS ARTS　　　T 020 7277 2880
2A Browning Street
Southwark
London SE17 1LN
E info@abacus-arts.org.uk
W www.abacus-arts.org.uk

ACTING SUITE LTD　　　T 020 7462 0792
Fully Equipped Film, Television, Commercial & Theatrical Casting & Rehearsal Studios
17 Percy Street
London W1T 1DU
E jimmy@actingsuite.com
W www.actingsuite.com

**ACTORS CENTRE
(LONDON) THE**　　　T 020 7632 8012
Auditioning. Casting. Rehearsals. Room Hire
1A Tower Street
London WC2H 9NP
T 020 7240 3940
E operations@actorscentre.co.uk
W www.actorscentre.co.uk

ACTOR'S TEMPLE THE　　　T 020 3004 4537
Basement, 13-14 Warren Street
London W1T 5LG
E bookings@actorstemple.com
W www.actorstemple.com

ALBANY THE　　　T 020 8692 0231
Douglas Way
Deptford
London SE8 4AG
F 020 8469 2253
E hires@thealbany.org.uk
W www.thealbany.org.uk

ALFORD HOUSE　　　T 020 7735 1519
Aveline Street
London SE11 5DQ
E tim@alfordhouse.org.uk
W www.alfordhouse.org.uk

ALLSTARS CASTING　　　T 0151 707 2100
66 Hope Street, Liverpool L1 9BZ
T 07739 359737
E sylvie@allstarscasting.co.uk
W www.allstarscasting.co.uk

**ALRA (ACADEMY OF LIVE
& RECORDED ARTS)**　　　T 020 8870 6475
The Royal Victoria Patriotic Building
John Archer Way
London SW18 3SX
E lynn.howes@alra.co.uk
W www.alra.co.uk

**AMERICAN INTERNATIONAL
CHURCH**　　　T 020 7580 2791
Contact: Monty Strikes
Whitefield Memorial Church
79A Tottenham Court Road
London W1T 4TD
F 020 7580 5013
E latchcourt@amchurch.co.uk
W www.latchcourt.com

ARCH 468 THEATRE STUDIO　　　T 07973 302908
Arch 468, 209A Coldharbour Lane
London SW9 8RU
E rebecca@arch468.com
W www.arch468.com

ARTSADMIN　　　T 020 7247 5102
Toynbee Studios, 28 Commercial Street
London E1 6AB
F 020 7247 5103
E admin@artsadmin.co.uk
W www.artsadmin.co.uk

AVIV DANCE STUDIOS　　　T/F 01923 250000
Watford Boys Grammar School
Rickmansworth Road
Watford WD18 7JF
E info@avivdance.com
W www.avivdance.com

**BATTERSEA ARTS
CENTRE (BAC)**　　　T 020 7326 8211
Lavender Hill, London SW11 5TN
F 020 7978 5207
E venues@bac.org.uk
W www.bac.org.uk/hires

BIG ACT THE　　　　　**T** 0117 2391274
14-16 Wilson Place
Bristol BS2 9HJ
E info@thebigact.com
W www.thebigact.com

BLOOMSBURY SPACE　　　**T** 020 7534 1740
Contact: Marion Vivien
The Undercroft of St George's Church
Bloomsbury Way
London WC1A 2PX
E rehearsalrooms@leicestersquaretheatre.com
W www.leicestersquaretheatre.com

**BREAK A LEG
MANAGEMENT LTD**　　**T/F** 020 7250 0662
The City College, University House, Room 33
55 East Road, London N1 6AH
E agency@breakalegman.com
W www.breakalegman.com

**BRIDGE THEATRE
TRAINING COMPANY THE**　　**T** 020 7424 0860
Various Large Studios & Meeting Rooms
90 Kingsway, Tally Ho Corner
North Finchley, London N12 0EX
E admin@thebridge-ttc.org　　**W** www.thebridge-ttc.org

Photo: David Andrew

17 Stukeley Street, Covent Garden
London, WC2B 5LT

020 7404 7274
bookings@dragonhall.org.uk
www.dragonhall.org.uk

Questors, Ealing's Playhouse

Rehearsal Rooms

For Hire **Daytimes** Monday – Friday
- Shaw Room 12m x 8.5m
- Emmet Room 11m × 9m *(sprung floor)*
- Redgrave Room 11m x 8.5m
- Piano available by arrangement
- See photos at ealingtheatre.com

Additional Facilities: On-Site Car Park, Café, Break-Out Spaces

Quiet and attractive location, opposite park with shopping centre nearby.
8 mins' walk from Ealing Broadway Tube and mainline station (District and Central lines).

The Questors Theatre

12 Mattock Lane, London W5 5BQ
020 8567 0011
enquiries@questors.org.uk

ealingtheatre.com

Registered Charity 207516

BRIXTON COMMUNITY BASE T 020 7326 4417
Formerly Brixton St Vincent's Community Centre
Talma Road, London SW2 1AS
T 07958 448690
E info@brixtoncommunitybase.org
W www.brixtoncommunitybase.org

**CALDER THEATRE
BOOKSHOP LTD THE** T 020 7620 2900
*Central London Rehearsal Space, Fringe Venue &
Theatre Bookshop*
51 The Cut, London SE1 8LF
E info@calderbookshop.com
W www.calderbookshop.com

CAROUSEL SPACES T 020 7487 5564
71 Blandford Street, Marylebone
London W1U 8AB
E nici@carousel-london.com
W www.carousel-london.com/hire.html#services

CASTING CABIN LTD THE T 020 7812 1399
Panther House, Unit 4, East Block
38 Mount Pleasant
Holborn, London WC1X 0AN
T 07767 445640
E thecastingcabin@gmail.com
W www.thecastingcabin.com

CASTING SUITE T 020 7427 5681
ROAR House, 46 Charlotte Street
London W1T 2GS
E info@castingsuite.net

CECIL SHARP HOUSE T 020 7241 8954
2 Regent's Park Road
London NW1 7AY
F 020 7284 0534
E hire@efdss.org
W www.cecilsharphouse.org

**CENTRAL LONDON
GOLF CENTRE** T 020 8871 2468
Burntwood Lane
London SW17 0AT
F 020 8874 7447
E info@clgc.co.uk
W www.clgc.co.uk

CENTRAL STUDIOS T 020 8698 8880
470 Bromley Road
Bromley, Kent BR1 4PQ
E info@dandbperformingarts.co.uk
W www.dandbperformingarts.co.uk

CHARING CROSS THEATRE T 020 7930 5868
Formerly New Players Theatre
The Arches
Off Villiers Street
London WC2N 6NL
E info@charingcrosstheatre.co.uk
W www.charingcrosstheatre.co.uk

CHATS PALACE T 020 8533 0227
42-44 Brooksby's Walk, Hackney
London E9 6DF
E info@chatspalace.com
W www.chatspalace.co.uk

CHELSEA THEATRE T 020 7349 7811
Contact: Francis Alexander
World's End Place, King's Road
London SW10 0DR
T 020 7352 1967
E admin@chelseatheatre.org.uk
W www.chelseatheatre.org.uk

CLUB FOR ACTS & ACTORS   T 020 7836 3172
Incorporating Concert Artistes Association
20 Bedford Street, London WC2E 9HP
E office@thecaa.org
W www.thecaa.co.uk

COLOMBO CENTRE THE   T 020 7261 1658
Audition & Rehearsal Space
34-68 Colombo Street, London SE1 8DP
E colombodm@jubileehalltrust.org
W www.colombo-centre.org

**COPTIC STREET
STUDIO LTD**   T 020 7636 2030
9 Coptic Street
London WC1A 1NH
E studio@copticstreet.com

**COVENT GARDEN
DRAGON HALL TRUST**   T 020 7404 7274
17 Stukeley Street, London WC2B 5LT
E bookings@dragonhall.org.uk
W www.dragonhall.org.uk

**CREATIVE KIDZ &
ADULTZ AGENCY**   T 07908 144802
Contact: Dani & Charlie
235 Foxglove House, Fulham Road
London SW6 5PQ
E agency@creativekidzandco.co.uk
W www.creativekidzandco.co.uk

CUSTARD FACTORY   T 0121 224 7777
Gibb Street, Digbeth
Birmingham B9 4AA
E info@custardfactory.co.uk
W www.custardfactory.co.uk

DANCE ATTIC STUDIOS   T 020 7610 2055
368 North End Road, Fulham
London SW6 1LY
E danceattic@hotmail.com
W www.danceattic.com

DANCE COMPANY STUDIOS   T 020 8402 2424
76 High Street
Beckenham BR3 1ED
E hire@dancecompanystudios.co.uk
W www.dancecompanystudios.co.uk

**DANCE STUDIO
LEEDS LTD THE**   T 0113 242 1550
Mill 6, 1st Floor, Mabgate Mills
Leeds, West Yorkshire LS9 7DZ
E katie@thedancestudioleeds.com
W www.thedancestudioleeds.com

DANCEWORKS   T 020 7318 4100
16 Balderton Street, London W1K 5TN
E info@danceworks.net
W www.danceworks.net

DAVIES, Siobhan STUDIOS   T 020 7091 9650
Rehearsal Studios, Meeting Rooms & Events Hires
85 St George's Road
London SE1 6ER
F 020 7091 9669
E info@siobhandavies.com
W www.siobhandavies.com

DIE-CAST STUDIOS   T 020 7494 4630
39A Berwick Street, Soho
London W1F 8RU
E studio@diecaststudios.co.uk
W www.diecaststudios.co.uk

DIORAMA ARTS STUDIOS   T 020 7383 0727
201 Drummond Street
Regents Place
London NW1 3FE
E info@diorama-arts.org.uk
W www.diorama-arts.org.uk

EALING STUDIOS   T 020 8567 6655
Ealing Green, London W5 5EP
F 020 8758 8658
E bookings@ealingstudios.com
W www.ealingstudios.com

**EASTSIDE EDUCATIONAL
TRUST**   T 020 7033 2380
Suite 16 Perseverance Works
37 Hackney Road
Shoreditch, London E2 7NX
E ktozer@eastside.org.uk
W www.eastside.org.uk

**ELMS LESTERS
PAINTING ROOMS**   T 020 7836 6747
1-3-5 Flitcroft Street, London WC2H 8DH
F 020 7379 0789
E info@elmslesters.co.uk
W www.elmslesters.co.uk

**ENGLISH FOLK DANCE
& SONG SOCIETY**   T 020 7485 2206
Cecil Sharp House, 2 Regent's Park Road
London NW1 7AY
F 020 7284 0534
E hire@efdss.org
W www.efdss.org

ENGLISH NATIONAL OPERA   T 020 7836 0111
Lilian Baylis House
165 Broadhurst Gardens
London NW6 3AX
E receptionlbh@eno.org
W www.eno.org

ENGLISH TOURING THEATRE   T 020 7450 1990
25 Short Street, Waterloo
London SE1 8LJ
E admin@ett.org.uk
W www.ett.org.uk

ETCETERA THEATRE   T 020 7482 4857
(Above the Oxford Arms)
265 Camden High Street
London NW1 7BU
E admin@etceteratheatre.com
W www.etceteratheatre.com

**EUROKIDS & EKA
CASTING STUDIOS**   T 01925 761083
Contact: Jodie Keith (Senior Casting Agent)
The Warehouse Studios, Glaziers Lane
Culcheth, Warrington, Cheshire WA3 4AQ
T 01925 761210
E jodie@eka-agency.com
W www.eka-agency.com

EXCHANGE THE   T 01258 475137
Old Market Hill, Sturminster Newton DT10 1FH
E info@stur-exchange.co.uk
W www.stur-exchange.co.uk

**FACTORY FITNESS &
DANCE CENTRE THE**   T 020 7272 1122
407 Hornsey Road, London N19 4DX
E info@factorylondon.com
W www.factorylondon.com

FSU LONDON STUDY CENTRE   T 020 7813 3223
99 Great Russell Street, London WC1B 3LH
F 020 7813 3270

GLASSHILL STUDIOS   T 020 7620 2141
Contact: Lori Ford
Kings Bench Street, London SE1 0QX
E lori@glasshillstudios.com
W www.glasshillstudios.com

**GRAEAE THEATRE
COMPANY**   T 020 7613 6900
Bradbury Studios
138 Kingsland Road
London E2 8DY
E info@graeae.org
W www.graeae.org

GROUNDLINGS THEATRE   T 023 9273 9496
42 Kent Street, Portsmouth
Hampshire PO1 3BS
E richard@groundlings.co.uk
W www.groundlings.co.uk

HAMPSTEAD THEATRE   T 020 7449 4200
Eton Avenue, Swiss Cottage
London NW3 3EU
F 020 7449 4201
E info@hampsteadtheatre.com
W www.hampsteadtheatre.com

HANGAR ARTS TRUST   T 020 3004 6173
Unit 7A, Mellish House
Harrington Way, London SE18 5NR
E info@hangarartstrust.org

JERWOOD SPACE

Excellent Central London Rehearsal Facilities for Theatre, Dance, Film & TV

- Magnificent Rooftop Studio (16.3m x 15.6m)
- 6 x Spaces (2 x 50 sq.m/2 x 108 sq.m/2 x 155 sq.m)
- 2 x Business Meeting Rooms with City views
- Production Offices + phones/wifi/photocopying
- Sprung floors/Lighting rig/Pianos/Mirrors/Audio
- Air-conditioned/Showers/Café 171/Gallery/Green Room
- Open 9am-9pm weekdays & 10am-6pm weekends
- Car parking (by arrangement)/security card access
- Fully accessible convenient Bankside location nr Southwark tube (Jubilee Line)/Borough/London Bridge/Waterloo

Call 020 7654 0171/fax 0172 **E-mail** space@jerwoodspace.co.uk **Visit** www.jerwoodspace.co.uk for rates & details
JERWOOD SPACE   171 UNION STREET   LONDON SE1 0LN   excellent facilities for the work of art

HEYTHROP COLLEGE   T 020 7795 6600
University of London, 23 Kensington Square
London W8 5HN
E conferences@heythrop.ac.uk
W www.heythrop.ac.uk

**HOLLY LODGE
COMMUNITY CENTRE**   T 020 8342 9524
Hall for Hire for Weekdays, Evenings & Weekends
30 Makepeace Avenue, London N6 6HL
E hollylodgelondon@hotmail.com
W www.hlcchl.org

HOLY INNOCENTS CHURCH   T 020 8748 2286
Paddenswick Road, London W6 0UB
E bookings@hisj.co.uk
W www.hisj.co.uk

HOLY TRINITY W6   T 020 7603 3832
Holy Trinity Parish Centre, 41 Brook Green
London W6 7BL
E brookgreen@rcdow.org.uk
W www.trinityfocus.org

HOPE STREET LTD   T 0151 708 8007
13A Hope Street, Liverpool L1 9BQ
E sarah@hope-street.org
W www.hope-street.org

**HOXTON HALL THEATRE &
YOUTH ARTS CENTRE**   T 020 7684 0060
130 Hoxton Street, London N1 6SH
E info@hoxtonhall.co.uk
W www.hoxtonhall.co.uk

IMT GALLERY   T 020 8980 5475
Unit 2, 210 Cambridge Heath Road
London E2 9NQ
E mail@imagemusictext.com
W www.imagemusictext.com

INVISIBLE DOT LTD THE   T 020 7424 8918
2 Northdown Street, London N1 9BG
E hire@theinvisibledot.com
W www.theinvisibledot.com

ISLINGTON ARTS FACTORY   T 020 7607 0561
2 Parkhurst Road, London N7 0SF
E info@islingtonartsfactory.org
W www.islingtonartsfactory.org

ISTD DANCE STUDIOS   T 020 7655 8801
346 Old Street, London EC1V 9NQ
E reception.istd2@istd.org
W www.istd.org

JACKSONS LANE   T 020 8340 5226
*Various Spaces including Rehearsal Rooms &
Theatre Hire*
269A Archway Road
London N6 5AA
E admin@jacksonslane.org.uk
W www.jacksonslane.org.uk

JAM THEATRE STUDIOS   T 01628 483808
Air-conditioned Studios
Archway Court
45A West Street
Marlow, Buckinghamshire SL7 2LS
E office@jamtheatre.co.uk
W www.jamtheatre.co.uk

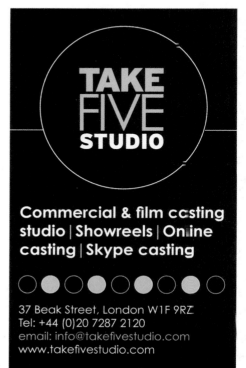

JERWOOD SPACE　　T 020 7654 0171
171 Union Street, London SE1 0LN
F 020 7654 0172
E space@jerwoodspace.co.uk
W www.jerwoodspace.co.uk

LARCA STUDIOS　　T 07779 321954
Studio Space with Adjustable Lighting. 7M x 4M
59 Mount Stuart Square, Cardiff
South Glamorgan CF10 5LR
E lizlarca@gmail.com
W www.larca.co.uk

**LEICESTER SQUARE
THEATRE REHEARSAL SPACE**　　T 020 7534 1740
Contact: Marion Vivien
6 Leicester Place
London WC1H 7BX
E rehearsalrooms@leicestersquaretheatre.com
W www.leicestersquaretheatre.com

LIVE THEATRE　　T 0191 261 2694
Broad Chare, Quayside
Newcastle upon Tyne NE1 3DQ
E info@live.org.uk
W www.live.org.uk

**LONDON BUBBLE
THEATRE COMPANY LTD**　　T 020 7237 4434
5 Elephant Lane, London SE16 4JD
E admin@londonbubble.org.uk
W www.londonbubble.org.uk

**LONDON SCHOOL
OF CAPOEIRA**　　T 020 7281 2020
Units 1 & 2 Leeds Place
Tollington Park
London N4 3RF
E studiohire@londonschoolofcapoeira.com
W www.londonschoolofcapoeira.com

LONDON THEATRE THE　　T 020 8694 1888
Lower Space, 443 New Cross Road
New Cross, London SE14 6TA
E thelondontheatre@live.co.uk
W www.thelondontheatre.com

LONDON WELSH CENTRE　　T 020 7837 3722
157-163 Gray's Inn Road
London WC1X 8UE
E roomhire@lwcentre.demon.co.uk
W www.londonwelsh.org

LS-LIVE　　T 01977 659888
Arena-sized Studio
Unit 53, Langthwaite Business Park
Lidgate Crescent, South Kirkby, Wakefield
West Yorkshire WF9 3NR
E sales@ls-live.com
W www.ls-live.com

LYRIC HAMMERSMITH　　T 020 8741 6850
King Street, London W6 0QL
E hires@lyric.co.uk
W www.lyric.co.uk

MA WORKS LTD　　T 07828 105125
Ground Floor, 6 Bakers Yard
London EC1R 3DD
E emily@modeladvice.info
W www.maworks.co.uk

**MACKINTOSH, Cameron
REHEARSAL STUDIO**　　T 020 7372 6611
The Tricycle, 269 Kilburn High Road
London NW6 7JR
F 020 7328 0795
E admin@tricycle.co.uk
W www.tricycle.co.uk

MAKEBELIEVE ARTS　　T 020 8691 3803
3 Spaces Available for Hire
The Deptford Mission, 1 Creek Road
London SE8 3BT
E info@makebelievearts.co.uk
W www.makebelievearts.co.uk

**MENIER CHOCOLATE
FACTORY**　　T 020 7378 1712
53 Southwark Street
London SE1 1RU
F 020 7234 0447
E office@menierchocolatefactory.com
W www.menierchocolatefactory.com

**MOBERLY SPORTS &
EDUCATION CENTRE**　　T 020 7641 4807
101 Kilburn Lane, Kensal Rise
London W10 4AH
E moberly@enquiries@gll.org

MOVING EAST STUDIO　　T 020 7503 3101
Harlequin Sprung Floor. Quadrophonic Sound System
St Matthias Church Hall
Wordsworth Road
London N16 8DD
E admin@movingeast.co.uk
W www.movingeast.co.uk

**NATIONAL YOUTH THEATRE
OF GREAT BRITAIN**　　T 020 7561 8661
Holloway Road Rehearsal Rooms
443-445 Holloway Road
London N7 6LW
E info@nyt.org.uk
W www.nyt.org.uk

**NEALS YARD
MEETING ROOMS**　　T/F 020 7436 9875
14 Neals Yard, Covent Garden
London WC2H 9DP
E info@walkinbackrub.co.uk
W www.meetingrooms.org.uk

NLPAC PERFORMING ARTS　　T 020 8444 4544
*Studio Hire, Casting & Production Office Facilities.
Performing Arts School*
76 St James Lane, Muswell Hill
London N10 3RD
E info@nlpac.co.uk
W www.nlpac.co.uk

**OBSERVATORY
STUDIOS THE**   T 020 7437 2823
45-46 Poland Street, London W1F 7NA
F 020 7437 2830
E info@theobservatorystudios.com
W www.theobservatorystudios.com

OCTOBER GALLERY   T 020 7831 1618
24 Old Gloucester Street, London WC1N 3AL
F 020 7405 1851
E events@octobergallery.co.uk
W www.octobergallery.co.uk

OLD VIC THEATRE THE   T 020 7928 2651
The Cut, London SE1 8NB
E hires@oldvictheatre.com
W www.oldvictheatre.com

OMNIBUS   T 020 7498 4699
1 Clapham Common North Side, London SW4 0QW
E hires@omnibus-clapham.org
W www.omnibus-clapham.org

ONLY CONNECT UK   T 0845 3707990
32 Cubitt Street, London WC1X 0LR
T 020 7278 8939
E info@oclondon.org
W www.onlyconnect.london

**OPEN DOOR
COMMUNITY CENTRE**   T/F 020 8871 8172
Beaumont Road
Wimbledon, London SW19 6TF
E publichalls@wandsworth.gov.uk
W www.wandsworth.gov.uk

Raindance Film Centre Rehearsal Rooms

10 Craven Street, Charing Cross, WC2N 5PE

Room 1 6.1m x 7.3m   **Room 2** 6.2m x 9.1m
Central Location | Free WiFi | Tea and Coffee Facilities | Piano
Perfect for castings, rehearsals and workshops.

T 020 7930 3412   **W** www.raindance.org/room-hire   **E** roombookings@raindance.co.uk

OUT OF JOINT   **T** 020 7609 0207
7 Thane Works, Thane Villas
London N7 7NU
E ojo@outofjoint.co.uk
W www.outofjoint.co.uk

OVALHOUSE   **T** 020 7582 0080
52-54 Kennington Oval, London SE11 5SW
E hire@ovalhouse.com
W www.ovalhouse.com/hire

PAINES PLOUGH REHEARSAL
& AUDITION SPACE   **T** 020 7240 4533
4th Floor, 43 Aldwych
London WC2B 4DN
F 020 7240 4534
E office@painesplough.com
W www.painesplough.com

PARK THEATRE   **T** 020 7167 6628
Morris Space available for Rehearsals
Clifton Terrace, Finsbury Park, London N4 3JP
E hire@parktheatre.co.uk
W www.parktheatre.co.uk

PEREGRINES PIANOS   **T** 020 7242 9865
Auditioning. Casting. Filming. Piano Hire
137A Gray's Inn Road, London WC1X 8TU
E info@peregrines-pianos.com
W www.peregrines-pianos.com

PHA CASTING SUITE   **T** 0161 273 4444
Tanzaro House, Ardwick Green North
Manchester M12 6FZ
F 0161 273 4567
E casting@pha-agency.co.uk
W www.pha-agency.co.uk/castingstudio

PINEAPPLE DANCE STUDIOS   **T** 020 7836 4004
7 Langley Street, Covent Garden
London WC2H 9JA
F 020 7836 0803
W www.pineapple.uk.com

PLACE THE   **T** 020 7121 1000
17 Duke's Road, London WC1H 9PY
F 020 7121 1142
E info@theplace.org.uk
W www.theplace.org.uk

PLAYGROUND STUDIO THE   **T/F** 020 8960 0110
Unit 8, Latimer Road, London W10 6RQ
E info@the-playground.co.uk
W www.the-playground.co.uk

POOR SCHOOL THE   **T** 020 7837 6030
242 Pentonville Road, London N1 9JY
E roomhire@thepoorschool.com
W www.thepoorschool.com

PRETZEL FILMS   **T** 020 7580 9595
2 Bermondsey Exchange
179-181 Bermondsey Street, London SE1 3UW
E info@pretzelfilms.com
W www.pretzelfilms.com

PRICE STUDIOS   **T** 020 7228 6862
110 York Road, London SW11 3RD
E info@pricestudios.co.uk
W www.pricestudios.co.uk

QUESTORS THEATRE
EALING THE   **T** 020 8567 0011
12 Mattock Lane, London W5 5BQ
E enquiries@questors.org.uk
W www.questors.org.uk

RAG FACTORY THE   **T** 020 7183 3048
16-18 Heneage Street, London E1 5LJ
E hello@ragfactory.org.uk
W www.ragfactory.org.uk

RAINDANCE FILM CENTRE
REHEARSAL ROOMS   **T** 020 7930 3412
10 Craven Street, London WC2N 5PE
E roombookings@raindance.co.uk
W www.raindance.org/london/roomhire

RAMBERT   **T** 020 8630 0600
99 Upper Ground, London SE1 9PP
F 020 8747 8323
E info@rambert.org.uk
W www.rambert.org.uk

REALLY USEFUL
THEATRES GROUP LTD   **T** 020 7379 4981
Contact: Jessica Nowell
65 Drury Lane, London WC2B 5SP
E jessica.nowell@reallyuseful.co.uk
W www.reallyusefultheatres.co.uk

RED HEDGEHOG THE   **T** 07817 109093
2 Spaces available for ad hoc Rehearsal Hire
255-257 Archway Road, Highgate, London N6 5BS
E clare.f@theredhedgehog.co.uk
W www.redhedgehog.co.uk

RIDGEWAY STUDIOS   **T** 01992 633775
Office: 106 Hawkshead Road, Potters Bar
Herts EN6 1NG
E info@ridgewaystudios.co.uk

RITZ STUDIOS   **T** 020 8870 1335
Provides Rehearsals/Backline & Sound Hire for
Musicians
The Courtyard, Esmond Street, Putney SW15 2LP
E lee@ritzstudios.com
W www.ritzstudios.com

ROCHELLE SCHOOL   **T** 020 7033 3539
Gallery. Conferences. Events. Venue Hire
Arnold Circus, London E2 7ES
E info@rochelleschool.org
W www.rochelleschool.org

ROOFTOP STUDIO THEATRE   **T** 01785 761233
Rooftop Studio, High Street Arcade
Stone, Staffordshire ST15 8AU
F 01785 818176
E laura@pssa.co.uk
W www.rooftopstudios.co.uk

SPOTLIGHT

The home of casting

Spotlight Rooms & Studios

Hold your auditions in the heart of central London

Spotlight Database & Website

Browse over 60,000 performers' CVs with photos, showreels, voicereels and contact details

Use Spotlight's award-winning search engine to find exactly the right performer for the part

E-mail casting calls to hundreds of UK agents and performers

www.spotlight.com/spaces
020 7440 5030

www.spotlight.com
020 7437 7631
casting@spotlight.com

REHEARSAL SPACE FOR HIRE KING'S CROSS

Studio 8.6m x 5.0m | **Blue Room** 4.9m x 4.9m

Competitive Rates for Rehearsals, Castings & Meetings

Northdown Street London N1 9BG
100m from King's Cross St Pancras Station

www.theinvisibledot.com   020 7424 8918   hire@theinvisibledot.com

---

ROOMS ABOVE THE   T 020 3503 0038
Westheath Yard, (Beside Davids Deli)
174 Mill Lane, West Hampstead
London NW6 1TB
E info@theroomsabove.org.uk
W www.theroomsabove.org.uk

ROOMS AT THE ARTS   T 020 7836 8463
6-7 Great Newport Street
London, WC2H 7JB
E rooms@artstheatrewestend.co.uk
W www.artstheatrewestend.co.uk/hire

ROSE GALLERY   T 020 8546 6983
Rose Theatre, Kingston, 24-26 High Street
Kingston upon Thames, Surrey KT1 1HL
E hireandevents@rosetheatrekingston.org
W www.rosetheatrekingston.org

ROYAL ACADEMY OF DANCE   T 020 7326 8000
36 Battersea Square, London SW11 3RA
F 020 7924 3129
E info@rad.org.uk
W www.rad.org.uk

ROYAL ACADEMY OF DRAMATIC ART   T 020 7908 4822
Including The RADA Studios
62-64 Gower Street, London WC1E 6ED
F 020 7307 5062
E venues@radaenterprises.org
W www.rada.ac.uk/venues

ROYAL SHAKESPEARE COMPANY   T 020 7819 8700
35 Clapham High Street, London SW4 7TW
F 020 7819 8708
W www.rsc.org.uk

RUDEYE STUDIOS   T 020 7014 3023
73 St John Street, Farringdon
London EC1M 4NJ
E info@rudeye.com
W www.rudeye.com

SADLER'S WELLS STUDIOS   T 020 7863 8065
Rosebery Avenue, London EC1R 4TN
E events@sadlerswells.com
W www.sadlerswells.com/venue-hire/studios

SANDS FILM STUDIOS   T 020 7231 2209
82 St Marychurch Street, London SE16 4HZ
F 020 7231 2119
E ostockman@sandsfilms.co.uk
W www.sandsfilms.co.uk

SOHO GYMS   T 020 7482 4524
Camden Town Gym, 193-199 Camden High Street
London NW1 7BT
F 020 7267 0500
E camden@sohogyms.com
W www.sohogyms.com

SOHO GYMS   T 020 7720 0321
Clapham Common Gym
95-97 Clapham High Street
London SW4 7TB
F 020 7720 6510
E clapham@sohogyms.com
W www.sohogyms.com

SOHO GYMS   T 020 7242 1290
Covent Garden Gym, 12 Macklin Street
London WC2B 5NF
F 020 7242 0899
E coventgarden@sohogyms.com
W www.sohogyms.com

SOHO GYMS   T 020 7370 1402
Earl's Court Gym
254 Earl's Court Road
London SW5 9AD
F 020 7244 6893
E earlscourt@sohogyms.com
W www.sohogyms.com

SOHO GYMS   T 020 7261 9798
Waterloo Gym, 11-15 Brad Street
London SE1 8TG
F 020 7928 8623
E waterloo@sohogyms.com
W www.sohogyms.com

SOHO THEATRE   T 020 7287 5060
21 Dean Street, London W1D 3NE
F 020 7287 5061
E hires@sohotheatre.com
W www.sohotheatre.com

SOUTH LONDON DANCE STUDIOS   T 020 7978 8624
130 Herne Hill, London SE24 9QL
E info@southlondondancestudios.co.uk
W www.southlondondancestudios.co.uk

SPACE @ CLARENCE MEWS   T 020 8986 5260
40 Clarence Mews
London E5 8HL
T 07871 190500
E 40cmews@gmail.com
W www.clarencemews.wordpress.com

SPACE ARTS CENTRE THE   T 020 7515 7799
269 Westferry Road, London E14 3RS
E info@space.org.uk
W www.space.org.uk

SPACE CITY STUDIOS   T 020 7371 4000
79 Blythe Road, London W14 0HP
F 020 7371 4001
E info@spacecity.co.uk
W www.spacecitystudios.co.uk

SPOTLIGHT ROOMS   T 020 7440 5030
Casting Studios. Room Hire. Twitter: @SpotlightUK
7 Leicester Place, London WC2H 7RJ
E rooms@spotlight.com
W www.spotlight.com/rooms

SPOTLIGHT STUDIOS   T 020 7440 5030
Casting Studios. Room Hire. Twitter: @SpotlightUK
7 Leicester Place, London WC2H 7RJ
E spaces@spotlight.com
W www.spotlight.com/spaces

ST AGNES CHURCH   T 020 7582 0032
St Agnes Place, Kennington Park
London SE11 4BB
E keith.potter@talk21.com

ST ANDREW'S CHURCH   T 020 7633 9819
*Casting Suites. Meetings. Rehearsal Room. Workshops
& Classes*
Short Street, Southbank
London SE1 8LJ
E bookings@stjohnswaterloo.org
W www.stjohnswaterloo.org

**ST GEORGE'S
CHURCH BLOOMSBURY**   T 020 7242 1979
Vestry Hall, 6 Little Russell Street
London WC1A 2HR
E hiring@stgb.org.uk
W www.stgeorgesbloomsbury.org.uk

**ST JAMES'S CHURCH,
PICCADILLY**   T 020 7292 4861
197 Piccadilly, London W1J 9LL
E roomhire@sjp.org.uk
W www.sjp.org.uk

ST MARTIN-IN-THE-FIELDS   T 020 7766 1130
Trafalgar Square, London WC2N 4JJ
E music@smitf.org
W www.smitf.org

ST MARY ABBOTS CENTRE   T 020 7937 8885
Vicarage Gate, Kensington
London W8 4HN
E adam.norton@stmaryabbotschurch.org
W www.smacentre.co.uk

**ST MARY MAGDALENE
ACADEMY**   T 020 7697 0123
475 Liverpool Road, Islington
London N7 8PG
E alistair.moulton@smmacademy.org
W www.smmacademy.org

STUDIO SOHO   T 020 7437 3175
*Large Air-Conditioned Spaces (1 with Piano) & 1 Smaller
Meeting Room. Wi-Fi. Reception. Kitchen. Changing
Room. Showers. Step-free Access via Stair-lift. HD Video
Recording/Projection Available. Twitter: @gilesForeman1*
Studio Soho, 2A Royalty Mews, (entrance by Quo Vadis)
22-25 Dean Street, London W1D 3AR
E info@gilesforeman.com
W www.gilesforeman.com

SUMMERS, Mark
CASTING STUDIOS   T 020 7229 8413
1 Beaumont Avenue
West Kensington, London W14 9LP
E louise@marksummers.com
W www.marksummers.com

SUMMIT STUDIOS   T 020 8840 2200
2-4 Spring Bridge Mews, Ealing, London W5 2AB
F 020 8840 2446
E info@summitstudios.co.uk
W www.summitstudios.co.uk

TAKE FIVE CASTING STUDIO   T 020 7287 2120
Casting Suite
37 Beak Street, London W1F 9RZ
F 020 7287 3035
E info@takefivestudio.com
W www.takefivestudio.com

THEATRE ALIBI   T/F 01392 217315
Emmanuel Hall, Emmanuel Road, Exeter EX4 1EJ
E info@theatrealibi.co.uk
W www.theatrealibi.co.uk/hire

THEATRE DELICATESSEN   T 020 7278 7694
Contact: Alex Guiney
119 Farringdon Road, London EC1R 3DA
E office@theatredelicatessen.co.uk
W www.theatredelicatessen.co.uk

THEATRE OF DEBATE   T 07534 067241
Flat 19, Battlebridge Court
Wharfdale Road, London N1 9UA
E info@theatreofdebate.co.uk
W www.theatreofdebate.co.uk

THEATRES TRUST THE   T 020 7836 8591
1st Floor Resource Centre with 2 Rooms for Day-time,
Evening & Weekend Hire
22 Charing Cross Road, London WC2H 0QL
E info@theatrestrust.org.uk
W www.theatrestrust.org.uk

THEATRO TECHNIS   T 020 7387 6617
26 Crowndale Road, London NW1 1TT
E info@theatrotechnis.com
W www.theatrotechnis.com

TOOTING & MITCHAM
COMMUNITY SPORTS CLUB   T 020 8685 6193
Imperial Fields, Bishopsford Road
Morden, Surrey SM4 6BF
F 020 8685 6190
E info@tmunited.org
W www.tmunited.org

TREADWELL'S   T 020 7419 8507
33 Store Street, Bloomsbury, London WC1E 7BS
E info@treadwells-london.com
W www.treadwells-london.com/london-shop/room-hire/

TRESTLE ARTS BASE   T 01727 850950
Home of Trestle Theatre Company
Russet Drive, St Albans, Herts AL4 0JQ
E admin@trestle.org.uk
W www.trestle.org.uk

TRICYCLE THE   T 020 7372 6611
269 Kilburn High Road, London NW6 7JR
F 020 7328 0795
E trish@tricycle.co.uk
W www.tricycle.co.uk

TT DANCE STUDIO   T 07904 771980
Parkwood Health & Fitness Centre
Darkes Lane, Potters Bar, Herts EN6 1AA
T 07930 400647
E info@talenttimetheatre.com
W www.talenttimetheatre.com

UNICORN THEATRE   T 020 7645 0500
147 Tooley Street, London SE1 2HZ
E stagedoor@unicorntheatre.com
W www.unicorntheatre.com

UNION CLUB SOHO   T 020 7734 4113
50 Greek Street, London W1D 4EQ
E bookings@unionclub.co.uk
W www.unionclub.co.uk

UNIT TWENTY THREE   T 01379 882200
Unit 23, Vince's Road
Court Industrial Estate, Diss, Norfolk IP22 4BF
E info@unittwentythree.co.uk
W www.unit23.co

URDANG ACADEMY THE   T 020 7713 7710
The Old Finsbury Town Hall
Rosebery Avenue, London EC1R 4RP
F 020 7278 6727
E studiohire@theurdangacademy.com
W www.theurdangacademy.com

VIVACE THEATRE SCHOOL   T 07740 585506
Contact: Joyce McLelland
243 Sauchiehall Street
Glasgow G2 3EZ
E info@vivacetheatreschool.co.uk
W www.vivacetheatreschool.co.uk

WATERMANS   T 020 8232 1019
40 High Street, Brentford TW8 0DS
E info@watermans.org.uk
W www.watermans.org.uk

WILSON, Miranda   T 07941 339612
Large Studio Space
47 Roundwood Road, Willesden
London NW10 9TP
E acting@mirandawilson.com

YOUNG, Sylvia
THEATRE SCHOOL   T 020 7258 2336
1 Nutford Place, London W1H 5YZ
T 020 7258 2339
E syoung@syts.co.uk
W www.syts.co.uk

YOUNG ACTORS THEATRE   T 020 7278 2101
70-72 Barnsbury Road
London N1 0ES
E info@yati.org.uk
W www.yati.org.uk

ACT UP　　　　　　　　　T 020 8767 7659
The Office, 93 Chasefield Road
London SW17 8LW
E info@act-up.co.uk
W www.act-up.co.uk

ACTIVATION　　　　　　　T 020 8783 9494
Riverside House
Feltham Avenue
Hampton Court
Surrey KT8 9BJ
F 020 8783 9345
E info@activation.co.uk
W www.activation.co.uk

APROPOS PRODUCTIONS LTD
53 Greek Street
London W1D 3DR
E info@aproposltd.com
W www.aproposltd.com/talent

BROWNE, Michael
ASSOCIATES LTD　　　　T/F 01462 812483
The Cloisters
168C Station Road
Lower Stondon
Bedfordshire SG16 6JQ
E enquiries@mba-roleplay.co.uk
W www.mba-roleplay.co.uk

CRAGRATS UK LTD　　　　T 0844 4774100
Vine Court, Chalk Pit Lane
Dorking, Surrey RH4 1AJ
E enquiries@cragrats.com
W www.cragrats.com

DRAMANON LTD　　　　　T 01753 647795
Langtons House
Templewood Lane
Farnham Common
Buckinghamshire SL2 3HD
F 01753 647783
E info@dramanon.co.uk
W www.dramanon.co.uk

FRANK PARTNERS LLP　　T 0117 908 5384
14 Brynland Avenue
Bristol BS7 9DT
E neil@frankpartners.co.uk
W www.frankpartners.co.uk

GLOBAL7　　　　　　　　T/F 020 7281 7679
Kemp House
152 City Road
Lodnon EC1V 2NZ
T 07956 956652
E global7castings@gmail.com
W www.global7casting.com

INTERACT　　　　　　　　T 020 7793 7744
138 Southwark Bridge Road
London SE1 0DG
E cv@interact.eu.com
W www.interact.eu.com

NORTH OF WATFORD　　　T 01422 845361
Twitter: @northofwatford
The Creative Quarter
The Town Hall
Hebden Bridge
Yorkshire HX7 7BY
T 020 3601 3372
E info@northofwatford.com
W www.northofwatford.com

NV MANAGEMENT LTD
Central Office
Minerva Mill Innovation Centre
Station Road
Alcester, Warwickshire B49 5ET
E hello@nvmanagement.co.uk
W www.nvmanagement.co.uk

PERFORMANCE
BUSINESS THE　　　　　T 01932 888885
The Coach House
78 Oatlands Drive
Weybridge, Surrey KT13 9HT
E lucy@theperformance.biz
W www.theperformance.biz

RADA IN BUSINESS　　　T 020 7908 4810
The Royal Academy of Dramatic Art
18-22 Chenies Street
London WC1E 7PA
F 020 7908 4811
E ask@radainbusiness.com
W www.radainbusiness.com

ROLEPLAY UK　　　　　　T 0333 121 3003
5 St Peters Street, Stamford
Lincolnshire PE9 2PQ
E bookings@roleplayuk.com
W www.roleplayuk.com

STEPS DRAMA
LEARNING DEVELOPMENT　T 020 7403 9000
Suite 10, Baden Place
Crosby Row
London SE1 1YW
F 020 7403 0909
E mail@stepsdrama.com
W www.stepsdrama.com

THEATRE& LTD　　　　　T 01484 664078
25 Queens Square Business Park
Huddersfield Road
Honley
West Yorkshire HD9 6QZ
F 01484 660079
E cmitchell@theatreand.com
W www.theatreand.com

WIZARD THEATRE　　　　T 0800 5832373
Blenheim Villa
Burr Street
Harwell
Oxfordshire OX11 0DT
E admin@wizardtheatre.co.uk
W www.wizardtheatre.co.uk

S →

**Set Construction, Lighting,
Sound & Scenery**

3D SET COMPANY LTD T 0161 273 8831
Construction. Exhibition Stands. Scenery Design. Sets
Unit 8 Temperance Street
Manchester M12 6HR
F 0161 273 6786
E twalsh@3dsetco.com
W www.3dsetco.com

**ALBEMARLE SCENIC
STUDIOS** T 0845 6447021
Suppliers of Scenery & Costumes Construction/Hire
Admin: PO Box 240, Rotherfield TN6 9BN
E albemarle.productions@virgin.net
W www.albemarleproductions.com

ALPHA CREW T 020 3691 9683
*Stage & Technical Crew for London & Midlands,
Festival Crew*
28 Grazebrook Road, Stoke Newington
London N16 0HS
E info@alphacrew.co.uk
W www.alphacrew.co.uk

AVW CONTROLS LTD T 01379 898340
Stage Automation Specialists
Unit 12 Willow Farm Business Centre
Allwood Green, Rickinghall, Diss, Norfolk IP22 1LT
F 01379 898386
E sales@avw.co.uk
W www.avw.co.uk

BONDINI LTD T 01763 852691
*Cabaret, Magic & Illusion. Scenery Construction. Venue
Decor. AV Equipment*
Low Farm, Brook Road
Bassingbourn, Royston, Herts SG8 5NT
F 01763 853946
E hello@bondini.co.uk
W www.bondini.co.uk

BOSCO LIGHTING T 020 8769 3470
Design/Technical Consultancy
47 Woodbourne Avenue
London SW16 1UX
E boscolx@lineone.net

BRISTOL (UK) LTD T 01923 779333
Scenic Paint
Unit 1, Southerland Court
Tolpits Lane, Watford WD18 9SP
F 01923 779666
E tech.sales@bristolpaint.com
W www.bristolpaint.com

**CAP PRODUCTION
SOLUTIONS** T 07973 432576
116 Wigmore Road, Carshalton
Surrey SM5 1RQ
E leigh@leighporter.com

CAROUSEL LIGHTS LTD T 07944 654349
86-90 Paul Street, London EC2A 4NE
E hello@carousellights.com
W www.carousellights.com

**CARTEY & CO LTD MANUFACTURERS
AGENT- UK & ITALY** T 07878 977970
*Film, Television & Theatre Lighting, Screen & Scenic
Solutions*
Suite 80, 26 The Hornet
Chichester, West Sussex PO19 7BB
E clivecartey@gmail.com
W www.cartey.co.uk

CCT LIGHTING UK LTD T 0115 985 8919
Lighting. Dimmers. Sound & Stage Machinery
33 Stoke Lane, Gedling, Nottingham NG4 2QS
E office@cctlighting.co.uk
W www.cctlighting.com

CLOCKWORK SCENERY T 01483 427531
*Hand-crafted Scenery for Theatres, Cruise Ships,
Exhibitions, Television & Film*
Secretts Farm, Chapel Lane, Milford, Surrey GU8 5HU
E enquiries@clockworkscenery.com
W www.clockworkscenery.com

COD STEAKS LTD T 0117 980 3910
*Costume. Design. Exhibitions. Model Making. Set
Construction. Exhibition Designers*
2 Cole Road, Bristol BS2 0UG
E mail@codsteaks.com
W www.codsteaks.com

DAP STUDIO T 07973 406830
55 Longdown Lane North, Epsom, Surrey KT17 3JB
E james@dapstudio.co.uk
W www.dapstudio.co.uk

DMN DESIGN BUILD T 0844 8711801
Unit 1, Calder Trading Estate, Lower Quarry Road
Bradley, Huddersfield HD5 0RR
E enquiries@dmndesignbuild.co.uk
W www.dmndesignbuild.com

eSTAGE LTD T 020 3514 3630
*Production Services including Set Construction, Lighting
& Sound Hire, Stage & Production Management,
Marketing & Online Design*
71-75 Shelton Street, Covent Garden
London WC2H 9JQ
E chat@estage.net
W www.estage.net

EVANS, Peter STUDIOS LTD T 01582 725730
Scenic Embellishment. Vacuum Forming
12-14 Tavistock Street, Dunstable
Bedfordshire LU6 1NE
F 01582 481329
E sales@peterevansstudios.co.uk
W www.peterevansstudios.co.uk

FULL EFFECT THE T 020 3553 5747
Event Designers & Producers
Millennium Studios, Bedford Technology Park
Thurleigh, Bedfordshire MK44 2YP
E mark.harrison@tfe.co.uk
W www.thefulleffect.co.uk

FUTURIST SOUND & LIGHT LTD **T** 0113 279 0033
Unit 1, White Swan Yard
Boroughgate, Otley LS21 1AE
F 0113 242 0022
E info@futurist.co.uk
W www.futurist.co.uk

GILL, Perry **T** 07815 048164
Installation. Production Management. Set Construction
E perry_gill100@hotmail.com

HALL STAGE LTD **T** 01582 439440
Unit 4, Cosgrove Way, Luton, Beds LU1 1XL
F 01582 720904
E sales@hallstage.com
W www.hallstage.com

HALO LIGHTING **T** 020 7607 4444
98-124 Brewery Road, London N7 9PG
E info@halo.co.uk
W www.halo.co.uk

HAND & LOCK **T** 020 7580 7488
Embroidery for Interiors & Costumes
86 Margaret Street, London W1W 8TE
F 020 7580 7499
E enquiries@handembroidery.com
W www.handembroidery.com

HARLEQUIN FLOORS **T** 01892 514888
Festival House, Chapman Way
Tunbridge Wells, Kent TN2 3EF
F 01892 514222
E enquiries@harlequinfloors.com
W uk.harlequinfloors.com/en

HENSHALL, John **T** 01793 790333
Director of Lighting & Photography
6 Divinity Close, Wanborough
Swindon SN4 0EH
E john@epi-centre.com

HERON & DRIVER **T** 020 7394 8688
Scenic Furniture & Structural Prop Makers
Unit 7, Dockley Road Industrial Estate
Rotherhithe, London SE16 3SF
E mail@herondriver.co.uk
W www.herondriver.co.uk

LEVIATHON WORKSHOPS **T** 01827 437652
Contact: Jake Linzey. Scenery & Prop Making Studio
40A Aldergate, Tamworth, Staffs B79 7DD
E info@leviathonworkshop.com
W www.leviathonworkshop.com

LIGHT WORKS LTD **T** 020 7249 3627
2A Greenwood Road, London E8 1AB
F 020 7254 0306

LS-LIVE **T** 01977 659888
*Arena-sized Studio. Set Design & Construction.
Equipment Rental*
Unit 53, Langthwaite Business Park
Lidgate Crescent, South Kirkby, Wakefield
West Yorkshire WF9 3NR
E sales@ls-live.com
W www.ls-live.com

MATTLX GROUP **T** 0845 6808693
Lighting. Design. Production Engineering. Safety. Training
Unit 3, Vinehall Business Centre
Vinehall Road, Robertsbridge
East Sussex TN32 5JW
E intray@mattlx.com
W www.mattlx.com

MODELBOX **T** 01837 810923
Computer Aided Design. Design Services
41C Market Street, Hatherleigh
Devon EX20 3JP
E info@modelbox.co.uk
W www.modelboxplans.com

MODERNEON LONDON LTD **T** 020 8650 9690
LED Lighting. Signage
Cromwell House
27 Brabourne Rise
Park Langley, Beckenham
Kent BR3 6SQ
F 020 8658 2770
E info@moderneon.co.uk
W www.moderneon-lite.co.uk

MOUNSEY, Matthew **T** 07941 355450
Scenic Artist
E mmounsey@yahoo.com

NEED, Paul J. **T** 020 8659 2558
Lighting Designer
5 Metro Business Centre
Kangley Bridge Road
London SE26 5BW
F 020 8778 9217
E paul@10outof10.co.uk
W www.pauljneed.co.uk

NORTHERN LIGHT **T** 0131 622 9100
Communications, Lighting, Sound & Stage Equipment
Assembly Street, Leith
Edinburgh EH6 7RG
F 0131 622 9101
E info@northernlight.co.uk
W www.northernlight.co.uk

ORBITAL SOUND LTD **T** 020 7501 6868
Sound Hire & Design
57 Acre Lane, Brixton
London SW2 5TN
F 020 7501 6869
E hire@orbitalsound.co.uk
W www.orbitalsound.co.uk

PANALUX **T** 020 8233 7000
12 Waxlow Road
London NW10 7NU
F 020 8233 7001
E info@panalux.biz
W www.panalux.biz

PMB THEATRE & EXHIBITION SERVICES LTD **T** 01763 852691
Low Farm, Brook Road
Bassingbourn, Royston, Herts SG8 5NT
F 01763 853946
E info@creatingtheimpossible.co.uk
W www.creatingtheimpossible.co.uk

REVOLVING STAGE COMPANY LTD THE **T** 024 7668 7055
Crondal Road
Bayton Road Industrial Estate
Coventry CV7 9NH
E enquiries@therevolvingstagecompany.co.uk
W www.therevolvingstagecompany.co.uk

RK RESOURCE **T** 01233 750180
2 Wyvern Way, Henwood, Ashford
Kent TN24 8DW
F 01233 750133
E rkresource2007@aol.co.uk
W www.rk-resourcekent.com

S + H TECHNICAL SUPPORT LTD   T 01271 866832
Starcloths. Drapes
Starcloth Way
Mullacott Industrial Estate
Ilfracombe, Devon EX34 8PL
F 01271 865423
E shtsg@aol.com
W www.starcloth.co.uk

S2 EVENTS   T 020 7928 5474
Design, Equipment Hire, Production, Scenery/Set Construction & Technical Services for Creative Live Events
141-143 Nathanway
London SE28 0AB
F 020 7928 6082
E info@s2events.co.uk
W www.s2events.co.uk

SCENA PRODUCTIONS LLP   T 020 7703 4444
Set Construction
12 Imperial Way
Croydon CR0 4RR
F 020 7703 7012
E info@scenapro.com
W www.scenapro.com

SCENIC WORKSHOPS LTD   T 0151 486 5979
9 Mayflower Avenue
Triumph Trading Park
Liverpool L24 9BA
E info@scenicworkshops.co.uk
W www.scenicworkshops.co.uk

SCOTT FLEARY PRODUCTIONS LTD   T 0870 4441787
Unit 1-4, Vale Industrial Park
170 Rowan Road
London SW16 5BN
F 0870 4448322
E info@scottfleary.com

SET CREATIONS LTD   T 01992 789759
Unit 14, Studio House
Delamare Road
Cheshunt EN8 9SH
F 01992 625180
E nash@setcreations.com
W www.setcreations.com

SPLINTER   T 0161 633 6787
Supplier of Touring Theatre Scenery
The Gasworks, Higginshaw Lane
Oldham, Greater Manchester OL1 3LB
F 0161 633 6851
E splintermail@aol.com
W www.splinterscenery.co.uk

STAGE MANAGEMENT COMPANY   T 01274 669259
Audio. Lighting. Production
Unit 12 Commerce Court
Challenge Way
Bradford BD4 8NW
E info@stagemanagementcompany.com
W www.stagemanagementcompany.com

STAGE SOLUTIONS   T 01273 555441
Portable Staging Sales & Consultancy
10 Second Avenue, Chatham
Kent ME4 5AU
E info@stagesolutions.uk.com
W www.stagesolutions.uk.com

STAGE SYSTEMS   T 01509 611021
Designers & Suppliers of Modular Staging & Tiering
2 Princes Court
Royal Way
Loughborough LE11 5XR
F 01509 233146
E info@stagesystems.co.uk
W www.stagesystems.co.uk

STAGECRAFT PRODUCTION SERVICES   T 01722 326055
Hire & Sales of Audio Visual, Lighting, Sound & Staging for Conferences & Live Events
F 01202 599900
E hire@cpsgroup.co.uk
W www.cpsgroup.co.uk

STAGEWORKS WORLDWIDE PRODUCTIONS   T 01253 342426
Lighting. Props. Scenery. Sound
525 Ocean Boulevard
Blackpool FY4 1EZ
F 01253 342702
E info@stageworksWWP.com
W www.stageworksWWP.com

STEWART, Helen   T 07887 682186
Theatre Designer
29C Hornsey Rise Gardens
London N19 3PP
E helen@helenstewart.co.uk
W www.helenstewart.co.uk

STORM LIGHTING LTD   T 01483 757211
Warwick House
Monument Way West
Woking, Surrey GU21 5EN
F 01483 757710
E hire@stormlighting.co.uk
W www.stormlighting.co.uk

TOP SHOW   T 01904 750022
Props. Scenery. Conference Specialists
North Lane, Huntington
York YO32 9SU

WELLINGTON SCENIC   T/F 01522 794260
Full Scenery Design & Build Services, also with Pantomime Sets for Hire
Units 1 & 2 Karglen Ind Est
Potterhanworth Road
Branston, Lincoln
Lincolnshire LN4 1HY
T 01636 636625
E info@wellingtonscenic.com
W www.wellingtonscenic.com

WEST, John   T 07753 637451
Art Director. Draughtsman
103 Abbotswood Close
Winyates Green
Redditch
Worcestershire B98 0QF
E johnwest@blueyonder.co.uk
W www.johnwest-artdirector.com

ZEAL   T 01256 359264
Contact: Steve Hough
Unit 6 Bessemer Park
Bessemer Road
Basingstoke, Hampshire RG21 3NB
E info@zeallive.com
W www.zeallive.com

T →

Theatre Producers

Theatre

- Alternative & Community
- Children, Young People & TIE
- English Speaking in Europe
- London
- Outer London,
  Fringe & Venues
- Provincial / Touring
- Puppet Theatre
  Companies
- Repertory (Regional)

Theatre Producers

What is a theatre producer?

A theatre producer is someone who oversees and organises a theatre show. They will find, or arrange for other professionals to find, a suitable script, design, director and cast for each production, while also managing all finances and marketing.

How should I use these listings?

Theatre producers tend to use casting directors to put forward suitable actors for the parts in forthcoming productions, but you could also try approaching them yourself.

Rather than sending your CV and headshot to every producer listed, it would be best to do some research first in order to target your search. You need to decide what type of work you want to do first, as there is no need to waste your time and the producer's time sending your CV to unsuitable companies. Then find out what each company has produced in the past, what they are currently working on and if possible what they are considering producing in the future, and only send your CV to those most relevant to the roles you want to play.

Don't forget to include a covering letter which states why you are contacting this producer in particular: for example, this could be because you feel you are perfect for a particular role in their next production. Personalising and targeting your correspondence in this way gives you the best chance of your CV being considered in a favourable light.

How should I approach theatre producers?

You should contact theatre producers by post or e-mail only. We would advise against calling them, especially when approaching them for the first time. Address your correspondence to an individual within the company, as this demonstrates that you have done your research. If you are unsure as to the best method of applying to theatre producers, as with other casting professionals it is safest to post your CV and headshot in the traditional way rather than e-mailing it.

Remember to put your name and telephone number on the back of the photo in case it gets separated from your CV. It would be a good idea to include a SAE big enough to contain your photo if you send hard copy and with sufficient postage to increase your chances of getting a reply. Do not enclose your showreel but you can mention that you have one available in your covering letter, and if the producer is interested in viewing it, they will contact you.

When should I approach theatre producers?

Listen to industry news and have a look at theatre producers' websites for forthcoming production details. The casting process usually takes place around three months prior to rehearsals, so bear this in mind when you are writing your covering letter.

How do I become a theatre producer?

The best way to learn about producing is to work in producing. Internships are a good way to get to grips with the industry; research the theatre producers listed over the following pages by checking their websites' jobs sections for vacancies. Remember to make sure they actually work in the area you are interested in before making contact. You should also try to build up a good general knowledge of the industry by going to see as many theatrical productions as you can and keeping track of which producers work on which types of shows.

Theatre Producers

CASE STUDY

The West Yorkshire Playhouse was established 25 years ago in Leeds. The Playhouse has two theatres, the Quarry with 750 seats and the smaller, more flexible Courtyard with 350 seats. Mimi Poskitt is the Senior Producer and has worked as a producer across several forms: with a career in TV and documentary film, site specific theatre work, new writing, as well as large scale touring, commercial theatre shows.

The job of the producer is varied and everyone enters into the role in a different way - usually it comes from wanting to make a certain show and then you ending up producing it. As a producer you are a fundraiser, an ideas generator, a networker, a friend, the HR department, a boss, an administrator, a prop maker, a van driver, a finance officer and anything else that needs your attention.

> **"As a producer you are a fundraiser, an idea generator, a networker, a friend, the HR department, a boss, an administrator, a prop maker, a van driver, a finance officer and anything else that needs your attention"**

No one producer works in the same way. A freelance producer may have a very different remit to an in house producer. An in house producer in one theatre will have a very different remit to another. By its nature, the role is incredibly diverse and changes on a day to day basis. This is a large part of why I love doing my job. I know quite a few actors who have become producers as they want to make their own work and don't want to wait around for someone to ask them. I think getting to understand the role of a producer and the process of making shows can be an invaluable experience for an actor.

> **"We aim to program dynamic, vital theatre that reflects our city and speaks to our audiences"**

The producers in regional theatres tend to work in cycles, mainly led by booking and planning seasons of work. Here at the Playhouse we plan in 6 month cycles - producing 2 brochures a year. We aim to program dynamic, vital theatre that reflects our city and speaks to our audiences. We work across all scales - making work for our smaller studio spaces right up to the 750 seater Quarry. We tour our work to local community venues around Leeds and develop and build large scale shows that tour all over the UK.

We have a number of producers in our team - each with a different focus. Our assistant producer leads on visiting work - looking to book the best touring work into our two spaces. We look for work we like, from companies we admire but also work we feel is going to complement and contrast with our own home produced shows. We like to see the work if possible before we book it and if this isn't possible then we usually like to read the script or watch footage of the show. Our associate producer is responsible for creating opportunities for early-career artists to develop and share their work with the public. The associate producer leads our Furnace development scheme and oversees artists, companies, theatre makers (across all art forms) to support and nurture this work in our building. The associate producer aims to work with these companies in a developmental capacity and supports them through a process, be that an early stage R&D or in the creation of a new show for one of our stages. As senior producer I oversee the artistic planning team - this includes the visiting work as well as the home produced work. Alongside the rest of the team and our Artistic Director James Brining, we develop projects that we want to see on our stages. These can be co-productions with other theatres and theatre companies as well as work we make only for our stages.

Getting in touch with theatres as a performer is often confusing, so we have a series of channels to make it clear to performers who want to work with us. For all of our in house produced shows we have a casting director. This person will coordinate auditions for us. Casting breakdowns will be posted on Spotlight and you can apply through there.

Once a year we hold auditions for local actors - those who live within 25 miles of the Playhouse - this is a chance for us to meet local talent so we can cast these actors in our shows, readings and workshops. We also run a scheme for graduate actors. Currently in its second year, Artistic Director James Brining and Associate Director Mark Rosenblatt hold auditions and select 2 actors from across UK accredited drama schools. They are here with us for 6-8 months performing in our in-house production as well as spending time around the building. The graduate scheme is just one part of a bigger drive by West Yorkshire Playhouse to expand our artist development strand. We want to create as many opportunities for lots of different artists from all disciplines and backgrounds to develop and work here, so that the theatre continues to be a major hub for Yorkshire based directors, writers, actors, designers and theatre makers.

"We want to create as many opportunities for lots of different artists from all disciplines and backgrounds to develop and work here"

Between acting in Playhouse shows, graduate actors are given the opportunity to work in the planning office, as well as doing secondments with stage management and Creative Engagement (our outreach team) to gain an insight into the day-to-day running of the building. It used to be that actors would work in rep, as well as having other company roles, and this process has contributed to the development of some of our greatest actors. The scheme we've developed here is about kick-starting someone's career, offering them a wide-ranging experience, allowing them to work with a range of directors and creative teams, to offer a unique

and rich perspective on a really competitive career choice. I'd urge graduates to seek out opportunities like our Graduate Actor Scheme, to give themselves an opportunity to see the range of what a regional theatre has to offer and discover the work that goes on away from the stage.

For more information about schemes and ways you can get in touch with the Playhouse team visit www.wyp.org.uk

10TH PLANET PRODUCTIONS
T/F 020 8442 2659
Contact: Alexander Holt
75 Woodland Gardens, London N10 3UD
E admin@10thplanetproductions.com
W www.10thplanetproductions.com

1505
T 020 7112 8750
3rd Floor, 20 Bedford Street
London WC2E 9HP
E hello@weare1505.co.uk
W www.weare1505.co.uk

30 BIRD PRODUCTIONS
T 01223 403362
Twitter: @30Bird
Cambridge Junction, Clifton Way
Cambridge CB1 7GX
E info@30bird.org
W www.30bird.org

ACORN ENTERTAINMENTS LTD
T 01285 644622
PO Box 64, Cirencester
Glos GL7 5YD
F 01285 642291
E info@acornents.co.uk
W www.acornents.co.uk

ACT PRODUCTIONS LTD
T 020 7484 5292
Golden Cross House, 8 Duncannon Street
London WC2N 4JF
E info@actproductions.co.uk
W www.actproductions.co.uk

ACTOR'S TEMPLE THE
T 020 3004 4537
Basement, 13-14 Warren Street
London W1T 5LG
E bookings@actorstemple.com
W www.actorstemple.com

ACTORS TOURING COMPANY
T 020 7930 6014
Contact: Nick Williams (Executive Director)
Institute of Contemporary Arts (ICA)
12 Carlton House Terrace
London SW1Y 5AH
E atc@atctheatre.com
W www.atctheatre.com

AGENCY:105
T 020 7205 2316
Twitter: @agency105
A105 Ltd, 64 Great Eastern Street
London EC2A 3QR
E lexi@international-collective.com
W www.agency105.com

AJTC THEATRE COMPANY
T/F 01483 232795
28 Rydes Hill Crescent, Guildford, Surrey GU2 9UH
W www.ajtctheatre.co.uk

AMBASSADOR THEATRE GROUP
T 020 7534 6100
39-41 Charing Cross Road, London WC2H 0AR
F 020 7534 6109
E azerajones@theambassadors.com
W www.atgtickets.com

ANTIC DISPOSITION
T 020 7284 0760
4A Oval Road, London NW1 7EB
E info@anticdisposition.co.uk
W www.anticdisposition.co.uk

AOD (ACTORS OF DIONYSUS)
T/F 01273 673691
Twitter: @aodtheatre
25 St Lukes Road, Brighton BN2 9ZD
E info@actorsofdionysus.com
W www.actorsofdionysus.com

APL THEATRE LTD
T 020 8655 7653
UK & International Theatre Producers
3B Nettlefold Place, West Norwood
London SE27 0JW
E info@apltheatre.com
W www.apltheatre.com

APROPOS PRODUCTIONS LTD
53 Greek Street, London W1D 3DR
E info@aproposltd.com
W www.aproposltd.com/events

ARDEN ENTERTAINMENT
T 020 7395 5433
Ambassadors Theatre
West Street
London WC2H 9ND
E info@arden-entertainment.co.uk
W www.arden-entertainment.co.uk

ARIA ENTERTAINMENT
T 07947 074887
7 Northiam, Cromer Street
London WC1H 8LB
E info@aria-entertainment.com
W www.aria-entertainment.com

ASHTON GROUP THEATRE THE
T 01229 430636
The Cooke's Studios, 104 Abbey Road
Barrow-in-Furness, Cumbria LA14 5QR
E theashtongroup@btconnect.com
W www.ashtongroup.co.uk

ATTIC THEATRE COMPANY (LONDON) LTD
T 020 8640 6800
Mitcham Library, 157 London Road
Mitcham CR4 2YR
E info@attictheatrecompany.com
W www.attictheatrecompany.com

AVVA LAFF! PRODUCTIONS
T 07798 692373
Family Entertainment Shows. Comedy. Children's Theatre
10B Harcourt Road, Windsor
Berkshire SL4 5NB
E jane@avvalaff.co.uk
W www.avvalaff.co.uk

BEE & BUSTLE ENTERPRISES
T 020 8450 0371
32 Exeter Road, London NW2 4SB
F 020 8450 1057
E info@beeandbustle.co.uk
W www.beeandbustle.co.uk

BIRMINGHAM STAGE COMPANY THE
T 020 7437 3391
Contact: Neal Foster (Actor/Manager), Philip Compton (Executive Producer), Roshni Savjani (General Manager)
Suite 228, The Linen Hall, 162 Regent Street
London W1B 5TB
E office@birminghamstage.com
W www.birminghamstage.com

BLUE BOX ENTERTAINMENT LTD
T 020 7395 7520
Top Floor, 80-81 St Martin's Lane
London WC2N 4AA
F 020 3292 1699
E info@newbluebox.com
W www.newbluebox.com

BLUE STAR PRODUCTIONS
T 020 7836 6220
Contact: Barrie Stacey, Keith Hopkins
7-8 Shaldon Mansions
132 Charing Cross Road
London WC2H 0LA
E bluestar.london.2000@gmail.com

BORDER CROSSINGS
T 020 8829 8928
13 Bankside, Enfield EN2 8BN
F 020 8366 5239
E info@bordercrossings.org.uk
W www.bordercrossings.org.uk

BOTELLO, Catalina
T 020 3286 1294
48 New Cavendish Street, London W1G 8TG
E contact@outoftheboxproductions.org
W www.outoftheboxproductions.org

**BRITISH THEATRE
SEASON IN MONACO**
T 020 8455 3278
1 Hogarth Hill, London NW11 6AY
E mail@montecarlotheatre.co.uk
W www.montecarlotheatre.com

BROOKE, Nick LTD
T 020 7240 3901
1st Floor, 62 Shaftesbury Avenue
London W1D 6LT
F 020 7494 4905
E nick@nickbrooke.com
W www.nickbrooke.com

**BRUNJES, Emma
PRODUCTIONS LTD**
T 020 7820 9332
Contact: Gemma Hardiker
1 Wardour Street, 4th Floor, London W1D 6PA
E info@emmabrunjesproductions.com
W www.emmabrunjesproductions.com

BUDDY WORLDWIDE LTD
T 020 7240 9941
PO Box 293, Letchworth Garden City, Herts SG6 9EU
F 01462 684851
E info@buddyshow.com
W www.buddythemusical.com

BUSH THEATRE
T 020 8743 3584
7 Uxbridge Road, Shepherd's Bush
London W12 8LJ
E info@bushtheatre.co.uk
W www.bushtheatre.co.uk

CAHOOTS THEATRE COMPANY
T 07711 245848
St Martin's Theatre, West Street
London WC2N 9NH
E denise@cahootstheatrecompany.com
W www.cahootstheatrecompany.com

**CAP PRODUCTION
SOLUTIONS LTD**
T 07973 432576
116 Wigmore Road, Carshalton
Surrey SM5 1RQ
F 07970 763480
E leigh@leighporter.com

**CENTRELINE PRODUCTIONS,
GALE KING PRODUCTIONS LTD &
THE TOURING CONSORTIUM
THEATRE COMPANY**
T 07710 522438
4th Floor, 80-81 St Martin's Lane
London WC2N 4AA
E jenny@centrelinenet.com
W www.touringconsortium.com

CHAIN REACTION
T/F 020 8981 9572
Millers House, Three Mills Lane
London E3 3DU
E admin@chainreactiontheatre.co.uk
W www.chainreactiontheatre.co.uk

**CHANNEL THEATRE PRODUCTIONS LTD &
CTP PANTOMIMES LTD**
T 01963 362937
5 Gold Street, Stalbridge
Dorset DT10 2LX
E info@scenethreecreative.co.uk
W www.scenethreecreative.co.uk

**CHAPMAN, Duggie
ASSOCIATES**
T/F 01253 403177
Concerts. Musicals. Pantomime
Clifton House, 106 Clifton Drive
Blackpool FY4 1RR
E info@duggiechapmanassociates.com
W www.duggiechapman.com

CHEEK BY JOWL
T 020 7382 2391
Contact: Beth Byrne
Stage Door, Barbican Centre
Silk Street, London EC2Y 8DS
E info@cheekbyjowl.com
W www.cheekbyjowl.com

**CHICHESTER
FESTIVAL THEATRE**
T 01243 784437
Oaklands Park, Chichester
West Sussex PO19 6AP
F 01243 787288
E admin@cft.org.uk
W www.cft.org.uk

CHICKENSHED
T 020 8351 6161
290 Chase Side, Southgate
London N14 4PE
E info@chickenshed.org.uk
W www.chickenshed.org.uk

CHOL THEATRE
T 01484 536008
Contact: Susan Burns (Director). Twitter: @choltheatre
48A Byram Arcade, Westgate
Huddersfield HD1 1ND
E info@choltheatre.co.uk
W www.choltheatre.co.uk

**CHURCHILL THEATRE
BROMLEY LTD**
T 020 8290 8210
Producing Theatre
The Churchill, High Street
Bromley, Kent BR1 1HA
W www.atgtickets.com/churchill

CLEAN BREAK
T 020 7482 8600
Theatre Education. New Writing
2 Patshull Road, London NW5 2LB
F 020 7482 8611
E general@cleanbreak.org.uk
W www.cleanbreak.org.uk

CODRON, Michael PLAYS LTD
T 020 7240 8291
Aldwych Theatre Offices
London WC2B 4DF
F 020 7240 8467

COLE KITCHENN
T 020 7427 5681
ROAR House, 46 Charlotte Street
London W1T 2GS
E info@colekitchenn.com

COMPLICITE
T 020 7485 7700
Twitter: @Complicite
14 Anglers Lane, London NW5 3DG
E email@complicite.org
W www.complicite.org

CONCORDANCE
T 020 7244 7439
Contact: Neil McPherson
Finborough Theatre, 118 Finborough Road
London SW10 9ED
E admin@concordance.org.uk
W www.concordance.org.uk

CONTEMPORARY STAGE COMPANY
9 Finchley Way, London N3 1AG
E contemp.stage@hotmail.co.uk

CREATIVE BLAST COMPANY T 01375 386247
2nd Floor, Viking House
Daneholes Roundabout
Stanford Road, Grays
Essex RM16 2XE
E info@creativeblastcompany.com
W www.creativeblastcompany.com

CREATIVE MANAGEMENT &
PRODUCTIONS (CMP) LTD T 020 7820 3655
3 Sharsted Street, London SE17 3TP
E nfrankfort@cmplimited.com
W www.cmplimited.com

DEAD EARNEST THEATRE T 07855 866292
15 Paternoster Row, Sheffield S1 2BX
E info@deadearnest.co.uk
W www.deadearnest.co.uk

DEAN, Lee T 020 7497 5111
PO Box 10703, London WC2H 9ED
E admin@leedean.co.uk

DISNEY THEATRICAL
PRODUCTIONS (UK) T 020 7845 0900
Lyceum Theatre, 21 Wellington Street
London WC2E 7RQ

DK PRODUKTIONS LTD T 01628 605981
42 Coalmans Way, Slough SL1 7NX
E info@dk-pro.co.uk
W www.dk-pro.co.uk

DONEGAN, David LTD T 07957 358909
PO Box LB689, London W1A 9LB
E daviddonegan@hotmail.co.uk

DRAMATIS PERSONAE LTD T 020 7834 9300
Contact: Nathan Silver
19 Regency Street
London SW1P 4BY
E ns@nathansilver.com

EASTERN ANGLES
THEATRE COMPANY T 01473 218202
The Sir John Mills Theatre
Gatacre Road, Ipswich
Suffolk IP1 2LQ
E admin@easternangles.co.uk
W www.easternangles.co.uk

ELDARIN YEONG STUDIO T 020 3714 9580
40 Gracechurch Street
London EC3V 0BT
E info@eldarin-yeong-studio.co.uk
W www.eldarin-yeong-studio.co.uk

ELLIOTT, Paul LTD T 020 3435 6439
4th Floor, 1 Wardour Street
London WC1D 6PA
E paul@paulelliott.ltd.uk

ENGLISH NATIONAL OPERA T 020 7836 0111
London Coliseum, St Martin's Lane
London WC2N 4ES
F 020 7845 9277
W www.eno.org

ENGLISH STAGE
COMPANY LTD T 020 7565 5050
Royal Court Theatre
Sloane Square
London SW1W 8AS
F 020 7565 5001
E info@royalcourttheatre.com
W www.royalcourttheatre.com

ENGLISH TOURING
THEATRE (ETT) T 020 7450 1990
25 Short Street, London SE1 8LJ
F 020 7633 0188
E admin@ett.org.uk
W www.ett.org.uk

ENTERTAINMENT
BUSINESS LTD THE T 07967 207573
Garden Studios, 71-75 Shelton Street
London WC2H 9JQ
E joanne.benjamin@entbiz.co.uk
W www.entbiz.co.uk

EUROPEAN THEATRE COMPANY THE
15 Beverley Avenue, London SW20 0RL
E europeanproductions@virginmedia.com
W www.europeantheatre.co.uk

EXCESS ALL AREAS T 020 8761 2384
3 Gibbs Square, London SE19 1JN
E admin@excessallareas.co.uk
W www.excessallareas.co.uk

FACADE T/F 020 8699 8655
Musicals
43A Garthorne Road, London SE23 1EP
E facade@cobomedia.com

FAIRBANK PRODUCTIONS
No CV's or Unsolicited Scripts
E info@fairbankproductions.co.uk
W www.fairbankproductions.co.uk

FEATHER PRODUCTIONS LTD
E anna@featherproductions.com
W www.featherproductions.com

FIELD, Anthony
ASSOCIATES LTD T 020 7240 5453
Top Floor, 80-81 St Martin's Lane
London WC2N 4AA
F 020 7240 2947
E info@anthonyfieldassociates.com
W www.anthonyfieldassociates.com

FIERY ANGEL LTD T 020 7734 9600
2nd Floor National House, 60-66 Wardour Street
London W1F 0TA
E mail@fiery-angel.com
W www.fiery-angel.com

FORBIDDEN THEATRE
COMPANY T 07852 942588
56 Handsworth Road, London N17 6DE
E info@forbidden.org.uk
W www.forbidden.org.uk

FORD, Vanessa
PRODUCTIONS T 01483 278203
Upper House Farm, Upper House Lane
Shamley Green, Surrey GU5 0SX
E vanessa.ford8@gmail.com

FOX, Robert LTD T 020 7584 6855
6 Beauchamp Place, London SW3 1NG
F 020 7225 1638
E info@robertfoxltd.com
W www.robertfoxltd.com

FRANK, Lina B. / AUSFORM
Circus & Theatre. Twitter: @ausform
Room 206, The Exchange, Corn Street
Bristol BS1 1JQ
E info@ausform.co.uk
W www.ausform.co.uk

FRIEDMAN, Sonia PRODUCTIONS   **T** 020 7845 8750
Duke of York's Theatre, 104 St Martin's Lane
London WC2N 4BG
F 020 7845 8759
E office@soniafriedman.com
W www.soniafriedman.com

GALLEON THEATRE COMPANY LTD   **T** 020 8310 7276
Contact: Alice De Sousa
Head Office, Greenwich Playhouse
50 Openshaw Road, London SE2 0TE
E boxoffice@galleontheatre.co.uk
W www.galleontheatre.co.uk

GBM PRODUCTIONS LTD   **T** 01837 871522
Bidlake Toft, Roadford Lake
Germansweek, Devon EX21 5BD
E gbm@bidlaketoft.com
W www.musicaltheatrecreations.com

GIANT CHERRY PRODUCTIONS LTD
Specialising in LGBT Productions for Theatre, Film
& Television
E info@giantcherryproductions.com
W www.giantcherryproductions.com

GIANT STEPS LTD   **T** 020 8567 5988
11 Chestnut Grove, London W5 4JT
T 07808 742307
E giantstepstheatre@googlemail.com
W www.giantsteps.info

GOUCHER, Mark LTD   **T** 020 7438 9570
1st Floor, 19 Garrick Street
London WC2E 9AX
E michael@markgoucher.com

GRADELINNIT COMPANY THE   **T** 020 7349 7222
Worlds End Studios, 132-134 Lots Road
London SW10 0RJ
E info@gradelinnit.com

GRAEAE THEATRE COMPANY   **T** 020 7613 6900
Bradbury Studios, 138 Kingsland Road
London E2 8DY
E info@graeae.org
W www.graeae.org

GRAHAM, David ENTERTAINMENT LTD   **T** 020 7175 7170
3rd Floor, 14 Hanover Street, London W1S 1YH
E info@davidgraham.co.uk
W www.davidgrahamentertainment.com

GRANDAGE, Michael COMPANY   **T** 020 3582 7210
4th Floor, Gielgud Theatre
Shaftesbury Avenue, London W1D 6AR
E info@michaelgrandagecompany.com

HALL & CHILDS LTD   **T** 07778 984365
Producers/General Managers
3 Thrifts Hall Farm Mews, Abridge Road
Theydon Bois, Essex CM16 7NL
E tc@hallandchilds.com
W www.hallandchilds.com

HAMPSTEAD THEATRE PRODUCTIONS LTD   **T** 020 7449 4200
Eton Avenue, Swiss Cottage
London NW3 3EU
F 020 7449 4201
E info@hampsteadtheatre.com
W www.hampsteadtheatre.com

HARDING, Andrew PRODUCTIONS LTD   **T** 07890 186213
71-75 Shelton Street, Covent Garden
London WC2H 9JQ
E info@andrewhardingproductions.co.uk
W www.andrewhardingproductions.co.uk

HARLEY PRODUCTIONS CONSULTANTS   **T** 020 8202 8863
78 York Street, London W1H 1DP
T 020 7486 2986
E harleyprods@aol.com

HARRISON, Garth   **T** 01508 530849
Michaelmas Barn, Long Stratton
Norfolk NR15 2PY
E garthsfp@hotmail.co.uk

HAYMARKET THE   **T** 01256 819797
c/o The Anvil Trust, Wote Street
Basingstoke, Hampshire RG21 7NW
F 01256 364179
E christine.bradwell@anvilarts.org.uk
W www.anvilarts.org.uk

HEADLONG THEATRE LTD   **T** 020 7478 0270
3rd Floor, 34-35 Berwick Street
London W1F 8RP
F 020 7438 1749
E info@headlong.co.uk
W www.headlong.co.uk

HENDERSON, Glynis PRODUCTIONS LTD   **T** 020 7580 9644
16-17 Little Portland Street
London W1W 8BP
F 020 7183 3298
E info@ghmp.co.uk
W www.ghmp.co.uk

HENDRY, Jamie PRODUCTIONS LTD   **T/F** 020 7183 5630
13 Regent Street, 6th Floor
London SW1Y 4LR
E office@jamiehendryproductions.com
W www.jamiehendryproductions.com

HENNEGAN, Nicholas ASSOCIATES   **T** 020 8090 5082
2nd Floor, 12 Fouberts Place
Carnaby Street, London W1F 7PA
E info@nicholashennegan.com
W www.nicholashennegan.com

HESTER, John PRODUCTIONS   **T/F** 020 8224 9580
Intimate Mysteries Theatre Company
105 Stoneleigh Park Road, Epsom
Surrey KT19 0RF
E hjohnhester@aol.com

HISS & BOO COMPANY LTD THE   **T** 01444 881707
Contact: Ian Liston. By Post (SAE). No Unsolicited
Scripts
Nyes Hill, Wineham Lane
Bolney, West Sussex RH17 5SD
E email@hissboo.co.uk
W www.hissboo.co.uk

HISTORIA THEATRE COMPANY   **T** 020 7837 8008
8 Cloudesley Square, London N1 0HT
T 07811 892079
E kateprice@lineone.net
W www.historiatheatre.com

HOLLOW CROWN PRODUCTIONS
T 07930 530948
Rose Cottage, Stone Street
Spexhall, Halesworth IP19 0RN
E peter.adshead@hollowcrown.co.uk
W www.hollowcrown.co.uk

HOLMAN, Paul ASSOCIATES LTD
T 020 8845 9408
Morritt House, 58 Station Approach
South Ruislip, Middlesex HA4 6SA
E enquiries@paulholmanassociates.co.uk
W www.paulholmanassociates.co.uk

HOLT, Thelma LTD
T 020 7812 7455
Noel Coward Theatre
85 St Martin's Lane, London WC2N 4AU
F 020 7812 7550
E thelma@dircon.co.uk
W www.thelmaholt.co.uk

HUGHES, Steve MANAGEMENT LTD
T 0844 5564670
E management@stevehughesuk.com
W www.stevehughesuk.com

HULL TRUCK THEATRE
T 01482 224800
50 Ferensway, Hull HU2 8LB
F 01482 581182
E admin@hulltruck.co.uk
W www.hulltruck.co.uk

HUNTLEY, Peter PRODUCTIONS
E info@peterhuntley.net
W www.peterhuntley.net

I&I PRODUCTIONS LTD
T 07875 461823
Contact: Ian Parsons
105 Leonard Street, Neath SA11 3HP
E iandiproductions@gmail.com
W www.iandiproductions.co.uk

IAN, David PRODUCTIONS
T 020 7427 8380
5th Floor, 53 Parker Street
London WC2B 5PT
F 020 7427 8381
E hello@davidianproductions.com
W www.davidianproductions.com

IBSEN STAGE COMPANY
T 07958 566274
72B Elmore Street
London N1 3FN
E ask@ibsenstage.com
W www.ibsenstage.com

ICARUS THEATRE COLLECTIVE
T 020 7998 1562
4 Ivor Court, 209 Gloucester Place
London NW1 6BJ
E info@icarustheatre.co.uk
W www.icarustheatre.co.uk

IMAGE MUSICAL THEATRE
T 020 8743 9380
197 Church Road, Northolt
Middlesex UB5 5BE
F 020 8181 6279
E admin@imagemusicaltheatre.co.uk
W www.imagemusicaltheatre.co.uk

INCISOR
T 07979 498450
41 Edith Avenue
Peacehaven
East Sussex BN10 8JB
E sarahmann7@hotmail.co.uk
W www.theatre-company-incisor.com

INGRAM, Colin LTD
T 020 7038 3906
Suite 526, Linen Hall
162-168 Regent Street, London W1B 5TE
F 020 7038 3907
E info@coliningramltd.com
W www.coliningramltd.com

INSIDE INTELLIGENCE
T/F 020 8986 8013
Theatre, including West End. New Writing. Contemporary Opera. Music Theatre
13 Athlone Close, London E5 8HD
E admin@inside-intelligence.org.uk
W www.inside-intelligence.org.uk

INSTANT WIT
T 0117 974 5734
Comedy Improvisation Theatre Show. Corporate/Conference Entertainment Show. Drama Based Training
6 Worrall Place, Worrall Road
Clifton, Bristol BS8 2WP
T 07711 644094
E info@instantwit.co.uk
W www.instantwit.co.uk

JAM THEATRE COMPANY
T 01628 483808
Jam Theatre Studios, Archway Court
45A West Street, Marlow
Buckinghamshire SL7 2LS
E office@jamtheatre.co.uk
W www.jamtheatre.co.uk

JERSEY BOYS UK LTD
T 020 3427 3720
Hudson House, 8 Tavistock Street
London WC2E 7PP
E jerseyboyslondon@dodger.com
W www.jerseyboyslondon.com

JEWELL, Jimmy LTD
T 020 7462 0790
17 Percy Street, London W1T 1DU
E jimmy@jwl-london.com
W www.jwl-london.com

JOHNSON, David
T 020 7284 3733
85B Torriano Avenue, London NW5 2RX
E david@johnsontemple.co.uk

JOHNSON, Gareth LTD
T 01239 891368
1st Floor, 19 Garrick Street
London WC2E 9AX
T 07770 225227
E gjltd@mac.com
W www.garethjohnsonltd.com

JORDAN, Andy PRODUCTIONS LTD
T 07775 615205
130 Newland Street West
Lincoln LN1 1PH
E andyjandyjordan@aol.com

JORDAN, Richard PRODUCTIONS
T 020 7243 9001
Mews Studios, 16 Vernon Yard
London W11 2DX
F 020 7313 9667
E info@richardjordanproductions.com

JORDAN PRODUCTIONS LTD
T 01323 417745
The Coach House, 5B Commercial Road
Eastbourne, East Sussex BN21 3XE
E info@jordanproductionsltd.co.uk

KEAN PRODUCTIONS
T 020 3151 2710
Communications House, 14 Stirrup Way
Crawley RH10 7RH
E info@keanprods.com
W www.keanprods.com

KELLY, Robert C. T 0141 533 5856
PO Box 5597, Glasgow G77 9DH
E office@robertckelly.co.uk
W www.robertckelly.co.uk

KENWRIGHT, Bill LTD T 020 7446 6200
BKL House, 1 Venice Walk
London W2 1RR
F 020 7446 6222
E info@kenwright.com
W www.kenwright.com

KING, Belinda
CREATIVE PRODUCTIONS T 01604 720041
BK Studios, 157 Clarence Avenue
Kingsthorpe, Northampton NN2 6NY
F 01604 721448
E casting@belindaking.com
W www.belindaking.com

KING'S HEAD THEATRE T 020 7226 8561
Contact: Adam Spreadbury-Maher (Artistic Director)
115 Upper Street, Islington
London N1 1QN
BO 020 7478 0160
E info@kingsheadtheatre.com
W www.kingsheadtheatre.com

LATCHMERE THEATRE T 020 7978 2620
Contact: Chris Fisher
Unit 5A, Spaces Business Centre
Ingate Place, London SW8 3NS
E latchmere@fishers.org.uk

LEIGH-PEMBERTON, David T 020 7112 8445
43-44 Berners Street, London W1T 3ND
E david@leigh-pemberton.co.uk
W www.davidleigh-pemberton.co.uk

LHK PRODUCTIONS LTD T 01744 808907
20 Maltby Close, St Helens WA9 5GJ
E info@lhkproductions.co.uk
W www.lhkproductions.co.uk

LHP LTD T 07973 938634
9 Coombe Court, Hayne Road
Beckenham, Kent BR3 4XD
E lhpltd@msn.com

LIMELIGHT PRODUCTIONS T 020 8853 9570
Unit 13, The io Centre, The Royal Arsenal
Seymour Street, London SE18 6SX
F 020 8853 9579
E enquiries@thelimelightgroup.co.uk

LINNIT PRODUCTIONS LTD T 020 7349 7222
Worlds End Studios, 132-134 Lots Road
London SW10 0RJ

LIVE THEATRE T 0191 261 2694
Broad Chare, Quayside
Newcastle upon Tyne NE1 3DQ
E info@live.org.uk
W www.live.org.uk

LONDON BUBBLE
THEATRE COMPANY LTD T 020 7237 4434
5 Elephant Lane, London SE16 4JD
E admin@londonbubble.org.uk
W www.londonbubble.org.uk

LONDON CLASSIC THEATRE T 020 8669 2221
The Production Office, 23 West Street
Carshalton, Surrey SM5 2PT
E admin@londonclassictheatre.co.uk
W www.londonclassictheatre.co.uk

Richard Jordan Productions Ltd

- **Producing**
- **General Management**
  UK and International Productions
  and International Festivals
- **Consultancy**

Richard Jordan Productions Ltd
Mews Studios, 16 Vernon Yard, London W11 2DX
T: 020 7243 9001 F: 020 7313 9667
e-mail: info@richardjordanproductions.com

LONDON MANAGEMENT
(UK) LTD T 01202 522711
The Old Dairy, Throop Road
Bournemouth BH8 0DL
F 01202 522311
E nicky@london-management.co.uk
W www.london-management.co.uk

LONDON PRODUCTIONS LTD T 020 7497 5111
PO Box 10703, London WC2H 9ED
E admin@leedean.co.uk

LONDON REPERTORY
COMPANY T/F 020 7258 1944
PO Box 59385, London NW8 1HL
E info@londonrepertorycompany.com
W www.londonrepertorycompany.com

LOVE & PRODUCE T 07455 011639 (UK)
*Contact: Corinne Wahlberg. Performance Art &
Devised Theatre*
T 001 401 830 4095 (US)
E info@loveandproduce.com
W www.loveandproduce.com

MACKINTOSH, Cameron LTD T 020 7637 8866
Contact: Melanie Watts (Casting Assistant)
1 Bedford Square, London WC1B 3RB
F 020 7436 2683
E melanie@camack.co.uk

MACNAGHTEN PRODUCTIONS T 01223 577974
19 Grange Court, Grange Road
Cambridge CB3 9BD

MALCOLM, Christopher
PRODUCTIONS LTD T 07850 555042
26 Rokeby Road, London SE4 1DE
T 020 8692 8563
E jl@christophermalcolmproductions.com

MANS, Johnny
PRODUCTIONS T 01992 470907
Incorporating Encore Magazine
PO Box 196, Hoddesdon
Herts EN10 7WG
T 07974 755997
E johnnymansagent@aol.com
W www.johnnymansproductions.co.uk

MASTERSON, Guy
PRODUCTIONS T 07979 757490
E guy@guymasterson.com
W www.guymasterson.com

MAYK T 0117 925 9999
c/o Bristol Old Vic, King Street
Bristol BS1 4ED
E matthewandkate@mayk.org.uk
W www.mayk.org.uk

**McCABE, Michael
PRODUCTIONS LTD** T 020 7831 7077
The Dutch House, 307-308 High Holborn
London WC1V 7LL
E mailbox@michaelmccabe.net
W www.michaelmccabe.net

McKITTERICK, Tom LTD T/F 001 212 431 7697
113 Greene Street
New York 10012, USA
E tommckitterick@aol.com

McLAUGHLIN, Dermot T 07957 491036
Freelance Producer
Brighton/London,
E dermotmclaughlin@me.com
W www.dermotmclaughlin.com

MEADOW, Jeremy T 020 7436 2244
26 Goodge Street, London W1T 2QG
F 0870 7627882
E info@jeremymeadow.com

MENZIES, Lee LTD T 020 7240 4070
19 Garrick Street, London WC2E 9AX
F 020 7681 3670
E leemenzies@leemenzies.co.uk
W www.leemenzies.co.uk

METAL RABBIT LTD T 07813 640858
London Based Commercial Theatre Producers
360A Clapham Road, London SW9 9AR
E gjwarren@metalrabbit.org.uk
W www.metalrabbit.org.uk

**MIDDLE GROUND
THEATRE CO LTD** T 01684 577231
3 Gordon Terrace, Malvern Wells
Malvern, Worcestershire WR14 4ER
F 01684 574472
E middleground@middlegroundtheatre.co.uk
W www.middlegroundtheatre.co.uk

MJE PRODUCTIONS LTD T 01536 560393
Contact: Carole Winter, Michael Edwards
The Enterprise Centre, Priors Hall
Weldon, Northants NN17 5EU
E info@mjeproductions.com
W www.mjeproductions.com

MOKITAGRIT T 07980 564849
75D Humber Road, London SE3 7LR
E mail@mokitagrit.com
W www.mokitagrit.com

MOVING THEATRE T 01323 815726
16 Laughton Lodge, Nr Lewes
East Sussex BN8 6BY
F 01323 815736
E info@movingtheatre.com
W www.movingtheatre.com

**MTP (MATTHEW TOWNSHEND
PRODUCTIONS LTD)** T 01394 384505
*Production & Management. Main & Small Scale Touring,
Community, Theatre in Education*
1 Fitzgerald Road, Woodbridge
Suffolk IP12 1EN
E mtproductions@btconnect.com
W www.mtproductions.co.uk

MUSIC THEATRE LONDON T 07831 243942
c/o Capriol Films, The Coach House
35 High Street, Holt, Norfolk NR25 6BN
T 01263 712600
E tony.britten@capriolfilms.co.uk
W www.capriolfilms.co.uk

NADINE'S WINDOW
Theatre Company
E nadineswindow@yahoo.co.uk
W www.nadineswindow.com

NATIONAL ANGELS T 020 7349 7060
Worlds End Studios
132-134 Lots Road
London SW10 0RJ
E admin@nationalangels.com

NATIONAL THEATRE T 020 7452 3333
Upper Ground, South Bank
London SE1 9PX
F 020 7452 3344
W www.nationaltheatre.org.uk

**NEAL STREET
PRODUCTIONS LTD** T 020 7240 8890
1st Floor, 26-28 Neal Street
London WC2H 9QQ
E post@nealstreetproductions.com

NEW PERSPECTIVES T 0115 927 2334
Park Lane Business Centre, Park Lane
Nottingham NG6 0DW
E info@newperspectives.co.uk
W www.newperspectives.co.uk

NEWPALM PRODUCTIONS T 020 8349 0802
26 Cavendish Avenue
London N3 3QN
F 020 8346 8257
E newpalm@btopenworld.com
W www.newpalm.co.uk

**NICHOLAS, Paul & IAN David
ASSOCIATES LTD** T 020 7427 8380
5th Floor, 53 Parker Street
London WC2B 5PT
F 020 7427 8381
E hello@davidianproductions.com
W www.davidianproductions.com

NITROBEAT
E info@nitro.co.uk
W www.nitro.co.uk

**NORDIC NOMAD
PRODUCTIONS** T 07980 619165
*Contact: Tanja Raaste (Creative Producer). Specialising
in New Writing, Site Specific & Interactive Work, Tango &
Dance Events & Festivals*
E info@nordicnomad.com
W www.nordicnomad.com

**NORTHERN BROADSIDES
THEATRE COMPANY** T 01422 369704
Dean Clough, Halifax HX3 5AX
E sue@northern-broadsides.co.uk
W www.northern-broadsides.co.uk

**NORTHERN STAGE (THEATRICAL
PRODUCTIONS) LTD** T 0191 242 7200
Barras Bridge
Newcastle upon Tyne NE1 7RH
F 0191 242 7121
E info@northernstage.co.uk
W www.northernstage.co.uk

NORTHUMBERLAND THEATRE COMPANY (NTC)   T 01665 602586
The Playhouse, Bondgate Without
Alnwick, Northumberland NE66 1PQ
F 01665 605837
E admin@northumberlandtheatre.co.uk
W www.northumberlandtheatre.co.uk

OLD VIC PRODUCTIONS PLC   T 020 7632 5200
Wellington House, 1st Floor
125 Strand, London WC2R 0AP
E becky.barber@oldvicproductions.com

OUT OF JOINT   T 020 7609 0207
7 Thane Works, Thane Villas
London N7 7NU
F 020 7609 0203
E ojo@outofjoint.co.uk
W www.outofjoint.co.uk

OVATION   T 020 8340 4256
Upstairs at The Gatehouse, Highgate Village
London N6 4BD
E events@ovationproductions.com
W www.ovationtheatres.com

PAINES PLOUGH   T 020 7240 4533
4th Floor, 43 Aldwych
London WC2B 4DN
F 020 7240 4534
E office@painesplough.com
W www.painesplough.com

PAPATANGO THEATRE COMPANY   T 07834 958804
360 Kingsland Road, London E8 4DA
E info@papatango.co.uk
W www.papatango.co.uk

PAPER MOON THEATRE COMPANY THE   T 020 8873 1901
Contact: Jan Hunt (Producer/Director). Specialising in Traditional 'Music Hall'
6 Thames Meadow, West Molesey
Surrey KT8 1TQ
E jan@papermoontheatre.co.uk

PASSWORD PRODUCTIONS LTD   T 020 7284 3733
Contact: John Mackay
85B Torriano Avenue, London NW5 2RX
E johnmackay2001@aol.com

PENDLE PRODUCTIONS LTD   T 01253 839375
Bridge Farm, 249 Hawes Side Lane
Blackpool FY4 4AA
F 01253 792930
E admin@pendleproductions.co.uk
W www.pendleproductions.co.uk

PENTABUS THEATRE   T 01584 856564
Bromfield, Ludlow, Shropshire SY8 2JU
E info@pentabus.co.uk
W www.pentabus.co.uk

PEOPLE SHOW   T 020 7729 1841
Brady Arts Centre, 192-196 Hanbury Street
London E1 5HU
E people@peopleshow.co.uk
W www.peopleshow.co.uk

PERFECT PITCH MUSICALS LTD   T 020 7930 1087
5A Irving Street, London WC2H 7AT
E info@perfectpitchmusicals.com
W www.perfectpitchmusicals.com

PERFORMANCE BUSINESS THE   T 01932 888885
78 Oatlands Drive, Weybridge
Surrey KT13 9HT
E info@theperformance.biz
W www.theperformance.biz

PILOT THEATRE   T 01904 635755
Performance Work across Platforms & National Touring
York Theatre Royal, St Leonard's Place
York YO1 7HD
E info@pilot-theatre.com
W www.pilot-theatre.com

PLAYFUL PRODUCTIONS   T 020 7811 4600
4th Floor, 41-44 Great Queen Street
London WC2B 5AD
F 020 7811 4622
E aboutus@playfuluk.com
W www.playfuluk.com

POLEROID THEATRE
c/o 32 Leigham Hall
Streatham Hill, London SW16 1DN
E molly@poleroidtheatre.co.uk
W www.poleroidtheatre.co.uk

POLKA THEATRE   T 020 8545 8323
240 The Broadway
Wimbledon SW19 1SB
F 020 8545 8365
E stephen@polkatheatre.com
W www.polkatheatre.com

POPULAR PRODUCTIONS LTD   T 020 8292 5305
79 Carlingford Road, London N15 3EJ
E info@popularproductions.com
W www.popularproductions.com

PORTER, Richard LTD   T 07884 183404
214 Grange Road, London SE1 3AA
E office@richardporterltd.com
W www.richardporterltd.com

POSTER, Kim   T 020 7240 3098
Stanhope Productions Ltd
4th Floor, 80-81 St Martin's Lane
London WC2N 4AA
F 020 7504 8656
E admin@stanhopeprod.com

PROMENADE PRODUCTIONS   T 020 7240 3407
20 Thayer Street, London W1U 2DD
E nnewton@promenadeproductions.com
W www.promenadeproductions.com

PUGH, David & ROGERS, Dafydd   T 020 7292 0390
David Pugh Ltd, Wyndhams Theatre
Charing Cross Road, London WC2H 0DA
F 020 7292 0399
E dpl@davidpughltd.com

PURSUED BY A BEAR PRODUCTIONS   T 01252 745445
Farnham Maltings, Bridge Square
Farnham GU9 7QR
E pursuedbyabear@yahoo.co.uk
W www.pursuedbyabear.co.uk

PW PRODUCTIONS LTD   T 020 7395 7580
2nd Floor, 80-81 St Martin's Lane
London WC2N 4AA
F 020 7240 2947
E info@pwprods.co.uk
W www.pwprods.co.uk

QDOS ENTERTAINMENT T 01723 500038
Qdos House, Queen Margaret's Road
Scarborough, North Yorkshire YO11 2YH
F 01723 361958
E info@qdosentertainment.co.uk
W www.qdosentertainment.co.uk

**QUAIFE, James
PRODUCTIONS**
Contact: James Quaife. Twitter: @JamesQuaife
E office@jamesquaifeproductions.com
W www.jamesquaifeproductions.com

QUANTUM THEATRE T 020 8317 9000
The Old Button Factory
1-11 Bannockburn Road
Plumstead, London SE18 1ET
E office@quantumtheatre.co.uk
W www.quantumtheatre.co.uk

**RAGS & FEATHERS
THEATRE COMPANY** T 020 8224 2203
80 Summer Road, Thames Ditton
Surrey KT7 0QP
T 07958 724374
E jilldowning.tls@gmail.com

**RAIN OR SHINE
THEATRE COMPANY** T 0330 660 0541
Twitter: @rainorshineUK
25 Paddock Gardens, Longlevens
Gloucester GL2 0ED
E theatre@rainorshine.co.uk
W www.rainorshine.co.uk

REAL CIRCUMSTANCE THEATRE COMPANY
50 Rectory Road, Wivenhoe
Colchester CO7 9ER
E info@realcircumstance.com
W www.realcircumstance.com

**REALLY USEFUL
GROUP LTD THE** T 020 7240 0880
Theatre Licensing & Production
17 Slingsby Place, London WC2E 9AB
F 020 7240 1204

RED ROOM THE T 020 7470 8790
The Garden Studio, 71-75 Shelton Street
London WC2H 9JQ
E admin@theredroom.org.uk
W www.theredroom.org.uk

RED ROSE CHAIN T 01473 603388
Gippeswyk Hall, Gippeswyk Avenue
Ipswich, Suffolk IP2 9AF
E info@redrosechain.com
W www.redrosechain.com

**RED SHIFT THEATRE
COMPANY** T/F 020 8540 1271
PO Box 60151, London SW19 2TB
E redshift100@gmail.com
W www.redshifttheatreco.co.uk

REDROOFS THEATRE SCHOOL T 01628 674092
Contact: By Post
Novello Theatre, 26 Bath Road
Maidenhead, Berkshire SL6 4JT
E info@redroofs.co.uk
W www.redroofs.co.uk

REDUCED CIRCUMSTANCES T 07585 155534
Contact: Emma Keele
E info@reducedcircumstances.co.uk
W www.reducedcircumstances.co.uk

REGENT'S PARK THEATRE LTD T 0844 3753460
Open Air Theatre
Stage Door Gate, Inner Circle
Regent's Park, London NW1 4NU
W www.openairtheatre.com

**REVEAL THEATRE
COMPANY LTD** T 07828 179614
72 Barnfield Road, Stoke on Trent ST6 3DH
E julia.barton@revealtheatre.co.uk
W www.revealtheatre.co.uk

RGC PRODUCTIONS T 07740 286727
260 Kings Road, Kingston, Surrey KT2 5HX
E info@rgcproductions.com
W www.rgcproductions.com

RHO DELTA LTD T 020 7436 1392
Contact: Greg Ripley-Duggan
26 Goodge Street, London W1T 2QG
E info@ripleyduggan.com

ROCKET THEATRE T 0161 969 1444
32 Baxter Road, Sale, Manchester M33 3AL
T 07788 723570
E martin@rockettheatre.co.uk
W www.rockettheatre.co.uk

ROSE THEATRE KINGSTON T 020 8546 6983
*Contact: Jerry Gunn (Executive Producer), Naomi Webb
(Assistant Producer)*
24-26 High Street, Kingston Upon Thames
Surrey KT1 1HL
F 020 8546 8783
E admin@rosetheatrekingston.org
W www.rosetheatrekingston.org

ROSENTHAL, Suzanna T 020 7436 2244
26 Goodge Street, London W1T 2QG
F 0870 7627882
E admin@meadowrosenthal.com
W www.meadowrosenthal.com

**ROYAL COURT THEATRE
PRODUCTIONS LTD** T 020 7565 5050
Sloane Square, London SW1W 8AS
F 020 7565 5001
E info@royalcourttheatre.com
W www.royalcourttheatre.com

ROYAL EXCHANGE THEATRE T 0161 833 9333
St Ann's Square, Manchester M2 7DH
W www.royalexchange.co.uk

**ROYAL SHAKESPEARE
COMPANY** T 020 7845 0500
1 Earlham Street, London WC2H 9LL
F 020 7845 0505
W www.rsc.org.uk

**ROYAL SHAKESPEARE
COMPANY** T 01789 296655
Royal Shakespeare Theatre, Waterside
Stratford-upon-Avon CV37 6BB
F 01789 403710
W www.rsc.org.uk

RUBINSTEIN, Mark LTD T 020 7021 0787
25 Short Street, London SE1 8LJ
F 0870 7059731
E info@mrluk.com

SCAMP THEATRE LTD T 01462 734843
44 Church Lane, Arlesey, Beds SG15 6UX
E admin@scamptheatre.com
W www.scamptheatre.com

SCENE THREE CREATIVE　T 01963 362937
*Creative Services. Project Management. Theatre
Production. Writing*
5 Gold Street, Stalbridge, Dorset DT10 2LX
E info@scenethreecreative.co.uk
W www.scenethreecreative.co.uk

**SEABRIGHT
PRODUCTIONS LTD**　T 020 7439 1173
Palace Theatre, Shaftesbury Avenue
London W1D 5AY
F 020 7183 6023
E office@seabrightproductions.com
W www.seabrightproductions.com

**SELL A DOOR THEATRE
COMPANY LTD**　T 020 3355 8567
Athelney House, 161-165 Greenwich High Road
London SE10 8JA
E info@selladoor.com
W www.selladoor.com

SHAKESPEARE'S MEN　T 01708 222938
10 Dee Close, Upminster, Essex RM14 1QD
E terence@terencemustoo.com
W www.terencemustoo.com

SHARED EXPERIENCE　T 01865 305321
c/o Oxford Playhouse, Beaumont Street
Oxford OX1 2LW
E admin@sharedexperience.org.uk
W www.sharedexperience.org.uk

SHOW OF STRENGTH　T 0117 902 0235
74 Chessel Street, Bedminster, Bristol BS3 3DN
E info@showofstrength.org.uk
W www.showofstrength.org.uk

**SHOWCASE ENTERTAINMENTS
INTERNATIONAL LTD**　T 01325 316224
*Contact: Geoffrey J.L. Hindmarch (Executive Producer),
Paul Morgan (Creative Director). Theatre. Cruises.
Hotels. Corporate*
2 Lumley Close, Newton Aycliffe
Co Durham DL5 5PA
E gjl@showcaseproductions.co.uk
W www.showcaseproductions.co.uk

SIMPLY THEATRE　T 00 41 22 8600518
Avenue de Choiseul 23A, 1290 Versoix
Switzerland
E info@simplytheatre.com
W www.simplytheatre.com

SINDEN, Marc PRODUCTIONS　T 020 8455 3278
1 Hogarth Hill, London NW11 6AY
E mail@sindenproductions.com
W www.sindenproductions.com

SIXTEENFEET PRODUCTIONS　T 020 7326 4417
25 Rattray Road, London SW2 1AZ
T 07958 448690
E info@sixteenfeet.co.uk
W www.sixteenfeet.co.uk

SOHO THEATRE COMPANY　T 020 7287 5060
21 Dean Street, London W1D 3NE
F 020 7287 5061
W www.sohotheatre.com

**SPARROW, Daniel
PRODUCTIONS**　T 07879 897900
Contact: Daniel Sparrow
3708/8 Walworth Road, London SE1 6EL
E daniel@danielsparrowproductions.com
W www.danielsparrowproductions.com

**SPARROW, Daniel
PRODUCTIONS**　T 07879 897900
Contact: Daniel Sparrow
44B Floral Street
London WC2E 9DA
E info@danielsparrowproductions.com
W www.danielsparrowproductions.com

SPHINX THEATRE COMPANY　T 07768 332564
Oval House, 52-54 Kennington Oval
London SE11 5SY
E info@sphinxtheatre.co.uk
W www.sphinxtheatre.co.uk

SPLATS ENTERTAINMENT　T 07944 283659
Contact: Mike Redwood
5 Denmark Street, London WC2H 8LP
E mike@splatsentertainment.com
W www.splatsentertainment.com

SPLITMOON THEATRE　T 020 7252 8126
PO Box 58891, London SE15 9DE
E info@splitmoontheatre.org
W www.splitmoontheatre.org

**SQUAREDEAL
PRODUCTIONS LTD**　T 020 7249 5966
Contact: Jenny Topper
24 De Beauvoir Square
London N1 4LE
T 07785 394241
E jenny@jennytopper.com

**STAGE ENTERTAINMENT
UK LTD**　T 020 7632 4700
Wellington House, 125 Strand
London WC2R 0AP
E info@seuk.uk.com
W www.stage-entertainment.co.uk

**STANHOPE
PRODUCTIONS LTD**　T 020 7240 3098
4th Floor, 80-81 St Martin's Lane
London WC2N 4AA
F 020 7504 8656
E admin@stanhopeprod.com

**STELLAR QUINES
THEATRE COMPANY**　T 0131 229 3851
30B Grindlay Street, Edinburgh EH3 9AX
E admin@stellarquines.co.uk
W www.stellarquines.com

**STEPHENSON, Ian
PRODUCTIONS LTD**　T 07960 999374
E soholondon@aol.com

**STRAIGHT LINE
PRODUCTIONS**　T 01737 535078
69 Shawley Way, Epsom Downs
Surrey KT18 5PD
E hilary@straightlinemanagement.co.uk

TALAWA THEATRE COMPANY　T 020 7251 6644
Ground Floor, 53-55 East Road
London N1 6AH
F 020 7251 5969
E hq@talawa.com
W www.talawa.com

**TAMASHA THEATRE
COMPANY**　T 020 7749 0090
RichMix, 35-47 Bethnal Green Road, London E1 6LA
F 020 7729 8906
E info@tamasha.org.uk
W www.tamasha.org.uk

TBA MUSIC T 0845 1203722
1 St Gabriels Road, London NW2 4DS
F 0700 607 0808
E peter@tbagroup.co.uk

TEG PRODUCTIONS LTD
See ROSENTHAL, Suzanna

THAT'S ENTERTAINMENT
PRODUCTIONS T 07803 050714
PO Box 223, Bexhill-on-Sea
East Sussex TN40 9DP
E chris@thatsentertainmentproductions.co.uk
W www.thatsentertainmentproductions.co.uk

THEATR NA NÓG T 01639 641771
Unit 3, Millands Road Industrial Estate
Neath SA11 1NJ
F 01639 647941
E drama@theatr-nanog.co.uk
W www.theatr-nanog.co.uk

THEATRE ABSOLUTE T 07799 292957
Shop Front Theatre
38 City Arcade
Coventry CV1 3HW
E info@theatreabsolute.co.uk
W www.theatreabsolute.co.uk

THEATRE ALIVE!
13 St Barnabas Road
London E17 8JZ
E andrew@andrewvisnevski.com
W www.theatrealive.org.uk

THEATRE OF COMEDY
COMPANY LTD T 020 7379 3345
Shaftesbury Theatre
210 Shaftesbury Avenue
London WC2H 8DP
F 020 7836 8181
E info@shaftesburytheatre.com

THEATRE ROYAL HAYMARKET
PRODUCTIONS T 020 7930 8890
Theatre Royal Haymarket
18 Suffolk Street
London SW1Y 4HT
E nigel@trh.co.uk

THEATRE ROYAL
STRATFORD EAST T 020 8279 1134
Gerry Raffles Square, Stratford
London E15 1BN
F 020 8534 8318
E theatreroyal@stratfordeast.com
W www.stratfordeast.com

THEATRE SANS FRONTIERES T 01434 603114
Queen's Hall, Beaumont Street
Hexham NE46 3LS
F 01434 607206
E info@tsf.org.uk
W www.tsf.org.uk

THEATRE TOURS
INTERNATIONAL LTD T 07979 757490
Contact: Guy Masterson
E admin@theatretoursinternational.com
W www.theatretoursinternational.com

THEATRE WORKOUT LTD T 020 8144 2290
13A Stratheden Road, Blackheath
London SE3 7TH
E enquiries@theatreworkout.com
W www.theatreworkout.com

THOMAS, Hazel PRODUCTIONS T 07948 211083
Flat 6, Highwood Manor
21 Constitution Hill
Ipswich, Suffolk IP1 3RG
E htproductions@live.co.uk
W www.hazel-thomas.wix.com/htproductions

TIATA FAHODZI T 07880 317889
Watford Palace Theatre
20 Clarendon Road
London WD17 1JZ
E info@tiatafahodzi.com
W www.tiatafahodzi.com

TOLD BY AN IDIOT T 020 7407 4123
Twitter: @toldbyanidiot93
Rada Studios, 16 Chenies Street
London WC1E 7EX
E info@toldbyanidiot.org
W www.toldbyanidiot.org

TOPPER, Jenny T 020 7249 5966
SquaredDeal Productions Ltd
24 De Beauvoir Square
London N1 4LE
T 07785 394241
E jenny@jennytopper.com

TOWER THEATRE
COMPANY T/F 020 7353 5700
Full-time, Non-professional
St Bride Foundation, Bride Lane
London EC4Y 8EQ
E info@towertheatre.freeserve.co.uk
W www.towertheatre.org.uk

TOWNSEND PRODUCTIONS T 07949 635910
5 Moorhills Road, Wing
Bucks LU7 0NG
E townsendproductions@hotmail.co.uk
W www.townsendproductions.org.uk

TRAFFIC OF THE STAGE T 020 8883 7817
Contact: John Cooper
154A East End Road, East Finchley
London N2 0RY
E trafficofthestage@aol.com
W www.trafficofthestage.com

TREAGUS, Andrew ASSOCIATES LTD
32-33 St James's Place
London SW1A 1NR
E admin@at-assoc.co.uk

TRENDS ENTERTAINMENT T 01253 396534
Unit 4, 9 Chorley Road, Blackpool
Lancashire FY3 7XQ
T 07506 171054
E info@trendsentertainment.com
W www.trendsentertainment.com

TRESTLE THEATRE COMPANY T 01727 850950
Visual/Physical Theatre. Music. Choreography. New
Writing. Various Spaces Available for Private Hire
Trestle Arts Base, Russet Drive
Herts, St Albans AL4 0JQ
E admin@trestle.org.uk
W www.trestle.org.uk

TRICYCLE THEATRE
COMPANY T 020 7372 6611
269 Kilburn High Road
London NW6 7JR
F 020 7328 0795
E admin@tricycle.co.uk
W www.tricycle.co.uk

TRIUMPH ENTERTAINMENT LTD
4th Floor, 1 Wardour Street
London W1D 6PA
E paul@paulelliott.ltd.uk
T 020 7379 4870

TRIUMPH PROSCENIUM PRODUCTIONS LTD
The Cottage, West Lavant
Chichester, West Sussex PO18 9AH
T 01243 527186

TURTLE KEY ARTS
Lyric Hammersmith, Lyric Square
King Street, London W6 0QL
E admin@turtlekeyarts.org.uk
W www.turtlekeyarts.org.uk
T 020 8964 5060

TWO'S COMPANY
244 Upland Road, London SE22 0DN
E graham@2scompanytheatre.co.uk
T 020 8299 3714

UK ARTS INTERNATIONAL
Theatre Royal Margate, Addington Street
Margate CT9 1PW
E janryan@ukarts.com
W www.ukarts.com

UK PRODUCTIONS LTD
Brook House, Mint Street
Godalming, Surrey GU7 1HE
E mail@ukproductions.co.uk
W www.ukproductions.co.uk
T 01483 423600

UNRESTRICTED VIEW
Above Hen & Chickens Theatre Bar, 109 St Paul's Road
London N1 2NA
E henandchickens@aol.com
W www.henandchickens.com
T 020 7704 2001

UPSTART CROWS THEATRE COMPANY
14 Chesnut Road, Raynes Park
London SW20 8EB
E upstartcrows@outlook.com
T 020 8543 4085

VANDER ELST, Anthony PRODUCTIONS
The Studio, 14 College Road
Bromley, Kent BR1 3NS
T 020 8466 5580

VOLCANO THEATRE COMPANY LTD
27-29 Hight Street, Swansea SA1 1LG
E mail@volcanotheatre.co.uk
W www.volcanotheatre.co.uk
T 01792 464790

WALKING FORWARD
29 Hampton Close, Fenstanton
Cambridgeshire PE28 9HB
E info@walkingforward.co.uk
W www.walkingforward.co.uk
T 01480 496309

WALLACE, Kevin LTD
Amadeus House, 27B Floral Street, London WC2E 9DP
E info@kevinwallace.co.uk
T 020 7812 7238

WAREHOUSE PHOENIX LTD
Formerly Warehouse Theatre Croydon. Producers of new work & The IInternational Playwriting Festival
87 Great Titchfield Street, London W1W 6RL
E warehousephoenix@outlook.com
W www.warehousephoenix.co.uk

WAX, Kenny LTD
3rd Floor, 62 Shaftesbury Avenue, London W1D 6LT
W www.kennywax.com
T 020 7437 1736

WELDON, Duncan C. PRODUCTIONS LTD
The Cottage, West Lavant
Chichester, West Sussex PO18 9AH
T 01243 527186

WESTENDFRONT PRODUCTIONS LTD
19A Goodge Street
London W1Y 2PH
E info@westendfrontproductions.co.uk
T 020 8150 7294

WHITALL, Keith
25 Solway, Hailsham
East Sussex BN27 3HB
T 01323 844882

WHITEHALL, Michael
6 Embankment, Putney
London SW15 1LB
E whitehallfilms@gmail.com
T/F 020 8785 3737

WILDER, David PRODUCTIONS
1 Elmlea Drive, Olney
Bucks MK46 5HU
E info@davidwilderproductions.co.uk
W www.davidwilderproductions.co.uk
T 07710 907221

WILLS, Newton MANAGEMENT
12 St Johns Road
Isleworth
Middlesex TW7 6NN
F 00 33 4 68218685
E newton.wills@aol.com
W www.newtonwills.com
T 07989 398381

WILSON, Jamie
Jamie Wilson Productions Ltd
4th Floor, 1 Wardour Street
Leicester Square
London W1D 6PA
E info@jamiewilsonproductions.com
W www.jamiewilsonproductions.com
T 020 7240 0748

WIZARD THEATRE
Blenheim Villa, Burr Street
Harwell, Oxfordshire OX11 0DT
E admin@wizardtheatre.co.uk
W www.wizardtheatre.co.uk
T 0800 5832373

WORD & MUSIC COMPANY THE
The Hub @ St Alban's Fulham
2 Margravine Road
London W6 8HJ
E info@associatedstudios.co.uk
W www.associatedstudios.co.uk
T 020 7385 2038

WORTMAN UK / POLESTAR PICTURES UK / US
Film & Television Productions
48 Chiswick Staithe
London W4 3TP
T 07976 805976
E neville@speakwell.co.uk
W www.speakwell.co.uk
T 020 8994 8886

YELLOW EARTH THEATRE
The Albany, Douglas Way
London SE8 4AG
E admin@yellowearth.org
W www.yellowearth.org
T 020 8694 6631

YOUNG VIC THEATRE
66 The Cut, London SE1 8LZ
E info@youngvic.org
W www.youngvic.org
T 020 7922 2800

Theatre

There are hundreds of theatres and theatre companies in the UK, varying dramatically in size and type. The theatre sections are organised under headings which best indicate a theatre's principal area of work. A summary of each of these is below.

Alternative & Community

Many of these companies tour to arts centres, small and middle-scale theatres, and non-theatrical venues which do not have a resident company, or they may be commissioned to develop site-specific projects. The term 'alternative' is sometimes used to describe work that is more experimental in style and execution.

Children, Young People & TIE

The primary focus of these theatre companies is to reach younger audiences. They often tour to smaller theatres, schools and non-theatrical venues. Interactive teaching – through audience participation and workshops – is often a feature of their work.

English Speaking Theatre Companies in Europe

These work principally outside of the UK. Some are based in one venue whilst others are touring companies. Their work varies enormously and includes theatre for young people, large-scale musicals, revivals of classics and dinner theatre. Actors are employed either for an individual production or a 'season' of several plays.

London Theatres

Larger theatres situated in the West End and Central London. A few are producing houses, but most are leased to theatre producers who take responsibility for putting together a company for a run of a single show. In such cases it is they and not the venue who cast productions (often with the help of casting directors). Alternatively, a production will open outside London and tour to provincial theatres, then subsequently, if successful, transfer to a London venue.

Outer London, Fringe & Venues

Small and middle-scale theatres in Outer London and around the country. Some are producing houses, others are only available for hire. Many of the London venues have provided useful directions on how they may be reached by public transport.

Provincial / Touring

Theatre producers and other companies sell their ready-made productions to the provincial/touring theatres, a list of larger venues outside London. A run in each theatre varies between a night and several weeks, but a week per venue for tours of plays is usual. Even if a venue is not usually a producing house, most provincial theatres and arts centres put on a family show at Christmas.

Puppet Theatre Companies

Some puppet theatres are one-performer companies who literally create their own work from scratch. The content and style of productions varies enormously. For example, not all are aimed at children, and some are more interactive than others. Although we list a few theatres with puppet companies in permanent residence, this kind of work often involves touring. As with all small and middle scale touring, performers who are willing, and have the skills, to involve themselves with all aspects of company life are always more valuable.

Repertory (Regional) Theatres

Theatres situated outside London which employ a resident company of actors (i.e. the 'repertory company') on a play-by-play basis or for a season of several plays. In addition to the main auditorium (usually the largest acting space) these theatres may have a smaller studio theatre attached, which will be home to an additional company whose focus is education or the production of new plays (see 'Theatre: Children, Young People & TIE'). In recent years the length of repertory seasons has become shorter; this means that a number of productions are no longer in-house. It is common for gaps in the performance calendar to be filled by tours mounted by theatre producers, other repertory theatres and non-venue based production companies.

CASE STUDY

Louis Hartshorn is the Executive Director of the Arts Theatre; a commercial theatre situated between London's Leicester Square and Covent Garden. The role of Executive Director includes overall responsibility for selecting productions, profitability, staffing and relationships with the rest of the theatre industry.

The Arts Theatre is the West End's smallest receiving house – it is one of the few remaining independent commercial theatres. The building, just by Leicester Square tube station, is a thriving hive of activity with a 350-seat auditorium over two levels, two rehearsal rooms, a studio theatre with bar, a cocktail club and a café.

The Arts is steeped in West End theatrical history. Built in 1927, it has hosted seminal plays by great writers such as Beckett, Stoppard and Pinter, was the original London venue for Monty Python and has been run by some of the country's finest artistic directors, such as Sir Peter Hall and Alec Clunes. Recent productions have been very varied, including a 13-month run of Ghost Stories, Green Day's American Idiot, Trevor Nunn's production of All That Fall by Samuel Beckett and Simon Callow in A Christmas Carol.

"because of the high demand for the venue it is possible to control the quality and style of the productions at the theatre with careful programming"

As a "receiving house", the Arts is available for hire by independent producers. Most West End theatres and many touring venues operate in this way. This means the Arts does not create and produce its own work, however because of the high demand for the venue, it is possible to control the quality and style of the productions at the theatre with careful programming.

Some theatres receive public funding – they may use this money to develop their own productions, pay in-house creative staff (such as an artistic director who may direct some of their own productions), or to attract certain types of show to their theatre for the cultural enrichment of the area they work in.

These theatres may accept script submissions, incubate and train creative individuals, develop work with partner companies and allocate resources to community and education projects. The cost of doing these things is borne by public funding, sponsorship, donations and ticket sales – in varying proportions from venue to venue.

The commercial theatre sector operates differently – the creative impetus comes from the producer who develops a production and then proposes it to the venue. The venue is there to facilitate their vision; to provide the resources for a first class production and customer experience.

The most common error in contacting theatres is not to have researched the way in which they work – it is no use sending a script to a receiving house which does not produce its own productions, and you could be wasting time by approaching a 'producing' venue about hiring their theatre for a production of your own.

The best approaches to the Arts Theatre include a synopsis, a copy of the script, details of the key creative team, information about the budget and marketing plan, and a proposed time-frame. Normal programming for the Arts is about 9-12 months in advance but occasionally gaps in the programme may appear sooner than that, or a particularly exciting production may be programmed further in advance.

"Nothing makes me happier than the days when every rehearsal room, dressing room and theatre space is in use and the café is full of people ready to entertain or be entertained. Knowing that all the facilities we offer are part of a sustainable ecosystem is immensely satisfying and I look forward to welcoming many people to the Arts Theatre in the years to come"

Theatre

Theatres, especially the old buildings, have high overheads and without funding to cover these, it's vital that programming decisions take the commercial position into account. This has driven many West End theatres into more and more mainstream shows, such as celebrity-focused productions and stage versions of successful films. Opening the studio theatre in 2015 has enabled the Arts to take a step in the opposite direction by participating in the creative process. Above the Arts provides a platform and environment for new work, emerging artists and small-scale productions which are looking for a home in the centre of London. Due to the infrastructure that already exists at the theatre, such as box office, administrative staff and technical department, it has been possible to offer the venue at an affordable rate. This encourages creative risk-taking and makes it accessible to developing artists who may not have the budget to work in some other central London venues.

This space is also the home of a new lunchtime theatre programme. Lunchtime theatre was very popular in the 1980s, however due to rising costs of central venues it was side-lined and ultimately vanished. Above the Arts is curating and supporting a year-round programme of lunchtime theatre. In keeping with its accessible ethos, these plays are affordably-priced, under an hour and encourage the audience to eat their lunch during the performance.

Every venue plays a unique role in its local and professional community. The Arts Theatre aims to straddle the divide between commercial entertainment and development for the artistic community without relying on public subsidy.

Nothing makes me happier than the days when every rehearsal room, dressing room and theatre space is in use and the café is full of people ready to entertain or be entertained. Knowing that all the facilities we offer are part of a sustainable ecosystem is immensely satisfying and I look forward to welcoming many people to the Arts Theatre in the years to come.

**For more information visit
www.artstheatrewestend.co.uk**

1623 THEATRE COMPANY   T 01332 285434
QUAD, Market Place
Cathedral Quarter, Derby DE1 3AS
E messages@1623theatre.co.uk
W www.1623theatre.co.uk

ABERYSTWYTH ARTS CENTRE   T 01970 621512
Penglais, Aberystwyth
Ceredigion SY23 3DE
F 01970 622883
E ggo@aber.ac.uk
W www.aber.ac.uk/artscentre

ADMIRATION THEATRE
Twitter: @theatre.com
E email@admirationtheatre.com
W www.admirationtheatre.com

**AGE EXCHANGE
THEATRE TRUST**   T 020 8318 9105
Contact: Suzanne Lockett (Director of Operations)
Number 11, Blackheath Village
London SE3 9LA
E administrator@age-exchange.org.uk
W www.age-exchange.org.uk

ALTERNATIVE ARTS   T 020 8800 6665
Top Studio, Montefiore Centre
Hanbury Street, London E1 5HZ
E info@alternativearts.co.uk
W www.alternativearts.co.uk

ANGLES THEATRE THE   BO 01945 474447
Alexandra Road, Wisbech
Cambridgeshire PE13 1HQ
E office@anglestheatre.co.uk

APELT, Steve PRODUCTIONS   T 01278 458253
20 Sandpiper Road, Blakespool Park
Bridgwater, Somerset TA6 5QU
E steve.apelt@virgin.net
W www.steveapelt.co.uk

ARUNDEL JAILHOUSE   T/F 01903 889821
Arundel Town Hall, Arundel, West Sussex BN18 9AP
E info@arundeljailhouse.co.uk
W www.arundeljailhouse.co.uk

**ASHTON GROUP
THEATRE THE**   T 01229 430636
The Cooke's Studios, 104 Abbey Road
Barrow-in-Furness, Cumbria LA14 5QR
E theashtongroup@btconnect.com
W www.ashtongroup.co.uk

ATTIC THEATRE COMPANY   T 020 8640 6800
Mitcham Library, 157 London Road
Mitcham CR4 2YR
E info@attictheatrecompany.com
W www.attictheatrecompany.com

BANNER THEATRE   T 0845 4581909
23 Endwood Court Road, Birmingham B20 2RX
E info@bannertheatre.co.uk

BECK THEATRE   T 020 8561 7506
Grange Road, Hayes
Middlesex UB3 2UE
BO 020 8561 8371
E enquiries@becktheatre.org.uk
W www.becktheatre.org.uk

**BLUEYED THEATRE
PRODUCTIONS**   T 07799 137487
13 Ancaster Road, Liverpool L17 9QE
E info@blueyedtheatreproductions.co.uk
W www.blueyedtheatreproductions.co.uk

**BLUNDERBUS THEATRE
COMPANY LTD**   T 01636 678900
The Old Painters Store, Cliff Nook Lane
Newark, Nottinghamshire NG24 1LY
E admin@blunderbus.co.uk
W www.blunderbus.co.uk

CARIB THEATRE COMPANY   T/F 020 8903 4592
73 Lancelot Road, Wembley
Middlesex HA0 2AN
E antoncarib@yahoo.co.uk

**CENTRE FOR
PERFORMANCE RESEARCH**   T 01970 622133
The Foundry, Parry Williams
Penglais Campus SY23 3AJ
F 01970 622132
E info@thecpr.org.uk
W www.thecpr.org.uk

CHAIN REACTION   T/F 020 8981 9527
Millers House, Three Mills Lane
London E3 3DY
E admin@chainreactiontheatre.co.uk
W www.chainreactiontheatre.co.uk

CHATS PALACE   T 020 8533 0227
42-44 Brooksby's Walk, Hackney
London E9 6DF
E info@chatspalace.com
W www.chatspalace.co.uk

CHICKENSHED   T 020 8216 2733
290 Chase Side, Southgate
London N14 4PE
BO 020 8292 9222
E susanj@chickenshed.org.uk
W www.chickenshed.org.uk

CHOL THEATRE   T 01484 536008
Contact: Susan Burns (Director)
Lawrence Batley Theatre, 8 Queen Street
Huddersfield, West Yorkshire HD1 2SP
F 01484 425336
E info@choltheatre.co.uk
W www.choltheatre.co.uk

CITIZENS LEARNING   T 0141 429 5561
Citizens' Theatre, 119 Gorbals Street
Glasgow G5 9DS
F 0141 429 7374
E info@citz.co.uk
W www.citz.co.uk

**CLOSE FOR COMFORT
THEATRE COMPANY**   T 07710 258290
34 Boleyn Walk, Leatherhead, Surrey KT22 7HU
T 01372 378613
E close4comf@aol.com
W www.closeforcomforttheatre.co.uk

COMPLETE WORKS THE   T 020 7377 0280
The Old Truman Brewery, 91 Brick Lane
London E1 6QL
F 020 7247 7405
E info@tcw.org.uk
W www.tcw.org.uk

CURZON KNUTSFORD   T 01565 633005
Primarily Cinema with Hire Spaces
Toft Road, Knutsford, Cheshire WA16 0PE
E manager.knutsford@curzon.com
W www.curzoncinemas.com

CUT-CLOTH THEATRE   T 07950 542346
41 Beresford Road, Highbury, London N5 2HR

EALDFAEDER   **T** 01787 238257
Anglo Saxon Living History & Re-enactment
12 Carleton Close Great Yeldham, Essex CO9 4QJ
E pete@gippeswic.demon.co.uk
W www.ealdfaeder.org

ELECTRIC CABARET   **T** 07714 089763
*Specialising in Physical Theatre, Mime, Street Theatre,
Clowns & Workshops*
50 Oakthorpe Road, Oxford OX2 7BE
E richard@electriccabaret.co.uk
W www.electricccabaret.co.uk

EUROPEAN THEATRE COMPANY THE
15 Beverley Avenue, London SW20 0RL
E admin@europeantheatre.co.uk
W www.europeantheatre.co.uk

**FEMME FATALE
THEATRE COMPANY**   **T** 07779 611414
30 Creighton Avenue, Muswell Hill, London N10 1NU
E dianelefley@yahoo.com
W www.femmefataletheatrecompany.com

**FOREST FORGE
THEATRE COMPANY**   **T** 01425 470188
The Theatre Centre, Endeavour Park, Crow Arch Lane
Ringwood, Hampshire BH24 1SF
E info@forestforge.co.uk
W www.forestforge.co.uk

FOUND THEATRE   **T** 01629 813083
The Byways, Church Street
Monyash, Derbyshire DE45 1JH
E found_theatre@yahoo.co.uk
W www.foundtheatre.org.uk

**FRANTIC THEATRE
COMPANY**   **T/F** 0870 1657350
32 Woodlane, Falmouth TR11 4RF
E bookings@frantictheatre.com
W www.frantictheatre.com

**GALLEON THEATRE
COMPANY LTD**   **T** 020 8310 7276
Head Office, Greenwich Playhouse
50 Openshaw Road, London SE2 0TE
E boxoffice@galleontheatre.co.uk
W www.galleontheatre.co.uk

GRANGE THEATRE   **T** 0161 785 4239
Rochdale Road, Oldham
Greater Manchester OL9 6EA
E grangetheatre@oldham.ac.uk
W www.oldham.ac.uk/grangetheatre

GREASEPAINT ANONYMOUS   **T** 020 8360 9785
Youth Theatre Company
13 Oak Lodge, 50 Eversley Park Road, London N21 1JL
T 07930 421216
E info@greasepaintanonymous.co.uk

**HEBE THEATRE
COMPANY THE**   **T** 01394 285669
Presents The Ruba'iya't of Omar Khayya'm
7 Harvest House, Cobbold Road
Felixstowe, Suffolk IP11 7SP
E c.mugleston672@btinternet.com
W www.thehebetheatrecompany.onesuffolk.net

HIJINX THEATRE   **T** 029 2030 0331
*Touring Theatre Company. Producers of Inclusive
Theatre*
Wales Millennium Centre, Bute Place, Cardiff CF10 5AL
E info@hijinx.org.uk
W www.hijinx.org.uk

**HISTORIA THEATRE
COMPANY**   **T** 020 7837 8008
8 Cloudesley Square, London N1 0HT
T 07811 892079
E kateprice@lineone.net
W www.historiatheatre.com

ICON THEATRE   **T** 01634 813179
The Brook Theatre, Old Town Hall
Chatham, Kent ME4 4SE
E nancy@icontheatre.org.uk
W www.icontheatre.org.uk

IMAGE MUSICAL THEATRE   **T** 020 8743 9380
197 Church Road, Northolt
Middlesex UB5 5BE
F 020 8181 6279
E admin@imagemusicaltheatre.co.uk
W www.imagemusicaltheatre.co.uk

ISOSCELES   **T** 020 8946 3905
7 Amity Grove, Raynes Park
London SW20 0LQ
E patanddave@isosceles.biz
W www.isosceles.biz

KING'S HEAD THEATRE   **T** 020 7226 8561
Contact: Adam Spreadbury-Maher (Artistic Director)
115 Upper Street, Islington
London N1 1QN
BO 020 7193 7845
E info@kingsheadtheatre.com
W www.kingsheadtheatre.com

KNEEHIGH   **T** 01872 267910
Twitter: @wearekneehigh
15 Walsingham Place, Truro
Cornwall TR1 2RP
E office@kneehigh.co.uk
W www.kneehigh.co.uk

KOMEDIA   **T** 01273 647101
44-47 Gardner Street, Brighton BN1 1UN
E info@komedia.co.uk
W www.komedia.co.uk

KORU THEATRE   **T** 020 8579 1029
11 Clovelly Road, London W5 5HF
E info@korutheatre.com
W www.korutheatre.com

LIVE THEATRE   **T** 0191 261 2694
New Writing
Broad Chare, Quayside
Newcastle upon Tyne NE1 3DQ
F 0191 232 2224
E info@live.org.uk
W www.live.org.uk

**LONDON ACTORS
THEATRE COMPANY**   **T** 020 7978 2620
Unit 5A, Imex Business Centre
Ingate Place, London SW8 3NS
E latchmere@fishers.org.uk

**LONDON BUBBLE
THEATRE COMPANY LTD**   **T** 020 7237 4434
5 Elephant Lane, London SE16 4JD
E admin@londonbubble.org.uk
W www.londonbubble.org.uk

**LONG OVERDUE THEATRE
COMPANY THE**   **T** 0845 8382994
16 Butterfield Drive, Amesbury
Wiltshire SP4 7SJ
E stefpearmain@hotmail.com
W www.tlots.co.uk

LSW JUNIOR INTER-ACT   T/F 020 7793 9755
PO Box 31855, London SE17 3XP
E londonswo@hotmail.com
W www.londonshakespeare.org.uk

LSW PRISON PROJECT   T/F 020 7793 9755
PO Box 31855, London SE17 3XP
E londonswo@hotmail.com
W www.lswproductions.co.uk

LSW SENIOR RE-ACTION   T/F 020 7793 9755
PO Box 31855, London SE17 3XP
E londonswo@hotmail.com
W www.lswproductions.co.uk

**LYRICS & LAUGHTER
PRODUCTIONS**   T 01425 612830
Music Hall. Comedy. Revues. Themed Shows.
Locally Based
35 Barton Court Avenue, Barton on Sea
Hants BH25 7EP
E lyricsandlaughter@outlook.com
W www.lyricsandlaughter.info

M6 THEATRE COMPANY   T 01706 355898
Studio Theatre, Hamer CP School
Albert Royds Street, Rochdale OL16 2SU
F 01706 712601
E admin@m6theatre.co.uk
W www.m6theatre.co.uk

MADDERMARKET THEATRE   T 01603 626560
Resident Community Theatre Company. Small-scale
Producing & Receiving House
St John's Alley, Norwich NR2 1DR
E office@maddermarket.org
W www.maddermarket.co.uk

MAGIC HAT PRODUCTIONS   T 07769 560991
Based in London
E general@magichat-productions.com
W www.magichat-productions.com

**MANCHESTER ACTORS
COMPANY**   T 0161 227 8702
c/o 31 Leslie Street, Manchester M14 7NE
E steve.boyes1411@gmail.com
W www.manactco.org.uk

**MAVERICK THEATRE
COMPANY LTD**   T 020 8090 5082
2nd Floor, 12 Fouberts Place
Carnaby Street, London W1F 7PA
T 07531 138248
E info@mavericktheatre.co.uk
W www.mavericktheatre.co.uk

**MIKRON THEATRE
COMPANY LTD**   T 01484 843701
Marsden Mechanics, Peel Street
Marsden, Huddersfield HD7 6BW
E admin@mikron.org.uk
W www.mikron.org.uk

NATURAL THEATRE COMPANY   T 01225 469131
Street Theatre. Touring. Corporate
Widcombe Institute, Widcombe Hill
Bath BA2 6AA
E info@naturaltheatre.co.uk
W www.naturaltheatre.co.uk

NEW PERSPECTIVES   T 0115 927 2334
Park Lane Business Centre, Park Lane
Basford, Nottingham NG6 0DW
E info@newperspectives.co.uk
W www.newperspectives.co.uk

NORTH COUNTRY THEATRE   T 01748 825288
3 Rosemary Lane, Richmond
North Yorkshire DL10 4DP
E office@northcountrytheatre.com
W www.northcountrytheatre.com

**NORTHERN STAGE (THEATRICAL
PRODUCTIONS) LTD**   T 0191 242 7200
Barras Bridge
Newcastle upon Tyne NE1 7RH
F 0191 242 7257
E info@northernstage.co.uk
W www.northernstage.co.uk

**NORTHUMBERLAND THEATRE
COMPANY (NTC)**   T 01665 602586
Touring Regionally & Nationally
The Playhouse
Bondgate Without
Alnwick, Northumberland NE66 1PQ
F 01665 605837
E admin@northumberlandtheatre.co.uk
W www.northumberlandtheatre.co.uk

**OPEN STAGE
PRODUCTIONS**   T/F 0121 777 9086
49 Springfield Road, Moseley
Birmingham B13 9NN
E info@openstage.co.uk
W www.openstage.co.uk

PASCAL THEATRE COMPANY   T 020 7383 0920
35 Flaxman Court, Flaxman Terrace
Bloomsbury, London WC1H 9AR
E pascaltheatrecompany@gmail.com
W www.pascal-theatre.com

PEOPLE'S THEATRE COMPANY THE
69 Manor Way, Guildford
Surrey GU2 7RR
E ptc@ptc.org.uk
W www.ptc.org.uk

**PLAYTIME THEATRE
COMPANY**   T 01227 266272
18 Bennells Avenue, Whitstable
Kent CT5 2HP
F 01227 266648
E playtime@circon.co.uk
W www.playtimetheatre.co.uk

**POWERHOUSE THEATRE
COMPANY**   T 01483 232690
Contact: Geoff Lawson (Artistic Director)
58 Oak Hill, Wood Street
Guildford GU3 3ER
T 07949 821567
E powerhousetheatre@hotmail.co.uk
W www.powerhousetheatre.co.uk

**PROTEUS THEATRE
COMPANY**   T 01256 354541
Multimedia & Cross-artform Work
Proteus Creations Space
Council Road
Basingstoke, Hampshire RG21 3DH
E info@proteustheatre.com
W www.proteustheatre.com

**PURSUED BY A
BEAR PRODUCTIONS**   T 01252 745445
Farnham Maltings
Bridge Square
Farnham GU9 7QR
E pursuedbyabear@yahoo.co.uk
W www.pursuedbyabear.co.uk

Q20 THEATRE LTD　T 01274 221360
Dockfield Road, Shipley
West Yorkshire BD17 7AD
E info@q20theatre.co.uk

**RIDING LIGHTS
THEATRE COMPANY**　T 01904 655317
Friargate Theatre, Lower Friargate
York YO1 9SL
F 01904 651532
E info@rltc.org
W www.ridinglights.org

**SALTMINE THEATRE
COMPANY (SALTMINE TRUST)**　T 01384 454807
61 The Broadway, Dudley DY1 3EB
E creative@saltmine.org
W www.saltminetrust.org.uk

SPANNER IN THE WORKS　T 020 7193 7995
95 Old Woolwich Road, Greenwich
London SE10 9PP
T 07850 313986
E info@spannerintheworks.org.uk
W www.spannerintheworks.org.uk

SPARE TYRE　T/F 020 7061 6454
*Contact: Arti Prashar (Artistic Director). Theatre Without
Prejudice. For Performers who are older, have learning
disabilities or have economic disadvantages*
Unit 3.22, Canterbury Court, Kennington Park
1-3 Brixton Road, London SW9 6DE
E info@sparetyre.org
W www.sparetyre.org

SPECTACLE THEATRE　T 01443 430700
Coleg y Cymoedd, Llwynypia
Tonypandy CF40 2TQ
F 01443 439640
E info@spectacletheatre.co.uk
W www.spectacletheatre.co.uk

SPONTANEITY SHOP THE　T 020 7788 4080
85-87 Bayham Street, London NW1 0AG
E info@the-spontaneity-shop.com
W www.the-spontaneity-shop.com

**TAKING FLIGHT
THEATRE COMPANY**　T 029 2023 0020
Chapter Arts Centre, Market Road
Canton, Cardiff CF5 1QE
E takingflighttheatre@yahoo.co.uk
W www.takingflighttheatre.co.uk

TANGLEHEAD PRODUCTIONS　T 07973 518132
*Film. Multimedia. Music Videos. Two Rock 'n' Roll
Musicals*
Flat 2, 76 Highdown Road
Hove BN3 6EB
E tarascas@btopenworld.com
W www.tanglehead.co.uk

THEATRE& LTD　T 01484 664078
25 Queens Square Business Park
Huddersfield Road
Honley, West Yorkshire HD9 6QZ
F 01484 660079
E cmitchell@theatreand.com
W www.theatreand.com

THEATRE PECKHAM　T 020 7708 5401
2nd Floor, Peckham Library
122 Peckham Hill Street
London SE15 5JR
E admin@theatrepeckham.co.uk
W www.theatrepeckham.co.uk

TMESIS THEATRE　T 07813 301517
Contact: Elinor Randle (Artistic Director)
13A Hope Street, Liverpool
Merseyside L1 9BQ
E admin@tmesistheatre.com
W www.tmesistheatre.com

**TOBACCO FACTORY
THEATRES**　T 0117 902 0345
1st Floor, Raleigh Road
Southville, Bristol BS3 1TF
E theatre@tobaccofactorytheatres.com
W www.tobaccofactorytheatres.com

TROY THEATRE COMPANY　T 07710 431741
New Plays Considered for Festivals & Fringe Venues
184 Wandle Road, Morden
Surrey SM4 6AB
E jane.sheraton@gmail.com

UPTKREEK THEATRE　T 07935 822939
82 St Stephens Road, Saltash
Cornwall PL12 6DA
E uptkreek@live.co.uk

WAREHOUSE PHOENIX LTD
Formerly Warehouse Theatre Croydon
87 Great Titchfield Street
London W1W 6RL
E warehousephoenix@outlook.com
W www.warehousephoenix.co.uk

**WOMEN & THEATRE
BIRMINGHAM LTD**　T 0121 449 7117
Twitter: @womenandtheatre
The Old Lodge, Uffculme
50 Queensbridge Road
Moseley, Birmingham B13 8QY
E info@womenandtheatre.co.uk
W www.womenandtheatre.co.uk

WYLLYOTTS THEATRE　T 020 8449 2342
Wyllyotts Place, Darkes Lane
Potters Bar, Herts EN6 2HN
T 07885 232414
E capitalarts@btconnect.com
W www.capitalarts.org.uk

YELLOW EARTH THEATRE　T 020 8694 6631
The Albany, Douglas Way
London SE8 4AG
E admin@yellowearth.org
W www.yellowearth.org

**YELLOWCHAIR PERFORMANCE
EXPERIENCE THE**
First Breaks on the London Fringe for New Talent
89 Birchanger Lane
Bishop Stortford CM23 5QF
E contacttype@gmail.com
W www.wix.com/yellowchair/type

**YORICK INTERNATIONALIST
THEATRE ENSEMBLE**　T/F 020 7836 7637
Yorick Theatre & Film
4 Duval Court
36 Bedfordbury
Covent Garden, London WC2N 4DQ
E yorickx@hotmail.com

YOUNG VIC THEATRE　T 020 7922 2800
66 The Cut, London SE1 8LZ
BO 020 7922 2922
E info@youngvic.org
W www.youngvic.org

A THOUSAND CRANES　　T 07801 269772
48 Brunswick Crescent, London N11 1EB
E kumiko@athousandcranes.org.uk
W www.athousandcranes.org.uk

ACTION STATION UK LTD THE　　T 0870 7702705
4-6 Canfield Place, London NW6 3BT
E info@theactionstation.co.uk
W www.theactionstation.co.uk

**ACTION TRANSPORT
THEATRE**　　T 0151 357 2120
New Writing. Professional Production for, by & with
Young People
Whitby Hall, Stanney Lane
Ellesmere Port, Cheshire CH65 9AE
E info@actiontransporttheatre.org
W www.actiontransporttheatre.org

**ACTIONWORK
WORLDWIDE LTD**　　T 01934 815163
Theatre & Film Productions with Young People. 25 Years
of Producing High Quality Theatre & Film
PO Box 433, Weston-super-Mare
Somerset BS24 0WY
E admin@actionwork.com
W www.actionwork.com

**AESOP'S TOURING
THEATRE COMPANY**　　T/F 01483 724633
Professional TIE Theatre Company Touring Nationally
The Arches, 38 The Riding
Woking, Surrey GU21 5TA
T 07836 731872
E info@aesopstheatre.co.uk
W www.aesopstheatre.co.uk

AKADEMI　　T 020 7691 3210
Hampstead Town Hall, 213 Haverstock Hill
London NW3 4QP
E info@akademi.co.uk
W www.akademi.co.uk

APELT, Steve PRODUCTIONS　　T 01278 458253
20 Sandpiper Road, Blakespool Park
Bridgwater, Somerset TA6 5QU
E steve.apelt@virgin.net
W www.steveapelt.co.uk

**ARTY-FACT THEATRE
COMPANY LTD**　　T 07020 962096
18 Weston Lane, Crewe, Cheshire CW2 5AN
F 07020 982098
E artyfact@talktalk.net
W www.arty-fact.co.uk

ASHCROFT YOUTH THEATRE　　T 0844 8005328
Ashcroft Academy of Dramatic Art
Harris Primary Academy Crystal Palace
Malcolm Road, Penge, London SE20 8RH
T 07799 791586
E info@ashcroftacademy.com
W www.ashcroftacademy.com

**BARKING DOG
THEATRE COMPANY**　　T 020 7117 6321
Building 3, Chiswick Park
566 Chiswick High Road, London W4 5YA
T 07803 773160
E mike@barkingdog.co.uk
W www.barkingdog.co.uk

BECK THEATRE　　T 020 8561 7506
Grange Road, Hayes, Middlesex UB3 2UE
BO 020 8561 8371
E enquiries@becktheatre.org.uk
W www.becktheatre.org.uk

BIG ACT THE　　T 0117 2391274
14-16 Wilson Place, Bristol BS2 9HJ
E info@thebigact.com
W www.thebigact.com

BIG WOODEN HORSE　　T 020 8567 8431
Twitter: @bigwoodenhorse1
30 Northfield Road, West Ealing
London W13 9SY
E info@bigwoodenhorse.com
W www.bigwoodenhorse.com

**BIRMINGHAM STAGE
COMPANY THE**　　T 020 7437 3391
Contact: Neal Foster (Actor/Manager), Philip Compton
(Executive Producer)
Suite 228, The Linen Hall, 162 Regent Street
London W1B 5TB
E office@birminghamstage.com
W www.birminghamstage.com

BITESIZE THEATRE COMPANY　　T 01978 358320
8 Green Meadows, New Broughton
Wrexham LL11 6SG
F 01978 756308
E admin@bitesizetheatre.co.uk
W www.bitesizetheatre.co.uk

**BLUNDERBUS THEATRE
COMPANY LTD**　　T 01636 678900
The Old Painter's Store, Cliff Nook Lane
Newark, Notts NG24 1LY
E hello@blunderbus.co.uk
W www.blunderbus.co.uk

**BOOSTER CUSHION
THEATRE LTD**　　T 01727 873874
75 How Wood, Park Street
St Albans, Herts AL2 2RW
F 01727 872597
E admin@booster-cushion.co.uk
W www.boostercushiontheatreforchildren.com

BRIDGE HOUSE THEATRE　　T 01926 776437
Professional & School Productions. Visiting Companies
Warwick School Site, Myton Road
Warwick CV34 6PP
E boxoffice@warwick.org
W www.bridgehousetheatre.co.uk

**CAMBRIDGE TOURING
THEATRE**　　T/F 01223 246533
29 Worts Causeway, Cambridge CB1 8RJ
E info@cambridgetouringtheatre.co.uk
W www.cambridgetouringtheatre.co.uk

CHAIN REACTION　　T/F 020 8981 9527
Millers House, Three Mills Lane
London E3 3DU
E admin@chainreactiontheatre.co.uk
W www.chainreactiontheatre.co.uk

CHICKENSHED　　T 020 8351 6161
290 Chase Side, Southgate
London N14 4PE
BO 020 8292 9222
E susanj@chickenshed.org.uk
W www.chickenshed.org.uk

**CLWYD THEATR CYMRU THEATRE
FOR YOUNG PEOPLE**　　T 01352 701575
Contact: Nerys Edwards (Administrator)
Raikes Lane, Mold
Flintshire CH7 1YA
F 01352 701558
E youngclwydifanc@clwyd-theatr-cymru.co.uk
W www.ctctyp.co.uk

COMPLETE WORKS THE   T 020 7377 0280
Contact: Phil Evans (Artistic Director)
The Old Truman Brewery, 91 Brick Lane
London E1 6QL
F 020 7247 7405
E info@tcw.org.uk
W www.tcw.org.uk

CRAGRATS   T 0844 4774100
Twitter: @cragratsuk
Head Office, Vine Court
Chalkpit Lane, Dorking, Surrey RH4 1AJ
E enquiries@cragrats.com
W www.cragrats.com

DAYLIGHT THEATRE   T 01453 763808
66 Middle Street, Stroud
Gloucestershire GL5 1EA

DONNA MARIA COMPANY   T 020 8670 7814
16 Bell Meadow, Dulwich
London SE19 1HP
E info@donnamariasworld.co.uk
W www.donna-marias-world.co.uk

DRAGON DRAMA   T 07590 452436
Theatre Company. Parties. Tuition. Workshops
347 Hanworth Road, Hampton TW12 3EJ
E askus@dragondrama.cc.uk
W www.dragondrama.co.uk

**EUROPA CLOWNS
THEATRE SHOW**   T 01892 537964
36 St Lukes Road, Tunbridge Wells
Kent TN4 9JH
T 07973 512845
E mikealan25@yahoo.com
W www.clownseuropa.co.uk

FUTURES THEATRE   T 020 7928 2832
St John's Crypt, 73 Waterloo Road
London SE1 8UD
F 020 7928 6724
E info@futurestheatre.co.uk
W www.futurestheatre.co.uk

GAZEBO THEATRE COMPANY   T 01902 497222
The Town Hall, Church Street
Bilston, West Midlands WV14 0AP
F 01902 497244
E admin@gazebotie.org
W www.gazebotie.org

**GREENWICH & LEWISHAM YOUNG PEOPLE'S
THEATRE (GLYPT)**   T 020 8854 1316
The Tramshed, 51-53 Woolwich New Road
London SE18 6ES
E info@glypt.co.uk
W www.glypt.co.uk

**GROUP 64 THEATRE FOR
YOUNG PEOPLE**   T 020 8788 6935
Putney Arts Theatre, Ravenna Road
London SW15 6AW
E group.64@virgin.net
W www.g64.org.uk

**HALF MOON YOUNG
PEOPLE'S THEATRE**   T 020 7265 8138
43 White Horse Road, London E1 0ND
F 020 7709 8914
E admin@halfmoon.org.uk
W www.halfmoon.org.uk

HOXTON HALL   T 020 7684 0060
130 Hoxton Street, London N1 6SH
E info@hoxtonhall.co.uk
W www.hoxtonhall.co.uk

IMAGE MUSICAL THEATRE   T 020 8743 9380
197 Church Road, Northolt
Middlesex UB5 5BE
F 020 8181 6279
E admin@imagemusicaltheatre.co.uk
W www.imagemusicaltheatre.co.uk

INDIGO MOON THEATRE   T 07855 328552
35 Waltham Court, Beverley
East Yorkshire HU17 9JF
E info@indigomoontheatre.com
W www.indigomoontheatre.com

INTERPLAY THEATRE   T 0113 263 8556
Armley Ridge Road, Leeds LS12 3LE
E info@interplaytheatre.co.uk
W www.interplaytheatre.co.uk

**KINETIC THEATRE
COMPANY LTD**   T 020 8286 2613
Suite H, The Jubilee Centre
10-12 Lombard Road
Wimbledon, London SW19 3TZ
F 020 8286 2645
E office@kinetictheatre.co.uk
W www.kinetictheatre.co.uk

KOMEDIA   T 01273 647101
44-47 Gardner Street, Brighton BN1 1UN
E info@komedia.co.uk
W www.komedia.co.uk

**LEAVENERS THE
(QUAKER COMMUNITY ARTS)**   T 0121 414 0099
1 The Lodge, 1046 Bristol Road
Birmingham B29 6LJ
E timi@leaveners.org
W www.leaveners.org

**LITTLE ACTORS
THEATRE COMPANY**   T 0151 336 4302
9 Carlton Close Road, Parkgate
Cheshire CH64 6TD
E mail@littleactorstheatre.com
W www.littleactorstheatre.com

M6 THEATRE COMPANY   T 01706 355898
Studio Theatre, Hamer CP School
Albert Royds Street
Rochdale OL16 2SU
F 01706 712601
E admin@m6theatre.co.uk
W www.m6theatre.co.uk

MAGIC CARPET THEATRE   T 01482 709939
18 Church Street
Sutton-on-Hull HU7 4TS
E jon@magiccarpettheatre.com
W www.magiccarpettheatre.com

**NATIONAL ASSOCIATION OF YOUTH
THEATRES (NAYT)**   T 07804 254651
*Works with Youth Theatres & other Organisations in
Regional Venues to Host Festivals & Events*
c/o Riding Lights Theatre Company
Friargate Theatre
Lower Friargate
York YO1 9SL
E info@nayt.org.uk
W www.nayt.org.uk

**NATIONAL STUDENT
DRAMA FESTIVAL**   T 020 7036 9027
Woolyard, 54 Bermondsey Street
London SE1 3UD
E info@nsdf.org.uk
W www.nsdf.org.uk

NATIONAL YOUTH MUSIC THEATRE T 020 7802 0386
Adrian House, 27 Vincent Square
London SW1P 2NN
F 020 7821 0458
E enquiries@nymt.org.uk
W www.nymt.org.uk

NATIONAL YOUTH THEATRE OF GREAT BRITAIN T 020 3696 7066
111 Buckingham Palace Road
London SW1W 0DT
F 020 7036 9031
E info@nyt.org.uk
W www.nyt.org.uk

NESTON'S INTERACT YOUTH THEATRE T 0151 336 4302
New Writing for Young People
9 Carlton Close, Parkgate
Neston, Cheshire CH64 6TD
E interact@littleactorstheatre.com
W www.littleactorstheatre.com

NOTTINGHAM PLAYHOUSE ROUNDABOUT T 0115 947 4361
Nottingham Playhouse, Wellington Circus
Nottingham NG1 5AF
F 0115 947 5759
E roundabout@nottinghamplayhouse.co.uk

OILY CART T 020 8672 6329
Creates Work for the under 6 yrs & for Young People 3-19 yrs with Profound & Multiple Learning Disabilities (PMLD) or ASD
Smallwood School Annexe
Smallwood Road
London SW17 0TW
E oilies@oilycart.org.uk
W www.oilycart.org.uk

ONATTI PRODUCTIONS LTD T 01594 562033
Contact: Andrew Bardwell (Artistic Director)
The Old Chapel, Yorkley
Gloucestershire GL15 4SB
F 0870 1643629
E info@onatti.co.uk
W www.onatti.co.uk

OUTLOUD PRODUCTIONS LTD T 07946 357521
Theatre Company. Drama Workshops. Children & Adult Classes
21-23 Glendale Gardens, Leigh on Sea
Essex SS9 2PA
E info@outloudproductions.co.uk
W www.outloudproductions.co.uk

PANDEMONIUM TOURING PARTNERSHIP T 029 2047 2060
228 Railway Street, Cardiff CF24 2NJ
T 07885 280635
E paul@pandemoniumtheatre.com

PIED PIPER THEATRE COMPANY T/F 01428 684022
1 Lilian Place, Coxcombe Lane
Chiddingfold, Surrey GU8 4QA
E twpiedpiper@aol.com
W www.piedpipertheatre.co.uk

PLAY HOUSE THE T 0121 265 4425
c/o Birmingham Repertory Theatre
Centenary Square, Broad Street, Birmingham B1 2EP
F 0121 233 0652
E info@theplayhouse.org.uk
W www.theplayhouse.org.uk

PLAYTIME THEATRE COMPANY T 01227 266272
TIE Company Touring Drama & Workshops Nationally & Internationally
18 Bennells Avenue, Whitstable
Kent CT5 2HP
T 01227 266648
E playtime@dircon.co.uk
W www.playtimetheatre.co.uk

POLKA THEATRE T 020 8545 8323
240 The Broadway, Wimbledon SW19 1SB
F 020 8545 8365
E stephen@polkatheatre.com
W www.polkatheatre.com

Q20 THEATRE LTD T 01274 221360
Creative Arts Hub, Dockfield Road
Shipley, West Yorkshire BD17 7AD
F 0871 9942226
E info@q20theatre.co.uk

QUANTUM THEATRE T 020 8317 9000
Contact: Michael Whitmore, Jessica Selous (Artistic Directors)
The Old Button Factory, 1-11 Bannockburn Road
Plumstead, London SE18 1ET
E office@quantumtheatre.co.uk
W www.quantumtheatre.co.uk

RAINBOW BIGBOTTOM T 01494 771029
84 Broadway, Chesham
Bucks HP5 1EG
T 07778 106552
E orrainebmays@aol.com
W www.mrpanda.co.uk

RAINBOW THEATRE LONDON EAST T 020 8331 6639
59 Prince John Road, Eltham
London SE9 6QB
F 07092 315384
E rainbowtheatrelondoneast@yahoo.co.uk
W www.rainbow-theatre.com

RESTLESS THEATRE COMPANY T 07915 666276
Contact: Sarah McCourt (Artistic Director)
7 Grosvenor Cottages
Belgrave Lane, Mutley
Plymouth, Devon PL4 7DB
E sarah@restlesstheatre.co.uk
W www.restlesstheatre.co.uk

ROYAL & DERNGATE T 01604 626222
19-21 Guildhall Road
Northampton NN1 1DP
E arts@royalandderngate.co.uk
W www.royalandderngate.co.uk

S4K INTERNATIONAL LTD T 01883 723444
Oxted Production Office, PO Box 287
Oxted, Surrey RH8 8BX
E carolyn@s4kinternational.com
W www.s4kinternational.com

SCOTTISH YOUTH THEATRE T 0141 552 3988
The Old Sheriff Court, 105 Brunswick Street
Glasgow G1 1TF
E info@scottishyouththeatre.org
W www.scottishyouththeatre.org

SHEFFIELD THEATRES TRUST T 0114 249 5999
Contact: Dan Bates (Chief Executive)
55 Norfolk Street, Sheffield S1 1DA
F 0114 249 6003
E info@sheffieldtheatres.co.uk
W www.sheffieldtheatres.co.uk/creativedevelopmentprogramme

SHOOTING STAR ENTERTAINMENTS   **T** 07708 390137
63 Charlton Street, Maidstone
Kent ME16 8LB
E enquiries@shootingstarents.co.uk
W www.shootingstarents.co.uk

SOLOMON THEATRE COMPANY   **T** 01725 518760
Penny Black, High Street
Damerham, Fordingbridge
Hants SP6 3EU
E office@solomontheatre.co.uk
W www.solomontheatre.co.uk

SOUTH WEST YOUTH THEATRE   **T** 0151 336 4302
New Writing for Young People. Based in London SW18.
Ages 10+
c/o 6 Carlton Close, Parkgate
Neston, Cheshire CH64 6TD
E swyt@littleactorstheatre.com
W www.littleactorstheatre.com

SPECTACLE THEATRE   **T** 01443 430700
Coleg y Cymoedd, Llwynypia
Tonypandy CF40 2TQ
F 01443 439640
E info@spectacletheatre.co.uk
W www.spectacletheatre.co.uk

STORYTELLERS THEATRE COMPANY THE   **T** 01253 839375
Bridge Farm, 249 Hawes Side Lane
Blackpool FY4 4AA
F 01253 792930
E admin@pendleproductions.co.uk
W www.pendleproductions.co.uk

TALEGATE THEATRE PRODUCTIONS   **T** 01302 771862
6 Ravenswood Drive, Auckley
Doncaster DN9 3PB
E info@talegatetheatre.co.uk
W www.talegatetheatre.co.uk

TALL STORIES   **T** 020 8348 0080
Jacksons Lane, 269A Archway Road
London N6 5AA
E info@tallstories.org.uk
W www.tallstories.org.uk

THEATR IOLO LTD   **T** 029 2061 3782
Courtesy of Chapter, Market Road
Canton, Cardiff CF5 1QE
E admin@theatriolo.com
W www.theatriolo.com

THEATRE& LTD   **T** 01484 664078
25 Queens Square Business Park
Huddersfield Road
Honley, West Yorkshire HD9 6QZ
F 01484 660079
E cmitchell@theatreand.com
W www.theatreand.com

THEATRE ALIBI   **T/F** 01392 217315
Adults & Young People
Emmanuel Hall, Emmanuel Road
Exeter EX4 1EJ
E info@theatrealibi.co.uk
W www.theatrealibi.co.uk

THEATRE CENTRE   **T** 020 7729 3066
National Touring. New Writing for Young Audiences
Shoreditch Town Hall, 380 Old Street
London EC1V 9LT
F 020 7739 9741
E admin@theatre-centre.co.uk
W www.theatre-centre.co.uk

THEATRE COMPANY BLAH BLAH BLAH   **T** 0113 380 5646
Roundhay Road Resource Centre
233-237 Roundhay Road
Leeds LS8 4HS
E admin@blahs.co.uk
W www.blahs.co.uk

THEATRE HULLABALOO   **T** 01325 352004
The Meeting Rooms, 5 Skinner Gate
Darlington, County Durham DL3 7NB
E info@theatrehullabaloo.org.uk
W www.theatrehullabaloo.org.uk

THEATRE WORKOUT LTD   **T** 020 8144 2290
13A Stratheden Road, Blackheath
London SE3 7TH
E education@theatreworkout.com
W www.theatreworkout.com

TRICYCLE THEATRE   **T/F** 020 7372 6611
Contact: Mark Londesborough (Creative Learning
Director)
269 Kilburn High Road, London NW6 7JR
E creativelearning@tricycle.co.uk
W www.tricycle.co.uk

UNICORN THEATRE   **T** 020 7645 0500
147 Tooley Street, London SE1 2HZ
F 020 7645 0550
E office@unicorntheatre.com
W www.unicorntheatre.com

WIZARD THEATRE   **T** 0800 5832373
Contact: Leon Hamilton (Artistic Director),
Emmy Bradbury (Company Manager), Oliver Gray
(Associate Producer)
Blenheim Villa, Burr Street
Harwell, Oxon OX11 0DT
E admin@wizardtheatre.co.uk
W www.wizardtheatre.co.uk

YOUNG ACTORS THEATRE   **T** 020 7278 2101
70-72 Barnsbury Road, Islington
London N1 0ES
E andrew@yati.org.uk
W www.yati.org.uk

YOUNG SHAKESPEARE COMPANY   **T** 020 8368 4828
Contact: Christopher Geelan, Sarah Gordon (Artistic
Directors)
213 Fox Lane, Southgate
London N13 4BB
E youngshakespeare@mac.com
W www.youngshakespeare.org.uk

ZEST THEATRE   **T** 01522 569590
The Terrace, Grantham Street
Lincoln, Lincolnshire LN2 1BD
E hello@zesttheatre.com
W www.zesttheatre.com

AUSTRIA, VIENNA:
Vienna's English Theatre T/F 01304 813330
UK Representative:, VM Theatre Productions Ltd
16 The Street, Ash, Canterbury
Kent CT3 2HJ
E vanessa@vmtheatre.demon.co.uk
W www.englishtheatre.at

DENMARK, COPENHAGEN:
The London Toast Theatre T 00 45 33228686
Contact: Vivienne McKee (Artistic Director), Soren Hall
(Administrator)
Kochsvej 18, DK-1812 Frb. C
Denmark
E mail@londontoast.dk
W www.londontoast.dk

FRANCE, LYON:
Theatre from Oxford
(Touring Europe & Beyond)
Contact: Robert Southam
B.P. 10, F-42750 St-Denis-de-Cabanne
France
E fm.oxford@gmail.com

GERMANY, FRANKFURT AM MAIN:
The English Theatre
Frankfurt T 00 49 69 24231615
Contact: Daniel Nicolai (Artistic & Managing Director)
Gallusanlage 7, 60329
Frankfurt am Main
Germany
F 00 49 69 24231614
E mail@english-theatre.de
W www.english-theatre.de

GERMANY, HAMBURG:
The English Theatre
of Hamburg T 00 49 40 2277925
Contact: Robert Rumpf, Clifford Dean
Lerchenfeld 14, 22081 Hamburg
Germany
BO 00 49 40 2277089
W www.englishtheatre.de

GERMANY, TOURING GERMANY:
White Horse Theatre T 00 49 29 21339339
Contact: Peter Griffith, Michael Dray
Boerdenstrasse 17, 59494 Soest, Germany
F 00 49 29 21339336
E theatre@white-horse-theatre.eu
W www.whitehorse.de

ICELAND, REYKJAVIK:
Light Nights -
The Summer Theatre T 00 354 5519181
Contact: Kristine G. Magnus (Artistic Director)
The Travelling Theatre, Baldursgata 37
IS-101 Reykjavik, Iceland
E info@lightnights.com
W www.lightnights.com

ITALY, SANREMO:
Theatrino & Melting Pot
Theatre - ACLE T 00 39 0184 506070
Via Roma 54, 18038 Sanremo (IM), Italy
F 00 39 0184 509996
E info@acle.org
W www.acle.org

SWEDEN, GOTHENBURG:
Gothenburg English Studio
Theatre (GEST) T 00 46 3142 5065
Chapmanstorg 10 BV, Gothenburg, Sweden 41454
E info@gest.se
W www.gest.se

SWITZERLAND, GENEVA:
Simply Theatre T 00 41 22 8600518
Avenue de Choiseul 23A, 1290 Versoix, Switzerland
E info@simplytheatre.com
W www.simplytheatre.com

UNITED KINGDOM, YORKLEY:
Onatti Productions Ltd T 01594 562033
Contact: Andrew Bardwell
The Old Chapel, Yorkley, Gloucestershire GL15 4SB
F 0870 1643629
E info@onatti.co.uk
W www.onatti.co.uk

ADELPHI   T 020 7836 1166
409-412 Strand
London WC2R 0NS
BO 0844 4124651

ALDWYCH   T 020 7836 5537
Aldwych
London WC2B 4DF
W www.aldwychtheatre.com

ALMEIDA   T 020 7288 4900
Almeida Street
London N1 1TA
BO 020 7359 4404
E info@almeida.co.uk

AMBASSADORS   BO 0844 8112334
West Street
London WC2H 9ND
E enquiries@theambassadorstheatre.co.uk
W www.theambassadorstheatre.co.uk

APOLLO   T 020 7851 2711 (Stage Door)
Shaftesbury Avenue
London W1D 7EZ
BO 0844 4124658
E enquiries@nimaxtheatres.com
W www.nimaxtheatres.com

APOLLO VICTORIA   T 020 7834 6318
17 Wilton Road
London SW1V 1LG
W www.apollovictorialondon.org.uk

ARTS   T 020 7836 8463 (T/BO)
6-7 Great Newport Street
London WC2H 7JB
E boxoffice@artstheatrewestend.co.uk
W www.artstheatrewestend.co.uk

BARBICAN   T 020 7628 3351
Barbican Centre, Stage Door
Silk Street, London EC2Y 8DS
BO 020 7638 8891
E theatre@barbican.org.uk
W www.barbican.org.uk

BLOOMSBURY   T 020 7679 2777
15 Gordon Street
London WC1H 0AH
BO 020 3108 1000
E admin@thebloomsbury.com
W www.thebloomsbury.com

BUSH   T 020 8743 3584
7 Uxbridge Road
London W12 8LJ
BO 020 8743 5050
E info@bushtheatre.co.uk
W www.bushtheatre.co.uk

CAMBRIDGE   T 020 7850 8710
Earlham Street, Seven Dials
Covent Garden, London WC2H 9HU
BO 020 7850 8715
W www.reallyuseful.com

CHARING CROSS THEATRE   T 020 7930 5868
The Arches
Villiers Street
London WC2N 6NL
E info@charingcrosstheatre.co.uk
W www.charingcrosstheatre.co.uk

CRITERION   T 020 7839 8811
2 Jermyn Street
Piccadilly
London SW1Y 4XA
BO 0844 8471778
E admin@criterion-theatre.co.uk
W www.criterion-theatre.co.uk

DOMINION   T 020 7927 0900
268-269 Tottenham Court Road
London W1T 7AQ
BO 0844 8471775
W www.dominiontheatre.com

DONMAR WAREHOUSE   T 020 7240 4882
41 Earlham Street
London WC2H 9LX
BO 0844 8717624
E office@donmarwarehouse.com
W www.donmarwarehouse.com

DRURY LANE   T 020 7850 8790
Theatre Royal
Catherine Street
London WC2B 5JF
BO 0844 8588877
W www.rutheatres.com

DUCHESS   T 020 7632 9600
Catherine Street
London WC2B 5LA
BO 0844 4829672
E general@nimaxtheatres.com

DUKE OF YORK'S   T 020 7565 6500
St Martin's Lane
London WC2N 4BG
BO 0844 8717623

EVENTIM APOLLO   T 020 8563 3800
45 Queen Caroline Street
London W6 9QH
BO 0844 2494300
E info@eventimapollo.com
W www.eventimapollo.com

FORTUNE   T 020 7010 7900
Russell Street
Covent Garden
London WC2B 5HH
BO 0844 8717627

GARRICK   T 020 7520 5692
2 Charing Cross Road
London WC2H 0HH
BO 020 7520 5693
E enquiries@nimaxtheatres.com

GIELGUD　T 020 7292 1320
Shaftesbury Avenue
London W1D 6AR
BO 0844 4825130

HACKNEY EMPIRE　T 020 8510 4500
291 Mare Street
London E8 1EJ
BO 020 8985 2424
E info@hackneyempire.co.uk
W www.hackneyempire.co.uk

HAMPSTEAD　T 020 7449 4200
Eton Avenue
Swiss Cottage
London NW3 3EU
BO 020 7722 9301
E info@hampsteadtheatre.com
W www.hampsteadtheatre.com

HAROLD PINTER　T 020 7321 5300 (SD)
Formerly Comedy Theatre
Panton Street
London SW1Y 4DN
BO 0844 8717622
E rachaellund@theambassadors.com
W www.atgtickets.com

HER MAJESTY'S　T 020 7850 8750 (SD)
Haymarket
London SW1Y 4QL

**LONDON COLISEUM
(ENGLISH NATIONAL OPERA)**　T 020 7845 9397
St Martin's Lane
London WC2N 4ES
BO 020 7845 9300
E theatre@eno.org
W www.eno.org

LONDON PALLADIUM　T 020 7850 8770
Argyll Street
London W1F 7TF
BO 0844 4122957

LYCEUM　T 020 7420 8100
21 Wellington Street
London WC2E 7RQ
BO 0844 8713000

LYRIC　T 020 7494 5840
29 Shaftesbury Avenue
London W1D 7ES
BO 0844 4124661
E general@nimaxtheatres.com

LYRIC HAMMERSMITH　T 020 8741 6850
Lyric Square
King Street
London W6 0QL
E hires@lyric.co.uk
W www.lyric.co.uk

NATIONAL　T 020 7452 3333
South Bank, Upper Ground
London SE1 9PX
BO 020 7452 3000
W www.nationaltheatre.org.uk

NEW LONDON　T 020 7242 9802
Drury Lane
London WC2B 5PW
BO 0344 4124654
E cuqui.rivera@reallyuseful.co.uk

NOËL COWARD　T 020 7812 7443
Formerly Albery
St Martin's Lane
London WC2N 4AU
BO 0844 4825140

NOVELLO　T 020 7759 9611
Formerly Strand
5 Aldwych
London WC2B 4LD
BO 0844 4825115

OLD VIC　T 020 7928 2651
The Cut, London SE1 8NB
BO 0844 8717628
E ovtcadmin@oldvictheatre.com
W www.oldvictheatre.com

PALACE　T 020 7434 0088
Shaftesbury Avenue
London W1D 5AY
BO 0844 4829676
W www.nimaxtheatres.com

PEACOCK　BO 0844 4124322
For Administration see SADLER'S WELLS
Portugal Street
Kingsway
London WC2A 2HT
E info@sadlerswells.com
W www.sadlerswells.com

PHOENIX　T 020 7438 9600
110 Charing Cross Road
London WC2H 0JP
BO 0844 8717629
E jaimebrent@theambassadors.com

PICCADILLY　T 020 7478 8800
Denman Street
London W1D 7DY
BO 020 7478 8805
E piccadillymanager@theambassadors.com

PLAYHOUSE　T 020 7839 4292
Northumberland Avenue
London WC2N 5DE
BO 0844 8717631

PRINCE EDWARD　T 020 7440 3021
28 Old Compton Street
London W1D 4HS
BO 0844 4825155
W www.delfont-mackintosh.co.uk

PRINCE OF WALES　T 020 7766 2100
Coventry Street
London W1D 6AS
BO 0844 4825110
E powmanagers@delmack.co.uk
W www.delfontmackintosh.co.uk

QUEEN'S　T 020 7292 1350
Contact: Nicolas Shaw (Manager)
51 Shaftesbury Avenue
London W1D 6BA
BO 0844 4825160

REGENT'S PARK OPEN AIR　T 0844 3753460
Inner Circle
Regent's Park, London NW1 4NU
BO 0844 8264242
W www.openairtheatre.com

RIVERSIDE STUDIOS　T 020 8237 1000
65 Aspenlea Road
London W6 8LH
BO 020 8237 1111
E info@riversidestudios.co.uk
W www.riversidestudios.co.uk

ROYAL COURT　T 020 7565 5050
Sloane SquarE
London SW1W 8AS
BO 020 7565 5000
E info@royalcourttheatre.com
W www.royalcourttheatre.com

ROYAL OPERA HOUSE　T 020 7240 1200
Bow Street
Covent Garden
London WC2E 9DD
BO 020 7304 4000

SADLER'S WELLS　T 020 7863 8034
Rosebery Avenue
London EC1R 4TN
BO 0844 4124300
E info@sadlerswells.com
W www.sadlerswells.com

SAVOY THEATRE　T 020 7845 6050
Savoy Court, Strand
London WC2R 0ET
BO 0844 8717637
E savoytheatremanagement@theambassadors.com
W www.atgtickets.com

SHAFTESBURY　T 020 7379 3345
210 Shaftesbury Avenue, London WC2H 8DP
BO 020 7379 5399
E info@shaftesburytheatre.com
W www.shaftesburytheatre.com

SHAKESPEARE'S GLOBE　T 020 7902 1400
21 New Globe Walk
Bankside, London SE1 9DT
BO 020 7401 9919
E info@shakespearesglobe.com
W www.shakespearesglobe.com

SHAW　T 020 7666 9037
100-110 Euston Road
London NW1 2AJ
BO 0844 2485075
E info@shaw-theatre.com
W www.shaw-theatre.com

SOHO THEATRE　T 020 7287 5060
21 Dean Street
London W1D 3NE
BO 020 7478 0100
E box1@sohotheatre.com
W www.sohotheatre.com

ST JAMES THEATRE　T 0844 2642140
12 Palace Street
London SW1E 5JA
E boxoffice@stjamestheatre.co.uk
W www.stjamestheatre.co.uk

ST MARTIN'S　BO 0844 4991515
West Street
London WC2H 9NZ
E enquiries@stmartinstheatre.co.uk
W www.the-mousetrap.co.uk

THEATRE ROYAL　T 020 7930 8890
Haymarket
London SW1Y 4HT
BO 020 7930 8800

TRICYCLE　T 020 7372 6611
269 Kilburn High Road
London NW6 7JR
BO 020 7328 1000
E info@tricycle.co.uk
W www.tricycle.co.uk

VAUDEVILLE　T 020 7836 3191 (Stage Door)
404 Strand
London WC2R 0NH
BO 020 7836 7969

VICTORIA PALACE　T 020 7828 0600
Victoria StreeT
London SW1E 5EA
BO 0844 2485000
E enquiries@victoriapalace.co.uk
W www.victoriapalace.co.uk

WYNDHAM'S　T 020 7759 8077
Charing Cross Road
London WC2H 0DA
BO 0870 9500925

YOUNG VIC　T 020 7922 2800
66 The Cut
London SE1 8LZ
BO 020 7922 2922
E info@youngvic.org
W www.youngvic.org

ALBANY THE BO 020 8692 4446
Douglas Way, Deptford
London SE8 4AG
E reception@thealbany.org.uk
W www.thealbany.org.uk

APROPOS PRODUCTIONS LTD
53 Greek Street, London W1D 3DR
E info@aproposltd.com
W www.aproposltd.com/events

ARCH 468 THEATRE STUDIO T 07973 302908
Arch 468, 209A Coldharbour Lane
London SW9 8RU
E rebecca@arch468.com
W www.arch468.com

ARCOLA THEATRE T 020 7503 1645
Contact: Mehmet Ergen (Artistic Director), Leyla Nazli
(Executive Producer). Route: Victoria Line to Highbury &
Islington, then Main Line to Dalston Kingsland or Dalston
Junction then 5 min walk. Buses: 38 or 242 from West
End, 149 from London Bridge
24 Ashwin Street, Dalston
London E8 3DL
BO 020 7503 1646
E info@arcolatheatre.com
W www.arcolatheatre.com

ARTSDEPOT T 020 8369 5454
5 Nether Street, Tally Ho Corner
North Finchley, London N12 0GA
E info@artsdepot.co.uk
W www.artsdepot.co.uk

BARONS COURT THEATRE T 020 8932 4747
'The Curtain's Up'. Route: Piccadilly or District Lines to
West Kensington or Barons Court
28A Comeragh Road, West Kensington
London W14 9HR
E londontheatre@gmail.com
W www.offwestend.com

BATES, Tristan THEATRE T 020 7632 3010
Contact: Ben Monks, Will Young (Creative Producers)
The Actors Centre, 1A Tower Street
London WC2H 9NP
BO 020 7240 6283
E tbt@actorscentre.co.uk
W www.tristanbatestheatre.co.uk

**BATTERSEA ARTS
CENTRE (BAC)** BO 020 7223 2223
Route: Victoria or Waterloo (Main Line) to Clapham
Junction then 5 min walk or Northern Line to Clapham
Common then 20 min walk
Lavender Hill, London SW11 5TN
E boxoffice@bac.org.uk
W www.bac.org.uk

BECK THEATRE T 020 8561 7506
Route: Metropolitan Line to Uxbridge then buses 427 or
607 or Paddington Main Line to Hayes Harlington then
buses 90, H98 or 195 (10 min)
Grange Road, Hayes
Middlesex UB3 2UE
BO 020 8561 8371
E enquiries@becktheatre.org.uk
W www.becktheatre.org.uk

BEDLAM THEATRE
11B Bristo Place, Edinburgh EH1 1EZ
E info@bedlamtheatre.co.uk
W www.bedlamtheatre.co.uk

BIKE SHED THEATRE THE T 01392 434169
162-163 Fore Street, Exeter EX4 3AT
E info@bikeshedtheatre.co.uk
W www.bikeshedtheatre.co.uk

BLACKHEATH HALLS T 020 8318 9758
23 Lee Road, Blackheath
London SE3 9RQ
BO 020 8463 0100
E k.murray@trinitylaban.ac.uk
W www.blackheathhalls.com

BLOOMSBURY THEATRE T 020 7679 2777
Route: Tube to Euston, Euston Square or Warren Street
15 Gordon Street, Bloomsbury, London WC1H 0AH
BO 020 7388 8822
E admin@thebloomsbury.com
W www.thebloomsbury.com

BRENTWOOD THEATRE T 01277 230833
Contact: David Zelly (Production Manager). Route:
Liverpool Street Main Line to Shenfield, then 15 min walk
15 Shenfield Road, Brentwood, Essex CM15 8AG
BO 01277 200305
E david@brentwood-theatre.org
W www.brentwood-theatre.org

BRIDEWELL THEATRE THE T 020 7353 3331
Route: Circle Line to Blackfriars. City Thameslink Capital
Connect. 15 different bus routes
St Bride Foundation, Bride Lane
Fleet Street, London EC4Y 8EQ
E info@sbf.org.uk
W www.sbf.org.uk

**BROADWAY STUDIO
THEATRE THE** T 020 8690 1000
Contact: Martin Costello (General Manager)
Route: Charing Cross to Catford Bridge
Catford, London SE6 4RU
BO 020 8690 0002
E martin@broadwaytheatre.org.uk
W www.broadwaytheatre.org.uk

BROADWAY THEATRE THE T 020 8507 5610
The Broadway, Barking IG11 7LS
BO 020 8507 5607
E admin@thebroadwaybarking.com
W www.thebroadwaybarking.com

**CALDER THEATRE
BOOKSHOP LTD** T 020 7620 2900
40 Seat Theatre Venue. Wide Selection of Plays on Sale
in Bookshop. Rehearsal Space for Hire
51 The Cut, London SE1 8LF
E info@calderbookshop.com

CAMDEN PEOPLE'S THEATRE T 020 7419 4841
Route: Victoria or Northern Line to Euston or Warren
Street, Hammersmith & City Line, Metropolitan or Circle
Line to Euston Square (2 min walk either way)
58-60 Hampstead Road, London NW1 2PY
E admin@cptheatre.co.uk
W www.cptheatre.co.uk

CANAL CAFE THEATRE THE T 020 7289 6056
Contact: Emma Taylor (Artistic Director)
The Bridge House, Delamere Terrace
Little Venice, London W2 6ND
BO 020 7289 6054
E mail@canalcafetheatre.com
W www.canalcafetheatre.com

CHARING CROSS THEATRE T 020 7930 5868
Formerly New Players Theatre
The Arches, Villiers Street, London WC2N 6NL
E info@charingcrosstheatre.co.uk
W www.charingcrosstheatre.co.uk

CHATS PALACE T 020 8533 0227
42-44 Brooksby's Walk, Hackney
London E9 6DF
E info@chatspalace.com
W www.chatspalace.co.uk

CHELSEA THEATRE
T 020 7352 1967
Route: District or Circle Line to Sloane Square then short bus ride 11 or 22 down King's Road
World's End Place
King's Road
London SW10 0DR
E admin@chelseatheatre.org.uk
W www.chelseatheatre.org.uk

CHICKENSHED
T 020 8216 2733
Contact: Susan Jamson (Press & PR). Route: Piccadilly Line to Oakwood, turn left outside tube & walk 8 min down Bramley Road or take 307 bus. Buses 298, 299, 699 or N19. Car Parking Available & Easy Access Parking by Reservation
290 Chase Side, Southgate
London N14 4PE
BO 020 8292 9222
E susanj@chickenshed.org.uk
W www.chickenshed.org.uk

CHRIST'S HOSPITAL THEATRE
T/BO 01403 247434
Box Office
Horsham, West Sussex RH13 0JD
E boxoffice@christs-hospital.org.uk

CHURCHILL THE
T 020 8290 8255
Contact: Chris Glover (General Manager)
High Street, Bromley
Kent BR1 1HA
BO 0844 8717620
W www.atgtickets.com/bromley

CLUB FOR ACTS & ACTORS THE
T 020 7836 3172
Contact: Malcolm Knight (Concert Artistes Association). Route: Piccadilly or Northern Line to Leicester Square then few mins walk
20 Bedford Street
London WC2E 9HP
E office@thecaa.org
W www.thecaa.co.uk

COCKPIT THE
T 020 7258 2925
Gateforth Street, Marylebone
London NW8 8EH
E mail@thecockpit.org.uk
W www.thecockpit.org.uk

COLOUR HOUSE THEATRE THE
T 020 8542 5511
Merton Abbey Mills, Watermill Way
London SW19 2RD
E info@colourhousetheatre.co.uk
W www.colourhousetheatre.co.uk

CORBETT THEATRE
T 020 8508 5983
Route: Central Line (Epping Branch) to Debden then 5 min walk
East 15 Acting School, Hatfields
Rectory Lane, Loughton IG10 3RY
E corbett@essex.ac.uk
W www.east15.ac.uk

COURTYARD THEATRE THE
T 020 7729 2202
Contact: June Abbott, Tim Gill (Joint Artistic Directors)
Bowling Green Walk
40 Pitfield Street
London N1 6EU
BO 0844 4771000
E info@thecourtyard.org.uk
W www.thecourtyard.org.uk

CUSTARD FACTORY
T 0121 224 7777
Gibb Street, Digbeth
Birmingham B9 4AA
E info@custardfactory.co.uk
W www.custardfactory.co.uk

DRILL HALL THE
See RADA: THE STUDIO THEATRE

EDINBURGH FESTIVAL FRINGE SOCIETY
T 0131 226 0026
180 High Street, Edinburgh EH1 1QS
E admin@edfringe.com
W www.edfringe.com

EMBASSY THEATRE & STUDIOS
T 020 7722 8183
Route: Jubilee Line to Swiss Cottage then 1 min walk
The Royal Central School of Speech & Drama
64 Eton Avenue
Swiss Cottage, London NW3 3HY
E enquiries@cssd.ac.uk
W www.cssd.ac.uk

EPSOM PLAYHOUSE THE
T 01372 742226
Contact: Elaine Teague (Assistant Manager). Main Auditorium Seats 450. Myers Studio Seats 80
Ashley Avenue, Epsom
Surrey KT18 5AL
BO 01372 742555
E eteague@epsom-ewell.gov.uk
W www.epsomplayhouse.co.uk

ETCETERA THEATRE
T 020 7482 4857
Hire Venue. In-house Productions
Twitter: @EtceteraTheatre
265 Camden High Street, London NW1 7BU
E admin@etceteratheatre.com
W www.etceteratheatre.com

FAIRFIELD HALLS
T 020 8681 0821
Route: Victoria & London Bridge Main Line to East Croydon then 5 min walk
Ashcroft Theatre & Concert Hall, Park Lane
Croydon CR9 1DG
BO 020 8688 9291
E info@fairfield.co.uk
W www.fairfield.co.uk

FINBOROUGH THEATRE
T 020 7244 7439
Contact: Neil McPherson (Artistic Director)
Route: District or Piccadilly Line to Earls Court then 5 min walk. Buses 74, 328, C1, C3 then 3 min walk
118 Finborough Road, London SW10 9ED
BO 0844 8471652
E admin@finboroughtheatre.co.uk
W www.finboroughtheatre.co.uk

GATE THEATRE
T 020 7229 5387
Route: Central, Circle or District Line to Notting Hill Gate (exit 3) then 1 min walk. Buses 23, 27, 28, 31, 52, 70, 94, 148, 328, 390, 452
11 Pembridge Road, Above Prince Albert Pub
Notting Hill, London W11 3HQ
BO 020 7229 0706
E gate@gatetheatre.co.uk
W www.gatetheatre.co.uk

GREENWICH PLAYHOUSE
T 020 8310 7276
Contact: Alice De Sousa
Head Office, 50 Openshaw Road
London SE2 0TE
E boxoffice@galleontheatre.co.uk
W www.galleontheatre.co.uk

GREENWICH THEATRE
T 020 8858 4447
Contact: James Haddrell (Artistic & Executive Director). Route: Jubilee Line (change Canary Wharf) then DLR to Greenwich Cutty Sark, 3 min walk or Charing Cross Main Line to Greenwich, 5 min walk
Crooms Hill, Greenwich
London SE10 8ES
BO 020 8858 7755
E info@greenwichtheatre.org.uk
W www.greenwichtheatre.org.uk

GROUNDLINGS THEATRE   T 023 9273 9496
42 Kent Street, Portsmouth
Hampshire PO1 3BT
E richard@groundlings.co.uk
W www.groundlings.co.uk

**GUILDHALL SCHOOL OF
MUSIC & DRAMA**   T 020 7628 2571
*Route: Hammersmith & City, Circle or Metropolitan Line
to Barbican or Moorgate (also served by Northern Line)
then 5 min walk*
Silk Street, Barbican
London EC2Y 8DT
E info@gsmd.ac.uk
W www.gsmd.ac.uk

HACKNEY EMPIRE THEATRE   T 020 8510 4500
Route: North London Line to Hackney Central
291 Mare Street, Hackney
London E8 1EJ
BO 020 8985 2424
E info@hackneyempire.co.uk
W www.hackneyempire.co.uk

HEN & CHICKENS THEATRE   T 020 7704 2001
*Route: Victoria Line or Main Line to Highbury & Islington,
directly opposite station*
Unrestricted View
Above Hen & Chickens Theatre Bar
109 St Paul's Road
Islington, London N1 2NA
E henandchickens@aol.com
W www.henandchickens.com

ICA THEATRE   T 020 7930 0493
No CVs. Venue only
Route: Nearest stations Piccadilly & Charing Cross
The Mall, London SW1Y 5AH
BO 020 7930 3647
W www.ica.org.uk

IVY ARTS CENTRE   BO 01483 636876
University of Surrey, Stag Hill
Guildford GU2 7XH
E boxoffice@surrey.ac.uk
W www.gsauk.org

JACK STUDIO THEATRE THE   T 020 8291 6354
410 Brockley Road
London SE4 2DH
E admin@brockleyjack.co.uk
W www.brockleyjack.co.uk

JACKSONS LANE   T 020 8340 5226
269A Archway Road, London N6 5AA
E admin@jacksonslane.org.uk
W www.jacksonslane.org.uk

**JERMYN STREET
THEATRE**   T 020 7434 1443 (Admin)
*Contact: Anthony Biggs (Artistic Director, Penny Horner
(General Manager)*
16B Jermyn Street
London SW1Y 6ST
BO 020 7287 2875
E info@jermynstreettheatre.co.uk
W www.jermynstreettheatre.co.uk

KING'S HEAD THEATRE   T 020 7226 8561
*Contact: Adam Spreadbury-Maher (Artistic Director).
Route: Northern Line to Angel then 5 min walk. Approx
halfway between Angel and Highbury & Islington tube
stations*
115 Upper Street, Islington
London N1 1QN
BO 020 7478 0160
E info@kingsheadtheatre.com
W www.kingsheadtheatre.com

**KING'S LYNN CORN
EXCHANGE**   T 01553 765565
Tuesday Market Place, King's Lynn, Norfolk PE30 1JW
BO 01553 764864
E cornexchangeadmin@liveleisure.co.uk
W www.kingslynncornexchange.co.uk

KOMEDIA   T 01273 647101
Contact: Marina Kobler (Programmer)
44-47 Gardner Street, Brighton BN1 1UN
BO 0345 2938480
E info@komedia.co.uk
W www.komedia.co.uk

LANDMARK ARTS CENTRE   T 020 8977 7558
Ferry Road, Teddington
Middlesex TW11 9NN
E info@landmarkartscentre.org
W www.landmarkartscentre.org

LANDOR THEATRE THE   T 020 7737 7276
*Contact: Robert McWhir (Artistic Director)
Route: Northern Line to Clapham North then 2 min walk*
70 Landor Road, London SW9 9PH
E info@landortheatre.co.uk
W www.landortheatre.co.uk

LEICESTER SQUARE THEATRE   T 020 7534 1740
6 Leicester Place, London WC2H 7BX
BO 020 7734 2222
E boxoffice@leicestersquaretheatre.com
W www.leicestersquaretheatre.com

LEIGHTON BUZZARD THEATRE   T 0300 3008130
Lake Street, Leighton Buzzard
Bedfordshire LU7 1RX
BO 0300 3008125
E lbtboxoffice@centralbedfordshire.gov.uk
W www.leightonbuzzardtheatre.co.uk

LIBRARY THEATRE THE   T 0114 273 4102
*260 Seat Civic Theatre for Hire. Traditional 1930s Art
Deco Style*
Central Library, Tudor Square
Sheffield, South Yorkshire S1 1XZ
E philip.repper@sheffield.gov.uk
W www.sheffield.gov.uk/libraries/librarytheatre

LILIAN BAYLIS STUDIO   T 020 7863 8065
Rosebery Avenue, London EC1R 4TN
BO 0844 4124300
E events@sadlerswells.com
W www.sadlerswells.com

LIVE THEATRE   T 0191 261 2694
Broad Chare, Quayside
Newcastle upon Tyne NE1 3DQ
BO 0191 232 1232
E info@live.org.uk
W www.live.org.uk

LONDON THEATRE THE   T 020 8694 1888
Lower Space, 443 New Cross Road
New Cross, London SE14 6TA
E thelondontheatre@live.co.uk
W www.thelondontheatre.com

LOST THEATRE   T 020 7622 9208
208 Wandsworth Road, London SW8 2JU
E info@losttheatre.co.uk
W www.losttheatre.co.uk

MADDERMARKET THEATRE   T 01603 626560
*Contact: Peter Beck, Stash Kirkbride (Joint Creative
Directors)*
St John's Alley, Norwich NR2 1DR
BO 01603 620917
E office@maddermarket.org
W www.maddermarket.co.uk

MECHANICS' THEATRE　　　**T** 01924 789815
Wood Street, Wakefield WF1 2EW
E c.lomas@wakefield.ac.uk
W www.facebook.com/mechanicstheatre

MENIER CHOCOLATE FACTORY　**T** 020 7378 1712
53 Southwark Street, London SE1 1RU
BO 020 7378 1713
E office@menierchocolatefactory.com
W www.menierchocolatefactory.com

MUSEUM OF COMEDY　　　**T** 020 7534 1744
Contact: Jo Rigg
The Undercroft of St George's Church, Bloomsbury Way
London WC1A 2PX
E boxoffice@museumofcomedy.com
W www.museumofcomedy.com

NEW DIORAMA THEATRE THE　**T** 020 7916 5467
Hire Venue. Route: Circle & District Line to Great
Portland Street then 5 min walk or Victoria & Northern
Lines to Warren Street then 5 min walk
15-16 Triton Street, Regents Place
London NW1 3BF
BO 020 7383 9034
E hello@newdiorama.com
W www.newdiorama.com

NEW WIMBLEDON
THEATRE & STUDIO　　　**T** 020 8545 7900
Route: Main Line or District Line to Wimbledon, then 3
min walk. Buses 57, 93, 155
The Broadway, Wimbledon
London SW19 1QG
BO 0844 8717646
W www.atgtickets.com/venue/new-wimbledon-theatre

NORTHBROOK THEATRE THE　**BO** 01903 273333
Contact: Theatre Co-ordinator
Northbrook College, Littlehampton Road
Worthing, West Sussex BN12 6NU
E box.office@nbcol.ac.uk
W www.northbrooktheatre.co.uk

NORWICH PUPPET THEATRE　**T** 01603 615564
St James, Whitefriars, Norwich NR3 1TN
BO 01603 629921
E info@puppettheatre.co.uk
W www.puppettheatre.co.uk

NOVELLO THEATRE THE　　**T** 01344 620881
Redroofs Theatre Company. Route: Waterloo Main Line
to Ascot then 1 mile from station
2 High Street, Sunninghill
Nr Ascot, Berkshire SL5 9NE

OLD RED LION THEATRE　　**T** 020 7837 7816
Contact: Stewart Pringle (Artistic Director)
Route: Northern Line to Angel, then 1 min walk
418 St John Street, Islington
London EC1V 4NJ
BO 0844 4124307
E info@oldredliontheatre.co.uk

ORANGE TREE　　**T** 020 8940 0141 (Admin)
Contact: Paul Miller (Artistic Director)
Route: District Line, Waterloo Main Line or Overground,
then virtually opposite station
1 Clarence Street, Richmond TW9 2SA
BO 020 8940 3633
E admin@orangetreetheatre.co.uk

ORCHARD THEATRE　　　**T** 01322 220099
Contact: Chris Glover (Theatre Director)
Route: Charing Cross Main Line to Dartford
Home Gardens, Dartford, Kent DA1 1ED
BO 01322 220000
E info@orchardtheatre.co.uk
W www.orchardtheatre.co.uk

OVALHOUSE　　　**T** 020 7582 0080
Route: Northern Line to Oval then 1 min walk, or Victoria
Line & Main Line to Vauxhall then 10 min walk
52-54 Kennington Oval, London SE11 5SW
BO 020 7582 7680
E info@ovalhouse.com
W www.ovalhouse.com

PARK THEATRE　　　**T** 020 7870 6876
Route: 1 min walk from Finsbury Park via tube (Victoria/
Piccadilly Lines), Main Line or bus
Clifton Terrace, Finsbury Park, London N4 3JP
E info@parktheatre.co.uk
W www.parktheatre.co.uk

PAVILION THEATRE　　**T** 00 353 1 2312929
Marine Road, Dun Laoghaire
County Dublin, Ireland
E info@paviliontheatre.ie
W www.paviliontheatre.ie

PENTAMETERS　　　**T** 020 7435 3648
Route: Northern Line to Hampstead then 1 min walk.
Buses 46, 268
(Theatre Entrance in Oriel Place, above The Horseshoe
Pub) 28 Heath Street
London NW3 6TE
W www.pentameters.co.uk

PLACE THE　　　**T** 020 7121 1101
Main London Venue for Contemporary Dance.
Route: Northern or Victoria Lines to Euston; Circle,
Hammersmith & City, Metropolitan, Northern, Piccadilly
or Victoria Lines to King's Cross St Pancras; Circle,
Hammersmith & City or Metropolitan Lines to Euston
Square; Piccadilly Line to Russell Square. All easy
walking distance
17 Duke's Road, London WC1H 9PY
BO 020 7121 1100
E theatre@theplace.org.uk
W www.theplace.org.uk

PLATFORM THEATRE
Central Saint Martins College of Arts & Design, University
of the Arts London
Handyside Street, King's Cross
London N1C 4AA
E platformboxoffice@arts.ac.uk
W www.csm.arts.ac.uk/platform-theatre

PLEASANCE ISLINGTON　　**T** 020 7619 6868
Contact: Anthony Alderson. 180-280 Seat Mainhouse
plus 60 Seat Studio. Route:
Piccadilly Line to Caledonian Road, turn left, walk 50 yds,
turn left into North Road, 3 min walk. Buses 17, 91, 259,
393, N91
Carpenters Mews, North Road
(Off Caledonian Road), London N7 9EF
BO 020 7609 1800
E info@pleasance.co.uk
W www.pleasance.co.uk

POLKA THEATRE　　　**T** 020 8545 8323
Route: Waterloo Main Line or District Line to Wimbledon
then 10 min walk. Northern Line to South Wimbledon
then 10 min walk. Tram to Wimbledon, Buses 57, 93,
219, 493
240 The Broadway, Wimbledon SW19 1SB
BO 020 8543 4888
E stephen@polkatheatre.com
W www.polkatheatre.com

PRINCESS THEATRE
HUNSTANTON　　　**T** 01485 532252 (T/BO)
13 The Green, Hunstanton
Norfolk PE36 5AH
E boxoffice@princesshunstanton.co.uk
W www.princesshunstanton.co.uk

**PRINT ROOM AT
THE CORONET**　T 020 3642 6606
103 Notting Hill Gate, London W11 3LB
E hello@the-print-room.org

PUTNEY ARTS THEATRE　T 020 8788 6943
Ravenna Road, Putney SW15 6AW
E info@putneyartstheatre.org.uk
W www.putneyartstheatre.org.uk

QUEEN'S THEATRE　T 01708 462362
*Route: District Line to Hornchurch. Main Line Train to
Romford or Gidea Park. 15 miles drive from West End via
A13, A1306 then A125, or A12 then A127*
Billet Lane, Hornchurch
Essex RM11 1QT
BO 01708 443333
E info@queens-theatre.co.uk
W www.queens-theatre.co.uk

**QUESTORS THEATRE
EALING THE**　T 020 8567 0011
*Route: Central or District Line to Ealing Broadway then 8
min walk. Buses 65, 83, 207, 427, 607, E2, E7, E8, E11*
12 Mattock Lane, London W5 5BQ
BO 020 8567 5184
E enquiries@questors.org.uk
W www.questors.org.uk

**RADA: THE CLUB
THEATRE**　T 020 7307 5060 (T/BO)
Formerly The Drill Hall
16 Chenies Street, London WC1E 7EX
T 020 7307 5075 (Theatre Hire)
E venues@radaenterprises.org
W www.rada.ac.uk/venues

**RADA: GBS THEATRE (GEORGE
BERNARD SHAW)**　T 020 7908 4800 (T/BO)
Malet Street, London WC1E 7JN
T 020 7307 5075 (Theatre Hire)
E boxoffice@rada.ac.uk
W www.rada.ac.uk/venues

**RADA: GIELGUD, John
THEATRE**　T 020 7908 4800 (T/BO)
Malet Street, London WC1E 7JN
T 020 7307 5075 (Theatre Hire)
E boxoffice@rada.ac.uk
W www.rada.ac.uk/venues

**RADA: JERWOOD
VANBRUGH THEATRE**　T 020 7908 4800 (T/BO)
Malet Street, London WC1E 7JN
T 020 7307 5075 (Theatre Hire)
E boxoffice@rada.ac.uk
W www.rada.ac.uk/venues

**RADA: THE STUDIO
THEATRE**　T 020 7307 5060 (T/BO)
Formerly The Drill Hall
16 Chenies Street, London WC1E 7EX
T 020 7908 4822 (Theatre Hire)
E venues@radaenterprises.org
W www.rada.ac.uk/venues

RED HEDGEHOG THE　T 07817 109093
255-257 Archway Road, Highgate
London N6 5BS
BO 020 8348 5050
E theatre@theredhedgehog.co.uk
W www.theredhedgehog.co.uk

**RED LADDER THEATRE
COMPANY LTD**　T 0113 245 5311
3 St Peter's Buildings, York Street
Leeds LS9 8AJ
E rod@redladder.co.uk
W www.redladder.co.uk

RICHMOND THEATRE　T 020 8332 4500
*Contact: Christiaan de Villiers (General Manager)
Route: 20 min from Waterloo (South West Trains)
or District Line to Richmond then 2 min walk*
The Green, Richmond
Surrey TW9 1QJ
BO 0844 8717651
E richmondstagedoor@theambassadors.com
W www.atgtickets.com/richmond

RIVERSIDE STUDIOS　T 020 8237 1000
*Route: District, Piccadilly or Hammersmith & City Line to
Hammersmith then 5 min walk. Buses 9, 10, 27, 33, 72,
190, 209, 211, 266, 267, 283, 295, 391, 419*
65 Aspenlea Road
London W6 8LH
BO 020 8237 1111
E info@riversidestudios.co.uk
W www.riversidestudios.co.uk

ROSE THEATRE KINGSTON　T 020 8546 6983
*Contact: Jerry Gunn (Executive Producer), Naomi Webb
(Assistant Producer)*
24-26 High Street
Kingston upon Thames
Surrey KT1 1HL
E admin@rosetheatrekingston.org
W www.rosetheatrekingston.org

**ROSEMARY BRANCH
THEATRE**　T 020 7704 6665
*Route: Tube to Bank, Moorgate or Old Street (exit 5),
then 21, 76 or 141 bus to Baring Street, or 271 bus from
Highbury & Islington*
2 Shepperton Road
London N1 3DT
E rosemarybranchtheatre@googlemail.com
W www.rosemarybranch.co.uk

SAGE GATESHEAD　T 0191 443 4661
St Mary's Square, Gateshead Quays
Gateshead NE8 2JR
F 0191 443 4551
E ticketoffice.mail@sagegateshead.com
W www.sagegateshead.com

**SCOTTISH STORYTELLING
CENTRE**　T 0131 556 9579
Netherbow Theatre
43-45 High Street
Edinburgh EH1 1SR
E reception@scottishstorytellingcentre.com
W www.tracscotland.org/scottish-storytelling-centre

**SHAW THEATRE @ PULLMAN
LONDON ST PANCRAS**　T 020 7666 9037
100-110 Euston Road, London NW1 2AJ
BO 0844 2485075
E info@shaw-theatre.com

**SOUTH HILL PARK
ARTS CENTRE**　T 01344 484858
*Route: Waterloo Main Line to Bracknell then 10 min bus
ride or taxi rank at station*
Bracknell, Berkshire RG12 7PA
BO 01344 484123
E enquiries@southhillpark.org.uk
W www.southhillpark.org.uk

SOUTH LONDON THEATRE　T 020 8670 3474
*Route: Victoria or London Bridge Main Line to West
Norwood then 2 min walk or Victoria Line to Brixton then
buses 2, 68, 196, 322*
Bell Theatre & Prompt Corner
2A Norwood High Street
London SE27 9NS
E southlondontheatre@yahoo.co.uk
W www.southlondontheatre.co.uk

SOUTHWARK PLAYHOUSE T 020 7407 0234
Contact: Chris Smyrnios (Chief Executive). Route: Trains to Borough or Elephant & Castle, Jubilee/Northern Line to London Bridge. Buses 47, 381, RV1, N47, N381. River service to London Bridge City
77-85 Newington Causeway, London SE1 6BD
E admin@southwarkplayhouse.co.uk
W www.southwarkplayhouse.co.uk

SPACE ARTS CENTRE THE T 020 7515 7799
269 Westferry Road, London E14 3RS
E info@space.org.uk
W www.space.org.uk

ST JOHN'S CHURCH T 020 7633 9819
Hosts Classical Concerts, Conferences, Large Meetings & Lectures
Waterloo Road, SouthbanK, London SE1 8TY
E bookings@stjohnswaterloo.org
W www.stjohnswaterloo.org

TABARD THEATRE T 020 8995 6035
Contact: Simon Reilly (Theatre Manager)
2 Bath Road, London W4 1LW
E info@tabardtheatre.co.uk
W www.tabardtheatre.co.uk

TARA ARTS THEATRE T 020 8333 4457
356 Garratt Lane, London SW18 4ES
E tara@tara-arts.com
W www.tara-arts.com

THEATRE503 T 020 7978 7040
Route: Main Line Train to Clapham Junction from Victoria or Waterloo then 10 min walk, or buses 44, 49, 319, 344, 345, or tube to South Kensington then buses 49 or 345 or tube to Sloane Square then bus 319
The Latchmere Pub, 503 Battersea Park Road
London SW11 3BW
E info@theatre503.com
W www.theatre503.com

THEATRE ALIBI T/F 01392 217315
Emmanuel Hall, Emmanuel Road, Exeter EX4 1EJ
E info@theatrealibi.co.uk
W www.theatrealibi.co.uk

**THEATRE ROYAL
STRATFORD EAST** T 020 8534 7374
Contact: Kerry Michael (Artistic Director)
Route: Central or Jubilee Lines, DLR, Overground or National Express trains to Stratford then 2 min walk
Gerry Raffles Square, London E15 1BN
BO 020 8534 0310
E theatreroyal@stratfordeast.com
W www.stratfordeast.com

THEATRO TECHNIS T 020 7387 6617
Contact: George Eugeniou (Artistic Director)
Route: Northern Line to Mornington Crescent then 3 min walk
26 Crowndale Road, London NW1 1TT
E info@theatrotechnis.com
W www.theatrotechnis.com

**TOBACCO FACTORY
THEATRES** T 0117 902 0345
Raleigh Road, Southville, Bristol BS3 1TF
E theatre@tobaccofactorytheatres.com
W www.tobaccofactorytheatres.com

TRICYCLE THEATRE T 020 7372 6611
Contact: Indhu Rubasingham (Artistic Director), Bridget Kalloushi (Executive Producer). Route: Jubilee Line to Kilburn then 5 min walk or buses 16, 32, 189, pass the door, 31, 98, 206, 316, 332 pass nearby
269 Kilburn High Road, London NW6 7JR
BO 020 7328 1000
E admin@tricycle.co.uk   W www.tricycle.co.uk

TRON THEATRE T 0141 552 3748
63 Trongate, Glasgow G1 5HB
BO 0141 552 4267
E box.office@tron.co.uk
W www.tron.co.uk

UNION THEATRE THE T 020 7261 9876
Contact: Sasha Regan (Artistic Director), Ben De Wynter (Associate Director), Michael Strassen (Resident Director), Iain Dennis (Technical Director). Route: Jubilee Line to Southwark then 2 min walk
204 Union Street, Southwark, London SE1 0LX
E sashareganunion@gmail.com
W www.uniontheatre.biz

**UPSTAIRS AT THE
GATEHOUSE** T 020 8340 4256
Route: Northern Line to Highgate then 10 min walk. Buses 143, 210, 214, 271
The Gatehouse, Corner of Hampstead Lane/North Road
Highgate, London N6 4BD
BO 020 8340 3488
E events@ovationproductions.com
W www.upstairsatthegatehouse.com

VINE ARTS LTD T 01442 818283
Contact: Corinna Chute
Northbridge Road, Berkhamsted
Hertfordshire HP4 1EH
E admin@berkhamstedartscentre.co.uk
W www.berkhamstedartscentre.co.uk

WATERLOO EAST THEATRE T 020 7928 0060
Brad Street, London SE1 8TN
E info@waterlooeast.co.uk
W www.waterlooeast.co.uk

WATERLOO EAST THEATRE T 020 7928 0060
Admin: 3 Wootton Street, London SE1 8TG
E info@waterlooeast.co.uk
W www.waterlooeast.co.uk

WATERMANS T 020 8232 1019
40 High Street, Brentford TW8 0DS
BO 020 8232 1010
E info@watermans.org.uk
W www.watermans.org.uk

WHITE BEAR THEATRE T 020 7793 9193
Favours New Writing & Classics
Route: Northern Line to Kennington (2 min walk)
138 Kennington Park Road, London SE11 4DJ
E info@whitebeartheatre.co.uk
W www.whitebeartheatre.co.uk

WILTON'S MUSIC HALL T 020 7702 2789
Route: Under 10 min walk from Aldgate East (exit for Leman Street) & Tower Hill Tube. DLR: Shadwell or Tower Gateway. Car: Follow the yellow AA signs to Wilton's Music Hall from the Highway, Aldgate or Tower Hill
Graces Alley, Off Ensign Street, London E1 8JB
E info@wiltons.org.uk
W www.wiltons.org.uk

WYCOMBE SWAN T 01494 514444
St Mary Street, High Wycombe
Buckinghamshire HP11 2XE
BO 01494 512000
E admin@wycombeswan.co.uk
W www.wycombeswan.co.uk

WYVERN THEATRE T 01793 535534
Theatre Square, Swindon, Wiltshire SN1 1QN
BO 01793 524481
E info@wyverntheatre.org.uk
W www.swindontheatres.co.uk

ABERDEEN:
His Majesty's Theatre   T 0845 2708200
Rosemount Viaduct, Aberdeen AB25 1GL
BO 01224 641122
E info@aberdeenperformingarts.com
W www.aberdeenperformingarts.com

ABERYSTWYTH:
Aberystwyth Arts Centre   T 01970 622882
Penglais, Aberystwyth
Ceredigion SY23 3DE
BO 01970 623232
E ggo@aber.ac.uk
W www.aber.ac.uk/artscentre

BACUP: Royal Court Theatre   BO 01706 874299
Rochdale Road, Bacup OL13 9NR
E managingdirector@bacuproyalcourttheatre.co.uk
W www.brct.co

BASINGSTOKE: The Haymarket   T 01256 819797
Churchill Way, Basingstoke RG21 7QR
BO 01256 844244
E box.office@anvilarts.org.uk
W www.anvilarts.org.uk

BATH: Theatre Royal   T 01225 448815
Sawclose, Bath BA1 1ET
BO 01225 448844
E forename.surname@theatreroyal.org.uk
W www.theatreroyal.org.uk

BELFAST: Grand Opera House   T 028 9024 0411
Great Victoria Street, Belfast BT2 7HR
BO 028 9024 1919
E info@goh.co.uk
W www.goh.co.uk

BILLINGHAM: Forum Theatre   T 01642 551389
Town Centre, Billingham TS23 2LJ
E forumtheatre@btconnect.com
W www.forumtheatrebillingham.co.uk

BIRMINGHAM: Hippodrome   BO 0844 3385000
Hurst Street, Southside, Birmingham B5 4TB
E info@birminghamhippodrome.com
W www.birminghamhippodrome.com

BIRMINGHAM:
New Alexandra Theatre   T 0121 230 9070
Station Street, Birmingham B5 4DS
BO 0844 8713011
W www.atgtickets.com/birmingham

BLACKPOOL: Grand Theatre   T 01253 290111
33 Church Street, Blackpool FY1 1HT
BO 01253 290190
E geninfo@blackpoolgrand.co.uk
W www.blackpoolgrand.co.uk

BLACKPOOL: Opera House   T 01253 625252
Church Street, Blackpool FY1 1HW
BO 0844 8561111
W www.wintergardensblackpool.co.uk

BOURNEMOUTH:
Pavilion Theatre   T 01202 456400
Westover Road, Bournemouth BH1 2BU
BO 0844 5763000
E paul.griffiths@bhlive.co.uk
W www.bic.co.uk

BRADFORD: Alhambra Theatre   T 01274 432375
Morley Street, Bradford BD7 1AJ
BO 01274 432000
E administration@ces.bradford.gov.uk
W www.bradford-theatres.co.uk

BRADFORD:
Theatre in the Mill   BO 01274 233200
University of Bradford Shearbridge Road
Bradford BD7 1DP
E theatre@bradford.ac.uk
W www.bradford.ac.uk/theatre

BRIGHTON: Brighton Dome
& Brighton Festivals   T 01273 700747
The Dome Corn Exchange & Studio Theatres
12A Pavilion Buildings, Castle Square
Brighton BN1 1EE
BO 01273 709709
E info@brightondome.org
W www.brightondome.org

BRIGHTON: Spymonkey   T 07766 712757
The Old Market, 11A Upper Market Street, Hove BN3 1AS
E info@spymonkey.co.uk
W www.spymonkey.co.uk

BRIGHTON:
Theatre Royal Brighton   T 01273 764400
New Road, Brighton BN1 1SD
BO 0844 8717650
W www.atgtickets.com/brighton

BRISTOL: Bristol Hippodrome   T 0117 302 3310
St Augustines Parade, Bristol BS1 4UZ
BO 0844 8713012
W www.atgtickets.com/bristol

BROXBOURNE: the Spotlight   BO 01992 441946
High Street, Hoddesdon
Herts EN11 8BE
E thespotlight@broxbourne.gov.uk
W www.broxbourne.gov.uk/thespotlight

BURY ST EDMUNDS:
Theatre Royal   T 01284 829944
Westgate Street, Bury St Edmunds IP33 1QR
BO 01284 769505
E admin@theatreroyal.org
W www.theatreroyal.org

BUXTON: Buxton Opera House
& Pavilion Arts Centre   T 01298 72050
Water Street, Buxton SK17 6XN
BO 01298 72190
E admin@boh.org.uk
W www.buxtonoperahouse.org.uk

CAMBRIDGE: Cambridge Arts
Theatre Trust Ltd   T 01223 578904
6 St Edward's Passage, Cambridge CB2 3PJ
BO 0 223 503333
E info@cambridgeartstheatre.com
W www.cambridgeartstheatre.com

CAMBERLEY:
Camberley Theatre   BO 01276 707600
Knoll Road, Camberley
Surrey GU15 3SY
E camberley.theatre@surreyheath.gov.uk
W www.camberleytheatre.biz

CAMBRIDGE: Mumford Theatre T 01223 417748
Anglia Ruskin University, East Road
Cambridge CB1 1PT
BO 0845 1962320
E mumford@anglia.ac.uk

CANTERBURY: Gulbenkian BO 01227 769075
Theatre & Cinema
University of Kent
Canterbury CT2 7NB
E boxoffice@kent.ac.uk
W www.thegulbenkian.co.uk

**CANTERBURY:
The Marlowe Theatre** BO 01227 787787
The Friars, Canterbury
Kent CT1 2AS
E marlowetheatre@marlowetheatre.com
W www.marlowetheatre.com

CARDIFF: New Theatre T 029 2087 8787
Park Place, Cardiff CF10 3LN
BO 029 2087 8889
E ntmailings@cardiff.gov.uk
W www.newtheatrecardiff.co.uk

**CARDIFF:
Wales Millennium Centre** T 029 2063 6400
Bute Place, Cardiff CF10 5AL
BO 029 2063 6464
E stagedoor@wmc.org.uk
W www.wmc.org.uk

**CHELTENHAM:
Everyman Theatre** T 01242 512515
Regent Street, Cheltenham GL50 1HQ
BO 01242 572573
E admin@everymantheatre.org.uk
W www.everymantheatre.org.uk

**CHICHESTER:
Festival Theatre** T 01243 784437
Oaklands Park, Chichester PO19 6AP
BO 01243 781312
E admin@cft.org.uk
W www.cft.org.uk

CRAWLEY: The Hawth T 01293 552941
Hawth Avenue, Crawley
West Sussex RH10 6YZ
BO 01293 553636
E hawthadmin@parkwoodtheatres.co.uk
W www.hawth.co.uk

CREWE: Lyceum Theatre BO 01270 638242
Heath Street, Crewe CW1 2DA
E admin@crewelyceum.co.uk
W www.crewelyceum.co.uk

DARLINGTON: Civic Theatre BO 01325 486555
Parkgate
Darlington DL1 1RR
E civictheatre.info@darlington.gov.uk
W www.darlingtoncivic.co.uk

DONCASTER: CAST T 01302 303950
Contact: Michael Cook
Waterdale, Doncaster
South Yorkshire DN1 3BU
E hello@castindoncaster.com
W www.castindoncaster.com

DUBLIN: Gaiety Theatre T 00 353 1 6795622
South King Street, Dublin 2, Ireland
BO 00 353 1 456 9569
E info@gaietytheatre.com
W www.gaietytheatre.com

DUBLIN: Gate Theatre T 00 353 1 8744368
1 Cavendish Row, Dublin, Ireland
BO 00 353 1 8744045
E info@gate-theatre.ie
W www.gatetheatre.ie

DUBLIN: The Olympia Theatre T 00 353 1 6725883
72 Dame Street, Dublin 2, Ireland
BO 00 353 1 6793323
E info@olympia.ie
W www.olympia.ie

**EASTBOURNE:
Congress Theatre** T 01323 415500
Admin Office: Winter Garden
Compton Street
Eastbourne BN21 4BP
BO 01323 412000
E theatres@eastbourne.gov.uk
W www.eastbournetheatres.co.uk

**EASTBOURNE:
Devonshire Park Theatre** T 01323 415500
Admin Office: Winter Garden, Compton Street
Eastbourne BN21 4BP
BO 01323 412000
E theatres@eastbourne.gov.uk
W www.eastbournetheatres.co.uk

EDINBURGH: King's Theatre T 0131 662 1112
2 Leven Street, Edinburgh EH3 9LQ
BO 0131 529 6000
E empire@edtheatres.com
W www.edtheatres.com

**EDINBURGH:
Playhouse Theatre** T 0131 524 3333
18-22 Greenside Place, Edinburgh EH1 3AA
BO 0844 8713014
E edinburghadministrator@theambassadors.com
W www.atgtickets.com/edinburgh

GLASGOW: King's Theatre T 0141 240 1300
297 Bath Street, Glasgow G2 4JN
BO 0844 8717648
E glasgowstagedoor@theambassadors.com
W www.atgtickets.com

GLASGOW: Theatre Royal T 0141 332 3321
282 Hope Street, Glasgow G2 3QA
BO 0844 8717647
W www.atgtickets.com/glasgow

**GRAYS THURROCK:
Thameside Theatre** T 01375 413981
Orsett Road, Grays Thurrock RM17 5DX
BO 0845 3005264
E thameside.theatre@thurrock.gov.uk
W www.thurrock.gov.uk/theatre

HARLOW: Harlow Playhouse T 01279 446760
Playhouse Square, Harlow CM20 1LS
BO 01279 431945
E playhouse@harlow.gov.uk
W www.playhouseharlow.com

HARROGATE: Harrogate International Centre   T 01423 500500
Kings Road, Harrogate HG1 5LA
E sales@harrogateinternationalcentre.co.uk
W www.hicyorkshire.co.uk

HASTINGS: White Rock Theatre   T 01424 462283
White Rock, Hastings TN34 1JX
BO 01424 462288
E enquiries@whiterocktheatre.org.uk
W www.whiterocktheatre.org.uk

HATFIELD: The Hawthorne Theatre   T 01707 330360
Campus West, Welwyn Garden City
Herts AL8 6BX
E guymasterson@hawthornetheatre.co.uk
W www.hawthornetheatre.co.uk

HAYES: Beck Theatre   T 020 8561 7506
Grange Road, Hayes
Middlesex UB3 2UE
BO 020 8561 8371
E enquiries@becktheatre.org.uk
W www.becktheatre.org.uk

HIGH WYCOMBE: Wycombe Swan   T 01494 514444
St Mary Street, High Wycombe HP11 2XE
BO 01494 512000
E enquiries@wycombeswan.co.uk
W www.wycombeswan.co.uk

HUDDERSFIELD: Lawrence Batley Theatre   T 01484 425282
Queen's Square, Queen Street
Huddersfield HD1 2SP
BO 01484 430528
E theatre@thelbt.org
W www.thelbt.org

HULL: Hull New Theatre   T 01482 613818
Kingston Square, Hull HU1 3HF
BO 01482 300300
W www.hullcc.gov.uk

HULL: Hull Truck Theatre   T 01482 224800
50 Ferensway, Hull HU2 8LB
BO 01482 323638
W www.hulltruck.co.uk

ILFORD: Kenneth More Theatre   T 020 8553 4464
Oakfield Road, Ilford IG1 1BT
BO 020 8553 4466
E admin@kmtheatre.co.uk
W www.kmtheatre.co.uk

IPSWICH: Sir John Mills Theatre   T 01473 218202
Eastern Angles Theatre Company
Gatacre Road, Ipswich IP1 2LQ
BO 01473 211498
E admin@easternangles.co.uk
W www.easternangles.co.uk

JERSEY: Jersey Opera House   T 01534 511100
Gloucester Street, St Helier
Jersey, Channel Islands JE2 3QR
BO 01534 511115
E admin@jerseyoperahouse.co.uk
W www.jerseyoperahouse.co.uk

KINGSTON: Rose Theatre   T 020 8546 6983
24-26 High Street
Kingston Upon Thames
Surrey KT1 1HL
E admin@rosetheatrekingston.org
W www.rosetheatrekingston.org

KIRKCALDY: Adam Smith Theatre   T 01592 583301
Bennochy Road
Kirkcaldy KY1 1ET
BO 01592 583302
E boxoffice.adamsmith@onfife.com
W www.onfife.com

LEATHERHEAD: The Leatherhead Theatre   T 01372 365130
7 Church Street, Leatherhead
Surrey KT22 8DN
BO 01372 365141
E info@the-theatre.org
W www.theleatherheadtheatre.org

LEEDS: City Varieties Music Hall   T 0113 391 7777
Swan Street, Leeds LS1 6LW
BO 0113 243 0808
E info@cityvarieties.co.uk
W www.cityvarieties.co.uk

LEEDS: Grand Theatre & Opera House   T 0113 245 6014
46 New Briggate
Leeds LS1 6NZ
BO 0844 8482705
E boxoffice@leedsgrandtheatre.com
W www.leedsgrandtheatre.com

LICHFIELD: The Lichfield Garrick   T 01543 412110
Castle Dyke, Lichfield WS13 6HR
BO 01543 412121
E garrick@lichfieldgarrick.com
W www.lichfieldgarrick.com

LINCOLN: LADA Productions   T 01522 775760
Sparkhouse Studios, Ropewalk
Lincoln, Lincs LN6 7DQ
F 01522 837201
E productions@lada.org.uk
W www.lada.org.uk

LINCOLN: Theatre Royal   T 01522 519999
Clasketgate
Lincoln LN2 1JJ
E boxoffice@lincolntheatreroyal.com
W www.lincolntheatreroyal.com

LIVERPOOL: Empire Theatre   T 0151 702 7320
Lime Street
Liverpool L1 1JE
BO 0844 8713017
W www.atgtickets.com/liverpool

LLANDUDNO: Venue Cymru   T 01492 879771
Promenade, Llandudno
Conwy, North Wales LL30 1BB
BO 01492 872000
E info@venuecymru.co.uk
W www.venuecymru.co.uk

MALVERN: Malvern Theatres   T 01684 569256
Festival & Forum Theatres
Grange Road, Malvern WR14 3HB
BO 01684 892277
E post@malvern-theatres.co.uk
W www.malvern-theatres.co.uk

**MANCHESTER: O2 Apollo
Manchester**   T 0161 273 6921
Stockport Road, Ardwick Green
Manchester M12 6AP
BO 0844 4777677
E o2apollomanchester@livenation.co.uk
W www.o2apollomanchester.co.uk

MANCHESTER: Opera House   T 0161 828 1700
Quay Street, Manchester M3 3HP
BO 0844 8713018
W www.atgtickets.com/manchester

MANCHESTER: Palace Theatre   T 0161 245 6600
Oxford Street, Manchester M1 6FT
BO 0844 8713019
E manchesterstagedoor@theambassadors.com
W www.palaceandoperahouse.org.uk

**MARGATE: Theatre Royal
Margate**   T 01843 296111
Addington Street, Margate, Kent CT9 1PW
BO 01843 292795
E box@theatreroyalmargate.com
W www.theatreroyalmargate.com

**MILTON KEYNES:
Milton Keynes Theatre**   T 01908 547500
500 Marlborough Gate, Central Milton Keynes MK9 3NZ
BO 0844 8717652
W www.atgtickets.com/miltonkeynes

NEWARK: Palace Theatre   T 01636 655750
Appletongate, Newark NG24 1JY
BO 01636 655755
E carys.coultonjones@nsdc.info
W www.palacenewark.com

**NEWCASTLE UPON TYNE: Northern Stage
(Theatrical Productions) Ltd**   T 0191 242 7200
Barras Bridge, Newcastle upon Tyne NE1 7RH
BO 0191 230 5151
E info@northernstage.co.uk
W www.northernstage.co.uk

**NEWCASTLE UPON TYNE:
Theatre Royal**   T 0191 244 2500
100 Grey Street, Newcastle upon Tyne NE1 6BR
BO 0844 8112121
W www.theatreroyal.co.uk

**NORTHAMPTON: Royal &
Derngate Theatres**   T 01604 626222
19-21 Guildhall Road, Northampton NN1 1DP
BO 01604 624811
E ashley.bishop@namtrust.co.uk
W www.royalandderngate.co.uk

**NORWICH:
Norwich Theatre Royal**   T 01603 598500
Theatre Street, Norwich NR2 1RL
BO 01603 630000
E info@theatreroyalnorwich.co.uk
W www.theatreroyalnorwich.co.uk

NOTTINGHAM: Royal Centre   T 0115 989 5500
Theatre Royal & Royal Concert Hall
Theatre Square
Nottingham NG1 5ND
BO 0115 989 5555
E enquiry@trch.co.uk
W www.trch.co.uk

OXFORD: New Theatre   T 01865 320760
George Street, Oxford OX1 2AG
BO 0844 8713020
E oxfordstagedoor@theambassadors.com

OXFORD: Oxford Playhouse   T 01865 305300
11-12 Beaumont Street
Oxford OX1 2LW
BO 01865 305305
E admin@oxfordplayhouse.com
W www.oxfordplayhouse.com

**PLYMOUTH: RESTLESS THEATRE
COMPANY**   T 07915 666276
Contact: Sarah McCourt
7 Grosvenor Cottages, Mutley
Plymouth, Devon PL4 7DB
E sarah@restlesstheatre.co.uk
W www.restlesstheatre.co.uk

**POOLE: Lighthouse,
Poole's Centre for the Arts**   BO 0844 4068666
Kingland Road
Poole BH15 1UG
W www.lighthousepoole.co.uk

READING: The Hexagon   T 0118 937 2123
Queen's Walk, Reading RG1 7UA
BO 0118 960 6060
E boxoffice@readingarts.com
W www.readingarts.com

**RICHMOND, N YORKS:
Georgian Theatre Royal**   T 01748 823710
Victoria Road, Richmond
North Yorkshire DL10 4DW
BO 01748 825252
E admin@georgiantheatreroyal.co.uk
W www.georgiantheatreroyal.co.uk

**RICHMOND, SURREY:
Richmond Theatre**   T 020 8332 4500
The Green, Richmond
Surrey TW9 1QJ
BO 0844 8717651
E richmondstagedoor@theambassadors.com
W www.atgtickets.com/richmond

**ROCHDALE:
Gracie Fields Theatre**   T 01706 716689
Hudsons Walk, Rochdale
Lancashire OL11 5EF
E enquiries@graciefieldstheatre.com
W www.graciefieldstheatre.com

**SHEFFIELD:
Sheffield Theatres Trust**   T 0114 249 5999
Crucible, Lyceum & Crucible Studio
55 Norfolk Street, Sheffield S1 1DA
BO 0114 249 6000
E info@sheffieldtheatres.co.uk
W www.sheffieldtheatres.co.uk

SHERINGHAM: Little Theatre   T 01263 822117
2 Station Road, Sheringham
Norfolk NR26 8RE
BO 01263 822347
E boxoffice@sheringhamlittletheatre.com
W www.sheringhamlittletheatre.com

SOMERSET:
Warehouse Theatre   T 01460 62739
Brewery Lane, Ilminster
Somerset TA19 9AD
E dave@downside.uk.com
W www.thewarehousetheatre.org.uk

SOUTHAMPTON:
The Mayflower Theatre   T 023 8071 1800
Empire Lane, Southampton SO15 1AP
BO 023 8071 1811
E info@mayflower.org.uk
W www.mayflower.org.uk

SOUTHEND:
Southend Theatres   T 01702 390657
Cliffs Pavilion, Palace Theatre & Dixon Studio
Southend on Sea, Station Road
Westcliff-on-Sea, Essex SS0 7RA
BO 01702 351135
E info@southendtheatres.org.uk
W www.southendtheatres.org.uk

ST ALBANS: Abbey Theatre   T 01727 847472
Holywell Hill, St Albans AL1 2DL
BO 01727 857861
E manager@abbeytheatre.org.uk
W www.abbeytheatre.org.uk

ST ALBANS: Alban Arena   T 01727 861078
Civic Centre, St Albans AL1 3LD
BO 01727 844488
E alban.arena@1life.co.uk
W www.alban-arena.co.uk

ST HELENS: Theatre Royal   T 01744 756333
Corporation Street, St Helens WA10 1LQ
BO 01744 756000
E info@sthelenstheatreroyal.co.uk
W www.sthelenstheatreroyal.com

STAFFORD: Stafford
Gatehouse Theatre   T 01785 253595
Eastgate Street, Stafford ST16 2LT
BO 01785 254653
E gatehouse@staffordbc.gov.uk
W www.staffordgatehousetheatre.co.uk

STEVENAGE:
Gordon Craig Theatre   T 01438 363200 (T/BO)
Stevenage Arts & Leisure Centre
Lytton Way
Stevenage SG1 1LZ
E enquiries@gordon-craig.co.uk
W www.gordon-craig.co.uk

SUNDERLAND:
Sunderland Empire   T 0191 566 1040 (Admin)
High Street West
Sunderland SR1 3EX
BO 0844 8713022
E sunderlandboxoffice@theambassadors.com
W www.atgtickets.com/sunderland

SWANAGE: Mowlem Theatre   BO 01929 422239
Shore Road, Swanage BH19 1DD
E mowlem.theatre@gmail.com

TAMWORTH: Assembly Rooms   T 01827 709619
Corporation Street, Tamworth B79 7DN
BO 01827 709618
E tarenquiries@tamworth.gov.uk
W www.tamworthassemblyrooms.gov.uk

TEWKESBURY:
The Roses Theatre   T 01684 853061 (Admin)
Sun Street, Tewkesbury GL20 5NX
BO 01684 295074
E assistant@rosestheatre.org
W www.rosestheatre.org

TORQUAY:
Babbacombe Theatre   BO 01803 328385
Babbacombe Downs, Torquay TQ1 3LU
E info@babbacombe-theatre.com
W www.babbacombe-theatre.com

TORQUAY: Princess Theatre   T 01803 206360
Torbay Road, Torquay TQ2 5EZ
BO 0844 8713023
E wendybennett@theambassadors.com
W www.atgtickets.com/torquay

TRURO: Hall For Cornwall   T 01872 321969
Contact: Rich Mason
Back Quay, Truro, Cornwall TR1 2LL
BO 01872 262466
E richm@hallforcornwall.org.uk
W www.hallforcornwall.co.uk

WAKEFIELD: Theatre Royal   T 01924 215531
Drury Lane, Wakefield, West Yorkshire WF1 2TE
F 01924 215525
E murray.edwards@theatreroyalwakefield.co.uk
W www.theatreroyalwakefield.co.uk

WINCHESTER: Theatre Royal   T 01962 844600
21-23 Jewry Street, Winchester SO23 8SB
BO 01962 840440
E kate.raines@theatreroyalwinchester.co.uk
W www.theatreroyalwinchester.co.uk

WORCESTER: Swan Theatre   T 01905 726969
The Moors, Worcester WR1 3ED
BO 01905 611427
E info@worcesterlive.co.uk   W www.worcesterlive.co.uk

WORTHING: Connaught Theatre,
Pavilion Theatre &
The Assembly Hall   BO 01903 206206
Union Place, Worthing BN11 1LG
E theatres@adur-worthing.gov.uk
W www.worthingtheatres.co.uk

YEOVIL: Octagon Theatre   T 01935 845900
Hendford, Yeovil BA20 1UX
BO 01935 422884
E octagontheatre@southsomerset.gov.uk
W www.octagon-theatre.co.uk

YORK: Grand Opera House   T 01904 678700
Cumberland Street, York YO1 9SW
BO 0844 8713024
E yorkboxoffice@theambassadors.com
W www.atgtickets.com/york

AUTHENTIC PUNCH & JUDY   T/F 020 8300 3579
Contact: John Styles. Booths. Presentations. Puppets
42 Christchurch Road, Sidcup
Kent DA15 7HQ
W www.johnstylesentertainer.co.uk

COMPLETE WORKS THE   T 020 7377 0280
Contact: Phil Evans (Artistic Director)
The Old Truman Brewery, 91 Brick Lane
London E1 6QL
F 020 7247 7405
E info@tcw.org.uk
W www.tcw.org.uk

**CORNELIUS & JONES
ORIGINAL PRODUCTIONS**   T/F 01908 612593
49 Carters Close, Sherington
Newport Pagnell, Buckinghamshire MK16 9NW
E admin@corneliusjones.com
W www.corneliusjones.com

**DNA PUPPETRY &
VISUAL THEATRE CO**   T 0161 408 1720
Hope Villa, 18 Woodland Avenue
Thornton Cleveleys, Lancashire FY5 4HB
E dna@dynamicnewanimation.co.uk
W www.dynamicnewanimation.co.uk

INDIGO MOON THEATRE   T 07855 328552
35 Waltham Court, Beverley
East Yorkshire HU17 9JF
E info@indigomoontheatre.com
W www.indigomoontheatre.com

JACOLLY PUPPET THEATRE   T 01822 852346
Redbar, Kirkella Road, Yelverton
West Devon PL20 6BB
E theatre@jacolly-puppets.co.uk
W www.jacolly-puppets.co.uk

LATIMER, Helyn   T 01446 790634
22 Starling Road, St Athan
Vale of Glamorgan CF62 4NJ
E info@puppettheatrewales.co.uk
W www.puppettheatrewales.co.uk

LITTLE ANGEL THEATRE   T 020 7226 1787
14 Dagmar Passage, Off Cross Street
London N1 2DN
E info@littleangeltheatre.com
W www.littleangeltheatre.com

**MAJOR MUSTARD'S
TRAVELLING SHOW**   T 0121 426 4329
1 Carless Avenue, Harborne
Birmingham B17 9EG
E mm@majormustard.com

NORWICH PUPPET THEATRE   T 01603 615564
St James, Whitefriars
Norwich NR3 1TN
F 01603 617578
E info@puppettheatre.co.uk
W www.puppettheatre.co.uk

**PROFESSOR PATTEN'S
PUNCH & JUDY**   T 01707 873262
Magic. Puppetry
14 The Crest, Goffs Oak
Herts EN7 5NP
E dennis@dennispatten.co.uk
W www.dennispatten.co.uk

PUPPET THEATRE WALES   T 01446 790634
22 Starling Road, St Athan
Vale of Glamorgan CF62 4NJ
E info@puppettheatrewales.co.uk
W www.puppettheatrewales.co.uk

**SLAPSTICK & TICKLE
PUPPET COMPANY**   T 07970 141005
14 Brackerns Way
Lymington SO41 3TL
E mike@eddowes.me.uk

TOPPER, Chris PUPPETS   T 0151 424 8692
Puppets & Costume Characters Created & Performed
75 Barrows Green Lane, Widnes
Cheshire WA8 3JH
E christopper@ntlworld.com
W www.christopperpuppets.co.uk

ALDEBURGH:
Summer Theatre   BO 01728 454022
July-August
The Jubilee Hall, Crabbe Street
Aldeburgh IP15 5BN
W www.southwoldtheatre.org

BELFAST: Lyric Theatre   T 028 9038 5685
Contact: Cat Rice (Admin Assistant), Jimmy Fay
(Executive Producer), Morag Keating (Admin Manager),
Ciaran McAuley (Chief Executive)
55 Ridgeway Street, Belfast BT9 5FB
E info@lyrictheatre.co.uk
W www.lyrictheatre.co.uk

BIRMINGHAM: Birmingham
Repertory Theatre   T 0121 245 2000
Contact: Roxana Silbert (Artistic Director), Stuart Rogers
(Executive Director)
Centenary Square
Broad Street, Birmingham B1 2EP
BO 0121 236 4455
E stage.door@birmingham-rep.co.uk

BIRMINGHAM:
Blue Orange Theatre   T 0121 212 2643
118 Great Hampton Street
Jewellery Quarter
Birmingham, West Midlands B18 6AD
E info@blueorangetheatre.co.uk
W www.blueorangetheatre.co.uk

BOLTON: Octagon Theatre   T 01204 529407
Contact: Elizabeth Newman (Artistic Director), Roddy
Gauld (Chief Executive), Vicky Entwistle (Administration
Manager), Olly Seviour (Head of Production)
Howell Croft South, Bolton BL1 1SB
BO 01204 520661
E info@octagonbolton.co.uk
W www.octagonbolton.co.uk

BRISTOL: BRISTOL OLD VIC
THEATRE & STUDIO   T 0117 949 3993
Contact: Tom Morris (Artistic Director), Emma Stenning
(Executive Director)
King Street, Bristol BS1 4ED
BO 0117 987 7877
E admin@bristololdvic.org.uk
W www.bristololdvic.org.uk

CARDIFF: Sherman Cymru   T 029 2064 6901
Contact: Rachel O'Riordan (Artistic Director), Margaret
Jones (General Manager)
Senghennydd Road
Cardiff CF24 4YE
E elin.partridge@shermancymru.co.uk

CHICHESTER: Chichester
Festival Theatre   T 01243 784437
Contact: Jonathan Church (Artistic Director), Alan Finch
(Executive Director), Janet Bakose (Theatre Manager)
Oaklands Park, Chichester
West Sussex PO19 6AP
BO 01243 781312
E admin@cft.org.uk
W www.cft.org.uk

CHICHESTER: Minerva Theatre at Chichester
Festival Theatre   T 01243 784437
Contact: Jonathan Church (Artistic Director), Alan Finch
(Executive Director), Janet Bakose (Theatre Manager)
Oaklands Park
Chichester
West Sussex PO19 6AP
BO 01243 781312
E admin@cft.org.uk
W www.cft.org.uk

COLCHESTER:
Mercury Theatre   T 01206 577006
Contact: Daniel Buckroyd (Artistic Director), Steve Mannix
(Executive Director)
Balkerne Gate
Colchester
Essex CO1 1PT
BO 01206 573948
E info@mercurytheatre.co.uk
W www.mercurytheatre.co.uk

COVENTRY: Belgrade Main
Stage & B2 Auditorium   T 024 7625 6431
Contact: Hamish Glen (Artistic Director/CEO), Joanna
Reid (Executive Director), Nicola Young (Director of
Communications)
Belgrade Square
Coventry
West Midlands CV1 1GS
BO 024 7655 3055
E admin@belgrade.co.uk
W www.belgrade.co.uk

DERBY: Derby LIVE   BO 01332 255800
Market Place
Derby DE1 3AH
E derbylive@derby.gov.uk
W www.derbylive.co.uk

DERBY: Derby Theatre   T 01332 593939 (BO)
Twitter: @derbytheatre
15 Theatre Walk
St Peters Quarter
Derby DE1 2NF
T 01332 593900 (SD)
E tickets@derbytheatre.co.uk
W www.derbytheatre.co.uk

DUBLIN: Abbey Theatre Amharclann
na Mainistreach   T 00 353 1 8872200
Contact: Fiach MacConghail (Director)
26 Lower Abbey Street
Dublin 1
Ireland
BO 00 353 1 8787222
E info@abbeytheatre.ie
W www.abbeytheatre.ie

DUNDEE: Dundee
Repertory Theatre   T 01382 227684
Tay Square
Dundee DD1 1PB
BO 01382 223530
E info@dundeereptheatre.co.uk
W www.dundeerep.co.uk

**EDINBURGH: Royal Lyceum
Theatre Company** T 0131 248 4800
Contact: Mark Thomson (Artistic Director)
30B Grindlay Street
Edinburgh EH3 9AX
BO 0131 248 4848
E info@lyceum.org.uk
W www.lyceum.org.uk

**EDINBURGH:
Traverse Theatre** T 0131 228 3223 (Admin)
*Contact: Orla O'Loughlin (Artistic Director), Linda Crooks
(Executive Producer). New Writing. Own Productions.
Touring & Visiting Companies*
10 Cambridge Street
Edinburgh EH1 2ED
BO 0131 228 1404
E rebecca.leary@traverse.co.uk
W www.traverse.co.uk

**EXETER: Exeter
Northcott Theatre** T 01392 223999
*Contact: Paul Jepson (Artistic & Executive Director)
Mid-Scale Receiving & Producing Theatre*
Stocker Road
Exeter
Devon EX4 4QB
BO 01392 493493
E info@exeternorthcott.co.uk
W www.exeternorthcott.co.uk

GLASGOW: Citizens Theatre T 0141 429 5561
*Contact: Dominic Hill (Artistic Director), Judith Kilvington
(Executive Director), Graham Sutherland (Head of
Production)*
Gorbals, Glasgow G5 9DS
BO 0141 429 0022
E info@citz.co.uk
W www.citz.co.uk

**GUILDFORD: Yvonne Arnaud
Theatre** T 01483 440077
Contact: James Barber (Director)
Millbrook
Guildford, Surrey GU1 3UX
BO 01483 440000
E yat@yvonne-arnaud.co.uk
W www.yvonne-arnaud.co.uk

**HARROGATE:
Harrogate Theatre** T 01423 502710
*Contact: David Bown (Chief Executive). Mainly
Co-productions. Touring & Visiting Companies*
Oxford Street
Harrogate HG1 1QF
BO 01423 502116
E info@harrogatetheatre.co.uk
W www.harrogatetheatre.co.uk

HULL: Hull Truck Theatre T 01482 224800
*Contact: Mark Babych (Artistic Director),
Janthi Mills-Ward (Executive Director)*
50 Ferensway, Hull HU2 8LB
E admin@hulltruck.co.uk
W www.hulltruck.co.uk

**IPSWICH:
The New Wolsey Theatre** T 01473 295900
*Contact: Peter Rowe (Artistic Director), Sarah Holmes
(Chief Executive)*
Civic Drive
Ipswich IP1 2AS
E info@wolseytheatre.co.uk
W www.wolseytheatre.co.uk

**KESWICK:
Theatre by the Lake** T 01768 772282
*Contact: Ian Forrest (Artistic Director), Patric Gilchrist
(Executive Director)*
Lakeside
Keswick
Cumbria CA12 5DJ
BO 01768 774411
E enquiries@theatrebythelake.com
W www.theatrebythelake.com

LANCASTER: The Dukes T 01524 598505
Contact: Joe Sumsion (Director)
Moor Lane
Lancaster
Lancashire LA1 1QE
BO 01524 598500
E info@dukes-lancaster.org
W www.dukes-lancaster.org

**LEEDS:
West Yorkshire Playhouse** T 0113 213 7800
*Contact: James Brining (Artistic Director/Chief
Executive), Robin Hawkes (Executive Director),
Mimi Poskitt (Senior Producer)*
Playhouse Square
Quarry Hill, Leeds LS2 7UP
E info@wyp.org.uk
W www.wyp.org.uk

LEICESTER: Curve T 0116 242 3560
*Contact: Verity Bartesch (Assistant Producer), Nikolai
Foster (Artistic Director), Fiona Allan (Chief Executive),
Chris Stafford (Executive Producer)*
Rutland Street
Leicester LE1 1SB
E c.stafford@curvetheatre.co.uk
W www.curveonline.co.uk

**LIVERPOOL: Everyman &
Playhouse Theatres** T 0151 708 3700
*Contact: Gemma Bodinetz (Artistic Director), Deborah
Aydon (Executive Director)*
Everyman: 5-11 Hope Street
Liverpool L1 9BH
Playhouse: Williamson Square
Liverpool L1 1EL
BO 0151 709 4776
E info@everymanplayhouse.com
W www.everymanplayhouse.com

MANCHESTER: Contact T 0161 274 0600
Oxford Road
Manchester M15 6JA
E info@contactmcr.com
W www.contactmcr.com

MANCHESTER: Home T 0161 228 7621
Contact: Dave Moutrey (Chief Executive), Walter Meierjohann (Artistic Director)
Cornerhouse & HOME, GMAC Ltd
2 Tony Wilson Place
First Street
Manchester M15 4FN
E admin@homemcr.org
W www.homemcr.org

MANCHESTER:
Royal Exchange Theatre T 0161 833 9333
Contact: Gregory Hersov, Sarah Frankcom (Artistic Directors), Richard Morgan (Producer/Studio), Jerry Knight-Smith (Casting Director)
St Ann's Square
Manchester M2 7DH
BO 0161 833 9833
W www.royalexchange.co.uk

MILFORD HAVEN:
Torch Theatre T 01646 694192
Contact: Peter Doran (Artistic Director)
St Peter's Road
Milford Haven
Pembrokeshire SA73 2BU
BO 01646 695267
E info@torchtheatre.co.uk
W www.torchtheatre.co.uk

MOLD:
Clwyd Theatr Cymru T 01352 756331
Repertoire. 4 Weekly. Also Touring
Mold, Flintshire
North Wales CH7 1YA
BO 0845 3303565
E admin@clwyd-theatr-cymru.co.uk
W www.clwyd-theatr-cymru.co.uk

MUSSELBURGH:
The Brunton T 0131 665 9900
Contact: Lesley Smith (General Manager). Annual Programme of Theatre, Dance, Music, Comedy & Children's Work. Also available for Private & Corporate Hire
Ladywell Way
Musselburgh EH21 6AA
BO 0131 665 2240
E mhegarty@eastlothian.gov.uk
W www.thebrunton.co.uk

NEWBURY:
Watermill Theatre T 01635 45834
Contact: Hedda Beeby (Artistic & Executive Director), Clare Lindsay (General Manager). 4-8 Weekly. February-January
Bagnor, Newbury
Berkshire RG20 8AE
BO 01635 46044
E admin@watermill.org.uk
W www.watermill.org.uk

NEWCASTLE-UNDER-LYME:
New Vic Theatre T 01782 717954
Contact: Theresa Heskins (Artistic Director), Fiona Wallace (Executive Director)
Etruria Road
Newcastle-under-Lyme
Staffordshire ST5 0JG
BO 01782 717962
E administration@newvictheatre.org.uk
W www.newvictheatre.org.uk

NEWCASTLE UPON TYNE: Northern Stage
(Theatrical Productions) Ltd T 0191 242 7210
Contact: Susan Cotter (Chief Executive)
Barras Bridge
Newcastle upon Tyne NE1 7RH
BO 0191 230 5151
E info@northernstage.co.uk
W www.northernstage.co.uk

NORTHAMPTON:
Royal & Derngate T 01604 626222
Contact: Martin Sutherland (Chief Executive), James Dacre (Artistic Director), John Manning (Producer)
19-21 Guildhall Road
Northampton NN1 1DP
BO 01604 624811
E arts@royalandderngate.co.uk
W www.royalandderngate.co.uk

NOTTINGHAM :
Nottingham Playhouse T 0115 947 4361
Contact: Stephanie Sirr (Chief Executive), Giles Croft (Artistic Director)
Nottingham Playhouse Trust Ltd
Wellington Circus, Nottingham NG1 5AF
BO 0115 941 9419
E enquiry@nottinghamplayhouse.co.uk
W www.nottinghamplayhouse.co.uk

OLDHAM: Coliseum Theatre T 0161 624 1731
Contact: Kevin Shaw (Chief Executive). 3-4 Weekly
Fairbottom Street, Oldham, Lancashire OL1 3SW
BO 0161 624 2829
E mail@coliseum.org.uk
W www.coliseum.org.uk

PERTH: Perth Theatre T 01738 472700
Contact: Kenny Miller (Creative Director) Graeme Wallace (Head of Planning & Resources), Colin McMahon (Chief Executive)
Horsecross Arts, 185 High Street, Perth PH1 5UW
BO 01738 621031
E info@horsecross.co.uk
W www.horsecross.co.uk

PETERBOROUGH: Key Theatre T 01733 207237
Touring & Occasional Seasonal
Embankment Road, Peterborough
Cambridgeshire PE1 1EF
BO 01733 207239
E key.theatre@vivacity-peterborough.com

**PITLOCHRY: Pitlochry
Festival Theatre**   **T** 01796 484600
Contact: John Durnin (Chief Executive/Artistic Director)
Pitlochry
Perthshire PH16 5DR
BO 01796 484626
E admin@pitlochryfestivaltheatre.com
W www.pitlochryfestivaltheatre.com

**PLYMOUTH: Theatre Royal &
Drum Theatre**   **T** 01752 668282
Contact: Simon Stokes (Artistic Director), Adrian Vinken
(Chief Executive)
Royal Parade, Plymouth
Devon PL1 2TR
BO 01752 267222
E info@theatreroyal.com
W www.theatreroyal.com

**READING: The Mill at
Sonning Theatre**   **T** 0118 969 6039
Contact: Sally Hughes (Artistic Director). 8 Weekly
Sonning Eye, Reading RG4 6TY
BO 0118 969 8000
E admin@millatsonning.com
W www.millatsonning.com

**SALISBURY: Playhouse &
Salberg (Studio)**   **T** 01722 320117
Contact: Gareth Machin (Artistic Director), Sebastian
Warrack (Executive Director). 3-4 Weekly
Malthouse Lane, Salisbury
Wiltshire SP2 7RA
BO 01722 320333
E info@salisburyplayhouse.com
W www.salisburyplayhouse.com

**SCARBOROUGH:
Stephen Joseph Theatre**   **T** 01723 370540
Contact: Chris Monks (Artistic Director), Matthew Russell
(Executive Director). Repertoire/Repertory
Westborough, Scarborough
North Yorkshire YO11 1JW
BO 01723 370541
E enquiries@sjt.uk.com
W www.sjt.uk.com

**SHEFFIELD: Crucible, Studio &
Lyceum Theatres**   **T** 0114 249 5999
Contact: Dan Bates (Chief Executive)
55 Norfolk Street
Sheffield S1 1DA
BO 0114 249 6000
E info@sheffieldtheatres.co.uk
W www.sheffieldtheatres.co.uk

**SHERINGHAM:
Sheringham Little Theatre**   **T** 01263 822117
Contact: Debbie Thompson (Theatre Director)
2 Station Road
Sheringham
Norfolk NR26 8RE
E debbie@sheringhamlittletheatre.com
W www.sheringhamlittletheatre.com

**SIDMOUTH:
Manor Pavilion Theatre**   **T** 01395 576798
Contact: Graham Whitlock (Theatre Manager). Weekly.
June-September
Manor Road, Sidmouth
Devon EX10 8RP
BO 01395 514413
E gwhitlock@eastdevon.gov.uk
W www.manorpavillion.com

SOUTHAMPTON: Nuffield   **T** 023 8031 5500
Contact: Sam Hodges (Director & Chief Executive)
University Road, Southampton SO17 1TR
BO 023 8067 1771
E info@nuffieldtheatre.co.uk
W www.nuffieldtheatre.co.uk

**SOUTHWOLD & ALDEBURGH
SUMMER THEATRE**   **T** 07030 530948
Contact: Suffolk Summer Theatres Ltd (Producer)
Unit 7, Southwold Business Centre, St Edmund's Road
Southwold, Suffolk IP18 6LB
E peter@southwoldtheatre.org
W www.suffolksummertheatres.org

**STRATFORD-UPON-AVON: Royal Shakespeare
Company**   **T** 0844 8001110 (T/BO)
Waterside, Stratford-upon-Avon
Warwickshire CV37 6BB
E info@rsc.org.uk
W www.rsc.org.uk

**WATFORD: Watford
Palace Theatre**   **T** 01923 235455
Contact: Brigid Larmour (Artistic Director/Chief
Executive)
20 Clarendon Road, Watford
Hertfordshire WD17 1JZ
BO 01923 225671
E enquiries@watfordpalacetheatre.co.uk
W www.watfordpalacetheatre.co.uk

WINDSOR: Theatre Royal   **T** 01753 863444
Contact: Robert Miles (Executive Director)
32 Thames Street, Windsor
Berkshire SL4 1PS
BO 01753 853888
E info@theatreroyalwindsor.co.uk
W www.theatreroyalwindsor.co.uk

**WOKING: New Victoria Theatre,
The Ambassadors**   **T** 01483 545999
Peacocks Centre, Woking GU21 6GQ
BO 0844 8717645
E wokingboxoffice@theambassadors.com
W www.atgtickets.com/woking

YORK: Theatre Royal   **T** 01904 658162
Contact: Damian Cruden (Artistic Director), Liz Wilson
(Chief Executive)
St Leonard's Place, York YO1 7HD
BO 01904 623568
E admin@yorktheatreroyal.co.uk
W www.yorktheatreroyal.co.uk

U

Unions, Professional Guilds
& Associations

Unions

What are performers' unions?

The unions listed in this section exist to protect and improve the rights, interests and working conditions of performers. They offer very important services to their members, such as advice on pay and conditions, help with contracts and negotiations, legal support and welfare advice. To join a performers' union there is usually a one-off joining fee and then an annual subscription fee calculated in relation to an individual's total yearly earnings.

Equity is the main actors' union in the UK. See www.equity.org.uk and their case study in this section for more details.

Do similar organisations exist for other sectors of the entertainment industry?

In addition to representation by trade unions, some skills also have professional bodies, guilds and associations which complement the work of trade unions. These include directors, producers, stage managers, designers and casting directors. These can also be found in the following listings.

What is the FIA?

The FIA (International Federation of Actors) www.fia-actors.com is an organisation which represents performers' trade unions, guilds and associations from all around the world. It tackles the same issues as individual actors' unions, but on an international rather than local level.

I'm a professionally trained actor from overseas and I want to work in the UK. How do I get started?

If you are a national of a country in the European Economic Area (EEA) or Switzerland (excluding Bulgaria and Romania) you do not need to apply for permission from the Home Office in order to work as an actor in the UK. You will be able to look for and accept offers of work without needing a visa. Visit www.ukba.homeoffice.gov.uk/eucitizens/rightsandresponsibilites for details of your rights to enter, live in and work in the UK.

If you are from a country outside the EEA you will need to apply for a visa before you can work as an actor in the UK. You might want to visit www.bia.homeoffi ce.gov.uk/visas-immigration/working for full information.

You may also wish to join the UK's actors' union, Equity. For more information please visit their website www.equity.org.uk. If you can prove that you have relevant professional acting training and/or experience, you can also apply to join Spotlight to promote yourself to casting opportunities.

I am a UK resident and I want to work as an actor elsewhere in Europe. Where do I start?

A good starting point would be to contact the actors' union in the country in which you are hoping to work for information on their employment legislation. Contact details for performers' unions in Europe can be found in the following listings or obtained from the FIA (www.fia-actors.com), who in most cases will be able to advise on what criteria you need to fulfil to be eligible for work.

As a UK national, you have the right to work in any country which is a member of the EEA without a work permit. You will be given the same employment rights as nationals of the country you are working in, but these rights will change according to the country you choose to work in and may not be the same as the UK.

For more general advice, the Foreign and Commonwealth Office (FCO) offers advice on living overseas and provides information on contacting the UK embassy in and relevant entry requirements for the country of your choice. Please see www.fco.gov.uk/en/traveland-living-abroad for details. You could also visit Directgov's website www.direct.gov.uk/en/BritonsLivingAbroad for further useful guidance for British citizens living abroad.

You should also go further and start researching agents, casting directors, production companies and so on which are based in the country you wish to live and work in. Begin your search online and then decide whether to approach a person or company for further information once you have found out more about them. Learning the culture and becoming as fluent as possible in the language of your chosen country would be advisable, as this opens up a far wider range of job opportunities.

What are English Speaking Theatres?

English Speaking Theatres can provide British actors with an opportunity to work abroad in theatre. These companies vary greatly in terms of the plays they put on and the audiences they attract: they may aim to teach English to schoolchildren; help audiences develop an appreciation of English plays; or may exist simply because there is a demand for English speaking entertainment. Some are based in one venue while others tour round the country. Actors may be employed for an individual production or, especially if touring, for a series of plays. Performers interested in the possibility of working for this type of theatre company should refer to the 'Theatre: English Speaking in Europe' section for listings.

I am a UK resident and I want to work as an actor in the USA. Where do I start?

To work in America you will need a Green Card – a visa which entitles the holder to live and work there permanently as an immigrant – but you will not qualify for one unless you are sponsored by a prospective employer in the US or a relative who is a US citizen. Visit the US Embassy's website http://london.usembassy.gov/visas.html or alternatively visit the US Department of State's Bureau of Consular Affairs' website http://travel.state.gov/visa for information about the criteria you must meet and the fees you will have to pay.

Don't expect to be granted immediate entry to the USA. There is a limit to the number of people who can apply for immigrant status every year, so you could be on the waiting list for several years depending on the category of your application. You could enter the Green Card Lottery at www.greencard.co.uk for a chance to fast-track the processing of your application, although your visa will still have to be approved.

Finding employment from outside the USA will be difficult. You might want to try signing with an American talent agent to submit you for work, although there is huge competition for agents. Try the Association of Talent Agents (ATA) www.agentassociation.com for US agent details. The most effective way to gain an American agent's interest would be to get a personal referral from an industry contact, such as a casting director or acting coach. You should also promote yourself as you would with Spotlight by signing up with casting services such as www.breakdownservices.com

Acting employment in America is divided into union work and non-union work. The major actors' unions are AEA www.actorsequity.org and SAG-AFTRA www.sagaftra.org. As with any other union they protect and enhance the rights of their members and offer various services and benefits. You will only become eligible for membership once you have provided proof of a contract for a job which comes under a particular union's jurisdiction. Non-members can work on union jobs if a producer is willing to employ them.

You can join more than one union, but once you have joined at least one you will be unable to accept any non-union work.

Unions

CASE STUDY

As you progress in the entertainment industry there will be all kinds of successes but also quite a lot of challenges. The industry is fast moving and changeable so it is helpful that there is an organisation, Equity, that is constant; committed to supporting performers and creative practitioners and also to campaigning for their rights and about their issues.

Equity is the only trade union in the UK to represent artists from across the entire spectrum of arts and entertainment. Formed in 1930 by a group of West End performers, Equity quickly spread to encompass the whole range of professional entertainment so the membership includes actors, singers, dancers, variety and circus artists, students, storytellers, street artists, models, choreographers, theatre directors, theatre designers, stage management, presenters, walk-on and supporting artists, stunt performers and fight directors and many other professional, creative practitioners. Being part of Equity is a statement of commitment to yourself and your profession.

Equity's main job is to negotiate minimum terms and conditions of employment throughout the industry and ensure these take account of social and economic changes. Equity looks to the future, negotiating agreements to embrace the new and emerging technologies so new platforms are covered, as are the more traditional areas such as theatre, film and television. At the heart of all of these is a fundamental position on decent treatment and equal opportunities to prevent exploitation and set standards across the industry.

"In a landscape of irregular work, Equity is a permanent fixture on which members can rely"

Equity Agreements covers such things as minimum rates of pay, health and safety, hours, breaks, holiday pay, grievance procedures and many other things which make working under

Equity terms the best protection you can have. However, the union also assists members if they are not working on Equity contracts and need advice or help.

At a national level the union lobbies government and other bodies on all kinds of issues e.g. Public Entertainment Licensing, funding for British filmmaking, theatre funding, the licence fee, unpaid work and other topics. In addition, the union operates at a global level through the International Federation of Artists, which Equity helped to establish, the International Committee for Artists' Freedom and through agreements with sister unions. Members get involved in national campaigns and also in local issues such as keeping venues open or promoting casting outside of London or fighting to maintain local government funding for the arts in their area.

There are lots of other ways that members get involved with Equity. There is an important network of branches throughout the UK where members meet to mutually support each other and put their views and ideas forward. There are specialist committees that make a genuine difference to the working life of performers and the ruling Council is also made up of elected members. Every member has a voice.

Finally there is a wide range of free services that are part of membership. There are a whole host of benefits which are continually being revised and developed. These include helplines, information about work opportunities, legal support, training, insurance cover, pension scheme and others.

In a landscape of irregular work, Equity is a permanent fixture on which members can rely.

For more information please visit www.equity.org.uk

UNITED KINGDOM: AMERICAN ACTORS UK
Contact: By e-mail only
E admin@americanactorsuk.com
W www.americanactorsuk.com

UNITED KINGDOM: BECTU - Broadcasting, Entertainment, Cinematograph & Theatre Union   T 020 7346 0900
373-377 Clapham Road, London SW9 9BT
F 020 7346 0901
E info@bectu.org.uk
W www.bectu.org.uk

UNITED KINGDOM: CDG - Casting Directors' Guild
Contact: Sophie Hallett
PO Box 64973, London SW20 2AW
E info@thecdg.co.uk
W www.thecdg.co.uk

UNITED KINGDOM: CPMA -Co-operative Personal Management Association
Contact: The Secretary
E cpmauk@yahoo.co.uk
W www.cpma.coop

UNITED KINGDOM: DGGB - DIRECTORS GUILD OF GREAT BRITAIN
E info@dggb.org
W www.dggb.org

UNITED KINGDOM: EQUITY inc Variety Artistes' Federation   T 020 7379 6000
Guild House, Upper St Martin's Lane
London WC2H 9EG
E info@equity.org.uk
W www.equity.org.uk

UNITED KINGDOM: EQUITY inc Variety Artistes' Federation (Wales & South West of England)   T 029 2039 7971
3rd Floor 1 Cathedral Road, Cardiff CF11 9HA
E southwestengland@equity.org.uk
W www.equity.org.uk

UNITED KINGDOM: EQUITY inc Variety Artistes' Federation (Northern Office)   T 0161 244 5995
Express Networks, 1 George Leigh Street
Manchester M4 5DL
F 0161 244 5971
E northwestengland@equity.org.uk
W www.equity.org.uk

UNITED KINGDOM: EQUITY inc Variety Artistes' Federation (Midlands)   T/F 024 7655 3612
Office 1 Steeple House
Percy Street, Coventry CV1 3BY
E tjohnson@midlands-equity.org.uk
W www.equity.org.uk

UNITED KINGDOM: EQUITY inc Variety Artistes' Federation (Scotland & Northern Ireland)   T 0141 248 2472
114 Union Street, Glasgow G1 3QQ
F 0141 248 2473
E scotland@equity.org.uk
W www.equity.org.uk

UNITED KINGDOM: FAA - Film Artistes' Association   T 020 7346 0900
Amalgamated with BECTU
373-377 Clapham Road, London SW9 9BT
F 020 7346 0925
E info@bectu.org.uk   W www.bectu.org.uk

UNITED KINGDOM:
MUSICIAN'S UNION T 020 7582 5566
60-62 Clapham Road, London SW9 0JJ
E info@themu.org
W www.musiciansunion.org.uk

UNITED KINGDOM: PMA - Personal Managers'
Association Ltd T 0845 6027191
E info@thepma.com
W www.thepma.com

UNITED KINGDOM: WRITERS' GUILD OF
GREAT BRITAIN T 020 7833 0777
134 Tooley Street, London SE1 2TU
E admin@writersguild.org.uk
W www.writersguild.org.uk

BELGIUM: CGSP - Centrale Générale
des Services Publics T 00 32 2 2261375
Rue de Congrès 17-19, 1000 Brussels
F 00 32 2 2261362
E dan.lecocq@cgsp.be
W www.fgtb-cgsp-culture.be

BELGIUM: CSC/TRANSCOM -
Cultuur T 00 32 22 890832
Galerie Agora, Rue du Marchè aux Herbes 150
Boîte 40, 1000 Brussels
F 00 32 25 141836
E dgilquin.transcom@acv-csc.be
W www.csctranscom-culture.be

BELGIUM: FIA - International
Federation of Actors T 00 32 2 2345653
40 Rue Joseph II, Box 4, 1000 Brussels
F 00 32 2 2350870
E office@fia-actors.com
W www.fia-actors.com

DENMARK: DAF -
The Danish Artist Union T 00 45 33326677
Dronningensgade 68, 4.sal, 1420 Copenhagen K
F 00 45 33337330
E artisten@artisten.dk
W www.artisten.dk

DENMARK: DSF -
Dansk Skuespillerforbund T 00 45 33 242200
Tagensvej 85, 3. sal, 2200 København, Denmark
F 00 45 33 248159
E dsf@skuespillerforbundet.dk
W www.skuespillerforbundet.dk

FINLAND: SNL -
Suomen Näyttelijäliitto T 00 358 9 25112135
Meritullinkatu 33, 00170 Helsinki
F 00 358 9 25112139
E toimisto@nayttelijaliitto.fi
W www.nayttelijaliitto.fi

FRANCE: SFA - Syndicat Français des
Artistes-Interprètes T 00 33 1 53250909
1 rue Janssen, 75019 Paris
F 00 33 1 53250901
E info@sfa-cgt.fr
W www.sfa-cgt.fr

GERMANY: GDBA - Genossenschaft Deutscher
Bühnen-Angehöriger T 00 49 40 43282440
HeinrichstraBe 23-25, 22769 Hamburg, Germany
F 00 49 40 432824428
E gdba@buehnengenossenschaft.de
W www.buehnengenossenschaft.de

GREECE: HAU -
Hellenic Actors' Union T 00 30 210 3817369
33 Kanigos Street, 10682 Athens
F 00 30 210 3808651
E support@sei.gr W www.sei.gr

IRELAND: IRISH EQUITY T 00 353 1 8586403
SIPTU
7th Floor, Liberty Hall
Dublin 1
E equity@siptu.ie
W www.irishequity.ie

ITALY: SLC - SINDICATO LAVORATORI
COMMUCAZIONE T 00 39 06 42048204
Piazza Sallustio 24, 00187 Rome
F 00 39 06 4824325
E segreteria.nazionale@slc.cgil.it
W www.slc-cgil.it/

LUXEMBOURG: OGB - L Onofhängege Gewerk-
schafsbond Lëtzebuerg T 00 352 496005
19 Rue d'Epernay, B.P. 2031
1020 Luxembourg, Luxembourg
F 00 352 486949
E leon.jenal@ogb-l.lu
W www.ogb-l.lu

NORWAY: NSF - Norsk Skuespillerforbund /
NORWEIGAN ACTORS'
EQUITY ASSOCIATION T 00 47 21027190
Welhavens Gate 1, 0166 Oslo
F 00 47 21027191
E nsf@skuespillerforbund.no
W www.skuespillerforbund.no

PORTUGAL: STE -
Sindicato dos Trabalhadores
de Espectáculos T 00 351 21 8852728
Rua da Fé 23, 2ºPiso
1150-149 Lisbon, Portugal
F 00 351 21 8853787
E stespectaculos@hotmail.com
W www.stespectaculos.com

SPAIN: CONARTE - Confederación
de Artistas -
Trabajadores del Espectáculo T 00 34 91 5222804
C/ Montera 34, 1ro Piso
28013 Madrid
F 00 34 91 5226055
W www.conarte.info

SPAIN: FSC-CC.OO. - Comisiones Obreras -
Comunicación, Artes,
Cultura y Deporte T 00 34 91 7572299
Calle Fernández de la Hoz 21
28010 Madrid
F 00 34 91 2733501
W www.fsc.ccoo.es

SWEDEN: TF -
Teaterförbundet T 00 46 8 4411300
Kaplansbacken 2A, Box 12 710
112 94 Stockholm
F 00 46 8 6539507
E info@teaterforbundet.se
W www.teaterforbundet.se

UNITED STATES:
SAG-AFTRA T 001 212 944 1030
1900 Broadway, 5th Floor
New York, NY 10023
E newyork@sagaftra.org
W www.sagaftra.org

UNITED STATES:
SAG-AFTRA T 001 855 724 2387
5757 Wilshire Boulevard, 7th Floor
Los Angeles, CA 90036-3600
F 001 323 549 6792
E sagaftrainfo@sagaftra.org
W www.sagaftra.org/home

Index To Advertisers

Alphabetical Listing Of Advertisers

TRAINING
(Schools, Companies & Workshops)

Q

R

S

T

U

V

W

N →

Notes